MOVEMENT IN SPECIAL POPULATIONS

Second Edition

DANIEL J. BURT

Texas A&M University—Kingsville

BETHANY L. HERSMAN

Wright State University

Cover images © Shutterstock.com

Kendall Hunt
publishing company

www.kendallhunt.com
Send all inquiries to:
4050 Westmark Drive
Dubuque, IA 52004-1840

Copyright © 2023 by Kendall Hunt Publishing Company

ISBN 979-8-7657-2217-6

All rights reserved. No part of this publication may be reproduced,
stored in a retrieval system, or transmitted, in any form or by any means,
electronic, mechanical, photocopying, recording, or otherwise,
without the prior written permission of the copyright owner.

Published in the United States of America

TABLE OF CONTENTS

FOUNDATIONS

CHAPTER 1 Introduction and History of Disability   3
Daniel J. Burt and Bethany L. Hersman

CHAPTER 2 Philosophical and Social Considerations   11
Justin A. Haegele

CHAPTER 3 Legal Issues and Disabilities   25
Daniel J. Burt

CHAPTER 4 Demystifying the Intersection Between Kinesiology, Therapy, and Public Health: Roles and Career Opportunities   55
Byron Lai, Heidi Stanish, Anne O Odusanya, Scott WT McNamara

CHAPTER 5 Therapeutic Recreation   65
Shelly Beaver

CHAPTER 6 Physical Activity and Exercise Recommendations   85
Robert Kowalsky

CHAPTER 7 Exercise Medicine and Programming   103
Robert Kowalsky

CHAPTER 8 Motor Development, Motor Learning, and Maturation   121
Nicholas Siekirk and Jody Langdon

CHAPTER 9 Measurement, Assessment, and Evaluation   165
Daniel J. Burt

CHAPTER 10 Sport for Individuals with Disabilities   175
Deborah Shapiro, Ashley Fallaize, and Cathy McKay

CHAPTER 11 Support Systems   201
Bethany L. Hersman, Luis Columna, and Wray Jean Connor

DISABILITIES

CHAPTER 12 Adult Onset and Lifestyle Diseases and Disabilities   223
Karen Wonders and Bethany L. Hersman

CHAPTER 13 Intellectual Disabilities   251
Kevin Casebolt and Bethany L. Hersman

CHAPTER 14 Autism Spectrum Disorder   271
Jihyun Lee

CHAPTER 15 Psychological and Behavioral Disorders, Disabilities, and Management   293
Daniel J. Burt

CHAPTER 16 Visual Impairments   323
T.N. Kirk and Justin A. Haegele

CHAPTER 17 Deafness and Deaf People in Sport, Physical Activity, and Physical Education 341
Anthony J. Maher

CHAPTER 18 Neuromuscular and Orthopedic Disabilities 353
T. N. Kirk and Larken Marra

CHAPTER 19 Spinal Cord Disabilities 375
Deborah Shapiro, Andrew Corbett, and Myung Ha Sur

CONTRIBUTING AUTHOR BIOS

Shelly Beaver, MS, CTRS, is a lecturer in park, recreation and tourism studies in the human movement sciences department at Old Dominion University, where she teaches courses in recreational therapy and recreation programming. She earned her BS in kinesiology and MS in leisure studies from Penn State University and is a certified therapeutic recreation specialist (CTRS). She has more than 10 years of clinical experience in long-term care, mental health, physical rehabilitation, and community settings and more than 10 years of teaching experience in higher education. She has received several awards recognizing her outstanding teaching, service, and advocacy for individuals with disabilities, including the Darden College of Education and Professional Studies Teaching Innovation and Excellence Award, the Kate Broderick Faculty Award for Excellence in Inclusive Education, the John R. Broderick Diversity Champion Award, and the HEALTHSOUTH of Altoona Rehabilitation Hospital National Rehab Week Advocate Award.
ORCiD: Beaver | 0000-0002-8717-629X
Email: sbeaver@odu.edu

Dr. Daniel J. Burt is an associate professor and associate department chair in the Department of Health and Kinesiology at Texas A&M University-Kingsville. He received his undergraduate degree in kinesiology from Ouachita Baptist University, master's degree from Henderson State University, and PhD in kinesiology pedagogy with a focus in movement for individuals with disabilities. He is currently completing his certified inclusive fitness trainer and autism exercise specialist certificate through the American College of Sports Medicine. He often hosts workshops and speaks with schools and daycares on behavior-related disabilities and behavior shaping. In his free time, he volunteers to serve as a parent advocate for special education school meetings and is the father of three children, two of whom have disabilities.
ORCiD: Burt | 0000-0001-6918-4862
Email: daniel.burt@tamuk.edu

Dr. Kevin Casebolt is a professor in the physical education teacher education (PETE) department and is a certified adapted physical educator (CAPE) specializing in programming individualized fitness programs to meet the unique needs of students with disabilities. His research is focused on the attitudes and perceptions of including individuals with disabilities into a regular physical education environment grounded in planned behavior theory. He has authored more than 25 publications and has delivered more than 45 presentations to support his profession. He currently teaches an adapted physical education course as well as a course titled recreation and leisure services for individuals with disabilities. He also directs a community swim and gym physical activity program for individuals with disabilities. He received a master of science degree in education specializing in motor learning and sport psychology from the University of Kansas (1995), a PhD in adapted physical education from the University of Kansas (1998), and was a postdoctoral fellow at Juniper Gardens Children's Project, an affiliate of the University of Kansas (1999).
ORCiD: Casebolt | 0000-0002-6381-9887
Email: kcasebolt@esu.edu

Dr. Luis Columna, a native of San Juan Puerto Rico, is an associate professor in the kinesiology department at the University of Wisconsin at Madison. He teaches in the new Health Equity and Health Promotion Program. He received a master's degree in physical education from the InterAmerican University of Puerto Rico in 2003 and a PhD in kinesiology (adapted physical education) from Texas Woman's University. He joined the UW-Madison Kinesiology faculty in January 2019.

Prior to coming to Madison, he was associate professor at Syracuse University, New York. His research focuses on ways to increase the participation of families (especially Hispanic) of children with disabilities into physical activity and also his research focuses on ways to better prepare physical activity professionals and physical education teachers to work with diverse populations. To address the physical activity needs of children with disabilities and their parents, he developed the Fit Families program. Fit Families is a physical activity program that brings together children with disabilities (e.g., visual impairments, autism spectrum disorders), their parents, college students, and in-service professionals in the fields of adapted physical education, special educators, psychologist, physical education, and exercise science, among others.
ORCiD: Columna | 0000-0003-3586-3191
Email: lcolumna@wisc.edu

Wray Jean Connor, MS Ed, who contributed to Chapter 19, is an adapted physical education teacher in an Ohio public school. She developed a mentoring program unifying adapted physical education students with peers without disabilities in an environment where all students can thrive. She holds a teaching license in health/physical education and intervention specialist (K-12). She received her master's degree from Xavier University. Her teaching philosophy is built on the premise "All students have abilities." She was named the Ohio Adapted Physical Education teacher of the year for 2022 by the Ohio Association for Health, Physical Education, Recreation, and Dance.
Email: connorwr@lovelandschools.org

Andrew Corbett is a doctoral student in the Department of Kinesiology and Health at Georgia State University and works as an exercise physiologist at the Shepherd Center in Atlanta, Georgia. His research focus lies in adaptive sports and sport, exercise, and performance psychology. He is a certified strength and conditioning specialist (CSCS) with the National Strength and Conditioning Association and certified mental performance consultant (CMPC) with the Association for Applied Sport Psychology.
ORCiD: Corbett | 0000-0003-1066-9835
Email: acorbett9@student.gsu.edu

Ashley Fallaize is the manager of training and education at BlazeSports America. She graduated with her bachelor of science in exercise science from Georgia State University and her master of science in kinesiology from the University of Georgia. In her role at BlazeSports, Ashley oversees the BlazeSports Institute for Adaptive Sports and Recreation, which includes their national certification program among other training initiatives. She has extensive experience teaching and coaching adaptive sports, both recreation and competitive. In addition, she teaches part time at Georgia State University courses on disability sports and coaching. She is a certified adaptive recreation and sports specialist II, certified adapted aquatics instructor, and certified inclusive fitness trainer.
ORCiD: Fallaize | 002-5149-1386
Email: Ashley.fallaize@gmail.com

Dr. Justin A. Haegele is an associate professor and director of the Center for Movement, Health, and Disability in the Department of Human Movement Sciences at Old Dominion University, United States. His research focuses within the interdisciplinary field of adapted physical activity, with a primary interest in examining how individuals with disabilities, in particular those with visual impairments, experience physical activity participation. He is a research fellow with the Research Council of SHAPE, and associate editor for *Adapted Physical Activity Quarterly* and *editor of Quest*.
ORCiD: Haegele | 0000-0002-8580-4782
Email: jhaegele@odu.edu

Dr. Bethany L. Hersman is a Professor and Department Chair in the Kinesiology and Health Department at Wright State University, teaching courses for the Adapted Physical Education endorsement, Health and Physical Education, and Sports Science programs. She is also a Certified Adapted Physical Educator through the National Consortium for Physical Education for Individuals with Disabilities and an Autism Exercise Specialist as well as a Certified Inclusive Fitness Trainer, both through the American College of Sports Medicine. She received her undergraduate and master's degrees in Physical Education at West Virginia University and her PhD in Adapted Physical Education from The Ohio State University. She is the past editor for the International Journal for Kinesiology in Higher Education, and spends her free time volunteering for various sporting events for individuals with disabilities.
ORCiD: Hersman | 0000-0002-4532-0409
Email: Bethany.hersman@wright.edu

Dr. T.N. Kirk is an assistant professor in the Department of Kinesiology at the University of Georgia, United States. Her research interest lies in investigating the motivational beliefs and lived experiences of individuals with visual impairments in the context of

physical activity, exercise, and sport. Currently, she is investigating objectively measured physical activity engagement, motivational beliefs, and health-related quality of life of adults with visual impairments. She is also an instructor in judo and other grappling sports, skills she puts to use in developing judo programming for youth with visual impairments.
ORCiD: Kirk | 0000-0002-8663-5589
Email: tnk51820@uga.edu

Dr. Robert Kowalsky received his Ph.D. in Exercise Physiology in 2017 from the University of Pittsburgh. He is currently an assistant professor in the Department of Public Health and Exercise Science at Appalachian State University in Boone, North Carolina. Dr. Kowalsky's principal research interest is improving cardiometabolic health in individuals with a focus on sedentary behavior strategies to interrupt prolonged sitting. He has published articles in this area while working with various populations including the elderly, college students, and adults with various cardiometabolic and musculoskeletal issues. Additionally, he is investigating sedentary behavior strategies that are specifically designed for populations with various disabilities. He is an active member of ACSM and the American Heart Association (AHA) Council on Lifestyle and Cardiometabolic Health.
ORCiD: Kowalsky | 0000-0001-9571-8223
Email: kowalskyrj@appstate.edu

Dr. Byron Lai is an assistant professor in the Department of Pediatrics at the University of Alabama at Birmingham, within the Division of Pediatric Rehabilitation Medicine. His research interests focus on incorporating technology to provide enjoyable and accessible, evidence-based exercise programs for people with disabilities. His particular areas of interest include active video gaming, wearable monitoring devices, and therapeutic exercise with music.
ORCiD: Lai | 0000-0002-5464-4720
Email: byronlai@uab.edu

Dr. Jody Langdon is a professor in the Department of Health Sciences and Kinesiology at Georgia Southern University. Along with her experience as a physical education teacher and coach, she teaches courses in coaching education and exercise science. Her research interests include self-determined motivation in a variety of contexts and the role that coaches play in supporting the needs of their athletes.
ORCiD: Langdon | 0000-0002-5589-1694
Email: jlangdon@georgiasouthern.edu

Dr. Jihyun Lee is an associate professor in the Department of Kinesiology at San José State University. She is a research fellow with the Research Council of the Society of Health and Physical Educators America and also received the David P. Beaver Adapted Physical Activity Professional Young Scholar Award from the National Consortium for Physical Education for Individuals with Disabilities. Her research focuses on mechanisms underlying the effects of physical activity on holistic development of children with disabilities and use of physical activity to assist effective transition and social inclusion of postsecondary transition students with disabilities. She is an accomplished athlete herself and shares her love of sports by directing many community-based and university-based physical activity programs for individuals with disabilities.
ORCiD: Lee | 0000-0002-5574-124X
Email: jihyun.lee@sjsu.edu

Dr. Anthony J. Maher is a professor of special educational needs, disability and inclusion in the Carnegie School of Education at Leeds Beckett University, United Kingdom. His research, consultancy and teaching expertise relate to centering the experiences and amplifying the voices of disabled children and young people, as well as supporting key stakeholders in schools to provide valuable and meaningful experiences of education for those children and young people. His research is sociological, psychological, and pedagogical in nature, using participatory, life history, (auto)ethnographical, and narrative approaches. He is the author of numerous research papers, organizational reports, book chapters, and books, including *Teaching physical Education to Pupils With Special Educational Needs and Disabilities* by Routledge.
ORCiD: Maher | 0000-0002-1628-0962
Email: Anthony.Maher@leedsbeckett.ac.uk

Dr. Larken Marra received her PhD in kinesiology and adapted physical activity from the University of Michigan. Her primary research interest lies in motor development and physical activity for individuals with physical disabilities. She has spent most of her career coordinating community-based adapted movement programs designed to meet the motor and fitness needs of a diverse population of individuals with disabilities across a wide variety of ages (3–65 years). She is currently working with adults with cerebral palsy to better understand the lifelong physical activity behaviors in this population.
ORCiD: Marra | 0000-0001-5177-3546
Email: lrmarra@umich.edu

Dr. Cathy McKay is an associate professor in the kinesiology department at James Madison University. She completed her doctoral degree at the University of Virginia and is a research fellow with the Research Council of SHAPE America. Her scholarly interests focus on social inclusion, changing attitudes and perspectives toward disability, and parasport education and awareness. She is passionate about contact theory and applying contact theory in educational settings.
ORCiD: McKay | 002-1802-2641
Email: mckayca@jmu.edu

Dr. Scott W. T. McNamara is an assistant professor at the University of New Hampshire within the kinesiology department. His primary areas of research include adapted physical education, research dissemination, and online learning.
ORCiD: McNamara | 0000-0003-4459-8633
Email: scott.mcnamara@unh.edu

Dr. Anne Odusanya is the Children and Youth with Special Health Care Needs director and unit supervisor in the Division of Public Health within the Wisconsin Department of Health Services. Her areas of interests include public health research, training, and education regarding health equity and maternal and child health, with an emphasis on children and youth with special health care needs. Her work aims to identify and resolve barriers and facilitators to engagement in healthy eating, physical activity, and positive social interactions for children.
ORCiD: Odusanya | 0000-0001-8783-1568
Email: anne.odusanya@dhs.wisconsin.gov

Dr. Deborah Shapiro is a professor in the Department of Kinesiology and Health at Georgia State University, United States. Her primary research focus has been in psychosocial factors of sport participation among youth athletes with disabilities and professional preparation. She has received several awards for her scholarship and leadership in the field of adapted physical activity.
ORCiD: Shapiro | 0002-5933-2638
Email: dshapiro@gsu.edu

Dr. Nicholas Siekirk obtained his PhD from Wayne State University (Detroit, Michigan) and is an assistant professor of motor behavior in the Department of Health Sciences and Kinesiology at Georgia Southern University (Statesboro, Georgia). He is a certified strength and conditioning coach (CSCS) through the National Strength and Conditioning Association. His research is centered on the optimization of human movement in clinical and performance-based applications.
ORCiD: Siekirk | 0000-0002-8762-4419
Email: nsiekirk@georgiasouthern.edu

Dr. Heidi Stanish is an associate professor of exercise and health sciences at the University of Massachusetts Boston and adjunct faculty in family medicine and community health at UMass Medical School. She has expertise in adapted physical activity with particular specialization in exercise and fitness promotion among individuals with intellectual and developmental disabilities. Her research efforts focus on developing strategies to meet the unique physical activity needs of this population in order to promote successful lifelong participation in inclusive community settings.
ORCiD: Stanish | 0000-0001-6688-0109
Email: heidi.stanish@umb.edu

Myung Ha Sur is a clinical assistant professor in the department of physical education at the University of South Carolina. His research focuses on physical activity and health-related quality of life promotion for individuals with disabilities. Myung Ha's research uses theoretical foundations to understand personal and environmental factors influencing motivation and intentions to engage in physical activity among individuals with physical disabilities and intellectual impairments.
ORCiD: Sur | 0000-0003-3432-4620
Email: msur@mailbox.sc.edu

Dr. Karen Wonders is the founder and CEO of Maple Tree Cancer Alliance and professor of exercise physiology at Wright State University. Her passion is to advocate for exercise as part of the national standard of care for cancer. Maple Tree provides free exercise training to thousands of cancer survivors every month at 43 clinical locations across the United States as well as four locations in Brazil. Maple Tree has been awarded *Best in Dayton* for Health and Fitness 7 years in a row. Dr. Wonders is committed to evidence-based practice in her facilities and has a robust research program that has published two text books, four book chapters, and more than 70 peer-reviewed manuscripts on the topic of exercise and cancer recovery. A gifted communicator, she has given numerous professional presentations on the national, state, and local levels, including a talk at TEDxDayton on Exercising through Cancer Care.
ORCiD: Wonders | 0000-0003-3233-4091
Email: karen.wonders@wright.edu

PART 1
FOUNDATIONS

CHAPTER 1
INTRODUCTION AND HISTORY OF DISABILITY

Daniel J. Burt and Bethany L. Hersman

At some point in our lives, most of us will experience a form of a disabling condition, whether it is temporary or permanent.[1] Similarly, as our population continues to age, people will experience difficulties that affect everyday life for them, and while most may consider this part of the aging process, these difficulties can be referred to as disabilities. Depending on where one looks, there are different definitions of the term **disability**, but for the purposes of this book, we will use the World Health Organization's definition, which is an umbrella term encompassing three dimensions: impairments, activity limitations, and participation restrictions. Among the three dimensions, **impairment** refers to problems within the body structure or function, **activity limitations** refer to individuals having difficulty completing certain activities such as getting out of bed or walking, and **participation restrictions** refer to problems within everyday life, many times due to limited accessibility or attitudes/discrimination by others. Within this definition, "disability" results from the interaction of a person with a health condition or impairment and the environment and attitudinal barriers that will keep them from being an equal member of society.[1] In this manner, viewing disability as an interaction means it is not an attribute of the person, but instead is generated from inaccessibility, environmental factors, and attitudes of others.

Disability itself is very diverse; some people who have disabilities may experience activity limitations, have trouble learning, or major health concerns, while others with disabilities may have none of those things and have what may be considered a *hidden disability* that is not evident by merely looking at someone. To add to the diversity of disability, it is also important to remember that no two people with the *same* disability may have the *same* characteristics or tendencies, so a practitioner will need to individualize and create plans according to the individual and not the disability. Each person with a disability will demonstrate individual needs and abilities, so we cannot create a one-size-fits-all exercise, therapy, or educational program that will work for everyone. The different authors and contributors of this textbook come from a variety of backgrounds and lines of work, some medical, some education, others in research, to work toward raising awareness and support for those with disabilities. Going forward, we have chosen to use the word **practitioner** for describing those who work with individuals with disabilities in various physical activity and movement settings.

STATISTICS: WHAT'S IN THE NUMBERS?

According to the U.S. Census Bureau, the total population of people living in the world today is just over 7.8 billion.[2] The World Health Organization (WHO) estimates that within the world population, about 1 billion individuals have disabilities.[1] Within the United States, there are an estimated 61 million adults with disabilities, which equals out to about 1 in 4 adults experiencing some form of disability.[3] Students with disabilities in the United States ages 3 to 21 receiving special education services under the Individuals with Disabilities Education Act (IDEA) totaled 7.3 million (or 14% of all students in public

Danile J. Burt, Texas A&M University—Kingsville and Bethany L. Hersman, Wright State University. © Kendall Hunt Publishing.

TABLE 1.1. Ethnicity and Disability in the United States

Ethnicity	Adults (%)[7]	Students ages 3–21 (IDEA) (%)[6]	Students ages 3–21 (504) (%)[5]
American Indian/Alaska Native	31	18	0.8
Asian	10.1	7	1.6
Black	22.7	17	13.8
Hispanic	17.7	14	15.9
Native Hawaiian/Pacific Islander	17.9	11	0.3
White	21.5	15	65.0

school) in the 2019–2020 academic year. It is important to note, though, that this number does not include the number of students who have 504 plans, as there are also students with documented disabilities who either do not qualify under IDEA or who do qualify for IDEA, but do not need full Individualized Education Plans (IEPs), so the school may utilize 504 plans instead.[4] It is estimated that the total percentage of students who have 504 plans is about 1.5% of the total population of students in public schools.[5] These numbers do not include those students with documented disabilities who do not need special education services, for example, someone with spina bifida who does not require any educational modifications. When broken down into ethnicities, American Indian/Alaska Native adults are more likely to be identified as having disabilities, while Asians are the least likely to be identified as having disabilities for both students and adults.[6,7] For a more specific listing of adults and students (served under IDEA and 504 out of the total population of students with disabilities) with disabilities specific to ethnicity, please refer to Table 1.1.

AWARENESS, ACCESSIBILITY, AND COMMUNICATION

As you will see in Chapter 2, stereotypes and attitudes toward individuals with disabilities can have a negative effect on the inclusion of individuals with disabilities in various settings. In instances where society is uninformed and/or inexperienced regarding individuals with disabilities, barriers can be intentionally or unintentionally created that will make it harder for an individual with a disability to become a part of society. Therefore, it is our job to help teach and prepare others to work successfully with individuals with disabilities in the various physical activity fields. In many cases, practitioners only receive one college course related to disability and movement,

Disability rights.

which is not enough time or information to fully prepare someone to successfully work with people with disabilities. Ongoing education and professional development is important to help continue the learning opportunities for practitioners who will work with individuals with disabilities in sport, physical activity, fitness, therapy, recreation, or education settings.

Communication and Common Courtesies

In many cases, when speaking of individuals with disabilities, mentioning the fact that they have a disability is irrelevant to a conversation, and may not need to be mentioned at all. In some cases, however, it is important when discussing modifications or needs of the individual, and when it is relevant, use person-first language. **Person-first language** is referring to the individual first, and then mentioning the disability second (see Chapter 2 for an in-depth discussion on person-first language). For example, in speaking of someone who is blind, do not refer to them as a "blind person," but instead as a "person who is blind." For individuals who are Deaf, and in some cases with individuals with autism, a community and culture may have formed around the shared experience and they prefer to be called a Deaf person", utilizing an upper case D, or "autistic person" (see Chapters 17 and 14, respectively, for more discussion).

When speaking with individuals with disabilities, communication is extremely important, but remember that there are different ways to communicate with someone so an emphasis should be placed on learning how they communicate best and utilizing that form of communication when speaking to them. The following is a list of tips for speaking and working with individuals with different disabilities.

- Make eye contact when speaking to them.
- Gain their attention before speaking to someone who is deaf/hard of hearing, and speak to the individual rather than to their interpreter.
- Do not turn your back (e.g., to demonstrate a skill or write on a board) when speaking to someone who is Deaf/hard of hearing.
- Learn key signs in sign language that are appropriate to your setting to aid in communication, or use a sign language app to help you communicate with a Deaf person.
- Learn how to use various communication devices like a Picture Exchange Communication System if that is how the individual communicates.
- Greet a person the same way you would anyone else such as shaking their hand, or in the way that is appropriate to their culture (e.g., in some cultures it is not acceptable for a male to shake hands with a female).
- If someone is having trouble finishing a sentence, be patient and let them finish their sentence, do not finish it for them or pretend that you understand if you do not understand.
- Place yourself at eye level to someone in a wheelchair rather than looking down at them in conversation.
- When beginning a conversation with someone who is blind or visually impaired, make sure to introduce yourself to them so that they know who is talking to them, and let them know when you are leaving the conversation so that they are not left talking to someone who is not there.
- Avoid using words like "over there" or pointing when speaking to someone who is blind/visually impaired since they may not be able to clearly see what you are pointing at.
- Make sure to gain approval for physical guidance—do not simply walk up to them and start moving their body through activities.
- Ask an individual if they need help rather than assuming they need help and wait for them to respond before jumping in to help. If they say no, let them be independent.
- A wheelchair, walker, and other assistive devices such as prostheses are considered part of the individual's body, so do not touch their devices without asking first.
- Do not come up behind someone in a wheelchair and start pushing them without asking if they need help (Imagine how you would feel if someone came up behind you and started pushing you in the back).
- Offer choices for equipment and let them choose what equipment they want to use rather than handing them something that may not be appropriate for them.
- Treat individuals age appropriately—do not treat an adult like a child regardless of intellectual functioning.
- Do not assume they cannot participate in physical activity—once you learn their abilities and gain medical clearance, find activities that are appropriate for them.

Most importantly, remember to treat people the way THEY want to be treated, rather than assuming we know how they want to be treated and treating them the way WE think they want to be treated. Get to know the individual and their preferences and abilities, and it can make your experiences with them more beneficial to you both.

Universal Design

Originally a term used in architecture and referring to accessibility for individuals with disabilities, **Universal Design** refers to designing products, environments, activities, or lessons that are made to be used by all people without any need for extra adaptation or modification.[8] As a practitioner, it is important to keep Universal Design principles in mind when creating a workout, practice, activity session, or lesson plan for individuals with and without disabilities. Essentially, utilizing Universal Design means the practitioner needs to be the flexible one, not the individual with a disability.[9] This means the practitioner should design the activity session with all individuals who will be participating in mind, and not creating a single plan that expects all individuals to conform to that plan. Not everyone has the same capabilities, movements, and needs, so when creating a plan, keep in mind that each individual should be able to be

6 CHAPTER 1: Introduction and History of Disability

successful within the activities in the plan. It might mean adding in several layers to an activity or having multiple plans or equipment options, but everyone should be able to participate at their own level. This is especially important in settings that are created inherently for people without disabilities; we cannot expect every individual to be able to successfully participate in settings that were not created for them.

HISTORY, SOCIETY, AND LEGAL DEVELOPMENT

If asked how society should support those with disabilities, most would respond in a positive manner to help provide anything needed to care for and allow all individuals to thrive. However, in reading this text, you will quickly see that this has not been the perspective taken by various societies and cultures throughout history. Even in modern society, how individuals with disabilities are not only treated but also exploited and used for marketing will be seen further in Chapter 2. Some societies did revere those with disabilities, in fact, several African cultures believed disability was a blessing from a supernatural entity or god in exchange for protection from evil. However, many cultures, and a good many western cultures, instead engaged in abandonment or outright hostility and infanticide when handling individuals with disabilities.[10] This has occurred many times due to the view that there was no worth in individuals with disabilities from an economic standpoint, who increase the needs on a family or local town.[11] However, religious and philosophical considerations on the treatment of individuals in western culture cannot be ignored either. This was seen through Plato's connection that a broken body would logically lead to a broken spirit, or the centuries-long Greek and Roman fear that disabilities were a punishment or curse from the gods,

Religious healing of the infirmed.
Source: LOC.gov, G. Eric and Edith Matson Photograph Collection

requiring atonement or removal. This often led to infants being smothered, strangled, or left for dead in the forest, a practice that carried into Judeo-Christian Europe up to the 1500s.[12] Combine this with Biblical Old Testament references denoting that sin was the cause of disability, reinforced by the New Testament curing of disabilities of those often referred to as blind or afflicted, several thousands of years passed with little change to the views of those with disabilities.

The New World through the Industrial Revolution

While colonies were developed in the new world (Canada, the United States, and Mexico) during the 1600 and 1700s, few changes occurred in perspectives

Factories were notorious for mass injuries to the populace during the Industrial Revolution.
Source: From loc.gov, c. 1910.

of morality, religion, and the place of those with disabilities. However, medicine had begun to see some changes in respect to the function of society and philanthropists such as Benjamin Franklin, who helped establish a hospital in the 1750s to treat everyone regardless of their "affliction,"[12] and started to show interests in supporting medical advancement. The industrial revolution during the 1800s caused a push of changes producing doctors and hospitals as new needs occurred for the sake of capitalism and the new labor force. Some views toward disabilities began to move away from societal beliefs that disabilities happened as a result of religious or moral issues, because of the increase of disabilities acquired due to factory work. Factory work was extremely dangerous, and quickly created nonproductive laborers who needed to work, but could not due to injuries. However, this began to leave those who were disabled (either due to injury or from birth) and not able to work in these prevalent jobs without a way to fend for themselves, creating a massive economic and survival gap between those with disabilities and those without.[13] During this time, some form of worker's compensation and medical coverage for injury-related disabilities began to develop by individual state governments as a mediation between laborers and companies. This is an example of some of the first laws that related to disabilities in the United States. While economics were then driving the suppression of those with disabilities, several religious groups began to provide services and support to individuals with certain disabilities. Notably, schools and programs for the blind and Deaf began to spring up in the United States, the UK, and Europe. However, it is worth mentioning that although many facilities were built for individuals with intellectual disabilities and mental illness during this time, it was often followed by merciless experimentation, treatments, and degrading living conditions as the field of psychology was espoused and explored.[11]

When Science Replaced Religion

The late 1800s and early 1900s saw a fascination with Darwin's *Origin of Species*, and led a follower named Herbert Spencer, who is credited with the phrase/idea "Survival of the Fittest," to push forward a new idea of Social Darwinism. This was a very ethnocentric theory where people believed that those who were not successful and who were poor were this way due to being genetically incapable of succeeding in life, and it would be better to let them perish than support them through any aid programs, delaying the inevitable. It is worth noting that those encouraging many of these beliefs in Social Darwinism were white and of northern European descent and who only found success really in other white, northern-descendant individuals, setting up a very racially charged belief.[14] This saw an advocacy for the concept of eugenics, a belief that human kind can be improved through either selectively mating individuals, or preventing the capability to produce through sterilization. By denoting that those "poor and unfortunate individuals" would never prosper because they were believed to be genetically incapable to do so, and tying together poverty, disabilities, and criminal activity, many individual states in the United States and several European countries allowed laws to be passed on individuals deemed "likely unable" to change.[10] This practice continued into the 1920s and began to slow and lose support across many countries until the rise of the Nazis in Germany, who took the idea of Social Darwinism and began extreme extermination.

Modern Hope and the 1970s

While there was at least a move away from sterilizing individuals with disabilities and some disabilities had more recognition like vision and hearing impairments, individuals with intellectual disabilities and mental health issues still suffered greatly. For example, Dr. Walter Freeman performed a lobotomy with an ice pick as late as 1967, which resulted in his last patient dying from a brain hemorrhage.[15]

Danvers state hospital, believed to have inspired the horror-oriented Lovecraft's asylum and Batman's arkham asylum.

Source: wikimedia.org, circa 1893

However, activism had become powerful throughout the 1960s and minority groups had begun to push forward for recognition of human rights and ending discrimination, eventually securing the passing of the Civil Rights Act of 1964. The power of advocacy, and more noteworthy, that individuals with disabilities who were suffering discrimination the most were ethnic and cultural minorities, led to a push for the government to act. Additional lawsuits brought against government organizations, universities, and companies led to a push for recognizing the need for independent living and legally ending discrimination through Congress passing the Rehabilitation Act of 1973. Education was heavily informed by the additional passing of the 1975 Education for All Handicapped Children Act[16] and subsequent reauthorizations of this Act, the most recent being the Individuals with Disabilities Education Improvement Act (IDEIA) in 2004. This leads to Chapter 3 of this textbook and where modern law and legislation has come to be today.

THE CHAPTERS TO COME

The following chapters in this textbook were developed through discussions between industry professionals, faculty, students, and alumni on what topics needed to be expanded in adapted physical activity/education textbooks. In a world that is more aware today than even 20 years ago, many expressed an interest in expanding the concepts on awareness, philosophy, and understanding the issues facing those with disabilities and not just knowing the disability and its effect on motor movement. Interestingly, this along with increased options for job potential in working with those with disabilities was the highest request from students and alumni. The following chapters reflect this and are designed to meet the needs for those in the exercise sciences, physical education, rehabilitation, fitness, and therapy-related fields.

Chapter 2 is designed to heighten awareness to the larger, current societal issues faced by those with disabilities and the philosophical underpinnings that form them, introducing both positive and concerning ideas and models that are currently employed in all fields that work with those with disabilities.

Chapter 3 introduces the laws that protect individuals with disabilities, and although it does have an extensive focus on the United States, many countries have similar laws when it comes to discrimination and protection of those with disabilities. What is unique to the United States in the chapter is the coverage of laws that expand protection into the public and private school systems, and the specific, almost contractual, documentation that is required.

Chapter 4 breaks down the roles and opportunities for employment in this field. Often classes covering these areas focus on physical or occupational therapy, or utilizing the information in physical education, but there are a variety of job options that can be found.

Chapter 5 focuses on the field of therapeutic recreation and breaks down the specific and often overlooked opportunities that can be found to not only provide therapy but also provide a positive and meaningful experience. This chapter will note the components of therapeutic recreation and why it is unique to the therapy setting.

Chapter 6 looks into the issues of physical activity and exercise needed in general. Often when discussing those with disabilities, it is ignored that many of the individuals will die from chronic illnesses and not the disability themselves. Additionally, the high risk due to possible physical or social limitations on individuals with disabilities created a need to understand the physical needs of the human body in terms of movement.

Chapter 7 brings forward an understanding of exercise model design and programming that can be used for individuals with disabilities. Keeping limitations in mind, the chapter raises the awareness of the readers on how to adapt and alter programming instead of a one-size-fits-all approach.

Chapter 8 emphasizes how the human body not only grows and matures but also the current theories on how it develops and learns new skills. This provides the foundation of understanding the human body functions as we know so far, before the subsequent chapters discuss the disruption of expected development and learning.

Chapter 9 focuses on the importance of assessment that plays a role in understanding functional capability, therapy, and educational needs. An emphasis is placed on the different assessment types, as well as the different domains to measure, and motor development categories needing to be considered with popular assessments demonstrating the critical points needing to be covered.

Chapter 10 reviews the motor capabilities for those with disabilities in an organized setting. Additionally, it looks at the opportunities, coaching training, and the organizations that provide awareness and options with those who have disabilities participating in sports. The chapter also reviews the organizational design and function of the Paralympic sports.

Chapter 11 breaks down the concepts and importance of support systems to work with individuals with disabilities. It provides categorization, training, and communication recommendations for developing strong individuals to assist in aiding participation in activities and skill development.

Chapter 12 reviews chronic illnesses in detail and the unique challenges facing those with disabilities, denoting issues that face them across the life span and major health concerns that could arise, exacerbated by disabilities.

Chapter 13 reviews the causes and issues facing those with intellectual disabilities. The chapter reviews the categorization and functional issues surrounding the impairment, as well as recommendations to aid and support in educational, therapy, and fitness settings.

Chapter 14 reviews the causes and issues facing those with autism spectrum disorder. The chapter reviews the function of the spectrum and social/behavioral issues surrounding the impairment, as well as recommendations to aid and support in educational, therapy, and fitness settings.

Chapter 15 reviews the causes and issues facing those with psychological, behavioral, and learning disabilities. The chapter reviews the various causes and tendencies of individuals with these types of disabilities. The chapter also reviews different approaches to working with individuals with these disabilities with regard to treatment and behavior management and how these can affect movement in physical activity settings.

Chapter 16 reviews the causes and issues facing those with visual impairment. The chapter reviews the various visual categorization and functional and daily-life issues surrounding the impairment, as well as recommendations to aid and support in educational, therapy, and fitness settings.

Chapter 17 reviews the causes and issues facing those with deafness and/or hearing impairments. The chapter reviews the commonality of impairment, as well as the categorization and issues surrounding the impairment of living in a world with hearing limitations, and recommendations to aid and support in educational, therapy, and fitness settings.

Chapter 18 reviews the causes and issues facing those with orthopedic and neuromuscular disabilities. The chapter reviews a broad range of limitations that may be found in this area, from amputations, to dwarfism, to various disabilities that break down the ability for the muscular motor units and central nervous system to communicate. Functional issues and motor risk surrounding the impairment are discussed, as well as recommendations to aid and support in educational, therapy, and fitness settings.

Chapter 19 reviews the causes and issues facing those with spinal cord disabilities. The chapter reviews the complication associated with damage to the spinal cord and how it will alter not only motor movement but also the autonomic nervous system. Additional complications from spinal cord deviations and the functional complications surrounding the impairment are also covered. Recommendations to aid and support in educational, therapy, and fitness settings are provided.

Every one belongs.

REFERENCES

1. World Health Organization. (2011). *World report on disability.* https://www.who.int/publications/i/item/9789241564182
2. United States Census Bureau. (2021). *U.S. and world population clock.* https://www.census.gov/popclock/
3. Centers for Disease Control and Prevention. (2020). *Disability impacts all of us.* https://www.cdc.gov/ncbddd/disabilityandhealth/infographic-disability-impacts-all.html
4. U.S. Department of Education. (2020). *Protecting students with disabilities.* https://www2.ed.gov/about/offices/list/ocr/504faq.html
5. The Advocacy Institute. (n.d.). *Public school students overall and those served solely under Section 504 by race/ethnicity, students with disabilities served under IDEA, by state: School Year 2011-12.* https://www.advocacyinstitute.org/resources/Overall.504StudentsCRDC2012.pdf
6. National Center for Education Statistics. (n.d.). *Students with disabilities.* https://nces.ed.gov/programs/coe/pdf/2021/cgg_508c.pdf
7. Courtney-Long, E. A., Romano, S. D., Carroll, D. D., & Fox, M. H. (2017). Socioeconomic factors at the intersection of race and ethnicity influencing health risks for people with disabilities. *Journal of Racial and Ethnic Health Disparities, 4*(2), 213–222.
8. Wing, C. (2012). *ACSM/NCHPAD resources for the inclusive fitness trainer.* American College of Sports Medicine.
9. Lieberman, L. L., Grenier, M., Brian, A., & Arndt, K. (2021). *Universal design for learning in physical education.* Human Kinetics.
10. Gallagher, H. G. (1995). *By trust betrayed: Patients, physicians, and the license to kill in the Third Reich* (rev. ed.). Vandamere.
11. Gostin, L. O. (2008). "Old" and "new" institutions for persons with mental illness: Treatment, punishment or preventive confinement?. *Journal of the Royal Institute of Public Health, 122,* 906–913.
12. Marini, I., Graf, N., & Millington, M. (2017). *Psychosocial aspects of disability: Insider perspectives and strategies for counselors* (2nd ed.). Springer Publishing Co.
13. Turner, D. M. (2006). Introduction: Approaching anomalous bodies. In D. M. Turner & K. Stagg (Eds.), *Social histories of disability in deformity* (pp. 1–16). Routledge.
14. Alemdaroglu, A. (2006). Eugenics, modernity and nationalism. In D. M. Turner & K. Stagg (Eds.), *Social histories of disability in deformity* (pp. 126–141). Routledge.
15. NPR (2005, November 16). 'My Lobotomy': Howard Dully's Journey. *All Things Considered Podcast.*
16. Wright, P., & Wright, P. (2007). *Special education law* (2nd ed.). Hartford House Law Press.

CHAPTER 2
PHILOSOPHICAL AND SOCIAL CONSIDERATIONS

Justin A. Haegele

INTRODUCTION

Adapted physical activity is a service delivery profession, focused on promoting active lifestyles and sport participation that is influenced by a cross-disciplinary body of practical and theoretical knowledge directed toward impairments and participation in physical activity. Given its cross-disciplinary nature, practitioners in adapted physical activity are influenced by a variety of philosophical and social considerations when making decisions about how to provide service for individuals with disabilities, what services to provide, and reasons why to provide them. In this chapter, I provide brief reviews of several philosophical and social considerations that practitioners in adapted physical activity should be mindful of when making decisions about practices. These considerations will span content pertaining to ethics, different understandings of what disability is, disability language use, ableism, intersectionality and inspiration porn, and inclusion. This chapter is not meant to be all-encompassing, and does not include all areas of philosophical or social thinking that practitioners should engage in when considering their practice. Rather, I provide pointed conversations about each of these aspects to help alert practitioners about considerations that should be made when considering, constructing, and implementing adapted physical activity practices.

ETHICAL THINKING AND PRACTICE IN ADAPTED PHYSICAL ACTIVITY

Ethics is a branch of philosophy concerned with how we should decide what is morally wrong and what is morally right. As an academic discipline, ethics tries to understand the reasoning behind moral life by analyzing the ways in which people think about and justify choices within particular situations.[1] In the field of adapted physical activity, ethical thinking, decision making, and practice must take into consideration a variety of complicated issues, including personal beliefs, potentially conflicting expectations, and organizational philosophies and complexities.[2] In this section, I will briefly engage with four ethical theories identified by Goodwin and Rossow-Kimball[3] that provide avenues for considering questions of what is morally right and morally wrong, and what is good and bad for the field: principilism, virtue ethics, ethics of care, and relational ethics.

The concept of **principlism** is derived from the field of biomedical ethics, and suggests that principles can be used to generate particular rules that are used to make moral judgments. The four principles that are associated with principlism are nonmaleficence (i.e., doing no harm and protecting others from harm), beneficence (i.e., helping others), autonomy (i.e., allowing others to choose freely and

---

Justin A. Haegele, Old Dominion University. © Kendall Hunt Publishing Company.

also accepting responsibility for choices), and justice (i.e., all persons are of equal moral worth and are to be treated fairly). While principlism appears to provide a simple framework or blueprint on how practitioners can understand what is morally right and wrong, it has also been questioned as perhaps being overly simplistic. For example, Clouser and Gert[4] suggest that

> At best, 'principles' operate primarily as checklists naming issues worth remembering when considering a biomedical moral issue. At worst 'principles' obscure and confuse moral reasoning by their failure to be guidelines and by their eclectic and unsystematic use of moral theory. (p. 220)

Goodwin and Rossow-Kimball[3] also criticized principlism, considering it a normalized framework that is distant from the everyday ethical issues that practitioners in adapted physical activity experience. As such, practitioners should reflect on their personal philosophical positions, and strongly consider whether relying on a predetermined checklist or recipe book for all situations is morally and ethically aligned with their philosophic position when engaging in this brand of moral reasoning.

It is logical to suggest that those working within the field of adapted physical activity are guided by ethical thinking. As noted by Goodwin,[5] "most practitioners and researchers in the area of adapted physical activity would think of themselves as motivated by good intentions, honest and caring, and as such adhere to core ethical dispositions that guide their daily and professional activities" (p. 173). This thinking is well aligned with the concept of **virtue ethics**, which is based on the idea that good people will make good decisions, and ethical behavior is what good or virtuous people do. It should be noted, though, that being virtuous is only virtuous if benefits received by the person being virtuous are also enjoyed by the person being helped.[3] As such, the good intentions held by practitioners and researchers in adapted physical activity are not enough to ensure that professional behavior is ethical. Rather, problematic outcomes, such as the creation of a false dichotomy between the benevolent and virtuous practitioner, and the vulnerable client or learner, can create services that unintentionally marginalize and exclude.[2] A false dichotomy is a logical fallacy, where a situation is presented as being an "either/or" option, when in reality, there are more than one choice available.

In this scenario, predefined roles (e.g., vulnerable client) are presented without the possibility of other roles (e.g., benevolent client, capable client) existing for each of the individuals involved. With that, although one may think they are acting virtuously, there can be consequences of help if it has a negative outcome for the person, such as denying independence, or if the help only benefits the person helping (that is, the belief that one is helpful because they help without caring if the help is desired).

The third ethical theory, **ethics of care**, emerged as a feminist alternative to the generally male dominated principlism. The defining attributes of ethics of care are care, involvement and maintaining harmonious relations, contextual and need-centered nature, and communicative rationality. According to Goodwin and Rossow-Kimball,[3] ethics of care is similar to virtue ethics, with a point of departure being a shift in care ethics from inner character (i.e., virtues) to relational qualities such as attunement. That is, ethics of care suggests that good practitioners are those who are attuned to a context and are skillful in intervening in ways that are responsive to the learner's interests and needs. Like other ethical theories, ethics of care is not without criticism. For example, ethics of care is characterized by a unidirectional nature where professionals are valorized as caregivers, and caring is always considered "to be good." The perspective that caring is always good is challenging, though, as the quality of care and fit of the offered care to the needed care are not considered within this theory. This is an important consideration within adapted physical activity, as practitioners cannot assume that what they are providing, while perhaps caring, is beneficial to the recipient within engaging and developing a personal relationship with those receiving the care.

A common theme in scholarship about ethics in adapted physical activity is a call for reflection on practice and increased reflexivity among professionals.[6] This, as mentioned earlier, should include engaging in critical conversations with clients or learners who are on the receiving end of practitioners' care or instruction. Highly related to this call is the final ethical theory, **relational ethics.** Relational ethics as an ethical theory centers on seeking to understand how people live in the world together in relationships with one another. This ethical theory places a high value on building relationships and contextually informing actions. As such, ethical moments become possible when people connect with one another and create a relational space of trust and authenticity.[3] Relational ethics has four components (a) engagement, which refers to being connected with one another, (b) mutual respect, which refers to an interdependent relationship between people while having respect for one another, (c) embodiment, which acknowledges that people live in specific social contexts, and (d) environment, which is created by everyday actions and is a space where ethical reflection can occur. Taken together, and according to Goodwin and Ebert,[7] "people come to understand their obligation and responsibility to themselves (service providers) and users (parents and children)" (p. 346) within physical activity contexts.

This section provided a brief overview of four different ethical theories and the importance they may have for practitioners within the field of adapted physical activity. Readers should keep in mind that this section is not intended to overly criticize any of these theories in favor of one or the other, but rather to provide a (very) brief overview for readers to consider the theories, and the way in which they approach ethical and moral decisions, on their own. Readers are strongly encouraged to engage with the writing of Donna Goodwin, who has contributed a considerable amount of literature to ethical considerations in thinking, research, and practice in adapted physical activity.

DISABILITY DISCOURSES

Over time, the meaning of disability has been understood in a variety of ways.[8,9] For example, early conceptualizations of disability were framed in religious discourses with the beliefs of Western Judeo-Christian society.[10] Within this conceptualization, disability was considered to be a product or act of a higher being and disability itself was viewed as an opportunity for miracles. This perspective toward disability was largely supplanted as religious leaders were replaced by doctors or scientists as the cognitive authority in developing societal perceptions and curing procedures.[10] In this context, a **cognitive authority** is a professional organization or collection of individuals who have the social power or capital to establish definitions in society and are key gatekeepers over knowledge in a particular field. As such, when authority over knowledge shifts between groups or individuals, societal knowledge and thinking can shift along with it. Like this religious discourse, several other disability models have undergone alterations or have been rejected due to perceptions of narrow-mindedness or prejudice as we, a society, progress with our thinking of what disability is.[11,12]

There is now an increasing variety of ways to conceptualize disability, and these various viewpoints have implications for individuals with disabilities, service providers, and society at large.[9,12,13] These conceptualizations provide frameworks for understanding disability that influence how society, including service providers in physical activity and exercise spaces, interact with and think about those with disabilities. For example, a service provider's orientation toward disability can influence (1) their expectations and interactions with persons with disabilities, (2) what is prioritized during activities, (3) the type and quality of instructions that service-providers provide, (4) the language used when discussing disability, and (5) what is considered competent in physical activity environments.[9,14,15]

In this section, I will outline three models of disability that are among the more dominant discourses internationally: the medical model, the social model, and the social relational model. In doing so, I will compare, contrast, and critique each of the models, and provide examples of how these various models can influence the way in which exercise, physical activity, or physical education practitioners interact with persons with disabilities. It is not my intention to suggest that one model represents "good practice" while others represent "bad practice," but rather to provide characteristics and information about these models and describe how those situating their beliefs in one of these perspectives view and interact with persons with disabilities.

Medical Model

The medical model of disability discourse emerged when doctors and scientists replaced religious leaders as the cognitive authority in society.[10,15] According to Brittain,[16] this role in society was gained when the medical field demonstrated the ability to define illnesses as well as heal injuries and cure illness. Because members of the medical community work from a biological perspective, they conceptualize disability as largely a biological product.[15,16] That is, in the medical model, disability is defined as a medical problem that resides in the individual as a defect, or failure, of a body system that is abnormal and pathological.[17] In this lens, disability is thought of as an individual phenomenon that results in limited functioning that is viewed as a problem or deficient.[8,18]

The medical model is strongly normative, meaning people are considered disabled on the basis that they are unable to function as a "normal person" would.[19] That is, the limitations associated with having a disability are largely viewed as a product of the impairment. Said another way, the medical model suggests that there is something inherently disabling about impairments, and that challenges faced by individuals with disabilities are independent of wider sociocultural, physical, or political environments.[16] Because disability is "caused" by parts of the body that are "abnormal," disability therefore should be "fixed" by psychological or medical interventions.[9] As such, this model aligns disability with the "sick role," where similar to ill health, disability is viewed as a problem that needs to be medically cured so that individuals can function "normally" within society.[12,15] Thus, to reduce disability, and therefore gain function and independence, one must eradicate the cause of or "fix" one's impairment. In instances where disabilities cannot be eliminated or "fixed," people with disabilities are often viewed as pitiful, helpless, or in need of help or charity.[19]

Historically, the medical model has underpinned many aspects of research and practice in adapted physical activity contexts. That is, a medical model understanding of disability influences language used in adapted physical activity contexts (e.g., individuals with special needs), as well as what types of interventions, and goals of those interventions, are favored or prioritized. Similarly, the medical model is characterized by a heavy reliance on medical professionals as being important gatekeepers who can restrict or provide access to resources or benefits. This is relevant in adapted physical activity contexts, which are often only offered when individuals have specific diagnoses. That is, adapted physical activity services (e.g., adapted physical education) are generally only available to those who present a medical diagnosis, therefore centralizing the role of medical professionals as gatekeepers to those services. This is one of the major criticisms of the medical model, where medical personnel seldom take into consideration what an individual wants or values, and rather tend to make decisions based on a psychological or physiological limitation.

Another issue with the medical model is the persistence of negative stereotypic beliefs about disabilities,[20] which is evident because disability is discussed as a deficit model.[18] For example, according to Haslett and Smith,[9] "the [medical] model relies on bio-physical assumptions of 'normality', and, in doing so, creates a problematic normal/abnormal binary: the disabled (not normal) become 'defective' and lose power and the able (normal) gain power" (p. 50). This language often influences how individuals interact with and talk about people with disabilities, including in sport contexts. For example, potential athletes with disabilities may find that their dreams and aspirations of being high level athletes may be mocked or disregarded by others because those without disabilities may believe that competitive sport is not something that individuals with disabilities are capable of. These conceptualizations may be attributed to the deficit-based definitions, language, and perceptions established by the medical model of disability discourse.

Social Model

The social model of disability discourse is often presented as a juxtaposition to the medical model (considered by some to be the "old" model). While the social model has been popular in academic circles for a number of years, language associated with this model is still being debated and the model itself has not gained universal acceptance.[21] To this effect, Mitra[18] identified nine different versions of the social model (see Figure 2.1). Similarities in these discourses exist in relation to defining and discussing disabilities. As such, in this chapter we will speak in general terms about the "social model," rather than explain small differences across the various models.

Versions of the Social Model for Disability Discourse

The Social Model of the United Kingdom

The Oppressed Minority Model

The Social Constructionist version of the United States

The Impairment Version

The Independent Living Version

The Postmodern Version

The Continuum Version

The Human Variation Version

The Discrimination Version

FIGURE 2.1. Versions of the social model for disability discourse (adapted from Mitra[18])

According to the social model, limitations associated with disability are not thought of as a product of impairment. Rather, social model advocates suggest that it is society that imposes disability on individuals with impairments.[22,23] It is important to note that the terms disability and impairment are considered separate within the social model. **Impairment** is perceived as an abnormality of the body, such as a restriction or malfunction of a limb.[24] On the other hand, **disability** is considered to be the disadvantages that are caused by social institutions that do not take into account people who have impairments and exclude them from community life.[25] This distinction is important to keep in mind, as advocates for the social model contest that there is nothing inherently disabling about having an impairment, rather, disability is imposed in addition to impairments by the way individuals with impairments are excluded from fully participating in their community. Exclusion and social isolation can both be a product of society's inability, unwillingness, or neglect to remove barriers encountered by those with disabilities or the perceptions toward individuals as being less able.[12,23]

The social model of disability discourse suggests that impairment should be considered as a form of diversity that offers a unique perspective which should be valued and celebrated.[19] Rather than attempting to "fix" individuals with disabilities, advocates of the social model assert that solutions should be directed toward society. The social model claims that with social change, having an impairment would not substantially reduce one's well-being, and that many problems typically associated with disability may disappear if people's attitudes toward individuals with disabilities would change. The overarching message of the social model is a call to move society from one that discriminates against those with impairments, to one of social inclusion.[23]

Like the medical model, there are also a number of critiques of the social model in the literature.[15] One notable critique is related to the social model's attempt to separate impairment from disability completely, which, according to Palmer and Harley,[23] does not fully account for the lived experiences of those with disabilities. That is, it appears that the social model fails to address impairment as an observable attribute of the individual. The social model has also been criticized for not accounting for differences between and among people with disabilities. Highlighting this, Fitzgerald[8] noted that the social model ignores intersectionality of different forms of oppressed states.

The concept of intersectionality is discussed in more depth later in this chapter, but this critique would suggest that the social model, in and of itself, does not lend itself well to understanding the experiences of an individual with a disability independently of other attributes, such as gender, race, or sexual orientation. A final notable critique of the social model is that, while problems associated with disability are identified to be within the minds of able-bodied individuals in the social model, others suggest that these problems may be located within practices in society. That is, discriminatory practices and policies that favor able-bodied individuals, and are unfavorable to individuals with disabilities are systematically embedded into the structures of society in the form of norms.[26] As such, changing attitudes or views toward disabilities isn't as simple as changing one's attitude, but rather changes must occur at the societal level.

Social-Relational Model

To date, the medical and social models of disability appear to have gained the most attention in kinesiology scholarship and practice. While there are many additional models of disability discourse,[9] one that has been identified as a conceptually progressive model that has emerged from criticisms of both the medical and social models is the social-relational model.[27] Within the social-relational model, impairments are considered to have direct and immediate effects that can simultaneously occur with socially engendered structural or attitudinal restrictions. Said another way, those subscribing to the social-relational model suggest that disability is something that is imposed on top of restrictions that are caused by one's impairment.[28,29] That is, as described by Martin,[30]

> According to the social-relational model of disability, restrictions of activity such as [physical activity] can be caused by social reasons (e.g. discrimination) and by impairments (e.g. lack of sight). Additionally, in different situations and different moments in time people's ability to engage in [physical activity] can be influenced by a host of different factors reflective of elements of medical and social model disability. (p. 2031)

As such, unlike the social and medical models, the social-relational model stresses the effects of both one's impairment as well as the social or structural limitations brought on by society.

According to the social-relational model, there are a number of social contexts in which the experience of disability can arise.[17,31] These can include restrictions that arise from (a) immediate everyday physical and social influences of impairments, (b) negative experiences of social/cultural ideas or attitudes toward disability, (c) structural disablism, which is being physically excluded from environments, opportunities, or services, or (d) self-imposition, when one's well-being is undermined by themselves.[31] The last context, self-imposition, is likely a result of *psycho-emotional oppression*, a form of social oppression that arises directly from negative social interactions between able-bodied persons and persons with disabilities.[31] Psycho-emotional oppression can either be indirect, which can include the psycho-emotional consequences of experiences with exclusion from opportunities, or direct, which constitute the consequences of explicit discriminatory negative social interactions. There are numerous examples of direct psycho-emotional disablism within literature that discuss persons with disabilities' experiences in integrated physical activity contexts, including experiences with marginalization, othering, and bullying by peers and teachers.[32] To note, **othering** is a term used to describe when some individuals or groups (e.g., persons with disabilities) are defined and labeled as not "fitting in" within the norms of a social group, such as a group of peers in a physical education class. This line of inquiry has exposed that ableism is likely embedded within the sociocultural fabric of these integrated contexts, and that although individuals with disabilities exist in the same pedagogical spaces as their peers without disabilities, they are experiencing these contexts in quite different ways.[33] Readers are encouraged to read more about this phenomenon later in this chapter, when integrated placements and inclusion as a subjective experience are discussed. These findings have practical implications, where practitioners must not assume that they are providing high-quality instruction, but rather must engage in dialogue with persons with disabilities as the experiential experts to understand the impact of decisions about how services are provided.

LANGUAGE

The language that we use to describe persons with disabilities reflects our beliefs about those with disabilities. As such, it is likely not surprising that disability models, like the medical, social, and social-relational models, have implications for the way we describe persons with disabilities. This section is dedicated to providing a brief overview of language related considerations when discussing disability. Regardless of the terminology that service providers and practitioners believe is the "correct" way to speak with and about persons with disabilities, they should first engage in critical and open discussions with members of that community to understand their values and positions. That is, as noted by Spencer and colleagues,[34] we have a responsibility to represent participants and communities using the words and descriptions they choose, with their consent. Readers are strongly encouraged to review seminal work by Peers and colleagues[35] to further familiarize themselves with disability-related language considerations.

Perhaps the most commonly recommended way to describe those with disabilities in the United States, and elsewhere, is **person-first language**. Person-first disability language (e.g., person with a disability) was popularized in the 1970s, 1980s, and 1990s, and is largely associated with the rights-based approach to disability activism. Using person-first terminology is intended to prioritize a person as a human being first, and impairment is considered to be one, of many, attributes of the person.[34] As such, person-first language is intuitive, where the term identifying the person is placed before the term identifying the disability. Examples can include student with a visual impairment, adult with autism spectrum disorder, and individual with cerebral palsy. It should be noted that, while commonly promoted in the United States, not all disability communities ascribe to person-first language. Highlighting this, Spencer and colleagues[34] note that arguments have been made that person-first language "reproduces the idea that disability is a characteristic of an individual (i.e., of the person *with* a disability) rather than something socially imposed, and also that it doesn't match other identitiarian languages (e.g., we do not say 'a person with femaleness')" (p. 135). Further consideration should be taken with groups, such as deaf/Deaf communities, who do not identify themselves without a disability rights framework, as noted later.

It is also important to note that person-first language is easily conflated with, and mistaken for, language associated with the medical model of disability. Medical model language generally centers on a specific diagnosis as a defining characteristic of a person (e.g., person with macular degeneration) and revolves around differences based on what is considered normal, acceptable, and valued compared to what is viewed as abnormal, unacceptable, or devalued.[34,35] An added feature of language rooted in the medical model is the ability–disability dichotomy, where comparative terms (e.g., average, or typically developing) are used to describe and compare persons with disabilities to nondisabled individuals. Comparisons like these, where persons are judged against normative standards, can be stigmatizing and harmful, and reinforces the view that disability is an undesirable difference to be corrected or eradicated.[35]

The most common alternative to person-first language comes from the social model of disability, where *disabled person* is used to refer to individuals who are oppressed by social barriers (that is, they are disabled by society). Said another way, in the social model, individuals do not *have* disabilities, but rather societies' activity *disable* people.[35] Those ascribing to the social model, and using disability first language, should keep in mind the conceptual distinction between an impairment and disability. As noted previously in this chapter, impairment is perceived as an abnormality of the body, such as a restriction or malfunction of a limb,[24] whereas disability is considered to be the disadvantages that are caused by social institutions that do not take into account people who have impairments and exclude them from community life.[25] Within this line of thinking, those using language associated with the social model may also select *person with an impairment* or *person experiencing disability*, although those two language terms are far less commonplace.

When considering language, practitioners and service providers must also be aware that there are communities that do not identify within any disability model, and therefore the language used within those models may be incongruent within that specific community. One notable example are Deaf people, where the capital D signifies membership in a cultural-linguistic group (see Chapter 17 for a discussion), that has deeply valuable languages and world-views, but does not identify as being disabled (although, those ascribing to the medical model may think otherwise). Other communities, such as autistic or neurodivergent individuals, have recently reclaimed impairment-related terminology that represent meaningful aspects of their identity (see Chapter 14 for a discussion).[34] According to Spencer and colleagues,[34] "such terms frame the ways their minds work as neutral or positive human variations, and frame their social and medical treatment as forms of oppression, eugenics, and genocide" (p. 137). That is, the reclamation of autism-related terminology is aligned with the idea that autism should not be considered as a detrimental feature of the human experience, but rather differences associated with autism are considered as positive, or neutral, features. In addition, autistic and neurodivergent individuals tend to disagree with the perceived need for research exploring the causes of autism, or services looking to reduce characteristics of autism, and rather seek for society to embrace and appreciate their unique particularities.

In addition to considerations regarding language about people with disabilities, service providers must also be cognizant of the way in which they use language to discuss exercise, physical activity, and exercise for persons with disabilities. In a recent editorial for the *British Journal of Sports Medicine*, Brett Smith and colleagues[36] made a call for inclusive messaging by providing recommendations for exercise and sedentary behaviors for persons with disabilities. Within this narrative, Smith and colleagues identified a litany of catchy exercise-related quotes that have ableist undertones, which included messages like "sit less, move more," "stand up, sit less," "chairs are killers," and "swap sitting for moving." While likely unintentional, these statements and others like these can create a perception of inability among those with disabilities, and can be stigmatizing, alienating, or excluding to those who don't meet these bodily standards (e.g., wheelchair users). Smith and colleagues recommend reconsidering some of these popular motivational quotes that may communicate messages consistent with the ability–disability dichotomy, which may also make them simpler. For example, rather than "sit less, move more," a more inclusive message may be simply, "move more."

ABLEISM AND INTERSECTIONALITY

Ableism is a form of prejudice and discrimination in which nondisabled people are viewed as superior or "normal" and people with disabilities are viewed as inferior or "abnormal."[36] Like sexism, racism, or heterosexism, ableism classifies an entire group of people as "less than." Ableism is inherent to legal, normative, educational, ethical, and political practices that are those associated with the promotion of persons without disabilities, and social demotion of those who do not fit normative ideologies.[37] That is, an ableist society treats people without disabilities as the standard (or as "normal"), which results in public places (such as sport, physical activity, and recreation facilities) that are built to serve standard people, inherently excluding those with disabilities. Ableism is largely rooted in the medical model of disability, in that people with disabilities require fixing and people are defined by their disability. That is, those with disabilities are viewed as needing to be changed (or to change themselves) in order to fit an existing society.

Ableism can be direct, indirect, or systemic. **Direct ableism** is both conscious and oppressive in nature. For example, the eugenics movement of the early 1900s or the mass murder of people with disabilities in Nazi Germany, would be considered extreme forms of direct ableism. Less extreme forms of direct ableism may include asking unnecessary invasive questions about personal life or medical history, or restricting participation in certain activities simply based on a disability diagnosis. This type of ableism is highly related to **asshole ableism**, a term used by the website *disabilitythinking.com*, which describes when people without disabilities purposely and maliciously dehumanize people with disabilities. Some examples include (1) feeling as though having to "deal with" people with disabilities is an inconvenience, (2) complaining that people with disabilities receive too many benefits or special privileges, (3) suspecting those with disabilities are "faking it" to get special attention, or (4) overprotecting or sheltering youth with disabilities. The final example, overprotection or sheltering youth with disabilities, is associated with the concept of **dignity of risk**, which suggests that youth with disabilities should not be prevented from opportunities to participate in activities, including sport or physical activities, because they are "risky," as taking away this option for risk devalues their human dignity.[38] **Indirect ableism**, which may also be labeled as ignorant or well-meaning ableism, is unconscious behavior that is not intended to cause harm. This may take the form of using verbal expressions that communicate a negative slight or insult in relation to someone's disability. For example, expressions such as "I'm really OCD about this," "You're acting bi-polar," or "You are so retarded" represent phrases that communicate that disability is a negative problem to be fixed and are rooted in ableism. **Systemic ableism**, or **institutional ableism**, is deeply rooted into our social structure as a result of centuries of misunderstanding and active discrimination against persons with disabilities. This form of ableism includes physical barriers, laws, and practices that restrict freedom and equality of persons with disabilities, as well as the ongoing failure of people to fix these issues. Like other forms of systemic prejudice, systemic ableism is often unnoticed and unquestioned by people without disabilities.

Ableism and the prejudice that it fosters against individuals with disabilities does not take shape independent of other forms of oppression, such as racism, sexism, and/or classism. The conceptual framework of **intersectionality** provides a lens through which we can understand how various differences among people with disabilities (e.g., racial, ethnic, cultural, gender differences) interact to influence experiences within society. The concept of intersectionality was developed by Black feminist scholars in the 1970s and 1980s who challenged mainstream feminists to think about how being a woman, and the oppression associated with being a woman, might "intersect" with being Black, and experiences of racism.[39,40] The term intersectionality is typically credited to the writing of critical race theorist Kimberlee Crenshaw,[39] who developed the concept to demonstrate how race/ethnicity, social class, disability, and gender/sex are not mutually exclusive and independent. Rather, intersectionality provides a tool that considers the meaning and consequences of membership in multiple social group categories, which includes providing a summary of the effects of multiple categories of difference.[41] As such, this framework suggests that inequalities are not the result of a single factor, but rather are "the result of intersections of dissimilar social locations, previous experiences, hierarchies, and power relations"[42] (p. 224). The concept of intersectionality has clear and important implications for practitioners and service providers in sport and physical activity contexts. That is, practitioners must not think of persons with disabilities through a monolithic lens as solely "a person with a disability," but rather in understanding that each of the identities that an individual with a disability has can be acting upon their experiences in important and varying ways. For example, Azzarito[43] explained that within the context of physical education that "ethnic minoritized students identified as having disabilities might not face only ableism as a unitary form of oppression; instead, they may occupy varying sites of oppression in school and, thus, must face and negotiate multiple disadvantaging factors" (p. 259).

INSPIRATION PORN

Inspiration porn is a relatively new concept in the disability studies literature.[44,45] Typically credited to Stella Young, the late comedian and former teacher with osteogenesis imperfecta, **inspiration porn** is a meme, video, or feel-good article that sensationalizes people with disabilities, particularly for audiences of those without disabilities in order to inspire.[46] More specifically, Grue[47] defined inspiration porn as having three components.

> Inspiration porn is a) an image of a person with visible signs of impairment who is b) performing a physical activity, preferably displaying signs of physical prowess, and is c) accompanied by a caption that directs the viewer to be inspired by the image in question. (p. 2)

Chief among the problems associated with inspiration porn is that images like this depict persons with disabilities in a way that objectifies them, devalues their experiences, and mystifies their place in the world.[47] Images deemed to be inspiration porn are rooted in ableism, and leverage images of persons with disabilities to "inspire" those without disabilities. While the opposite argument could be made, that positive depictions of person with disabilities is a good thing in and of itself, but this argument would ignore the substantial amount of work exploring how ostensibly positive portrayals of marginalized groups, like those with disabilities, contribute to that marginalization.

Unsurprisingly, images considered to be inspiration porn have gained negative attention from disability rights advocates and scholars. This phenomenon is articulated by Martin,[45] who describes that

> Inspiration porn is viewed negatively by many people, especially individuals with disabilities, because it is seen as co-opting a disabled persons' impairment and as objectifying because the person is equated with his or her disability. The purpose of the image is to inspire able-bodied individuals by giving them perspective by encouraging them to feel better by thinking "at least I am not as bad off as that person in a wheelchair." (p. 199)

Images like these are disappointingly common in sport, exercise, and physical activity contexts, and are regularly used by service providers to attempt to motivate learners. That is, a quick Google search of "inspiration porn" returns a variety of images of athletes with disabilities, including young children and elite athletes, with phrases such as "the only disability in life is a bad attitude," "your excuse is invalid," or "so … what's your excuse again?" These images, undoubtedly, are intended to motivate persons without disabilities to exercise or train harder, by objectifying persons with disabilities in images of them "overcoming" disability. Service providers in these spaces must be aware of the images they are using when attempting to motivate learners, and must understand that despite the intentions of their use of these images to motivate, there are hidden and unnoticed consequences of leveraging images of persons with disabilities to motivate. The author of this chapter would encourage readers to refrain from utilizing images like these, because, as noted by Stella Young, "I'm not your inspiration, thank you very much."

INCLUSION AND INTEGRATION

Within sport, physical activity, and physical education scholarship, the term *inclusion* is used in a variety of different ways, oftentimes without explicit or clear definitions or conceptualizations of what it means.[48-50] This is problematic, as without providing clarity on the term's use, *inclusion* can be interpreted in a variety of different ways, which can ultimately affect the way in which practitioners decide to provide services, and the sport, physical activity, and physical education experiences of individuals with disabilities. This has been exemplified throughout the adapted physical activity literature, where several scholars have identified that *inclusion* is commonly mistaken for a physical space or setting whereby individuals with disabilities are expected to *fit into* existing activities without regard for their experiences within those settings.[48] As such, many sport and physical activity programs are advertised as being "inclusive" but merely pay lip service to the prospect of "inclusion" while simply enrolling individuals with and without disabilities together.

Recent years have seen a movement toward the differential utilization of the terms *integration* and *inclusion* to help reduce clarity around what *inclusion* means.[48] According to Haegele and colleagues,[48,51,52] the term **integration** should be used to describe a physical place or space in which individuals with and without disabilities receive services together. That is, *integration* (and not *inclusion*) is the physical location where the service is being provided. On the other hand, adapted physical activity scholars have begun to conceptualize *inclusion* by centering the experiences of individuals with disabilities, rather than referring to government or organizational policy and practices. That is, **inclusion** should be conceptualized as a subjective experience of individuals with disabilities that fosters feelings of belonging, acceptance, and value. This conceptualization is an emerging trend in the field of adapted physical activity[48,53] that is well aligned with calls to amplify the voices of individuals with disabilities about their subjective experiences[54] as well as the "nothing about us, without us" movement that emphasizes the importance of empowering individuals with disabilities through centering their experiences when constructing experiences.[55] Within this conceptualization, *inclusion* extends beyond an individual's physical presence within a context, space, or activity to consider the individual's experience within that space. As such, the feelings that individuals with disabilities experience within the space are more valued, within this conceptualization of *inclusion* than the perceptions of service providers, who act as a conduit to providing experiences that may, or may not, facilitate feelings of inclusion.

There are a number of important implications for practice that can be derived from these conceptualizations of *integration* and *inclusion*. First, and foremost, receiving services within integrated contexts does not guarantee that individuals with disabilities will experience *inclusion*. In fact, it is reasonable to suggest that many policies and practices intended to promote service delivery in integrated contexts may, unintentionally, create forms of exclusion at the individual level.[56] This has been highlighted specifically in the physical education literature, where although individuals with disabilities are likely to be enrolled in integrated placements, their experiences in those placements appear to be riddled with marginalization, bullying, and exclusion.[32,33] Relatedly, since inclusion is conceptualized as a subjective experience, feelings associated with inclusion (acceptance, belonging, and being valued) can be available in any host of settings. That is, *integration* is not necessary for *inclusion*. Rather, individuals with disabilities can experience a sense of belonging, acceptance, and value within homogenous groups of persons with disabilities who participate in adapted sports together as well as those settings that have persons with and without disabilities participating together. Finally, I would argue that observational methods, such as "inclusion" checklists or predetermined "inclusive" strategies, have no place in understanding the inclusiveness of contexts or settings. Rather, it is more likely that these types of materials deprioritize the voices of individuals with disabilities in favor of creating simple boxes to check so that practitioners can create the "illusion of inclusion." As such, utilizing any observational method or rating scale to measure the inclusiveness of a program or experience would be incongruent with what *inclusion* means. Rather, practitioners should be encouraged to engage in active conversations with individuals with disabilities to guide service delivery. That is, rather than making a priori decisions about program features and expecting those with disabilities to fit into those programs, practitioners should move away from these practices and place the voices of individuals with disabilities at the center of their decision making.

CHAPTER SUMMARY

- Ethics is a branch of philosophy concerned with how we should decide what is morally wrong and what is morally right.
- In the medical model of disability discourse, disability is defined as a medical problem that reside in the individual as a defect, or failure, of a body system that is abnormal and pathological.[1] In this lens, disability is thought of as an individual phenomenon that results in limited functioning that is viewed as a problem or deficient.
- In the social model of disability discourse, impairment is perceived as an abnormality of the body, such as a restriction or malfunction of a limb, whereas disability is considered to be the disadvantages that are caused by social institutions that do not take into account people who have impairments and exclude them from community life.
- Whereas person-first terminology may be the most recommended way to address individuals with disabilities in the United States, it is not the only appropriate way to do so. Practitioners should reflect upon their philosophical orientation toward disability, as well as

- cultural particularities concerning disability, when choosing language preferences.
- Ableism a is a form of prejudice and discrimination in which nondisabled people are viewed as superior or "normal" and people with disabilities are viewed as inferior or "abnormal."
- Inspiration porn is a meme, video, or feel-good article that sensationalizes people with disabilities, particularly for audiences of those without disabilities in order to inspire.
- Inclusion is a subjective experience of individuals with disabilities that foster feelings of belonging, acceptance, and value, whereas integration is the physical space where those with and without disabilities exist together.
- To ensure that experiences are inclusive, practitioners should center their decision making on the voices of individuals with disabilities by actively communicating with them about their experiences.

WEB RESOURCES

Stella Young's TED Talk about Inclusion Porn
https://www.ted.com/talks/stella_young_i_m_not_your_inspiration_thank_you_very_much?language=en

DISABILITY THINKING

https://disabilitythinking.com/
What's New in Adapted Physical Education Podcast | This podcast includes several episodes about inclusion and disability models that are relevant to this chapter.
http://mrmcnamaras.blogspot.com/

BOOKS AND PRINTED MATERIALS

Goodley, D. (2016). *Disability studies: An interdisciplinary introduction.* Sage

Haegele, J. A., Hodge, S. R., & Shapiro, D. R. (2020). *Routledge handbook of adapted physical education.* Routledge.

Martin, J. J. (2018). *Handbook of disability sport & exercise psychology.* Oxford.

REFERENCES

1. Reiss, M. (2010). Ethical thinking. In A. Jones, A. McKim, & M. Reiss (Eds). *Ethics in the science and technology classroom: A new approach to teaching and learning.* (pp. 7–15). Sense Publishers.
2. Goodwin, D. L., & Howe, P. D. (2016). Framing cross-cultural ethical practice in adapt(ive) physical activity. *Quest, 68*(1), 43–54.
3. Goodwin, D. L., & Rossow-Kimball, B. (2012). Thinking ethically about professional practice in adapted physical activity. *Adapted Physical Activity Quarterly, 29,* 295–309.
4. Clouser, K. D., & Gert, B. (1990). A critique of principlism. *The Journal of Medicine and Philosophy, 15,* 219–236.
5. Goodwin, D. L. (2008). Self-regulated dependency: Ethical reflections on interdependence and help in adapted physical activity. *Sport, Ethics, & Philosophy, 2*(2), 172–184. https://www.doi.org/10.1080/17511320802223477
6. Standal, O. F., & Rugseth, G. (2016). Experience, intersubjectivity, and reflection: A human science perspective on preparation of future professionals in adaptive physical activity. *Quest, 68*(1), 29–42.
7. Goodwin, D. L., & Ebert, A. (2018). Physical activity for disabled youth: Hidden parental labor. *Adapted Physical Activity Quarterly, 35*(4), 342–360.
8. Fitzgerald, H. (2006). Disability and physical education. In D. Kirk, D. MacDonald, & M. O'Sullivan (Eds.), *The handbook of physical education* (pp. 752–766). SAGE Publications.
9. Haslett, D., & Smith, B. (2020). Viewpoints toward disability: Conceptualizing disability in adapted physical education. In J. A. Haegele, S. R. Hodge, and D. R. Shapiro, *Routledge Handbook in Adapted Physical Education* (pp. 48–64). Routledge.
10. Humpage, L. (2007). Models of disability, work and welfare in Australia. *Social Policy & Administration, 41*(3), 215–231.
11. Donoghue, C. (2003). Challenging the authority of the medical definition of disability: An analysis of the resistance to the social constructionist paradigm. *Disability & Society, 18*(2), 199–208.
12. LoBianco, A. F., & Sheppard-Jones, K. (2008). Perceptions of disability as related to medical and social factors. *Journal of Applied Social Psychology, 37*(1), 1–13.
13. Watson, N., & Vehmes, S. (2020). Disability studies: Into the multidisciplinary future. In N. Watson and S. Vehmes, *Routledge Handbook of Disability Studies* (pp. 3–13). Routledge.
14. Barton, L. (2009). Disability, physical education and sport: Some critical observations and questions. In H. Fitzgerald (Ed.), *Disability and your sport* (pp. 39–50). Routledge Publishing.
15. Haegele, J. A., & Hodge, S. R. (2016). Disability discourse: Overview and critiques of the medical and

16. Brittain, I. (2004). Perceptions of disability and their impact upon involvement in sport for people with disabilities at all levels. *Journal of Sport & Social Issues, 28*, 429–452. https://www.doi.org/10.1177/0193723504268729
17. Goodley, D. (2016). *Disability studies: An interdisciplinary introduction.* SAGE.
18. Mitra, S. (2006). The capability approach and disability. *Journal of Disability Policy Studies, 16*(4), 236–247.
19. Roush, S. E., & Sharby, N. (2011). Disability reconsidered: The paradox of physical therapy. *Physical Therapy, 91*(12), 1715–1757.
20. Smith, B., & Bundon, A. (2018). Disability models: Explaining and understanding disability sport in different ways. In I. Brittain (Ed.), *The Palgrave handbook of Paralympic studies* (pp. 15–34). Palgrave Macmillan.
21. Barney, K. (2012). Disability simulations: Using the social model of disability to update an experiential educational practice imprint. *SCHOLE: A Journal of Leisure Studies and Recreation Education, 27*(1), 1–11.
22. Coles, J. (2001). The social model of disability: What does it mean for practice in services for people with learning difficulties? *Disability & Society, 16*(4), 501–510.
23. Palmer, M., & Harley, D. (2012). Models and measurement in disability: An international review. *Health Policy and Planning, 27*(5), 357–364. https://www.doi.org/10.1093/heapol/czr047\
24. Forhan, M. (2009). An analysis of disability models and the application of the ICF to obesity. *Disability and Rehabilitation, 31*(16), 1382–1388.
25. Goodley, D. (2001). Learning difficulties, the social model of disability and impairment: Challenging epistemologies. *Disability & Society, 16*(2), 207–231.
26. Oliver, M., & Barnes, C. (2012). *The new politics of disablement.* Palgrave Macmillan.
27. Thomas, C. (2007). *Sociologies of disability, "impairment", and chronic illness: Ideas in disability studies and medical sociology.* Palgrave
28. Reindal, S. M. (2008). A social relational model of disability: a theoretical framework for special needs education? *European Journal of Special Needs Education, 23*(2), 135–146.
29. Reindal, S. M. (2009). Disability, capability, and special education: Towards a capability-based theory. *European Journal of Special Needs Education, 24*(2), 155–168.
30. Martin, J. J. (2013). Benefits and barriers to physical activity for individuals with disabilities: A social-relational model of disability perspective. *Disability and Rehabilitation, 35*(24), 2030–2037.
31. Haslett, D., Fitzpatrick, B., & Breslin, G. (2017). The psychological influences on participation in wheelchair rugby: A social relational model of disability. *AUC Kinanthropologica, 53*(1), 60–78.
32. Holland, K., & Haegele, J.A. (2021). Perspectives of students with disabilities toward physical education: A review update 2014-2019. *Kinesiology Review, 10*(1), 78–87. https://www.doi.org/10.1123/kr.2020-002
33. Haegele, J. A., Hodge, S. R., Zhu, X., Holland, S. K., & Wilson, W. J. (2020). Understanding the inclusiveness of integrated physical education from the perspectives of adults with visual impairments. *Adapted Physical Activity Quarterly, 37*(2), 141–159.
34. Spencer, N. L. I., Peers, D., & Eales, L. (2020). Disability language in adapted physical education: What is the story? In J. A. Haegele, S. R. Hodge, and D. R. Shapiro, *Routledge Handbook in Adapted Physical Education* (pp. 131–144). Routledge.
35. Peers, D., Spencer-Cavaliere, N., & Eales, L. (2014). Say what you mean: Rethinking disability language in Adapted Physical Activity Quarterly. *Adapted Physical Activity Quarterly, 31*, 265–282.
36. Smith, B., Mallick, K., Monforte, J., & Foster, C. (2021). Disability, the communication of physical activity and sedentary behaviour, and ableism: A call for inclusive message. *British Journal of Sports Medicine.* https://www.doi.org/10.1136/bjsports-2020-103780
37. Campbell, F. K. (2009). *Contours of ableism: Territories, objects, disability, and desire.* Palgrave Macmillan.
38. Ball, L., Lieberman, L. J., & Haibach-Beach, P. (2021). Dignity of risk in physical education for students with visual impairments. *EC Ophthalmology, 12*(3), 2021.
39. Crenshaw, K. (1989). Demarginalizing the intersection of race and sex: A Black feminist critique of antidiscrimination doctrine, feminist theory and antiracist politics. *The University of Chicago Legal Forum, 140*, 139–167.
40. Crenshaw, K. (1991). Mapping the margins: Intersectionality, identity politics, and violence against women of color. *Stanford Law Review, 43*(6), 1241–1299.
41. Cole, E. R. (2009). Intersectionality and research in psychology. *The American Psychologist, 64*(3), 170–180.
42. Dagkas, S. (2016). Problematizing social justice in health pedagogy and youth sport: Intersectionality of race, ethnicity, and class. *Research Quarterly for Exercise and Sport, 87*(3), 221–229.
43. Azzarito, L. (2020). Re-thinking disability and adapted physical education: An intersectionality perspective. In J. A. Haegele, S. R. Hodge, and D. R. Shapiro, *Routledge Handbook in Adapted Physical Education* (pp. 252–265). Routledge.
44. Martin, J. J. (2018). *Handbook of disability sport & exercise psychology.* Oxford.
45. Martin, J. J. (2019). Mastery and belonging or inspiration porn and bullying: special populations in youth sport. *Kinesiology Review, 8*(3), 195–203.

46. Darrow, A.-A., & Hairston, M. (2016). Inspiration porn: A qualitative analysis of comments on musicians with disabilities found on international YouTube posts. *Proceedings of the 21st International Seminar of the ISME Commission on Special Music Education and Music Therapy*. International Society for Music Education.
47. Grue, J. (2016). The problem with inspiration porn: A tentative definition and provisional critique. *Disability & Society, 31*, 838–849.
48. Haegele, J. A. (2019). Inclusion illusion: Questioning the inclusiveness of integrated physical education. *Quest, 71*(4), 387–397. https://www.doi.org/10.1080/00336297.2019.1602547
49. Spencer-Cavaliere, N., Thai, J., & Kinsley, B. (2017). A part of and apart from sport: Practitioners' experiences coaching in segregated youth sport. *Social Inclusion, 5*(2), 120–129.
50. Smith, A. (2004). The inclusion of pupils with special educational needs in secondary school physical education. *Physical Education & Sport Pedagogy, 9*(1), 37–54.
51. Haegele, J. A., & Maher, A. (2021). Autistic youth experiences of belonging in integrated physical education. *Autism*.
52. Haegele, J. A., Kirk, T. N., Holland, S. K., & Zhu, X. (2020). 'The rest of the time I would just stand there and look stupid': Access in integrated physical education among adults with visual impairments. *Sport, Education & Society*. https://www.doi.org/10.1080/13573322.2020.1805425
53. Spencer-Cavaliere, N., & Watkinson, E. J. (2010). Inclusion understood from the perspectives of children with disability. *Adapted Physical Activity Quarterly, 27*(4), 275–29. https://www.doi.org/10.1123/apaq.27.4.275.
    Pellicano, E., Dinsmore, A., & Charman, T. (2014). What should autism research focus upon? Community views and priorities from the United Kingdom. *Autism, 18*(7), 756–770. https://www.doi.org/10.1177/1362361314529627
54. Charlton, J. I. (2000). *Nothing about us, without us: Disability oppression and empowerment*. University of California Press.
55. Slee, R. (2018). *Inclusive education isn't dead, it just smells funny*. Routledge.

CHAPTER 3
LEGAL ISSUES AND DISABILITIES

Daniel J. Burt

WHY KNOW THE LEGAL ISSUES?

There is a long history of how disabilities have been addressed, including in the United States, as covered in Chapter 1. However, the law has changed extensively over the past century, especially in protection of active discrimination and an increase in activism and equality. While it is illegal now to engage in most forms of blatant discrimination against someone with a disability, passive and systematic discrimination does occur and can be seen in the legislative changes occurring progressively and not revolutionarily in a single legal victory.

The reason it is important for readers of this textbook to know this is knowing it is first and foremost for their students, clients, participants, or patients. They should be a priority and knowing the law will not only help keep them safe but will also help ensure you protect yourself from liability risk and lawsuits. In the United States, civil lawsuits can easily be filed, it does not mean they will stand up in court, but it puts a lot of stress and financial burden on the individual involved. Additionally, a priority needs to be made because it is the law. While civil lawsuits from other people are definitely a concern, so is violating federal law in which you will have to answer for. Even though there may not have been an intent to disobey the law, since it is the law, you are expected to know the law and are held responsible for following it.[1] An example can be seen in if you pass a speed limit sign without seeing it and are now going too fast; this is not an excuse if you get pulled over. You are still responsible for the speed you were going and whether or not you knew the legal speed limit.

EARLY LEGISLATION IN THE UNITED STATES

Just as World War I was ending, the implementation of the Smith–Hughes Act of 1917 of Congress denotes the shift away from the concept of social Darwinism in the United States. As noted in Chapter 1, increased concern was facing an industrial labor force that had high injury, and therefore high disability rates. The Smith–Hughes Act provided federal funding to allow vocational training to be provided for laborers and workers who had become displaced from their employment for one reason or another. It quickly helped veterans who were returning from war with disabilities and were unable to readily find work without some tradecraft skill or knowledge.[1] This act was not about disabilities specifically, but the ability to return people to economically capable individuals in society became a prime point. The issue of returning veterans and their high rate of acquired disabilities was formally recognized with the passing of the Soldier's Rehabilitation Act of 1918 to specifically address specialized vocational training for those returning from the war with disabilities, and emphasis on the same idea for civilians born, or who acquired disabilities, occurred in the Smith–Fess Act of 1920. While many of the societal views and interviews done during this time recorded by newspapers were ones of pity and the need to be protective of those who might be in need, there was now at least a positive developing attitude toward individuals with disabilities, especially when associated with veterans.[2]

Daniel J. Burt, Texas A&M University-Kingsville. © Kendall Hunt Publishing.

World War II had a profound effect on the views of individuals with disabilities, along with continued advances in the medical sciences, specifically orthopedics and spinal cord complications. The war caused millions of regularly employed laborers to leave the country and created a massive labor demand in the country for factory work. This provided an opportunity for hiring those with disabilities, who were often passed over as hiring options. While this did not continue once the war ended, it is worth noting that again the individuals showed they were economically capable of being tax paying members of society. The Barden–La Follette Act of 1943 and the Vocational Rehabilitation Act Amendments of 1954 begun to extend services to those with mental illnesses opening additional rehabilitation and vocational services. In 1968, the Architectural Barriers Act was put into place, requiring that all federal buildings, or buildings designed, built, or leased with federal dollars be accessible. It also established the international accessibility symbol be used in all public buildings.[3]

Veteran learning vocational skills like sewing.

REHABILITATION ACT OF 1973

One of the most historic and altering legislative pieces for individuals with disabilities, the Rehabilitation Act of 1973, won support through tireless activism and the Civil and Women's Rights movements. The primary focus worth noting on the bill was under Title V and in Sections 501-504. Section 501 attempted to end discrimination found in hiring or promoting in the public sector. The private sector was also limited if they received federal funding of $2,500 or above in Section 503, however, most private entities did not use federal funds. Section 502 created a compliance board to review and enforce the Architectural Barriers Act. Section 504 focused on equality and reducing discrimination in specific industries like health care, housing, and education. It is worth noting that entities are required to make reasonable accommodations to meet these standards; however, if they are deemed unreasonable or causes undue hardship, than they are legally not required to comply with the request. However, the law is broad in its original formation and case law through lawsuits has built an understanding about how it applies to various situations over the decades. The primary reason for legal noncompliance is typically costs being too high for an individual or business to be able to afford making the changes.[4]

AMERICANS WITH DISABILITIES ACT (ADA) OF 1990

Almost two decades later, another landmark legislation was passed after increased activism and with significant support and input from the disability community. It is often considered the primary human and civil rights act in bringing equality to those with disabilities, especially with Congress acknowledging the amount of discrimination and continued segregation suffered by those with disabilities. It is worth noting that Congress acknowledged that not only was this a suppressed minority group, but that with few exceptions like WWII, continuing to not create support structures for individuals with disabilities would cost the United States billions in economic dollars. Research provided for the preparation of the legislative bill denoted that there were 43 million Americans with known disabilities at the time, and the population was living longer, meaning the number was expected to continue to grow as people aged. This law did have a lot of pushback from businesses and corporations who worried over the cost to stay compliant for these requirements. However, on July 1, 1990 the Americans with Disabilities Act was signed by President George H. W. Bush.[4]

TITLES OF THE AMERICAN DISABILITIES ACT

There are five guiding titles, or codes of law that are classifications covered under ADA. The titles did well to assist ending broad holes that were left uncharted in previous legislation over disabilities. However, these titles are written broadly, and the advancement of time and technology do cause them to have to be reconsidered in how they sometimes apply in the modern era. Without legislation being reviewed and updated, it often falls to lawsuits to challenge their meaning in areas that are not clearly stated.

Title I Employment provided protection from the public sector into the privately owned sector by noting that any employer or company with 15 or more employees may not engage in any behaviors that would be considered discriminating in the hiring/firing process. Examples of this can be seen in the types of questions that can be asked in an interview, and employers must consider reasonable accommodation in terms of a disability, or if they are actively affiliated with someone who has a disability, such as having a child with a disability at home. Reasonable accommodations in this case often refer to allowing some flexibility in scheduling and potential assistive technology, like screen reader software or a specialized chair. However, a request cannot be made of the employer for excessive absences, technology, or equipment of great expense such that it creates undue hardship, or restructuring of the job so much that it no longer resembles the job that the person was originally hired for.

Title II State/Local Governmental Entities and Transportation is a focus on individuals with disabilities having equal opportunities in all local or state government programs. This is an adjustment from previous legislation that said only the federal government may have control of discrimination of those with disabilities. This extends to preventing discrimination regarding state aid programs, policies, and communication of information. Additionally, it specifically references the need for public transportation to be accessible. This is due to a number of important rights tied to transportation, like buying food at the grocery store or the ability to vote. This is only excused if the governmental entity can show that they would not be able to financially support the cost, and thereby, it would then be considered unreasonable.

Title III Public Accommodations denotes that many public and commercially opened facilities, as in locations that serve the public, are run by private individuals and groups. The title emphasizes that businesses must make reasonable modifications and minimum following of ADA standards to provide those with disabilities the same experiences as those without disabilities. This is reflected often in places like as stadiums, gyms, and stores. Notably it is usually present in the emphasis of Accessible Design (the idea that access is created for normative access, this has been replaced with a focus on Universal Design in recent years), specifically the creation of access for all if a new building, or the renovation of an older building. It is worth noting that the ADA designs were updated from 1991 to 2010, and that is what the existing building standards are held to when they are being renovated.[5]

Title IV Telecommunications formed the telecommunication relay service to specifically allow individuals who are Deaf, hard of hearing, struggle with speech, or who are deaf-blind. This allows communication assistance operators or some automated speech-recognizing programs to use accessible phone services without additional cost. Examples could be using text-based software to translate and the operator or software would then interpret for the person on the other side and vice versa. While this is still offered as a public service so all have access, the adoption of cell phones and texting, as well as many companies utilizing chat-based programs have limited the number of individuals who take advantage of it. However, it needs to be remembered that this is a free service and plenty of individuals do not have or cannot afford cell phones and computers to access chat services with companies.[6]

Title V Misc. Provisions allows for some protection and service considerations in provisions that were not covered in the previous titles. Additionally, it provides protections for whistleblowing on those who report discrimination, and prevent businesses or government entities from coercing or retaliating against individuals from reporting.[5]

Part of the Americans with Disabilities Act is providing access through a variety of ways, including access ramps, seen here.

AMERICANS WITH DISABILITIES AMENDMENTS ACT (ADAA) OF 2008

Numerous lawsuits have tried to guide decisions and create legal clarity over the five titles of the ADA over the period of several decades. This includes issues like how many accessible rooms should be in a hotel, should an international cruise ship be required to be accessible, and how various sport applications work to meet equality for those with disabilities.

WORKFORCE INNOVATION AND OPPORTUNITY ACT (WIOA, PL 113-128) OF 2014

While it did not activate until 2016, this act signed into law by President Obama took the Vocational Rehabilitation Program that assists individuals with disabilities in receiving job assistance and preparedness, as well as counseling services and placed it all into one organization to streamline the process. However, previous to this law, most of the services had been required to be provided by specialized and educationally relevant individuals, typically individuals with master's degrees with emphasis in counseling, disabilities, and social support. Under the previous legal design, all employed in the program were required to understand and know the nature of how a disability might affect working in various environments. In the new legislation, specialties are no longer required, the education requirement was reduced to a bachelor's degree with a specialty in anything now allowed, including fields not necessarily relevant, such as Marketing.[7]

EARLY LEGISLATION OVER EDUCATION

Education has had a long and fraught history for any minority group in the United States, and individuals with disabilities are no exception. Multiple lawsuits, and eventual legislation, have assisted to create equality, but moving beyond the spirit of the law and what duties are owed by the school to the student in actual related services and functional capability through modifications and accommodations, has been accomplished by numerous legal challenges

Disability sport.

and lawsuits. As mentioned previously some schools were specifically developed for individuals who were blind, deaf, and who had intellectual disabilities, but they were rare and had minimum impact on the population with disabilities at large. Noteworthy cases to know tend to begin with the U.S. Supreme Court case *Brown v. the Board of Education (1954)*. Prior to the case, *Plessy v. Ferguson (1896)* is how most public schools functioned, with the concept "separate but equal" historically meaning that African American children were educated in a segregated environment, but the education value would be the same. *Brown* highlighted that this was not the case; while there was certainly segregation, there was not equality in materials, instruction, and access. This case and its emphasis on minorities being segregated and lack of equality led to more legislation and lawsuits being brought by parents of individuals with disabilities. Congressional legislation created the Elementary and Secondary Education Act (1965), and it held an emphasis on creating federal resources to assist in helping disadvantaged students receive a quality education. Two lawsuits stand out when discussing early educational law and disabilities. The first is the *Pennsylvania Assn. for Retarded Citizens v. Commonwealth of Pennsylvania (1971)*, known often as PARC, where a lawsuit was brought on behalf of students with intellectual disabilities. While a settlement was eventually reached, it included the need for parents to be able to participate and a due process to be established and occur if the parents disagrees with the decisions made by the school district. The second is the *Mills v. Board of Education of District of Columbia (1972)*, known often as *Mills,* this legal case focused on the removing, suspending, and exclusion of students with disabilities. Schools relied heavily on the cost factors associated with educating individuals with disabilities as the primary defense against the suit. This is the time that Congress decided to investigate the economic ramifications of individuals with disabilities and found that the cost with creating individuals dependent on the government would cost billions of dollars, which could be better spent on creating educational opportunities for meaningful and economically beneficial lives. This led to the Congressional action of Public Law 94-142: The Education for All Handicapped Children Act.[8]

INDIVIDUALS WITH DISABILITIES EDUCATION ACT (IDEA)

With previous Congressional action highlighting the needs of minorities, along with findings on economic outcomes and increased activism and lawsuits, Public Law 94-142: The Education for All Handicapped Children Act (1975) was approved. Its primary function was to note that education was a right for those with disabilities and that educational agencies at the state and local level should be held responsible for educating individuals with disabilities. This law has been updated and reauthorized several times with major revisions occurring in the Individuals with Disabilities Education Act (1990) and the Individuals with Disabilities Education Improvement Act (2004) to help with clarification on school district responsibility, parental and student protections, use of funds, and eligibility. Typically, the law and its reauthorizations are known as IDEA. IDEA defined the concept of Special Education, referring to the modification or adaptation of skills, knowledge delivery, or curriculum for individuals who differ mentally, socially, physically, or behaviorally to the point it inhibits their educational learning. An example of this applying in this chapter would be Physical Education, which is directly impacted by IDEA as it is curriculum. Major components can be seen in the broad concepts known as Child Find, Free and Appropriate Public Education (FAPE), and Least Restrictive Environment (LRE). **Child Find** is the requirement that schools have a duty to locate, identify, and evaluate all children with disabilities. This includes children who may be in private or charter schools, homeschooled, or even homeless. This makes the reporting of suspected disabilities paramount for schools so that they know which students to evaluate and consider if they may or may not have a disability. **Free and Appropriate Public Education (FAPE)** focuses on the idea that if states and local educational agencies are going to continue to receive federal funding then they must guarantee that students are provided an opportunity for not only a free education but also one that is appropriate for their needs to match all students being provided for. This concept includes students with disabilities who have been suspended or expelled. The concept of **Least Restrictive Environment (LRE)** mandates that schools keep students with disabilities together and educated with those who do not have disabilities to the maximum extent appropriate, based on learning disruption for the student with disabilities and those learning around them. Often called mainstreaming, only when disability severity is high enough and/or other related services are needed is it recommended to change the placement of a student with disability away from their peers. Instead, expectations are for the use of modifications and accommodations so that students with disabilities may remain in the classroom to create as close to an equitable experience as possible and for the improved social and emotional interaction with peers. Additionally, the law provided the opportunity for *parental participation* as part of the IEP team. While the school may move forward with the IEP if a parent chooses to not participate, the parent, and the concerns they express, are to be addressed and considered to be a priority during an IEP meeting. It also established **procedural safeguards,** creating guidelines so that parents and the students with disabilities have a right to notice of meetings, ability to review documentation at any time, and a due process to resolve complaints or disagreements, as well as file mediation with the state. The legislation also emphasized the right to an **appropriate evaluation**, this means that a student with disabilities has the right to an evaluation over their potential disability and how it may affect their educational capability. This is required to be done by a qualified individual in the relevant field. This has been an area of some contention and the case for several legal battles since some school districts have taken positions that an elementary teacher would be qualified to know if handwriting deficiencies exist since they teach the grade, instead of having an occupational therapist evaluate it. It should come as no surprise that often these occurrences happen when a district is choosing to not evaluate. Additionally, districts have been known to accept the rationale that a student has a specific disability as a reason to skip performing an evaluation (since they just decided to agree the disability exists); however, this is merely trying to step around the intent of the law from Congress. Evaluations do more than denote a disability exists, they are key components in identifying deficiencies and helping aid in creating appropriate recommendations for accommodating those deficiencies. This allows for optimal success in the classroom, and not merely performing the minimum effort. The final major point of legislation is the requirement of an **Individualized Education Plan (IEP)** a written legal document, developed

Photograph of a school historically known as a School for the Crippled before *inclusion* became a policy.
Source: ca. 1909. Photograph. https://www.loc.gov/item/2002711180/.

by an IEP team, which draws upon existing evaluation information in order to meet a student's unique educational needs. The written IEP should contain information related to the student's present levels of educational performance and evaluations, planned annual goals and measurable benchmarking objectives, related services and supplementary aids to be received (transportation, counseling services, rehabilitation, physical or occupational therapy, etc.), and should include a detailed explanation of instances where a student is not participating in the general classroom and is instead receiving services or coursework elsewhere, how often, and the rationale for this to occur.[8]

Qualifying Categories for Special Education

In qualifying for special education according to IDEA, the IEP team must determine that a child has a disability in one of 13 categories, listed below; however, several are not easily determined and continue to be reviewed by the Department of Education, releasing recommendations in their "Dear Colleague" letters. It also must be demonstrated that the disability itself adversely affects the student's learning and educational components.

- Autism spectrum disorder
- Deaf-blindness
- Deafness
- Emotional disturbance
- Hearing impairment
- Intellectual disability
- Multiple disabilities
- Orthopedic impairment
- Other health impairment
- Specific learning disability
- Speech or language impairment
- Traumatic brain injury
- Visual impairment, including blindness[9]

OTHER IMPORTANT CASES TO NOTE

Multiple cases have reached the U.S. Supreme Court over the last fifty years for clarification over what is legally owed to a child with disabilities, and more specifically what constitutes FAPE. In the case of *Board of Education v. Rowley (1984)*, the Court noted a Deaf student was passing their classes and so refused them an interpreter, but found that the student did not always understand what was going on and therefore would benefit and potentially perform better academically if one was provided. In *Irving School District v. Tatro (1984)*, a quick catheterization that took a few minutes was needed to manage a child's spina bifida every few hours. The school refused since they believe it constituted a medical procedure. However, the Court disagreed, noting that the procedure did not require any medical setting, a person could be trained to complete the procedure in minutes, and that it would fall under a related service since the child would not be able to attend school or benefit from special education if they did not do the catherization. This was further extended when a nurse was required full-time in school for a student who had been paralyzed from the neck down, *Cedar Rapids v. Garret F. (1999)*. The question was if the nurse should be considered a related service due to the extensive nature and cost. The Court ruled that it was a related service based on its necessity to allow a student with disabilities to attend school and have access to educational opportunities. A key case over discipline guidance is *Honig v. Doe (1985)*, in which the district removed is a joint lawsuit in which districts expelled two separate students with emotional disturbance as a diagnosis permanently for engaging in disruptive behavior and acting violent. This was at the heart of one of the original points of the law when Congress created it, that districts had consistently found ways to remove students who had disabilities by creating categories or terms denoting a student is beyond the capabilities of education. Since the behavior was related to their disability, the Court stated that they would not be removed and prevented from having educational access, instead they were to engage in additional interventions. Unfortunately, schools tend to continue to find ways to remove students with disabilities, more specifically over behavior and intellectual disabilities, with parents unaware of options they may have. Even the year of this textbook being written, numerous cases are ongoing for removal or in some case using physical force or police officers

Case law, law creating legal precedent, is one of the key methods of clarifying and understanding laws governing disability.

to handle a child. While the term "violent" may be used, it includes screaming, pushing, throwing items against a wall, and so on. The student having an intent to harm others often is very unconvincing in most of these cases; however, the use of force by school officials and police has resulted in multiple injuries, broken bones, and several deaths of children in various school settings, including at the elementary level. Continued student success and what a school district legally owes the student has been settled in additional Supreme Court case law. Often these specific lawsuits occur due to a district offering low, or minimum, effort for student success. An example is Zachary Deal v. Hamilton Board of Education (2003), where it was district was determined that it was not required to provide the maximum benefits for the student, but it was considered a denial of FAPE if an alternative program that demonstrates much higher levels of progress to be made is available. A final and more recent case garnered unanimous support from the Supreme Court in *Endrew F. v. Douglas County School District (2017)*. In the case, the Court targeted the consistent minimum efforts by schools to provide for students with disabilities, denoting that tactics provided to reach the lowest level of success to merely be able to state a student with disabilities was achieving success was unacceptable. The accusation included referencing the high dropout rate of students with disabilities and that schools were merely waiting them out until they stop attending altogether. Instead, schools needed to provide intervention and services to help these students make progressive success in their educational endeavors.[8] In the case of Doug C. v. Hawaii Department of Education (2013), the Supreme Court noted that parents are to be active members of the IEP committee and can only be excluded if they affirmatively refuse to attend. This placed the expectation that the parents are to be included in IEP meetings and decisions. Additionally, school districts are to be flexible to the parent's needs on scheduling, as well as concerns they may have.

INDIVIDUAL EDUCATION PROGRAM (IEP)

An **Individual Education Program (IEP)** is defined as a written document that outlines the student's present level of educational achievement, identifies goals and objectives for the near future, and lists the educational services to be provided to meet those goals. Note that educational capability and achievements for all students are determined by the state that a student lives in and not the federal government. The U.S. Department of Education has pointed out that educational achievement cannot be determined by grades alone, and that educational achievement and services are not merely related to academics, but also to the social and emotional development of a child. The IEP is considered a legal document, but teachers are not legally held accountable for a child's progress.[8,10]

Eligibility Process for Special Education

- A child is identified with a potential disability (may be referred by a daycare center or worker, their parents, doctor or medical professional, etc.).
- Parents/Guardians give consent for any evaluations.
- Child is referred to an evaluation team.
- Child evaluated to determine their present level of performance.
- Determine child's eligibility for special education services.
- Develop child's IEP (review the Present Level of Performance and Goals/Objectives).
- Determine placement for education and services.

Participants on an IEP Team

The original intent of the Congressional design was a cooperative effort between the schools and the parents. However, while schools are required to give good faith effort to work with parents on assessment and services, they are allowed to continue to make decisions since parents may not choose to participate, and parents can choose to file a complaint with the state if they disagree with decisions made. This leads to parents being considered as unequal members in committees and has led to numerous legal issues in individual states. Additionally, if a parent wants to change or disagrees with a part of the proposed IEP from the school, then the school may choose to disagree and not provide any services while the disagreement is happening. Sadly, the legal review process with the state could take months, denying a child access to needed services during that time. Conflict can arise from the parents for a number of reasons, often because they are not informed on the nature of disabilities or the law surrounding them. They may have more expectations on services than a school is legally required to give, or they may truly believe their child does not have a disability or are concerned with them carrying a "label" if they receive services.

The individuals who should be present in an IEP meeting are:

- A general education teacher (preferably the student's actual teacher) to help with understanding the general educational progress required.
- A local education agency (LEA) representative is also required to denote how finances and services are able to be distributed. Usually, the LEA role is filled by a principal or vice principal, but may be filled by anyone with administrative authority.
- A special education teacher is the third and last person required by the school's side of the IEP process. Typically, this a certified special education teacher who can help decide what accommodations a student might need for their coursework and provide feedback to general education teachers on how to adapt their work for a specific student's needs. However, it has occurred that contracted specialists in a child's disability can fill this role. An example could be a speech therapist filling this role, and if this is the only deficit a student has then this is fine. The issues that parents have been facing is when students are diagnosed with multiple disabilities, an example could be autism, and then there is no one there to speak on assisting accommodations or modifications for the other disabilities in the general coursework. It is also not recommended for the school district since an actual special education teacher should have had courses and continued education in special education laws and guidelines, other specialists being present may not have a similar background, and therefore put the district at risk through poor recommendations or denial of services.
- While multiple people could be discussed in the remainder of the IEP team, the emphasis required by law is that they bring special knowledge and expertise about the student, disability, or situation to provide input. An exception to this would be a parent choosing to bring another family member or friend as support or as an advocate. The school is required to notify a parent of anyone that they will have attend the meeting, although it can just be the position/role not the actual name of the individuals, but parents are not required to do the same. It is recommended that parents do notify the district on who they plan to have attend since this may reduce surprise, which may cause a lot of contention in an IEP meeting.[10]

Due Process when Disagreement Occurs

- Parents disagree with school system or vice versa
- Impartial hearing conducted with hearing officer (decision made within 45 days)
- Continued disagreement or no resolution found
- Appeal to a state's education department
- Reviewed by state appointed hearing officer (decision within 45 days)
- Continued disagreement
- Appeal through court action[10]

Overall Components in an IEP

- Present level of performance (PLOP)
- Annual goals and short-term objectives
- Statement of services (including assistive technology and/or other special equipment) and extent child will not participate in regular education program
- Transition services (for children 14–16 or older)
- Procedures and scheduling for evaluation

Present Level of Performances (PLOP)

This section may have several different names depending on the state or software program a school decides to utilize. The PLOP is where many of the assessments performed on the child will report the summarized results and identification of disabilities and tendencies. Additionally, it is used to describe the unique needs of the child that should be provided services through special education (including physical education) and/or related services (like physical or occupational therapy). It will also establish a measurable baseline for the creation of annual goals and benchmarks. This section may also include information provided from outside the IEP members, or the parents, to help understand the unique needs, strengths, or concerns that may surround the child.

Annual Goals

Annual goals describe what a child can reasonably be expected to accomplish within a 12-month time span with their educational and specialized services.

IEPs are intended to be individualized to the student's specific needs and provides guidance for instruction and related services needed.

All annual goals are to be designed to enable the child to be involved in and continue to progress in the general curriculum. Annual goals are also to be designed to help meet other educational needs that result from the child's disability, this may include social and emotional needs that affect them in school or in the classroom as well. These are legally required to be reviewed yearly at the annual meeting and progress reported to the state educational agency.

Short-Term Instructional Objectives

Short-term instructional objectives (STIOs) are designed to create measurable, intermediate steps between a student's PLOP and their annual goal. The STIOs are to be benchmarks and milestones leading up to the annual goal, allowing changes if things are not making process instead of letting an entire academic year pass.

Statement of Services

The statement of services defines what services will be provided (e.g., special education, physical therapy, adapted physical education), who will provide these services, and where will services be provided (e.g., pull-out, inclusion). Additionally, it denotes the minutes and percentage of time that will be pulled out of the general curriculum. It might also note when the service program will begin and end. Located in this section of the IEP will be the noting of Direct and Indirect Services. **Direct Services** are in-person services, usually hands-on components between the provider and the student. These are seen with Occupational and Physical Therapy. Nursing Services are also considered here after the Supreme Court case Cedar Rapids v. Garret F (1999). Adapted Physical Education is considered a direct service, and the details on that service will be listed here, however, due to direct school curriculum impact it may have a dedicated section detailing if it is being used and why it is needed at the beginning of an IEP. **Indirect Services** are usually supervision, consulting, or skill teaching that may occur adjacent to the work with a student. An example could be an Occupational Therapist teaching a paraprofessional how to correct a student in holding a pencil. A Licensed Professional Counselor assisting a family in creating better transitions to school from home would be an example of a indirect service. It is also worth noting that there is a delineation between special education, as it is part of curriculum, and services not linked to the curriculum. Which is what physical education would fall under, just as would math, literature, science, etc. Compared to **Related Services**, which are services provided that may impact learning, but are not associated to the curriculum, but are related to the learning process or their development. This is the categorization of occupational and physical therapy, as well as counseling, would fall. Only after identifying the need would you assign it as direct or indirect services.

Transition Services

Transition services are not on every IEP due to the section being designed for preparing students to move from school to being an adult. Legally, this is required to be addressed at 16 years old, but in some cases a state may begin earlier. The student is often included in these meetings, and the activities provided through this section teaches them skills to reach their postsecondary goals, whether this is about independent living, postsecondary education, vocational education, community participation, or integrated employment.

Procedures and Scheduling for Evaluation

This section outlines how often evaluations will take place depending on specific needs. Additionally, it may include sections that require consistent review of benchmarks and how they will be tested, like a communication review of benchmark measures every 9 weeks for a student who has speech therapy.[10]

Example of a Notice of an IEP Meeting

MO STATE SAMPLE

Student's Name _____

NOTIFICATION OF MEETING

To: _____

☐ Parent(s)/Guardian(s)   ☐ Adult Student (age 18+ or emancipated minor)

☐ Student (required when postsecondary transition is a purpose of the meeting)

This is to confirm that a meeting with you has been scheduled for _____ (Date)

at _____ (Time) at _____ (Location)

The purpose of this meeting is to: (check all that apply)

☐ Review existing data as part of an initial evaluation or reevaluation
☐ Determine initial or continued eligibility
☐ Develop initial IEP
☐ Review/Revise IEP
☐ Consider Post-secondary Transition
☐ Conduct Manifestation Determination
☐ Consider/conduct Functional Behavioral Assessment
☐ Other:_____

The following individuals have been invited to participate in this meeting:

Role	Position within Public Agency	Name (optional)
☐ Local Education Agency (LEA) Representative*		
☐ Special Education Teacher*		
☐ Individual to interpret instructional implications of evaluation results*		
☐ General Education Teacher*		
☐ Student		
☐ Agency representative(s) for post-secondary transition (must have appropriate consent to invite)		
Agency Name_____		
Agency Name_____		
☐ Part C Representative (if applicable)**		
☐ Parent(s)		
☐ _____		
☐ _____		

* For IEP and Review of Existing Data meetings, required participant. Participation in Review of Existing Data meeting does not have to be in person. Parent LEA may agree/consent in writing to excusal of IEP team members for IEP team meetings only.

This agency **AND** the parents have the right to invite any other participants they feel have knowledge or special expertise of the child. The determination of knowledge or special expertise shall be made by the party (parent or public agency) who invited the individual to be a participant at the meeting. The Family Educational Rights and Privacy Act (FERPA) requires a written Release of Information **MUST** be obtained for other persons invited by the parent or LEA to share confidential information at the IEP meeting

**For the initial IEP meeting of children served in First Steps, the public agency must, at the request of the parent, send an invitation to the First Steps Service Coordinator or other representatives of the First Steps system to assist with the smooth transition of services at the initial IEP meeting.

If you are unable to attend this meeting, please contact me at _____ as soon as possible.
(Phone)

Sincerely,

_____ _____ _____
         Name   Title   Date

Updated 10/13/2017

Example of a Notice of an IEP Meeting

RECORD OF DISTRICT ATTEMPTS TO SCHEDULE MEETING

☐ 1st Attempt

Date of contact: _____

☐ Parent waived notification requirement*

Method of contact:

☐ Written:
    ☐ Hand carried by student
    ☐ Regular mail
    ☐ Certified mail
    ☐ Fax
    ☐ E-mail
    ☐ Other: _____

☐ Verbal:
    ☐ Phone
    ☐ Voice mail/answering machine
    ☐ Face to face contact
    ☐ Other: _____

<u>PARENT/GUARDIAN RESPONSE</u>

☐ Do not want to attend (proceed with IEP meeting).
☐ Cannot attend, please reschedule (proceed with 2nd attempt).
☐ No response (proceed with 2nd attempt).
☐ **Yes, I'll be there.

* In general, reasonable notification is 10 days.

**If parent does not attend meeting, proceed to 2nd attempt

☐ 2nd Attempt (must be a direct contact with parent)

Date of contact: _____

☐ Parent waived notification requirement*

Method of contact: (must be a direct contact)

☐ Written:
    ☐ Regular mail
    ☐ Certified mail

☐ Verbal:
    ☐ Phone
    ☐ Face to face contact

<u>PARENT/GUARDIAN RESPONSE</u>

☐ Do not want to attend (proceed with meeting).
☐ Cannot attend (proceed with meeting).
☐ No response (proceed with meeting).
☐ **Yes, I'll be there.

* In general, reasonable notification is 10 days

**If parent does not attend, agency may proceed with meeting.

Updated 10/13/2017

Source: https://dese.mo.gov/

Example of a IEP Document

DATE OF MEETING	TEC §29.005(b-1)(1)

I. STUDENT IDENTIFYING INFORMATION

The school district may include in this section student identifying information (such as name, address, date of birth, etc.).

Student Name
Home Campus
Age (assuming 8 years of age) and Date of Birth
Current Full Evaluation 1/5/2020 and next due date 1/5/2023
Evaluations:
Functional Behavioral Assessment
Counseling Evaluation
Autism
Occupational Therapy Evaluation

Duplicate sections II – VII, as needed.

II. ANNUAL GOAL AREA

Content, skill, and/or service:

Goal 1: Occupational Therapy as a related services
Skill/Focus Area 1: Sensorimotor

In 36 instructional weeks, James will demonstrate measurable progress towards the development of fine motor and sensory processing skills as evidenced by mastery of OT objectives at target mastery level. Success will be measured using observation, work samples, teacher report/feedback, and data collection during therapy sessions.

Goal 2: Behavioral
Skill/Focus Area 2: Behavior

Within 36 instructional weeks, using 1 to 2 step directions and check for understanding with specific feedback from student, James will Choose to complete coursework 80% of the time during the assigned task with co-regulating skills with prompting by teacher and paraprofessional.

Goal 3: Behavioral
Skill/Focus Area 2: Behavior

Within 36 instructional weeks, using 1 to 2 step directions and check for understanding with specific feedback from student, James will choose alternate ways to emotionally regulate, rather than become angry, yelling, hitting, or throwing things at individuals (teachers, administrators and/or peers/students). Success will be measured using 3 out of 4 trials.

Goal 4: Behavioral
Skill/Focus Area 2: Behavior

Within 36 instructional weeks, using 1 to 2 step directions and check for understanding with specific feedback from student, James will demonstrate appropriate use of de-escalation techniques when becoming frustrated (e.g. hears a negative comment, told no, requested to transition, requested to do work, or stop something, etc.).

Goal 5: Counseling
Skill/Focus Area 3: Emotional

Within 36 instructional weeks, using 1 to 2 step directions and check for understanding with specific feedback from student, James will identify and label physical characteristics of basic negative emotions (sad, frustrated, mad, or scared)

Goal 6: Counseling
Skill/Focus Area 3: Emotional

Within 36 instructional weeks, using 1 to 2 step directions and checking for understanding with specific feedback from student, James will use a variety of relaxation techniques/self-regulation techniques in counseling sessions.

Goal 7: Adapted Physical Education
Skill/Focus Area 3: Functional Movement

Within 36 instructional weeks, using instructional cues, James will engage in functional motor skills improving age-level appropriate skills by 70%, James will use a variety of motor pedagogical techniques while in adapted physical education sessions.

III. PRESENT LEVEL OF ACADEMIC ACHIEVEMENT AND FUNCTIONAL PERFORMANCE 34 CFR §300.320(a)(1)

Including how student's disability affects involvement and progress in the general education curriculum, or, for a preschool child, how student's disability affects participation in appropriate activities:

Physical
Health/Physical: James' vision and hearing were screened by the school nurse. His Vision is Normal (R20/20, L20/25). His Hearing is also
Normal (Sweep at 25db, passed 1000/2000/4000). His Gross Motor and Fine Motor skills appear to be poor. Based on the above information Adapted Physical Education is required for Fundamental Motor Skill development. James' is physically fit and can participate in Physical Education class, recess and sports with developed accommodations and close monitoring.
James' has been diagnosed with ADHD, ODD and ASD
On 07/27/2020 James' was diagnosed with Autism by Dr. Penser (Pediatrician) and Dr. Cap (Psychologist).
Currently James' is prescribed Zoloft 25 mg daily and Focalin XR 5mg daily
James' was evaluated on 09/08/2020 for OT (outside evaluation). James will be attending OT therapy an hour biweekly for fine motor skill
training and sensory input.
James' was evaluated by the LSSP; Assessment results determine that James' falls under the guidelines of Autism.
Evaluation for Occupational Services was completed on 02012020

Behavioral
Emotional/Behavioral: James' has had emotional/behavioral issues over the last year. Current issues include leaving the classroom
(remotely and face to face), frustration issues during remote learning that required using breakout rooms with the paraprofessional. Providing
breaks frequently in order to keep on task. Currently while face to face James' has run out of the classroom multiple times. James' still exhibits
issues with transitions from one activity to another.
James' has improved with behavioral issues. Using the support tools in the classroom have been effective. James' has had more successful
days in the classroom and less incidents of elopement. Using the safe space in the classroom was observed by the LSSP during the evaluation.
Documentation has been submitted and James' is in need of a behavior intervention plan.

Discipline
Behavior impedes learning or that of others
Behavioral strategies, including positive interventions and supports are included in the class accommodations and/or IEP goals

Functional
James functional abilities are within normal limits. (Cognitive)

Academic
James' academic skills are consistently developed with classmates/peers. James was nominated to be tested for the GT program. No academic issues noted.

IV. MEASURABLE ANNUAL GOAL(S) 34 CFR §300.320(a)(2)(i)

Goal 1: Occupational Therapy as a related services

In 36 instructional weeks, James will demonstrate measurable progress towards the development of fine motor and sensory processing skills as evidenced by mastery of OT objectives at target mastery level. Success will be measured using observation, work samples, teacher report/feedback, and data collection during therapy sessions.

Goal 2: Behavioral

Within 36 instructional weeks, using 1 to 2 step directions and check for understanding with specific feedback from student, James will Choose to complete coursework 80% of the time during the assigned task with co-regulating skills with prompting by teacher and paraprofessional.

Goal 3: Behavioral

Within 36 instructional weeks, using 1 to 2 step directions and check for understanding with specific feedback from student, James will choose alternate ways to emotionally regulate, rather than become angry, yelling, hitting, or throwing things at individuals (teachers, administrators and/or peers/students). Success will be measured using 3 out of 4 trials.

Goal 4: Behavioral

Within 36 instructional weeks, using 1 to 2 step directions and check for understanding with specific feedback from student, James will demonstrate appropriate use of de-escalation techniques when becoming frustrated (e.g. hears a negative comment, told no, requested to transition, requested to do work ,or stop something, etc.).

Goal 5: Counseling

Within 36 instructional weeks, using 1 to 2 step directions and check for understanding with specific feedback from student, James will identify and label physical characteristics of basic negative emotions (sad, frustrated, mad, or scared)

Goal 6: Counseling

Within 36 instructional weeks, using 1 to 2 step directions and checking for understanding with specific feedback from student, James will use a variety of relaxation techniques/self-regulation techniques in counseling sessions.

Goal 7: Adapted Physical Education

Within 36 instructional weeks, using instructional cues, James will engage in functional motor skills improving age-level appropriate skills by 70%, James will use a variety of motor pedagogical techniques while in adapted physical education sessions.

V. HOW PROGRESS TOWARD MEETING ANNUAL GOAL(S) WILL BE MEASURED 34 CFR §300.320(a)(3)(i)-(ii)

Goal 1:
Objective/Benchmark:
1. In 36 instructional weeks, James will demonstrate developed complex in hand manipulation of objects and utensils, with average dexterity speed and motor response time, in 9 out of 10 trials or observations.

Objective/Benchmark:
2. In 36 instructional weeks, with provided verbal, visual, and gestural cues, James will be able to tie shoe laces independently in 9 out of 10 trials or observations.

Objective/Benchmark:
3. In 36 instructional weeks, with provided verbal, visual, and gestural cues, James will be able to recall and replicate a 4-5 step motor task/obstacle course that incorporates projected action sequences, heavy work/deep proprioceptive activities, and bilateral coordination tasks with 80% accuracy, within a 5 second motor and fewer than 3 redirections.

Objective/Benchmark:
4. In 36 instructional weeks, with provided verbal, visual, and sensory strategies and cues, James will be able to maintain upright trunk and pelvic alignment when seated in a conventional classroom chair and engaged in fine motor tasks for 8-10 consecutive minutes.

Responsible for Implementing Goal:
Occupational Therapist/OT Assistant

Frequency of Progress Reporting:
Concurrent with report cards

Goal 2:
Objective/Benchmark:
A. James will demonstrate on task behavior and complete coursework during the assigned time in each subject category (math, language arts. etc.) 80% of the time.
B. When given a non-preferred task paired with the use of self-regulation strategies and rewards systems, James will begin the task within 10 minute(s), and complete the appropriately modified version of the task (i.e. all even numbers on worksheet, dictated answers, etc.) within a predesignated appropriate amount of time (with use of timer) 80% of the time.

Goal 3:
Objective/Benchmark:
Within 36 instructional weeks, using 1 to 2 step directions and check for understanding with specific feedback from student, James will choose alternate ways to emotionally regulate, rather than become angry, yelling, hitting, or throwing things at individuals (teachers, administrators and/or peers/students). Success will be measured using 3 out of 4 trials.

Goal 4:
Objective/Benchmark:
A, When James becomes upset, frustrated, or angry he will use a co or self-regulation/coping strategy (movement break, deep breathing, pick from tool bin, quiet space break, requesting to sit out with paraprofessional, drink water, headphones, using feelings chart, cards, or thermometer, using appropriate language to explain feelings, asking for help, secret hand symbol, etc.) 3 out of 4 trials.
B. When given a frustrating situation (e.g. undesired task, demand, and/or undesired peer behaviors), with 1-2 prompts James will communicate how he feels (using emotion rating cards) and utilize coping strategies (e.g. take a break, walk, drink of water, deep breath, pick from tool bin, etc.) and return to and remain on task with a calm body and mind for a minimum of 10 minutes and an average of 3 out of 4 trials across all classroom environments.
C. When James is presented with a problem (non-preferred task, frustrating situation, criticism/correction), James will accurately determine the size of the problem (big vs. little) and determine the appropriate emotional response (take a break, talk with teacher, paraprofessional or counselor, deep breath, pick from tool bin, replace frustration with good thoughts, use of headphones, etc.) and return to task at hand in all classroom environments 3 out of 4 trials.

Goal 5:
Objective/Benchmark:
A. When given scenarios of social conflicts, James will demonstrate problem solving skills by identifying the problem and generating two solutions appropriate to the situation 70% of the time.
B. In counseling sessions, James will accurately identify feelings and appropriate coping strategies when presented with real or imagined situations70% of the time.
C. James will demonstrate successful debriefing (ABC's-antecedent, behavior, and consequences) after feelings of anger or outburst with the counselor 70% of the time.
D. With the use of learning to regulate thoughts and beliefs during counseling sessions, James will reduce instances of negative or anxious thoughts and comments (e.g. "they are looking at me", "I can't", "they are laughing at me", etc.) in all classroom environments 3 out of 4 trials

Goal 6:
Objective/Benchmark:
A. James will demonstrate 3 different relaxation/self-regulation techniques
B. James will cite his preferred technique
C. James will use his preferred technique to self-regulate when negative emotions and inappropriate behaviors arise

Goal 7:
Objective/Benchmark:
Within 36 instructional weeks, cueing and specific feedback on fundamental movement skill performance will be

provided to the student on locomotor, non-locomotor, and object control skills. James will improve and success will be measured in trials at 75% completion rate.

VI. BENCHMARKS OR SHORT-TERM OBJECTIVES 34 CFR §300.320(a)(2)(ii)

For students with disabilities who take alternate assessments aligned to alternate achievement standards (in addition to the annual goals), a description of benchmarks or short-term objectives:

N/A

VII. SPECIAL EDUCATION AND RELATED SERVICES DESIGNED TO MEET THE STUDENT'S NEEDS RELATED TO THE ABOVE OUTLINED GOAL(S) 34 CFR §300.320(a)(4)(i),(ii), 34 CFR §300.320(a)(7), 19 TAC §89.1075(e)

A statement of the special education and related services and supplementary aids and services, based on peer-reviewed research to the extent practicable, to be provided to the student, or on behalf of the student, and a statement of the program modifications or supports for school personnel that will be provided to enable the student to advance appropriately toward attaining the annual goals, and to be involved in and make progress in the general education curriculum:

Type of Services	Frequency of Services	Amount of Time	Beginning / Ending Date	Location of Services
Special Education	Adapted PE	Direct: 50 minutes per 2 weeks	8/22/22-5/16/23	Auxiliary Gymnasium
Related Services	OT Services	Direct: 1x/week 30 minutes Consult/Indirect: 1x/6 weeks 30 minutes	8/22/22-5/16/23	In reserved classroom
	Counseling/LSSP	Direct: 1x/week	8/22/22-5/16/23	Counselor office
Supplementary Aids and Services				
Program Modifications	Modifications in section XXVI	420 minutes a day	8/22/22-5/16/23	In classrooms and learning locations.
Supports for Personnel	Paraprofessional Support for English, Math, Science, Social Studies, Physical Education	420 minutes a day	8/22/22-5/16/23	In classrooms and learning locations.

Key: Include as appropriate

VIII. FREQUENCY FOR REPORTING THE STUDENT'S PROGRESS TO PARENTS 34 CFR §300.320(a)(3)(ii)

Behavioral updates will be sent home every end of the school week.

All other measured updates will be sent home every 9 weeks with school reports.

IX. DETERMINATION OF PARTICIPATION IN STATE AND DISTRICTWIDE ASSESSMENTS

34 CFR §300.320(a)(6)

Assessment/Content Area	Justification for Alternate Assessment or for Alternate English Language Proficiency Assessment	Detail of Accommodations
34 CFR §300.320(a)(6)(ii)(B) 19 TAC §101.1003(b) 19 TAC §101.1005(a)	34 CFR §300.320(a)(6)(ii)(A) 19 TAC §89.1055(b)(2) 19 TAC §101.1003(b) 19 TAC §101.1005(a)	34 CFR §300.320(a)(6)(i) 19 TAC §89.1055(b) 19 TAC §101.5 19 TAC §101.1003(c) 19 TAC §101.1005(e)
N/A	N/A	N/A

X. OPPORTUNITIES TO PARTICIPATE IN EXTRACURRICULAR AND NONACADEMIC ACTIVITIES

34 CFR §300.320(a)(4)(ii), (iii)

Provide a statement of the special education and related services and supplementary aids and services, based on peer-reviewed research to the extent practicable, to be provided to the student, or on behalf of the student, and a statement of the program modifications or supports for school personnel that will be provided to enable the student to participate in extracurricular and other nonacademic activities and to be educated and participate with other students with disabilities and students without disabilities in extracurricular and other nonacademic activities.

James is provided every opportunity to participate in extracurricular and nonacademic activities.

XI. JUSTIFICATION FOR NONPARTICIPATION

34 CFR §300.320(a)(5)

Provide an explanation of the extent, if any, to which the student will not participate with students without disabilities in the regular class, extracurricular and other nonacademic activities.

N/A

XII. INSTRUCTIONAL SETTING AND LENGTH OF STUDENT'S SCHOOL DAY

19 TAC §89.1005, 19 TAC §89.1075(e)

XIII. MEETNG PARTICIPANTS

TEC §29.005(b-1)(2)

The IEP must include the name, position, and signature of each member participating in the meeting.

Position	Printed Name	Signature
Parent		
Parent		
Student (if appropriate)		
District Representative		

General Education Teacher		
Special Education Teacher or Provider		
Interpreter of Evaluation Results		
Career and Technical Education Representative (if appropriate)		
Language Proficiency Assessment Committee Representative (if appropriate)		
Visual Impairment Teacher (if appropriate)		
Auditory Impairment Teacher (if appropriate)		
Representative from Transition Services Agency (if appropriate)		
Other		
Other		

XIV. INDICATION OF AGREEMENT OR DISAGREEMENT TEC §29.005(b-1)(3)

The IEP must indicate whether the student's parents, the adult student, if applicable, and the district representative/administrator agreed or disagreed with the decisions of the IEP committee.

	Yes	No	N/A
Did the student's parent agree with the decisions of the IEP committee?			
Did the student's other parent agree with the decisions of the IEP committee?			
Did the adult student agree with the decisions of the IEP committee?			
Did the district representative/administrator agree with the decisions of the IEP committee?			

XV. STATEMENT OF DISAGREEMENT TEC §29.005(c)

If the IEP was not developed by agreement of all IEP committee members, the IEP must include a written statement of the basis of the disagreement. Each IEP committee member who disagrees with the IEP is entitled to include his or her own statement of disagreement.

Duplicate section XV, as needed.

XVI. THE IEP MUST DOCUMENT THE DECISIONS OF THE IEP COMMITTEE WITH RESPECT TO THE ISSUES DISCUSSED AT THE MEETING. TEC §29.005(b-1)

Decisions regarding issues that are included in another section of the IEP do not have to be restated below.

XVII. REQUIREMENTS FOR TRANSITION SERVICES TEC §29.011

Appropriate state transition planning under the procedure adopted under TEC §29.011 and 19 TAC §89.1055(h) must begin for a student not later than when the student reaches 14 years of age.

The IEP committee must consider, and if appropriate, address the following issues in the student's IEP and must annually review these issues.   19 TAC §89.1055(h)-(i)
Appropriate student involvement in the student's transition to life outside the public school system
N/A
If the student is younger than 18 years of age, appropriate parental involvement in the student's transition by the student's parents and other persons invited to participate by the student's parents or the school district in which the student is enrolled.
N/A
If the student is at least 18 years of age, involvement in the student's transition and future by the student's parents and other persons, if the parent or other person: is invited to participate by the student or the school district in which the student is enrolled or has the student's consent to participate pursuant to a supported decision-making agreement under Texas Estates Code, Chapter 1357.
N/A
Appropriate postsecondary education options, including preparation for postsecondary-level coursework.
N/A
An appropriate functional vocational evaluation
N/A
Appropriate employment goals and objectives
N/A
If the student is at least 18 years of age, the availability of age-appropriate instructional environments, including community settings or environments that prepare the student for postsecondary education or training, competitive integrated employment, or independent living, in coordination with the student's transition goals and objectives.
N/A
Appropriate independent living goals and objectives
N/A
Appropriate circumstances for facilitating a referral of a student or the student's parents to a governmental agency for services or public benefits, including a referral to a governmental agency to place the student on a waiting list for public benefits available to the student such as a waiver program established under the Social Security Act (42 U.S.C. Section 1396n(c)), §1915(c).
N/A
The use and availability of appropriate supplementary aids, services, curricula, and other opportunities to assist the student in developing decision-making skills and supports and services to foster the student's independence and self-determination, including a supported decision-making agreement under Texas Estates Code, Chapter 1357.
N/A

CHAPTER 3: Legal Issues and Disabilities   47

Beginning not later than the first IEP to be in effect when the student turns 16, or younger if determined appropriate by the IEP committee, and updated annually thereafter, the IEP must include: 34 CFR §300.320(b)(1)

Appropriate measurable postsecondary goals based upon age-appropriate transition assessments related to:
Training
N/A
Education
N/A
Employment
N/A
Independent Living Skills (where appropriate)
N/A
The transition services (including courses of study) needed to assist the student in reaching the postsecondary goals 34 CFR §300.320(b)(2)
N/A

XVIII. TRANSFER OF RIGHTS AT AGE OF MAJORITY   34 CFR §300.320(c), 19 TAC §89.1049(a)

☐ **Beginning not later than one year before the student reaches the age of 18:**
The student has been informed of the student's rights under the IDEA, if any, that will transfer to the student on reaching the age of 18.

☐ **The IEP must include the following statement:**
The student has been provided information and resources regarding guardianship, alternatives to guardianship, including a supported decision-making agreement under Texas Estates Code, Chapter 1357, and other supports and services that may enable the student to live independently.

XIX. REQUIREMENTS FOR A STUDENT WHO IS BLIND OR VISUALLY IMPAIRED
19 TAC §89.1055(d), TEC §30.002(e)

Provide a detailed description of the arrangements made to provide the student with the requirements in TEC §30.002(c)(4).

Evaluation of the Impairment	N/A

Instruction in an expanded core curriculum, including instruction in:	
Compensatory skills such as braille and concept development, and other skills needed to access the rest of the curriculum	N/A

Orientation and mobility	N/A
Social interaction skills	N/A
Career planning	N/A
Assistive technology, including optical devices	N/A
Independent living skills	N/A
Recreation and leisure enjoyment	N/A
Self-determination	N/A
Sensory efficiency	N/A

The student was provided with a detailed explanation of the various service resources available in the community and throughout the State, as follows: TEC §30.002(e)(3)

N/A

Describe the plans and arrangements made for contacts with and continuing services to the student beyond regular school hours (if needed) to ensure the student learns the skills and receives the instruction specified above: TEC §30.002(e)(5)

N/A

In the development of the individualized education program for a student with a visual impairment, the IEP must include instruction in braille and the use of braille unless the student's admission, review, and dismissal committee determines and documents that braille is not an appropriate literacy medium for the student. TEC §30.002(f)

N/A

XX. REQUIREMENTS FOR TRANSPORTATION 34 CFR §300.320(a)(4)

Transportation as a related service will be provided in the following manner:

Transportation is currently provided by parents, due to their choice.

XXI. REQUIREMENTS FOR EXTENDED SCHOOL YEAR (ESY) SERVICES 19 TAC §89.1055(c)

If the IEP committee determines that the student is in need of ESY services, then the IEP must identify which of the goals and objectives in sections IV and VI will be addressed during ESY services.
Duplicate section XXI page, as needed.

The IEP committee has determined that ESY services are necessary for the following goals and objectives. 19 TAC §89.1055(c)	
Counseling Services during the summer to take place at District Administration Offices 2xweek for 50 minutes each.	

ESY Special Education and Related Services

A statement of the special education and related services and supplementary aids and services, based on peer-reviewed research to the extent practicable, to be provided to the student, or on behalf of the student, and a statement of the program modifications or supports for school personnel that will be provided to enable the student to advance appropriately toward attaining the annual goals and to be involved in and make progress in the general education curriculum.

34 CFR §300.320(a)(4)(i),(ii), 34 CFR §300.320(a)(7), 19 TAC §89.1075(e)

Type of Services	Frequency of Services	Amount of Time	Beginning / Ending Date	Location of Services
Special Education				
Related Services				
Supplementary Aids and Services				
Program Modifications				
Supports for Personnel				

Key: ▨ Include as appropriate

XXII. REQUIREMENTS FOR A STUDENT WITH AUTISM OR OTHER PERVASIVE DEVELOPMENTAL DISORDER
19 TAC §89.1055(e)

Based on peer-reviewed research-based educational programming practices, to the extent practicable, the IEP committee determines whether the following strategies are needed.

Extended Educational Programing   19 TAC §89.1055(e)(1)

The IEP committee has considered extended educational programming (e.g., extended day and/or extended school year services that consider the duration of programs/settings based on assessment of behavior, social skills, communication, academics, and self-help skills) and determined that the student needs extended educational programming as part of the IEP.
Describe below:

N/A

Daily Schedules Reflecting Minimal Unstructured Time   19 TAC §89.1055(e)(2)

The IEP committee has considered the use of daily schedules reflecting minimal unstructured time and active engagement in learning activities (for example: lunch, snack, and recess periods that provide flexibility within routines; adapt to individual needs skill levels; and assist with schedule changes, such as changes involving substitute teachers and pep rallies) and determined that the student needs services as part of the IEP.
Describe below:

N/A

In-Home and Community-Based Training	19 TAC §89.1055(e)(3)

The IEP committee has considered in-home and community-based training or viable alternatives that assist the student with acquisition of social/behavioral skills (for example: strategies that facilitate maintenance and generalization of such skills from home to school, school to home, home to community, and school to community) and determined that the student needs services as part of the IEP.
Describe below:

In-Home Training Evaluation and Services to be completed and provided by Therapeutic and Wellness Connections. One evaluation a semester and two in-home consultations per semester.

Positive Behavior Support Strategies	19 TAC §89.1055(e)(4)

The IEP committee has considered the use of positive behavior support strategies based on relevant information, for example:
(A) antecedent manipulation, replacement behaviors, reinforcement strategies, and data-based decisions; and
(B) a behavioral intervention plan (BIP) developed from a functional behavioral assessment (FBA) that uses current data related to target behaviors and addresses behavioral programming across home, school, and community-based settings and determined that the student needs services as part of the IEP.
Describe below:
- 1 to 2 step directions
- Behavior parent log
- Check for understanding
- Clearly defined/consistent limits
- Cool down corner, square or spot
- Frequent breaks
- Frequent reminder of the rules
- Paraprofessional support
- Preferential seating / Proximity control
- Reduced assignments and appropriate activities
- Reference Tool
- List (see attached) for teacher/staff
- Timed warnings
- Visual cues

Futures Planning	19 TAC §89.1055(e)(5)

Beginning at any age, the IEP committee has considered futures planning for integrated living, work, community, and educational environments that considers skills necessary to function in current and post-secondary environments and determined that the student needs services as part of the IEP.
Describe below:

N/A

Parent/Family Training	19 TAC §89.1055(e)(6)

The IEP committee has considered parent/family training and support provided by qualified personnel with experience in Autism Spectrum Disorders (ASD) that, for example:
(A) provides a family with skills necessary for a student to succeed in the home/community setting;
(B) includes information regarding resources (for example: parent support groups, workshops, videos, conferences, and materials designed to increase parent knowledge of specific teaching/management techniques related to the student's curriculum; and
(C) facilitates parental carryover of in-home training and determined that services are needed as part of the student's IEP.
Describe below:

In-Home Training Evaluation and Services to be completed and provided by Therapeutic and Wellness Connections. One evaluation a semester and two in-home consultations per semester.

Staff-to-Student Ratio	19 TAC §89.1055(e)(7)
The IEP committee has considered the suitable staff-to-student ratio appropriate to identified activities and as needed to achieve social/behavioral progress based on the student's developmental and learning level (acquisition, fluency, maintenance, generalization) that encourages work towards individual independence as determined by, for example: (A) adaptive behavior evaluation results; (B) behavioral accommodation needs across settings; and (C) transitions within the school day and determined that the student needs specified staff-to-student ratio as part of the IEP. Describe below:	
N/A	

Communication Interventions	19 TAC §89.1055(e)(8)
The IEP committee has considered the use of communication interventions, including language forms and functions that enhance effective communication across settings (for example: augmentative, incidental, and naturalistic teaching) and determined that the student needs services as part of the IEP. Describe below:	
N/A	

Social Skills Supports and Strategies	19 TAC §89.1055(e)(9)
The IEP committee has considered the use of social skills supports and strategies based on social skills assessment/curriculum and provided across settings (for example: trained peer facilitators (e.g., circle of friends), video modeling, social stories, and role playing) and determined that the student needs services as part of the IEP. Describe below:	
Provided in BIP	

Professional Educator and Staff Support	19 TAC §89.1055(e)(10)
The IEP committee has considered professional educator/staff support (for example: training provided to personnel who work with the student to assure the correct implementation of techniques and strategies described in the IEP) and determined that services are needed and should be specified in the IEP. Describe below:	
Paraprofessional for all classes to support in emotional and behavioral goals.	

Teaching Strategies	19 TAC §89.1055(e)(11)
The IEP committee has considered teaching strategies based on peer reviewed research-based practices for students with ASD (for example: those associated with discrete-trial training, visual supports, applied behavior analysis, structured learning, augmentative communication, or social skills training) and determined that the student needs teaching strategies specified in the IEP. Describe below:	
N/A	

If the IEP committee determines that services are not needed in one or more of the areas listed above, the IEP must include a statement to that effect and the basis upon which the determination was made.
Describe below: 19 TAC §89.1055(f)

N/A

XXIII. REQUIREMENTS FOR A STUDENT PLACED IN A RESIDENTIAL EDUCATIONAL PLACEMENT OR OFF-CAMPUS PROGRAM PLACEMENT   19 TAC §§89.1092; 89.1094

Describe the services which the school district is unable to provide and which the facility will provide.
19 TAC §§89.1092(a)(4)(B); 89.1094(b)(3)(A)

N/A

Describe the criteria and estimated timelines for the student's return to the school district.
19 TAC §§89.1092(a)(4)(C); 89.1094(b)(3)(B)

N/A

Describe the appropriateness of the facility for the student.
19 TAC §§89.1092(a)(4)(D); 89.1094(b)(3)

N/A

XXIV. REQUIREMENTS FOR A STUDENT PLACED AT THE TEXAS SCHOOL FOR THE BLIND AND VISUALLY IMPAIRED (TSBVI) OR THE TEXAS SCHOOL FOR THE DEAF (TSD)   19 TAC §89.1085(c)

Describe the services in the student's IEP that the TSBVI or the TSD can appropriately provide.
19 TAC §89.1085(c)(1)

N/A

Describe the criteria and estimated timelines for the student's returning to the resident school district.
19 TAC §89.1085(c)(3)

N/A

XXV. REQUIREMENTS FOR BEHAVIOR IMPROVEMENT PLAN OR BEHAVIORAL INTERVENTION PLAN
TEC §29.005(g), 19 TAC §89.1055(g)

If the IEP committee determines that a behavior improvement plan or a behavioral intervention plan is appropriate for the student, that plan must be included as part of the student's IEP.

BIP is attached to the end of the IEP.

XXVI. SUPPLEMENTAL ACCELERATED INSTRUCTION — 19 TAC §104.1001(f)(5)

The IEP committee, serving as the accelerated learning committee, must document decisions regarding supplemental accelerated instruction in writing included in the IEP deliberations or as a supplemental attachment to the student's individualized education program, and a copy must be provided to the student's parent or guardian in accordance with TEC, §28.0211(f-1).

Tools for Transition/Prevention
1. Provide 23 choices (firm calm voice) instead of "no"
2. Timer or time warning (explain what will be doing in 5 minutes and setting timer, what expectations are, etc. so it's not a surprise) with academic activity for chances to change behavior
3. Offer him to assist preparing classroom for next activity (opportunity to help)
4. Reinforce compliant behaviors (detailed reinforcehow)
5. Positive verbal praise & encouragement

James' Optional Emotional Regulation Tools
**He must be rewarded if he co or selfregulates appropriately and in a timely manner BEFORE melting down and/or using any techniques during a meltdown to come back around & debriefs appropriately*
1. Counting
2. Deep breathing (use hand going up and down around fingers)
3. Drink of water
4. Draw for 5 minutes
5. A short walk
6. Laying head down for 2 minutes
7. Using yellow index card to request a "break" with paraprofessional
8. Blanket
Tool bin: squeeze balls & snap toys

Comprehensive Tool List
- Complete minor tasks before providing new directions & transitions
o Build up compliance
- Planned movement breaks between tasks
- Provide 2-3 choices (firm calm voice) instead of "no"
- Avoid confrontational tones
- Reinforce compliant behaviors (detailed reinforce)
- High interest reinforcers/tracked or charted
- Immediate reinforce (i.e. extra recess)
- Validate & recognize feelings "James, I see you are frustrated…"
- Focus on +, when correcting begin sentences with a +
- Reward when replacement behaviors are appropriately used
- Counting
- Breathing
- Feelings chart
- Positive verbal praise & encouragement
- Opportunity to help
- Feelings chart
- Drink of water
- Choices to complete work (pencil, crayon, dictation to para)
- Remind of positive reward opportunities & options
- Putting head on desk
- Secret hand symbol to signal para or teacher
- Break cards (to hold up)
- Encourage use of tools and appropriate behavior/coping
- Use social skills tools (thermometer or feelings cards throughout the day to check in)
o Emotional range recognition (annoyed < frustrated < mad < angry)
- Snacks
- Timer
- Headphones
- Blanket?
- Leave classroom with para with one sheet of work to complete in a quiet area, immediate reward for completing

- Designated cool down area or walk
- Debrief of behavior (ABC of incident to be documented)
- Offer tool bin: sand, monkey noodle, glitter bottle, squeeze balls, snap toys, dominos, cards to pick something

Deescalation
- Validate & recognize feelings "James, I see you are frustrated…"
- Focus on +, when correcting begin sentences with a +
- Encourage use of tools and appropriate behavior/coping
- Offer firm choices (bin, etc. and reemphasize hitting, etc. is **not** an option)
- Offer tool bin: sand, monkey noodle, glitter bottle, squeeze balls, snap toys, dominos, cards to pick something
- Reward when replacement behaviors are appropriately used
- High interest reinforcers/tracked or charted
- Immediate reinforce (i.e. extra recess, drawing for x amount of time))
- Counting
- Breathing
- Drink of water
- Putting head on desk
- Snacks
- Timer
- Headphones
- Remove to quiet area with para (walk, errand, etc.)
- Designated cool down area or walk (sensory room?)
- Debrief of behavior (ABC of incident to be documented)

Source: https://tea.texas.gov/media/document/333431

REFERENCES

1. Kelly, L. (2020). *Adapted Physical Education National Standards* (3rd ed.). Human Kinetics.
2. Chubon, R. A. (1994). *Social and psychological foundations of rehabilitation*. Charles C. Thomas.
3. Rubin, S. E., & Roessler, R. T. (1995). *Foundations of the vocational rehabilitation process* (4th ed.). Pro-Ed.
4. Marini, I., Graf, N., & Millington, M. (2017). Psychosocial aspects of disability: Insider perspectives and strategies for counselors (2nd ed.). Springer Publishing Co.
5. Wing, C. (2012). *ACSM/NCHPAD Resources for the inclusive fitness trainer.* ACSM and NCHPAD.
6. Federal Communications Commission. (2021). *https://www.fcc.gov/trs*
7. McClanahan, M. L., & Sliger, S. R. (2015). Adapting to WIOA 2014 minimum education requirements for vocational rehabilitation counselors. *Journal of Rehabilitation, 81*(3), 3–8.
8. Wright, P., & Wright, P. (2007). *Special Education Law* (2nd ed.). Hartford House Law Press.
9. Wright, P., & Wright, P. (2019). *From emotions to advocacy: The special education society.* (2nd ed.) Harbor House Law Press.
10. Wright, P., Wright, P., & O'Connor, S. (2020). *All about IEPs: Answers to frequently asked questions about IEPs.* Harbor House Law Press.

CHAPTER 4

DEMYSTIFYING THE INTERSECTION BETWEEN KINESIOLOGY, THERAPY, AND PUBLIC HEALTH: ROLES AND CAREER OPPORTUNITIES

Byron Lai, Heidi Stanish, Anne O Odusanya, Scott WT McNamara

Kinesiology is a broad field with many undergraduate and graduate degree career paths and subspecialties related to helping people with disabilities to improve their health and function through exercise. **Kinesiology** is a human discipline[1] involving the study of "physical activity and its impact on health, society, and quality of life" (para 1).[2] This chapter summarizes how the field of kinesiology branches off into three related fields that aim to help people with disabilities through exercise, namely, rehabilitation, adapted physical activity and education (APA&E), and public health. Within this chapter, we describe a continuum of exercise services for people with disabilities. The continuum includes three phases displayed in Figure 4.1, where a person with a disability will transition from exercise services that emphasize restoration, fitness, and then lifelong physical activity participation, which is based upon a transformative exercise framework for people with disabilities.[3] These phases are supported by three fields: rehabilitation, APA&E, and public health. The figure presents career opportunities and certifications, degrees, and subspecialities, within each of the three fields. The flow of the model is described here, and each of the three fields are described within the remaining subsections of this chapter, along with career opportunities that are available to an aspiring kinesiologist.

In summary, people may acquire a disability (e.g., spinal cord injury), an injury, or have an exacerbation of a condition (e.g., spasticity, illness, pressure ulcer, loss of mobility) that might require rehabilitation services. In the restoration phase, the focus on exercise is to *restore* as much physical function as possible through rehabilitation to help an individual maintain or regain physical independence and perform their activities of daily living, which may include self-care activities such as showering, bathing, changing clothes, transferring into and out of a wheelchair, and household chores. The restoration phase includes the fields of physical and occupational therapy. After being discharged from rehabilitation, the focus is to engage an individual in suitable (i.e., adapted) exercises that can improve and maintain health and function, which leads to the second phase of the continuum: fitness. In the second phase, the field of APA&E plays a critical role in adapting and developing exercise programs to suit the unique needs of the individual so that they can engage in exercise at an intensity that can improve and maintain their health-related fitness (e.g., cardiovascular, musculoskeletal, metabolic, and mental or brain health). This area includes the development and testing of school- or community-based exercise programs for people with disabilities. The final phase, participation, includes the field of public health, where the focus is on the *promotion of adapted exercise* and dissemination of knowledge among as many people living in the community as possible. Each of these three phases provides several

---

Byron Lai, Department of Pediatrics, Division of Rehabilitation Medicine, University of Alabama at Birmingham; Heidi Stanish, Department of Exercise and Health Sciences, University of Massachusetts Boston; Anne Odusanya, Division of Public Health, Wisconsin Department of Health Services; and Scott W.T. McNamara, Kinesiology Department, University of New Hampshire. © Kendall Hunt Publishing Company.

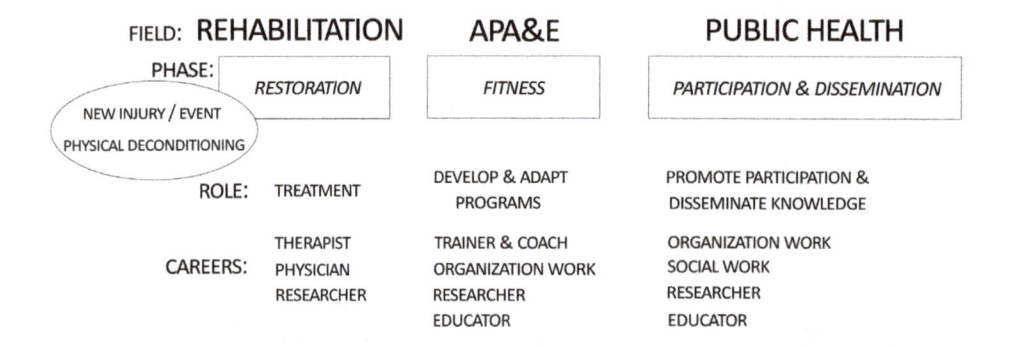

FIELD:	REHABILITATION	APA&E	PUBLIC HEALTH
PHASE:	RESTORATION	FITNESS	PARTICIPATION & DISSEMINATION
	(NEW INJURY / EVENT PHYSICAL DECONDITIONING)		
ROLE:	TREATMENT	DEVELOP & ADAPT PROGRAMS	PROMOTE PARTICIPATION & DISSEMINATE KNOWLEDGE
CAREERS:	THERAPIST PHYSICIAN RESEARCHER	TRAINER & COACH ORGANIZATION WORK RESEARCHER EDUCATOR	ORGANIZATION WORK SOCIAL WORK RESEARCHER EDUCATOR

FIGURE 4.1 Exercise continuum for people with disabilities.
Source: Byron Lai, Heidi Stanish, Anne O Odusanya, Scott WT McNamara

unique opportunities to help people with disabilities through exercise. However, we strongly recommend that, should you choose to learn how to provide services within one of the three phases, you engage within the appropriate fields as soon as possible, because many of these opportunities will require specialized degrees or experience.

There are a few assumptions that should be understood before delving into the chapter. First and foremost, we strongly believe that exercise can be performed by everyone, regardless of physical or cognitive ability, assuming that the exercises are adapted appropriately for the needs of the individual. Indeed, reviews of the literature demonstrate that exercise is beneficial on many aspects of health for people with various disabilities and functional abilities.[4,5] Second, for the purpose of this chapter, we define people with disabilities in a broad sense to include physical (e.g., stroke, spinal cord injury, multiple sclerosis), cognitive (e.g., traumatic brain injury and intellectual disability), and other developmental disabilities (e.g., cerebral palsy and spina bifida). Finally, it is important to note that we present the three exercise-related fields within phases as opposed to sequential stages. The reason for this is to convey that the transition from exercise services between the three fields is not always a clear, stepwise progression. Exercise services can blend between fields. For example, an exercise professional might deliver a program that aims to both restore physical function and enhance fitness. An APA&E researcher might aim to promote a program on a large scale using public health strategies. Moreover, some people might experience an injury or health condition that might regress them from a need for fitness to restoration. Some individuals in rehabilitation may never progress to the point where they can participate in exercise at appropriate intensities to be termed fitness.[3] Some people may never find physical activities that they enjoy and can maintain over a long term. Understand that this chapter provides a simplified depiction of three rich fields and how they intertwine.

REHABILITATION

Rehabilitation encompasses a variety of therapeutic fields that aim to improve a person's physical and cognitive function, functional independence, and activities of daily living (daily and self-care activities). For the purpose of this chapter, we emphasize three exercise-related therapeutic fields: physical therapy, occupational therapy, and rehabilitation medicine (also called physical medicine and rehabilitation or psychiatry). **Rehabilitation Medicine** is a specialty field for physicians who aim to treat conditions associated with a disability and help an individual maximize their recovery. **Physical therapy** provides services aimed at restoring physical function of the human body. **Occupational therapy** focuses on improving a person's ability to perform *occupation*, which is defined as meaningful or purposeful tasks for the individual (e.g., activities of daily living).[6]

Career Opportunities and Training

As for the difference between physical and occupational therapy, occupational therapy emphasizes a holistic perspective that accounts for the individual, their roles, and their environment, whereas physical therapy emphasizes a more targeted approach through mechanistic neural pathways (e.g., reflex pathways). Both physical and occupational therapy services can be inpatient (therapy for people staying in the hospital, which could include intensive or acute care) or outpatient (services people who are not staying at the hospital but may come to the hospital or clinic for therapy or have these therapies at home) in nature. Additionally, professionals in both fields can choose to specialize in providing services for a specific population, which could include pediatrics, adults, older adults, athletes, or specific disability groups (e.g., spinal cord injuries, cerebral palsy, and traumatic brain injury). Of note, a graduate degree (either master's or doctorate) is typically required in most developed countries to obtain a license to practice as a physical or occupational therapist. In the United States, physical therapy schools generally no longer offer a master's level education. A graduate degree will generally require 2 to 3 years to complete, depending on the program. Nevertheless, becoming a professional in either field will provide a livable salary and job flexibility, since therapists are needed across the globe. Furthermore, being able to directly observe a client's improvement is a truly rewarding experience. Deciding on attending graduate school early is critical for pursuing a career in rehabilitation, because schools often have different prerequisite requirements that must be completed prior, such as hours of internship at specific clinics, and additional core basic science classes (and are often not required for pursuing careers in APA&E or public health).

Know that, compared to the two other phases of the continuum (APA&E and public health), rehabilitation is a more structured field in terms of transitioning from education to employment: completion of a graduate degree and license exam leads to a specific type of job. For this reason, this chapter gives a greater emphasis toward the latter two phases of the continuum (APA&E and public health), both of which may be just as rewarding of a career path but may have less traditional avenues to attain them.

Research Opportunities

Research and academic careers are available within both therapeutic fields (as well as APA&E and Public Health), and sometimes physical and occupational therapy are combined within a single field or area of study referred to as rehabilitation medicine. Research in rehabilitation is critical for advancing therapeutic practice. Since physical and occupational therapy are relatively new fields, practices and techniques are constantly evolving scientific knowledge. If an individual decides to pursue research, they can further pursue a doctorate in philosophy (PhD) in a related field, such as rehabilitation science. Research can involve surveys, observations, reviews, and clinical trials to understand and resolve questions that further knowledge in the field. Research projects, especially large projects, are usually funded by research institutions (such as the National Institutes of Health [NIH]) or organizations. A PhD is not absolutely necessary to participate in research, but will make an individual highly marketable to general clinics, universities, and research institutions. A PhD will be necessary for obtaining grants from research institutions and organizations to the lead investigator and to conduct projects. A PhD will generally take 4 to 6 years, but will lead to a higher salary after graduation, especially when combined with a therapy degree. Of note, a PhD is typically obtained after completing a graduate therapy degree, which equates to roughly 6 to 9 years of graduate education. However, some schools offer a dual degree education that will include both a DPT and PhD.

ADAPTED PHYSICAL ACTIVITY AND ADAPTED PHYSICAL EDUCATION

Adapted physical activity (APA) and adapted physical education (APE) are separate, but closely associated, fields. This chapter respectfully unites the two (APA&E) while acknowledging their individuality. A consistent and clear definition of APA is hard to find, perhaps because the field continues to grow and expand at a rapid rate in many directions. The International Federation of Adapted Physical Activity (IFAPA), a scientific organization dedicated to promoting APA, defines the **Adapted Physical Activity** field as:

> a cross-disciplinary body of practical and theoretical knowledge directed toward impairments, activity limitations, and participation restrictions in physical activity. It is a service delivery profession and an academic field of study that supports an attitude of acceptance of individual differences, advocates access to active lifestyles and sport, and promotes innovative and cooperative service delivery, supports, and empowerment.[7]

More simply, APA is considered a subdiscipline of kinesiology that focuses on individual differences in physical activity that require adaptation or special attention.[8]

APE focuses on the context of physical education where modifications are made to the regular program

Adapted group aquatics class.
Source: © Lakeshore Foundation

in order to meet the needs of students with disabilities.[9] Some might contend that APE is a branch of APA, while others consider it to be a subdiscipline of physical education. Regardless of the published definitions of APA&E, the field is grounded by a commitment to ensuring that people with disabilities have equal opportunities to engage in physical activity safely and successfully across the life span. Through creative planning, APA&E can lead to increased access to sport, exercise, physical education, and recreation for all. Those who have pursued clinical and research careers in APA&E know well what the work entails, the positive impact on the health and function of people with disabilities, and the professional fulfillment it brings.

Roles of the Field/s

It is easy to understand why those with a background in kinesiology might be highly motivated to pursue APA&E. The field offers extensive opportunities to use physical activity as a means to promote integration and a feeling of inclusion, celebrate individual differences, and transform lives. An interest in APA&E is often driven by a commitment to overall health and fitness that is directed toward a group of people with disabilities that has traditionally been underserved and marginalized. APA&E professionals aim to promote participation in physical activity among both children and adults and will typically specialize in one of these age groups.

Disappointingly, a wealth of research has demonstrated that many people with disabilities are not participating in sufficient levels of exercise to improve their health, and levels of participation are far lower than people without disabilities.[10–13] As a result, people with disabilities are at risk for a multitude of chronic/primary health conditions[14] (e.g., cardiovascular disease, metabolic syndrome, obesity) and secondary health conditions[15] (e.g., pain, severe chronic fatigue, and low mobility). This knowledge drives both the field of APA&E and Public Health because the significant disparities in health and fitness experienced by people with disabilities are troubling and have gained attention from public health authorities. As one example, the *Healthy People 2030* initiative in the United States includes a goal "to improve health and well-being in people with disabilities,"[16] which represents a commitment to addressing the gaps that exist. For this reason, APA&E professionals often work closely with professionals in public health or transition into public health roles.

Physical inactivity among people with disabilities is not a direct outcome of the disabling condition itself. While the functional limitations associated with some conditions create challenges to activity participation, there is no reason to assume that because a person has a disability they cannot, or will not, engage in physical activity. The most effective ways to intervene on physical inactivity and promote full participation by people with disabilities are still

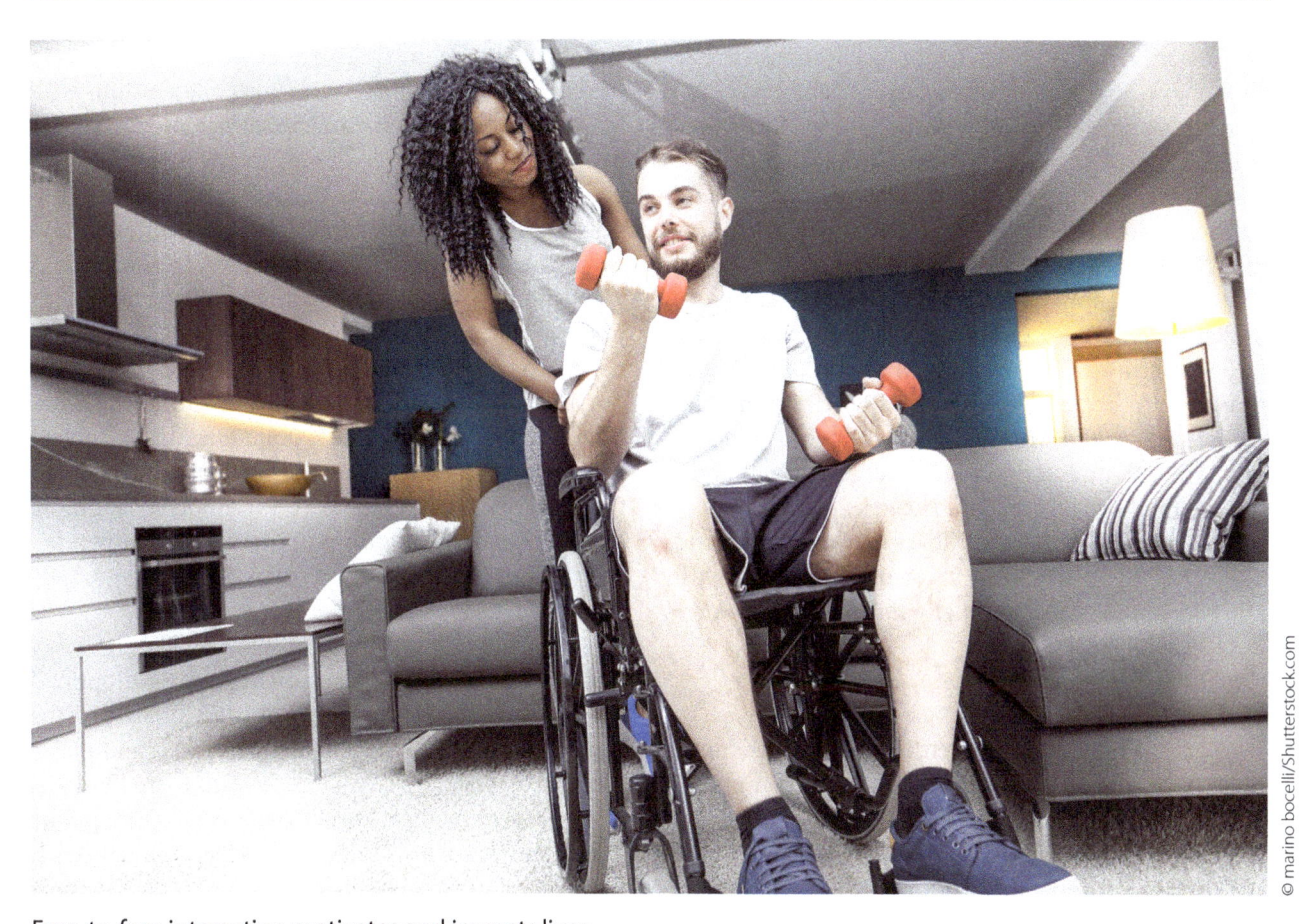

Face-to-face interaction motivates and impacts lives.

unknown and require further exploration. This presents an exciting opportunity for current and prospective APA&E professionals and researchers to make impactful discoveries and advance the field. It is not uncommon for APA&E professionals to be active as both researchers and clinicians. There is a shared, deep dedication to people with disabilities and to their full inclusion that underpins APA&E and drives those who practice in the field.

Career Opportunities and Training

An undergraduate degree in kinesiology provides an important foundation in exercise, fitness, and health promotion that is needed for a career in APA&E. For some professional opportunities, there is a need for special expertise in disability and/or a graduate degree (Masters or PhD). However, there are still a range of options for clinical careers related to APA&E that hold potential for those with an undergraduate education.

A clinical career in the field of APA&E will be appealing to those with an interest in providing direct services to people with disabilities in a variety of contexts and settings. Similar to Rehabilitation, regular, face-to-face interactions with the population and the ability to directly impact lives are what motivate people to work in APA&E. People want to make a difference and great professional satisfaction can come from implementing adapted exercise programming in a variety of settings and contexts. One example of a clinical career opportunity is a Certified Inclusive Fitness Trainer (CIFT) available to those with a bachelor's degree or accredited fitness certification. The American College of Sports Medicine (ACSM) and National Center on Health, Physical Activity, and Disability (NCHPAD) collaborated to create the CIFT program to qualify professionals to work with people with health risks and/or physical limitations. Similarly, the National Strength and Conditioning Association offers the Certified Special Population Specialist (CSPS) certification to qualified candidates. These specialists are certified to train, educate, motivate, and assess individuals with chronic or temporary health conditions who require special exercise interventions. Examples of other professional roles in APA&E include: disability sport coach, inclusive community program coordinator/facilitator (e.g., YMCA, summer camps), disability sport administrator, adapted aquatics specialist, and local or state government positions in disability and health branches.

Becoming an APE teacher or teaching assistant is also an exciting and rewarding career path for people who desire face-to-face interactions with the population. Of note, some schools or states require APE teachers to be certified. Certification options for APE teachers can include the Adapted Physical Education National Standards (APENS) Certified Adapted Physical Educator (CAPE) designation in addition to obtaining state APE endorsements (when required). In order to be eligible for the CAPE exam, candidates must have a bachelor's degree in PE or related field, completed a course in APE, a minimum of 200 hours providing PE instruction to individuals with disabilities, and hold a valid teaching license. Career opportunities in APA&E are likely to expand as the demand and expectation for integration of individuals with and without disabilities in these settings is realized.

Research Opportunities

Research in APA&E is interdisciplinary and aims to understand a diverse array of topics commonly centered on exercise, sport, physical education, and recreation for people with various disability types. APA&E researchers often work with teams comprised of scholars in other disciplines such as nutrition, psychology, epidemiology, social work, biostatistics, and education who engage collaboratively and contribute unique expertise. Interestingly, APA&E researchers may find themselves playing a central role on the team because of their general knowledge in each of these disciplines (and others) accompanied by specific knowledge and skills in disability and function, modification/adaption strategies, individualized instruction, and inclusive practices that anchor the research.

Research career opportunities within APA&E are likely to require specialization that comes from a graduate degree in the field. There are master's and doctoral programs throughout the U.S. and around the world that train future professionals for research careers in APA&E. The Office of Special Education and Rehabilitation Services (OSERS) in the U.S. Department of Education has supported the training of many APA&E professionals through grant funding to academic programs. This investment by the federal government in the U.S. is indicative of the commitment to promoting integration, equity, and opportunity for all children and adults with disabilities.

Research career opportunities can exist within universities, health and/or disability branches of state, local and federal government (e.g., NIH, Centers for Disease Control and Prevention [CDC]), disability and/or sport organizations (e.g., Special Olympics), and health care institutions. A research career in APA&E affords opportunities for collaboration with families, community members, service providers, and people with disabilities themselves who can play an important role in driving meaningful research questions. APA&E research can lead to discoveries around effective exercise programming for children and adults with disabilities that have lasting positive effects. It is important to mention that there are *funded* graduate degrees across the globe, particularly for individuals pursuing a PhD. This applies to all fields (Rehabilitation Science, APA&E, and Public Health). A funded program means that tuition will be paid for by either the mentoring professor or the school. In addition, the program may provide a yearly salary or stipend.

PUBLIC HEALTH

The field of **public health** aims to *promote* optimal health and protect the health of individuals and the communities where they live, learn, work, and play.[15] Medical professionals diagnose and treat illnesses, diseases, and medical conditions. In contrast, public health professionals utilize a whole person approach and place a greater emphasis on *prevention* (i.e., proactively taking steps to prevent issues). Additionally, public health professionals strive to encourage wellness and the adoption of healthy behaviors for individuals and their communities.[17] Public health includes a variety of methods to ensure people and their communities stay healthy, such as surveillance (i.e., surveying issues and methods of resolving issues), advocation for program or policy changes, and promotion of programs or knowledge (i.e., dissemination, which is explained later in this subsection). Public health professionals recognize that there are many inequities that contribute to a single issue on many different levels, and these inequities need to be limited and disrupted.[17] This multilevel method of viewing an issue can be referred to as a *system*, but resolving one level of the system may not be sufficient to promote widespread change. However, tackling an issue on multiple levels will enhance the likelihood of success. Regarding exercise, public health professionals view people with disabilities as a group who are systematically excluded (discussed in Research Opportunities) from participating in health-enhancing exercise.

Career Opportunities and Training

In contrast to the fields of Rehabilitation and APA&E that primarily focus on individual change, public health is aimed at emphasizing change among many societal levels, so that change occurs among as many people's lives as possible and as effectively as possible. Accordingly, public health is a rewarding career path for a young kinesiologist looking to make an impact on a community or population wide level. Pursuing physical activity as a specific career role in public health may require certification (Certified Health Education Specialist, Master Certified Health Education Specialist, and Certified in Public Health), graduate education, as well as experience working with people with disabilities. In addition to an academic career as a professor (which can be pursued in all fields along the exercise continuum with a graduate degree), receiving a master's, PhD, or doctor of public health degree can make an individual marketable toward jobs provided by health-related government institutions and community organizations, such as the U.S. health departments within each state, the CDC, the NIH or any one of its many agencies, and one of numerous disability-specific organizations that favor healthy living through exercise (e.g., the Cerebral Palsy Foundation or Craig H. Neilsen Foundation).

Research Opportunities

Research is a core piece of tackling a public health issue and will thus be pertinent in many public health careers. Public health professionals will often have to present research evidence with regard to surveillance, advocation, and dissemination, in order to inform health professionals and policy makers of issues that need to be resolved and ensure that programs are being maximally disseminated to people at large (with as minimal exclusion as possible). The stronger the level of evidence is, the easier it will be to ensure public health issues have been comprehensively evaluated and effectively addressed through large-scale programs.

Using exercise as an example, public health professionals recognize that there are many barriers as well as different types of barriers that result in systemic exclusion preventing people with disabilities from engaging in exercise. To dissolve, convey, and address these barriers, public health professionals will utilize models such as the social ecological model,[18,19] which takes into account multiple levels of influence: intrapersonal, interpersonal, organizational, community, and public policy.[20] The intrapersonal level pertains to individual characteristics encompassing knowledge, beliefs, motivation, attitudes, self-concept, skills, and past experience. The interpersonal level centers on the individual's relationships and social networks, such as family members, friends, physicians, and more. The organizational level concerns institutions including but not limited to schools, worksites, and clinics.[20] At the community level, there is the built environment, community norms, social capital within the community, and relationships among organizations. Public policy encompasses national, state, and local laws or regulations.[19,21]

Disappointingly, people with disabilities still today experience several barriers on each level of the Social Ecological Model.[22,23] At the intrapersonal level, barriers can include little to no knowledge of accessible exercise programs and facilities within the community, and negative self-conscious thoughts while in fitness facilities. Barriers at the interpersonal level may be lack of support from family members and peers, or overprotective family members or caregivers. At the organizational level, barriers comprise high cost and maintenance associated with adapted equipment for organizations and people with disabilities, membership fees of recreation groups and facilities, little to no accessible recreational facilities, lack of staff who are knowledgeable about working with people with disabilities. Barriers at the community level can entail geographic location (rural vs urban), lack of transit planning and accommodations, and negative attitudes and behavior of the general population directed toward people with disabilities. Finally, at the public policy level, barriers pertaining to recreation organizations include: noncompliance of fitness facilities with minimum access standards (e.g., the Americans with Disabilities Act); lack of sufficient time for people with disabilities to use recreation facilities; not allowing the entry of service animals; and not adopting a maintenance plan to ensure accessibility to facilities and equipment. Approximately three decades of research underpinned the barriers that we presented to you within this paragraph, were obtained from a systematic review (published in 2016) of studies that examined barriers and facilitators to exercise among people with disabilities.[23] Now that researchers and health professionals have a comprehensive understanding of the issue, further research and public health efforts are needed to resolve the issue, which leads us to a unique section within this public health subsection: *dissemination*.

Dissemination

Often the goal of public health initiatives, in the broad sense, is to develop and modify systems using a breadth of evidence to positively impact outcomes for specific populations. However, one of the barriers that prevents public health initiatives from reaching their goals is the inadequate dissemination of *knowledge* to key stakeholders[24] (e.g., policy makers or the target disability group/population). For the purposes of this chapter, we refer to *knowledge* as 1) effective programs that have strong research evidence to support their dissemination on a large scale; and 2) knowledge in the traditional sense, which primarily includes research knowledge. The dissemination of knowledge requires the highest levels of evidence, to enhance the likelihood that the knowledge is well received among stakeholders. Examples of high-level evidence include meta-analyses, systematic reviews, and large-scale surveillance studies. Indeed, knowledge dissemination itself is a scientific field with theoretical and evidence-based practices and approaches, also known as knowledge translation.[25] Utilizing a systematic approach of knowledge dissemination to educate those within and outside of a field is a crucial element of growing awareness, building positive public opinion, and correctly implementing evidence within practitioner settings.[26,27]

Dissemination Along the Exercise Continuum

Dissemination is a core element for advancement of scientific knowledge and practice of all three phases of the exercise continuum. Once researchers identify safe and beneficial breakthrough treatments or programs in research studies, the knowledge of the program benefits must be spread to key stakeholders that will lead directly to changes in practice or the community. For example, research in rehabilitation is always in continuous cycles of discovery that lead to new treatments or techniques every 5 to 10 years. As a result of this process, older techniques should be discarded as quickly as possible among therapists. However, the reality is that many treatments that are outdated or have been debunked through scientific investigation are still being used by therapists across the globe. Disappointingly, the average time it takes for health research to make a widespread impact for clinical practice is 17 years,[28] and this underscores the need for public health professionals to address dissemination.

The fields of APA&E are no different in their need to effectively communicate to key stakeholders and the public. Without the support of the general public, these areas, as well as the scholars and practitioners within them, are unlikely to receive the resources needed to provide meaningful physical activity opportunities to individuals with disabilities. Indeed, strong attitudes from the public have often been shown to effect legislation, which, in turn, results in an accumulation of trained professionals and additional resources. This has been seen within various fields and disciplines, such as the rise of special education during the 1960s and 1970s.[29]

Bridging the Knowledge Gap

To reduce the knowledge disparities that may exist, or have yet to be fully acknowledged in the field, rehabilitation, APA&E and public health professionals, researchers, and well-informed practitioners need to serve as "knowledge-brokers."[30] This means these experienced individuals need to make concerted efforts to educate others in their field about best practices and guiding theories. In addition, these individuals could develop comprehensible information about the importance of exercise for individuals with disabilities, as well as the beneficial outcomes exercise programs can have on society as a whole. For instance, there is a need to communicate how well-designed exercise programs can result in positive health outcomes that benefit both the individual with the disability (e.g., enhanced fitness, physical function, and health) and the community at large (e.g., reduced use of health care systems). It is also important to communicate the barriers that often prevent individuals with disabilities access to quality exercise opportunities, such as inadequate training of health and fitness professionals, availability of programs, transportation (or lack thereof), and cost.[22,23] Regarding program dissemination, program developers should keep in mind these barriers when developing their programs, and package their program so that it can be more readily accessible and reproducible. Examples of ways to make exercise programs for individuals with disabilities more accessible include reducing: program cost, burden (on both participants and the practitioners), and complexity. By creating a less expensive and more easily implemented program, this increases the chances individuals with disabilities participate in the program, as well as may allow health and fitness practitioners with little experience working with individuals with disabilities the ability to still be successful.

A public health professional who aims to bridge knowledge gaps on the exercise continuum could find a career in academia or working for government institutions and organizations that want to ensure that program benefits are widespread among the community (e.g., NCHPAD; and the National Institute on Disability, Independent Living, and Rehabilitation Research). A career in this area will be rewarding to an individual who wants to make an impact on as many people's lives as possible. Specific strategies that a public health professional might utilize could include creating regular newsletters about specific exercises individuals with disabilities can perform at home; disseminating fact sheets that provide physical activity tips for specific disabilities or policy makers; developing short videos that describe the benefits of physical activity for individuals with disabilities and distributing them via social media; or sending out evidence-based, already-created resources (e.g., podcasts, research articles).

CONCLUSION

This chapter demystified how three key exercise-related fields for people with disabilities are connected on a continuum of services, from which aspiring students can find the niche they aim to pursue. Rehabilitation professionals are often the first guides in a person's journey toward restoring their health and function. APA&E professionals are meant to extend a person's journey into performing exercise and fitness to maintain and improve health. Public health professionals may not always be noticed or directly seen by the person who is on this journey, but the public health professionals do their best to ensure that there are no societal obstacles that prevent people from receiving the services they deserve. Dissemination is an important area of study for public health professionals and supports knowledge advancement along all fields on the continuum. Together, rehabilitation, APA&E, and public health professionals can band together to ensure that people with disabilities are adequately supported by exercise services on their journey to live healthy, physically active lifestyles. Of course, it is important to mention that people with disabilities should be included in the development, implementation, evaluation, and dissemination of all exercise programs (i.e., they should inform or directly participate in the entire process because they are the experts of their own lived experiences).

A Note from the Chapter Contributors

In all of our undergraduate and graduate education, we did not receive such guidance on possible career choices that stemmed from a kinesiology-related degree. Our careers resulted from walking blindly along paths we paved mostly by ourselves, with the help of our mentors who were at too early of a stage in their careers to witness the burgeoning and convergence of the three exercise fields presented within this chapter. We hope that the exercise continuum within this chapter provides you with guidance and a clear path for pursuing a career in helping people with disabilities through exercise.

CHAPTER SUMMARY

- Rehabilitation, adapted physical activity, adapted physical education, and public health offer many exciting career opportunities for kinesiologists who are interested in helping people with disabilities through exercise.
- Rehabilitation focuses on restoring function among people with disabilities.
- Adapted physical activity and education focus on promoting inclusive exercise to improve health-related fitness among people with disabilities.
- Public health emphasizes survey and dissemination work to make a meaningful impact on as many people with disabilities as possible.
- Most career paths will require a graduate degree or specialty training (certification).

REFERENCES

1. Twietmeyer, G. (2012). What is kinesiology? Historical and philosophical insights, *Quest, 64*(1), 4–23.
2. American Kinesiology Association. (n.d.). *The undergraduate core in kinesiology 2021.* https://americankinesiology.org/SubPages/Pages/Statement%20on%20Undergraduate%20Core
3. Rimmer, J., & Lai, B. (2015). Framing new pathways in transformative exercise for individuals with existing and newly acquired disability. *Disability and Rehabilitation, 39*(2), 173–180. https://doi.org/10.3109/09638288.2015.1047967.

4. Lai, B., Lee, E., Wagatsuma, M., Frey, G., Stanish, H., Jung, T., & Rimmer, J. H. (2020). Research trends and recommendations for physical activity interventions among children and youth with disabilities: A review of reviews. *Adapted Physical Activity Quarterly, 37*(2), 211–234. https://doi.org/10.1123/apaq.2019-0081.
5. Lai, B., Young, H. J., Bickel, C. S., Motl, R. W., & Rimmer, J. H. (2017). Current trends in exercise intervention research, technology, and behavioral change strategies for people with disabilities: A scoping review. *American Journal of Physical Medicine and Rehabilitation, 96*(10), 748–761. https://doi.org/10.1097/phm.0000000000000743.
6. Nelson, D. L. (1996). Therapeutic occupation: A definition. *American Journal of Occupational Therapy, 50*(10), 775–782. https://doi.org/10.5014/ajot.50.10.775.
7. International Federation of Adapted Physical Activity. (2021). What is APA. https://ifapa.net/what-is-apa/.
8. Hutzler, Y., & Sherrill, C. (2007). Defining adapted physical activity: International perspectives. *Adapted Physical Activity Quarterly, 24*(1), 1–20.
9. Block, M. E. (2016). *A teacher's guide to adapted physical education*: Paul H. Brookes Publishing.
10. Carlon, S. L., Taylor, N. F., Dodd, K. J., & Shields, N. (2013). Differences in habitual physical activity levels of young people with cerebral palsy and their typically developing peers: A systematic review. *Disability and Rehabilitation, 35*(8), 647–655. https://doi.org/610.3109/09638288.09632012.09715721
11. Dairo, Y. M., Collett, J., Dawes, H., & Oskrochi, G. R. (2016). Physical activity levels in adults with intellectual disabilities: A systematic review. *Preventive Medicine Reports, 4*, 209–219.
12. Diaz, K. M. (2020). Physical activity and sedentary behavior among U.S. children with and without down syndrome: The National Survey of Children's Health. *American Journal on Intellectual and Developmental Disabilities, 125*(3), 230–242. https://doi.org/10.1352/1944-7558-125.3.230.
13. McGuire, D. O., Watson, K. B., Carroll, D. D., Courtney-Long, E. A., & Carlson, S. A. (2018). Using two disability measures to compare physical inactivity among U.S. adults with disabilities. *Preventing Chronic Disease, 15*, E08. https://doi.org/10.5888/pcd15.170261.
14. Carroll, D. D., Courtney-Long, E. A., Stevens, A. C., Sloan, M. L., Lullo, C., Visser, S. N., Fox, M. H., Armour, B. S., Campbell, V. A., Brown, D. A., Dorn, J. M., & Centers for Disease Control and Prevention (CDC) (2014). Vital signs: Disability and physical activity--United States, 2009-2012. *Morbidity and Mortality Weekly Report, 63*(18), 407–413.
15. Rimmer, J. H., Chen, M. D., & Hsieh, K. (2011). A conceptual model for identifying, preventing and treating secondary conditions in people with disabilities. *Physical Therapy, 91*(12), 1728–1738.
16. U.S. Department of Health and Human Services. Healthy People 2030, Office of Disease Prevention and Health Promotion. (n.d.). *People with disabilities.* https://health.gov/healthypeople/objectives-and-data/browse-objectives/people-disabilities
17. American Public Health Association. (n.d.). What is public health? 2020 www.apha.org/What-is-Public-Health
18. Bronfenbrenner, U. (1992). *Ecological systems theory.* Jessica Kingsley Publishers.
19. Sallis, J., Owen, N., Fisher, E., Glanz, Z., Rimer, B., & Viswanath, K (2008). Ecological models of health behavior. In K. Glanz, B. K. Rimer, & K. Viswanath (Eds.), *Health behavior and health education: Theory, research, and practice.* Jossey-Bass.
20. Butterfoss, F. D., Kegler, M. C., & Francisco, V. T. (2008). Mobilizing organizations for health promotion: Theories of organizational change. In K. Glanz, B. K. Rimer, & K. Viswanath (Eds.), *Health behavior and health education: Theory, research, and practice* (pp. 335–361). Jossey-Bass.
21. Heaney, C.A., & Israel, B.A. (2008). Social networks and social support. In K. Glanz, B. K. Rimer, & K. Viswanath (Eds.), *Health behavior and health education: Theory, research, and practice* (pp. 189–210). Jossey-Bass.
22. Shields, N., Synnot, A. J., & Barr, M. (2012). Perceived barriers and facilitators to physical activity for children with disability: A systematic review. *British Journal of Sports Medicine, 46*(14), 989–997.
23. Martin Ginis, K. A., Ma, J. K., Latimer-Cheung, A. E., & Rimmer, J. H (2016). A systematic review of review articles addressing factors related to physical activity participation among children and adults with physical disabilities. *Health Psychology Review, 10*(4), 478–494.
24. Green, L. W., Ottoson, J. M., García, C., & Hiatt, R. A (2009). Diffusion theory and knowledge dissemination, utilization, and integration in public health. *Annual Review of Public Health, 30*, 151–174.
25. Choi, B. C. K (2005). Understanding the basic principles of knowledge translation. *Journal of Epidemiology and Community Health, 59*(2), 93.
26. Kingston, J. (2012). Choosing a knowledge dissemination approach. *Knowledge and Process Management, 19*(3), 160–170.
27. Ordonez, M., & Serrat, O. (2017). *Disseminating knowledge products. Knowledge solutions: Tools, methods, and approaches to drive organizational performance.* Springer Singapore, pp. 871–878.
28. Morris, Z. S., Wooding, S., & Grant, J. (2011). The answer is 17 years, what is the question: Understanding time lags in translational research. *Journal of the Royal Society of Medicine, 104*(12), 510–520.
29. Spaulding, L. S., & Pratt, S. M .(2015). A review and analysis of the history of special education and disability advocacy in the United States. *American Educational History Journal, 42*, 91.
30. Meyer, M. (2010). The rise of the knowledge broker. *Science Communication, 32*(1), 118–127.

CHAPTER 5
THERAPEUTIC RECREATION

Shelly Beaver

An active leisure lifestyle is an essential component of health, wellness, and quality of life. Participation in recreational activities enhances our physical, psychological, social, and spiritual well-being. Through leisure, we can learn new skills, socialize with others, relieve stress, experience a sense of freedom, and simply have fun. In addition, our favorite pastimes are a part of who we are and contribute to our self-identity. Leisure is a key ingredient in life satisfaction.

The value and importance of leisure are the same for all people regardless of ability. However, individuals with disabilities, illnesses, and chronic health conditions experience increased barriers preventing them from engaging in meaningful leisure participation. Health related limitations, lack of leisure knowledge or skill, decreased confidence, and inaccessible environments may inhibit their ability to pursue leisure activities of choice and experience the benefits. To overcome these barriers, professional support from a recreational therapist may be required.

This chapter will explore the field of therapeutic recreation (TR) and the role of the recreational therapist in promoting lifelong health and wellness in individuals with disabilities, illnesses, and health impairments through active participation in recreation and leisure. The history of the field, its foundational principles, and the scope of recreational therapy (RT) practice will be presented. Professional practice settings, populations served, and therapeutic interventions will be explained. RT as a career path and opportunities for interprofessional collaboration will also be discussed.

DEFINING THERAPEUTIC RECREATION

Throughout the field's history, a common definition of therapeutic recreation (TR) has been difficult to find, as various scholars, professional organizations, service agencies, and practitioners have explained the term differently to reflect their personal philosophies and perspectives. However, despite their nuances, all descriptions of TR share the same core characteristics. The following themes create the building blocks of therapeutic recreation.

- TR is purposeful and goal-oriented.
- TR uses recreation-based interventions to achieve desired outcomes.
- TR seeks to maintain or improve health, wellness, and quality of life.
- TR is holistic, focusing on physical, cognitive, emotional, social, and spiritual well-being.
- TR is provided to all individuals who may benefit from services but focuses primarily on the needs of individuals with disabilities, illnesses, and health conditions.

These foundational concepts have led to a more formalized definition for the profession and serve to distinguish TR from other related disciplines.

Today, the most comprehensive explanation of TR comes from the American Therapeutic Recreation

Shelly Beaver, Old Dominion University. © Kendall Hunt Publishing Company

Association (ATRA). ATRA is the national professional organization for recreational therapists and promotes the following definition.

> **Recreational therapy**, also known as **therapeutic recreation**, is a systematic process that utilizes recreation and other activity-based interventions to address the assessed needs of individuals with illnesses and/or disabling conditions, as a means to psychological and physical health, recovery and well-being. Further, "Recreational Therapy" means a treatment service designed to restore, remediate and rehabilitate a person's level of functioning and independence in life activities, to promote health and wellness as well as reduce or eliminate the activity limitations and restrictions to participation in life situations caused by an illness or disabling condition.[1]

While this definition acknowledges the interchangeable use of the terms therapeutic recreation and recreational therapy (RT) within the discipline, ATRA endorses the following clarifications.

- Therapeutic Recreation is the field.
- Recreational Therapy is the practice.
- Recreational Therapists are the practitioners.
- The CTRS (Certified Therapeutic Recreation Specialist) is the qualified provider.[2]

ATRA's terminology will be applied in this chapter to distinguish between the field (i.e., TR), the practice (i.e., RT), and the practitioner (i.e., recreational therapist).

FOUNDATIONAL CONCEPTS OF THERAPEUTIC RECREATION

To further one's understanding of therapeutic recreation, it is important to explore the foundational concepts that drive the field. This section examines key terms such as disability, health, well-being, recreation, and leisure and discusses their relevance to recreational therapy practice. The relationships between these concepts are highlighted to demonstrate the value and importance of recreational therapy in the lives of people with disabilities, illnesses, and health conditions.

Disability

Recreational therapy professionals and their practice serve individuals with disabilities. According to the Americans with Disabilities Act (ADA), a person with a disability is defined as one who has, has a record of, or who is regarded as having a physical or mental impairment that substantially limits one or more daily life activities.[3] A wide variety of physical, cognitive, intellectual, and psychological health conditions may be classified as disabilities if their symptoms hinder one's ability to perform common functional tasks including but not limited to seeing, hearing, standing, speaking, reading, and working. The field of TR also considers one's ability to successfully participate in meaningful recreation and leisure when defining disability. Conditions such as spinal cord injury, traumatic brain injury, cerebral palsy, autism spectrum disorder, dementia, and post-traumatic stress disorder are disabilities often treated and supported with RT services.

It is important to note, though the ADA defines individuals with disabilities by their limitations, RT practice uses a strengths-based approach to meet the needs of this population. With clients' input, recreational therapists develop treatment plans, therapeutic interventions, and recreational programs that acknowledge and reflect the capabilities and strengths of their clients. This approach promotes self-confidence, self-determination, optimism, and resiliency leading to an increased sense of happiness and overall well-being.[4]

Health and Well-Being

RT practice strives to enhance the health and well-being of individuals with disabilities. According to the commonly used medical model, health is defined as the absence of illness or disease. This definition directly conflicts with the core values of the field of TR, as it suggests individuals with disabilities live in a constant state of infirmary and are incapable of achieving optimal health. To better align with TR's foundational principles, beliefs, and strengths-based approach, RT professionals apply the World Health Organization's (WHO) definition of health to their practice. The WHO describes **health** as "a state of complete physical, mental, and social well-being and not merely the absence of disease or infirmity."[5] This holistic perspective implies individuals with disabilities *can* achieve an overall state of health by managing their condition and its life impact. Recreational therapy supports individuals with disabilities in reaching holistic health by enhancing their physical, cognitive, social, and emotional functioning; developing their leisure-related skills; and providing opportunities for recreation participation.

Related to health is the concept of well-being. **Well-being** is "a subjective state of successful,

Couple exercising together on a bicycle and in a wheelchair.

satisfying, and productive engagement with one's life and the realization of one's full physical, cognitive, and social-emotional potential."[6] This sense of well-being is influenced by a variety of factors including one's perception of their physical, psychological, social, and spiritual health. People who consider themselves healthy in these domains report higher levels of well-being and overall life satisfaction. For people with disabilities, additional factors such as self-acceptance, sense of belonging, level of independence, autonomy, and environmental features may also contribute to one's sense of well-being.

It is important to note that well-being is a dynamic concept. Just as one's health status fluctuates or life circumstances change, so too their level of perceived wellness may change. Individuals with disabilities and chronic illnesses may be more susceptible to these inconsistencies depending on the nature of their condition. However, both individuals with and without disabilities can positively influence their state of wellness by actively engaging in all aspects of their lives while making intentional choices to create a healthier lifestyle and cope with environmental variables. Recreational therapists can be instrumental in this process, specifically for individuals with disabilities, by teaching healthy decision making skills, leisure-based coping strategies, and stress management techniques to positively influence clients' well-being.

Recreation and Leisure

RT professionals strategically utilize recreation and leisure to improve the overall health and wellness of their clients with disabilities and illnesses. Though the general public uses these terms interchangeably, recreation and leisure have distinguishable definitions in the field of TR. These distinctions are important in guiding RT practice and service delivery.

Recreation is defined as an enjoyable, nonwork *activity* chosen by the participant for the purpose of obtaining some type of intrinsic or extrinsic benefit. **Leisure**, however, is a *subjective state of mind* where the activity is irrelevant and one's individual perception of their experience is paramount. While recreation does not consider how the person feels while participating in the activity, one's personal feelings about their participation are the only thing that matters in leisure. For example, a new college student may go for a daily run to burn off excess energy after classes, to relieve the stress of final exams, or to train for a campus 5K race. They may or may not find pleasure in the activity of running but are motivated to achieve their desired outcome. In this case, running is considered recreation. However, if this same student freely chooses to run after class simply for the sake of running (not because of expected results or external rewards), they are engaging in leisure. In leisure, the participant's optimal state of pleasure gained from the experience itself is most salient while the focus on the activity itself is minimal. For the experience to be considered leisure, a sense of perceived freedom and intrinsic motivation must be present. Additionally, perceived competence, an internal sense of control, and strong feelings of enjoyment are characteristics distinguishing leisure from recreation.

Though distinct, the concepts of recreation and leisure are closely connected. One can experience leisure by actively participating in meaningful recreation.[7] Consider the student in the previous scenario who has been running since their first year of college. While running initially served only as a means of achieving extrinsic reward, the same activity may now bring a sense of leisure satisfaction to the participant. Ongoing participation in this recreation activity likely results in increased skill, self-confidence, and gratification causing a shift in motivation from the tangible outcomes originally sought (e.g., energy release, reduced stress, fitness) to the feelings elicited by the experience itself. To achieve the most satisfying lifestyle, it is advisable to choose and participate in recreation activities experienced as leisure.

These foundational concepts of recreation and leisure are applied in RT practice to meet the wide array of needs presented by clients with disabilities. Through the implementation of goal-driven recreation activities, interventions, and programs, clients may experience a variety of desired outcomes. Measurable improvements in physical, cognitive, social, and emotional functioning may be gained as a result of participation in intentionally designed recreation activities. In addition, RT professionals may use recreation activities to elicit leisure experiences for their clients. Through these leisure experiences, individuals with disabilities may realize feelings of relaxation, rejuvenation, competence, and satisfaction. For example, the RT professional may facilitate a small-group card game to improve clients' fine motor skills, enhance their ability to problem-solve, build peer relationships, and develop leisure-based coping strategies. The very same small-group card game can also provide opportunities to experience fun, escape from daily stressors, and build social capital. These extrinsic and intrinsic benefits obtained through recreation and leisure serve to enhance clients' overall health, well-being, and quality of life.

Senior people playing lotto at care home.

Benefits of Recreation and Leisure Participation through the Life Span

In the field of TR, recreation and leisure are used as therapeutic tools to treat the effects of disability and enhance quality of life. However, one does not have to have a disability or receive RT services to experience the therapeutic benefits of recreation and leisure participation. The value of play is experienced by individuals with and without disabilities during each and every life stage from both structured and informal activities. The benefits of recreation and leisure participation presented in this section are applicable to both clients engaged in RT services and the general population.

Leisure plays an important role in physical development and healthy functioning throughout the life span. Through play, children develop physical strength, endurance, motor skills, motor control, and coordination. Adolescents and young adults can enhance and perfect these skills through recreation participation resulting in peak physical health and performance. As adults age, continued leisure participation helps to maintain good physical health and increase their life expectancy. Regular physical activity has been shown to lower blood pressure and cholesterol, assist with weight management, strengthen muscles and bones, and reduce risk of acquiring a variety of chronic secondary health conditions.[8]

Social well-being is also enhanced through recreation and leisure, assisting in learning about, accomplishing, and adjusting to life's social norms. Children develop social skills such as communication, empathy, self-control, and sharing through play. Recreation and leisure enable adolescents and young adults to explore social groups, develop a self-identity, and establish their independence. Adults and older adults use recreation and leisure to adjust to transitions in family structure, work responsibilities, and living situations while maintaining meaningful social connections with their communities.[9]

Recreation and leisure participation positively impact the emotional domain as well, enhancing one's emotional development and ability to cope with life's ups and downs. Through play, children become skilled in controlling their emotions and expressing them in appropriate ways. For adolescents and young adults, recreation and leisure provide healthy and constructive outlets to manage and reduce feelings of stress and anxiety. Older adults use recreation and leisure to cope with emotional stressors associated with aging and reduce the feelings of loneliness and isolation often prevalent during this life stage.

Child with disability participating in theraputic drumming.
Source: Shelly Beaver

In addition to the tangible physical, social, and emotional impacts of recreation and leisure participation, engagement in one's favorite pastimes can result in other important outcomes influencing well-being. Leisure provides a sense of freedom that is often elusive in everyday life. In these moments, participants are truly free—free to choose any activity deemed personally satisfying and free from any and all obligations. This sense of freedom is quite valuable, as many seek an antidote to their high-pressured careers and demanding personal lives. Leisure provides this reprieve while promoting feelings of happiness, pleasure, and relaxation. Experiencing these emotions helps to refresh and restore both the body and the mind from daily stressors. Lastly, participation in leisure can result in spiritual outcomes, including feelings of connectedness and a state of transcendence. This promotes harmony and a sense of peace with oneself and the world around them.[9]

The many benefits of leisure, as described in this section, demonstrate its importance and value to all. However, recreation and leisure have additional significance for individuals with disabilities and chronic illnesses. Leisure plays an important role in this population's adjustment to the onset of their condition and regaining a sense of optimal health and well-being.[10]

Barriers to Recreation and Leisure Participation

The value of recreation and leisure participation for all people is clear and undeniable—so much so that Article 24 of the United Nations' Universal Declaration of Human Rights identifies leisure as a basic human right.[11] However, due to a variety of leisure constraints, not everyone has the same opportunity to experience the benefits that come from engaging in free-time activities. A variety of environmental, communication, and intrapersonal barriers may limit individuals, particularly those with disabilities, in their pursuit of a satisfying leisure lifestyle. Therefore, goals of recreational therapy practice include decreasing leisure barriers and increasing opportunities for meaningful recreation participation in clients with disabilities.

Environmental leisure barriers are the physical and social factors present or absent within the environment that impede one's ability to access and participate in activities of choice. For individuals with disabilities, inaccessible spaces, insufficient accommodations, and a lack of accessible transportation present significant obstacles to recreation participation.[12] Structural barriers such as stairs, narrow doorways, and high countertops prevent people who use wheelchairs for mobility from accessing and using recreational spaces. The absence of Braille, closed captions, or a sign-language interpreter restrict recreation participation by individuals with sensory impairments. And the inability to drive oneself to recreational sites may inhibit individuals experiencing paralysis, visual impairment, and intellectual disability.

Individuals with disabilities may also experience social leisure constraints. Individuals with an impaired ability to express or receive language may find it challenging to participate in recreation and leisure due to communication barriers. Some pastimes require the skills of reading and writing to successfully participate. Thus, individuals with intellectual, cognitive, or visual impairments may have difficulty engaging in activities such as table games, word puzzles, and baking. Activities requiring verbal communication, such as social gatherings and team sports, may be challenging for members of the Deaf community and individuals with speech impairments. In addition, many recreational activities tend to be social in nature, encouraging a variety of interactions between participants. Appropriate social skills like initiating conversation, active listening, cooperation, and turn-taking are needed for successful participation. Decreased social skills resulting from conditions like autism spectrum disorder (ASD), attention deficit hyperactivity disorder (ADHD), and conduct disorders may hinder these individuals' successful participation.

Lastly, individuals with disabilities may experience **intrapersonal** barriers that negatively impact their participation in recreation and leisure activities. Intrapersonal barriers reside within the individual and create constraints resulting from one's own physical, emotional, or cognitive limits.[13] For individuals with disabilities, symptoms related to their condition (e.g., pain, fatigue, decreased mobility, cognitive deficits) may negatively impact their ability to pursue preferred pastimes, and some recreation activities may be contraindicated due to the risk of medical complications or injury. Additionally, individuals with disabilities may be constrained by a lack of knowledge. This is particularly applicable to individuals who have recently acquired their condition, as they are often unaware of recreation programs, facilities, transportation, adapted equipment, and support services that meet their new needs as individuals with disabilities.

Recreational therapists implement a variety of interventions to reduce leisure barriers experienced by clients with disabilities. Activity-based interventions are used to improve functional abilities (e.g., mobility, problem-solving, communication, appropriate public behavior) and decrease undesired symptoms (e.g., pain, fatigue, weakness) to combat condition-related intrapersonal, communication, and social constraints. In addition, clients engage in leisure education to increase their awareness of leisure resources and develop activity-specific skills to reduce knowledge-related barriers. Finally, skills related to assertiveness, self-advocacy, use of adapted equipment, and disability rights are taught by recreational therapists to ensure clients with disabilities can independently pursue a healthy, active, and meaningful leisure lifestyle. These and other related interventions will be discussed in more depth later in this chapter.

HISTORY OF THERAPEUTIC RECREATION

History shapes what we understand today. Therefore, to truly appreciate how recreational therapy is currently defined and practiced, it is important to review its historical roots. This section will identify the key people, events, themes, and values of various historical periods that were integral to the development of the field of TR in the United States.

Historical Values of Recreation and Leisure

People have engaged in recreation and leisure since the beginning of time. In early societies, free time activities were used for various purposes. For some tribes, play was utilitarian in nature, as it was used to train young warriors for battle and develop essential survival skills. Leisure also served as a necessary means for rest and recouperation from work given the harsh conditions and rigorous tasks associated with survival. Additionally, a sense of solidarity and harmony to communities was achieved through activities such as music, dancing, festivals, and religious ceremonies.[14]

For the Greeks, leisure had a different purpose. Engagement in a variety of virtuous and constructive leisure pursuits was thought to be the secret to reaching "the good life." Men participated in athletic competitions, and those who were socially privileged participated in music, poetry, theater, and philosophical contemplation. A well-rounded leisure lifestyle was considered ideal in this culture.[14]

The Romans implemented a more organized approach to recreation with government sponsored events, including public baths, parades, and gladiator combat in the Colosseum. These activities were used as public entertainment in an attempt to control the masses and reduce community unrest. The purpose of leisure shifted once again during the Renaissance period, as people believed leisure to be a time for self-expression to bring about feelings of happiness and holistic wellness of the mind, body, and spirit.[9,14] This brief review of historical leisure values demonstrates the use of leisure to produce both personal and social benefits.

Historical Treatment of Individuals with Disabilities

Just as leisure has been present since the beginning of time, so too has disability. Both evolutionary and biblical perspectives present evidence of disability, as Neanderthals were thought to have experienced chronic impairments such as arthritis and the Old Testament suggested disability was a punishment from God. In ancient Greece and Rome, illness, injury, and impairment were common due to poor sanitation, pervasive disease, and the effects of war.

During the Middle Ages, cases of mental illnesses, intellectual disability, and leprosy were documented and often addressed with institutionalization.[15]

Residential institutionalization and incarceration of individuals with mental illnesses continued during the Renaissance and Enlightenment periods. It is important to note the overarching purpose of institutionalization at this time was for confinement, not therapy or rehabilitation. This led to the inhumane treatment of individuals with mental illnesses through the early 18th century in both Europe and the United States. In the 19th century, efforts focused on the moral treatment of individuals with mental illnesses were futile due to significant overcrowding and understaffing in the institutions.[15]

During this same time period, some individuals with physical and intellectual disabilities were living in their communities and receiving primary care and support from their families. An emerging healthcare system comprised of general hospitals and almshouses provided treatment to people with illnesses and chronic health conditions. Residential schools were established to educate youth with hearing and visual impairments, while training schools taught job skills to individuals with physical and intellectual disabilities.[15] The humane and inhumane treatment of individuals with disabilities through the 19th century inspired visions for the rehabilitation and integration of individuals with disabilities, particularly in the United States.

Humanism through Recreation

During the Renaissance and Enlightenment periods, humanism became the dominant philosophy, giving prime importance to the worth of human beings. Individual happiness, quality of life, and holistic wellness of the mind, body, and spirit were prioritized, as were human rights and social justice. While this era's leisure values clearly reflected a humanistic ideology, the inhumane treatment of individuals with disabilities in asylums and institutions was in direct conflict with these emerging tenets. In an effort to reform institutional care for individuals with disabilities, several key advocates turned to recreation and leisure to promote a more humanistic approach to treatment and foster holistic wellness of the body and the mind.

In the late 18th and early 19th centuries, Philippe Pinel and William Tuke were instrumental in using recreational activities to provide moral treatment to individuals with mental illnesses. Pinel, the director of the Bicêtre insane asylum, and Tuke, the founder of the York Retreat, promoted the use of outdoor activities like walking and gardening to improve physical and mental health. Benjamin Rush, known as the Father of American Psychiatry, held a prominent position on the board of Pennsylvania Hospital in Philadelphia. He, too, encouraged his clients to use activities such as sewing, music, and exercise to treat their mental illnesses. This purposeful use of recreation and leisure as rehabilitation was a precursor to the field of TR.[16,17]

Community Health through Recreation

The purposeful use of recreation to achieve positive outcomes continued in the late 19th and early 20th centuries with the emergence of settlement houses. Built in response to increasing immigration and unfair labor practices caused by industrialization, settlement houses were social welfare agencies located within impoverished neighborhoods dedicated to improving urban issues through education, recreation, socialization, and advocacy. One of the most well-known settlement houses was Chicago's Hull-House, established by Jane Addams, Ellen Gates Starr, and Mary Keyser in 1889.

In addition to other social services, Hull-House offered a variety of recreational opportunities intended to improve the health and well-being of community members. Sports, dances, boys and girls clubs, and summer camps were developed to engage youth in moral activities while reducing their participation in delinquent behaviors (e.g., street gangs). Playgrounds, recreation centers, and a coffeehouse were built to serve as social centers for the neighborhood. The coffeehouse in particular not only provided a community space for social gatherings and relaxation after work but a healthy alternative to saloons for individuals who experienced alcohol dependency.[18,19] This strategic use of recreation furthered the notion that meaningful engagement can be therapeutic for both individuals and their communities.

Recreation as Therapy for Soldiers

Another important advocate of recreation as therapy was Florence Nightingale, the founder of modern nursing. While working in British hospitals during the Crimean War, Nightingale was profoundly disturbed by the poor conditions and minimal care given to injured soldiers. She was dismayed to observe soldiers turning to alcohol and other drugs to cope with the harsh realities of war. Nightingale criticized hospital leaders for their poor service provision and worked tirelessly to improve quality of care, in part through the therapeutic use of leisure. She recommended soldiers listen to and make music, write, play games, and care for pets as healthy coping mechanisms. In 1855, Nightingale also established the Inkerman Café on hospital grounds, which served as a recreation center and coffee shop where soldiers could gather to play and socialize.[16,17]

Amidst World War I, the American Red Cross recognized leisure's value to recuperating soldiers. The organization constructed recreation huts near military hospitals providing veterans access to movies, entertainment, table games, music, reading, and more to aid in their recovery. This practice continued during World War II, as women, later known as the Gray Ladies, were trained and hired by the Red Cross to provide recreation-based services to wounded soldiers. This practice was called hospital recreation. They implemented activities like gardening, crafts, dances, and educational classes to enhance soldiers' functional skills and improve their physical and mental health.[20] Similar programs were eventually established in the Veterans' Administration (VA) Hospital system and are still widely used today (see Chapter 10 for further information). These initiatives clearly paved the way for the development of Recreational therapy as a profession. One example is depicted in the photo below, recreation for wounded soldiers at 159th US General Hospital in 1945.

(1919) The best form of recreation that has been offered the American soldiers in the big Base Ports has been a new occupation that leaves them no spare time. They have been taught handicrafts of all kinds in the Red Cross Recreation Huts. At St. Nazaire, they specialized on bead work under the direction of Miss Gertrude Farrel of New York City. France, 1919. [29 July date received] [Photograph] Retrieved from the Library of Congress, https://www.loc.gov/item/2017669722/.

The Emergence of Therapeutic Recreation as a Profession

By the 1940s, RT was being used in various settings including hospitals, psychiatric institutions, military facilities, residential schools, and even prisons. This prompted the need for an organized profession with trained specialists. As a result, various professional organizations focused on the purposeful use of recreation for individuals with disabilities and health impairments were developed. The Hospital Recreation Section of the American Recreation Society (HRS/ARS) was established in 1948 for professionals working in military and VA hospitals. The Recreation Therapy Section of the American Association for Health, Physical Education, and Recreation (AAHPER) was established in 1952 for professionals focused on the benefits of physical activity. And, in 1953, the National Association of Recreational Therapists (NART) was established for people employed by state psychiatric hospitals and state schools for individuals with intellectual disabilities. Shortly thereafter, representatives of these three organizations collaborated to form the Council for Advancement of Hospital Recreation and created a credentialing program for RT professionals. This early credentialing program eventually led to the development of the National Council on Therapeutic Recreation Certification (NCTRC) in 1981. NCTRC remains the national credentialing body for recreational therapists today.[21]

In 1966, HRS/ARS, the Recreation Therapy Section of AAHPER, and NART merged to become the National Therapeutic Recreation Society (NTRS), a branch of the newly established National Recreation and Park Association (NRPA). The organization's name reflected the newly established umbrella term *therapeutic recreation* and intended to encapsulate the differing philosophies of the founding organizations. Prior to the merge, the HRS/ARS assumed a leisure orientation to TR (i.e., recreation for all) while both the Recreation Therapy Section of AAHPER and NART followed a therapy orientation (i.e., recreation as a tool for treatment and rehabilitation). After decades of discussion within the field about the true purpose of TR, a group of clinically minded figures within the field initiated a movement to create an independent organization focused on "TR as clinical practice" to address rapid changes in the healthcare industry and represent the interests of many practicing recreational therapists. Thus, in 1984, the American Therapeutic Recreation Association (ATRA) was established and continues to serve as the nation's primary organization representing the interests of recreational therapists today.[16,21,22]

An Increased Need for Therapeutic Recreation

As recreational therapists worked diligently to establish their profession, significant social changes occurring in the United States emphasized the growing need for the field of TR. One significant trend of the late 1950s was the deinstitutionalization of individuals with psychiatric conditions. Because of the development of psychotropic medicines, the establishment of nursing homes, and the emergence of a community mental health philosophy, individuals with mental illnesses and intellectual disabilities were leaving state institutions and reintegrating into their communities.[23] This resulted in a significant need for community-based care, support, and free-time activities to maintain and improve the holistic health of these populations. In response, a variety of human services organizations were established, several of which focused specifically on recreation participation for individuals with disabilities. Special recreation associations, often staffed by recreational therapy professionals, were created among municipal park districts to develop and provide leisure services specifically for individuals with disabilities in community settings. Additionally, the National Wheelchair Athletic Association was developed to engage athletes with a disability in recreational and competitive sports, while Special Olympics offered summer camps and large-scale athletic events for individuals with intellectual disabilities (see Chapter 10 for more discussion on these organizations).

In the early 1970s, the Disability Rights Movement picked up steam and resulted in the passing of key legislation focused on the inclusion of individuals with disabilities. The Architectural Barriers Act of 1968 and the Rehabilitation Act of 1973 mandated physical accessibility and the elimination of environmental barriers for individuals with disabilities in any entity receiving federal funds (e.g., national parks). The Rehabilitation Act of 1978 provided amendments to the 1973 act and secured federal funding for the initiation of recreation programs for individuals with disabilities to assist with mobility and socialization. Also, the Education for All Handicapped Children Act of 1975 was established to guarantee children with disabilities a free and appropriate public education. This law was reauthorized and renamed in 1990 as the Individuals with Disabilities Education Act (IDEA), which mandated children with disabilities receive a free and appropriate public education in the least restrictive environment. Under this law, the provision of physical education for students with disabilities is required and TR may be included in a child's Individualized Education Plan if this related service is necessary.[13]

The Americans with Disabilities Act (ADA) of 1990 was the hallmark of the Disability Rights Movement. The ADA aimed to protect the civil rights of individuals with disabilities while preventing discrimination in the areas of employment; state and local government services (including public transportation); public accommodations and commercial facilities; and telecommunications. As a result, opportunities for individuals with disabilities to obtain jobs and engage in community-based recreation dramatically increased. The services of recreational therapy professionals were in demand as agencies sought expertise in revamping existing programs to ensure accessibility by and the integration of community members with disabilities.

Therapeutic Recreation Today

Today, the professional field of therapeutic recreation is alive and well. There are more than 20,000 recreational therapists practicing in the United States, and over 19,000 have earned the Certified Therapeutic Recreation Specialist (CTRS) credential from NCTRC.[24,25] The U.S. Bureau of Labor Statistics projects the employment of recreational therapists to grow 10 percent over the next 10 years.[25] With an aging population, an increase in the number of individuals with chronic health conditions, and the ongoing needs of veterans with disabilities, the demand for RT services remains strong to treat and manage these conditions while promoting an active and healthy leisure lifestyle for all individuals with disabilities.

RECREATIONAL THERAPY—THE PRACTICE

As characterized throughout this chapter, recreation and leisure have therapeutic powers. Engaging in one's favorite pastimes can restore the body and the mind and promote an enhanced sense of holistic wellness. However, though it is beneficial to individuals with and without disabilities, everyday participation in recreational activities does not constitute recreational therapy. This section will serve to delineate recreational therapy as a professional practice serving the health and leisure needs of clients with disabilities, illnesses, or other health conditions.

Underlying Principles of Recreational Therapy

As previously defined, recreational therapy is a systematic process that uses goal-directed recreation and activity-based interventions to enhance the functional abilities, holistic health, and overall well-being of individual clients. This definition embodies three important underlying principles that guide RT practice and service delivery:

- RT follows a systematic process.
- RT interventions are goal-directed.
- RT uses a person-centered approach.

Each key principle will be explored to provide further insight into the work of the recreational therapist.

The Recreational Therapy Process

To ensure the highest quality of service delivery, recreational therapists follow a systematic process to build programs and provide individualized services to clients. This process, known as the recreational therapy process, is composed of five major components.

- **A**ssessment—obtain pertinent information about the client
- **P**lanning—develop an individualized intervention plan and client goals
- **I**mplementation—carry out the intervention plan
- **E**valuation—determine whether client goals were met
- **D**ocumentation—record client information, participation, and progress

These five components are referred to as APIED (pronounced "a-pied") in the field. Recreational therapists in all practice settings follow this process to ensure their services are effective and efficient in meeting clients' individual needs and achieving predetermined outcomes. Therefore, it can be argued that professionals not following the APIED process are not truly providing RT, as each stage of this process is essential to reaching therapeutic outcomes.[26]

Assessment. The first step in the APIED process is assessment. During this stage, the recreational therapist gathers essential information about the

CHAPTER 5: Therapeutic Recreation 75

```
Assessment → Planning → Implementation → Evaluation
                    ↓   ↓   ↓   ↓
                    Documentation
```

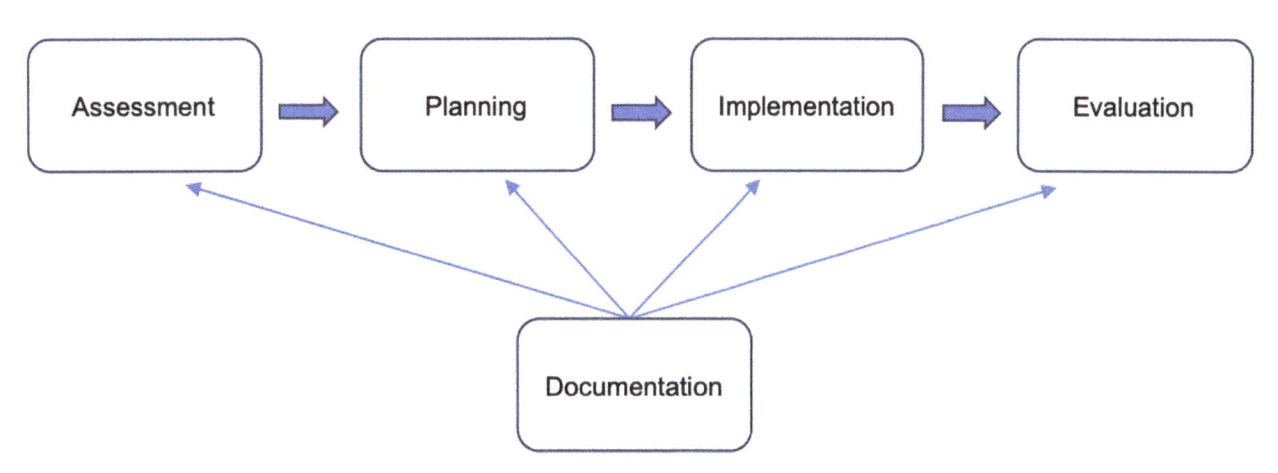

FIGURE 5.1 The RT process.
Source: Shelly Beaver

client to inform the development of an appropriate and individualized intervention plan. A variety of assessment methods are used to learn about a client's strengths, areas of need, leisure interests, participation patterns, and preferences. The recreational therapist may conduct their assessment by reviewing existing medical documents, administering a standardized assessment tool or leisure interest inventory, conducting an interview, or simply observing the client. Because this step is so crucial to the effectiveness of the RT process, most recreational therapists use multiple approaches to ensure their assessment is thorough and accurately representative of the needs, goals, and lifestyle of the client.

Planning. The second step in the APIED process is planning. During this stage, the recreational therapist uses information gathered during the assessment process to prioritize the client's needs and develop an individualized intervention plan (also called a program plan or treatment plan). The recreational therapist, in collaboration with the client, develops a set of goals and objectives to clearly identify the intended outcomes of RT services. Then, based on the client's strengths, needs, and leisure interests, appropriate evidence-based RT strategies, interventions, and programs are prescribed to achieve the desired outcomes. A projected schedule is also outlined to include the frequency, duration, and intensity of the client's participation in the selected interventions. Lastly, during the planning stage, the recreational therapist identifies how client progress will be evaluated and measured.

Implementation. The third step in the APIED progress is implementation. During this stage,

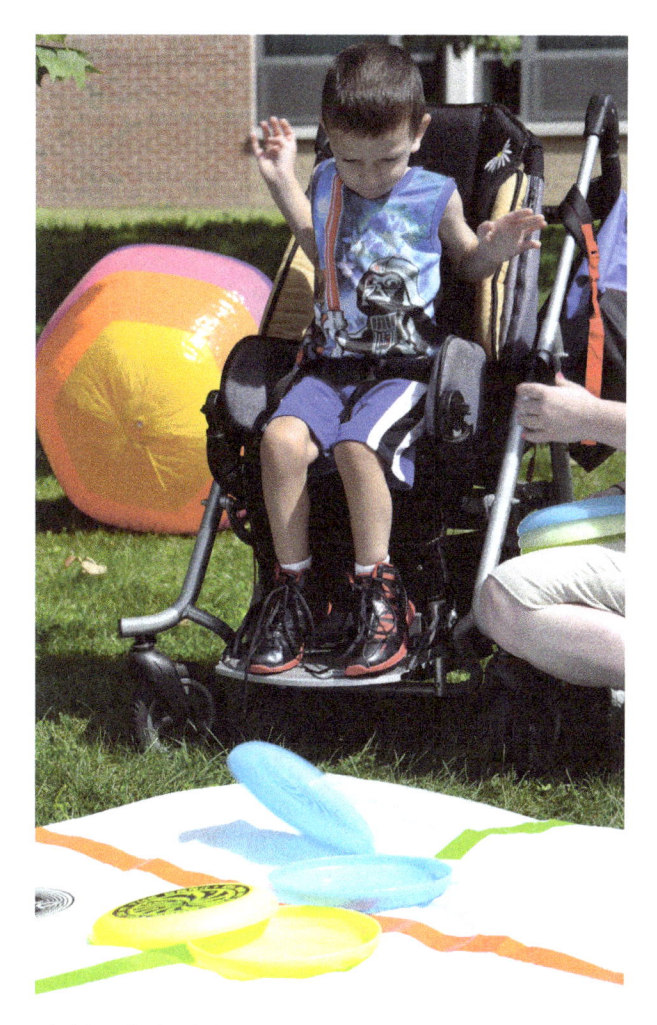

Child with disability playing a yard game.
Source: Shelly Beaver

the recreational therapist puts the individualized intervention plan into action by engaging the client in their prescribed interventions and programs. A one-to-one, small group, or large group approach may be utilized depending on the client's goals, needs, and preferences as well as the nature of the activity or program. The recreational therapist facilitates the interventions while maintaining a therapeutic environment in which the client feels welcomed, comfortable, encouraged, and pressure-free.[7] Client behaviors and progress are continually monitored and feedback is provided to the client throughout the RT experience. Modifications to the client's treatment plan are made as needed.

Evaluation. The final step in the APIED process is evaluation. During this stage, the recreational therapist uses a variety of methods to determine how effective the intervention plan was in achieving the client's goals. Standardized tools may be used to measure client progress by comparing the client's post-intervention scores to those obtained during the assessment process. Observations conducted by the recreational therapist and other members of the treatment team can determine whether the intended outcomes were achieved. Most importantly, the thoughts, feelings, and perceptions of the client are also used to analyze the client's level of success. At this point, the recreational therapist will determine if additional RT services are needed or if the client will be discharged. Referrals to other programs or services may also be made at this time.

Documentation. Documentation is an essential component of the RT process. It is completed by the recreational therapist during each and every stage of APIE. Key information about the client and their progress is recorded in the client's medical record or client file to provide evidence of RT services and to track client progress. Documents completed by RT professionals include assessment summaries, client goals and objectives, individualized intervention plans, treatment protocols, participation records, client observations, evaluation summaries, and discharge/transition plans. Care team members use these artifacts to communicate across disciplines and ensure continuity of care. Additionally, RT documentation is used to demonstrate accountability and compliance with regulations imposed by the agency, governmental agencies, and accrediting bodies.

A Goal-Directed Approach

Recreational therapy utilizes a goal-directed approach to service delivery. During the planning phase of the RT process, a set of client goals is established based on the results of the initial assessment. These goals guide the development and implementation of the intervention plan. To ensure the client's participation in RT is meaningful and of value, the established goals must be individualized, have relevance and importance to the client, and reflect the client's desired outcomes.[7] To achieve this, the recreational therapist and client work together to develop and select the most appropriate goals. Through this approach, clients experience a greater sense of autonomy and motivation during their participation in RT services and, as a result, realize greater outcomes.

A Person-Centered Approach

Recreational therapy uses a person-centered approach to service delivery. The goal of person-centered care is to ensure the RT experience is meaningful and valuable to each individual client. Recognizing the uniqueness of each client and their circumstances, clients are empowered to take an active role in the RT process to ensure services received align with their individual needs, preferences, values, cultural traditions, and goals. Family, friends, and other members of a client's support network may collaborate as well. The recreational therapist molds the intervention plan to account for and reflect the client's input while maintaining the client's senses of autonomy, self-determination, and freedom of choice.[7,27] Additionally, the TR environment created by the recreational therapist demonstrates genuineness, empathy, and unconditional positive regard for the client, promoting more positive therapeutic outcomes.[28]

Recreational Therapy Practice Models

Recreational therapy practice models provide additional insight into the purpose, scope, and delivery of RT services. RT professionals can select from a variety of field-specific models to structure and guide their practice. Two of the most widely used models, the Leisure Ability Model and the Health Protection/Health Promotion Model, will be discussed in detail, as they are most reflective of the philosophies presented in this chapter.

Leisure Ability Model

According to the **Leisure Ability Model,** the purpose of recreational therapy is to improve an individual's ability to "engage in a successful, appropriate, and meaningful independent leisure lifestyle that, in turn, leads to improved health, quality of life, and well-being."[29] The model suggests three major categories of RT service (i.e., functional intervention, leisure education, and recreation participation) can assist clients in achieving this outcome. Each category of service has a distinct purpose, and the role of the recreational therapist is modified to ensure therapeutic goals are met. Clients may participate in one, two, or all three categories of service depending on their assessed needs.

The first category of RT service is functional intervention. During this phase, the RT professional acts as a therapist to improve the client's physical, cognitive, social, and emotional abilities necessary for successful leisure participation. The client's functional needs are assessed, and specific activity-based interventions are prescribed by the recreational therapist to target the identified needs. For example, a client with a spinal cord injury who wants to pursue wheelchair sports may participate in therapeutic activities designed to improve strength, endurance, and mobility, as these skills are required for successful participation. A client who experienced a stroke may engage in interventions focused on improving memory and problem solving to successfully play table games with their family. While the client contributes to the development of the intervention plan in this phase of RT, the recreational therapist exerts significant control over the therapeutic process.[30]

The second category of RT service, leisure education, focuses on developing a client's leisure-related skills, attitudes, and knowledge to promote a healthy and independent leisure lifestyle. The role of the RT professional is an instructor, as they teach the client a variety of leisure-related concepts and skills. Through leisure awareness modalities, the client gains knowledge of the benefits of leisure, identifies goals for their leisure participation, and learns healthy decision-making skills to ensure their free time pursuits are valuable. The recreational therapist may also teach the client specific leisure and social skills to reduce leisure barriers and promote active participation. Finally, as part of leisure education, clients increase their knowledge of and ability to use community-based leisure resources (e.g., recreation programming, accessible transportation). Though the RT professional maintains a fair amount of control over the therapeutic process during this phase, the client takes a more active role by applying the knowledge and skills gained to their personal leisure pursuits.[30]

The final category of RT service is recreation participation. "Recreation participation programs are structured activities that allow the client to practice newly acquired skills, and/or experience enjoyment and self-expression."[30] The recreational therapist organizes and facilitates the activity while the client is responsible for their own engagement as well as the outcomes of their participation. Through recreation participation, the client gains competence and confidence in their leisure pursuits leading to an independent and satisfying leisure lifestyle.[30] Refer to the leisure ability model case scenario (Figure 5.2) to see how this model is applied in RT practice.

Health Protection/Health Promotion Model

The Health Protection/Health Promotion Model also serves to describe and guide RT practice in the context of three components of service. However, while the Leisure Ability Model focuses on leisure functioning, the Health Protection/Health Promotion Model centers around optimal health.[26] Under the **Health Protection/Health Promotion Model**, the purpose of recreational therapy is twofold. RT can assist clients in restoring a state of health after experiencing disability or illness (i.e., health protection), and it can help clients experiencing disability or chronic illness to maintain a high level of health and well-being (i.e., health promotion).[31]

This model identifies three broad interventions used by RT professionals to move clients through a continuum of health ranging from poor health to optimal health. When a client is experiencing poor health, the RT professional implements prescriptive activities to combat feelings of depression, helplessness, and a lack of control. The structure and direction provided by the recreational therapist in this intervention allow clients to regain a sense of autonomy and competence over their well-being. Once a sense of stability is achieved, clients enter the second intervention in the model, recreation. The recreational therapist and client act as partners to identify activities of intrinsic value to the client and set goals for their participation. The RT professional supports the client's participation in these activities to promote mastery of skills, an enhanced self-concept, and a restored level of health. The final component of the continuum is leisure during which the focus shifts from health protection to health promotion. The client exhibits self-determination in their selection of and participation in leisure activities, and their full potential is realized with the continued support of the RT professional. At this point, the client is capable of achieving optimal health through independent leisure participation, and RT services are no longer needed.[26]

> Mr. James is 80 years old and recently experienced a stroke resulting in mild memory loss and paralysis of the right leg. Recreational therapy services were ordered as part of his treatment plan. To provide the best outcomes, the CTRS followed the RT process and used the Leisure Ability Model to guide Mr. James' treatment.
>
> - Assessment: The CTRS met with Mr. James to conduct an initial assessment. Through the interview process and use of standardized assessment tools, the CTRS identified Mr. James' strengths, leisure interests, and functional needs.
> - Planning: Based on the information gathered during the initial assessment and with input from Mr. James, the following goals were created by the CTRS: (1) increase upper extremity strength; (2) enhance short-term memory; and (3) maintain an active leisure lifestyle. Mr. James was scheduled to engage in RT three times per week for eight weeks. Each session had a duration of 45 minutes.
> - Implementation: The CTRS addressed Mr. James' assessed needs using a variety of RT interventions reflective of the client's leisure interests and focused on functional intervention, leisure education, and recreation participation.
>   - Functional Intervention: For the first four weeks, the CTRS, in collaboration with the physical therapist, engaged Mr. James in a small group fitness class with basic exercises using light weights and resistance bands. Additionally, Mr. James participated in a large group drum circle facilitated by the CTRS which required gross motor movements of the upper extremities and recall of simple drumming patterns. Both interventions targeted Mr. James' functional goals of increased upper extremity strength and enhanced short-term memory.
>   - Leisure Education: During weeks five and six, the CTRS focused on developing Mr. James' leisure-related skills through leisure education. Using a one-to-one approach, the CTRS assisted Mr. James in identifying his personal leisure goals, potential barriers to participation, and strategies for overcoming those barriers. The CTRS assisted Mr. James in researching community-based programs and accessible transportation. Mr. James practiced reserving van transport and registered for two programs at the senior center. The CTRS facilitated a community outing to the local senior center to allow Mr. James to practice accessing and using the leisure resources in his area.
>   - Recreation Participation: The last two weeks of RT focused on maintaining Mr. James' active leisure lifestyle. The CTRS offered several activity programs, and Mr. James selected and engaged in those that aligned with his interests and current skill levels. The CTRS provided encouragement and positive reinforcement as Mr. James worked to increase his independence in pursuing leisure activities of choice.
> - Evaluation: Throughout the eight weeks, the CTRS monitored Mr. James' progress. Upon conclusion of the treatment period, the CTRS reviewed all documented observations and administered the same standardized assessments that were conducted at the start of treatment. Progress was measured, and Mr. James was discharged from RT services as all goals were met.

FIGURE 5.2 Leisure ability model case scenario.
Source: Shelly Beaver

Recreational Therapy Interventions

The primary goals of recreational therapy are to enhance functional skills, decrease leisure barriers, and promote a state of optimal health that includes a satisfying leisure lifestyle. To realize these therapeutic outcomes, recreational therapists implement a plethora of modalities focused on the physical, cognitive, social, emotional, and spiritual domains. Activities such as aquatics, tai chi, table games, music, creative arts, guided imagery, aromatherapy, and meditation are frequently used in the field to achieve client goals. The field of TR also utilizes a host of unique interventions to target specific client needs. This section will present a sample of the specialized evidence-based interventions used in RT practice.

Adapted Sports

Adapted sports are recreational or competitive sports activities that have been modified for individuals with disabilities. While any sport can be adapted, some of the most popular are wheelchair basketball, adapted skiing, goalball, wheelchair rugby, and

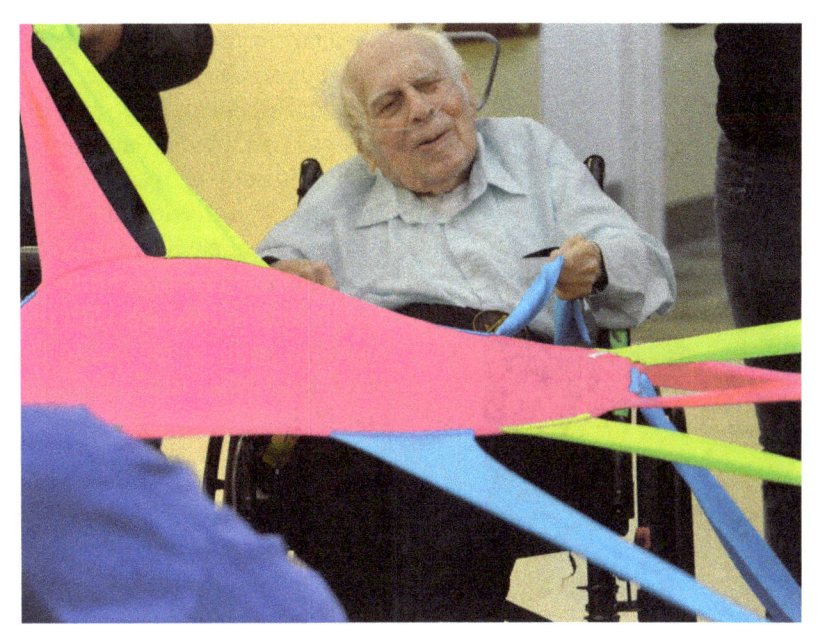

Older adult engaging in upper-extremity fitness activity.
Source: Shelly Beaver

adapted cycling. Recreational therapists prescribe this intervention for a variety of populations including youth, young adults, and veterans with physical, intellectual, and psychological disabilities. Specific sports are selected based on a client's assessed leisure interests and needs. Therapeutic outcomes include improved physical skills (e.g., strength, endurance, mobility), social skills (e.g., teamwork, emotional control), health (e.g., decreased blood pressure, depression management), self-confidence, and quality of life.

Animal Assisted Interventions (AAI)

"**Animal-assisted interventions** are goal-oriented and structured interventions that incorporate animals in health, education, and human service for the purpose of therapeutic gains and improved health and wellness."[32] Specially trained therapy animals are used in one-to-one or small group sessions to elicit therapeutic outcomes in both medical and community settings. Target populations include individuals with traumatic brain injury, ASD, dementia, depression, behavioral disorders, and developmental disability. Older adults in long-term care settings also benefit from AAI. Recreational therapists engage their client with the therapy animal in a variety of ways such as petting the animal, talking or reading to the animal, providing care for the animal (e.g., walking, brushing, feeding), and teaching the animal tricks. Therapeutic outcomes of AAI include lowered blood pressure, reduced anxiety, increased tolerance for pain, reduced isolation, increased alertness, increased motivation, and improved speech.[33]

Reminiscence

Reminiscence therapy is a cognitive intervention used to stimulate clients' memory and review past life events to promote feelings of life satisfaction. This intervention is most often implemented with older adults but can be beneficial for individuals with memory impairments and mental health conditions as well. One to one or in small groups, the recreational therapist guides a meaningful discussion using photos, stories, music, props, and aromas to prompt clients' reflection on their past. Topics may include holidays, weddings, children, historical eras, or leisure interests. Therapeutic outcomes of reminiscence include increased socialization, decreased anxiety and depression, improved self-esteem, and an enhanced sense of well-being.[33]

Adventure Therapy

Adventure therapy (AT) is rapidly growing in popularity for youth and adults with behavioral and mental health conditions. AT uses an experiential approach to actively engage clients in activities perceived as challenging or risky to evoke personal growth and

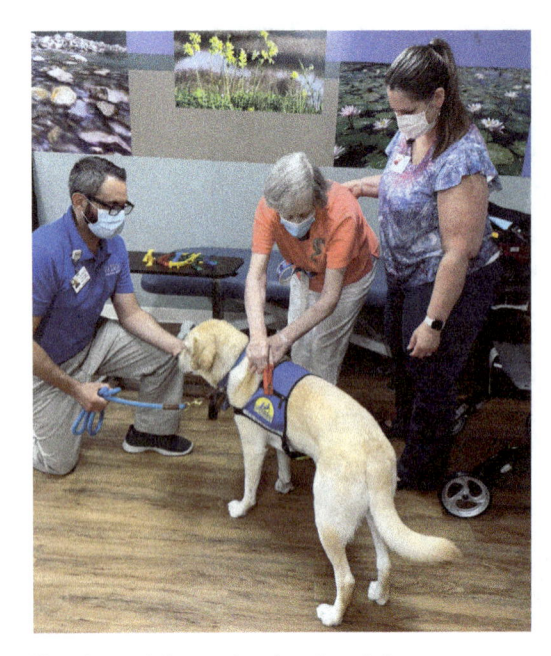

Yanni providing animal assisted therapy.
Source: Photo © Dana Hayner

behavioral change. These activities may occur indoors or outdoors and include cooperative tasks, trust activities, ropes courses, outdoor adventure activities, expeditions, and more. The recreational therapist uses strong leadership skills to guide clients through the adventure-themed tasks, encouraging them to engage physically, socially, emotionally, cognitively, and spiritually.[33,34] Following the activity, the RT professional facilitates a debrief where the participants process their experiences and discuss what they have learned as a result. Lessons learned are then aligned with clients' individual goals and applied to their everyday lives. Therapeutic outcomes include increased self-esteem, improved emotional control, decreased anxiety and depression, and reduced deviant behavior.

Community Reintegration

Community integration is an important RT intervention to promote the inclusion of individuals with disabilities. Its primary purpose is to ensure individuals with newly acquired conditions can successfully return to and actively engage in all aspects of their environment including work, education, recreation, and socialization.[33] The recreational therapist collaborates with the client to plan a community outing where the client practices skills acquired through therapy such as wheelchair mobility, healthy decision making, effective communication, and self-advocacy. Additionally, the client acquires knowledge of community resources and supports including accessible transportation, recreational opportunities, and advocacy and support groups. Therapeutic outcomes of community reintegration include increased confidence, independence, and perceived freedom as well as decreased isolation and perceived environmental and psychological barriers. Populations benefiting from this intervention can include individuals with physical disabilities, individuals with mental health conditions, individuals impacted by the justice system, and veterans.

Collaborative Practice

In many settings, recreational therapists work as members of interdisciplinary teams, collaborating with a variety of professionals to deliver the most effective and efficient services to clients. According to the World Health Organization, interprofessional practice can improve client health outcomes, reduce length of treatment, and increase client satisfaction.[35] Therefore, RT professionals may implement therapeutic interventions and services in partnership with members of their team.

In acute care and physical rehabilitation settings, the RT professional may collaborate with physical therapists, occupational therapists, speech-language pathologists, social workers, and nurses to facilitate therapeutic activities. In psychiatric settings, psychologists and mental health workers may colead treatment sessions with the recreational therapist. In long-term care, the RT staff regularly collaborate with dieticians and pastoral care professionals, and, in community settings, vocational rehabilitation counselors, athletic trainers, coaches, and teachers are partners in care.

A CAREER IN THERAPEUTIC RECREATION

According to the U.S. Bureau of Labor Statistics, the number of recreational therapists employed in the United States is expected to grow over the next decade.[25] This is good news for those interested in pursuing a career as an RT professional. To secure one of the many jobs in the field of TR, employment candidates must have the proper knowledge, training, and credentials to be successful. This section outlines the education and certification requirements for work as a recreational therapist and discusses the various settings in which one may work. Professional organizations that support and advance the field are featured as well.

Education Requirements

Recreational therapists must be competent in the foundational concepts of therapeutic recreation. Therefore, a bachelor's degree in recreational therapy or a related field (e.g., leisure studies, parks and recreation, recreation and sport management) with a concentration in RT is typically required to enter the field.[36] Academic courses teaching the basic concepts of human development, recreation and leisure, disability, and all components of the RT process are essential for professional preparation. Most bachelor's degree programs also require a TR-specific internship experience. If desired, professionals-in-training may pursue a supporting minor, such as psychology, gerontology, kinesiology, youth development, or special education, to enhance their knowledge of specific populations.

Professional Certification

Though not all employment opportunities in TR require professional certification, the Certified Therapeutic Recreation Specialist (CTRS) is considered the qualified provider of RT services. The National Council for Therapeutic Recreation Certification (NCTRC) is responsible for certifying RT professionals and does so through a rigorous credentialing process. Applicants who have successfully completed required TR and supportive (e.g., anatomy and physiology, abnormal psychology) courses, as well as a field-based internship or extensive TR paid work experience, are eligible to sit for the CTRS exam. Those who meet all requirements and pass the certification exam may use the CTRS credential. To maintain their certification, CTRSs are required to complete a total of 50 hours of continuing education every 5 years.

Professional Settings and Populations Served

One of the most attractive aspects of TR as a career is the many settings in which an RT professional can work. Since RT services are provided to individuals of all ages with a variety of conditions and needs, a wide array of professional opportunities exists with diverse client populations. According to NCTRC's 2014 Job Analysis Report, nearly 38% of RT professionals work in behavioral and mental health, 30% work in settings serving older adults, 20% work in physical medicine, and nearly 12% work with individuals with developmental disabilities.[37]

Recreational therapists are employed in acute care and physical rehabilitation hospitals, psychiatric treatment facilities (including drug treatment programs), long-term care facilities, and community agencies, such as municipal parks and recreation departments, adapted sports programs, adult day services, and summer camp programs. Additionally, a CTRS may find employment in schools, correctional facilities, and military-affiliated agencies. Services provided may be specific to individuals with disabilities, or they may occur in inclusive settings. Therefore, job titles may be RT-specific (e.g., CTRS, recreational therapist, therapeutic recreation specialist) or reflect a broader scope of service (e.g., inclusion specialist, life enrichment coordinator, adapted recreation specialist).

Professional Organizations

Various professional organizations support the needs of practicing recreational therapists. The national professional organization for RT professionals in the United States is the American Therapeutic Recreation Association (ATRA), and the Canadian Therapeutic Recreation Association (CTRA) represents the interests of recreational therapists in Canada. Regional and state-level professional organizations also exist to support those in the field. Such organizations provide opportunities for continuing education, professional networking, and advocacy. Their overarching purpose is to strengthen both the field and the practice.

CHAPTER SUMMARY

This chapter explored the field of TR and the role of the recreational therapist in promoting lifelong health and wellness in individuals with disabilities, illnesses, and health conditions through active participation in recreation and leisure. Key points include:

- Recreation and leisure participation contribute to the holistic health and overall well-being of individuals with and without disabilities throughout the life span.
- Individuals with disabilities often experience a variety of environmental, communication,

and intrapersonal barriers to successful recreation and leisure participation.
- The field of therapeutic recreation was established to assist individuals with disabilities in overcoming leisure constraints, achieving a meaningful leisure lifestyle, and reaching a state of optimal health.
- Recreational therapists follow a systematic process (i.e., APIED) that uses goal-directed activity-based interventions to enhance clients' functional abilities, provide leisure education, and encourage independent recreation participation.
- A person-centered approach is utilized by recreational therapists to empower clients and maximize therapeutic outcomes.
- A variety of therapeutic interventions (e.g., adapted sports, animal assisted interventions, reminiscence, adventure therapy, community reintegration) are implemented to meet the physical, cognitive, social, emotional, and spiritual needs of diverse populations in clinical, community, and agency settings.
- While practitioners in the field of TR may hold a variety of professional titles, the certified therapeutic recreation specialist (CTRS) is the qualified provider of recreational therapy services.

REFERENCES

1. American Therapeutic Recreation Association. (n.d.). *About recreational therapy.* www.atra-online.com/page/AboutRecTherapy.
2. American Therapeutic Recreation Association. (2015) *Who we are.* www.atra-online.com/page/WhoWeAre.
3. ADA.gov. (n.d.) *Americans with disabilities act of 1990, as amended.* www.ada.gov/pubs/adastatute08.htm#12102.
4. Heyne, L. A., & Anderson, L. S. (2012). Theories that support strengths-based practice in therapeutic recreation. *Therapeutic Recreation Journal, 46*(2), 106–128.
5. World Health Organization (WHO). (2022). *Constitution.* https://www.who.int/about/governance/constitution.
6. Hood, C., & Carruthers, C. (2007). Enhancing leisure experience and developing resources. *Therapeutic Recreation Journal, 41*(4), 298–325.
7. Kunstler, R., & Stavola Daly, F. (2010). *Therapeutic recreation leadership and programming.* Human Kinetics.
8. Centers for Disease Control and Prevention (CDC). (2021). *Benefits of Physical Activity.* www.cdc.gov/physicalactivity/basics/pa-health/index.htm.
9. Russell, R. (2020). *Pastimes: The context of contemporary leisure* (7th ed.). Sagamore-Venture.
10. Caldwell, L. L. (2005). Leisure and health: Why is leisure therapeutic?. *British Journal of Guidance and Counselling, 33*(1), 7–26.
11. United Nations. (n.d.). *Universal declaration of human rights.* https://www.un.org/en/about-us/universal-declaration-of-human-rights
12. Dattilo, J. (2017). *Inclusive leisure services* (4th ed.). Sagamore-Venture.
13. Austin, D. R., & Lee, Y. (2013). *Inclusive and special recreation* (6th ed.) Sagamore Publishing.
14. Genoe, M. R., Kennedy, D., Singleton, J. F., Hopper, T., & Sturts, J. (2019). History of recreation. In Tapps, T., & Wells, M. S. (Eds.), *Introduction to recreation and leisure* (3rd ed., pp. 23–41). Human Kinetics.
15. Braddock, D. L., & Parish, S. L. (2001). An institutional history of disability. In Albrecht, G. L., Seelman, K., & Bury, M. (Eds.), *Handbook of disability studies* (pp. 11–68). SAGE. http://dx.doi.org/10.4135/9781412976251.n2.
16. Long, T., & Robertson, T. (Eds.), *Foundations of therapeutic recreation* (2nd ed.). Human Kinetics.
17. Carter, M. J., & Van Andel, G. E. (2011). *Therapeutic recreation: A practical approach* (4th ed.). Waveland Press, Inc.
18. Addams, J. (1910). *Twenty years at Hull House.* The MacMillan Company.
19. Reynolds II, J. F. (2017). Jane Addams' forgotten legacy: Recreation and sport [Special Issue]. *Journal of Issues in Intercollegiate Athletics*, July, 11–18.
20. Bedini, L. (1995). The play ladies: The first therapeutic recreation specialists. *Journal of Physical Education, Recreation & Dance, 66*(8), 32–35.
21. Austin, D. R. (2004). Therapeutic recreation: A long past, but a brief history. *Palaestra, 20*(1), 37–42.
22. American Therapeutic Recreation Association (ATRA). (n.d.). *History of ATRA.* www.atra-online.com/page/HistoryofATRA.
23. Talbott, J. A. (2004). Deinstitutionalization: Avoiding the disasters of the past. *Psychiatric Services, 55*(10), 1112–1115. https://doi.org/10.1176/appi.ps.55.10.1112.
24. National Council for Therapeutic Recreation Certification. (2022). *About NCTRC.* www.nctrc.org/about-ncrtc/.
25. U.S. Bureau of Labor Statistics. (2022). *Occupational outlook handbook: Recreational therapists.* www.bls.gov/ooh/healthcare/recreational-therapists.htm.
26. Austin, D. R. (2018). *Therapeutic recreation processes and techniques: Evidence-based recreational therapy* (8th ed.). Sagamore-Venture Publishing LLC.
27. Hebblethwaite, S. (2013). "I think that it could work but…": Tensions between the theory and practice of person-centered and relationship-centered care. *Therapeutic Recreation Journal, 47*(1), 13–34.

28. Rogers, C. R. (1981). The foundations of the person-centered approach. *Dialectics and Humanism, 8*(1), 5–16. https://doi.org/10.5840/dialecticshumanism19818123.
29. Stumbo, N. J., & Peterson, C. A., (2021). *Therapeutic recreation program design: Principles and procedures* (6th ed.). Sagamore-Venture.
30. Stumbo, N. H., & Peterson, C. A. (1998). The leisure ability model. *Therapeutic Recreation Journal, 32*(2), 82–96.
31. Austin, D. R. (1998). The health protection/health promotion model. *Therapeutic Recreation Journal, 32*(2), 109–117.
32. Pet Partners. (2021). *Terminology*. https://petpartners.org/learn/terminology/.
33. Porter, H. R. (Ed.). (2016). *Recreational therapy basics, techniques, and interventions*. Idyll Arbor, Inc.
34. Associaton for Experimental Education (n.d.). Adventure therapy best practice. https://assets.noviams.com/novi-file-uploads/aee/TAPG_Adventure_Therapy_Best_Practices_1_.pdf
35. World Health Organization. (2010). *Framework for action on interprofessional education & collaborative practice*. https://www.who.int/publications/i/item/framework-for-action-on-interprofessional-education-collaborative-practice
36. National Council for Therapeutic Recreation Certification. (2021). *NCTRC certification standards: Information for the Certified Therapeutic Recreation Specialist® and new applicants*. www.nctrc.org/wp-content/uploads/2019/08/CertificationStandards.pdf.
37. National Council for Therapeutic Recreation Certification. (2020). *2014 CTRS® job analysis report: NCTRC report on the international job analysis of Certified Therapeutic Recreation Specialists*. www.nctrc.org/wp-content/uploads/2019/05/JobAnalysisReport.pdf.

CHAPTER 6
PHYSICAL ACTIVITY AND EXERCISE RECOMMENDATIONS

Robert Kowalsky

PHYSICAL ACTIVITY AND HEALTH

The World Health Organization (WHO) defines **health** as a state of complete physical, mental, and social well-being, not merely the absence of disease or infirmity.[1] An important behavior to improve or maintain health, recognized by the WHO, is the engagement of regular physical activity due to its ability to improve health benefit of one's heart, body, and mind.[2] Many other organizations follow suit with this, including the American Heart Association (AHA), National Institute of Health (NIH), Centers for Disease Control and Prevention (CDC), and the U.S. surgeon general, all clearly providing guidelines or recommendations for physical activity participation. With so many organizations recognizing the importance of physical activity, this provides strong evidence that getting individuals to engage in physical activity can lead to a cascade of health benefits. However, the challenge becomes actually getting those individuals to engage in physical activity. Fortunately, health professionals can provide clear and concise exercise and physical activity guidance to individuals that results in the health benefits desired. Even for individuals with disabilities, physical activity participation can lead to a plethora of health benefits and is highly encouraged.

What should also be highlighted is that the benefit from physical activity participation is for *everyone*. Regardless of gender, race, ethnicity, age, population, and the presence or elevated risk of conditions, diseases or disorders, the benefit of regular physical activity is well documented. Though the point of this chapter is not to discuss all the benefits of physical activity in depth, it should be recognized that the benefit of physical activity comes in the form of both acute and chronic (long-term) benefits. The benefit of physical activity begins immediately following activity participation and continues to be enhanced with regular participation. Even a single bout of physical activity can help with blood pressure, insulin sensitivity, decreased low-density blood lipids, cognition, and improving sleep.[3-7] Furthermore, many health-related benefits follow a dose-response relationship, meaning the more physical activity participation, the greater the benefit. This holds true for cardiorespiratory health, metabolic health, weight loss, bone health, joint health, muscular health, depression, and all-cause mortality.[8]

In light of these extensive potential benefits, and when evaluating and implementing physical activity recommendations, one should take into consideration the individual's current health status, their likes and dislikes, as well as equipment availability and space. Choosing activities that are enjoyable is important and will help the individuals adhere to the programming that is provided to them.[9] Fortunately, most physical activity and exercise recommendations are typically broad, allowing for the health professionals to manipulate and adapt them to meet the individual's needs and desires. Having a solid understanding of the general guidelines though will allow you to quickly adapt and find unique and fun ways to meet the recommended levels of physical activity.

Robert Kowalsky, Appalachian State University. © Kendall Hunt Publishing Company

Another important consideration when following physical activity guidelines is the potential risk that is involved with participation. In almost every case, the benefit of physical activity outweighs the potential risk, even in individuals with clinical complications such as those with cardiovascular disease, metabolic disease, or musculoskeletal conditions.[10] However, having a full understanding of that risk can help practitioners interpret the guidelines and make appropriate decisions when it comes to physical activity participation in their clients. Making appropriate decisions based on the guidelines and other recommendations helps eliminate risk when possible, and keep any remaining risk extremely low. This risk from physical activity is mostly focused on musculoskeletal injuries and complications relating to the cardiovascular system; such as sudden cardiac death, myocardial infarctions, and cardiac arrest.[11] Limiting these occurrences and keeping the risk of these events low ensures that individuals can lead long and healthy lives. The published physical activity and exercise guidelines consider this idea of weighing risk versus the benefit as per scientific evidence and base their decisions on optimizing benefit while minimizing risk. Due to this, health professionals can implement these guidelines and recommendations with confidence that the benefits will be achieved while also reducing risk of an adverse event in either children or adults with and without disabilities.

PHYSICAL ACTIVITY VERSUS EXERCISE

In advance of discussing recommendations, it is important to understand the difference between the domains of physical activity and exercise. **Physical activity** is a broad term to describe muscular contraction resulting in bodily movement that raises energy expenditure above resting values.[12] With this definition, being physically active happens in all aspects of daily life. Transportation such as walking, manual labor for work, chores and activities around the house such as lawn care and cleaning, and leisurely activities such as golf and walking your dog can all be considered physical activity pursuits. Increasing physical activity throughout the day can easily be achieved for most individuals without disabilities through a variety of behavioral decisions, such as choosing to engage in active forms of transportation such as walking versus passive forms like riding in a car or train, deciding to take the stairs instead of the elevator, and parking farther away from the store in the parking lot. Notably, increasing daily physical activity can be done without needing a gym membership or purchasing expensive exercise equipment and should be able to be widely implemented for any given population. However, in certain populations with disabilities, some of the most obvious ways to incorporate physical activity into daily life are not feasible, potentially due to mobility limitations or lack of access/accessibility. Therefore, even simple strategies that frequently alter posture from sitting to standing or another posture should be encouraged. Based on functional capacity, promoting engagement in daily household chores, even if modified, can still be considered physical activity, so activities of daily living that can help develop independence should be promoted when possible.

Though being physically active can provide health benefits, engaging in regular exercise optimizes that health benefit. **Exercise** is a subcategory of physical activity, and is defined as planned, structured and repetitive movement that is reoccurring in an effort to improve one's health or fitness.[12] Exercise can be activities such as, but not limited to; playing a sport, going for a walk, run, or roll in a wheelchair/sport chair, going to the gym to lift weights, or engaging in a yoga session. As a health professional, many individuals with diverse ability levels may seek you out to provide specific recommendations to meet their exercise needs, so it is the responsibility of a health professional to be prepared to provide specific guidelines and programming along with modifications to address any limitations of the individual.

With these two domains in mind, practitioners should seek to encourage engagement in both exercise and physical activity throughout their clients' or students' daily lives to enhance their health status. As a practitioner, you are in a unique position to provide the professional guidance and instruction that can ensure reliable results and continuing adherence to the programming. In populations with disabilities, it is your responsibility to design programming that is accessible and meets the needs of the individual.

PHYSICAL ACTIVITY INTENSITY AND THE PHYSICAL ACTIVITY CONTINUUM

Physical activity and exercise participation should be thought of as a continuum as individuals transition from lower to higher levels of physical activity and exercise. There are several ways to describe exercise intensity, such as heart rate intensity, percent of maximal volume of oxygen consumed (VO_{2max}), rating of perceived exertion (RPE), as well as the **metabolic**

equivalent of tasks (METs). In general terms, physical activity can be considered light-, moderate-, or vigorous-intensity. Above vigorous-intensity is considered maximal-intensity. These general intensities can be described further as follows, per the U.S. physical activity guidelines.[11]

- **Light-intensity physical activity** is nonsedentary waking behavior that requires only a slight increase above resting values of energy expenditure with a slight increase in heart rate and include activities such as household work, shopping at a store, or moving around an office.
- **Moderate-intensity physical activities** require an increased level of effort with an increased rate of breathing, heart rate, and energy expenditure, but still allows the individual to talk while doing them. These include activities such as brisk walking/pushing in a wheelchair, mowing the grass, or playing a sport in a social setting like golf or tennis.
- **Vigorous-intensity physical activities** lead to a substantial increase in heart rate and breathing, including the potential for panting depending on fitness level, and include activities such as aerobics on land or in the water, swimming, jogging or running, playing sports competitively, or yardwork that includes lifting or carrying heavy items.

With these general definitions in mind, the physical activity continuum begins to take shape, but provides more distinct cut points for where the transition from one level of intensity to the next occurs. These cut points are typically described in METs, but other variables could be used (such as heart rate, VO_2, and RPE). METs are a ratio of energy expenditure relative to the mass of the person during a task compared to the energy expenditure relative to the mass of the person at rest.[13] One MET is the value assigned to an individual at rest (sitting quietly) and a MET value of six would be an example of an activity that would require six times greater than what is used at rest. Using METs, we can see in Figure 6.1 the full physical activity continuum. You can see that this continuum ranges from no activity (sedentary behavior) to vigorous-intensity (which includes max intensity). Briefly, anything from 1.5 to less than 3 METs is considered light-intensity, 3 to less than 6 METs is considered moderate-intensity, and anything from 6 or higher is considered vigorous-intensity. Understanding this continuum and how certain activities can fall along this line can help individuals and practitioners provide guidance when it comes to encouraging exercise and physical activity engagement. Changing behaviors in individuals' daily lives that shifts more of their daily activities further to the right on this continuum should be the focus of recommendations and guidance. However, this shift should be done in a gradual manner over time. Individuals who are previously inactive should start low and slow, and build up their tolerance to higher levels of physical activity over time.

Aside from METs, Table 6.1 breaks down each of the methods used to describe intensity levels based on the activity continuum and general definitions

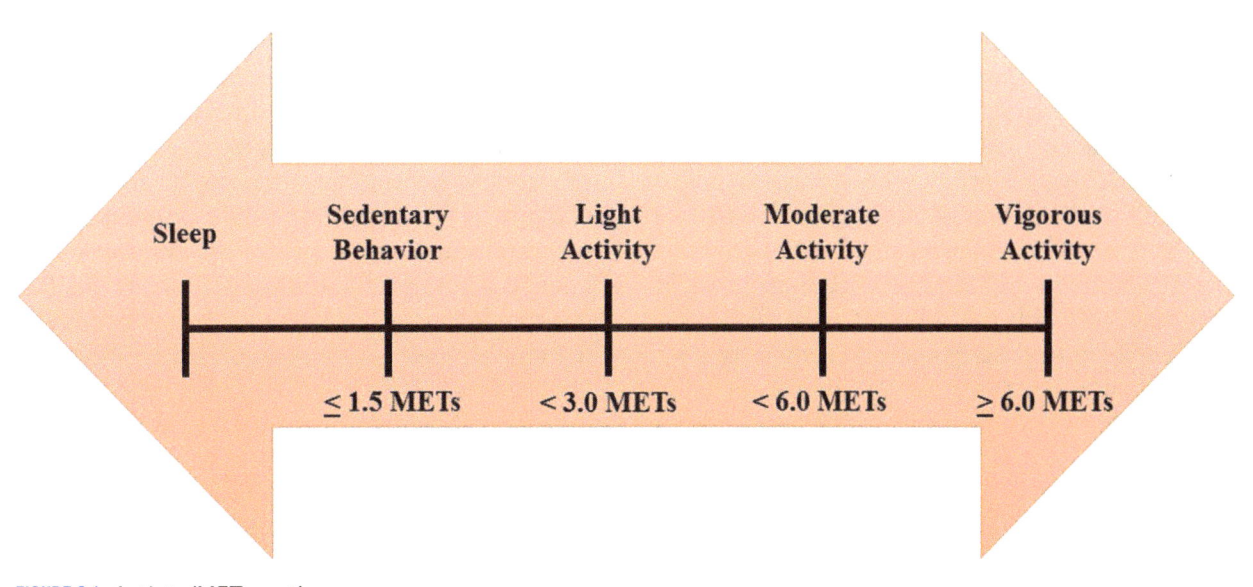

Sleep	Sedentary Behavior	Light Activity	Moderate Activity	Vigorous Activity
	≤ 1.5 METs	< 3.0 METs	< 6.0 METs	≥ 6.0 METs

FIGURE 6.1 Activty/MET continuum.
Source: Robert Kowalsky

TABLE 6.1 Methods to describe exercise intensities

Method	Light Intensity	Moderate Intensity	Vigorous Intensity	Maximal Intensity
% VO$_{2max}$	≤45	46–63	64–90	≥91
% of HR$_{max}$	≤63	64–76	77–95	≥96
% of VO$_2$R or HRR	≤39	40–59	60–89	≥90
RPE	≤11	12–13	14–17	≥18
METs	1.5 to <3.0	3.0 to <6.0	≥6.0	>8.8

VO$_{2max}$, maximal volume of oxygen consumed per unit of time; HR$_{max}$, maximal heart rate; VO$_2$R, oxygen uptake reserve; HRR, heart rate reserve; RPE, rating of perceived exertion; METs, metabolic equivalents.

Source: Robert Kowalsky

or intensity levels. Having several ways to describe intensity allows for you to overcome challenges that may limit use of one or more of these definitions. For example, describing intensity with percentage of VO$_{2max}$ may be limited if you do not have an available way to directly analyze or track VO$_2$ such as a metabolic cart. A metabolic cart allows for the measure of oxygen being consumed during exercise and carbon dioxide being produced, which allows for the calculation of energy being produced via aerobic energy pathways, a marker of exercise intensity. Though methods exist to estimate current level of VO$_2$ during exercise, these methods rely on using measures of speed, incline, and resistance gathered from exercise equipment such as stationary cycles and treadmill. Many populations, including those with disabilities, are limited or unable to use these types of equipment, making this method or predicting VO$_2$ invalid as well. Heart rate (HR) is relatively easy to measure through palpitation or using a heart rate monitor worn on the wrist or chest. However, these methods can also be limited if someone is on a medication that alters heart rate response such as a beta blocker or in certain clinical populations such as those with spinal cord injuries that result in chronotropic responses. An additional limitation of palpitation of heart rate is the potential for strength of pulse to be asymmetrical. Practitioners are recommended to palpate HR using locations with the strongest pulse. RPE provides a subjective description of the intensity on a scale, but each person needs to be familiarized to the lowest and highest levels of the scale before using this method, so the individual can relate to the appropriate levels. The scale ranges from 6, representing no exertion, all the way up to 20, representing maximal exertion. Values that fall between 6 and 20 represent light, moderate, and high intensities of exertion. This approach has been validated for use in adult and youth populations as well as with those with disabilities.[14–16] Other RPE scales range from 0 (no exertion) to 10 (max exertion). Regardless of method, deciding which way to describe intensity can be decided on by equipment availability, health status of the individual (including medications), and what works best for each person.

SEDENTARY BEHAVIOR

One of the subcategories of physical activity, or rather lack of physical activity, not covered in detail yet is at the far left of the physical activity continuum. This is termed sedentary behavior. **Sedentary behavior** is defined as any waking behavior in a seated, reclined, or lying posture that is <1.5 METs.[17] This is a two-pronged definition, defined by (1) energy expenditure as well as (2) posture. If only one definition is met, it does not necessarily constitute as sedentary behavior. For example, if someone is in a wheelchair (a seated posture), but has a sufficient energy expenditure level above 1.5 METs for a given activity, then it would not be classified as sedentary. In general, guidelines encourage the reduction of prolonged time spent in sedentary behavior, but there are no specific recommendations similar to those for physical activity concerning duration, frequency, and intensity due to limited current research evidence. However, the U.S. Health Guidelines, Canadian Health Guidelines, and the WHO Guidelines all recommend limiting prolonged sedentary behavior.[8,18,19] These guidelines recommend limiting time in sedentary activities such as sitting at work or school, watching TV, reading, playing video games, or sitting while riding in a car, train, or bus where energy expenditure is typically very low. Sedentary behavior has seen an accumulation in recent years and could be linked to the modernization of the office space with adults needing to be positioned at a desk 8 hours a day for their job with little to no movement, or the high prevalence of youth engaging in sedentary leisure time activities such as watching television or playing video games. It is reported that adults and youth spend a large portion of their day (about 7.7 hr/day) engaging in sedentary behaviors.[20] This highlights the ongoing issue of sedentary behavior and the need to limit the amount of time engaging in such behaviors. However, it should be recognized that certain activities may need to be carried out in postures that promote sedentary behavior (certain jobs, schooling situations, travel), yet efforts should still be made to limit sedentary time when interruption to sedentary time is feasible.

Research studies regarding the high accumulation of sedentary behavior have identified sedentary behavior as a risk factor for negative health consequences.[21] Most individuals accumulate sedentary behavior during transportation (driving a car), at work (sitting at a desk), or during leisure time pursuits (watching television).[22] With this in mind, researchers have attempted to replace these activities with more active pursuits with varying levels of success. Figure 6.2 displays several different strategies that have been demonstrated to reduce time spent sedentary in a variety of settings including the workplace, schools, and at home. Furthermore, other studies have demonstrated that several of the behaviors listed in Figure 6.2 result in benefits to various health risk factors. For example, the use of a sit–stand desk in the office or school setting can help to lower blood pressure,[23] lower blood glucose levels,[24] and decrease the severity of muscular discomfort.[25,26] Other strategies such as brief resistance exercise breaks (such as

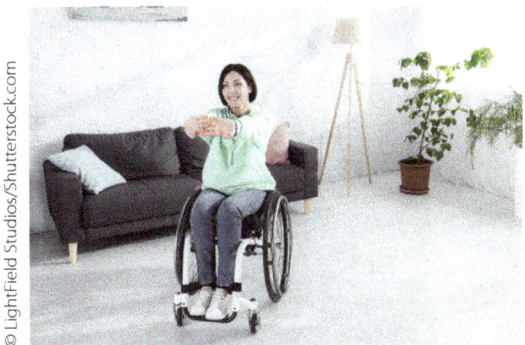

FIGURE 6.2 Examples of increasing movement and activity at work, home, and for recreation.

body-weight squats up and down from a chair) or going for a brief walk can have similar benefits for the cardiovascular, metabolic, and musculoskeletal systems.[27-29]

Yet it should be noted with the 2021 release of the WHO's Physical Activity Guidelines for Individuals with Disabilities,[30] the organization highlighted that the majority of strategies developed are not geared for those with limitations stemming from disabilities, and unique strategies are needed to help reduce sedentary behavior and improve health. For example, many disabilities limit one's ability to be in a standing posture, such as those utilizing wheelchairs. Therefore, strategies such as walking breaks and sit–stand desks are not practical. Developing unique strategies that aid these populations, such as desk-based arm cycles or seated exercise breaks, are needed. Being able to fully assess your client's or student's abilities and any functional limitations will aid you in your choices for exercises and strategies to incorporate physical activity into their daily lives while limiting sedentary behavior.

RELATIONSHIP BETWEEN SEDENTARY BEHAVIOR AND PHYSICAL ACTIVITY

The concept of reducing sedentary behavior aside from physical activity participation is relatively new. Fortunately, there has been an increasing interest in the study of sedentary behavior and the role it plays in health status. This expanding interest has resulted in an increasing amount of research allowing for experts to establish in the most recent guidelines (2018 U.S. guidelines for Physical Activity) that sedentary behavior was strongly linked to hazardous health effects and should be included separate from physical activity recommendations.[31] However, based on current evidence available, the experts could not determine an exact target of sedentary behavior reduction. This resulted in a more generalized recommendation to just limiting sedentary behavior without any time component. This lack of a more detailed and established recommendation is in part due to the dependent nature of sedentary behavior and physical activity. The negative health impact of sedentary behavior can at least in part, be offset by participating in sufficient levels of physical activity.[32] This concept is demonstrated in Figure 6.3. The colors represent level of risk, with red representing the highest risk of all-cause mortality and green representing the lowest risk. It can be seen that those with the accumulation of high volumes of moderate-to-vigorous physical activity remove the excess risk of all-cause mortality associated with high amounts of sedentary behavior. However, a very low amount of moderate-to-vigorous physical activity does not completely remove the risk of participating in sedentary activities. Regardless, it is suggested that individuals would receive benefit for both the participation in moderate-to-vigorous physical activity and limiting sedentary behavior; this holds true regardless of limitations.

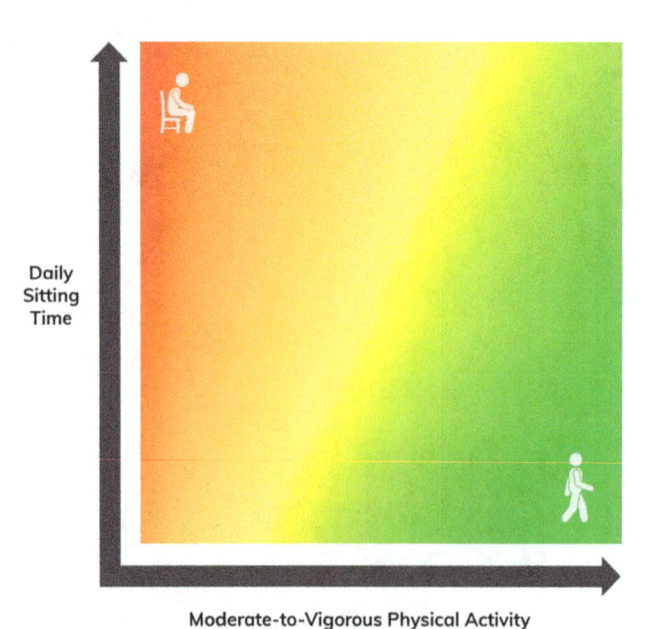

FIGURE 6.3 Activity levels and mortality slide scale.
Source: U.S. Department of Health and Human Services

TYPES OF PHYSICAL ACTIVITY

The main types of physical activity an individual can engage in include muscle and bone strengthening, aerobic activity, and stretching. Each of these categories should be engaged in on a regular basis to promote overall health improvement. Because of this, physical activity guidelines promote all types of activities in a balanced effort. Engaging in each of these behaviors results in specific benefits to a variety of human systems including the cardiovascular, pulmonary, metabolic, nervous, and musculoskeletal systems. While engaging in any form of physical activity will result in benefit to most if not all of the systems, certain activity types should be the focus when attempting to target a specific system. For example, both aerobic and muscle strengthening exercises can result in a similar beneficial response for blood pressure,[33] yet beneficial changes to metabolic outcomes (such as weight loss) are more realized in aerobic training.[34] It is up to the practitioner, along with the individual they are working with, to determine needs, interests, and goals, which will allow the practitioner to choose which type of physical activity would be best for all training sessions. Furthermore, this helps the practitioner know when it would be best to mix in different types of exercises to keep things interesting and to meet evolving goals. Along with developing a plan to meet goals, practitioners need to consider the individual's fears or hesitations with physical activity that could stem from limitations with certain limbs or body parts, fear of reinjury, or the potential of discomfort or pain with physical activity. These fears can lead to a cycle of continuous avoidance of participation in physical activity which can result in further decline in health status.

GENERAL PHYSICAL ACTIVITY AND EXERCISE RECOMMENDATIONS

Based on the 2nd edition of the Physical Activity Guidelines for Americans,[8] there are several key takeaways for the adult population. Practitioners should stress that some physical activity is better than none and that physical activity can begin the process to gaining health benefits. Another key takeaway is that for substantial health benefits, individuals should be engaging in aerobic activity of at least 150 to 300 minutes per week of moderate-intensity physical activity, or 75 to 150 minutes per week of vigorous-intensity physical activity. Individuals should also strive to accumulate these minutes throughout the week so that they are being physically active on most, if not all, days of the week. A third take away of the recommendations is that additional health benefits are gained by engaging in moderate-intensity physical activity beyond 300 minutes per week. Lastly, the fourth takeaway is that adults should engage in muscle strengthening activities of moderate or greater intensity that involve all major muscle groups for 2 or more days per week due to their additive benefit from aerobic activity participation alone. As for the sedentary behavior component, the current recommendation was established as "sit less and move more", unfortunately this statement is a bit insensitive to those who are unable to avoid sitting due to impairments. However, and as discussed in chapter 2, is not inclusive to all individuals with disabilities, it still provides guidance that sedentary behavior should be taken into consideration and that efforts should be made to limit the amount of overall daily sedentary behavior. With these guidelines in mind, a recent study estimates individuals who meet these guidelines in the United States falls at roughly 51.6% meeting the aerobic guidelines, 29.3% meeting the muscle strengthening guidelines, and only 20.6% meeting both.[35] This highlights the ongoing work for health professionals to actively engage the general population in exercise participation, and to educate them on the benefits.

As for children and adolescents, the general physical activity recommendations are broken down to preschool-aged children and a separate recommendation for children and adolescents. For preschool-aged children (ages 3–5 years), engagement in physical activities is recommended throughout the day and those activities should contain various types. This is all in an effort to promote growth and development. As for children and adolescents (age 7 through 17) the guidelines recommend 60 minutes of daily moderate-to-vigorous–intensity activity. Of these daily 60 minutes, most activity should include moderate-intensity aerobic activity. They should also strive to get at least 3 days per week of vigorous-intensity aerobic activity. As part of their daily 60 minutes, children and adolescents should also engage in bone and muscle-strengthening activities at least 3 days per week. Recommended levels of physical activity participation in U.S. youth (6–17 years old) during 2018–2019 was at 22.3% (60 minutes, every day of moderate-to-vigorous–intensity physical activity),[36] with a highest percentage of youth (40.5%) participating in 1 to 3 days of the recommended levels. This parallels what we see in the adult population, that more can be done to encourage physical activity participation to achieve health benefits.

Regardless of the population, steps should be taken to ensure safety during physical activities. This includes choosing appropriate activities for individuals' current fitness levels and health goals. Safety also includes appropriate progression. Those starting out from low or no physical activity should progress slowly and gradually increase intensity, frequency, and duration. Individuals should also implement safety equipment as needed, such as bicycle helmets or other equipment as the activity dictates.

PHYSICAL ACTIVITY AND EXERCISE RECOMMENDATIONS FOR INDIVIDUALS WITH DISABILITIES

Concurrent with the physical activity and exercise recommendations reported in the previous section that are geared for the general adult and youth populations, are the guidelines geared toward those with disabilities. However, these guidelines are relatively new, and even in the early 21st century, these guidelines did not exist. A disability is a broad term and can have a varying degree of impact on the functionality of an individual from a mild disruption to a severe limitation, as discussed throughout this book. Furthermore, this degree of limitation can be acute (lasting a day or a week) or long lasting (a few months to years). It is reported that there are 1.5 billion people currently living with a disability worldwide,[37] highlighting the likelihood that a practitioner will at some point be providing exercise and physical activity recommendations to an individual who currently has some degree of disability. Having appropriative recommendations for this population would provide guidance and direction to benefit their level of health while also considering their disability.

Published in 2021, a report from the WHO established the first global physical activity recommendations for individuals with disabilities for both adults as well as children and adolescents.[30] Based on the evidence reviewed by the organization, they recognized the disparity in the evidence for a variety of disabilities. Those with conditions such as multiple sclerosis and Parkinson's were most represented in the research, and those with schizophrenia, clinical depression, and attention deficit hyperactivity disorder (ADHD) were the least represented. Regardless of disability, the WHO considered any study that evaluated the impact on comorbidities, physical function, quality of life, and cognition in individuals with disabilities. This resulted in evidence ranging from high-certainty to low-certainty for the benefit of physical activity participation. In summary, the experts concluded that the evidence indicated an overall benefit to those with disabilities from participation in physical activity and exercise while interrupting sedentary behavior. Furthermore, they reported that based on the evidence, the benefit from physical activity and exercise and the limiting of sedentary behavior would result in the same health benefits for those with disabilities as it does for the general population. Due to this, the experts felt that the guidelines provided for the general populations also fit those individuals with disabilities at the adult or child and adolescent levels. They also concluded that this recommendation could be used broadly, even for those disabilities not included specifically in the review.

Additionally, several "good practice" statements emerged from the WHO guidelines, which are reported in Table 6.2. These statements provide further guidance toward working with those individuals with disabilities in an effort to meet the physical activity guidelines for the general population. Taken together, the good practice statements and the general guidelines provide ample direction for the implementation of physical activity and exercise.

Several gaps in the research emerged and should be taken into consideration as well. These gaps include the scarcity of evidence used to develop these guidelines as well as substantial lack of evidence for a variety of disabilities, with substantial evidence only existing for specific disabilities. Furthermore, there is insufficient data on reduction of incidence rates for several key outcomes such as cardiovascular, metabolic, cancer, bone, and obesity as well as mortality rates. Another gap is the dearth of interventions, strategies, and built environments to allow for physical activity engagement in those with disabilities. Therefore, the practitioner needs to be able to adapt the recommendations to meet individual needs and functionality in pursuit of the health benefits from physical activity and exercise. Another important gap is the communication aspect of the guidelines. Individuals with learning disabilities or those with disabilities that are limiting to visual or hearing capacities may find difficulties in gathering and interpreting recommendations from printed sources or from discussing them with their practitioner. Therefore, you may be required to be unique in your delivery of information that best suits the population you are working with at that time.

PHYSICAL ACTIVITY PARTICIPATION LEVELS

Part of following the physical activity and exercise recommendations from the Physical Activity Guidelines for Americans[8] is understanding current status

TABLE 6.2 The WHO guidelines on physical activity and sedentary behavior for children, adolescents, and adults living with disabilities

Children and adolescents (aged 5–17 years) living with disability

It is recommended that:

- Children and adolescents living with disability should do at least an average of 60 minutes per day of moderate to vigorous intensity, mostly aerobic, physical activity, across the week.

Strong recommendation, moderate certainty evidence

- Vigorous-intensity aerobic activities, as well as those that strengthen muscle and bone should be incorporated at least 3 days a week.

Strong recommendation, moderate certainty evidence
Good practice statement:

- *Doing some physical activity is better than doing none.*
- *If children and adolescents living with disability are not meeting these recommendations, doing some physical activity will bring benefits to health.*
- *Children and adolescents living with disability should start by doing small amounts of physical activity and gradually increase the frequency, intensity, and duration over time.*
- *There are no major risks for children and adolescents living with disability engaging in physical activity when it is appropriate to an individual's current activity level, health status, and physical function; and the health benefits accrued outweigh the risks.*
- *Children and adolescents living with disability may need to consult a health care professional or other physical activity and disability specialist to help determine the type and amount of activity appropriate for them.*

In children and adolescents, higher amounts of sedentary behavior are associated with the following poorer health outcomes: increased adiposity, poorer cardiometabolic health, fitness, behavioral conduct/prosocial behavior, and reduced sleep duration.
It is recommended that:

- Children and adolescents living with disability should limit the amount of time spent being sedentary, particularly the amount of recreational screen time.

Strong recommendation, low-certainty evidence

Adults (aged 18 years and over) living with disability

It is recommended that:

- All adults living with disability should undertake regular physical activity.

Strong recommendation, moderate-certainty evidence

- Adults living with disability should do at least 150–300 minutes of moderate-intensity aerobic physical activity, or do at least 75–150 minutes of vigorous intensity aerobic physical activity, or an equivalent combination of moderate- and vigorous-intensity activity throughout the week for substantial health benefits.

Strong recommendation, moderate-certainty evidence

- Adults living with disability should also do muscle-strengthening activities at moderate or greater intensity that involve all major muscle groups for 2 or more days a week, as these provide additional health benefits.

Strong recommendation, moderate-certainty evidence

- As part of their weekly physical activity, older adults living with disability should do varied multicomponent physical activity that emphasizes functional balance and strength training at moderate or greater intensity for 3 or more days a week, to enhance functional capacity and prevent falls.

Strong recommendation, moderate-certainty evidence

- Adults living with disability may increase moderate-intensity aerobic physical activity to more than 300 minutes, or do more than 150 minutes of vigorous-intensity aerobic physical activity, or an equivalent combination of moderate- and vigorous-intensity activity throughout the week for additional health benefits.

(continued)

TABLE 6.2 The WHO Guidelines on physical activity and sedentary behavior for children, adolescents, and adults living with disabilities (*continued*)

Conditional recommendation, moderate-certainty evidence
Good practice statement:

- *Doing some physical activity is better than doing none.*
- *If adults living with disability are not meeting these recommendations, doing some physical activity will bring benefits to health.*
- *Adults living with disability should start by doing small amounts of physical activity and gradually increase the frequency, intensity, and duration over time.*
- *There are no major risks to adults living with disability engaging in physical activity when it is appropriate to the individual's current activity level, health status, and physical function; and when the health benefits accrued outweigh the risks.*
- *Adults living with disability may need to consult a health care professional or other physical activity and disability specialist to help determine the type and amount of activity appropriate for them.*

In adults, higher amounts of sedentary behavior are associated with the following poor health outcomes: all-cause mortality, cardiovascular disease and cancer mortality, and incidence of cardiovascular disease, cancer, and type 2 diabetes.
It is recommended that:

- Adults living with disability should limit the amount of time spent being sedentary and replacing sedentary time with physical activity of any intensity (including light intensity) has health benefits.

Strong recommendation, low-certainty evidence

- To help reduce the detrimental effects of high levels of sedentary behavior on health, adults living with disability should aim to do more than the recommended levels of moderate-to-vigorous physical activity.

Source: Carty C, van der Ploeg HP, Biddle SJH, Bull F, Willumsen J, Lee L, Kamenov K, Milton K.

of your clients, students, athletes, or patients. The guidelines use four classifications for adults to describe their level of physical activity participation. These include inactive, insufficiently active, active, and highly active.

- **Inactive**: Not getting any moderate- or vigorous-intensity physical activity beyond basic movement in daily life.
- **Insufficiently active**: Some moderate- or vigorous-intensity physical activity, but less than 150 minutes per week of moderate-intensity physical activity or 75 minutes per week of vigorous-intensity physical activity, or the equivalent combination.
- **Active**: meeting the recommended levels of moderate-intensity physical activity per week (150–300 minutes). This includes minutes of vigorous-intensity physical activity as well.
- **Highly active**: Exceeding the recommended minutes of moderate-intensity physical activity each week of 300 minutes, or equivalent vigorous-intensity physical activity.

Though these classifications focus on the use of aerobic activity, the Physical Activity Guidelines for Americans[8] still stresses that all individuals should engage in other types of physical activity like muscle strengthening, and does not diminish the importance of these other areas. Similar classifications are used in children and adolescents to describe current activity levels—those who are not meeting the guidelines, who meet the guidelines, and who exceed the guidelines.

INITIATING PHYSICAL ACTIVITY IN INDIVIDUALS WITH DISABILITIES

In determining current physical activity status of your clients, students, athletes, or patients, it may become clear that they fall in the inactive, insufficiently active, or does not meet recommendation categories. In these instances, the physical activity recommendations may appear as a massive barrier and the suggested level of activity participation may seem largely out of reach for their current health status. Due to this, you may want to approach the initiation of physical activity participation with more reasonable and obtainable guideline recommendations. The American College of Sports Medicine has published recommendations for those with chronic diseases and disorders that may be useful for those with disabilities who are just starting out.[38] These guidelines provide recommendations in similar categories as the general guidelines (aerobic, strength, and flexibility) but with an accessible approach. Table 6.3

CHAPTER 6: Physical Activity and Exercise Recommendations 95

TABLE 6.3 American College of Sports Medicine's (ACSM) basic physical activity guidelines for persons with chronic conditions

Mode	Frequency	Duration	Intensity	Progression
Aerobic	4–5 days/week	Start any duration, build to 40 minutes per session. 20 if combined with strength	Start self-selected walking speed, at an intensity meeting talk test. Gradually increase to RPE of 3–5/10	Over 4 weeks, gradually increase time to 40 minutes, increasing intensity as tolerated.
Strength	2–3 days/week	Body weight exercises: Functional exercises of 1 set. For weights: 1 set of 8–12 reps to fatigue	• Sit to stand: 8 reps • Alternating stair steps • Arm curls: 8 reps with ~4 kg • 50%–70% of 1 rep max	Build gradually to as many sets a day as tolerated. For curls and weight training: increase to 2 sets over ~8 weeks
Flexibility	3 days/week	20 seconds per stretch	Maintain stretch below discomfort point	Discomfort point should occur at a ROM that does not cause instability. This discomfort point will vary between people and joints.
Warm-up and cool-down	Before and after each session	10–15 minutes	Easy RPE <3/10	Should be maintained

RPE, rating of perceived exertion; ROM, range of motion

Source: Geoffrey E. Moore, J. Larry Durstine, Patricia L. Painter

details these recommendations. Overall, there is special focus on providing a small stimulus at the start of an exercise program, but working toward increasing that stimulus over time. The end goal is to be able to transition that individual to follow the general guidelines, once sufficient adaptation has occurred that makes the higher level of physical activity able to be tolerated with minimal risk to the health of the individual.

PREPHYSICAL ACTIVITY HEALTH EVALUATION

Prior to initiating any physical activity with anyone, it is the responsibility of any practitioner to assess the current health status of the individual they will be working with. This provides an overarching picture of the person's health and will help guide the decisions made regarding physical and exercise recommendation. This will also help address any concerns and areas of needed attention regarding their health status. The following questions should be answered before engaging in any testing of physical activity levels or programming.

1. Should this individual seek the clearance of a medical doctor (MD or DO) before engaging in physical activity?
2. Which types of exercise tests should you consider and what should the intensity level of those tests be to ensure safety?
3. What intensity of physical activity and exercise should the individual start at to limit any risk of an adverse event occurring (i.e., myocardial infarction or other cardiovascular complication) when you begin their programming?
4. Are there any special considerations you may need to address throughout your programming for the individual?

Completing a detailed health history and assessment will aid you in answering these questions. The American College of Sports Medicine has developed an algorithm[39] that helps you determine the answers to these questions and how to proceed with the individual. Details from the individual that you will need include the following information.

- YES/NO are they currently physically active? Physically active is defined as participating in moderate-to-vigorous aerobic physical activity for 30 minutes, 3 times per week, for the past 3 months.
- YES/NO do they have a current known cardiovascular, metabolic, or renal disease? This focuses on the mentioned diseases and others such as cancer, asthma or arthritis do not qualify.
- YES/NO do they display any signs or symptoms suggestive of cardiovascular, metabolic, or renal disease? All these signs and symptoms are listed in Table 6.4.

TABLE 6.4 Signs and symptoms of suggestive of cardiovascular, metabolic, and renal disease*

Sign or Symptoms	Clarifications/Significance
Pain; discomfort (or other angina equivalent) in the chest, neck, jaw, arms, or other areas resulting from myocardial ischemia.	One of the cardinal manifestations of cardiac disease; in particular, coronary artery disease Key features favoring an ischemic origin include the following: • *Character:* constricting, squeezing, burning, "heaviness," or "heavy feeling" • *Location:* substernal, across midthorax, anteriorly; in one or both arms, shoulders; in neck, cheeks, teeth; in forearms, fingers in interscapular region • *Provoking factors:* exercise or exertion, excitement, other forms of stress, cold weather, occurrence after meals Key features against an ischemic origin include the following: • *Character:* dull ache; "knifelike," sharp, stabbing; "jabs" aggravated by respiration • *Location:* in left submammary area; in left hemithorax • *Provoking factors:* after completion of exercise, provoked by a specific body motion
Shortness of breath at rest or with mild exertion	Dyspnea (defined as an abnormally uncomfortable awareness of breathing) is one of the principal symptoms of cardiac and pulmonary disease. It commonly occurs during strenuous exertion in healthy, well-trained individuals and during moderate exertion in healthy, untrained individuals. However, it should be regarded as abnormal when it occurs at a level of exertion that is not expected to evoke this symptom in a given individual. Abnormal exertional dyspnea suggests the presence of cardiopulmonary disorders; in particular, left ventricular dysfunction or chronic obstructive pulmonary disease.
Dizziness or syncope	Syncope (defined as a loss of consciousness) is most commonly caused by a reduced perfusion of the brain. Dizziness and, in particular, syncope during exercise may result from cardiac disorders that prevent the normal rise (or an actual fall) in cardiac output. Such cardiac disorders are potentially life-threatening and include severe coronary artery disease, hypertrophic cardiomyopathy, aortic stenosis, and malignant ventricular dysrhythmias. Although dizziness or syncope shortly after cessation of exercise should not be ignored, these symptoms may occur even in healthy individuals as a result of a reduction in venous return to the heart.
Orthopnea or paroxysmal nocturnal dyspnea	Orthopnea refers to dyspnea occurring at rest in the recumbent position that is relieved promptly by sitting upright or standing. Paroxysmal nocturnal dyspnea refers to dyspnea, beginning usually 2–5 hours after the onset of sleep, which may be relieved by sitting on the side of the bed or getting out of bed. Both are symptoms of left ventricular dysfunction. Although nocturnal dyspnea may occur in individuals with chronic obstructive pulmonary disease, it differs in that it is usually relieved following a bowel movement rather than specifically by sitting up.
Ankle edema	Bilateral ankle edema that is most evident at night is a characteristic sign of heart failure or bilateral chronic venous insufficiency. Unilateral edema of a limb often results from venous thrombosis or lymphatic blockage in the limb. Generalized edema (known as anasarca) occurs in individuals with the nephrotic syndrome, severe heart failure, or hepatic cirrhosis.
Palpitations or tachycardia	Palpitations (defined as an unpleasant awareness of the forceful or rapid beating of the heart) may be induced by various disorders of cardiac rhythm. These include tachycardia, bradycardia of sudden onset, ectopic beats, compensatory pauses, and accentuated stroke volume resulting from valvular regurgitation. Palpitations also often result from anxiety states and high-cardiac-output (or hyperkinetic) states, such as anemia, fever, thyrotoxicosis, arteriovenous fistula, and the so-called idiopathic hyperkinetic heart syndrome.
Intermittent claudication	Intermittent claudication refers to the pain that occurs in the lower extremities with an inadequate blood supply (usually as a result of atherosclerosis) that is brought on by exercise. The pain does not occur with standing or sitting, is reproducible from day to day, is more severe when walking upstairs or up a hill, and is often described as a cramp, which disappears within 1–2 minutes after stopping exercise. Coronary artery disease is more prevalent in individuals with intermittent claudication. Patients with diabetes are at increased risk for this condition.
Known heart murmur	Although some may be innocent, heart murmurs may indicate valvular or other cardiovascular disease. From an exercise safety standpoint, it is especially important to exclude hypertrophic cardiomyopathy and aortic stenosis as underlying causes because these are among the more common causes of exertion-related sudden cardiac death.
Unusual fatigue or shortness of breath with usual activities	Although there may be benign origins for these symptoms, they also may signal the onset of or change in the status of cardiovascular disease or metabolic disease.

*These signs or symptoms must be interpreted within the clinical context in which they appear because they are not all specific for cardiovascular, metabolic, or renal diseases.

Source: American College of Sports Medicine

Once you have the yes or no response to these points, you can use the information to guide yourself to answering the foregoing questions 1 through 4. Doing so aids in lowering risk of any adverse events occurring. For example, medical clearance by a doctor is recommended for anyone who is currently experiencing signs or symptoms suggestive of cardiovascular, metabolic, or renal disease, regardless if they were previously active or not. Following clearance, the individual should begin with light-to-moderate intensity exercise testing and programming, or return to what intensity they were previously doing. However, medical clearance is not needed for anyone who is not currently experiencing signs or symptoms and does not have a known disease, regardless if they were physically active before. The practitioner though would begin with the exercise testing and programming intensity at light-to-moderate for those not previously active, but would use moderate-to-vigorous intensity for those who previously were physically active. A more comprehensive description of this can be found in the American College of Sports Medicine's Guidelines for Exercise Testing and Prescription, 11th edition.[40] If working with an individual with a disability you are unfamiliar with or do not have extensive background knowledge in, it is advised that you seek out medical clearance before developing a program for the individual to avoid any unnecessary risk.

PHYSICAL FITNESS TESTING

Once you have determined that your client is cleared for exercise, you should begin with physical fitness testing to determine current status and identify any areas that need addressed. **Physical fitness** is a combination of both skill and health-related fitness outcomes, as described here. Typically for the general population, the focus of most exercise programming focuses on the health-related outcomes. This holds true for populations with disabilities as well. However, depending on the individual's limitation, there may be an emphasis to spend some time with your programming focused on one or more of the skill-related outcomes, such as coordination. Improving and focusing on coordination could be beneficial for specific disabilities who are at increased risk of falling, or specific disabilities where fluidity of fine motor controls is reduced. **Health-related fitness** outcomes include the following.

- Cardiorespiratory endurance
- Muscular strength and endurance
- Body composition
- Flexibility

However, the **skill-related fitness domains** have their importance as well. Typically, they are reserved for athletes and sport-specific training; however, these skill-related fitness domains can have their purpose for the general population as well as for individuals with disabilities. Still, most individuals engaging in activity that promotes changes the health-related domains will improve skill-related domains to some degree as well. Skill-related domains include the following.

- Coordination
- Reaction time
- Speed
- Agility
- Power

The goal of physical fitness testing is to determine current status of one or multiple fitness domains, as well as identifying limitations and disease risk status. By completing fitness testing, health practitioners are able to classify level of risk of certain diseases and to recognize domains that should be maintained versus improved upon with your programming. This allows for a targeted approach, ensuring that the programming you utilize impacts your outcomes of interest (e.g., aerobic capacity).

To determine current physical fitness status, many physical fitness tests have been developed to assess these health and skill-related domains in both adult and youth populations. These tests can range from complicated laboratory tests that utilize specialized equipment to obtain accurate measurements, or field-based assessments that can be done anywhere with minimal to no equipment that can give you relatively accurate estimations of these outcomes. Furthermore, plenty of submaximal intensity assessments are available in each domain, including specific tests for individuals with disabilities. These submaximal assessments rely on estimations that predict the full potential of each individual. When choosing a test, you will need to take into consideration what the individual has been cleared to participate in, what their goals and interests are, what their abilities are, and what equipment you have available that is appropriate for them. For example, if determining aerobic capacity is of interest, you can choose from simple walking tests that collect information such as time and heart rate, to more complex tests that utilize a treadmill or cycle operated by the arms or legs of the individual.

It should be noted that though some of these more complex tests can be used with certain disabilities, some protocols may be unsafe to complete in certain populations. These treadmill and cycle tests can also include the measurement of respiratory gasses by capturing oxygen and carbon dioxide via respiratory gases entering and leaving the body each breath, which is referred to as indirect calorimetry. Regardless of the method chosen, you will be able to determine current aerobic capacity, which can also be used to track progression over time to determine if the program you are using for the individual is sufficient to improve outcomes or if you need to modify your programming. Practitioners should implement regular intervals of testing to ensure progression is occurring.

In working with individuals with disabilities, the disabilities themselves may also limit the utilization of certain tests. Certain exercise tests require complex steps to be carried out by the individual, mostly given via instruction prior to starting the test. If the individual has a hard time remembering instructions or has difficulty staying on task, a practitioner may choose to avoid these more complex assessments. This consideration may hold true for children as well, as more complex tasks may be difficult for them to understand. In children and adults with disabilities, allowing the individual to practice the assessment or test first, may help alleviate some of the complications with the test, allowing for a more representative measurement. Furthermore, certain physical limitations from disabilities may make certain tests inappropriate to complete for that individual. For example, if an individual has issues with balance, a step test would not be ideal, due to the high risk of falls. If hand grip is impacted, certain assessments may be difficult to complete if it requires the person to hold on to a weight or handle.

Fortunately, several exercise tests have been developed to help assess health- and skill-related fitness outcomes in many populations including children and those with disabilities. For example, the FITNESSGRAM[41] is a battery of assessments that include aerobic, strength, flexibility, and muscular endurance. Though many youth populations with a disability could potentially complete this assessment, the Brockport Physical Fitness Test[42] is accessible version of the FITNESSGRAM, and allows for customization of the testing battery, based on the individual's disability. The Brockport has a total of 27 different fitness tests to choose from in areas of muscular strength/endurance, aerobic capacity, body composition, and flexibility. Additionally, these assessments can be completed with minimal equipment and allows for substitution of equipment if something is not available. As for adults, existing protocols with a modification are most often utilized in those with disabilities. For example, standard protocol may be completing a test in a standing position, but having the person sit during the test addresses the disability while allowing the person to complete the test. Another example is aerobic capacity assessments. Many tests assess how long an individual can walk over a given time, how fast they can cover a given distance. If working with someone who uses a wheelchair, these same principles can be used to assess how fast they can push over a given distance, or how far they can push for a given time. Regardless of the individual you are attempting to test, always consider the abilities of individuals, which should become apparent during the preparticipation screening, and choose the best test available. It may also require the practitioner to be creative and think outside the box in their assessments to successfully complete an assessment.

CHAPTER SUMMARY

Physical activity and exercise are viewed as an important lifestyle behavior and is encouraged for youth, adults, and even those with many clinical conditions including disabilities. Several key takeaways are:

- In daily activity, all individuals are encouraged to be both physically active while also setting aside time to engage in regular exercise.

- With both physical activity and exercise, monitoring the intensity of such activity can ensure safety while also focusing on implementing the desired adaptations to the body systems (i.e., cardiovascular, metabolic, etc.).

- Prior to engaging in any exercise, it is important to engage in a preparticipation screening to recognize any potential issues or limitations

- that allows for a more tailored and safe approach to exercise recommendations.
- Exercise programming recommendations suggest adults should participate in 150 minutes per week of moderate-to-vigorous–intensity physical activity, and this holds true for those individuals with disabilities.
- Youth are recommended to participate in 60 minutes per day of moderate-to-vigorous-intensity activity that includes aerobic, muscle-strengthening, and bone-strengthening exercises. This again holds true for those with disabilities.
- Any activity time counts. Activity can be broken into any amount of time spread throughout the week to help meet recommended levels. This is important for those with disabilities where sustained activity participation may not be feasible.
- Consider utilizing physical fitness testing to determine current status of the individual and to track progression. Be sure to choose tests that fit the individual's needs and goals, and that you have the necessary equipment available. Certain disabilities may require different types of tests.

REFERENCES

1. Constitution of the World Health Organization. (2005). *World Health Organization: Basic documents* (45th ed.). World Health Organization.
2. Bull, F. C., Al-Ansari, S. S., Biddle, S., Borodulin, K., Buman, M. P., Cardon, G., Carty, C., Chaput, J. P., Chastin, S., Chou, R., Dempsey, P. C., DiPietro, L., Ekelund, U., Firth, J., Friedenreich, C. M., Garcia, L., Gichu, M., Jago, R., Katzmarzyk, P. T., Lambert, E., Leitzmann, M., Milton, K., Ortega, F. B., Ranasinghe, C., Stamatakis, E., Tiedemann, A., Troiano, R. P., van der Ploeg, H. P., Wari, V., & Willumsen, J. F. (2020). World Health Organization 2020 guidelines on physical activity and sedentary behaviour. *British Journal of Sports Medicine*, 54(24), 1451–1462.
3. Ferguson, M. A., Alderson, N. L., Trost, S. G., Essig, D. A., Burke, J. R., & Durstine, J. L. (1998). Effects of four different single exercise sessions on lipids, lipoproteins, and lipoprotein lipase. *Journal of Applied Physiology*, 85(3), 1169–1174.
4. Mikines, K. J., Sonne, B., Tronier, B., & Galbo, H. (1989). Effects of acute exercise and detraining on insulin action in trained men. *Journal of Applied Physiology*, 66(2), 704–711.
5. Seals, D. R., Silverman, H. G., Reiling, M. J., & Davy, K. P. (1997). Effect of regular aerobic exercise on elevated blood pressure in postmenopausal women. *The American Journal of Cardiology*, 80(1), 49–55.
6. Roig, M., Skriver, K., Lundbye-Jensen, J., Kiens, B., & Nielsen, J. B. (2012). A single bout of exercise improves motor memory. *PloS One*, 7(9), e44594.
7. Wang, X., & Youngstedt, S. D. (2014). Sleep quality improved following a single session of moderate-intensity aerobic exercise in older women: Results from a pilot study. *Journal of Sport and Health Science*, 3(4), 338–342.
8. Piercy, K. L., Troiano, R. P., Ballard, R. M., Carlson, S. A., Fulton, J. E., Galuska, D. A., George, S. M., & Olson, R. D.. (2018). The physical activity guidelines for Americans. *JAMA*, 320(19), 2020–2028.
9. Jekauc, D. (2015). Enjoyment during exercise mediates the effects of an intervention on exercise adherence. *Psychology*, 6(01), 48.
10. Melzer, K., Kayser, B., & Pichard, C. (2004). Physical activity: The health benefits outweigh the risks. *Current Opinion in Clinical Nutrition and Metabolic Care*, 7(6), 641–647.
11. Garber, C. E., Blissmer, B., Deschenes, M. R., Franklin, B. A., Lamonte, M. J., Lee, I. M., Nieman, D. C., Swain, D. P., & American College of Sports Medicine. (2011). American College of Sports Medicine position stand. Quantity and quality of exercise for developing and maintaining cardiorespiratory, musculoskeletal, and neuromotor fitness in apparently healthy adults: Guidance for prescribing exercise. *Medicine and Science in Sports and Exercise*, 43(7), 1334–1359.
12. Caspersen, C. J., Powell, K. E., & Christenson, G. M. (1985). Physical activity, exercise, and physical fitness: Definitions and distinctions for health-related research. *Public Health Reports (Washington, D.C.: 1974)*, 100(2), 126–131.
13. Jetté, M., Sidney, K., & Blümchen, G. (1990). Metabolic equivalents (METS) in exercise testing, exercise prescription, and evaluation of functional capacity. *Clinical cardiology*, 13(8), 555–565.
14. Borg, G. (1998). *Borg's perceived exertion and pain scales*. Human Kinetics.
15. Robertson, R. J., Goss, F. L., Dube, J., Rutkowski, J., Dupain, M., Brennan, C., & Andreacci, J. (2004). Validation of the adult OMNI scale of perceived exertion

for cycle ergometer exercise. *Medicine and Science in Sports and Exercise, 36*(1), 102–108.

16. Utter, A. C., Robertson, R. J., Nieman, D. C., & Kang, J. (2002). Children's OMNI Scale of Perceived Exertion: Walking/running evaluation. *Medicine and Science in Sports and Exercise, 34*(1), 139–144.

17. Tremblay, M. S., Aubert S., Barnes, J. D., Saunders, T. J., Carson, V., Latimer-Cheung, A. E., Chastin, S. F. M., Altenburg, T. M., & Chinapaw, M. J. M. (2017). Sedentary behavior research network (SBRN)—terminology consensus project process and outcome. *International Journal of Behavioral Nutrition and Physical Activity, 14*(1), 75.

18. Ross, R., Chaput, J. P., Giangregorio, L. M., Janssen, I., Saunders, T. J., Kho, M. E., Poitras, V. J., Tomasone, J. R., El-Kotob, R., McLaughlin, E. C., Duggan, M., Carrier, J., Carson, V., Chastin, S. F., Latimer-Cheung, A. F., Chulak-Bozzer, T., Faulkner, G., Flood, S. M., Gazendam, M. K., Healy, G. N., Katzmarzyk, P. T., Kennedy, W., Lane, K. N., Lorbergs, A., Maclaren, K., Marr, S., Powell, K. E., Rhodes, R. E., Ross-White, A., Welsh, F., Willumsen, J., & Tremblay, M. S. (2020). Canadian 24-hour movement guidelines for adults aged 18–64 years and adults aged 65 years or older: An integration of physical activity, sedentary behaviour, and sleep. *Applied Physiology, Nutrition, and Metabolism, 45*(10), S57–S102.

19. Dempsey, P. C., Biddle, S. J., Buman, M. P., Chastin, S., Ekelund, U., Friedenreich, C. M., Katzmarzyk, P. T., Leitzmann, M. F., Stamatakis, E., van der Ploeg, H. P., Willumsen, J., & Bull, F.. (2020). New global guidelines on sedentary behaviour and health for adults: Broadening the behavioural targets. *International Journal of Behavioral Nutrition and Physical Activity, 17*(1), 1–12.

20. Matthews, C. E., Chen, K. Y., Freedson, P. S., Buchowski, M. S., Beech, B. M., Pate, R. R., & Troiano, R. P. (2008). Amount of time spent in sedentary behaviors in the United States, 2003–2004. *American Journal of Epidemiology, 167*(7), 875–881.

21. Wilmot, E. G., Edwardson, C. L., Achana, F. A., Davies, M. J., Gorely, T., Gray, L. J., Katzmarzyk, P. T., Leitzmann, M. F., Stamatakis, E., van der Ploeg, H. P., Willumsen, J., & Bull, F. (2012). Sedentary time in adults and the association with diabetes, cardiovascular disease and death: Systematic review and meta-analysis. *Diabetologia, 55*(11), 2895–2905.

22. Owen, N., Healy, G. N., Matthews, C. E., & Dunstan, D. W. (2010). Too much sitting: The population-health science of sedentary behavior. *Exercise and Sport Sciences Reviews, 38*(3), 105.

23. Barone Gibbs, B., Kowalsky, R. J., Perdomo, S. J., Taormina, J. M., Balzer, J. R., & Jakicic, J. M. (2017). Effect of alternating standing and sitting on blood pressure and pulse wave velocity during a simulated workday in adults with overweight/obesity. *Journal of Hypertension, 35*(12), 2411–2418.

24. Thorp, A. A., Kingwell, B. A., Sethi, P., Hammond, L., Owen, N., & Dunstan, D. W. (2014). Alternating bouts of sitting and standing attenuate postprandial glucose responses. *Medicine and Science in Sports and Exercise, 46*(11), 2053–2061.

25. Kowalsky, R. J., Perdomo, S. J., Taormina, J. M., Kline, C. E., Hergenroeder, A. L., Balzer, J. R., Jakicic, J. M., & Gibbs, B. B. (2018). Effect of using a sit-stand desk on ratings of discomfort, fatigue, and sleepiness across a simulated workday in overweight and obese adults. *Journal of Physical Activity and Health, 15*(10), 788–794.

26. Ee, J., Parry, S., IR de Oliveira, B., McVeigh, J. A., Howie, E., & Straker, L. (2018). Does a classroom standing desk intervention modify standing and sitting behaviour and musculoskeletal symptoms during school time and physical activity during waking time? *International Journal of Environmental Research and Public Health, 15*(8), 1668.

27. Kowalsky, R. J., Jakicic, J. M., Hergenroeder, A., Rogers, R. J., & Gibbs, B. B. (2019). Acute cardiometabolic effects of interrupting sitting with resistance exercise breaks. *Applied Physiology, Nutrition, and Metabolism, 44*(10), 1025–1032.

28. Dempsey, P. C., Larsen, R. N., Sethi, P., Sacre, J. W., Straznicky, N. E., Cohen, N. D., Cerin, E., Lambert, G. W., Owen, N., Kingwell, B. A., & Dunstan, D. W. (2016). Benefits for type 2 diabetes of interrupting prolonged sitting with brief bouts of light walking or simple resistance activities. *Diabetes Care, 39*(6), 964–972.

29. Dempsey, P. C., Sacre, J. W., Larsen, R. N., Straznicky, N. E., Sethi, P., Cohen, N. D., Cerin, E., Lambert, G. W., Owen, N., Kingwell, B. A., & Dunstan, D. W. (2016). Interrupting prolonged sitting with brief bouts of light walking or simple resistance activities reduces resting blood pressure and plasma noradrenaline in type 2 diabetes. *Journal of Hypertension, 34*(12), 2376–2382.

30. Carty, C., van der Ploeg, H. P., Biddle, S. J., Bull, F., Willumsen, J., Lee, L., Kamenov, K., & Milton, K. (2021). The first global physical activity and sedentary behavior guidelines for people living with disability. *Journal of Physical Activity and Health, 18*(1), 86–93.

31. Katzmarzyk, P. T., Powell, K. E., Jakicic, J. M., Troiano, R. P., Piercy, K., Tennant, B. & 2018 Physical Activity Guidelines Advisory Committee. (2019). Sedentary behavior and health: Update from the 2018 Physical Activity Guidelines Advisory Committee. *Medicine and Science in Sports and Exercise, 51*(6), 1227–1241.

32. Ekelund, U., Steene-Johannessen, J., Brown, W. J., Fagerland, M. W., Owen, N., Powell, K. E., Bauman, A., Lee, I. M., Lancet Physical Activity Series 2 Executive Committee, & Lancet Sedentary Behaviour Working

Group. (2016). Does physical activity attenuate, or even eliminate, the detrimental association of sitting time with mortality? A harmonised meta-analysis of data from more than 1 million men and women. *Lancet (London, England)*, *388*(10051), 1302–1310.
33. Collier, S. R., Kanaley, J. A., Carhart, R., Frechette, V., Tobin, M. M., Hall, A. K., Luckenbaugh, A. N., & Fernhall, B. (2008). Effect of 4 weeks of aerobic or resistance exercise training on arterial stiffness, blood flow and blood pressure in pre-and stage-1 hypertensives. *Journal of Human Hypertension*, *22*(10), 678–686.
34. Willis, L. H., Slentz, C. A., Bateman, L. A., Shields, A. T., Piner, L. W., Bales, C. W., Houmard, J. A., & Kraus, W. E. (2012). Effects of aerobic and/or resistance training on body mass and fat mass in overweight or obese adults. *Journal of Applied Physiology*, *113*(12), 1831–1837.
35. Centers for Disease Control and Prevention. (2013). Adult participation in aerobic and muscle-strengthening physical activities--United States, 2011. *MMWR. Morbidity and Mortality Weekly Report*, *62*(17), 326–330.
36. Child and Adolescent Health Measurement Initiative. (n.d.). 2018-2019 National Survey of Children's Health (NSCH) data query. Data Resource Center for Child and Adolescent Health supported by the U.S. Department of Health and Human Services, Health Resources and Services Administration (HRSA), Maternal and Child Health Bureau (MCHB). www.childhealthdata.org.
37. World Health Organization & World Bank. (2011). *World report on disability 2011*. World Health Organization. https://apps.who.int/iris/handle/10665/44575
38. American College of Sports Medicine. (2003). *ACSM's exercise management for persons with chronic diseases and disabilities*. Human Kinetics.
39. Riebe, D., Franklin, B. A., Thompson, P. D., Garber, C. E., Whitfield, G. P., Magal, M., & Pescatello, L. S. (2015). Updating ACSM's recommendations for exercise preparticipation health screening. *Medicine and Science in Sport and Exercise*, *47*(11), 2473–2479.
40. Liguori, G., Feito, Y., Fountaine, C., & Roy, B. A. (2022). *ACSM's guidelines for exercise testing and prescription* (11th ed.). Wolters Kluwer.
41. Cooper Institute. (2017). *Fitnessgram and activitygram test administration manual-updated* (5th ed.). Human Kinetics.
42. Winnick, J. P., & Short, F. X. (2014). *The Brockport physical fitness test manual* (2nd ed.). Human Kinetics.

CHAPTER 7
EXERCISE MEDICINE AND PROGRAMMING

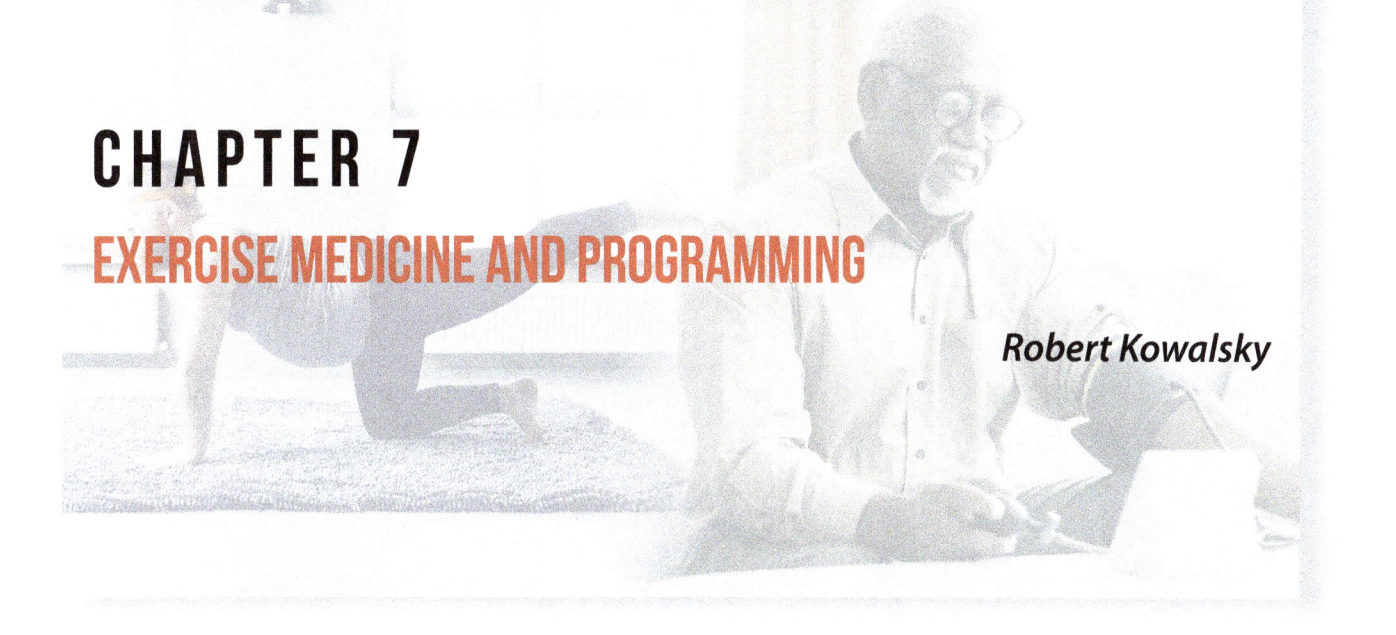

Robert Kowalsky

Medicine is defined as the science and art of the maintenance of health and the prevention, alleviation, or cure of disease.[1] If needed, this applies to treating any injury or disease that becomes present as well. Historically, this is done through the care of a doctor relying on practices of surgical intervention or drug therapies. Many surgical options and drug therapies can provide immediate and long-lasting relief. Yet both these approaches can potentially lead to various degrees of side effects or adverse events; however, usually the benefits of these options outweigh the negatives.

An alternative view to medicine is the use of behavior adaptations to prevent and treat certain medical conditions. Behavioral adaptations may include altering an individual's diet, but of specific interest to this chapter are adaptations using exercise and physical activity. This concept entails that by using exercise, you can treat and prevent many chronic health conditions while improving physical function and quality of life. In this chapter, we will review the ranging benefit of exercise and how it can be "medicine" to both prevent and manage many medical conditions. This includes aiding in the treatment and management of the chronic conditions that can develop in those with disabilities. Furthermore, we will discuss the appropriate programming considerations for the general adult and youth populations, while also discussing considerations with programming for individuals with disabilities.

PREVENTION VERSUS TREATMENT

The presence of two or more conditions or diseases is referred to as a **comorbidity**. Whether it is individuals with or without disabilities, the prevalence of comorbidities and other chronic conditions such as cardiovascular, metabolic, and musculoskeletal diseases are relatively high.[2-6] It is not uncommon for those with disabilities to develop another condition or disease on top of the disability, such as obesity.[7] Not only do complications arise from obesity, such as high blood pressure and insulin resistance, but this can also result in further mobility issues, depression, and fatigue.[8] Therefore, there is a need for a targeted plan to prevent the development of comorbidities as well as treat any comorbidities that have developed in individuals with disabilities. Three terms to understand that relate to this process are primary prevention, secondary prevention and tertiary prevention. **Primary prevention** refers to any efforts made to prevent an individual from developing a disease in the first place, whereas **secondary prevention** is the act of detecting a disease early enough in its development and preventing it from getting worse. A third term that is utilized is **tertiary prevention**, which focuses on improving the quality of life in an individual while also attempting to reduce the symptoms of the disease. Regardless of the stage, exercise can play a key role in efforts made to treat and prevent conditions.

Robert Kowalsky, Appalachian State University. © Kendall Hunt Publishing Company.

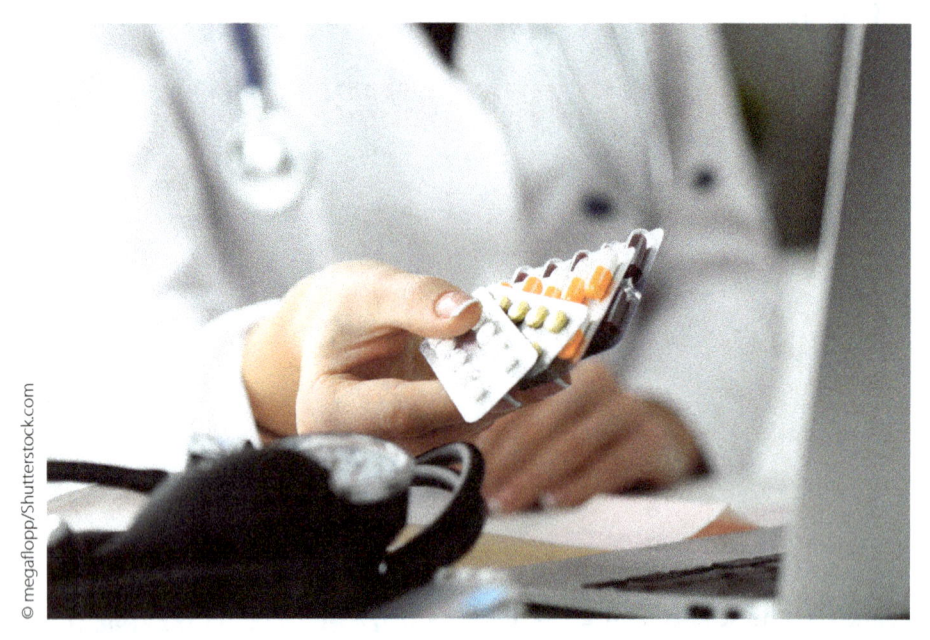

Exercise can be preventative and also potentially reduce the need for pharmacological treatment.

Aside from the treatment of comorbidities, exercise can be used as a direct treatment for many risks and complications associated with disabilities. This includes lessening symptoms and severity of disabilities, while also improving physical functioning and mobility of an individual. Engaging individuals in physical activity and exercise should follow evidence-based and population-specific recommendations and be tailored to address the general benefits of physical activity while also addressing any functional limitations an individual may have. An example of this would be an individual who has suffered a stroke and now has limitations to their gait and physical function. Participation in exercise can be geared toward improving those outcomes specifically by strengthening leg muscles and improving endurance to enhance their ability to sustain walking over a given duration. Additionally, programming that targets other muscles and other domains of physical activity (e.g., flexibility, reaction time, upper body strength) can provide a range of benefits discussed throughout this chapter.

CARDIORESPIRATORY BENEFITS OF PHYSICAL ACTIVITY AND EXERCISE

One of the major benefits to participation in exercise and physical activity is the improvement to the cardiovascular and respiratory systems. This includes benefit to the lungs and corresponding muscles, heart, blood, and arteries.[9] In turn, improvements to these systems via exercise or physical activity will result in enhancing the body's ability to supply oxygen to all areas throughout the body that can be used in the formation of usable energy.[10] Within certain disabilities, the respiratory or cardiovascular pathways may be compromised which, in turn, diminishes the body's ability to provide oxygen to the necessary areas to produce energy. Examples of this are those with asthma, spinal cord injuries, multiple sclerosis, and even those with severe scoliosis. These conditions can alter the function of the lungs and their ability to fully expand to bring oxygen from the external environment into the body. However, regular aerobic exercise can help improve the respiratory muscles used to expand the lungs and can result in improved lung function for these populations.[10-13]

Other cardiorespiratory benefits from aerobic exercise include improved blood pressure, heart rate, cardiac output, and arterial compliance.[14,15] This, in turn, reduces the risk of complications such as cardiovascular disease, diabetes, and mortality.[16-19] Though aerobic training is typically relied upon for cardiorespiratory benefit, resistance training can provide benefit in this area as well. For example, resistance training has demonstrated meaningful reduction in blood pressure.[20] Resistance training has also demonstrated its potential positive impact on lung function, specifically in clinical populations, such as those with chronic

Cardiorespiratory exercise increases the quality of life.

obstructive pulmonary disease (COPD).[21] Yet significant amounts of resistance training can have a negative impact on cardiorespiratory health, such as reduced arterial compliance, or reduced elastic property of the artery.[22] Other benefits can be achieved from resistance training though, as described later in this chapter. These benefits hold true for those with disabilities as well. For example, regular exercise participation in individuals with Down syndrome improves cardiovascular outcomes and reduces their cardiometabolic risk profile.[23] Another example is the benefit from exercise for stroke survivors, resulting in reduction in blood pressure and arterial function, important markers for reducing a reoccurrence of a stroke.[24]

METABOLIC BENEFIT OF PHYSICAL ACTIVITY AND EXERCISE

Metabolic health relates to the body's ability to develop usable energy, which is a requirement for almost all biological processes that are carried out within the human body. Several metabolic systems are involved in the development of the compound adenosine triphosphate (ATP), which is developed from the breakdown of carbohydrates, fats, and proteins ingested in the diet as well as from their stored forms found in adipose (fat) tissue, the muscle, and liver. The stored energy in ATP is then used to carry out many biological processes in the body.

The metabolic process is directly controlled via three main categories.

- Delivery
- Uptake
- Metabolism

The delivery of these food sources to be converted into energy is done primarily through the cardiovascular system, and those benefits are previously discussed. As for uptake, this is the process of moving the substrates that will be used in the metabolism process from the blood to inside the cell. For examples, blood glucose's uptake into muscle is facilitated by insulin binding to their target receptors, opening channels to allow glucose into the muscle. As for metabolism, this is the act to form ATP from glucose and free fatty acids, and occurs within the cytosol of the muscle or within the mitochondria.

Regular physical activity has demonstrated wide ranging benefit to the metabolic process. One of the greatest benefits is the improvement in insulin sensitivity.[25] This improvement to insulin sensitivity holds true for both aerobic and resistance exercise participation, even after just one bout of activity.[26] Improving insulin sensitivity can be beneficial for individuals dealing with obesity, diabetes, and even cardiovascular disease.[27]

Aside from improving insulin sensitivity, other metabolic benefits can be realized from the improvement of body weight. This is achieved through

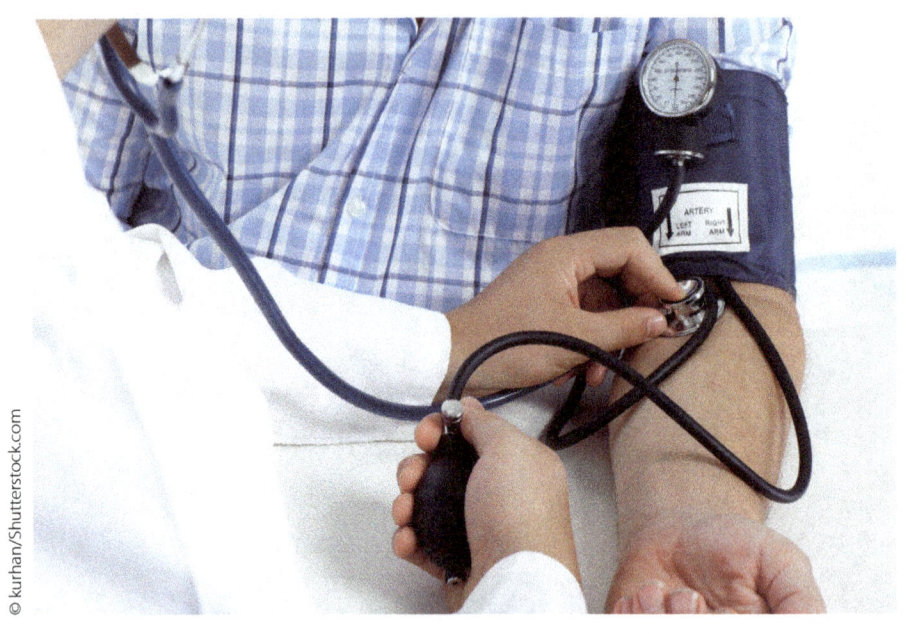

Blood pressure, along with heart rate, respiratory rate, and temperature are essential in monitoring health.

the reduction in excessive adipose tissue. A meta-analysis conducted on exercise training and its impact on those with metabolic syndrome demonstrated that exercise can result in improvements to body composition as well as beneficial changes to blood lipoprotein levels, triglycerides, and body mass index.[28] Weight loss can reduce the risk of conditions such as cardiovascular disease, diabetes, and cancer.[29] The management of weight gain, or the promotion of weight loss if overweight/obese, in those with disabilities is also important, as this can compound health issues in those with disabilities. Due to many disabilities having mobility issues, excess weight gain is a very common problem. However, recommendations encourage greater than 150 minutes per week, and promote greater than 250 minutes per week in the management of obesity,[30] yet in certain disabilities this can be difficult. Fortunately, studies have demonstrated that even in populations with disabilities, weight loss interventions can be successful. For example, those with intellectual disabilities can still have successful weight loss utilizing a group-based approach that includes

Successful weight loss relies on a healthy balance of diet and exercise.

the involvement of the caregiver in both exercise and diet interventions,[31] yet more research is needed.

NEUROMUSCULAR BENEFIT OF PHYSICAL ACTIVITY AND EXERCISE

The nervous system and muscular system work jointly to initiate and carry out movement in the human body. The role of the nervous system is to carry conscious or somatic signaling to the muscles to carry out muscle contractions. This electrical signal must move down from the brain, through the spinal cord and arrive at the muscle. At the muscle, this electrical signal results in the release of calcium, which initiates the sliding filament model. This model explains how the individual muscle filaments (known as actin and myosin; see Figure 7.2) can interact with each other and result in muscle shortening, muscle staying the same length, or muscle lengthening (muscle contraction). The quality of muscle contraction for any given muscle is determined in the number of muscle fibers being recruited, the frequency of electrical signals coming from the brain, and how active opposing muscles are to the muscle in question. With many disabilities, this pathway from the brain, to the spinal cord, and in the muscle can be impacted and result in improper signaling, no signaling, or impaired muscle contraction. Fortunately, physical activity and exercise can play an important role in the prevention and treatment of these limitations.

Participation in exercise can result in muscle growth or **hypertrophy**. Though some hypertrophy is achieved from aerobic exercise,[32] resistance exercise is the most potent stimulus for muscle growth.[33] Increasing muscle mass allows for individuals to move their own body as well as external weights more effectively. This can be a very important concept for those with disabilities. For example, those who use wheelchairs may need to transfer themselves in and out of their chair throughout their day to use the restroom, for transportation, and other activities of daily living. This would require substantial amount of upper body strength, which can be achieved with increasing muscle size. It has been demonstrated that resistance training can result in significant improvements in strength and power outcomes which can translate to improvement in physical function in daily life.[34]

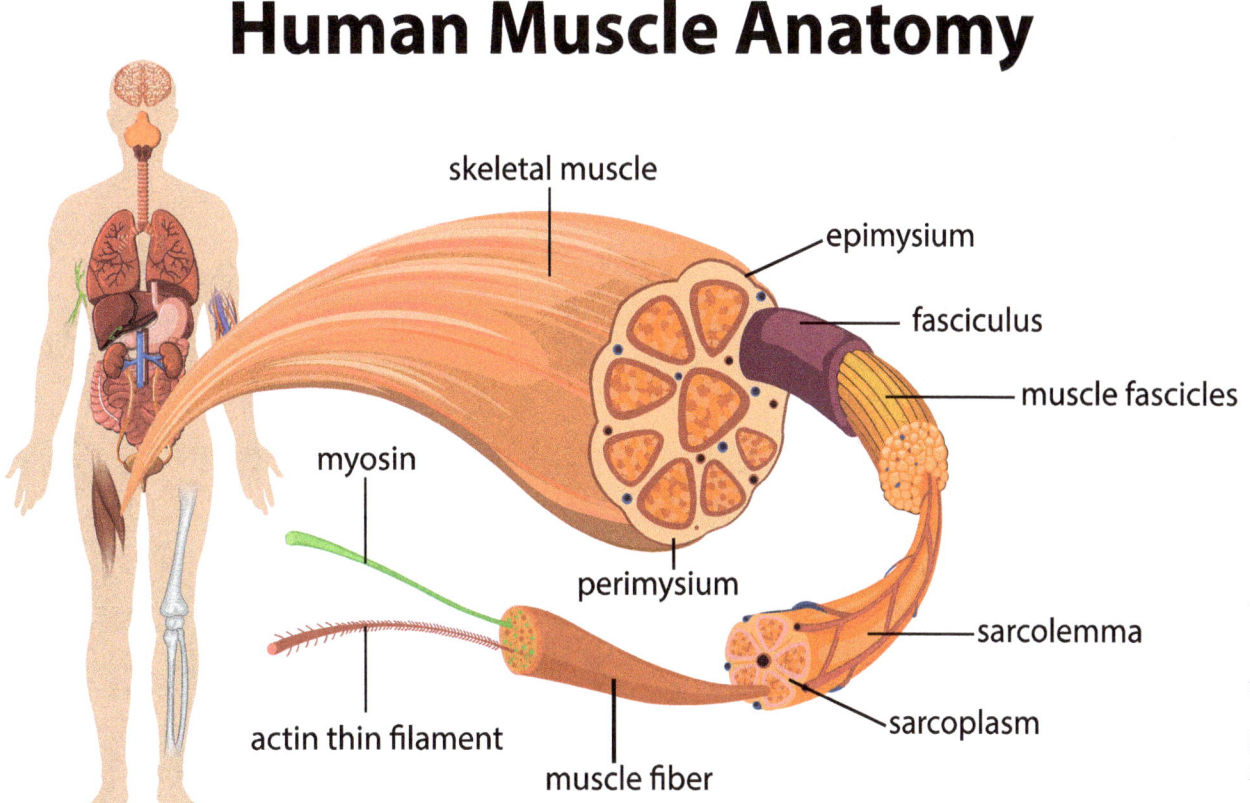

FIGURE 7.2 Anatomical model of actin and myosin in muscle that are responsible for muscle contraction.

As for the neurological pathways, exercise can play an important role in disabilities such as Parkinson's disease, multiple sclerosis, or amyotrophic lateral sclerosis (ALS). These conditions all are results in impairment to the nerve pathways, though they are pathologically different. Multiple sclerosis is an autoimmune disease that attacks the myelin sheaths that protect and insulate the nerves. Exercise, including yoga, can be beneficial combating some of the symptoms of the condition, such as fatigue.[35] Other benefits include improvements to muscular strength, aerobic capacity and ambulatory performance, and may improve fatigue, gait, balance, and quality of life.[36] Many of these benefits from exercise can be applied to all populations, regardless of disease or disability, and is attributed to better coordination between the primary moving muscle (agonist), the opposing muscle (antagonist), and the aiding muscles (synergists) as well as an increase in firing frequency.[37]

BONE HEALTH BENEFITS OF PHYSICAL ACTIVITY AND EXERCISE

Bone provides the structural support for the body. It gives the body its shape, and acts as a medium for muscles to engage with to perform movement. Bone development and growth occurs throughout childhood into early adulthood, where it reaches its peak and then slowly declines throughout life.[38] Good bone health is a result of proper nutrition and physical activity. Bone growth relies on calcium and vitamin D intake, yet an important stimulant for bone growth, or osteogenesis, is stress on the bone. This stress is applied through regular physical activity and exercise, highlighting the importance of all individuals with and without disabilities participating in activity throughout the life span.

As an example of the benefit of exercise, research has demonstrated an 8%–10% increase in bone mineral content in adulthood for those who exercised regularly throughout their lives compared to more sedentary individuals.[38] This is attributed to the activity participation that occurs within the youth and adolescent years, highlighting the importance for all youth, including those with disabilities, to engage in regular physical activity to set themselves up for a life span of beneficial bone health. As for adults, beneficial changes still occur from regular exercise participation, yet at reduced levels from childhood, and at least in part contribute to bone preservation.[38]

© ALPA PROD/Shutterstock.com

Decline in mobility capability from many disabilities becomes a major concern for bone health.

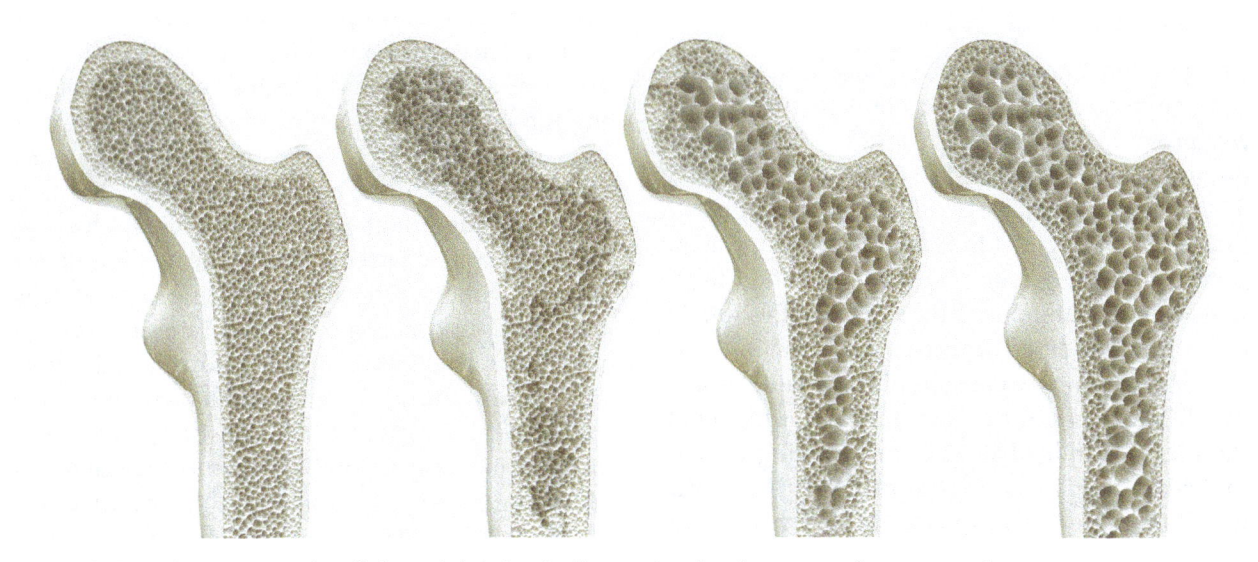

FIGURE 7.3 Bone loss progression (left to right) that indicates the development of osteoporosis.

In certain clinical populations, exercise plays a key role in the treatment process of the disease. For example, in those who are diagnosed with osteoporosis, a disease with progressive bone loss making bones hollow and brittle (see Figure 7.3), exercise at low, moderate, and vigorous intensities can at least maintain bone levels, with higher levels of activity promoting bone growth in this population.[39] The key message with exercise for the prevention and treatment of bone health issues is to ensure that the exercise is weight-bearing.[39] That is, the individual is supporting their own body weight while exercising, such as walking. Though those with more severe degrees of osteoporosis may need to begin with exercise that is not weight-bearing, such as swimming or using an arm or leg cycle, the goal is to eventually transition them to more weight-bearing activities.

COGNITIVE BENEFITS OF PHYSICAL ACTIVITY AND EXERCISE

One of the newest areas of research for the benefit of physical activity and exercise is the potential benefit it can provide to arguably the most important organ in the entire body: the brain. The U.S. 2018 Physical Activity Guidelines determined that there is evidence that exercise influences the brain as well as that those who experience brain-related disorders, such as dementia, can benefit from regular exercise participation.[40] This evidence on the benefit of exercise for brain health is most important for individuals in the early and late stages of life (children and elderly) because these periods are where we observe substantial growth or decline in cognitive outcomes and markers of academic performance. Exercise can help facilitate that growth in young individuals while counteracting or at least slowing the decline in cognitive function observed in older adults.

The benefit of exercise and physical activity for children and adolescents ranges in improvements for executive function, attention, memory, language, and academic achievement.[40] Yet this is still an emerging area and more research is needed to fully understand how exercise and physical activity in youth populations can impact brain health, but currently the evidence is promising. As for adults, both middle- and older-aged individuals observe improvements in cognition, attention, and executive function when engaging in regular physical activity.[40]

In populations with clinical diagnoses, such as dementia or other cognitive disabilities, there is strong evidence that increasing levels of physical activity and exercise reduces risk of dementia and cognitive decline.[40] As for those with dementia, including Alzheimer's disease, physical activity and exercise may help improve cognition.[40] Other conditions such as attention deficit hyperactivity disorder (ADHD), Parkinson's disease, schizophrenia, multiple sclerosis, and stroke have all demonstrated moderate evidence that physical activity and exercise improves cognition.[40] Further evidence in individuals with ADHD reveals that attention and executive function (impulsivity) are improved, and these findings are also similar for children with social, emotional, and behavioral problems.[40]

TRAINING PRINCIPLES

Now that the benefits of exercise have been reviewed, and before discussing the general structure of exercise programs and prescriptions, it is important to discuss several training principles and how they dictate decisions made regarding programming. The first is the principle of **individuality**. This principle states that each person responds differently to the same training stimulus. This holds true for individuals with disabilities in that no two disabilities are the same, and no two people with the same disability will respond in the same manner. This highlights the need for individualized programming to meet individual needs. The second principle is **specificity**. This states that adaptions to the human body will be specific to the type of exercise, intensity, and duration engaged in. As an example, you cannot expect vast improvements to the strength of your arms if you are only engaging in aerobic activity such as running. The next principle is the principle of **reversibility**. This states that any improvements you see from training can only be maintained if you continue to participate in activity. If you decide to stop being physically active, the benefits you gained will be lost, forcing. Even with a reduced volume of training, the continuation activities in similar patterns will allow the gains and benefits of the training to remain. The key is to not stop activity all together. The last training principle is **progressive overload**. This principle states that the body will respond and adapt to any stresses you place on it (such as exercise), but those adaptations will only change until they meet the demand being placed on the body. Progression does not happen when someone becomes complacent in their physical activity. Thus, if a desire to see continual improvement is there for the individual, then you must continuously increase the stress placed on the body system. Increases in intensity, duration, or frequency of exercise are easy ways to achieve this.

DESIGNING AN EXERCISE PROGRAM: FITT-VP PRINCIPLES OF EXERCISE PRESCRIPTION

When approaching the development of an exercise program for any individual, it is important to have a starting point to work from and manipulate to meet the abilities, needs, and goals of the individual. In general terms, all exercise training sessions should follow a basic format of three to four phases. This includes the use of a warm-up phase, the conditioning phase, the cool-down phase, and as needed based on goals and needs, the stretching phase.[41] The warm-up and cool-down phases are responsible for transitioning the body from a resting state to an exercising state and back down to a resting state. These transitional phases allow the body to adapt to the demands placed on the body's physiological, biomechanical, and bioenergetic systems. Sudden demands on these systems without proper transitioning can result in the increased occurrence of adverse events such as musculoskeletal injury as well as myocardial infarctions (heart attack) or other similar cardiovascular events.[41] These phases should consist of movements and activities that are similar in nature to what is employed in the conditioning phase. The conditioning phase includes the use of aerobic, resistance, or neuromuscular activities or exercises designed to target one or more of the physical fitness domains discussed in Chapter 6. The stretching phase is distinct from the other phases and should follow either the warm-up or cool-down phases, which will increase the overall temperature within the musculature, which, in turn, results in increased range of motion achieved while stretching.

In all phases, the employment of the FITT-VP principles of exercise prescription aids in the development of program to help individuals achieve the various health benefits from regular exercise participation.[41] The acronym FITT-VP serves as a reminder to the various details that should be considered for all exercise sessions. The following is a description of what each of the letters in FITT-VP stand for with a description.

- Frequency
- Intensity
- Type (mode)
- Time
- Volume
- Progression

Frequency

Frequency refers to how often the exercise session will be carried out. Typically, it is reported as the number of days per week you engage in the specific programming. When determining the frequency, you will need to consider the amount of time available to the individual to devote to exercise each week, while also ensuring that there is sufficient recovery time between training sessions so that the body systems taxed during each session can recover.

Intensity

Intensity relates to the degree of difficulty or how hard you work during the exercise session. When providing programming for an individual, you need to instruct them on how hard they should be working during the session. This can be evaluated using various techniques as discussed in Chapter 6, such as the percentage of VO_{2max}, heart rate, rating of perceived exertion (RPE), or METs. Typically, the goal of the intensity portion is to achieve either moderate- or vigorous-intensity levels; however, light-intensity physical activity can be utilized in warm-ups/cool-downs as well as with those with lower fitness levels or those new to exercise who are not yet ready for higher intensity and must build up to the higher intensities. As for resistance training, the intensity is typically defined by the amount of weight you are moving with each repetition. This could include just your body weight, the thickness of the resistance band, or the amount of weight for a dumbbell, plate, or setting on a machine.

Type (mode)

The **type** of activity utilized will rely largely on the goals, functional abilities, and needs of the individual. Additionally, personal preferences, equipment availability and accessibility, space, and weather may also dictate the type of activity employed. The focus should be on using activities that target the specific muscles and body systems you are wanting to target regardless of whether the focus is aerobic or resistance training. For aerobic training, the activities should be rhythmic and continuous such as walking running and swimming, whereas resistance training exercises could utilize body weight, free weights, machines, exercise bands, or a mixture of styles.

Time

Time is how long each individual training session should take or more specifically, the duration you will spend completing each exercise. This is an important factor and corresponds directly with frequency to help individuals with disabilities in achieving the physical activity recommendations. As you may recall, the recommended physical activity levels include a minimum of 150 minutes per week for adults, that is spread out over several days per week. For youth, the goal is a total of 60 minutes or more every day of the week.

Volume

Volume is considered the weekly amount of activity that the individual will be engaging in. It is actually a product of the frequency, time, and intensity components of the FITT-VP principle. This can be expressed as MET-minutes per week (MET·min·wk^{-1}) or kilocalories burned per week (kcal·wk^{-1}). MET·min is a product of the MET level for a certain activity multiplied by the minutes of that activity. For example, if you are walking at a MET level of three for 30 minutes, your MET·min would be 90 (30 × 3). If you are doing that for 5 days per week, then your MET·min·wk^{-1} equates to 450. Research indicates an association of 500 to 1,000 MET·min·wk^{-1} with lower rates of cardiovascular disease and premature death, including for those with disabilities.[42] Kcal·wk^{-1} can be derived from MET levels of activities, and is another way to express volume. As for resistance training, the volume refers the number of repetitions and sets you have the individual engage in. An example would be having an individual complete 2 sets with 8 to 10 repetitions per set.

Progression

Progression refers to knowing when to advance the individual so that the programming you are offering them continues to be challenging to their body systems in an effort to continue positive adaptations. Several factors play into the rate of progression including how they are responding to training, their current health status, and the goals of the client. You are able to progress the individual by increasing one or more of the other factors such as frequency, duration, or intensity. Utilizing frequent assessments of physical fitness domains including aerobic, strength, flexibility and other measures of physical function will provide detailed information regarding if progression is needed, or if what you are doing is not a large enough stimulus to create progression. However, caution must be taken to ensure that the level of progression is not too rapid, as this can lead to overtraining and in those with disabilities progressing too fast may elicit symptoms and adverse reactions relating to their disability. Overtraining occurs when the stimulus and progression creates too large of a stress on the body, without appropriate rest and recovery between training periods. Figure 7.4 demonstrates the concepts of appropriate progressive overload and inappropriate progression that can lead to overtraining.

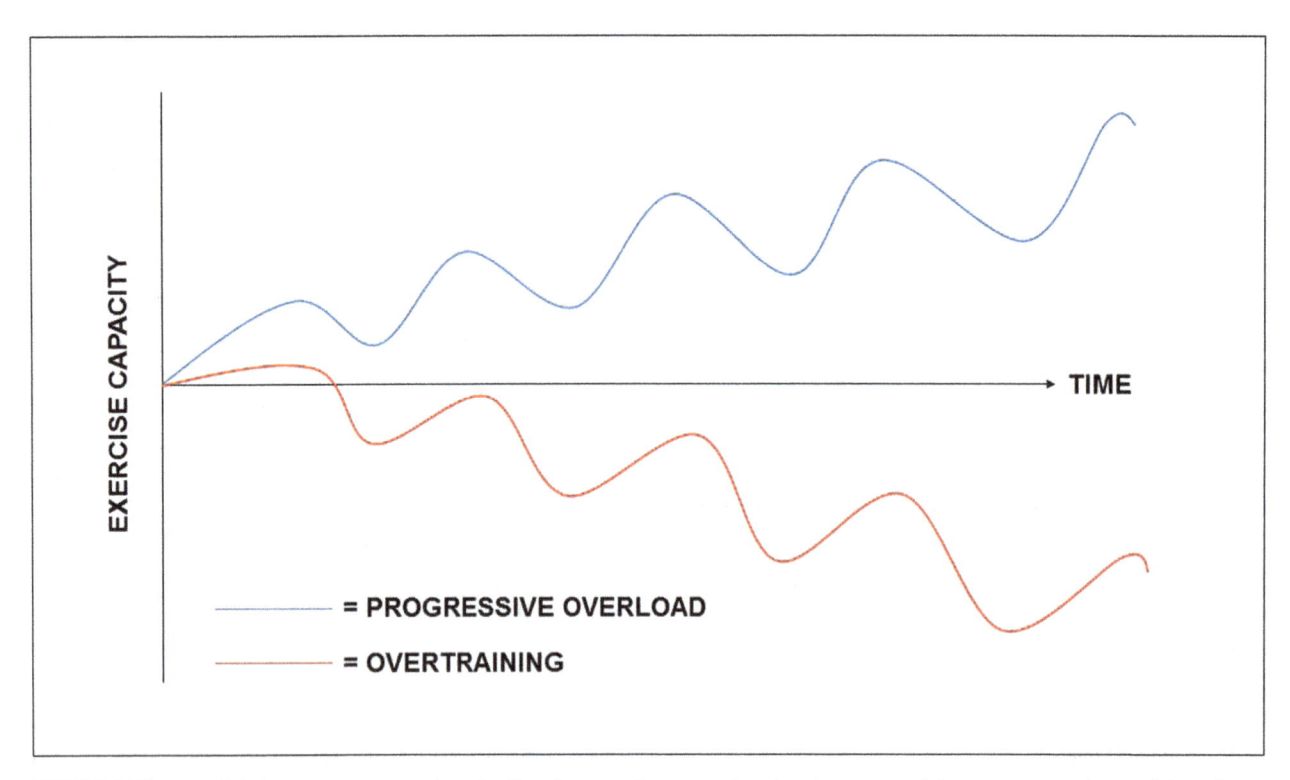

FIGURE 7.4 The model shows a progressive decline in exercise capacity due to overtraining compared to safely using the progressive overload principle.
Source: Robert Kowalsky

PROGRAMMING CONSIDERATIONS FOR CHILDREN AND ADOLESCENTS

When designing an exercise plan for a child or adolescent with a disability, several items need to be taken into consideration to provide a safe and effective program. Most programming should still be based on what is recommended for the general youth population as discussed in this section. Though you may employ a similar FITT-VP approach to their program, several other adaptations should be considered. For example, children have a specific recommendation to limit the amount of screen time daily (<2 hours per day), due to its link to decreased fitness, increased adiposity, increased blood pressure, lipids and glycohemoglobin levels.[43] The participation in physical activity and limitation of sedentary behavior is important to promote and form healthy habits and behaviors that will carry over to adulthood. For physical activity participation, it is acceptable for youth to participate in aerobic, strength training, and bone loading exercises. Though the general expectation is that most youth are healthy enough to participate in light to moderate intensity activity without preexercise screening, it is recommended to undergo preexercise screening for those with disabilities to determine if they should seek further medical clearance from a doctor before starting any physical activity. This screening also allows the practitioner to identify any contraindications for the individual they are working with before starting so they can adjust their programming accordingly.

The first area for consideration in youth is with exercise testing. Typical testing procedures that are implemented in an adult population can be done in a youth population as well. However, there are several items to consider including the following.

- The setting: Testing in youth is typically not done in a clinical or formal setting unless absolutely necessary, therefore, field-based testing is typically utilized. When working with individuals with limitations, consider settings that are quiet and distraction free as much as possible, as well as considering the accessibility of the space being utilized.
- Type of protocol: You want to choose a protocol that meets the reason for you needing to test, as well as considering the functional capacity of the individual. Also consider picking tests that have been designed for individuals with disabilities such as the Brockport Physical Fitness Test (as appropriate).

- Familiarization: Prior to testing, you want to fully explain the test to the individual in their preferred mode of communication and be sure that they understand all aspects. This may require demonstration of the test on your part as youth typically need more instruction than adults.
- Providing extra motivation: Youth compared to adults are usually not as strong at self-motivation, therefore, to ensure the test elicits the responses you are looking for, be prepared to supply ample motivation to keep them on task and committed until the test is over. Also, keeping the test fun and engaging is key.

Practitioners may also consider implementing one of several developed youth fitness testing batteries. For example, the FITNESSGRAM, and its accessible counterpart, the Brockport, is a test battery designed to be implemented in a school setting and can assess youth ages 10 to 17 for areas relating to the components of health-related fitness.[44] The FITNESSGRAM and Brockport Physical Fitness Test[45] are cost-friendly, with minimal equipment needed and allows for testing multiple children very quickly. Along with exercise testing considerations, practitioners should consider the altered physiological response to exercise youth have compared to adults. The altered responses should be considered when choosing the appropriate testing procedures as well as tracking of intensity for programming. These altered responses include the following but are not limited to; higher respiratory rate due to smaller lung size, lower systolic and diastolic blood pressures, and lower stroke volume and cardiac output, even though their heart rate response is higher compared to adults.

As for exercise prescription considerations in a general youth population, the goal should be to obtain the appropriate levels of physical activity engagement via multiple avenues. In younger children, the focus should be on unstructured play. That is, exercise should be disguised or hidden inside of a game or fun activity that is enjoyable to the child. This should include bursts of moderate-to-vigorous–intensity activity. You may also engage youth populations in strength training exercises, but youth should receive proper instruction and supervision before and during activity to avoid injury. The focus of resistance exercise training should be toward proper form

When working with children, field-based testing, and not clinical, becomes a priority.

and control of the body and not on adding weight/resistance. Begin with using body weight exercises and progress to resistance bands and lighter free weights as they begin to gain control of bodily movements. You should also consider that some youth may be overweight or physically inactive, so this will come into play when designing a program that meets their needs and abilities. These individuals will require you as the practitioner to start slow and low, and build up their tolerance to activity over time to meet the daily 60 minutes of activity requirement. Lastly, due to the underdeveloped thermoregulation capacity of youth, sustained heavy intensity activity, specifically in hot and humid climates should be limited and the use of proper hydration protocols should be employed.

ADDITIONAL PROGRAMMING CONSIDERATIONS FOR ADULTS AND YOUTH WITH DISABILITIES

The general recommendations for testing and exercise programming in adults and youth discussed earlier still apply in most situations when working with those with disabilities; however, there are a few additional considerations to implement. These considerations could be related directly to the disability, or related to any comorbidity they may have developed. In general, exercise testing and prescription for individuals with disabilities is highly individualized and no two disabilities in individuals are the same. The good news is that the approach to exercise for any condition is relatively simple due to the overwhelming benefit of exercise and that most individualized considerations are geared toward safety and functional abilities of the individual.

With any disability, a preexercise health screening should help identify any considerations you may need to address before choosing an exercise test or exercise program. These limitations could address any physical impairments, addressing issues with balance or inability to get their body into a certain posture to complete an exercise, or even a limitation with comprehension, making it difficult to understand complex instructions. Furthermore, the preexercise health screening will help to identify medication usage for the management of a disability or comorbidity that may alter decisions with testing and programming. Lastly, this preexercise screening allows for the identification of individual goals of the client and previous history with exercise participation, which include identifying disability-related outcomes as well as general health and fitness outcomes. Therefore, ingenuity of the practitioner is essential to be able to take all information gathered during the screening and to adapt to any situation that arises. To help in this, practitioners should consider preparing several approaches to exercise and having a toolbox of exercises that can be interchanged with each other to target the same muscle groups. This adaptability should also be considered with testing procedures. Practitioners should have at their disposal multiple methods for assessing each of the health-related fitness domains.

In adult populations with disabilities, an additional assessment to the preexercise health screening includes understanding the individual's levels of exertion that exhibits symptoms or contraindications of physical activity. This can include a questionnaire with simplified questions that individuals can answer with yes or no responses, which is important for those with disabilities impacting cognition. Examples of these questions include:

- Are you able to walk for 10 minutes before having to stop?
- Are you able to walk up 10 steps without needing to stop?
- Are your physical activity-limiting symptoms relieved after 5 minutes of rest?

When transitioning into evaluation of physical fitness and function, individuals with various disability types are still able to engage in a formal type of exercise testing that would be used in the general adult population with only slight modification to address their limitations. An example is using a graded treadmill test to assess aerobic capacity for an individual with visual impairment; in most cases they would just need a treadmill with handrails to ensure balance. In disabilities with more substantial impact of physical function, a practitioner may consider a more basic assessment such a 6-minute walk test or a short assessment of gait speed along with their ability to sit and stand out of a chair or their ability to lift household items for multiple repetitions, like a laundry basket from the floor to a table. This may also include modification to common exercise tests like push ups, which can be altered to standing wall push ups. In those who are unable to walk or those who need assisted devices to ambulate, consider seated assessments such as seated bicep curls, seated one-leg flexibility, or a wheelchair shuttle test. For exercise programming, many considerations will end up being specific to the individual, but some general considerations include keeping the environment clean and open to avoid any hazards that could cause an individual to trip or hurt themselves, frequent assessments of heart rate, blood pressure, or other markers of health status to understand the impact of the exercise on their safety status, and focusing the programming on exercise and movements that aid the individual in overcoming any limitations of their disability while enhancing mobility and physical function. At the initiation of any program, the focus will not be on improving markers of health-related fitness outcomes such as aerobic fitness, strength, and flexibility, though improvements in these outcomes will still take place.

In youth with disabilities, many considerations with adults who have disabilities stay the same with the addition of a few population-specific considerations. With exercise testing, you may consider using the Brockport Physical Fitness Test as mentioned before, which is a youth fitness test battery designed for those with individuals. Aside from this, consider using disability specific assessments of physical fitness. For example, those with cerebral palsy have the ability to engage in a ten-meter shuttle test that allows for the use of an assisted device like a rollator. For younger individuals with disabilities, it is important to allow for multiple trials of any testing so that the individual can practice and become familiar with the protocol before attempting it for assessment or score. Consider basing any assessment around activities that the individual identifies as enjoyable during their preexercise health screening. For youth, a big factor in the willingness to engage in exercise is that they find the activity fun and enjoyable, so use this when designing fitness tests, as well as with exercise programming.

CASE STUDY EXAMPLES OF PROGRAMMING FOR SELECTED DISABILITIES

Here are several example case studies of hypothetical people with a disability that provide a general guide as to what an exercise program may look like for an individual. This includes relative background information as well as items to consider when evaluating and making decisions for the client. Attempt to follow the general template for the FITT-VP principle along with any specific considerations with the client:

Case Study 1

A middle-aged male who suffers from chronic low back pain. A detailed medical history provides

An example of a modified push up for testing or programming purposes.

information that he exercises regularly (walks 5 times a day for 45 minutes each day) unless his back-pain symptoms flare up. Additionally, his cholesterol is high, but he is on a statin to help lower it. Though his BMI is classified as overweight, he attributes this mostly due to his poor diet. He is seeking help to manage his back pain symptoms and hopefully lose some weight. His doctor attributes his chronic back pain to weak back muscles and his poor posture at work (desk job >50 hours week).

Consider: Aside from the man's disability, prescribing exercise that fits most adult populations is appropriate. However, because on his own, he already engages in an appropriate amount aerobic exercise (225 total minutes per week), the focus of your program should be on strength training and flexibility while managing his symptoms. Though there may be a tendency to target his back muscles with your programming, you want to make sure that you are not neglecting other muscle groups and other areas of his body. Focusing too much of your programming on one area of the body can result in muscle imbalances that may result in increases of his symptoms instead of helping him. With any of the exercises you use with him, it is highly important he maintains proper form throughout each repetition. Additionally, you may want to discuss with him his daily routine and ways he can change certain behaviors in his life to offset his high exposure to sedentary behavior. Discussing methods to break up his sitting with activity breaks or modifying his workstation may be key to reducing his back-pain symptoms.

Case Study 2

A 22-year-old female diagnosed with Down syndrome, an intellectual disability. Her mother is her caregiver and reports that last year, her daughter became highly interested in watching the Olympic Games and is potentially interested in participating in the Special Olympics, but has not been physically active in recent years. She works part time at the local library, but on her days off her mother reports that she spends a lot of her time watching TV. She does help out with chores around the house including laundry, walking the family dog, and some cleaning activities. Her medical history reveals no immediate cause for concern. She is slightly overweight (BMI: 25.8 kg/m^2), inactive, and has a slightly elevated blood pressure (128/78 mmHg).

Consider: Due to her being previously inactive, it is important to start slow and low with her and build up as she progresses. Because of her interest in Special Olympics, you may consider building your programming around the types of events that she is interested in, so it would be important to discuss with her what sports and events interest her. However, your programming should still focus on all health-related fitness domains until it becomes clear what type of events she likes and can excel at. Additionally, because of the importance of physical function and her responsibilities with her job and chores, you should ensure the exercise she engages in can help aid her in these activities. When considering appropriate exercise tests and exercises for her program, choose protocols that are simpler to describe and carry out. Due to her being previously inactive, you will want to start out with activities such as walking, jogging (if applicable), and swimming along with stretching and engaging in body weight resistance exercises to ensure she is able to move her body appropriately for each exercise. However, you should take into consideration that individuals with Down syndrome tend to have hypermobile joints, low muscle tone, and may have atlantoaxial instability so being familiar with their medical history, and ensuring direct supervision and care by the practitioner is highly encouraged when starting new exercises. By engaging in exercise including aerobic, strength, and flexibility, she should be easily able to improve her body composition, blood pressure, and be prepared for the future when she is ready to engage in various events at the Special Olympics.

Case Study 3

A 10-year-old boy, who has a visual impairment due to vision loss that started at the age of 5. His parents want him to continue to be a healthy and growing boy and though his vision issues sometimes limit his ability to participate in sports and games with friends, they still want him to be physically active. Aside from his vision impairment, he is healthy and does not have any other limitations. He enjoys playing in the backyard with his younger sister where they have a tree fort that includes monkey bars and a rope swing. He also enjoys swimming, but is hesitant to be on his own in a pool.

Consider: At this age, formal testing is not really necessary and with him presenting no other conditions other than his visual impairment, more formal testing can be overlooked. However, you may consider implementing a fitness test battery designed for children to determine where he classifies compared to his peers, such as the Brockport Physical Fitness Test. With his visual impairment, any exercises implemented into his programming should begin with a focus on simpler movement patterns and should be able to be verbally cued with ease. Avoid more complex activity starting out that would be difficult to explain without being able to visually see what is happening. However, over time, more complex movement patterns can be used as the individual becomes more comfortable with exercise. Consider implementing exercises that incorporate his favorite things like swimming and consider getting his younger sister involved as well in group-based exercise to build his confidence.

CHAPTER SUMMARY

In summary, regular exercise and physical activity participation can provide benefit to youth and adult populations with and without disabilities. Other key points include:

- Exercise and physical activity can be viewed as a behavioral therapy for both the treatment and prevention of many disabilities as well as many comorbidities that may develop.
- Benefits from being physically active and engaging in exercise are wide-ranging and contribute to positive changes to all body systems including: cardiorespiratory, metabolic, neuromuscular, bone, and the brain. This holds true for youth and adult populations.
- As a practitioner, when providing exercise programming you should begin with a general template for the program, such as FITT-VP, that targets the multiple facets of health-related fitness while also addressing the goals and abilities of the client while considering any functional limitations or other needs.
- Overtraining can occur if not monitored for, and any programming should be constantly evaluated for volume of activity and how it relates to your population.
- Practitioners need to be highly adaptable to individualize any programing to the specific needs of the individual.
- For any individualized approach, consider safety of the individual as well as their individual abilities and limitations. Keep in mind that no two people are the same.
- Any modifications to your program should be sure to not overlook any limitations or considerations with comorbidities.

REFERENCES

1. Merriam-Webster. (n.d.). Medicine. In *Merriam-Webster.com dictionary*. Retrieved May 29, 2021, from https://www.merriam-webster.com/dictionary/medicine.
2. Sidney, S., Quesenberry, C.P., Jaffe, M.G., Sorel, M., Nguyen-Huynh, M.N., Kushi, L.H., . . . & Rana, J.S. (2016). Recent trends in cardiovascular mortality in the United States and public health goals. *JAMA Cardiology, 1*(5), 594–599.
3. Aguilar, M., Bhuket, T., Torres, S., Liu, B., Wong, R.J. (2015). Prevalence of the Metabolic Syndrome in the United States, 2003-2012. *JAMA, 313*(19), 1973–1974. doi:10.1001/jama.2015.4260.
4. Cheng, Y.J., Kanaya, A.M., Araneta, M.R.G., Saydah, S.H., Kahn, H.S., Gregg, E.W., . . . & Imperatore, G. (2019). Prevalence of diabetes by race and ethnicity in the United States, 2011-2016. *JAMA, 322*(24), 2389–2398.
5. Deyo, R.A., Mirza, S.K., & Martin, B.I. (2006). Back pain prevalence and visit rates: estimates from U.S. national surveys, 2002. *Spine, 31*(23), 2724–2727.
6. Nahin, R.L. (2015). Estimates of pain prevalence and severity in adults: United States, 2012. *The Journal of Pain, 16*(8), 769–780.
7. Rimmer, J.H., Rowland, J.L., & Yamaki, K. (2007). Obesity and secondary conditions in adolescents with disabilities: addressing the needs of an underserved population. *Journal of Adolescent Health, 41*(3), 224–229.
8. Liou, T.H., Pi-Sunyer, F.X., & Laferrere, B. (2005). Physical disability and obesity. *Nutrition Reviews, 63*(10), 321–331.
9. Nystoriak, M.A., & Bhatnagar, A. (2018). Cardiovascular effects and benefits of exercise. *Frontiers in Cardiovascular Medicine, 5*, 135.

10. Avallone, K.M., & McLeish, A.C. (2013). Asthma and aerobic exercise: A review of the empirical literature. *Journal of Asthma*, *50*(2), 109–116.
11. Akkurt, H., Karapolat, H.U., Kirazli, Y., & Kose, T. (2017). The effects of upper extremity aerobic exercise in patients with spinal cord injury: A randomized controlled study. *European Journal of Physical Rehabilitation Medicine*, *53*(2), 219–227.
12. Mostert, S., & Kesselring, J. (2002). Effects of a short-term exercise training program on aerobic fitness, fatigue, health perception and activity level of subjects with multiple sclerosis. *Multiple Sclerosis Journal*, *8*(2), 161–168.
13. Athanasopoulos, S., Paxinos, T., Tsafantakis, E., Zachariou, K., & Chatziconstantinou, S. (1999). The effect of aerobic training in girls with idiopathic scoliosis. *Scandinavian Journal of Medicine & Science in Sports*, *9*(1), 36–40.
14. Nystoriak, M. A., & Bhatnagar, A. (2018). Cardiovascular effects and benefits of exercise. *Frontiers in Cardiovascular Medicine*, *5*, 135.
15. Tanaka, H., Dinenno, F.A., Monahan, K.D., Clevenger, C.M., DeSouza, C.A., & Seals, D.R. (2000). Aging, habitual exercise, and dynamic arterial compliance. *Circulation*, *102*(11), 1270–1275.
16. Agarwal, S.K. (2012). Cardiovascular benefits of exercise. *International Journal of General Medicine*, *5*, 541.
17. Liu, Y., Lee, D.C., Li, Y., Zhu, W., Zhang, R., Sui, X., ... & Blair, S.N. (2019). Associations of resistance exercise with cardiovascular disease morbidity and mortality. *Medicine and Science in Sports and Exercise*, *51*(3), 499.
18. Colberg, S.R., Sigal, R.J., Yardley, J.E., Riddell, M.C., Dunstan, D.W., Dempsey, P.C., ... & Tate, D.F. (2016). Physical activity/exercise and diabetes: a position statement of the American Diabetes Association. *Diabetes Care*, *39*(11), 2065–2079.
19. Paffenbarger Jr, R.S., Hyde, R., Wing, A.L., & Hsieh, C.C. (1986). Physical activity, all-cause mortality, and longevity of college alumni. *New England Journal of Medicine*, *314*(10), 605–613.
20. Cornelissen, V.A., & Smart, N.A. (2013). Exercise training for blood pressure: a systematic review and meta-analysis. *Journal of the American Heart Association*, *2*(1), e004473.
21. Strasser, B., Siebert, U., & Schobersberger, W. (2013). Effects of resistance training on respiratory function in patients with chronic obstructive pulmonary disease: A systematic review and meta-analysis. *Sleep and Breathing*, *17*(1), 217–226.
22. Miyachi, M., Kawano, H., Sugawara, J., Takahashi, K., Hayashi, K., Yamazaki, K., ... & Tanaka, H. (2004). Unfavorable effects of resistance training on central arterial compliance: a randomized intervention study. *Circulation*, *110*(18), 2858–2863.
23. Barnard, M., Swanepoel, M., Ellapen, T.J., Paul, Y., & Hammill, H.V. (2019). The health benefits of exercise therapy for patients with Down syndrome: A systematic review. *African Journal of Disability*, *8*(1), 1–9.
24. Saunders, D.H., Greig, C.A., & Mead, G.E. (2014). Physical activity and exercise after stroke: Review of multiple meaningful benefits. *Stroke*, *45*(12), 3742–3747.
25. Borghouts, L.B., & Keizer, H.A. (2000). Exercise and insulin sensitivity: A review. *International Journal of Sports Medicine*, *21*(01), 1–12.
26. Koopman, R., Manders, R.J., Zorenc, A.H., Hul, G.B., Kuipers, H., Keizer, H.A., & van Loon, L.J. (2005). A single session of resistance exercise enhances insulin sensitivity for at least 24 h in healthy men. *European Journal of Applied Physiology*, *94*(1), 180–187.
27. Abbasi, F., Brown, B.W., Lamendola, C., McLaughlin, T., & Reaven, G.M. (2002). Relationship between obesity, insulin resistance, and coronary heart disease risk. *Journal of the American College of Cardiology*, *40*(5), 937–943.
28. Ostman, C., Smart, N.A., Morcos, D., Duller, A., Ridley, W., & Jewiss, D. (2017). The effect of exercise training on clinical outcomes in patients with the metabolic syndrome: A systematic review and meta-analysis. *Cardiovascular Diabetology*, *16*(1), 1–11.
29. Fruh, S.M. (2017). Obesity: Risk factors, complications, and strategies for sustainable long-term weight management. *Journal of the American Association of Nurse Practitioners*, *29*(S1), S3–S14.
30. Donnelly, J. E., Blair, S. N., Jakicic, J. M., Manore, M. M., Rankin, J. W., & Smith, B. K. (2009). American College of Sports Medicine Position Stand. Appropriate physical activity intervention strategies for weight loss and prevention of weight regain for adults. *Medicine and Science in Sports and Exercise*, *41*(2), 459–471.
31. Hamilton, S., Hankey, C. R., Miller, S., Boyle, S., & Melville, C. A. (2007). A review of weight loss interventions for adults with intellectual disabilities. *Obesity Reviews*, *8*(4), 339–345.
32. Konopka, A. R., & Harber, M. P. (2014). Skeletal muscle hypertrophy after aerobic exercise training. *Exercise and Sport Sciences Reviews*, *42*(2), 53.
33. Schoenfeld, B. J. (2010). The mechanisms of muscle hypertrophy and their application to resistance training. *The Journal of Strength & Conditioning Research*, *24*(10), 2857–2872.
34. Turbanski, S., & Schmidtbleicher, D. (2010). Effects of heavy resistance training on strength and power in upper extremities in wheelchair athletes. *The Journal of Strength & Conditioning Research*, *24*(1), 8–16.
35. Oken, B. S., Kishiyama, S., Zajdel, D., Bourdette, D., Carlsen, J., Haas, M., Lawrence, J., & Mass, M. (2004). Randomized controlled trial of yoga and exercise in multiple sclerosis. *Neurology*, *62*(11), 2058–2064.

36. Motl, R. W., & Pilutti, L. A. (2012). The benefits of exercise training in multiple sclerosis. *Nature Reviews Neurology, 8*(9), 487–497.
37. Folland, J. P., & Williams, A. G. (2007). Morphological and neurological contributions to increased strength. *Sports Medicine, 37*(2), 145–168.
38. Santos, L., Elliott-Sale, K. J., & Sale, C. (2017). Exercise and bone health across the lifespan. *Biogerontology, 18*(6), 931–946.
39. Todd, J. A., & Robinson, R. J. (2003). Osteoporosis and exercise. *Postgraduate Medical Journal, 79*(932), 320–323.
40. Erickson, K. I., Hillman, C., Stillman, C. M., Ballard, R. M., Bloodgood, B., Conroy, D. E., Macko, R., Marquez, D. X., Petruzzello, S. J., & Powell, K. E. (2019). Physical activity, cognition, and brain outcomes: A review of the 2018 physical activity guidelines. *Medicine and Science in Sports and Exercise, 51*(6), 1242.
41. Garber, C. E., Blissmer, B., Deschenes, M. R., Franklin, B. A., Lamonte, M. J., Lee, I. M., Nieman, D. C., & Swain, D. P. (2011). American College of Sports Medicine position stand. Quantity and quality of exercise for developing and maintaining cardiorespiratory, musculoskeletal, and neuromotor fitness in apparently healthy adults: Guidance for prescribing exercise. *Medicine and Science in Sports and Exercise, 43*(7), 1334–1359.
42. Piercy, K. L., Troiano, R. P., Ballard, R. M., Carlson, S. A., Fulton, J. E., Galuska, D. A., George, S. M., & Olson, R. D. (2018). The physical activity guidelines for Americans. *JAMA, 320*(19), 2020–2028.
43. Tremblay, M. S., LeBlanc, A. G., Kho, M. E., Saunders, T. J., Larouche, R., Colley, R. C., Goldfield, G., & Gorber, S. C. (2011). Systematic review of sedentary behaviour and health indicators in school-aged children and youth. *International Journal of Behavioral Nutrition and Physical Activity, 8*(1), 1–22.
44. Cooper Institute. (2017). *Fitnessgram and activitygram test administration manual-updated* (5th ed.). Human Kinetics.
45. Winnick, J. P., & Short, F. X. (2014). *The Brockport physical fitness test manual* (2nd ed.). Human Kinetics.

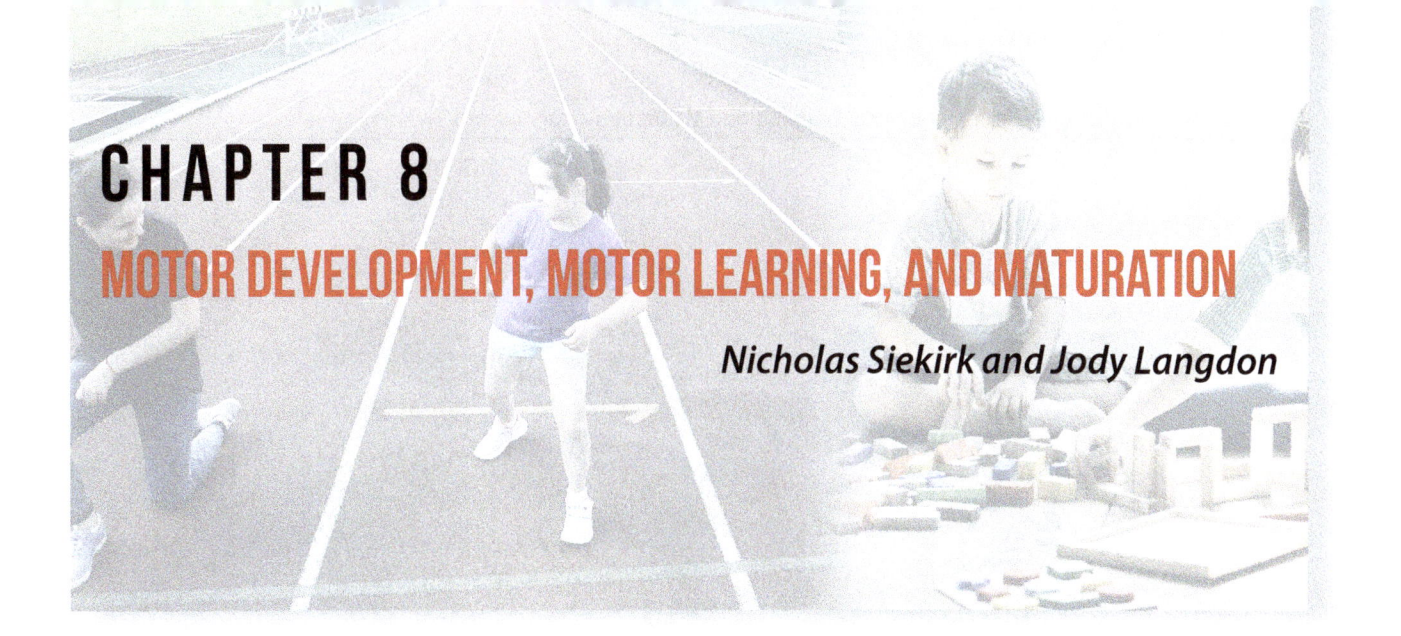

CHAPTER 8
MOTOR DEVELOPMENT, MOTOR LEARNING, AND MATURATION

Nicholas Siekirk and Jody Langdon

Movement is a vehicle for environmental exploration and social interaction. We must foster opportunities for early movement. Our inherent goal is to prepare the practitioner to cultivate early movement competence. Fundamental movement competence encourages the development of more complex and coordinated skills. Ultimately, we propose that movement expression is rooted in the first opportunity and refinement through practice supervised by a qualified practitioner. Our collective goal is to equip society to (1) value movement but (2) optimize possible movement. First, we examine human motor development from both nature and nurture perspectives. Nurture extends beyond the immediate family and is further influenced by larger social and cultural constructs. If mindful of the social and cultural lens, the future practitioner may cultivate meaningful changes in movement adherence over the life span. Inclusive approaches deemphasize focus on normative comparisons and allow the individualized expression of movement to unfold. We discuss factors that influence the control of human movement while considering widely supported theories. Also included in this chapter is an examination of motivation and its influence on movement throughout the life span. The chapter concludes by outlining how the practitioner can use interventions to support skill development.

WHY IS THERE VALUE IN MOVEMENT? A VIEW OF PHYSICAL LITERACY, PHYSICAL ACTIVITY AND STRUCTURED EXERCISE

Movement is inherent to life and is the culmination of nature (e.g., genetics) and nurture (i.e., life experience, social interjections, and cultural norms). Practitioners should empower learners first to explore movement and later to find how to move effectively and routinely. It is the practitioner's job to guide movement exploration and the development of a skilled movement. As stated, movement expression is merely an exploratory experiment between bodily action and sensory consequence. Movement exploration should be encouraged and celebrated throughout one's life span. Therefore, we must sustain the capacity to perform movement experiments over our life span. However, notably, not all will learn to move effectively or move with adaptability. Developing fundamental skills improves the likelihood of acquiring more advanced or complex skills. Practice can help shape whether the mover is prepared to execute the skill. Notably, the capacity to move is constrained by the mover's characteristics (e.g., prior experiences, characteristics of their physical structures, their capacity to use their systems), the task's characteristics, and the environment in which the task takes place.

Nicholas Siekirk and Jody Langdon, Georgia Southern University. © Kendall Hunt Publishing Company.

Physical activity is often informed by external sources, like playing with friends and family.

Independence is not conditional on birth. Early human life is dependent on external sources of care. We must depend on others to retrieve and provide, feed, clothe, and bathe us. The proximity of a supportive care system is vital to satisfy immediate physiological needs (see Maslow's Hierarchy of Needs). Observation and interaction with the dynamic world can encourage our curiosity to explore further. Novel environmental stimuli capture our attention, and as bodily control is developed, we are increasingly capable of furthering our interaction with the environment and its enticing incentives. With continued systemic support, the capacity for active control is cultivated and will evolve to advance exploration and play.

Early interactions between body and space may be elicited through primitive reflexes. **Primitive reflexes** are involuntary motor responses originating in the brainstem present after birth in early child development that facilitate survival.[1] Under this ideology, sensory input triggers stereotyped and hardwired motor networks. With time, the ability to hone or regulate the sensitivity of these reflexive circuits is improved. However, that is not to say early motor actions cannot be deliberate and based upon perception.

Active postural control is an early independent goal. The capacity to resist and overcome gravity's stabilizing force can be considered an early foundation for developing independence. Our reliance on passive (e.g., external to the body) forces, such as parents or caregivers, for stability is gradually reduced as our active strategies evolve. Active strategies are thought to develop with head control and radiate progressively downward. Active control of the head and proximal torso allows for early but deliberate evaluation and processing of the environment. This model of using passive support and increasingly active strategies is commonplace. This may occur within each of the below posture advancements:

Supine posture
↓
Prone posture
↓
Seated posture
↓
Quadruped posture
↓
Bipedal posture

Postural selection is, in part, determined by our actual or perceived capacity to control our body. Increased body control can increasingly free the limbs from providing stability and invite them to be mobile. Mobile limbs lend themselves to the exploration of bodily transportation. The capacity to transition between postures can also influence postural decisions and environmental interactions. We should not assume that perceptual decision-making is carried forward with each advancement in postures. That is, an understanding of body and space is less transferable. The development of perceptual-based movement decisions through trial and error needs to be developed in each posture. In addition, novel external stimuli may promote psychological inquiry. If physical distance prevents direct interaction, we may be persuaded to transition postures that allow us to move toward the stimulus. Thus, the organization of bodily transport may evolve from innate curiosity to interact and satisfy our expanding desires. We can become increasingly aware that we can rely on others less. Early movement strategy depends on opportunity and can evolve with time and experience. That is, our perceptions shape our actions. Actions serve to modify perceptions then. It's important to note that self-organizing movement is subject to rate limiters (e.g., physical strength and coordination). Movement becomes increasingly competent and later progressively complex. Consequently, movement may be considered synonymous with the development of independence.

The motivation to move may evolve from an inherent desire to explore. However, physical interactions can also be cultivated through observable examples or demonstrations. Movement exploration is now interwoven with informal social and cultural exchanges. These informal ecosystems may evolve to include more formal, structured, and organized experiences (e.g., recess, physical education class, sports, and after-school activities).

Knowing that movement and physical activity (PA) are essential features of our development across the life span, learning which movements we enjoy and how to express that movement is imperative. Knowing this, we argue that early physical competency should be established. This competence can encourage a person to be more physically active, whether in sports, leisure, or activities of daily living. As a result, foundational skills (e.g., running, jumping, kicking, catching, striking) can underpin the acquisition of more complex skills.

Skill acquisition is formally defined as a consequence of motor learning. Learning is a construct. Therefore, **motor learning** is indirectly quantified through measured changes in performance over time. Performance improvement is a function of deliberate practice. When motivated, the exerciser is attentive and provides an effort to practice the skill. Keep in mind that performance improvements are not linear. Motor skill performance can fluctuate because effort and motivation are not constants. Remember, practice causes physical and psychological stress from which we must recover. Recovery and, therefore, adaptation are increasingly possible when sleep (both quality and quantity) is sufficient and nutritional intake is prioritized. Not to mention, motor skill performance is also subject to critical factors such as anxiety and arousal. The rate of improvement may differ among learners, and as a result, the practitioner should evaluate and value performance improvements longitudinally.

Skilled movers can perform skills consistently. Consistency is rooted in how one practices and the design of that practice. Therefore, skill acquisition is influenced by the quality and quantity of practice experiences. In theory, practice should prepare the learner for employing their skill in the desired environment. Like exercise, practices should adhere to progressive overload and specificity. Moreover, practitioners should design practice to adequately transfer to skill tests (e.g., the game). Over time, practice can evolve to resemble how skills will be later performed. Although, it's unrealistic to think practice can sufficiently mimic all aspects or circumstances of performance tests. Training in sports can become increasingly variable to reflect circumstances where motor strategies must conform to the situation. With time, our capacity to, in real-time, interact and adapt movement strategy is a positive consequence of advancing skills. Essentially, the practitioner's role is to equip learners to solve problems.

Practice results in the formation or consolidation of procedural memories. In subsequent practices, these motor memories are recalled and used. After practice, motor memories are again consolidated but susceptible to practice-driven updates. Motor memories are malleable but are refined and stabilized with time. The continuation of this refinement process is thought to explain how stored movement instructions can be generalized and applied to varying circumstances. Feedback during practice from internal or external sources guides this reformation of motor memory. In other words, coordinated movement results from updating and stabilizing

Environment has a major impact on motor competency.

procedural memory through training. In theory, this is complemented by an increased capacity to perceive environmental cues and organize real-time movements. When coordinated, we have optimized the possible range of motion (ROM) to maximize output while not unnecessarily increasing metabolic costs. Collectively, coordination is symbiotic with motor learning. When we become more proficient in our movement, we are more likely to engage in activities because of a built sense of competence. Unlike the novice performer, who may depend on external sources of motivation, the skilled performer often finds inspiration from a developed and internalized valuation from practice experience. It is worth noting that interactions with the environment are also social, allowing us to establish a sense of belonging and motivation, advancing movement strategy.

Sensory experiences form internalized models that allow the skilled to decipher and understand their performance without external feedback. This chapter aims to highlight how these features combine to direct motor development. For our purposes, we identify the following differences in terms. **Development** examines the progressive and regressive changes incurred across one's life span. **Growth** refers to an increase in body size or structure. For example, bone growth can occur longitudinally, where the bone will grow in length during the fetal to adolescence period. Bones can also grow laterally, where this increase in diameter is a response to repeated bouts of loading. Finally, **maturation** describes physical and psychological changes and interaction with the world during puberty. As such, this chapter is focused on the following guiding questions:

- *How can we increase the likelihood of lifelong movement?*
- *Can early competency improve our ability to move over our life span?*

HUMAN DEVELOPMENT: NATURE VERSUS NURTURE AND ITS IMPLICATIONS ON MOVEMENT

The study of twins is widely utilized to understand the relationship between nature and nurture. Under this model, the study of identical twins controls for genetics and allows researchers to tease away the effect of the environment. Major conclusions from the wide variety of studies conducted suggest that certain

Identical twins.
Source: Jody Langdon

traits are genetically predisposed, such as personality, cognitive abilities, and weight.[2] Seemingly, genetics can define the scope for which nurture can bias. Early exposure can result in an earlier acquisition of skills. However, earlier skill acquisition does not seem to allude to greater absolute performance outcomes over one's life span. Recent advances in genetic testing reveal that genes are expressed differently depending on one's environment.[1] Understanding this, we present information on how nature and nurture influence the development and maintenance of motor skills.

Origin of the Central Nervous System

Both the father and mother produce distinct gametes termed haploids through **meiosis**. These distinct haploids (with a single set of unpaired chromosomes) combine during fertilization. The fertilized egg (i.e., diploid zygote with 46 chromosomes) is formed from the combination of two haploids, the father's sperm (n = 23 chromosomes) and the mother's egg (n = 23 chromosomes), in the fallopian tube. After fertilization (i.e., conception), the early embryo is formed due to **mitosis** (i.e., somatic cell division). As mitosis continues, the original diploid zygote will evolve into a blastocyst that will embed itself into the endometrium of the uterus. Pregnancy consists of three trimesters: first (weeks 1–12), second (weeks 13–26), and third (weeks 27–40 or the end of pregnancy).

The first two weeks of pregnancy constitute the **Germinal Period**. Following the germinal period, the next 6 weeks constitute the **Embryonic Period** (see figure 8.1). During these periods, the central nervous system will begin to form. The early neural plate will fold to create a neural groove, and when the track closes, it will become the neural tube. The neural tube is the basis for the central nervous system and will later differentiate to form brain regions, including the hindbrain, forebrain, and spinal cord. Teratogens (e.g., alcohol, certain medications, and tobacco products) and nutritional deficits can result in abnormal development. For example, a lack of folic acid in the mother's diet can cause spina bifida in the embryo. Other abnormal developments, such as learning disabilities and child psychiatric disorders, also stem from poor material nutrition or teratogen exposure.[3,4]

Between weeks 4 and 8 after conception, the cerebral hemispheres will differentiate into distinct hemispheres. The cerebral cortex will grow through the generation of new neuronal cells (i.e., neurogenesis) during weeks 8–26. These newly formed neurons migrate away from their origin to more distal locations. Neurons acquire location-based roles that are respective to brain regions. As the process continues, neurogenesis drives a layering effect of the cortex. The layering can be compared to the structure of an onion. *Gyri* are the superficial hills, whereas *sulci* are the superficial valleys of the cerebral cortex. Conditions like Attention Deficit Hyperactivity Disorder (ADHD) are thought to be the result of abnormal

Timeline (Weeks)	Conception	2	4	8	12	13	16	20	24	28	29	32	36	40
Period	Germinal Period			Embryonic Period		Fetal Period								
Trimesters	1st						2nd				3rd			

FIGURE 8.1 Categorizations of the human gestational period.

neuronal migration. Abnormal migration can increase the porosity of brain regions involved with executive function.

Nature

Neurogenesis is the formation of neurons from the more generalized stem cell. Neuronal connections are shaped by experience-driven reshaping called **synaptic pruning**. In essence, neuronal connections are created and eliminated as they are not used. Regions of the brain have location-based functions (i.e., Broadman Areas). However, the brain's networks are subject to ongoing experience-driven plasticity. Plasticity involves the growth and reorganization of neurons and the formation of new synapses (i.e., synaptogenesis). Movements can serve to retain the brain's ability to rewire. Neural pathways are stabilized by their continued use and summarized by the mantra "if you fire together, you wire together."[5] The synapses are not physical; instead, the connections between neurons are bridged by neurotransmitters. Neurons can also project onto visceral organs in the autonomic nervous system and skeletal muscle in the somatic nervous system. As such, *neurons* are specialized cells facilitating electrical communication and bodily functions.

Take-Home Messages
- The central nervous system (CNS) begins developing during the embryonic stage of pregnancy.

Muscle Contraction and the Nervous System

The **CNS** comprises the brain, brain stem, and spinal cord. In addition to neurons, the CNS also contains glial cells, whose responsibility is to support neurons. Cerebrospinal fluid, a clear and colorless liquid, removes waste and provides the CNS nourishment and protection.

The cerebral cortex is the first in command and is considered at the top of the CNS hierarchy. The brain stem, responsible for driving less conscious and more automated motor and homeostatic functions (e.g., cardiovascular function, breathing mechanics), is a middle-level controller. Concerning hierarchy, the spinal cord is at the lowest level and houses the simplest hardwired and stereotyped circuits.

The CNS excites skeletal muscles. Skeletal muscles convert that excitation to mechanical force. This force is transmitted through the muscle's connective tissue (i.e., fascia) into the muscle's tendinous attachments to bone. To move a joint, a muscle must cross that joint. Therefore, muscles are often classified by

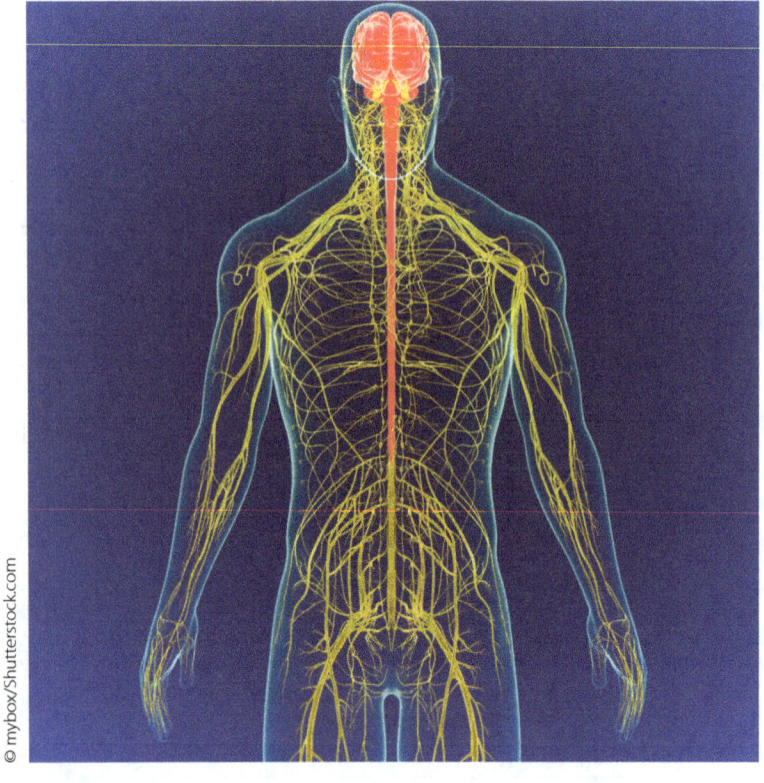

3D Illustration of the human brain with nervous system anatomy.

the number of joints they cross. This pull can create a rotary force called torque. When muscle excitation and the resultant mechanical tension are sufficient, joint rotation is possible. Muscle recruitment is an active metabolic process. However, passive structures can also contribute to the generation of force. When landing, the skeletal muscle acts to absorb the landing force. Passive muscle properties also undergo extension, and their recoil can assist during immediate active force generation.

Whole-body movement requires a balanced expression of mobility and stability. Coordinated movement is a result of delicate balance between mobility (the capacity to display active movement) and stability (the ability to control position or resist perturbative forces). We learn to harness physical laws to control momentum and reduce metabolic demand. Therefore, the center of mass (COM) movement is dynamically controlled. Whole-body movement is coupled, rhythmic, and reciprocal. For instance, consider contact of the right foot and how the opposite hand is also forward during walking gait. Perturbations can be of external (e.g., gravity, opposing players) or internal (i.e., fatiguing metabolic byproducts) origin. Coordination evolves through firsthand movement experience and the refinement of movement strategy over time. Coordination, by definition, is a reduction in the co-contraction of muscles surrounding a joint. Seemingly, co-contraction stabilizes a joint, so it is understandable when advancing motor strategies are tuned to what muscles should be recruited, the order for which they are recruited, and the intensities at which they are recruited. Mobility is possible by reducing co-contraction.

Afferent sensory information arrives from the periphery. When specialized receptors detect a sufficient stimulus, an electrical signal will relay that information to the brain stem and spinal cord. Initial processing of sensory information from muscles can occur in the spinal cord. Still, it also ascends to the brain stem and hindbrain (e.g., cerebellum), where it is processed less consciously. More conscious processing occurs when sensory information reaches the cerebral cortex's hemispheres (i.e., front lobe, parietal lobe, occipital lobe, and temporal lobe). Notably, the conscious processing of most ascending sensory projections is to the cortex using the thalamus. The only exception is olfaction or smell. Information from olfaction bulbs is relayed to the frontal cortex and deeper brain structures, including the amygdala and hippocampus. Sensory input can shape the frontal lobe's outgoing and descending movement instructions.

Humans tend to move according to the path of least resistance. When mobility is compromised, movement strategies are shaped by this constraint. To achieve task goals, joints above or below the constraint may provide additional range of motion. Therefore, where ROM is obtained is essential for the practitioner to consider.

Take-Home Messages
- Stability is the capacity to resist the perturbation of external forces (e.g., gravity) or internal processes (e.g., fatigue).
- Joint mobility is the capacity to move a joint, influenced by the joint structure and the extensibility of the surrounding musculature.
- Mobility can also refer to whole-body locomotion or the combined actions of multiple joints required for a particular movement pattern.

Neuromuscular Control of Movement

The below table 8.1 highlights structures or regions of the CNS involved in the movement.

TABLE 8.1 Brian sections and their functional applications.

Structure or Region	Functions
Primary Motor Cortex (Frontal)	• Directs the force and speed of movement • Determines movement direction • Outlines the extent of movement (ROM or distance traveled)
Premotor Cortex (Frontal)	• Involved with movement preparation • Signals the sensory expectations for a particular movement task • Outlines behavioral context of a task (e.g., clearing the table vs. eating from the table) • Helps identify correct vs. incorrect movements
Supplementary Motor Area (Frontal)	• Involved in preparatory actions (e.g., mental rehearsal of motor actions) • Helps transform coordinated force generation to appropriate bodily behavior

(continued)

TABLE 8.1 Brian sections and their functional applications (*contined*).

Structure or Region	Functions
Association Cortex (Prefrontal + Posterior Parietal)	• Plans and sequence movements according to behavioral contexts • Responsible for executive function during movement • Gives rise to a perceptual understanding of movement's sensory consequences
Primary Somatosensory Cortex (Parietal)	• High-level processing of pain, temperature, and touch information • Processing of peripheral and ascending sensory input to guide the use of feedback during movement

Primary Visual Cortex (Occipital)	• Initial high-level processing of visual information
	   ○ The temporal lobe assists in secondary processing to help us identify objects in the environment.
	   ○ The parietal lobe assists in secondary processing to help us identify environmental movement.
	• The combined input of both eyes allows us to understand changes in our environment relative to our body's position.
	• Visual feedback on our movement's progression and confirmation of movement results.

Primary Auditory Cortex (Temporal)	• Involved with the production of speech and processing of auditory cues related to movement
Basal Ganglia	• Helps identify and select desired motor memory through inhibitory signaling to the motor cortex • Works in conjunction with the cerebellum to balance motor output
Cerebellum	• Involved with the smoothing of motor movements and over-time motor learning through excitatory signaling to the motor cortex • Identifies and executes real-time corrections in movement • Less conscious output to control and correct posture
Hippocampus	• Important for the consolidation of memory
Amygdala	• Processing emotional responses—specifically fear, anxiety, and aggression

Each neuron has a resting electrical state called **resting membrane potential**. The collective input upon that neuron influences its electrical state. **Upper motor neurons** of the primary motor cortex can initiate movement voluntarily by sending efferent (i.e., brain to bodily target) and descending motor action potentials to the **lower motor units** in the anterior (ventral) side of the spinal cord. An **alpha motor unit (AMN)** comprises the lower motor neuron and the muscle fibers it innervates. As the number of innervated muscle fibers by a single AMN increases, that movement incorporates larger muscles and produces movement that is considered grosser or of a larger scale. When multiple muscles work together, more significant bodily movement is possible. Therefore, **gross motor movement** is a coordinated action of large physical segments. These muscle groups tend to be of a larger cross-section area and are controlled by fewer AMNs. **Fine motor movements** tend to involve smaller structures capable of more precise movements like the dexterity of hands and refined actions of the eyes. We must also consider the reduced number of muscle fibers the AMNs innervate. AMNs responsible for fine motor control project their axons toward a lower number of muscle fibers, allowing precise motor action to unfold.

Skeletal muscle responds to the **depolarization** of AMNs, whose resultant action potential travels down the AMN's axon. All AMNs will excite muscle fibers through the terminal end of their axon. The presence of an electrical signal results in the release of a neurotransmitter. This neurotransmitter, acetylcholine, bridges the physical gap between the axon terminal and the muscle cell. The neurotransmitter's crossing of the synapse is analogous to the axon directing a "spritz" of acetylcholine upon the muscle's external wall.

In the CNS, myelinated axons of larger diameters send faster signals than those of smaller diameters and without myelination. Myelination serves to insulate the axon. The time between sending a signal and receiving the electrical signal is also dictated by the distance between the presynaptic neuron and its target.

Brain's Plasticity

Neuronal connections are established through generation of synapses. Synaptogenesis is most prominent during the third trimester of pregnancy (i.e., approximately weeks 29–40) and continues steadily into the first year postnatally. Connections are therefore proactively assembled and later subject to experience-based changes called **synaptic pruning**. This process is comparable to trimming plants and landscaping a yard. Neural connections not reinforced are more likely to be disassembled or trimmed. With use, connections are strengthened and less subject to decay. Therefore, this process is highly dependent on emotions and environmental interactions. Movement enhances our interactions with the environment. Social and cultural influences shape whether and how we move.

Generation of Mechanical Force

The binding of neurotransmitters on the motor end plate triggers the opening of sodium channels. Sodium enters the muscle cell and spreads through elevator-like structures called *t-tubules*. Sodium's target is the Sarcoplasmic Reticulum (SR). Sodium triggers the release of calcium from the SR. Calcium migrates and binds to a protein among the thin filament (i.e., troponin C). Once bound, tropomyosin undergoes a confirmatory change in shape, exposing actin's binding site. With its affinity to actin, the myosin head binds the thick filament to the thin filament. The electrical signal is now converted to mechanical tension, and force generation is now possible. The muscle can now move bones by shortening (i.e., concentric contraction), slowing a limb's acceleration, or stabilizing a joint.

AMNs are recruited according to the **size principle**. Notably, AMN size is probably best described as a continuum. To simplify, we present them as a trilogy. The smallest AMNs are recruited first and innervate muscle fibers with the greatest oxidative capacity (e.g., slow-twitch muscle). These **slow-twitch muscle fibers** are more fatigue-resistant but cannot produce high levels of absolute force. The **intermediate muscle fibers** are recruited second and, relative to slow-twitch fibers, are innervated by slightly larger AMNs. The largest AMNs have the largest thresholds for depolarization and innervate the **fast-twitch muscle fibers**. Their recruitment and the movement's resultant force depend on the frequency of the depolarizing signal. **Rate coding** is the number of depolarizing signals per unit of time. Frequent signals combine or summate to recruit larger AMNs. The largest AMNs are recruited last when descending signals are frequent. Increased frequency, also known as rate coding, results in signal summation. When electrical signals are summed, the largest AMNs can be recruited. The recruitment order does not change whether the muscle fiber is contracting (e.g., actively and concentrically shortening), maintaining its length, or controlling the rate at which it lengthens (i.e., eccentric action).

Take-Home Messages
- Our somatic nervous system is responsible for exciting skeletal muscles.
- Skeletal muscles convert that excitation to mechanical tension.
- Muscle fiber types are recruited according to the size principle, and alpha motor neurons projecting onto fast-twitch muscle fibers require a sufficient frequency to depolarize.
- The CNS is capable of experience-based changes called neural plasticity.

Muscle Action

The orientation of stacked contractile units called sarcomeres defines a muscle's line of pull. The muscle's architecture determines this orientation. The repeated **power stroke** (attached → detach → attach) of the myosin head can shorten the sarcomere to produce **concentric** muscle action. When the sarcomere shortens, actin filaments move toward the sarcomere's middle to reduce the distance between the polar ends. This active shortening is coined a concentric contraction. Although characterized as a pushing action, the overhead press results from skeletal muscle pulling upon its attachments. Muscle recruitment is dictated mainly by prior task experience and the body's position relative to gravity.

Counter to popular opinion, muscles do not remember the movement instructions, nor are they capable of being confused. The phrase "muscle confusion" is a misrepresentation of the practitioner (1) using progressive overload by strategically manipulating the frequency, intensity, time, and type (FITT) equation or (2) introducing novel exercise stress (e.g., a new exercise or variation of a planned exercise). The operational role of skeletal muscle is less complicated. Skeletal muscle responds to any excitation of the CNS. The CNS will recruit muscles in a position of mechanical advantage, a process referred to as **neuromechanical matching**. Mechanical advantage is dictated by muscle length and the body's position relative to the muscle's pull line. Lengthened muscles are under extension and are considered not in a mechanically advantageous position to produce torque. This is also related to the exerciser's position relative to gravity and whether the muscle's proximal attachment (*origin*) or the more distal attachment (*insertion*) attaches to the moving segment. Muscle functions are also relative to the pull line within separate compartments within the muscle belly. For instance, the gluteus medius can be divided into a more forward compartment (i.e., anterior fibers) and a rear compartment (i.e., posterior fibers). The initial position of the thigh can dictate the function of each compartment.[6,7] See table 8.2 below

TABLE 8.2 Anatomical movements and how they are classified.

Starting Position	Glute Medius Anterior Compartment	Glute Medius Posterior Compartment	Anatomical Plane	Movement Goal
Anatomical Position	• Abduct the thigh • Assist in flexing and internally rotating the thigh	• Abduct the thigh • Assist in extending and laterally rotating the thigh	• Frontal plane • Sagittal plane and Transverse plane	• Unilateral Movement of the thigh on a fixed pelvis
Hip Flexion	• Internal rotation of the thigh	• Internal rotation of the thigh	• Transverse plane	• Unilateral Movement of the thigh on a fixed pelvis
Walking	• Stabilization of the pelvis		• Frontal plane	• Prevention of hip drop during gait

Co-contraction of opposing muscles (i.e., agonist and antagonist) surrounding a joint can stabilize the joint and produce stability but no net movement. Repeated practice is thought to reduce co-contraction. Skilled movement can, in part, unfold because of this reduced co-contraction. Consider the actions of hip flexors and quadriceps in running gait. The resulting forward movement of the thigh (hip flexion) can be slowed or offset with recruitment of the hamstring group. Thus, neurological recruitment can slow a muscle's stretch by **eccentric** muscle actions. Eccentric action is vital for absorption during landing, change of direction, or slowing down. Another protein, titin, is thought to uncoil during eccentric contraction. The recoil of titin may assist concentric muscle contractions that immediately follow eccentric action. In combination with fascia, titin forms a spring-like feature that can recoil to assist concentric muscle contraction under stretch. To illustrate this further, consider the vertical jump using both legs. The jumper's COM will move toward the ground by flexing the hip, knee, and ankle (triple flexion). When the desired ROM is found, the muscles are under a controlled stretch. This recoil assists coordinated and rapid contractions to produce forward or upward propulsion by extending the hip, knee, and plantar-flexing the ankle (triple extension). During walking or running, the hip abductors can act on both sides to stabilize the pelvis from excessive movement in the frontal plane. Muscle action is considered **isometric** when a muscle responds to neurological excitement but maintains constant length after initial tension development.

Defining the Involved Muscles

During task analysis, the recruitment of skeletal muscle can be described by its relative role. **Agonists** are considered the prime movers, and the **antagonist** is the muscle opposite in concentric function to the agonist. However, the practitioner should be aware that body position relative to gravity, the muscle architecture, and attachment location can influence the categorization of the prime movers. For example, a commonly known elbow flexor is the biceps brachii. The elbow flexors are joint position dependent. Take, for example, bending the elbow in a standing posture. Early elbow flexion is possible through excitation of brachialis and brachioradialis. Recruitment of the biceps brachii is upregulated later in the ROM when its lever arm (i.e., the distance between attachment and axis of rotation) is longer and the muscle's attachment and lengths are in a position of mechanical advantage. **Synergist** muscles can assist in joint actions produced through contraction of the agonist. A synergist may also assist the movement of a related joint action. For example, the triceps brachii acts upon the elbow to help the pectoralis major's (agonists) actions on the shoulder to coordinate the concentric phase of the bench press.

The practitioner should remain aware that the initial joint position can influence the role of muscle. For example, in a bipedal anatomical stance, the hamstrings can synergistically assist the gluteus maximus in performing unilateral hip extension. However, suppose the hip is initially forward (i.e., the forward swing of gait). In that case, the adductor magus is in a position of mechanical advantage and provides early hip extension. As a result, multiple muscles can work together to extend the hip. Coordinated actions of multiple muscles are often described as a synergy. The degree to which these muscles contribute depends on the initial thigh position and desired terminal position. It is, therefore, advantageous for practitioners to hone their understanding of how joint position dictates muscle recruitment.

It is important to note that neurological recruitment and consequential change in muscle length will help determine the movement's ROM. However, the position of the external load and the mover's motor strategy should also be considered when designating a muscle's role. Muscle contractions and actions create a tautness in the tendon, which applies force to the attachment site on the bone. As a result, bone can remodel along that line of force application to improve its structural integrity.

Nurture

Human movement begins in the buoyant environment in the womb. As the infant grows, the extent of movement becomes constrained.[8] The median gestation period in humans, approximately 38 weeks, is shorter than in other species.[9] The gestation period of the Northern Giraffe may be as long as 60 weeks, whereas the African Bush Elephant has a typical gestation period of 22 months.[10] Therefore, a shorter gestational period may be, in part, why humans early in life are heavily dependent on caretakers.

Theoretical explanations of why we move in different life stages are traditionally organized by several cognitive, psychosocial, and motor domains. Furthermore, many current textbooks identify theories related to moral development and psychosexual development. One of the more popular theories is driven by the work of Jean Piaget, a Swiss psychologist specializing in child development. According to Piaget,[11] humans undergo four stages that occur in succession (i.e., sensorimotor, preoperational, concrete operational, and formal-operational stages). Although they are not age-dependent, many of the characteristics of the stages are seen in children of a certain age. For example, children aged 2–7 years typically exhibit behaviors of the preoperational stage, including representing objects by intuition (e.g., pretending a ball is a dinosaur egg), but are not quite able to rely on logical reasoning. Children at this stage also exhibit an inability to see situations from another's perspective, often termed **egocentrism**.

Like Piaget's cognitive development stages, social development theories also encompass goals met by specific age ranges. Work by Erikson[12] suggests that proximal and influential figures, such as parents, teachers, significant others, friends, and the community, can influence the psychosocial development of an individual over time. Within each stage, an individual is confronted by a stage-specific conflict, and how the individual navigates that conflict may have a long-term residual effect. A successful resolution helps move individuals into the next stage. Unlike the cognitive stages, Erikson's stages[12] of social-emotional development comprise eight stages, all of which are tied to play, exploration, and self-expression. For example, in early adulthood (stage 6), individuals are driven by intimacy versus isolation. During this time, a person will rely on forming intimate relationships. Across both theories, movement seems to aid in fostering independence.

Exploration, Play, and Social Interaction

It is important to remember that although changes are related to different life stages, they are supported by several factors that appear during those life stages. Play is a primary factor influencing socialization, coordination, movement competency, and daily living.[13] According to Eberle,[13] play consists of six essential elements: anticipation, surprise, pleasure, understanding, strength, and poise. Movement and PA can catalyze many of these elements while improving general health and well-being. Practitioners seeking to work with kids are encouraged to incorporate play elements in practice and exercise programs. Often, practitioners dictate how a skill should be performed.

Conversely, the practitioner may designate individualized or collaborative outcomes but reduce the constraints on how they are pursued. This can enrich the mover's autonomy and enhance the mover's or movers' ability to self-organize. Play also plays a crucial role in brain development, helps develop social skills and varied relationships, and fuels creativity and innovation.

Motor development literature provides a strong foundation on the importance of play to develop

Children preparing for independent movement.

procedural and social skills at an early age. However, it can be argued that play is a vital rationale for movement across one's entire life span. For example, highly successful intramural sports programs on college campuses indicate the importance of continuous PA for young adults. Adult recreational leagues outside of college campuses are also becoming increasingly popular. In older adults, programs such as Silver Sneakers provide an opportunity for supervised physical activities with strong social emphasis. The desire to play influences PA levels and community interactions within all these life stages, which can have numerous health-related benefits.[14]

Socialization through play is also a strong driver of motor development as individuals develop a sense of independence. It is often one of the critical objectives of engaging in movement and PA in early childhood. A strong focus on the interaction between individuals can influence more autonomous and collaborative decision-making regardless of physical ability. Arguably, this skill set extends to many facets of life.

Aside from social aspects, movement can give an individual a sense of purpose. Structured practice without play may be viewed as mundane by children. The child may view practice negatively if it is free of choice. Under autonomy, children are allowed to make decisions. Whether successful or erroneous, the consequences of these decisions may drive motor learning (a stabilized ability to execute motor skills). Often, motor learning is described as "muscle memory." However, we argue that the capacity to display previously learned skills is a function of the brain's cerebral cortex. Thus, we agree with **motor memory** to describe this execution of an earlier stored procedural memory. Learning through movement may also allow an individual to find purpose and contribute positively to the larger group.

Take-Home Messages
- Early movement exploration is an early form of experimentation.
- Social, cognitive, and motor domains are integral to motor development.
- The practitioner should look for opportunities to incorporate play into movement practice across the learner's life span. Motor memory and not "muscle memory" should be used to describe the consolidated procedural memory we must recall to move initially.

WHAT ARE THE EARLY LIFE FACTORS THAT MOTIVATE US TO MOVE?

Paillard[15] described our need to permanently reestablish balance. An ongoing reestablishment is **postural control**. When we control our COM, we can maintain postural control. When postural control is compromised, we are at risk of falling. Recurrent falls increase the risk for morbidity and increased dependency in the elderly.[16] Under such control, we can manage any perturbation (i.e., internal and external forces) to improve our likelihood of exploration and successful task completion. Movement exploration is increasingly possible when basic needs (e.g., food, water, shelter, touch) are met. Experientially based interactions are a potent vehicle for learning.

The Romanian Orphanage Story: What Happens When Infants and Young Children Experience Neglect?

Early perceptual-motor experiences drive an infant's interaction with the world around them. The infant's interactions with parents and caretakers are familiar drivers. In 1989, after the Romanian government was overthrown, thousands of children were discovered living in overcrowded orphanages. The absence of sufficient caretaker–infant interactions compounded this situation. Infants were only held while being fed or bathed on a fixed schedule. As a result of this neglect, they displayed developmental deficits, including cognitive impairment and maladaptive socio-emotional behaviors.[17] Children within this group were more likely to develop psychiatric disorders or demonstrate inconsistent attachments to adults. In addition, later MRI evidence showed reduced brain size and increased porosity compared to children adopted from orphanages in the United Kingdom. While children who were eventually adopted seemed to fare better than those who did not, this situation highlights the importance of nurture and the potential consequences of limited movement opportunities and social interactions.

Self-driven movement is possible when we can control our axial skeleton. This proximal control reduces our tendency to use our limbs to stabilize the body (e.g., just like the outriggers of a crane). Under this limb-assisted strategy for stabilization, we forgo limb dexterity for postural control. In theory, this

Children on balance beam.

lack of dexterity can reduce the extent to which we can move from point to point. Without this bodily translation, environmental exploration and interactions are reduced.

Visual study of the environment can drive early social and cultural understanding. Demonstrations are often provided to those attempting to learn a skill. Consider how an early visual search of the environment may serve as an active search for demonstrations of environmental interaction. Mirrored neurons may serve as a structural and physiological explanation. Mirrored neurons are in the motor and sensory areas of the brain and are thought to respond to actions we observe in others.[18] Furthermore, our movement will provide additional sensory information to strengthen our perceptual understanding if we attempt to recreate the once observed interactions.

Sensory Integration

Proprioceptive information originates from tautness in tendons or muscle. This musculoskeletal tension, in conjunction with tactile interaction, is integrated into understanding the use of our body and how changes in our body's position influence our interaction with the environment. The vestibular apparatus can detect changes in our body's acceleration and whether we are upside down or right-side up. Visual information can reaffirm and help solidify our understanding and processing of these sensory inputs. Interestingly, early vision lacks clarity and can help explain why contrasting shapes and colors are so intriguing to infants in the first months of life. In the infamous moving room experiment, we understand that visual information predominates during 13–16 months of age compared to nonvisual input. The movement of walls resulted in the fall of these early walkers. This effect is reduced with time as we can better use, integrate, and make sense of incoming nonvisual sensory information.[19] With experience, the use of vision can translate to an evaluation of the environment and not serve, to the same degree, as confirmation that movement occurred.

Pain can help direct behavior and strategies for movement. Accidentally hitting your hand with a hammer can direct you to approach that task with an alternative movement strategy. For instance, you may use the opposite hand to hold a nail with pliers. Or when children fall and scrape their arm, they may hold on to something stable with their hands to dimmish future risk of falling again. Repetitive tasks are fatiguing and, thus, can trigger a pain-related burning sensation. As a result, an alternative motor strategy may be utilized to continue the task. In part, perceptual understanding of the task can be attributed to a relationship between motor action and sensory consequences.

Objects in the environment are variable and have different sizes, shapes, textures, and tastes. Attempts to manipulate and interact with environmental objects can encourage or discourage how we organize a movement. For instance, object shape or weight (perceived or actual) can drive the adoption of motor strategies. For example, whether we need to use one hand or two to lift and whether the involvement of larger muscles of the legs can ease the task's burden. Therefore, interaction and manipulation produce a sensory experience that can help shape our understanding of their use(s). How and why we use objects gives rise to an account of the object's potential variations in use. Rudimentary understanding of cause and effect begins to blossom, and life unfolds by trial and error. Variations in either motor output or sensory experience can help develop a nuanced and contextual-based understanding of the surrounding world.

Active visual search can lead to locomotive strategies when an enticing object is absent or when we seek to gain clarity of the source or meaning of auditory information. Therefore, it is fair to say that our environment influences our need for locomotive strategy. For example, many studies on locomotive strategies in various settings show that infants use exploratory movements to find the best way to move in multiple environments.[20] Their locomotive strategy depends on their body's initial position, environmental **constraints**, and what movement is possible at that stage (i.e., individual constraints). As an illustration, an infant attempting to move downhill will try a variety of positions to be successful, including crawling headfirst, sitting, scooting, sliding while prone, and backing down while prone.[20]

Decisions on how to move are developed through experimentation and guided by examples (e.g., demonstration) from one's environment. In essence, locomotive strategies may be inherent to the task's goal and the imposed situational constraint. Therefore, it is plausible that varying conditions can produce different movement strategies. This is important to remember even beyond infancy as developing children, adults, or individuals with disabilities navigate their environments and learn how to move in them. In many cases, an individual's perception of their environment dictates how they interact with it. For example, what to an adult may seem to be a

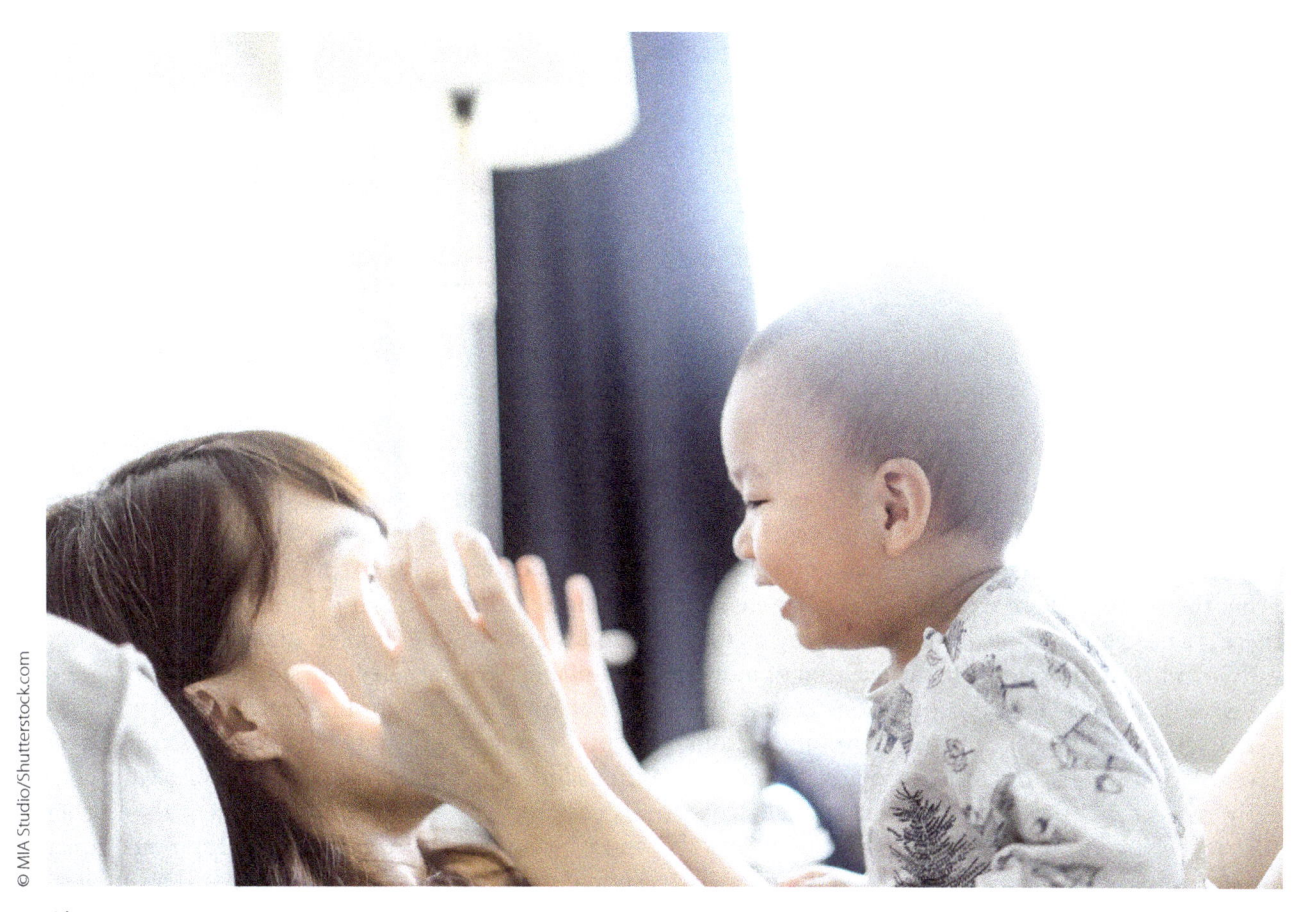

Object permanence.

simple table and chair may seem like a fort to a child. An adult capable of bipedal walking can strategically adopt a crawling strategy to reduce exposure to smoke while exiting a burning building. A firefighter can also adopt a crawling approach to perform an ice rescue. However, in this instance, the strategy is not to avoid smoke but to distribute their mass over a larger area, reducing the risk of falling through the ice. In children, understanding one's body and environment may be part of how object permanence is developed. The child can move away from an object, so it is no longer visible. A strategic return to the initial position can make that object visual again to reinforce object permanence.

Later, we learn to better distinguish between our movement, an object's movement, or a combination thereof. Early training is thought to require more visual information to complete the skill. That is, early catching may require vision to track a thrower's ball into the baseball glove. In contrast, skilled movers hone early or periodic visual information to predict the ball's final location. Therefore, skilled movers rely less on visual confirmation to confirm that the ball will enter the glove. At this point, the visual gaze may shift toward the target they must throw toward.

IS THERE A NEED TO ESTABLISH EARLY PHYSICAL COMPETENCY?

Motor skill acquisition can be seen detailed in several long-term athlete development models and curriculum standards in physical education. Several position statements, including those distributed by SHAPE America, ACSM,[21] the U.S Government, and others, outline the importance of daily PA. They emphasize that PA can be facilitated through play in various forms, engaging individuals in the process of motor skill acquisition that facilitates PA. Although these statements concern athletes, exercisers, students, or other groups, the ideas presented here apply to practitioners in many fields.

The remainder of this chapter considers how movement is organized, the transfer of foundational skills, and the idea that sensitive periods of development (periods where specific skills are said to develop) are presented here, with particular attention to how each contributes to the overall importance of early physical competency.

According to **dynamic systems theory (DST)**, movement is self-organized through many subsystems within the body. When combined with an

ACSM and CDC Guidelines for Physical Activity

Moderate-intensity aerobic activity every week for 150 minutes

Muscle-strengthening activities 2 or more days a week working all major muscle groups

ACSM and CDC Guidelines for Physical Activity.
Source: Data based on ACSM and CDC.

ecological approach, movement results from our interaction with physical and psychological constraints. These constraints include personal, task, and environmental factors that impact movement. From the perspective of early physical competency, there is a need to examine the idea of self-organizing movement related to competent execution of motor skills. At later ages, neural connections are reorganized, displayed as coordinated movements from several joints.[22] Taking the example of running, early movers will develop an organizational structure to, relative to walking, move their body at an enhanced pace. Comparison between individuals should consider how individual differences (e.g., maturation, genetics, disability, body type, body shape, or experience level) may explain how self-organized motor strategies can vary among peers of matched or similar ages.

Furthermore, psychological factors (e.g., rationale to run) and external factors (e.g., space to run) can influence development. Novel movement, however, is possible without prior experience because we can self-organize. Self-organization is a function of one's ability to develop an understanding of constraints. A well-rounded physical literacy program will accept variations in movement strategy but assist the development and refinement of strategy over time. Individualized progress is possible with consistent practice. To practice deliberately, the learner must be motivated to make effort. The practitioner should aim to find a balance between their predesignated ideal and what is possible as dictated by the individuals' constraints. Our goal here is not to deter movement exploration through various forms or exile including but not limited to the unjust use of subjective labels or publicized scrutiny.

TABLE 8.3 Fundamental Movement Skills

Fundamental Movement Skill	Definition	Transfer Examples
Running	A form of locomotion where rhythmic movement of arms and legs are contralaterally coupled. Running involves a flight phase (i.e., a period where both feet are off the ground simultaneously).	• Most sports and physical activities require translation of the body or locomotion to exceed the velocity possible by walking.
Hopping	A single-legged forward or backward movement involving the propulsion and landing of the same leg (i.e., leaving the ground on one foot and landing on the same foot.)	• Hopscotch and integrated into skipping
Skipping	Forward or backward movement involves stepping and hopping on the same foot, then alternating and hopping to the opposite foot.	• Integration into dynamic warm-ups that precede sport or PA with running requirements • Single-leg jumping • Squats with an asymmetrical posture
Jumping	It can include jumping for horizontal distance or height. It involves propulsion with both feet. Propulsion can occur with feet in a symmetrical or asymmetrical position. Both feet leave the ground and land at the same time.	• Vertical Jumping is a strategy for vertical displacement. It can be used for blocking (e.g., volleyball). • Horizontal jumping is a strategy to translate the body over a potential barrier (e.g., a puddle).

(continued)

TABLE 8.3 Fundamental Movement Skills (*continued*)

Fundamental Movement Skill	Definition	Transfer Examples
Galloping	A rhythmic movement of legs where the hip of the front leg moves first, followed by the trailing leg to propel the body forward. The front knee is extended, and the trailing leg's foot is most often pointed laterally. In this movement, the back leg remains behind the lead leg.	• A strategy to reduce the BOS width but maintain elevated forward velocity • Used in games and play
Leaping	A forward, single-legged jumping movement where the individual lands on the opposite foot (i.e., leaving the ground on one foot and landing on the opposite foot).	• Horizontal jumping is a strategy to translate the body when ground contact is not possible and the individual needs to avoid an object on the ground. • This strategy can increase flight time when attempting more considerable horizontal distances than a hop.
Cycling	A rhythmic-alternating movement of the legs is applied to the bicycle while the exerciser is seated.	• Wingate tests (Test for Anaerobic Power) • Triathletes • Riding a bike (i.e., playing) • Aerobic exercise on elliptical
Freestyle Swimming	In a prone position, forward movement in the water involves alternating overhead arm movement and short, fast kicks with the legs.	• Quadruped locomotion • Swimming (e.g., breaststroke, butterfly, backstroke) • Water polo • Synchronized swimming
Lunging	This involves single step forward or backward where the leading leg undergoes hip flexion, knee flexion, and ankle dorsiflexion. A stationary lunge returns the exerciser to an upright position through hip extension, knee extension, and ankle plantarflexion. A walking lunge involves bodily translation with alternating steps in the desired direction.	• Single-leg jumping • Sport
Overhead Press	Upward movement of arm(s) over one's head involves the coordination and mobility of the shoulders, scapulas, and elbows. The lumbar spine does not need to extend. In addition to thoracic extension, the scapula should adequately protract to assist the overhead movement of arms. During a single-arm press, the thoracic spine must rotate in the transverse plane toward the arm moving overhead.	• Overhead carry • Lifting overhead
Push-up	In a prone position, hands and feet are in contact with the floor. Upper body upward movement is generated by pressing down on the hands.	• Prone to standing transition • Getting out of bed or off the floor • Basketball chest pass
Scooting	A locomotive strategy to translate the body while seated. The pelvis is moved through a coordinated action to lift the pelvis through hip extension and knee flexion.	• Navigating obstacles • Locomotion under objects while requiring dexterity of the hands
Squatting	From a bipedal stance, the movement involves lowering their COM using the hip, knee, and ankle joints. Each joint's ROM is complementary and coordinated to achieve the desired or tolerated depth. The downward action requires sufficient internal rotation at the hip to perform hip flexion. The knees can go over the toes to achieve terminal depth. The arch of the foot should be maintained. The knees should translate forward in the direction of the toes.	• Transiting from sitting to standing • Sport and play • Vertical jumping

TABLE 8.3 Fundamental Movement Skills

Fundamental Movement Skill	Definition	Transfer Examples
Treading Water	A kicking pattern is alternated in water to keep the head above water.	• Integrated into swimming • Leisure water activities • Water survival
Striking	The task is coordinated by directing a held object (e.g., bat, stick) and contacting a target with sufficient force. However, accuracy is also important because a successful strike result reaches and contacts the target.	• Sport and play (e.g., tennis, softball) • Martial arts and self-defense
Throwing	It can include overhand and underhand motions whereby an object is projected forward or backward. Both arms can be used to throw overhead (e.g., soccer throw-in), or an underhand strategy can be used. Early single-arm throwing often fixes the body toward the target. Skilled throwing uses transverse rotation to rotate away from and then toward the target. The arm will follow.	• Sport and play (e.g., football, baseball, cricket, ultimate frisbee)
Catching	To gain possession of an object by stopping the object's motion with the hands or glove. Vision is used to track the projectile during early catching. Early catching may trap the ball with the body. As skill improves, the arms can meet the object. Advanced catching techniques may only involve one hand as compared to two.	• Used in sport and play (e.g., softball, baseball, basketball, football, ultimate frisbee, guts [flying disk sport])
Punching	One arm moves forward or sideways while the other is bent near and protecting the face. The goal here is often to contact a target with sufficient force. Jabs sacrifice ROM for speed. The torso can be rotated to produce greater power.	• Strategy used in sport and play (e.g., boxing) • Martial arts and self-defense
Grasping	Arm and hand movement to hold an object can be with one hand or both. Advanced grasping uses less of the palm and increasingly fewer fingers. The actions of the thumb are essential to complement the efforts of the fingers.	• Writing • Object manipulation (e.g., dexterity) • Getting dressed • Picking up small items
Reaching	Forward arm movement, usually directed toward an object, can be unimanual or bimanual (i.e., with one arm or two). Reaching can be involved in strategies for catching or grasping. The goal here is to locate an object visually and direct the body toward the object to close the physical distance between the body's position and the object.	• Integrated with grasping to move objects • Interaction with environments • Occupational tasks • Catching in sport
Kicking	The leg is accelerating toward the ball to contact the foot. The opposite leg provides stability. Early kicking is often self-organized to strike the ball with the toe. The advancing strategy uses the inside of the foot, the top of the foot, and the outside of the foot. The kicker may emphasize force development to kick a ball with distance or attempt to target the kick with a specified direction or spin.	• Kicking is commonly integrated into dynamic warm-ups that precede sport or PA. • Strategy used in sport and play (e.g., soccer, kickball) • Running

BOS, base of support; COM, center of mass; PA, physical activity; ROM, range of motion.

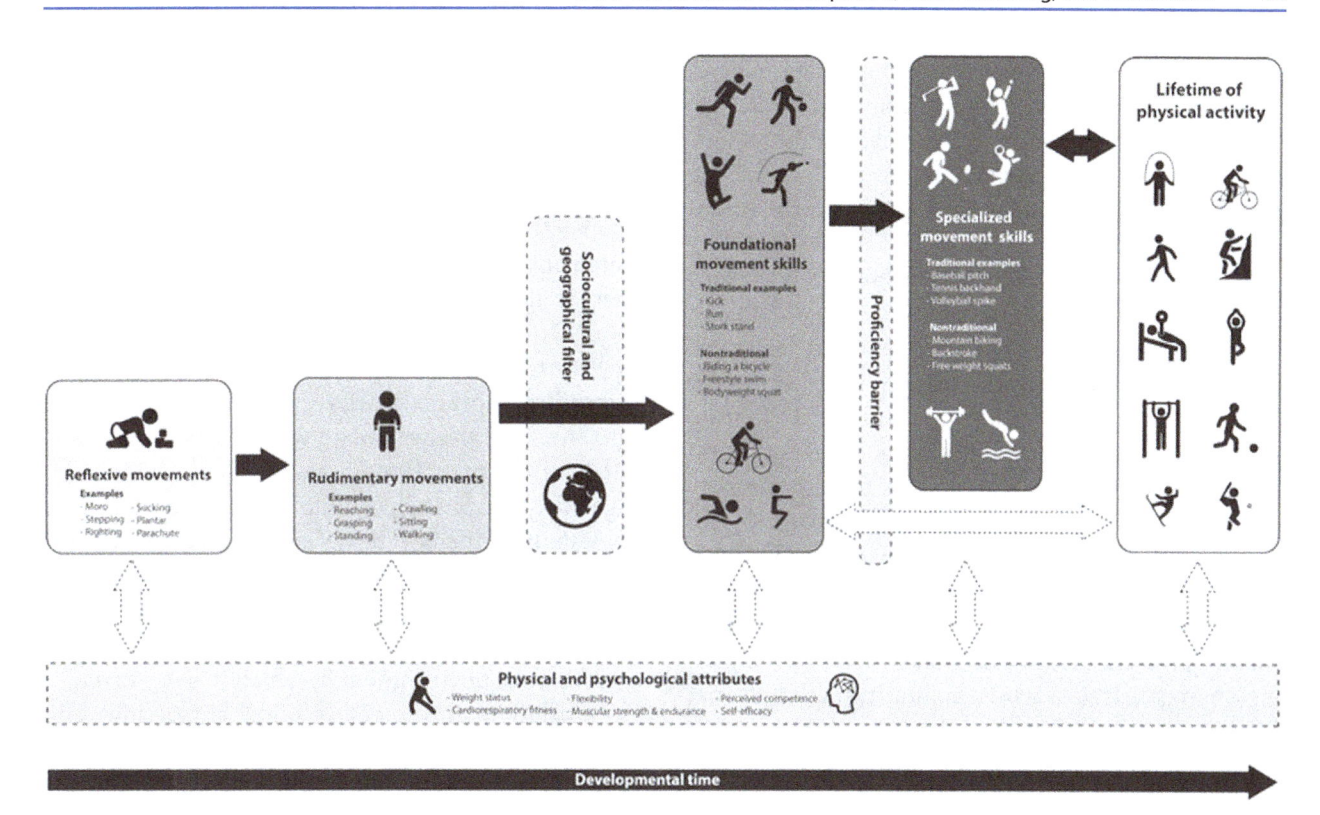

FIGURE 8.2 Development of foundational movement skills: A conceptual model for physical activity across the life span.

Source: Hulteen, R. M., Morgan, P. J., Barnett, L. M., Stodden, D. F., & Lubans, D. R. (2018). Development of foundational movement skills: A conceptual model for physical activity across the lifespan. *Sports Medicine, 48*, 1533–1540. https://link.springer.com/article/10.1007/s40279-018-0892-6

Fundamental movement skills are thought to be fostered, modified, and transferred to advancing skills in different contexts (see table 8.3). These include locomotor and object control skills. Hulteen and colleagues[23] argue that standard lists of fundamental movement skills should be expanded to include cycling, freestyle swimming, lunging, overhead presses, push-ups, scootering, squatting, and treading water.

It is important to reintroduce the idea of sensitive periods of development. While the term is a part of many long-term athlete development models, many assume that these sensitive periods are critical, meaning that individuals will not acquire a specific skill after the period has passed.[24] Within their new conceptual model, Hulteen et al.[23] outline that health-related physical fitness components, perceived competence, and self-efficacy shape movement across one's life span. Collectively, these skills are referred to as foundational movement skills, representing a broader range of activities in which individuals can engage across their life span. Additionally, connections are made directly between these foundational movement skills and lifetime PA, indicating that competence in transfer movements is needed to promote PA throughout one's life span. It could be argued that individuals should be exposed to various movement types involving object manipulation and bodily translation in evolving and dynamic environments.

The Need for Self-Exploration Is Apparent. But Why Do Practitioners Still Exist?

Ecological Theory outlines three constraints (i.e., individual, task, and environment) that shape and ultimately influence the emergence of behavior. The perceptual understanding of these constraints can interact with the body's systems to self-organize behavior. **Affordances** (specific opportunities for movement) can permit or suggest certain strategies for object–environmental interaction. **Body scaling** matches an object to the individual's size. It can provide a foundation for a strategy's perceived difficulty or usefulness with the tools or equipment on hand. However, notably, self-organization of movement does not serve to rid us of coaches. Instead, the DST may modify common coach-centered approaches and replace them with athlete-centered strategies. After all, the coach cannot play in place of the athlete. Instead, the coach's role is to mentor and prepare the athlete to adapt and independently organize strategies effectively.

However, developing complex and efficient motor patterns requires practice and refinement. To do this, an individual relies on external feedback, usually from a caregiver, teacher, coach, or therapist. Their performance also depends on **deliberate practice**. Deliberate practice is a systematic and repetitive rehearsal of motor skills to help improve performance. Regardless of the skill involved, deliberate practice increases performance.[25] However, practice does not inherently make skills perfect. A practitioner's role is to provide an environment for meaningful deliberate practice, balancing the provision of constraints while facilitating activities that increase opportunities for autonomy-driven movement exploration. This is independent of the skill level or ability of the individual. The practitioner creates an environment that actively encourages self-initiation, experimentation, and individual responsibility. Practitioners exist within these environments to connect previously learned skills to new ones and provide purpose and rationales for skill development. This may include strategies including peer demonstrations (i.e., demonstrations by others closer in skill to the individual) and simplifying the instruction of movement patterns to include key features of the skill or outlining common errors in strategy. In short, self-exploration is vital to proper development, but practitioners provide the means to facilitate this process. Knowing how critical a practitioner's role is in the development and maintenance of movement, it is common to see more tailored approaches to learning movement, which is facilitated by certified or appropriately credentialed professionals, whether it be as an adapted physical education teacher, certified inclusive fitness professional, or strength and conditioning coach.[26] Although we need to value experience, practitioners should seek appropriate credentials for legal and ethical reasons. Those with specialized training are generally more prepared to navigate the constraints of targeted populations. For example, former athletes who never sought additional credentials to become a coach may just replicate what they did as an athlete. This appeal to antiquity is a logical heuristic and may not align with updated standards or scientific consensus.

CLASSIFICATION OF MOVEMENT

Early skill acquisition is cognitively demanding. The skilled are subjectively viewed to perform with fluidity and reduced effort. This ease of movement is often attributed to "natural ability." However, this statement does not give credit to the 6,000 hours, on average, it may take to master a motor skill.[27]

We must first walk through the evolution of the novice's movement and how it progresses to becoming skilled movement. Here, we provide an insight into the **task analysis** (e.g., what the task requires) and how the practitioner's analysis and understanding of the task can help facilitate practice design. Task analysis may include but is not limited to examining the musculature, joint actions, and the involved planes of motion. In addition, task analysis may examine the energy systems' contribution, the task's goal, and the environment in which it is performed.

Unskilled movement is often rigid, slow, and abrupt. The ROM is constrained. Over time and with practice, this rigidity can be reduced. The expressed **degrees of freedom** (i.e., the range of motion) are released and later optimized for movement efficiency. There is a transition to add the use of more **distal** (i.e., further from the body's origin) joints. In other words, movement strategy advances when the ROM requirements are distributed through multiple joints. As part of this learning process, the individual begins to understand that an increased ROM can increase force production and, thus, improve movement speed. However, there is an inherent risk. Movement can become variable with increased range of motion. This variability can occur because, with an increased number of contributing joints, the movement has more degrees of freedom from start to finish. Thus, novice individuals can struggle when motor patterns require an unaccustomed level of force (e.g., throwing a football 50 yards when only accustomed to passes <30 yards). A novice moving with "haste" will produce "waste." Under this "haste," the accuracy of movement is compromised. Movers can increase their ROM by perceptually releasing and correctly identifying the extent of their release. Through trial and error, advancing movers will note how their freedom must be timed appropriately.

Mental rehearsal and physical action seem to be subject to Fitts' law.[28] **Fitts' law** describes the inverse relationship between movement speed and accuracy. As a novice moves faster than accustomed, the coach should expect accuracy to be compromised. As we previously noted, movement time is also increased when the ROM is increased (i.e., to produce higher levels of force). However, there is an unsung advantage; increased ROM allows refining or correcting errors using real-time sensory feedback. This, however, assumes sensory information can be processed in time to update the movement. Keep in mind that increased movement time is not always strategic. The longer it takes for a hockey player to wind up and take a slapshot, the greater risk of that puck being stolen by the opposition. Moreover, in theory, the goalie has more time to prepare for a shot, which allows for gauging and predicting the shot's characteristics. The longer it takes to pass a basketball, the more likely it is intercepted. Therefore, skilled movers attempt to move quickly by balancing the movement's ROM with the task's force requirements without unnecessarily increasing the total movement time.

Locomotion

Continuous motion is a poetic combination of muscular action and exploitation of physical law. Nevertheless, a continuous dynamic motion has discrete characteristics. Postural control during dynamic movements requires ongoing reestablishment of balance. Manipulating one's COM is vital for propulsion and control of posture during gait. To stay in control, the COM must say within or near our **base of support (BOS)**. Any deviation is usually short and used strategically to take advantage of the momentum. In early gait, stability is emphasized at the expense of speed. Early rudimentary gait requires a more frequent cycle than mature gait because each stride is shorter. Relative to more mature gait patterns, stability is more reliant on passive structures (e.g., longitudinal axes of bones) and less on the surrounding muscle's coordination. The BOS is broad, and the hips are externally rotated. This combination can improve frontal plane stability but compromises the step length. Reduced step length requires high cadence (i.e., step cycles per unit distance). Since the knees (i.e., extended) and ankles (i.e., neutral) are more so fixed, the movement pattern is predominated by the ROM at the hip. Forward lean is limited.

As gait becomes more advanced, the COM is manipulated because of the growing capacity to control it. The COM translates toward the foot accepting weight (i.e., heel contact) and upward during that foot's midstance. The opposite arm moves to complement the action of the foot in part to control the extent of the COM's movement. An overview of maturing gait is outlined in the below table:

Gait Characteristic	1-Year-old	7-Year-old
The BOS Width	Greater percentage of pelvic width	Reduced percentage of pelvic width
Step Length	Reduced	Increased
Cadence	Increased	Reduced
Reciprocal Arm Swing	Reduced	Complements leg action
Hip Extension	Reduced	Increased

BOS, base of support.

Multitasking

A skilled individual can complement a primary locomotion-based task with manual dexterity or object manipulation. With time, the primary task of locomotion is stabilized. Locomotion is optimized, and a secondary task becomes possible. The secondary task is often skill-specific but can involve the manipulation of an object. For instance, dribbling (i.e., secondary object manipulation) a basketball while running (i.e., primary locomotive task) is a dual task. However, it is essential to note that task performance is defined by both the body's locomotion and manipulation of the object. Novice players rarely dribble at sprint speeds. The skilled, in theory, should be able to manipulate an object with both hands with similar proficiency. In sports, proficient use of both hands or feet is a competitive advantage. The capacity to multitask is reduced when two simultaneous tasks require the same cognitive processes. These tasks are cognitively competing, resulting in reduced capability to perform tasks simultaneously.

Limb Preference

This is not to say that a task-specific limb preference does not exist. For instance, movers prefer to balance their left leg and kick with their right.

FIGURE 8.3 Limb preference is often seen in ball handling sports like Basketball.

Most people are genetically biased to be right-handed, but the role of nurture (e.g., social and circumstantial reinforcement) should not be disregarded. Whether a bias toward right-handedness is expressed or not is part of nurture.[29] The practitioner should consider how demonstrating with their preferred hand may affect the viewer with an opposing preference.

Open Versus Closed Environment

To adequately prepare the learner, practitioners must evaluate the task at hand, its requirements, and its integrated elements. Predictability of the environment is on a continuum where predictable or **closed** environments are more controlled and may lack environmental variability from trial to trial (i.e., no changes in wind, playing surface is highly similar). Conversely, **open** environments are highly variable and incorporate elements outside one's control. Thus, an open environment is less predictable. However, because of prior experience, skilled athletes can increasingly and successfully predict characteristics within an open environment (e.g., when third base gravitates toward home plate to field the batter's bunt in softball). Open environments, although less predictable, are constrained by the parameters and rules of the sport or social/cultural expectations of the domain.

Movement Time

Discrete tasks have an identifiable beginning and end (e.g., the act of injecting a vaccination). Serial tasks are longer in duration than discrete tasks because they string discrete tasks together to form a more elongated element (i.e., piano keys struck in a particular order per the music's script). A **continuous task** is a repetitive movement outside of the constraints of an event (e.g., race), having no beginning or end. For example, rollerblading is an ambiguous description of forwarding locomotion on wheels. It generically lacks basic descriptors, such as location, duration, or weather. Keep in mind that the rollerblading stride can be described by discrete elements. Like running, the lower extremities work in opposition and repetitively, alternating between providing propulsive hip extension.

Boy rollerblading.

Reaction Time

Movement actions often require the processing of an environmental stimulus. Experimentally, when respondents must process which stimulus is presented, they are tasked with matching that stimulus with a particular action. Under these circumstances, the processing is more complex; thus, the processing time is increased and the reaction time (RT) is measurably longer. The time for the brain to consciously process sensory information, select a response, and send an efferent signal is **premotor reaction time**. Often, the brain's involvement is analogous to central processing. The time between peripheral receipt of a signal and the start of observable movement is the **motor reaction time**. Here, the muscle is receiving and converting the signal to a mechanical tension (e.g., peripheral processing). **Movement time** begins with observable behavior and ends with the cessation of movement. **Response time** combines RT (premotor RT + motor reaction time) and movement time. Compared to single-choice RT, choice RT tasks demonstrate **Hick's law**. Under Hick's law, RTs increase when the task is more difficult due to increased choice options. Please note how reduced RT is favorable because the unit of measurement, often milliseconds, is quantifiably shorter.

Planned Movements

A dancer's routine is a choreographed performance. The routine is meticulously planned, and as a result, dancers perform as a cohesive unit. Each movement is timed following a complementary song or musical number. The dancer may use visual or auditory cues to confirm the timing of each sequence, but the dancer's following action is set.

Reactive Movements—Externally Paced Tasks

The initiation of a movement can be self-generated or dependent on an outside factor. Movement initiation to external factors is often reactionary, where action responds to a particular stimulus. In these circumstances, the individual, with time and experience, may want to predict the timing or location of a specific stimulus. False start in sprinting is a prime example of rules to reduce the prediction of the starting gun.

Foreperiods, the time between a stimulus warning (e.g., starter yelling "sprinters ready") and the stimulus (i.e., starter's pistol) should vary between races. Reaction times are constrained to the CNS's ability to receive the signal, process the signal, and execute movement instructions. When the sprinter's first movement occurs faster than this physiological constraint (≤105 milliseconds), it is considered a fault. When an athlete can predict and anticipate a stimulus or cue, instead of having to react randomly to something like an auditory stimulus, then it provides an advantage. One way to prevent this is to continue to vary the time between providing a warning to sprinters to start, and the actual go signal for them to begin, lowering their ability to predict when to start.

We shall now compare how a target's characteristics shape a task's requirements. A stationary target (e.g., a baseball placed on a tee) is a fixed target. A target swinging on a rope is, by comparison, more variable. However, the target's possible locations are constrained by the length of the string, its arc, and the initial velocity. The swinging target is a task progression relative to a stationary target. In contrast, the stationary target is considered a task regression. **Regressions** are more straightforward or less complex variations. The moving target could be swung at an increased angular velocity to progress the ball on the string task. Aside from all else, we can also increase the target size to regress this task. When we are addressing a larger target, we can improve the speed of our actions because our targeting no longer requires the same level of precision.

Let us consider two similar but distinct striking tasks. In the first example, consider the striking task of hitting a piñata where the hitter is not blindfolded, and the piñata is not repeatedly manipulated. The initial swinging target is on a string, eventually slowing and becoming increasingly stationary. If not otherwise confined, the hitter could merely wait and attempt to strike a slowing and, ultimately, a stationary target. In contrast, the machine-pitched ball only provides a "small window" for a successful swing and striking. The pitched ball is considered a more externally paced task, whereas the piñata in the previous example is considerably more self-paced. Let us reexamine the batting cage example and compare it to a baseball game. The ball must be hit forward in gameplay and stay within the allotted field's dimensions. When the ball is pitched, the pitcher's intent must be considered. Conversely, when the pitcher opposes the batter (e.g., opposing teams), the pitcher will pitch with highly variable speeds, movement paths, and resultant locations. When the pitching action is consistent, the pitcher's (e.g., fastball, curve, change-up) ball actions are deceptive, and part of the in-game strategy often called "the game within the game." Granted, in high levels of competition, opposing teams are aware of the pitcher's available pitches. The pitcher interjects strategy, and as a result, trial-to-trial (i.e., pitch to pitch) variability in speed, ball movement, and location (when crossing plate) is often employed. A skilled batter may attempt to form predictions based on the circumstances of the encounter. Factors like pitch count (i.e., balls vs. strikes), pitch availability, and the game situation can influence their prediction. Furthermore, coaches on both teams may communicate with a myriad of hand signals, using nonverbal communication to help their own respective athletes perform. This may occur when the pitcher has a consistent "tell" and unknowingly provides insight into the next pitches' type.

When the pitching action (i.e., pitcher's windup) is identical, the batter's ability to predict is negatively affected. Predictability is reduced when pitchers can disguise their pitch by employing a consistent windup. This task will, on some level, rely on predictive "tells" or preferences of the batter because the ball's velocity is often too fast for real-time adjustments to occur. A skilled batter's movement time is often considered constant. When the swing is initiated depends on the pitcher's windup and ball release and the hitter's prediction. In theory, the swing's initiation is delayed with a slower velocity pitch and sped up with faster velocities. The batter can pull the ball by initiating the swing early or increasing the bat's velocity. Collectively, we can now begin to dissect how a striking task can be progressed in difficulty.

When a drill is progressed, the mover is challenged by the drill's modification. In exercise programs, a widely used progression is increasing load. However, the coach is not limited to load to progress the exercise. Examples include reducing the rest time between sets, adding repetitions or sets (i.e., increased volume), and changing postures that provide less passive stability. In practicing motor skills, a coach can add variability to the environment (e.g., adding a defender in an offensive drill) or reduce the time for a motor skill to be successfully performed. Progressions to drill can also challenge the mover psychologically by asking the mover to perform under-elevated states of anxiety or arousal.

In weight training, the acronym FITT [Frequency (F), Intensity (I), Time (T), and Type (T)] can be altered according to the needs of the individual and the goals of the exercise program. The use of **progression** and **regression** in exercise programs is highlighted below.

Examples of Exercise Progressions	• Decreased points of contact with supporting surface
	• Increased influence of gravity
	• Increased intensity
	    ○ +% of 1 rep max (1RM)
	    ○ +% HR peak
	    ○ +% Vo2 peak
	    ○ +Rating of perceived exertion (RPE)
	• Increased volume (e.g., sets or reps)
	• Increased frequency per week
	• Decreased rest between sets
	• Increased speed of execution
	• Increased ROM

Examples of Exercise Regressions	• Increased points of contact with supporting surface
	• The reduced influence of gravity
	• Reduced intensity
	    ○ -% of 1 rep max (1RM)
	    ○ -% HR peak
	    ○ -% Vo2 peak
	    ○ - RPE
	• Reduced volume (e.g., sets or reps)
	• Reduced frequency per week
	• Reduced rest between sets
	• Reduced speed of execution
	• Reduced ROM

ROM, range of motion; RPE, rating of perceived exertion.

Appropriate challenges or modifications are those inclusive of individuals' differences and the acute states of the learner. Practitioners should be conscious of the learner's current motivation state and incorporate the learner's sources of motivation. Successive and stepwise **drill progressions** are part of the "art" or craft of coaching and applying general principles. **The principle of specificity** states that practice should be specific to how the skill will be tested. Secondly, **progressive overload**, frequently discussed in exercise, can be applied to motor skill practice.

Internally Paced Tasks

Compared to an externally paced task, internally paced tasks give movers greater autonomy to start movement sequences. However, this can be governed by the rules of the sport. Please see the example below:

Shot Clock in Golf

The caddy serves to help the golfer make decisions on strategy, including, but not limited to, which club to hit (distance), ball flight/trajectory, and tee location. According to etiquette, the golfer farthest from the hole hits first while the other golfers prepare to hit. The golfer may wait for ideal environmental conditions (e.g., wind, noise) to match strategy with needs before addressing their ball and swinging the club. Ultimately, the golfer will address the ball and initiate their swing when they have decided to swing. However, notably, the individualized actions of a golfer can influence the pace of play on the entire hole, and that influence can extend beyond their hole. For this reason, the Professional Golfers Association[30] has implemented an informal shot clock of 40–60 seconds.

Movement Error

To react efficiently, individuals must (1) successfully process and (2) select the correct motor action. Feedback can help stop incorrect actions. However, feedback is not always integrated until after repetition or trial. The learner may also not incorporate feedback because of inadequate attention to the feedback's source. Alternatively, perhaps, heightened arousal has considerably narrowed their attention. In other circumstances, feedback reinforces incorrect behavior. This can be seen when automobile drivers, rather than appropriately stopping their vehicle, accelerate into a storefront because they have mistaken their gas pedal for their brake. The feedback (e.g., combined visual and vestibular input) necessitates correcting the vehicle's forward trajectory. The pedal (thought to be the brake) is pressed harder to fix the vehicle's course. If we retrospectively evaluate this driver error, they were confident their actions were correct and were confused as to why there was a mismatch between a sensory experience (i.e., continued forward trajectory of a vehicle) and motor action (e.g., pressing of what they perceived the brake to be). Have you ever turned into a parking spot and misinterpreted your vehicle as moving forward if the car next to you, unbeknownst to you, begins to back out? This is another example of how sensory information can be misinterpreted and how driving errors can be explained.

Body Translation Versus Stationary Body

Movement is often related to or depends on a goal-directed task or environmental influence. Movements are considered more complex as the number of required elements is increased. For instance, a frisbee thrown directly at the recipient does not require a change in the recipient's location. When the recipient must change their body's locations to meet the frisbee's trajectory, the task goal to catch the frisbee remains. Still, the required elements to successfully catch the frisbee now need bodily translation to be synchronously integrated into the catching action.

Static Versus Dynamic Postural Control

The static heel-to-toe stance requires exercisers to maintain control of their body without translation. However, a static balance test may be progressed by evaluating postural control during movement. This is demonstrated when police officers ask a driver suspected of being influenced by alcohol or drugs to perform a field sobriety test.

Strategic changes in posture, if sufficiently controlled, are thought to be advantageous. For instance, the exerciser's COM will move during walking. The COM will rise during midstance and fall during the swing phase to harness gravity's effect and reduce metabolic costs. The exerciser can also shift their COM toward the left to prepare the left leg to bear weight during stance. This frees the opposite limb (i.e., the right leg) to express movement and swing forward.

Postural sway will exist despite the seemingly static nature of the position. We will remain in control of the posture if our ability to actively resist perturbations is present and retained. However, we expect the postural sway to increase with time as fatigue becomes increasingly present. This is increasingly true when active muscle actions are the source of stability. For example, if we were to hold the bottom position of a single-leg squat, we can expect deviations in the exerciser's COM. When mobility is coupled with a reduced BOS, the task requires elevated levels of coordination.

Open Chain Versus Closed Chain Movement

Movement can also be described as **closed chain** when the limbs are weight-bearing (e.g., squat, push-ups). However, during a seated single-leg extension, a unilateral exercise of the right leg, the distal shank (i.e., the lower leg below the knee) is not

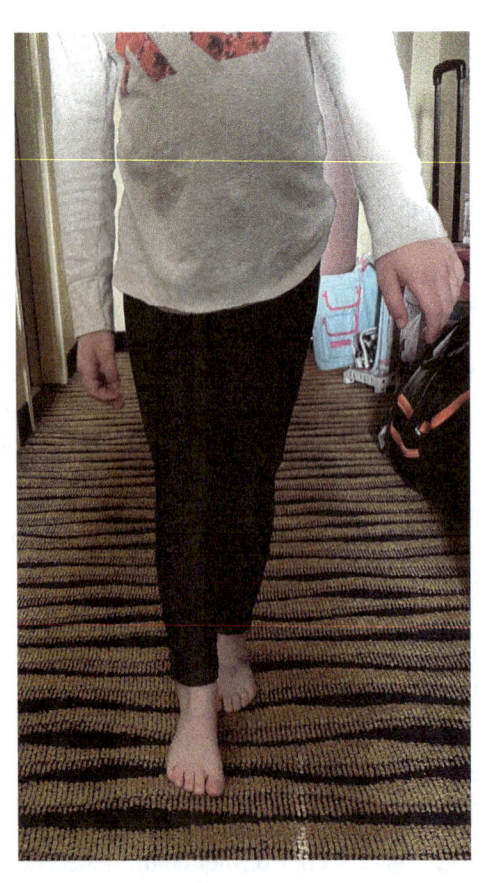

FIGURE 8.4 Static heel-to-toe stance.

FIGURE 8.5 Single-leg knee flexion.

weight-bearing. The shank can move upon the proximal and stable femur. The right leg is under an **open chain** or non–weight bearing condition.

THEORETICAL NEED FOR INTERVENTION

The Problem With Norms

Movement development can be considered the refinement and recalibration of movements throughout one's life span. Under typical development, humans have similar constraints. Interventions are warranted when development is "atypical" at certain ages. There is also a concern if previously obtained movements are lost. However, much of the current information on motor development operates on the assumption of "typical," although many argue that certain stages of development are not exclusively age-dependent. This implies that anyone who does not reach certain milestones at an exact age is characterized as "atypical" or "abnormal." Oversimplification through a false dichotomy does not lend itself to individual differences. That is, caution should be utilized when interpreting norms because norms are often represented by measures of central tendency (e.g., averages) and may forgo typical or expected ranges. In addition, whether normative values can adequately capture variations between cultures, geography, and societal expectations is questioned. Therefore, practitioners should consider the consequences of this label. Arbitrary labeling can create unwarranted concerns. Individuals and their social and cultural factors should be considered.[31] Practitioners should distinguish between clinically meaningful deviations from the expected range.

Geographical and Cultural Considerations

To further this point, Hulteen et al.[23] suggested the need to consider sociocultural and geographic factors that influence the acquisition and maintenance of foundational movement skills. Swimming, for example, may only be taught in some geographic regions due to locations near bodies of water. In some instances, children as young as 6 months old are taught swimming skills, while in other areas, swimming may not be a focus until adulthood. In cultures where PA is promoted, individuals tend to have higher health-related fitness levels and healthy weight status.[32] From this perspective, even those specializing in a sport early could have deficits in broader motor skills that are not required for that activity.

Scaling as a Constraint

A key feature of most physical activities is the idea of scaling. Simply put, scaling allows a practitioner to modify the available field dimensions (e.g., drill area), or equipment size, enabling an individual to learn a game, activity, or sport more efficiently. For example, small children learning to throw a football might have an easier time doing so with a ball sized to fit their hand, allowing for a better grip. While learning volleyball, young children can use balloons or beach balls to increase the amount of time the ball is in flight. This gives the individual more time to decide how to strike the ball.

In a recent systematic review, Buszard et al.[33] indicated evidence across multiple studies that suggest benefits to using scaling, including increased engagement and feelings of self-efficacy, better hitting accuracy, and improved skill acquisition. Biomechanically speaking, using scaled equipment can also lead to more efficient movement patterns in certain situations.[33] Similarly, modifying the net height and court size in badminton also improved player skills in competition, including observing various stroke and play patterns not seen when net regulation height and court sizes were used.[34] Keeping this in mind, using scaling as an intervention technique makes sense in PA environments, especially during early skill acquisition and regardless of age. Doing so may improve skill acquisition and encourage higher-level cognitive processing during specific tasks.[33]

To extrapolate this theory further, practitioners should consider how reduction in the drill's area can keep players involved by keeping them engaged. Rather than using an entire soccer field, a drill limited to one-half of the field can increase the number of interactions, decisions, and the ball touches a player may have in a 10-minute drill. As a result, the player will likely adapt well to game situations where open space is at a premium. Creativity to find space (e.g., to become available for a pass) becomes a good strategy.

Small-Sided Games

Small-sided games are used across many PA contexts, from physical education spaces to professional sport practices. Originally a key feature of various instructional models, small-sided games are included even in direct instruction situations.[35] The significant advantage of using small-sided games is that they allow full practice time for individuals, increasing overall PA levels. Davids et al.[36] also highlight

Seniors playing volleyball.

how small-sided games enhance movement and decision-making skills development. Unlike individual skill drills, small-sided games allow flexibility in constraints, providing a more practical application of technical and tactical skills in a highly variable environment.

Simply put, small-sided games allow individuals to work on a combination of skills more directly related to full-game play. As an intervention strategy, some researchers have noted an increase in overall training workload in soccer, especially when the small-sided games involve fewer players per game.[37] The same was found in rugby, with longitudinal studies showing improved physiological adaptations due to small-sided games.[38] From this perspective, small-sided games are ideal for introducing constraints in an unstable environment. This can challenge individuals learning sport-specific skills to execute various movements simultaneously, representing what they might experience in a real game.[39] Aside from increasing PA and requisite physiological responses, small-sided games allow practitioners to adjust tactical skill learning to the needs of the individual. Small-sided games can be utilized for team sports at any age level.

Equipment

Why do athletes use different cleats on grass as compared to turf? Cleats are equipped with studs of varying lengths. The longer the stud, the greater the contact area between shoe and ground. Combined with the cleat's piercing of the ground, the increased contact area creates necessary friction, and the athlete's capacity to change directions is improved. It is not uncommon for athletes to switch shoes with longer studs during halftime during inclement weather. This strategy can help offset such environmental conditions. Notably, weather can influence performance and is accounted for by alterations of strategy that aim to control its effects. However, it's important to note that too much friction is not advantageous, like walking in wet concrete. Transitions between force absorption and propulsive actions are increasingly tricky, and change of direction is no longer fluid.

MOTOR DEVELOPMENT: FOCUS ON MOTIVATING FOR MOVEMENT

Traditional motor development textbooks present development separately in the cognitive, social, and motor domains. As we have shown, movement is derived from nature and nurture, which drive development and maturation. Furthermore, consistent training is based on motivation, which is tied to all domains simultaneously. Considering this, various theoretical explanations for movement help rationalize how and why we move. There is no single theoretical perspective that explains all movement. Therefore, this section will explain motor development at different life stages, utilizing a more collective approach.

The desire to move is based on motivation. In the early stages of life, external motivation drives individuals to satisfy their basic needs. In this case, we refer to being fed, clothed, and having shelter. Infants display their rationale for these needs by communicating with caretakers through body language and audible crying. Over time, the caretaker begins to understand the infant's different types of expression and can increasingly satisfy those needs.

Further along, children begin to prepare to explore their environment to fulfill these needs independently. This exploration is possible after gaining head movement and trunk control, which are the precursors for limb exploration. Locomotive strategies unfold and often are selected according to perception and capacity. As they learn more about the environment and grow, motivation becomes more intrinsic, as evidenced in young children's play. While external sources of motivation are not always present, the need to move grows more and more intrinsic as we age. These intrinsic goals aid in establishing purpose and can satisfy the need for social interaction and feelings of competence across one's life span.

Along with motivation, the individual's complexity of movement evolves with time. What starts as a simple movement, such as a belly roll, turns into more complex movements, like log rolls and forward rolls. Learning these movements allows us to be more aware of moving in different spaces and is also a precursor to complex movements. For example, understanding how to roll enables the body to absorb forces better during and after a fall. A soccer goalie can use a roll to fall to the ground, trap a ball, and return to standing quickly. Given this evolution over time, it is essential to remember that as movement complexity increases, we must be lenient to variations that might exist. Again, the goal is to have the individual move in the most efficient way possible. This may mean that they do not achieve the ultimate level of complexity but still can reach a level that satisfies their motivation for movement. We may only be interested in having an individual be comfortable with rolling to keep them from injuring themselves, or

Belly roll.

Forward roll.

Early Movement Expression

The capacity to move depends on our capacity to stabilize the torso and move our limbs. Attention must also be paid to the infant's ability to transition to a particular locomotive strategy from a posture. In the following section, we examine motor skill development holistically, combining explanations of the different domains of development simultaneously. It is vital to note how stability is a precursor for limb mobility. Stability is first dependent on passive sources (i.e., external sources) and is later possible through muscle contraction (i.e., active stability). This theme is apparent in various postures and actions. Over time, the movements become more coordinated as perceptual information is learned and remembered.[20]

Passive Stability for Distal Mobility

In the womb, myogenic actions are possible around week 20, when the fetus can take advantage of the buoyant environment. After birth, primitive reflexes can produce the baby's first examples of cause and effect. At this stage, reflective (e.g., rooting and suckling) and deliberate movements are highly related to basic needs. Vision at this stage is present, but it lacks clarity. Rudimentary vision combined with the hand's mechanical input can help guide environmental search. For example, hands may be used to search for the mother's breast to eat. Passive head control allows for early visual exploration of the environment. With time, head control is increasingly active and less reliant on passive support. Active management of the torso is progressively observed. This can be seen when an infant is in prone position and combines extension of the head and trunk. This action is eventually coupled to and assisted by congruent arm action.

Movement and reach of the extremities show the infant how transitions may be increasingly possible. Prone and supine postures can encourage the use of limbs. Continued use of limbs can demonstrate how their use can have an axial effect. Limb manipulation can be combined with active use of one's torso. This early experimentation helps note the impact and influence of gravity. When supine, the infant can use vision to guide the greater ROMs observed at the shoulders and hips. This may explain why supine to prone rolls are thought to occur first. To roll, the infant uses its arms and legs to manipulate its COM. This manipulation of the COM can create momentum to produce postural transition successfully.

When infants can sit up, either passively or actively, their hands are free to reach and grasp objects. Seated postures may originate passively (e.g., placement by an adult) or be sought when the infant's coordination is sufficient and desires more significant interaction with the environment. In early active strategies, the hands are used as part of the BOS. As trunk control is improved, one or both hands are freed for arms to reach and perform manual actions. Passively supported postures can also increase the time the posture is observed. The more they practice these skills, the more sensorimotor input they receive, which impacts the coordination of effort on subsequent attempts to sit and explore objects.[20]

Take-Home Messages
Expected antigravity progressions of the head and torso:
1. The head must be passively stabilized.
2. Improved active control of the head control = reduced need for passive stability
3. Successful active head control against the force of gravity (i.e., anti-gravity)
4. Active head control with dissipating need for passive control of the torso
5. Increased active torso control

Early Locomotion

Included in this phase of the movement is the manual exploration of objects. Infants move beyond just reaching and grasping for an object to using one hand to hold the object and the other to palpate and manipulate it. They can also transfer an object from one hand to the other. In this stage, an infant may be motivated to move in space in the way described previously to reach, grasp, or otherwise manipulate an object actively. This way, locomotor patterns allow infants to expand their exploratory space.

Locomotive strategies unfold as an infant is motivated to move from point A to point B. Early strategies keep the COM close to the ground in a general sense. The seated scoot often precedes quadruped strategies (e.g., crawling or creeping). However, remember that not all kids will crawl before exploring the bipedal strategy. Locomotive strategies are often highly dependent on the starting position.

Highlighted in the following table are examples of locomotive strategies:

Scoot	• Active control of one or both legs can extend and flex the knees, dragging the body to the destination

Quadruped Strategy in Prone Position	• Crawl
	  ○ Lowered COM
	  ○ Belly in contact with the ground
	  ○ Moving forward with belly on the floor, pulling with arms and pushing with legs
	• Creep
	  ○ The elevated COM (relative to crawl)
	  ○ Belly not in contact with the ground
	  ○ 6 points of contact (hands, knees, feet)
	  ○ Moving on hands and knees in a rhythmic-alternating and opposing locomotion pattern.
	• Bear crawl
	  ○ The elevated COM (relative to creep)
	  ○ Belly not in contact with the ground
	  ○ 4 points of contact (hands, feet)
	  ○ Moving on hands and feet in a rhythmic-alternating and opposing locomotion pattern

COM, center of mass.

With passive help transitioning from a seated posture, the infant can begin to bear weight while standing (i.e., bipedal posture). As strength develops, the infant may be able to right themselves into a bipedal posture. In early bipedal posture, the infant will use passive support (e.g., chair, walls, tables, couches) to remain upright. A high level of postural sway is expected. There is an expected lack of reactivity or timely corrective mechanisms. Loss of postural control can be expected. Actively controlled standing posture will be possible in short durations with gradual removal of passive supports. On an inclined path to better remain in control, we can use our hands in an alternating reach-and-hold strategy. One hand provides an additional source of stability where the opposite arm can be mobile. The once mobile component is now the added source of stability, as the rest follows.

Further manual control is impacted by introducing tools, such as utensils, writing implements, or toys, that serve as extensions of hands. Coordinated movements continue to develop as toddlers learn how to use these tools effectively. Adolph and Franchak[20] indicate that toddlers must be willing to see value in using the device for further manual exploration.

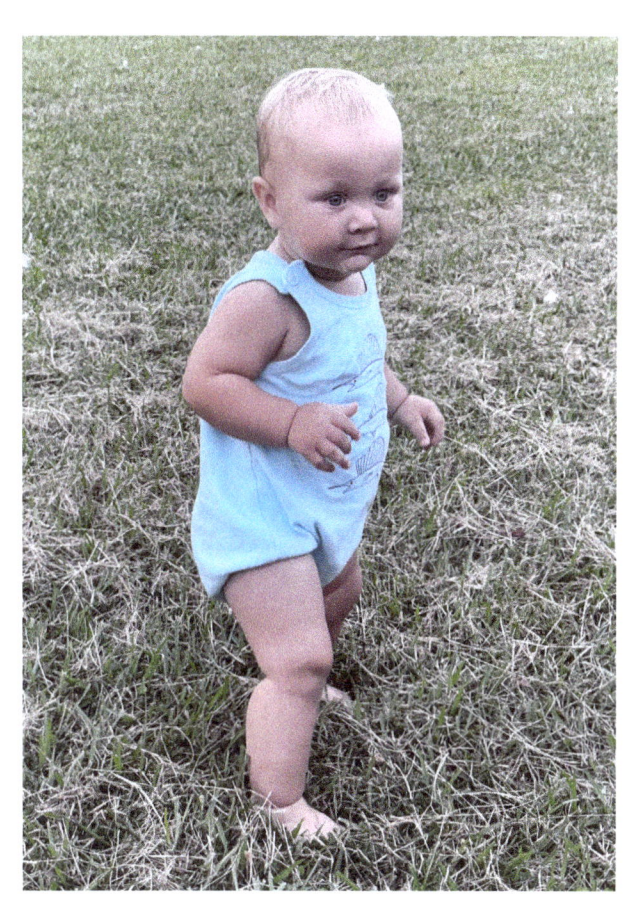

Early standing.

Foundational Motor Skills

In early childhood, bipedal locomotion improves and the need to establish competency in foundational motor skills is increasingly apparent.[23] It is important to note that the foundational skills described previously are not an exhaustive list, nor do they indicate that each skill must be mastered to engage in PA. Depending on the individual's situation, various foundational skills can be taught to reveal more PA options later in life. Practitioners must know each skill and how it develops to be applied to individual situations. An individual's movement is driven by several factors, including their desire to participate in peer groups and explore their environment. Therefore, motor skills are typically taught with a particular game or activity.

In this stage, motor skills continue to be refined based on the activity choices of the individual. These decisions are influenced by the family, social and cultural norms, peer influence, and availability of opportunities (e.g., community programs). In some cases, specific movements become more specialized to match demand. However, we recommend various activities at this stage for primarily two reasons: (1) to differentiate the physical stresses on one's body and (2) to improve the scope of motor skill competence. Physical changes and neurophysiological maturation allow for continued movement and social-cognitive development. This impacts the way individuals move as they grow.

Considering this information, we recommend the reader examine the pillars for *Long-Term Athletic Development*.[40] In addition, we consider the question, "Is weight training safe for the growing child and adolescent?". Bluntly stated, weight training does not stunt growth. Furthermore, qualified practitioners should supervise the athlete engaging in resistance training. As a rule of thumb, exercise form should be prioritized over the exercise's absolute load. Regardless of the developmental stage, weight-training programs should adhere to progressive overload and employ specificity. Remember, how we exercise is how we adapt. Exercise programs should, when possible, be specific to the needs of the individual or, at the very least, address common needs. When developing weight training programs, practitioners should consider how best to keep the program enticing to the developing athlete. Practitioners should be well rehearsed in how an exercise can be progressed or regressed. Outlined below are advanced examples of how exercises can be progressed and regressed.

Regression	Progression
1. Time Between Sets	

• *Increased rest time between sets
   ○ 2 sets × 15 reps (near 15 rep max) with 30 seconds between a Good Morning exercise set with a barbell
	• *Reduced rest time between sets
	   ○ 2 sets × 15 reps with 25 seconds between a Good Morning exercise set with a barbell

*The above example for progression assumes the individual can successfully perform the assigned regression. Regressions and progressions are relative to the individual's current fitness status and the intra-person changes that influence the capacity to exercise (i.e., motivation, sleep, nutritional intake before exercise), and caloric sufficiency. Current fitness status does not equate to "what they could do when they were younger" or "before the injury."	
2. Degrees of Freedom: +/- # of Moving Joints	

• ^Reduced number of moving joints that are changing in a coordinated or synchronous fashion
   ○ Multi-joint exercise → single-joint exercise
	• ^Increased coordination requirements by increasing the number of moving joints used in an asynchronous and coordinated fashion
	   ○ Single-joint exercise → multi-joint exercise

^It's important to note differences in absolute load between the multi-joint and single-joint exercises. We assume that muscles crossing each moving joint contribute to the collective movement.	
3. Removal of Passive Support	

• Increased passive support of trunk (i.e., less muscle recruitment in lumbopelvic hipcomplex [LPHC]) for axial stability
   ○ Seated shoulder press with trunk support vs. seated shoulder press with reduced or absent, passive trunk support
	• Increased reliance on active muscle recruitment and coordination of the LPHC (i.e., muscles that attach to the pelvis or lumbar spine) for axial stability
	   ○ Seated (with knees extended) Z-press

4. Increased Percentage of Repetition Max	

• Use 90% of the predicted weight or measured as your max repetition weight.
   ○ 65 lb × 15 reps = 15 rep max
   ○ 92% of 65 lb ~ 60 lb
	• Increasing the % of a rep max or using 100% of the predicted or measured rep max
	   ○ 100% rep max for as many reps as possible (AMRAP)

Exercise readiness or the capacity to handle particular exercise stress can ebb and flow with factors outside of the practitioner's control. Therefore, programs should be malleable to match better what the developing athlete can do on that given day. Recovery should be emphasized by reinforcing the importance of sleep schedules. Many factors affect our capacity to perform motor skills. It is vital for the coach to understand how regressions in the skilled may still be warranted under conditions of compromised recovery (e.g., reduced sleep) or motivation (e.g., external stresses unrelated to the sport).

Practitioners who wish to incorporate resistance training into the PA of a child or adolescent should first check whether the child or adolescent agrees with the decision. Future concerns should be directed to the American Academy of Pediatrics[41] position statement on resistance training for children and adolescents. Practitioners are essential facilitators of **self-exploration**. First, practitioners must monitor deliberate practice demands while accounting for exercise readiness or recovery variations. This is balanced with the provision of instruction and necessary feedback for performance. In this case, the practitioner is also responsible for providing more individualized attention. This often complements the realistic need to employ strategies that fit a more extensive group where individualized attention is less necessary or feasible.

As we consider the importance of skill practice and how to facilitate movement, attention must be paid to transferring skills in different situations. In weight training, proper form is emphasized under additional external load. However, in sports or play, the body is not always aligned, movements lack tempo, and breathing patterns are not consciously driven.

The physical and mental adaptations learned through strength training can improve the athlete's likelihood of being structurally resilient and available to practice sport-specific skills. Furthermore, well-rounded athletes are exposed to circumstances that require various psychological needs (i.e., arousal differences), motor strategies (i.e., memory), and physical stresses. When movement requirements are variable, the individual produces and absorbs force in multiple planes of motion and axes. Movement on these axes and within planes are, in theory, across more significant degrees of ROM. Motor competencies are less fixed to the demands of that sport or activity.

Adulthood and Aging

Physical inactivity is a growing public health concern. Tyndall et al.[42] have reported that nearly 60% of older adults are not engaging in PA and exercising, both of which can promote maintenance and improvements in cognitive and brain health. Recent evidence shows a relationship between poor health and all-cause mortality, independent of the time spent in moderate- to vigorous-intensity PA (MVPA).[43] During adulthood, exercise and PA are opportunities for continued social and cognitive development. As of 2018, an estimated 117 million American adults (nearly half) have at least one preventable chronic condition, most of which are exacerbated by a lack of regular PA. Regular PA reduces chronic disease risk and provides additional health benefits resulting in a longer life span than in the case of sedentary adults.

Evidence suggests that regular PA can improve health and reduce the risk of common chronic diseases such as type 2 diabetes, coronary heart disease, hypertension, obesity, anxiety, and depression. For health benefits, it is recommended that, at minimum, adults get 150 minutes of moderate-intensity PA or 75 minutes of vigorous PA per week.[21] Research has shown that moderate to vigorous aerobic exercise improves sleep quality and perceived quality of life and can delay disease-specific and all-cause mortality progression. As a form of PA, exercise has also been shown to improve cognition or slow decline related to aging.[44] Individuals who meet the equivalent of 300 minutes of moderate aerobic exercise per week prevent excessive weight gain and see reductions in the risk for obesity and type 2 diabetes.

Although the minimum recommendations are typically met with these improvements, substantial health benefits are seen when PA levels surpass the minimum recommendations. This includes focusing on moderate to vigorous strength training, which provides adults with benefits not achieved by aerobic exercises, such as improving bone strength and maintaining muscle mass during weight loss.

FACILITATING MOVEMENT PRACTICE

Considerations for Motor Learning

Along with constraining movement, deliberate practice is required for **skill acquisition**. To be deliberate, training must be conducted with **effort**. Performance is positively affected by the accumulation of trials during practice. Effort can help instill a selective focus on or attention to the demonstration's main components. However, to provide sustained effort, an individual needs to be motivated. Deliberate motor skill practice depends on an underlying knowledge of what to do.[28] Injecting the proposed differences between strategic knowledge and strategic control

Seated exercise.

may be essential. **Strategic knowledge** may result from active practice but can also be acquired through testimony or study. This may speak to the coach who never played but acquired an understanding of rules through only observation. **Strategic control** describes the application of knowledge through its action. Practice improves performance; hence, strategic control can progress through practice. It is argued that strategic decisions extend beyond the knowledge of a skill that directs how the skill is approached. For instance, Fridland[28] cites examples where emotion may further characterize how the skill is performed. "We may, for example, decide to perform the skill aggressively, defensively, or energetically" (n.p.).

The practitioner can help serve in this capacity by carefully designing practice experiences. For our purposes, we believe practice design is a continuum that validates the need for an athlete-centered approach to promoting independence while maintaining appropriate structure. This aligns with the idea that movement patterns evolve with age, development, experience, and multiple "right ways" to move. Small variability in movement is expected. As the mover learns to move optimally, variability is optimized. Furthermore, a skilled mover may use variability to offset fatigue during repetitive tasks.

Regardless of the movement desired, individuals may be more motivated to engage in goal-directed behavior. **Goal-directed behavior** focuses on the goal rather than its qualitative or subjective opposition.

Instructional Considerations

Along with constraints, how skills are taught profoundly affects how they are executed. As part of this consideration, practitioners must also be aware of the feedback after a specific skill is completed. Various instructional methods have highlighted feedback as an integral part of the teaching process. In some cases, feedback is given directly, with corrective language intended to modify movement. In other cases, feedback can be more indirect, given through questioning, which can help promote the independent learning of the mover. Aligned with motivational theory, the need for supportive feedback has gained attention in sports and physical education instruction because of its impact on the acquisition, learning, and maintenance of skills.[45] Supporting a learner's need for autonomy, instructors consider their perspective and find ways to work with their prior knowledge. The instructor also actively encourages self-initiation and experimentation, ultimately giving the responsibility of movement correction to the learner. This also impacts a learner's competence and sense of belonging.[46]

Demonstrations

During skill learning, it is suggested to simultaneously provide visual demonstrations (from at least two different angles) with verbal instructions. Then, the individual should be allowed to practice the skill using verbal cues to direct attentional focus. As part of this process, there must also be time for reflection on the mover's part. Questioning techniques rather than telling movers what should be corrected can allow for more critical consideration. This includes allowing the mover to explore all options to determine which version of the skill works best for them. Reflection time is often forgotten, as instructors must quickly move from skill to skill.

The extent to which we can **focus** is limited by our **attentional capacity** (the amount of information we can pay attention to at one time). Attention is thought to restrict similar tasks from being performed simultaneously. We often navigate circumstances that can overwhelm our ability to filter the copious amounts of sensory information entering our CNS. That input may be processed consciously, through the cerebral cortex or in the deeper, subconscious structures of our brain stem or reticular formation. Information is, therefore, centrally filtered. We filter according to the importance, and what is essential is often dictated by prior experience and our evolving bias. However, our ability to filter may be overrun by intense and sudden changes in our environment. Practitioners must know how to direct attention to observe demonstrations and execution of motor skills.

Effective Use of Demonstrations

When performing demonstrations, practitioners should provide learners with multiple angles of demonstration. If teaching a larger group, practitioners must ensure all participants can see each demonstration and hear the verbal instructions and will need to adjust accordingly for individuals with hearing or vision impairments. If possible, practitioners should relate the instructions of a novel drill or task to a previously understood concept. This use of analogies can aid the learner's acquisition. Lastly, practitioners should consider the consequences of providing visual demonstrations without considering handedness or preference. Consider teaching the softball strike. A right-handed visual demonstration may be less informative if the learner prefers to bat left-handed.

A practitioner will often integrate verbal instructions into a visual demonstration. Consider the following interaction: You are tasked with teaching a 5-year-old who is blind and does not know how to tie their shoes. In this circumstance, you cannot rely on visual demonstration. Instead, you can depend on tactile demonstrations coupled with verbal instructions. The practitioner can also serve to help shape sensorial expectations. The 5-year-old can use these (nonvisual) sensory experiences to form an internalized model. This evolving model is known and actively used for comparison during practice. Simply stated, each discrete step is being compared to this known sensory experience and allows the 5-year-old to see if they are progressing successfully or if an error has been made. As a result of trial and error, performance during practice progresses.

Verbal Cues

Verbal cues prime the mover for the upcoming component of the task. They can also serve to remind movers of the task goal or the main elements of the task. These **verbal cues** are short in length (≤3 words) and can prompt movement strategy before movement. Verbal cues can also be integrated into the coach's supervision to remind the individual of the critical features of the task.

During exercise, posture seems to matter most while the individual is under a load or the posture is held chronically over time. **Proximal stability** can be accomplished through breathing and muscular recruitment that ultimately increases intra-abdominal pressure. This rigidity helps to offset the axial load and how it may move. The movement of this load creates a rotational torque that perturbs the neutral spine. Proximal stability can be cued using an externalized analogy. For example, a "brace for punch" is thought to appropriately

Application of Motor Learning in Personal Training

As noted by Smith,[47] personal training certifications often focus on content, not teaching or applying it. Early personal training interaction can help frame the session's agenda. A plan that outlines the purpose and events (e.g., new movements and their purpose) can help the client's investment. At this time, clients can also help direct the session by noting any want or need. A task description, including its critical features and safety requirements, is necessary. The practitioner should provide insight into equipment, set it up, and individualize adjustments. A supervised practice[48] follows a demonstration of the skill.

Postural Cues During Resistance Training

In the weight room, our instructions often revolve around maintaining body alignment and the neutrality of the axial spine. We fear movement extremes as a cautionary tale to avoid injury. This is demonstrated in the controversial dichotomy between the standing Jefferson Curl and the need for coaches to emphasize spinal neutrality during the squat. It is important to note; the Jefferson Curl is often performed with a lower absolute load. Often, we assume that spinal neutrality, as confirmed by visual examination, does not contain small levels of spinal movement. Previous research demonstrated that when the squat is performed to depth (i.e., increased range of motion), the squat requires spinal flexion.[50] High levels of the compressive axial load seem to be best offset by maintaining spinal alignment and restricting large degrees of spinal flexion and extension through the creation of intra-abdominal pressure.

transfer to tension development in the core musculature (i.e., the lumbopelvic hip complex). In addition to increasing intra-abdominal pressure, the client is often reminded to rhythmically breathe. These separate but related tasks are integrated into resistance training. This complicates the exerciser's experience if they are unaccustomed to performing both simultaneously. We caution against excessive use of verbal instructions in early acquisition. The exerciser may be unable to effectively integrate or provide attentional focus on all these directives. Of course, the practitioner must help shape early movement. However, ultimately, the individual needs to depend less on these external origins of instruction.

Verbal cues can be phase or ROM-dependent. For example, the barbell deadlift is often broken into two phases: In *Phase 1*, the barbell moves from floor to knee. The coach can instruct the weightlifters to "push away from the floor." Over time, the longer cues can be shortened to "push away" as the lifter has already understood the cue and the coach's intent. Whereas, in *Phase 2*, the barbell moves from knee to the final (i.e., terminal) position. "Hips forward to hold" can facilitate hip extension and remind the lifter to end movement in a neutral spine (i.e., maintaining the normal spine curve). In summary, early foci should include explicit directions on rhythmic breath and axial stability (see Sands et al.[49] for further information). Coaches should avoid using multiple verbal cues that overwhelm their ability for adequate attention. To be effective, verbal cues should be contextually appropriate and interpreted correctly. The same verbal cue may evoke different movement strategies. Therefore, practitioners should also confirm a clear understanding of what the cue is meant to elicit.

Feedback

Instructions often accompany visual demonstration. Practitioners provide a recipe (i.e., instructions) and demonstrate how the task is performed. Feedback is provided during or after the movement has concluded. An understanding of error originates from external sources of feedback (e.g., coach); over time, learners can depend more on their sources (e.g., proprioception, visual feedback). Feedback can be provided in two generic forms: (1) knowledge of results and (2) knowledge of performance.[56] Practice is ultimately shaped by active trial and error. Learning is enhanced when practitioners delay extrinsic feedback, allowing the mover to self-reflect. This helps the learner become less dependent on external sources of feedback. External sources of feedback can redirect the exerciser toward a cognitive state advantageous to the performance of the task. Coaches may provide external sources of feedback, including auditory (i.e., verbal feedback) and visual (e.g., video of the participant, reflective demonstration), to help shape skill acquisition.

Attentional Focus

During the learning process, it is often thought that an internal attentional focus,[51] conscious thought, or deliberate thought can disrupt an autonomous organization of that movement.[28] The novice mover practices explicitly under direct and active mannerisms.[52,53] An external focus of attention is advantageous for motor skill acquisition (see Optimal Theory[54]). This attentional focus is external to the body. It may evolve from a proximal-external focus (e.g., tennis racket handle) to a more distal-external focus (e.g., the resultant landing area for the tennis ball). The mover relies on self-organizing mechanisms when the attentional focus is directed outside the body. In theory, the reduced cognitive load (the amount of information a person must process) allows the learner to dedicate consciousness to other stimuli, additional tasks, or open environments. This type of automatic organization is less conscious and less susceptible to emotional interference. This is not to say, skilled movement is devoid of higher-level cerebral thought.[28] When automatized, rehearsed and stable skill frees cognitive processes for a secondary task[55] or expressive variations of the primary task. For example, a pianist wants to add a whole-body expression to emphasize a particular note. As such, we may consider a need for pianists to divert attention to an upcoming difficult section of a song.[28] Cognitive load is seemingly reduced with accumulating experience. However, Fridland[28] compellingly argues that the automatic skill is not devoid of thought, even if we accept skilled actions are primarily automatic and can be disrupted by certain kinds of thinking or attention, such as a novel internal or external stimulus.

Anxiety and Arousal

The Optimal Theory further outlines a need to combine deliberate practice with an external focus of attention.[51] An external focus drives autonomic organization and reduces the effect of acute-psychological characteristics like negative self-talk (i.e., cognitive anxiety) that can disrupt proficient movers. However, skilled movers often employ strategies like imagery to optimize arousal and attention and, thus, increase the likelihood of competent performance. When an experienced performer acutely chokes (i.e., has an acute decrease in

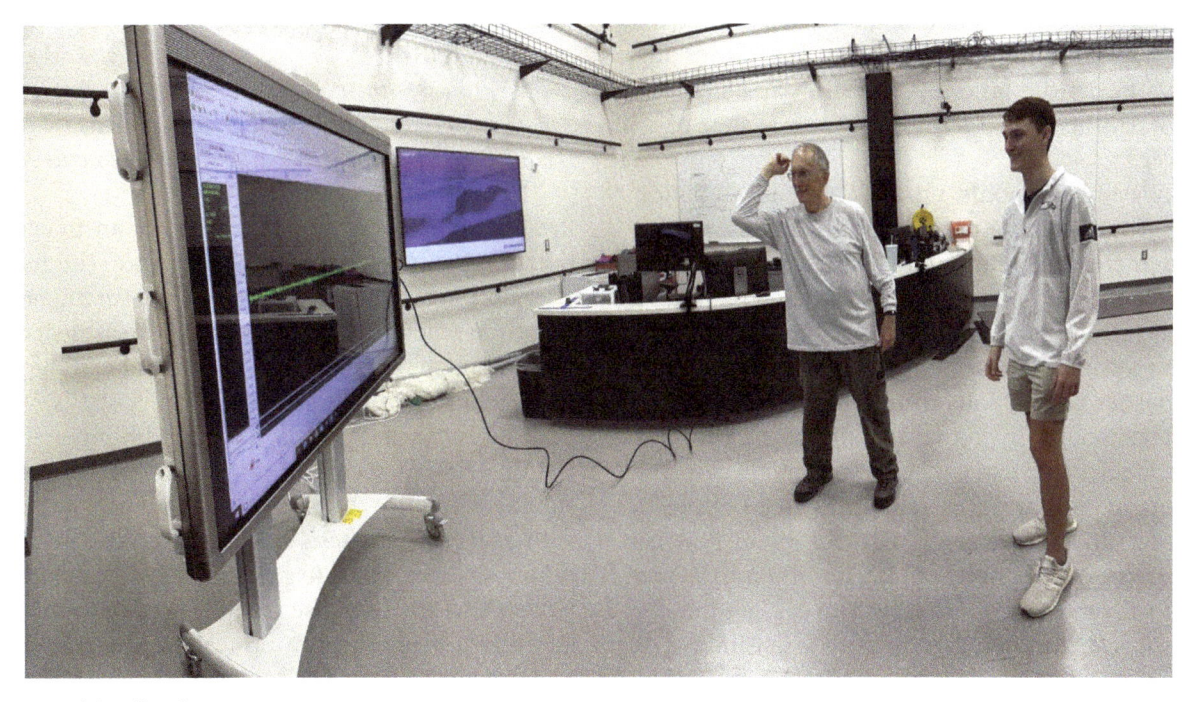

Visual feedback.

performance), it is viewed as a unique and rare spectacle. Notably, the ramifications of this can be pretty severe. Take, for instance, a skilled airline pilot who lines up the aircraft to land on the wrong (occupied) runway. For this reason, the origin of errors and how to reduce the likelihood of error is a widespread communized agenda. It's important to note that a redirection of cognitive states may be required between tasks. For instance, if the first task requires maximal force production (e.g., maximal effort 20-yard sprints while dribbling) but the second task requires accuracy (e.g., passing drill), an intervention to lower arousal levels is desired.

Movement Preparation—Warm-Up

Practitioners must consider how best to transition the mover from rest before practice. A warm-up should consider addressing the upcoming task's mental and physical needs. Furthermore, the mover's cognitive state at arrival can help determine the cognitive strategies implemented during movement preparation. Remember, each task has an optimal level of arousal. Therefore, the practitioner should consider the upcoming task(s) and at what arousal levels the task is best performed. Movement preparation may consider reducing arousal states if the mover arrives at an arousal level above task requirements. Notably, gradual reduction of arousal states can occur throughout the warm-up. At the end of the warm-up, one should find a cognitive state that matches the task's requirements. The mover may arrive below the task's optimal arousal state. Here, the warm-up helps increase the arousal state of the mover.

Warm-ups should upregulate bodily functions to match upcoming needs. Mobility drills can gradually increase a joint's ROM to match the ROM requirements, recruitment sequence, and joint actions of the upcoming task. In part, mobility drills can improve the muscle and connective tissue's thixotropic properties and its tolerance to stretch through the heat generated by movement (e.g., via the muscle's metabolism) and the directed blood flow that brings oxygen and fuel (e.g., stored carbohydrates and fat) to the exercising muscle. Blood flow can also remove the metabolic waste products associated with movement. Thus, warm-ups can improve the muscle and connective tissue's extensibility (i.e., tolerated elongation) and elasticity (i.e., capacity to recoil) and enhance the robustness of instructions sent by the CNS.

Take-Home Messages
- The warm-up should be specific to the upcoming demands on the body.
- The warm-up should transfer the mover from resting to "movement-ready" states by including physical and mental preparation.
- The warm-up should not prematurely fatigue the athlete.

Assessments—Tests of Performance

Motor learning is best defined as performance over time. We expect to improve performance with practice and to have some performance decay between practices. Successful early performance is not necessarily indicative of learning. Experimentally, practice is often referred to as skill acquisition. An assessment of performance will follow. When time separates the last practice trial, the **retention test** is a learning performance assessment. The retention test is a performance assessment that mimics or replicates how the skill was practiced. Whereas a **transfer test** is a test of task performance that is incongruent with the context for which the skill was practiced (i.e., right-hand [practice and retention] → left hand [transfer]). This can also be extrapolated to different tasks (i.e., tennis serves → ping pong serve) with similar or overlapping mechanics.

The assessment aims to define the mover's performance at a certain point in time. A simplified model follows the below order:

1. *Pre-assessment or battery of assessments*
2. *Intervention (e.g., practice, treatment)*
3. *Post-assessment or battery of assessments*

Pre-assessments are conducted before an intervention. In contrast, post-assessments are conducted after an intervention. To improve measurement validity, the practitioner must perform assessments under similar circumstances (e.g., exact time of the day, sleep habits before assessment, recovery status).

The National Strength and Conditioning Association (NSCA) recommends that to improve measurement validity, test batteries should be conducted with non-fatiguing tests first, followed by short duration discrete tests (e.g., agility tests, maximum power, and strength assessments), localized muscular endurance (e.g., push up-test), and whole-body assessments of anaerobic (e.g., 100-yard dash) capacity. Finally, aerobic capacity tests (e.g., 1.5-mile run) are performed last.

Purpose of the Intervention

The construct of motor learning is routinely defined by one's improved motor skill performance over time.[56] To acquire a new skill, the exerciser must practice it deliberately. Deliberate practice can be a mental (i.e., mental rehearsal, mental imagery) or an active, physical practice.[28] Coaches can help shape the exerciser's learning experience by providing visual demonstrations and verbal instructions. The verbal instructions can teach the learner about the skill or explain the mechanical sequences and intricacies involved.[54] Coaches may also provide verbal encouragement, often targeted to optimize motivational or emotional states. The learner's attentive observation then evolves to active participation (i.e., deliberate practice). The coach can reinforce the movement's main elements by using verbal cues to redirect the exerciser's attention to critical task elements, initiate a movement sequence, or recall a series of motor activities.[57] Mastering a skill is more likely when deliberate physical and mental practice is performed over time in various environments. The exerciser is intrinsically motivated and capable of emotional and cognitive regulation. Practice under a motivated state is ideal because the exercise can better shape concerted efforts.[58] Over time, the challenges presented to movers need to be skillfully modified.

Organization—Physical Practice and Intra-Task Variability

Practice design is heavily influenced by coaches' availability, the setup of the facilities, and the number of learners (e.g., individual coaching vs. team coaching). When considering how to design practice, practitioners must consider the skill and how variation in practice challenges benefits the learner. This section acknowledges that a single practice contains separate drills or tasks. Each task can be comprised of blocks and trials.

Each task is practiced, and the tasks are combined to constitute one structured practice. The practice of each task may be comprised of **blocks** (e.g., groups of attempts) and **trials** (e.g., individualized attempts). **Constant trials** of each task maintain the conditions across trials. Let us consider an example from soccer. When practicing a corner kick, under constant practice, the goal would be to repeatedly aim for the ball to land in the same position, travel with the same trajectory (e.g., ball spin, ball trajectory), and under the same defensive (e.g., marking of offensive players or zones) and offensive strategies (e.g., offensive runs in the box). Depending on the player's conditioning, rest between trials may be less necessary (i.e., massed practice) or more necessary (i.e., distributed practice).

Massed Organization	• Repeated trials with no or little rest between trials • It may be best for discrete skills or implemented when skills need to be performed under fatigue.
Distributed Organization	• Rest intervals separate trials. • Rest may be necessary for more complex skills. • Furthermore, when the risk for injury is elevated, rest intervals may be appropriate for skills that pose a risk of injury. • Learners with short attention spans or little motivation to practice may benefit from distributed practice.

When the coach implements **variable trials**, there is variability in how a particular trial is repeated. Each trial may vary the task's parameters to integrate variability in the soccer corner kick. For example, the ball's target (i.e., targeted teammate) may differ. For instance, the first trial may ask the kicker to aim for the offensive player running to the far post (i.e., the lateral and upright aspect of the net most distant from the kicker) and the second trial to aim for the near post-run. Trial-to-trial variability can also originate from how the ball was kicked (e.g., part of the foot that contacts the ball, the ball's spin, and the kick's height). The trial-to-trial variability can be dictated by the coach or chosen because of the kicker's perception of the defensive strategy.

Constant Trials	There is no trial-to-trial variability within a practice block. No changes are made from trial to trial.
Variable Trials	They involve trial-to-trial variability within each practice block. Each trial will comprise slightly different variations (e.g., speed, distance, velocity, technique, target).

Organization—Physical Practice

When structured practice comprises three tasks, the order in which the tasks are performed becomes increasingly relevant. The serial organization follows a predetermined order of multiple tasks. For example, volleyball practice may include the following tasks: serve, bump, and spike. The following sections provide insight into what practitioners should consider when designing an intervention or practice with multiple tasks.

Practice (1/3/2022)	1. **Task A (e.g., serve)**
	   a. (n = 4) blocks
	   b. Each block consists of (n = 4) trials
	 2. **Task B (e.g., bump)**
	   a. (n = 4) blocks
	   b. Each block consists of (n = 4) trials.
	 3. **Task C (e.g., spike)**
	   a. (n = 4) blocks
	   b. Each block consists of (n = 4) trials.

	Total Time = 60 minutes
	Total Volume (n = 3) tasks × (n = 4) blocks × (n = 4 trials) = **48**

This order is predetermined. After completing Task A, the learner does not return to the serve during Task B or Task C. The total practice volume can be mathematically described as (tasks × blocks × trials). Here, (n = 3) tasks × (n = 4) bocks × (n = 4 trials) equal volume of (n = 48). We should note that a coach could theoretically reduce the volume (i.e., blocks × trials). This would then require multiple rounds within the same practice.

Practice (1/3/2022)	1. **Round 1**
	   a. **Task A (e.g., serve)**
	     i. (n = 2) blocks
	     ii. Each block consists of (n = 4) trials.
	   b. **Task B (e.g., bump)**
	     i. (n = 2) blocks
	     ii. Each block consists of (n = 4) trials.
	   c. **Task C (e.g., spike)**
	     i. (n = 2) blocks
	     ii. Each block consists of (n = 4) trials.
	 2. **Round 2**
	   a. **Task A (e.g., serve)**
	     i. (n = 2) blocks
	     ii. Each block consists of (n = 4) trials.
	   b. **Task B (e.g., bump)**
	     i. (n = 2) blocks
	     ii. Each block consists of (n = 4) trials
	   c. **Task C (e.g., spike)**
	     i. (n = 2) blocks
	     ii. Each block consists of (n = 4) trials.

	Total Time = 60 minutes
	Total Volume = (n = 3) tasks × [(n = 2) rounds × (n = 2) blocks] × (n = 4) trials = **48**

However, this assumes the coach can successfully reorganize the players and equipment to return to each task. In the previous example, the calculated volume remains 48; (n = 3) tasks × [(n = 2) rounds) × (n = 2) blocks] × (n = 4) trials. Although logically organized, the order of the tasks is still predetermined. Arguably, the practiced order of tasks does not have the contextual specificity to the more random expression of skill during a volleyball match. Here, the learner is still preplanning movement and repeating the same tasks.

An alternative arrangement is **Random Practice**. Here, practice blocks would comprise multiple tasks presented in random order. The learner does not practice the same task on two consecutive trials in random practice. This requires the player to perform tasks in a less predictable order that mimics the volleyball match.

Practice (1/3/2022)	1. **Block 1 (n = 6 trials)**
	   a. *Randomized order of tasks*
	     i. *Task C*
	     ii. *Task A*
	     iii. *Task B*
	     iv. *Task A*
	     v. *Task C*
	     vi. *Task B*
	 2. **Block 2 (n = 6 trials)**
	 3. **Block 3 (n = 6 trials)**
	 4. **Block 4 (n = 6 trials)**
	 5. **Block 5 (n = 6 trials)**
	 6. **Block 6 (n = 6 trials)**
	 7. **Block 7 (n = 6 trials)**
	 8. **Block 8 (n = 6 trials)**

	Total time = 60 minutes
	Total volume = (n = 8) blocks × (n = 6) trials = **48**

A serial organization may result in early improvements in task performance. Unfortunately, performance on retention and transfer tasks is reduced. The reduced performance displayed during random practice is thought to enhance performance at retention and transfer. However, the practitioner should show caution in implementing random practice. It may be best reserved for those in an advanced acquisition state.

Alternative Forms of Practice: Mental Practice

Mental rehearsal or practice can aid in preparing and performing a skill. Perhaps, mental practice's effect is most potent when the skill is complex.[28] Furthermore, a mental practice may be best employed with physical practice.[59] However, mental practice cannot replace physical practice but is viewed as a valued addition to physical practice or implemented when physical practice is not possible.

Practice and Motor Learning

Practice design is indicative of the mover's stage of competence. The goal is for the learner to display increasingly consistent performance over time. An overview of motor learning and how it relates to practice is outlined below:

Cognitive States of Skill Acquisition	
Performance of Skill	Novice → developing skill → skill proficiency
Cognitive States	Cognitive state → associative state → autonomous stage
	Practice Considerations • The individual must be focused on the performance of the task. • The individual must be motivated to provide effort. • Feedback should enhance the capacity to recognize the error. • The coach should allow the learner to make and recognize errors.

	Novice	**+Time**	**Skill Proficient**
Practice Design	This design is less complex (e.g., fewer stages, slower pace) and focused on all skills. However, all skills are not necessarily integrated into all drills.	→	More complex and highly specific to needs
Learner's Attentional Focus	External Proximal Attentional Focus	→	External distal attentional focus
Learner's Motivation	External sources (e.g., social or team dynamic)	→	Internalized sources (e.g., the skilled may inherently value the skill)
Learner's Autonomy	The novice does not want to depend on externalized feedback. However, the beginner needs to understand errors.	→	The skilled learner may want to have control of decisions on how and what to practice.
Coach's Total Amount of Feedback	Novices may require more feedback.	→	Skilled learner requires a less absolute amount of feedback.
Frequency of Feedback	There may be a greater need for more frequent feedback.	→	Feedback is required less frequently.
Feedback Precision (Bandwidth)	Feedback may be more specific.	→	Feedback may be less specific and more generalized.

With accumulating experience, the learner begins developing an intrinsic understanding of the task's requirements. This is in conjunction with a deepened intrinsic value of practice itself. This is partly due to the skilled mover having accumulated positive results in performance as a result of continued practice. Although this may not hold true for all experienced movers, the skilled are often less dependent on external sources of motivation. Independent practice is also increasingly possible because the skilled are increasingly less dependent on practitioners for feedback. The skilled are better at operating within their constraints. As a result, self-assessment is increasingly possible. The goal is for the learner to be increasingly aware of their strengths and limitations. Movers should learn to self-reflect to understand the evolving demands of the skill better.

Sport Specialization

In considering the development and maintenance of motor skills, we must also present information on sports specialization, as it is a popular topic of study concerning the adverse effects of sport participation. Early specialization is physically and mentally problematic, increasing an individual's risk of developing overuse injuries and burnout. There is merit in continuous motor skill practice from a development perspective, but more of something is not always better.

The development of motor skills works best when applied in various contexts, especially in childhood and early adolescence. This is reflected in position statements and government reports, such as the U.S. National Youth Sport Strategy[60] and the Canadian Long Term Athlete Development Model,[61] which stress the importance of sport sampling rather than sport specialization. The NSCA and sport-specific national governing bodies have also adopted such approaches. Across the board, there is broad support for allowing individuals to participate and become competent in various sports and activities, with specialization occurring in later adolescence. Doing so allows for appropriate transfer of skills, reduces repetitive movements that can lead to overuse injuries, and reduces the mental strain of focusing solely on performing at a high level in one sport.

REFERENCES

1. Modrell, A.K., & Tadi, P. (2022). *Primitive reflexes*. StatPearls Publishing. https://www.ncbi.nlm.nih.gov/books/NBK554606/
2. Guo, G. (2005). Twin studies: What can they tell us about nature and nurture? *Contexts, 4*(3), 43–47. https://doi.org/10.1525/ctx.2005.4.3.43
3. Alliance, G. (2010). Understanding genetics: A District of Columbia guide for patients and health professionals. https://www.ncbi.nlm.nih.gov/books/NBK132140/
4. Purandare, C. N. (2012). Maternal nutritional deficiencies and interventions. *Journal of Obstetrics and Gynaecology of India, 62*(6), 621–623. https://doi.org/10.1007/s13224-013-0347-9
5. Shatz, C. J. (1992). The developing brain. *Scientific American, 267*(3), 60–67.
6. Reiman, M. P., Bolgla, L. A., & Loudon, J. K. (2012). A literature review of studies evaluating gluteus maximus and gluteus medius activation during rehabilitation exercises. *Physiotherapy Theory and Practice, 28*(4), 257–268.
7. Palastanga, N., & Soames, R. (2012). *Anatomy and human movement: Structure and function* (6th ed.). Churchill Livingstone.
8. Chen, H., Song, Y., Xuan, R., Hu, Q., Baker, J. S., & Gu, Y. (2021, August). Kinematic comparison on lower limb kicking action of fetuses in different gestational weeks: A pilot study. In *Healthcare* (Vol. 9, No. 8, p. 1057). Multidisciplinary Digital Publishing Institute.
9. Jukic, A. M., Baird, D. D., Weinberg, C. R., McConnaughey, D. R., & Wilcox, A. J. (2013). Length of human pregnancy and contributors to its natural variation. *Human Reproduction, 28*(10), 2848–2855.
10. Laws, R. M. (1970). Biology of African elephants. *Science Progress, 58*(230), 251–262.
11. Piaget, J. (1932). *The moral judgment of the child*. Routledge & Kegan Paul.
12. Erikson, E. H. (1963). *Childhood and society* (2nd ed.). Norton.
13. Eberle, S. G. (2014). The elements of play: Toward a philosophy and a definition of play. *American Journal of Play, 6*(2), 214–233.
14. Warburton, D. E. R., Nicol, C. W., & Bredin, S. S. D. (2006). Health benefits of physical activity: The evidence. *Canadian Medical Association Journal, 174*(6), 801–809. https://doi.org/10.1503/cmaj.051351
15. Paillard, T. (2012). Effects of general and local fatigue on postural control: a review. *Neuroscience & Biobehavioral Reviews, 36*(1), 162–176.
16. Appeadu, M. K., & Bordoni, B. (2022). Falls and fall prevention in the elderly. In *StatPearls [Internet]*. StatPearls Publishing.
17. Nelson, C. A., Fox, N. A., & Zeanah, C. H. (2014). *Romania's abandoned children: Deprivation, brain development, and the struggle for recovery*. Harvard University Press.
18. Acharya, S., & Shukla, S. (2012). Mirror neurons: Enigma of the metaphysical modular brain. *Journal of Natural Sciences, Biology, and Medicine, 3*(2), 118–124. https://doi.org/10.4103/0976-9668.101878
19. Lee, D. N., & Aronson, E. (1974). Visual proprioceptive control of standing in human infants. *Perception & Psychophysics, 15*(3), 529–532.
20. Adolph, K. E., & Franchak, J. M. (2017). The development of motor behavior. *Wiley Interdisciplinary Reviews: Cognitive Science, 8*(1–2), e1430.
21. American College of Sports Medicine. (2013). *ACSM's guidelines for exercise testing and prescription*. Lippincott Williams & Wilkins.
22. Davids, K., Araújo, D., Correia, V., & Vilar, L. (2013). How small-sided and conditioned games enhance acquisition of movement and decision-making skills. *Exercise and Sport Sciences Reviews, 41*(3), 154–161.
23. Hulteen, R. M., Morgan, P. J., Barnett, L. M., Stodden, D. F., & Lubans, D. R. (2018). Development of foundational movement skills: A conceptual model for physical activity across the lifespan. *Sports Medicine, 48*(7), 1533–1540.

24. Van Hooren, B., Fuller, J. T., Buckley, J. D., Miller, J. R., Sewell, K., Rao, G., Barton, C., Bishop, C., & Willy, R. W. (2020). Is motorized treadmill running biomechanically comparable to overground running? A systematic review and meta-analysis of cross-over studies. *Sports Medicine, 50*(4), 785–813.
25. Ericsson, K. A. (2006). The influence of experience and deliberate practice on the development of superior expert performance. In K. Ericsson, N. Charness, P. Feltovich, & R. Hoffman (Eds.), *The Cambridge handbook of expertise and expert performance* (pp. 683–704). Cambridge University Press. https://doi.org/10.1017/cbo9780511816796.038
26. Johnson, M., Nocera, V., Kaushal, N., Simon, L., Hasson, R., & the ACSM Strategic Health Initiative on Health Equity. (2021, March 22). Why we must prioritize equitable access to physical activity for children with disabilities. *ACSM Blog.* https://www.acsm.org/blog-detail/acsm-blog/2021/03/22/prioritize-equitable-access-to-physical-activity-for-children-with-disabilities
27. Coutinho, P., Mesquita, I., & Fonseca, A. M. (2016). Talent development in sport: A critical review of pathways to expert performance. *International Journal of Sports Science & Coaching, 11*(2), 279–293.
28. Fridland, E. (2021). Skill and strategic control. *Synthese, 199*, 5937–5964. https://doi.org/10.1007/s11229-021-03053-3
29. Corballis, M. C. (2014). Left brain, right brain: Facts and fantasies. *PLoS Biology, 12*(1), e1001767.
30. PGA Tour. (2013). Pace of play rules for TOUR, masters. https://www.pgatour.com/tourreport/2013/04/12/pace-of-play-rules-for-PGA-TOUR-and-Masters.html
31. Lobo, M. A., Harbourne, R. T., Dusing, S. C., & McCoy, S. W. (2013). Grounding early intervention: Physical therapy cannot just be about motor skills anymore. *Physical Therapy, 93*(1), 94–103. https://doi.org/10.2522/ptj.20120158
32. Cattuzzo, M. T., Henrique, R. dos S., Ré, A. H. N., Oliveira, I. S., Melo, B. M., Moura, M., Araújo, R. C., & Stodden, D. (2016). Motor competence and health related physical fitness in youth: A systematic review. *Journal of Science and Medicine in Sport, 19*(2), 123–129. https://doi.org/10.1016/j.jsams.2014.12.004
33. Buszard, T., Reid, M., Masters, R., & Farrow, D. (2016). Scaling the equipment and play area in children's sport to improve motor skill acquisition: A systematic review. *Sports Medicine, 46*(6), 829–843. https://doi.org/10.1007/s40279-015-0452-2
34. Ortega-Toro, E., Blanca-Torres, J. C., Giménez-Egido, J. M., & Torres-Luque, G. (2020). Effect of scaling task constraints on the learning processes of under-11 badminton players during match-play. *Children, 7*(10), 164. https://doi.org/10.3390/children7100164
35. Petersen, S., & Cruz, L. (2000). Using small-sided games in traditional activities. *Strategies, 14*(2), 19–21. https://doi.org/10.1080/08924562.2000.10591476
36. Davids, K., Glazier, P., Araújo, D., & Bartlett, R. (2003). Movement systems as dynamical systems. *Sports Medicine, 33*(4), 245–260. https://doi.org/10.2165/00007256-200333040-00001
37. Aguiar, M., Botelho, G., Lago, C., Maças, V., & Sampaio, J. (2012). A review on the effects of soccer small-sided games. *Journal of Human Kinetics, 33*(2012), 103–113. https://doi.org/10.2478/v10078-012-0049-x
38. Zanin, M., Ranaweera, J., Darrall-Jones, J., Weaving, D., Till, K., & Roe, G. (2021). A systematic review of small-sided games within rugby: Acute and chronic effects of constraints manipulation. *Journal of Sports Sciences*, 1–28. https://doi.org/10.1080/02640414.2021.1891723
39. Ramirez-Lizana, C. J., Reverdito, R. S., Brenzikofer, R., Macedo, D. V., Misuta, M. S., & Scaglia, A. J. (2015). Technical and tactical soccer players' performance in conceptual small-sided games. *Motriz Revista De Educ Física, 21*, 312–320.
40. Ford, P., De Ste Croix, M., Lloyd, R., Meyers, R., Moosavi, M., Oliver, J., Till, K., & Williams, C. (2011). The long-term athlete development model: Physiological evidence and application. *Journal of Sports Sciences, 29*(4), 389–402. https://doi.org/10.1080/02640414.2010.536849
41. Stricker, P. R., Faigenbaum, A. D., McCambridge, T. M., LaBella, C. R., Brooks, M. A., Canty, G., Diamond, A. B., Hennrikus, W., Logan, K., Moffatt, K., Nemeth, B. A., Pengel, K. B., & Peterson, A. R. (2020). Resistance training for children and adolescents. *Pediatrics, 145*(6), e20201011. https://doi.org/10.1542/peds.2020-1011.
42. Tyndall, A. V., Clark, C. M., Anderson, T. J., Hogan, D. B., Hill, M. D., Longman, R. S., & Poulin, M. J. (2018). Protective effects of exercise on cognition and brain health in older adults. *Exercise and Sport Sciences Reviews, 46*(4), 215–223. https://doi.org/10.1249/jes.0000000000000161
43. Lerma, N. L., Cho, C. C., Swartz, A. M., Maeda, H., Cho, Y., & Strath, S. J. (2020). Acceptance and feasibility of seated elliptical pedaling to replace sedentary behavior in older adults. *Journal of Aging and Physical Activity, 28*(6), 844–853.
44. Bademli, K., Lok, N., Canbaz, M., & Lok, S. (2019). Effects of Physical Activity Program on cognitive function and sleep quality in elderly with mild cognitive impairment: A randomized controlled trial. *Perspectives in Psychiatric Care, 55*(3), 401–408.
45. Wulf, G., & Lewthwaite, R. (2016). Optimizing performance through intrinsic motivation and attention for learning: The OPTIMAL theory of motor learning. *Psychonomic Bulletin & Review, 23*(5), 1382–1414.
46. Niemiec, C. P., & Ryan, R. M. (2009). Autonomy, competence, and relatedness in the classroom: Applying self-determination theory to educational practice. *Theory and Research in Education, 7*(2), 133–144.

47. Smith, A. (2021). Teaching for skill acquisition in fitness: Best practices for fitness pedagogy. *NSCA Coach*, 74(4), 22–27.
48. (Magill, R., & Anderson, D. (2010). *Motor learning and control*. McGraw-Hill Publishing.
49. Sands, W. A., Wurth, J. J., & Hewit, J. K. (2012). *Basics of strength and conditioning manual*. National Strength and Conditioning Association.
50. McKean, M., & Burkett, B. J. (2012). Does segment length influence the hip, knee and ankle coordination during the squat movement? *Journal of Fitness Research, 1*(1), 23–30.
51. Wulf, G. (2013). Attentional focus and motor learning: a review of 15 years. *International Review of Sport and Exercise Psychology, 6*(1), 77–104. https://doi.org/10.1080/1750984x.2012.723728
52. Fitts, P. M., & Posner, M. I. (1967). *Human performance*. Brooks/Cole.
53. Anderson, J. R. (1993). Problem-solving and learning. *American Psychologist, 48*(1), 35–44.
54. Schmidt, R. A., Lee, T. D., Winstein, C., Wulf, G., & Zelaznik, H. N. (2018). *Motor control and learning: A behavioral emphasis*. Human Kinetics.
55. Wulf, G., McNevin, N., & Shea, C. H. (2001). The automaticity of complex motor skill learning as a function of attentional focus. *Quarterly Journal of Experimental Psychology, 54*(4), 1143–1154. https://doi.org/10.1080/713756012
56. Fairbrother, J. T. (2010). *Fundamentals of motor behavior*. Human Kinetics.
57. Landin, D. (1994). The role of verbal cues in skill learning. *Quest, 46*, 299–313.
58. Wulf, G., & Schmidt, R. A. (1997). Variability of practice and implicit motor learning. *Journal of Experimental Psychology: Learning, Memory, and Cognition, 23*(4), 987.
59. Madan, C. R., & Singhal, A. (2012). Using actions to enhance memory: effects of enactment, gestures, and exercise on human memory. *Frontiers in Psychology, 3*, 507. https://doi.org/10.3389/fpsyg.2012.00507
60. Office of Disease Prevention and Health Promotion. (2018). *U.S. National Youth Sport Strategy*. https://health.gov/sites/default/files/2019-10/National_Youth_Sports_Strategy.pdf
61. Athletics Canada. (2015). Canadian long term athlete development model. https://athletics.ca/wp-content/uploads/2015/01/LTAD_EN.pdf

CHAPTER 9
MEASUREMENT, ASSESSMENT, AND EVALUATION

Daniel J. Burt

WHY MEASURE

How are decisions to be made for the benefit of an individual engaging in motor interventions and strategies? As the field at large, including the medical community, has begun to take a more functional approach to viewing individuals with disabilities, how do we make safe and advantageous recommendations for improving function and quality of life for them? This requires going through the decision-making process, and at the heart of this process is the collection of data. Specifically gathering information, data, to make an informed decision is the basis of assessment. **Assessment** is the evaluation or estimation of the nature, quality, or ability of someone or something and is looked at in two parts—measurement and evaluation. **Measurement** is the act of assessing or the act of comparing something to a set standardized unit. This allows the collection of information or data, such as the time it takes to complete an activity and therefore how proficient someone is at a task. Measuring someone's ability to bend or move a joint's range of motion may inform us of damage done by trauma or a progressive disease, and may further inform on much needed and appropriate therapies and activities. This then leads to **evaluation**, where judgments or decisions are made about the quality, nature, or value of an item being assessed through measurement. Often, tools are developed to know what the particular nature of an item (a question or activity) is, and are often referred to individually as **tests** in assessments.[1]

Norm and Criterion-Referencing Standards comparing something to a set standardized unit

Typically, evaluation decisions are categorized into two types of reference standards. The first reference type is **norm-referenced standards**, this compares an individual's gathered data to that of a specific sample. Hospitals and doctors do this often, comparing weight, height, heart rate, and blood pressure to what has been recorded as the population norm. This can sometimes help determine that a disability or issue may be present due to a norm-referenced standard not being met. An example could also be seen in a child who is always at the bottom of normative height expectations; this might cause a pediatrician to see if there is a deficiency in a growth hormone. One of the issues that have been facing norm-referenced standards is that they do very little to help with the issues surrounding an individual with a known disability who might be continuously facing capabilities outside the expectation of the normative. Therefore, the authors of several tests, namely, the Bruininks-Oseretsky Test of Motor Proficiency-2 (BOT-2) and the Brockport Physical Fitness Test (BPFT), in recent years have been working on improving expectations by creating norms for developmental deficiencies. **Criterion-referenced standards** are used to compare a performance or action against a set criterion. Sometimes, criteria are developed around norm-referenced expectations, but often a skill or performance is broken

Daniel Burt, Texas A&M University-Kingsville. © Kendall Hunt Publishing Company

EVALUATION

ASSESSMENT — ANALYSIS — PERFORMANCE — IMPROVEMENT — RESULTS — FEEDBACK

Evaluation is a process that requires a number of components to complete.

down into components and then assessed if those items are done at all or the quality of how they may have been performed. Many fitness tests have begun taking this approach for ease of mass testing, and it is often seen in educational tests, due to the increase in speed of assessing very complex items along social, cognitive, and behavior functions.[2,3]

Formative Versus Summative Assessment

Formative assessment measures how an activity is being performed currently and how well the activity is developing toward the planned outcome. The purpose of formative assessment allows for there to be a change in the activity if there is not adequate progress being made toward the end goal. It allows for correction before the end of the activity arrives. **Summative assessment** is to determine if the end goal or planned benchmarks/intervals are being met. This is typically compared to a previous and deliberately set of standards.

Process Versus Product Measures

Most types of measurement that occur in activity settings tend to look at either the process or the product of a movement. **Product measures** will look at the outcome of a movement activity. Examples of this might be how many repetitions, or the amount of times, a specific activity movement is performed, or could be the amount of time it takes to complete an activity. Another example could be making a basket 8 out of 10 times, or hitting a target a specific number of times out of a total. Oftentimes, this is attached to a number and is considered an objective measurement. **Process measures** usually look at how well a movement activity was performed. This can often be tied to how a ball was thrown, if feet were placed in the right

An example of product measurement would be whether the ball went into the basket or not.

Process measures are used to review the performance of an action, an giving a chance to make a changes for improvement.

position or legs bent appropriately, whether there was a follow-through after the ball had been shot, and so on. It is common that the process measures are subjective in how they are recorded and therefore are often matched with criterion-referenced standards and are considered a formative assessment.[4]

Assessment Considerations and Types

Multiple forms of assessment exist to aid and help professionals decide on the best way for a motor movement skill or activity to be measured toward reaching a goal.

Authentic versus Alternative Assessment. Authentic assessments are often used to measure performance of individuals in "authentic" real-world situations, providing a more accurate sense of measurement for a specific skill or activity. Oftentimes, these are based on learning objectives that require higher level thinking and applying concepts across a variety of situations. An example of how this may help can be seen in some individuals with specific learning disabilities such as dyscalculia, where an individual will struggle with concepts involving numbers such as using money to pay for items. **Alternative assessment** is a focus on assessments that move away from what is considered traditional assessment and look at other ways to measure accomplishments. Traditional assessments are focused items like matching terms and definitions, and items that are often seen in school tests. This can be seen in true/false questions, matching, selection, short answer, and essay questions. An alternative assessment moves more into application use; they include the use of rubrics, presentations, checklists, and breaking down skills via task analysis, the focus being still on the content covered, but allowing for more capability to not only use higher levels of Bloom's taxonomy but also to allow students who may work better in nontraditional ways a chance to expand and show their abilities.

Curriculum-based assessment is often viewed as the assessment of short-term benchmarks or measurements to assist toward specific goals or objectives that relate to educational topics or units. So long as an individual is engaged in the educational unit, the assessment is continuous to provide a method that the lesson objectives are being accomplished over time.[5,6]

Intervention-based assessment is usually used when creating a model around solving a problem and to determine if a person meets eligibility criteria, say, for special education qualifications or unique placements. Usually the first step is to define the issue or problem, then collect data around the issue for a baseline, create goals or expected achievements, measure the progress of the individual, and finally compare this to the data from the baseline. An example could be handwriting capability before and after utilizing a pencil grip to remove strain on the hand and improve writing legibility. This pre/post method of assessment allows for a strong consideration if intervention strategies being used are working as intended or if additional/alternative interventions should be used.

Functional assessment is based on the concept that people with individual specific needs may not always follow what is expected in development. This can be readily apparent in therapy-related fields, where there are expected progressions in both gross and fine motor skills, with examples able to be seen in fundamental motor skills like throwing and kicking. The assessment is for looking at what they are actually capable of, and not where we expect them to be. Not only is this assessment key in recognizing individuals as actual individuals, but it may also help at focusing on developing specific skills and techniques that they are in dire need of improving.[5,6]

WHY TEST

A need exists to decide what tools and interventions are best for helping evaluate and understand a motor or cognitive performance. It allows us to understand the specific needs of the individuals, as well as create accountability toward meeting intervention goals.

Placement: Oftentimes, assessment and testing need to occur to help determine the optimal instructional setting for individuals to learn based on their specific needs. This also will take the least restrictive environments (LRE) into consideration as they apply to the goals and objectives set for the individual.

Diagnosis: Assessment can serve as an excellent way to identify issues or deficiencies that may affect an individual's physical, mental, or behavioral health. Increased risk of sedentary behaviors in those with disabilities continues to place a need for diagnostic assessments not only for issues related to disabilities, but also chronic diseases like diabetes and various cardiovascular illnesses.

Prediction: Many assessments used in research and in measuring deficits may help in determining where a future result or performance should be, often without intervention. Specific learning tests may inform where an individual is at in academic capability compared to others of a similar age. This allows assessors to determine how close, or how far, a person's trajectory will be in comparing to specific developmental expectations.

Motivation: While we may not publicize an individual's scores in health or school work, it may benefit the individual to see where they fall when compared to the overall data collected. This may let them choose to make healthier decisions if they realize they are dropping into what society considers high health risks. An individual engaging in therapy to improve motor movement may be inspired to keep working harder and staying with performing their therapy modalities when seeing their progress reach closer toward their goals. They may also choose to work harder in their academics, or with techniques that help in keeping focus on academic work, when being able to see their progress compared to their peers.

Achievement: In order for assessment to be successful, there have to be clear objectives to show that progress has been accomplished. This may be seen in achieving specific motor capabilities with physical impairments, or it may be accomplishing academic achievement goals set by a school special education team. It helps to show if interventions are working and goals are being attained. While this is usually a summative evaluation method, it is harder to utilize if the finalization of data tends to be more subjective or a criterion-referenced standard.

Program evaluation: Various program types are designed to be beneficial and part of the intervention process for those who have needs. In reality, continuous development of a program or interventions need to be consistently considered. Finding room for improvement allows for increased benefit and better understanding of the needs for individuals. This could be dealing with improving curriculum in classes, updating protocols on motor movement therapy, or even how education team handles selecting who can or cannot be eligible for their services.[2]

DOMAINS IN KINESIOLOGY

In kinesiology and the pre-therapy training fields, assessment methodology tends to fall into three domains that are considered for human performance measurement. The **psychomotor domain** often gets the most attention in kinesiology, and it focuses on locomotor movement, physical abilities, skilled motor movement, perceptual motor skills, and reflexive movements. These are often seen in discrimination of perceptual motor skills; an example could be visual discrimination and telling the difference between foregrounds and backgrounds. It can include manipulative skills, for example, how you use and interact with your hands, often measured by occupational therapists. Locomotor movement, safely being able to navigate across a room or up a set of stairs, are often developed with a physical therapist. The second domain is the **cognitive domain**, which often deals with knowledge-based information, and plays a role

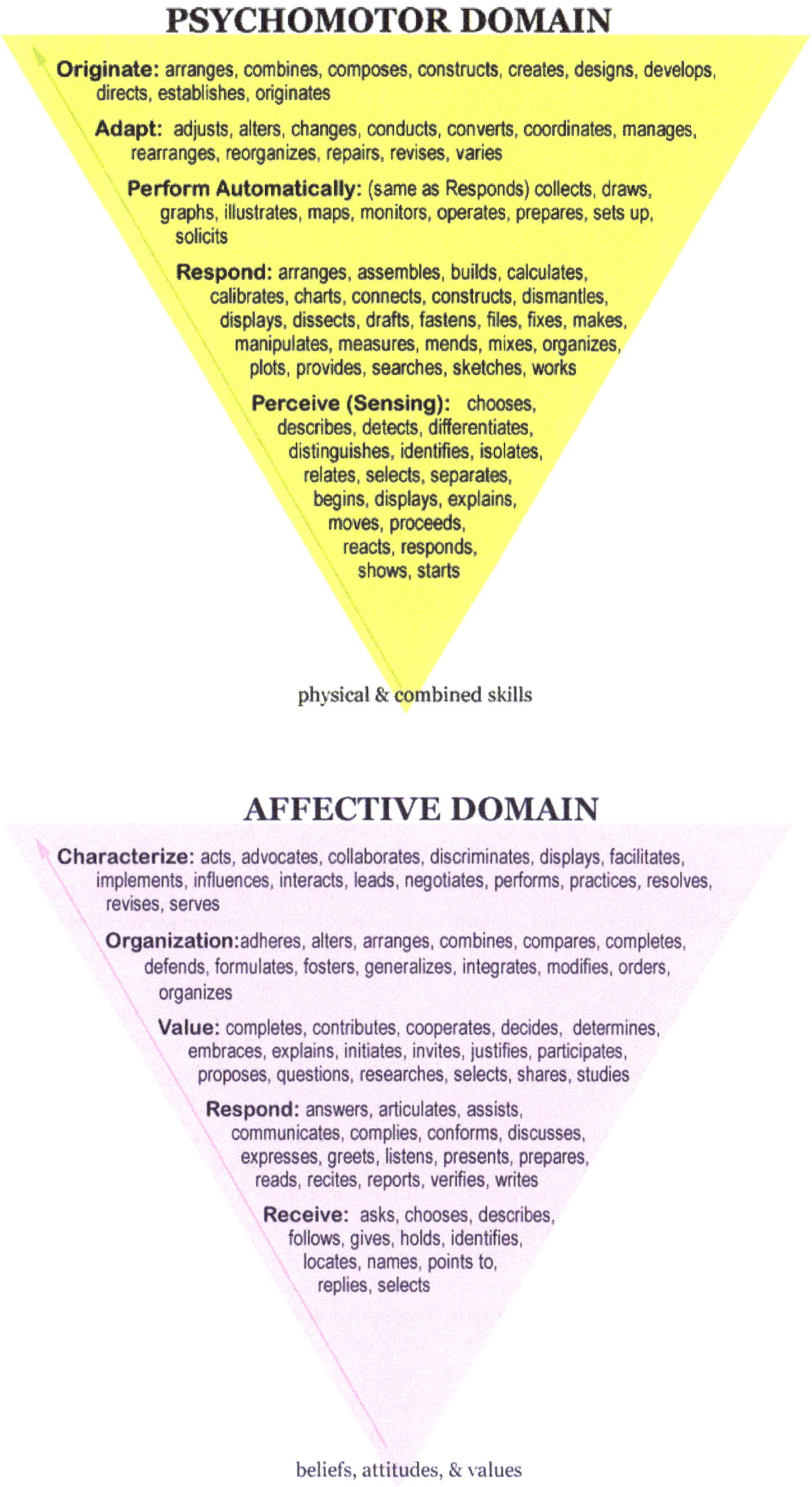

PSYCHOMOTOR DOMAIN

Originate: arranges, combines, composes, constructs, creates, designs, develops, directs, establishes, originates

Adapt: adjusts, alters, changes, conducts, converts, coordinates, manages, rearranges, reorganizes, repairs, revises, varies

Perform Automatically: (same as Responds) collects, draws, graphs, illustrates, maps, monitors, operates, prepares, sets up, solicits

Respond: arranges, assembles, builds, calculates, calibrates, charts, connects, constructs, dismantles, displays, dissects, drafts, fastens, files, fixes, makes, manipulates, measures, mends, mixes, organizes, plots, provides, searches, sketches, works

Perceive (Sensing): chooses, describes, detects, differentiates, distinguishes, identifies, isolates, relates, selects, separates, begins, displays, explains, moves, proceeds, reacts, responds, shows, starts

physical & combined skills

AFFECTIVE DOMAIN

Characterize: acts, advocates, collaborates, discriminates, displays, facilitates, implements, influences, interacts, leads, negotiates, performs, practices, resolves, revises, serves

Organization: adheres, alters, arranges, combines, compares, completes, defends, formulates, fosters, generalizes, integrates, modifies, orders, organizes

Value: completes, contributes, cooperates, decides, determines, embraces, explains, initiates, invites, justifies, participates, proposes, questions, researches, selects, shares, studies

Respond: answers, articulates, assists, communicates, complies, conforms, discusses, expresses, greets, listens, presents, prepares, reads, recites, reports, verifies, writes

Receive: asks, chooses, describes, follows, gives, holds, identifies, locates, names, points to, replies, selects

beliefs, attitudes, & values

FIGURE 9.1 Psychomotor, cognitive, and affective domains.
Source: CDC

COGNITIVE DOMAIN

Evaluate: appraises, compares, concludes, contrasts, criticizes, discriminates, explains, justifies, interprets, relates, summarizes, supports

Synthesize: categorizes, combines, compiles, composes, devises, generates, interprets, modifies, organizes, plans, rearranges, reconstructs, relates, reorganizes, revises, rewrites, summarizes, translates

Analyze: assesses, breaks down, defines, diagrams, differentiates, discriminates, distinguishes, identifies, illustrates, infers, outlines, points out, selects, separates, subdivides

Apply: changes, computes, demonstrates, discovers, locates, manipulates, modifies, operates, predicts, prepares, produces, relates, shows, solves, uses

Comprehend: coverts, defends, distinguishes, estimates, explains, extends, generalizes, gives, examples, infers, paraphrases, recognizes, writes

Know: defines, describes, identifies, lists, matches, names, reproduces

knowledge & thinking skills

FIGURE 9.1 Continued.

in what we know and how well we comprehend and apply the information we are learning. This is an extremely important domain not only in how we learn information, but also how we evaluate when to adjust and then apply that knowledge to motor movement changes or new skills being developed. The third domain is the **affective domain**, and prioritizes the emotional and psychological components of an individual. The emphasis of this domain is on value creation and how we form and maintain values for things that are cared about. They are often extremely difficult to create measurements for and should be used with care when considering to base "success" or completion on. Examples are often seen in situations where individuals with autism or behavioral issues may struggle with recognizing and processing their own emotions, being able to control attention to emotional cues, or conceptualizing and organizing a value framework from which to operate and work with others.[7]

ROLES IN THE ASSESSMENT PROCESS

As technology has advanced and allowed for increased sharing of information and more convenient and immediate methods of assessment, individuals with disabilities have seen more of a team approach to assessing and the sharing of information. This has allowed expert medical professionals to create medical teams over specific issues, like an individual struggling with growth hormone deficiencies resulting in inhibited motor movement development and who may have separate assessments and ultimately, shared plans put together by an endocrinologist and a physical therapist. This now addresses the medical issue and the functional one of daily living facing the individuals. Schools have seen the biggest benefit of this, with physical therapists handling major gross movement issues, occupational therapists assessing and assisting in how to write, speech specialists developing methods to improve speech communication, and licensed specialists in school psychology (LSSP) who assess and work with issues in behavioral and social interaction. These individuals are now able to work through quick messaging and video conferencing to be active participants in improving diagnostics and plans for forward development. This holistic approach allows for progress to be supported in all areas of an individual's life and not just the few hours they are in therapy or rehabilitation as it allows parents, teachers, administrators, and other professionals to ask questions and make recommendations to each other.[8]

ASSESSING MOTOR DEVELOPMENT

While Chapter 7 focused on assessment of fitness-related skills from a medical and chronic illness perspective, this section focuses on the movement patterns and landmarks across the human life span. It is worth noting that the life span is a spectrum and most of our movement development continues in one direction; however, age and disabilities may cause some development to stop, or even regress.

Reflex Tests

Commonly seen the most in measuring the responses of infants, these assessments measure **reflex movements**, which are automatic reactions when presented with various stimuli, like touch, sound, or light. It is believed that the purpose of these reflex movements is to better protect individuals in the infant stage and help develop the responsive nature of skeletal muscles and the central nervous system. Assessments for reflexes are most common in the stages of infancy and young childhood and often are reviewing the possibility of neurological development problems. This is first to be determined by the reflexes existing, and then further by testing to see if some of the reflexes persist into older childhood. This is worth noting since the higher brain takes over as a child ages, and reflex responses are expected to be less common. Responses are often categorized into several categories with the first being **righting reactions**, which involve keeping the head in alignment with their body. The second is **balance reactions**, where reactions are based on keeping an individual from falling over when there is a loss of balance. The third is **protective reactions**, where limbs are outstretched to avoid injury in case of a fall or loss of balance.[8]

Examples of Reflexive Tests
- Apgar Scoring
- Neonatal Neurological Examination
- Primitive Reflex Profile

Motor Development Tests

The prevailing belief that specific behavioral milestones are reached during motor development is the reason for developing this specific type of assessment.

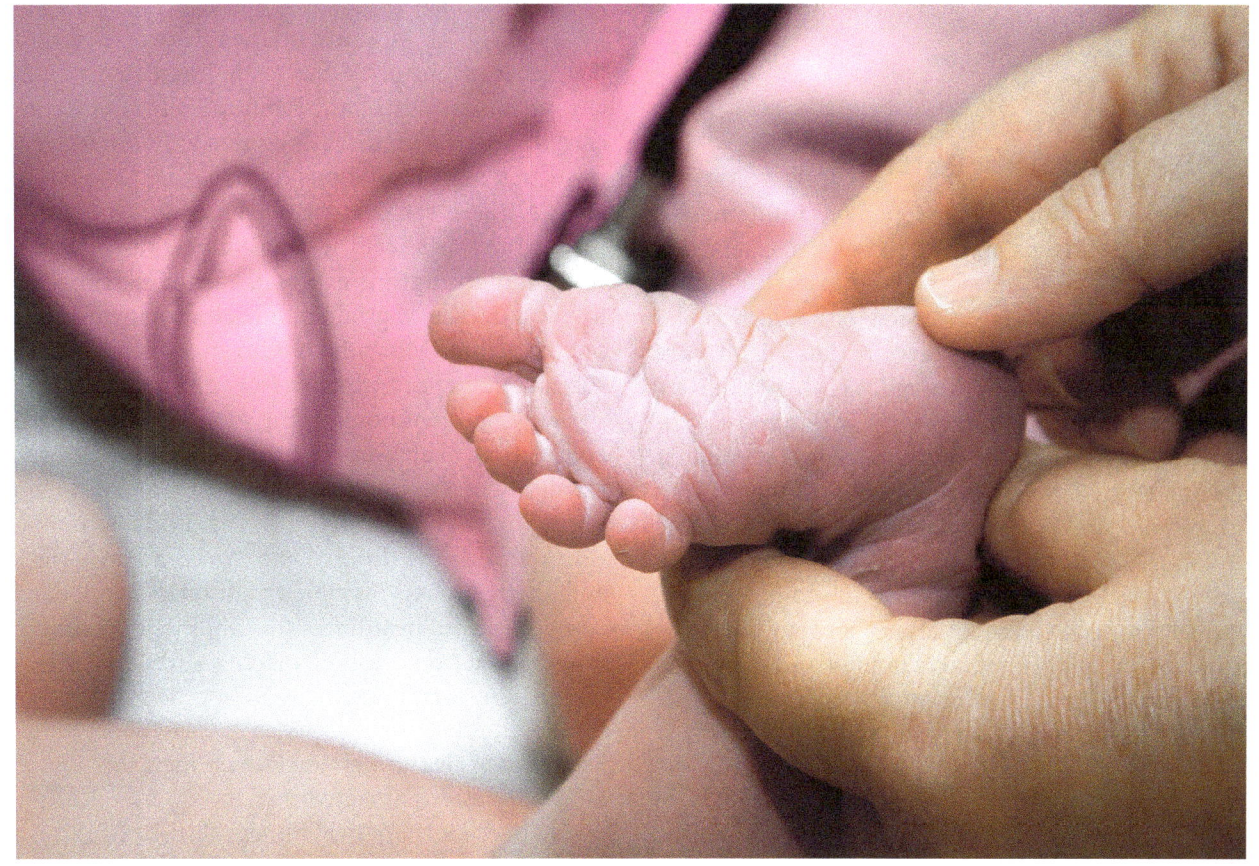

Reflex testing often occurs immediately after birth.

The milestones themselves and the theory behind their developmental emergence is covered under Chapter 8. While it is possible to see many milestones occur, an example could be a child developing from creeping to walking to running, however, there is also the comparison to what is typical, or "normative" for an individual in that age range. Practitioners often perform motor development tests not only to have a baseline, but also to see if an individual is making appropriate progress in their development based on what we know is expected in motor movement. Motor development is placed into two categories. The first is **gross motor skills**, the skills that occur due to large muscles or muscle groups like the legs and arms. Gross motor skills are often measured in physical therapy and physical education. The second is **fine motor skills**, the skills that occur due to smaller muscles or muscle groups, primarily focused on items with the hands. Examples might be writing, manipulating objects, and are typically assessed by an occupational therapist.[4]

Examples of Motor Development Tests
- Peabody Developmental Motor Scales 2 (PDMS-2)
- Development Assessment of Young Children 2 (DAYC-2)
- Assessment, Evaluation, and Programming System (AEPS)

Fundamental Motor Pattern Tests

While part of motor development, **fundamental movement patterns** are patterns of movement that we are expected to develop over our early life and which are believed to be essential for neuromuscular integration. Additionally, these are patterns that are also seen in sport skills. Examples of these skills are running, jumping, and throwing. While most individuals will develop these skills to some degree either naturally or by observation, mastery of them is not guaranteed and requires training and practice. Due to the nature of skills, there are two categories typically focused on. The first category is locomotor skills, moving from one point to another, and emphasize on running, jumping, hopping, skipping, galloping, and so on. The second is ball control, with examples like throwing, catching, kicking, and striking.

Example of a Fundamental Motor Pattern Test
- Test of Gross Motor Development 3 (TGMD-3)

Motor Ability Tests

Motor abilities are the characteristics that are related to the previously discussed motor skills. While skills like throwing, running, and so forth are looked at from a developmental lens, motor abilities are the items that support their accuracy and mastery, like balance, bilateral coordination, or hand-eye coordination. Motor abilities are often generalized and when developed could help in various motor skill areas, for example, balance being developed would assist in both an individual running or an individual trying to play hopscotch. Note that many assessments do not use traditional skill movements for assessment, like picking pennies up with fingers and moving them from one hand to another, because it is possible to be excellent at a skill due to practice, but have low generalized motor ability.[4]

Examples of Motor Ability Tests
- Bruininks-Oseretsky Test of Motor Proficiency 2 (BOT-2)
- Movement Assessment Battery for Children 2 (Movement ABC-2)

Health-Related Fitness Tests

In the field of kinesiology, health-related fitness has become a priority due to the increased risk of chronic illness. This has become an additional concern for those with disabilities due to increased risk from potential limitations as noted in Chapters 6 and 12. There are currently five components often focused on in health-related fitness assessment. **Muscular strength** is expressed as the maximal effort of a muscle or group of muscles when performing an action. **Muscular endurance** relates to the submaximal effort when performing an action repeatedly or when holding the muscles in sustained contraction. **Cardiorespiratory endurance** is the capability of the respiratory and circulatory system to oxygenize muscles when in use. **Body composition** refers to the difference between adipose (fat), and fat free mass. **Flexibility**, an often-overlooked component in health, is the ability to maintain range of motion without placing additional stress on the joints and body.[9]

Examples of Health-Related Fitness Tests
- FitnessGram/ActivityGram
- Brockport Physical Fitness Test (BPFT)

Perception and Cognition Tests

The ability to receive feedback and make sense of incoming sensory information is essential to motor movement and skill performance. It allows for the understanding of the environment and the individual's body in the environment for the initial movement, but also how to make corrections as the skill continues. **Perception** is how we receive, organize, and interpret the sensory-related information from the five senses into an integrated use for our central nervous system. **Cognition** is the higher functioning brain capabilities of memory, motivation, attention selection, and planning aptitude. Perception receives and sorts the sensory information while cognition determines how to react to it. This then allows us to focus certain components of motor skills, like our ability to concentrate or the ability to recall information and how fast we can do either. Oftentimes, intelligence tests are measuring these various components as well. A small selection of examples are provided here; however, assessment in this area has flourished due to concerns over early-onset dementia, concussions and the effects of post-traumatic stress disorder (PTSD).[8]

Examples of Perception and Cognition Tests
- Wechsler Adult Intelligence Scale 4 (WAIS-IV)
- Trail Making Test (TMT)
- Sport Concussion Assessment Tool 5 (SCAT5)

REFERENCES

1. Crocker, L., & Algina, J. (2008). *Introduction to classical & modern test theory.* Cengage Learning.
2. Morrow, J., Jackson, A., Disch, J., & Mood, D. (2011). *Measurement and evaluation in human performance* (4th ed.). Human Kinetics.
3. Allen, M., & Yen, W. (2002). *Introduction to measurement.* Waveland Press, Inc.
4. Schmidt, R., & Lee, T. (2011). *Motor control and learning* (5th ed.). Human Kinetics.
5. Winnick, J., & Porretta, D. (2017). *Adapted physical education and sport* (6th ed.) Human Kinetics.
6. Hodge, S., Lieberman, L., & Murata, N. (2012). *Essentials of teaching adapted physical education.* Holcomb Hathaway Publishing Inc.
7. SHAPE America. (2015). *The essential components of physical education guidance document.* https://www.shapeamerica.org/upload/TheEssentialComponentsOfPhysicalEducation.pdf.
8. Horvat, M., Kelly, L., Block, M., & Croce, R. (2019). *Development and adapted physical activity assessment* (2nd ed.). Human Kinetics.
9. Hoffman, J. (2006). *Norms for fitness, performance, and health.* Human Kinetics.

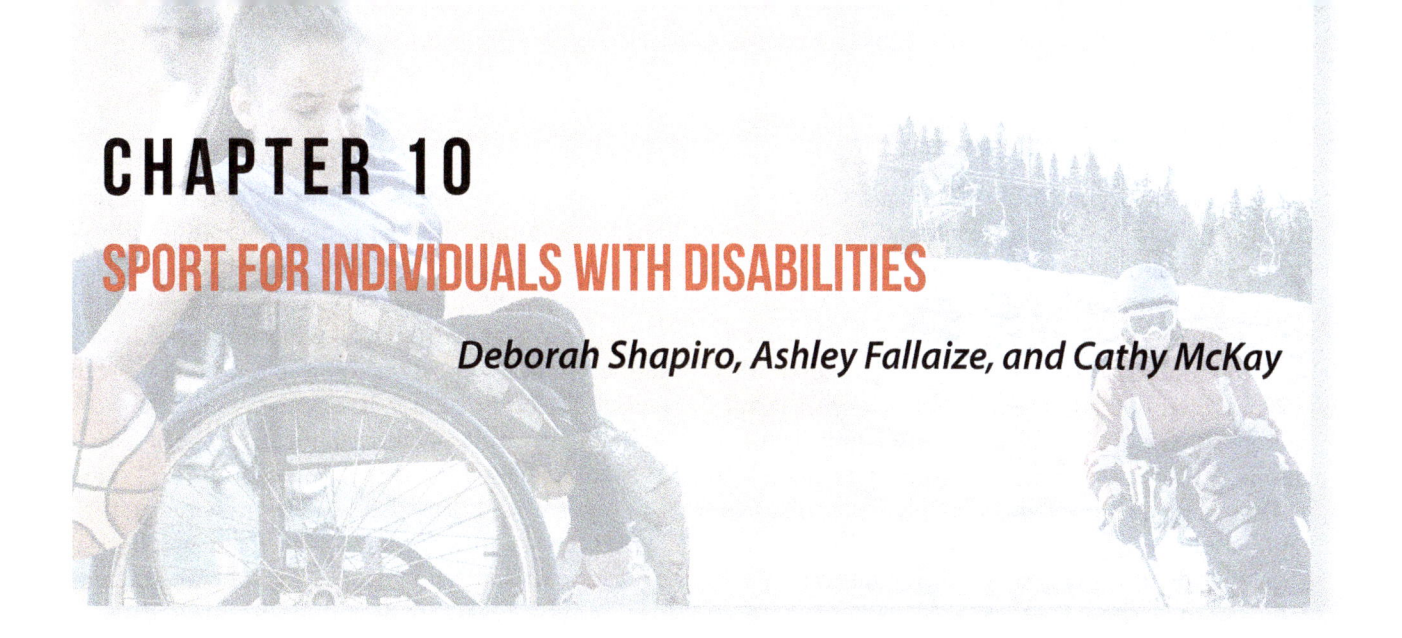

CHAPTER 10
SPORT FOR INDIVIDUALS WITH DISABILITIES

Deborah Shapiro, Ashley Fallaize, and Cathy McKay

INTRODUCTION TO DISABILITY AND DISABILITY SPORT

Individuals with disabilities participate in sport at all levels—recreational, competitive club, intramural and interscholastic (high school and college), and elite level. Elite competition includes the Paralympic Games, Pan American and Parapan American Games, Far East and South Pacific Games, Commonwealth Games, Special Olympics World Games, and the Deaflympics. To understand the scope of opportunities in sport for individuals with disabilities, it is important to first understand the language surrounding disability and sport.

As seen in Chapter 2, disability has traditionally been considered through the lens of a medical model as a problem, a defect, or failure of the body structure or mind to function "normally." In this regard, the medical model sets up a dichotomy labeling those without a disability as normal, while those with a disability are perceived to be abnormal.[1] *Disability*, under a medical model, is perceived to reside within an individual requiring medical interventions and/or technological advances to improve the life of the person living with a disability. A more nuanced approach using the *social relational model* considers disability the result of the interaction between the individual (person with an *impairment)*, with impairment defined as the absence of or difference in a person's body structure, body function, or mental functioning (e.g., the loss of a limb, or nerve damage in the eye causing loss of vision), and that individual's contextual barriers that hinder equal opportunity and access to participation in society (i.e., physically inaccessible environments such as lack of curb cuts, inaccessible bathrooms, inaccessible transportation, lack of knowledge of others, and negative attitudes).[2] As a society, disability can be improved upon by challenging and removing structural, political, social, economic, and cultural barriers, and improving attitudes and behaviors that act as barriers to integrating individuals with disabilities in sport and society.[3-6]

Disability is not homogeneous, and should not be considered as dichotomous or in opposition to people without a disability (i.e., able-bodied). Two people with the same impairment (e.g., cerebral palsy), and people with different impairments, are as unique and heterogeneous as people without a disability.[7] People can be born with a congenital disability (e.g., Down syndrome) or acquire their disability at any point in life through trauma (e.g., car accident, war) or disease (e.g., cancer). People can have invisible disabilities (e.g., traumatic brain injury, PTSD, deaf), minor, or more severe disabilities, static/permanent (e.g., amputation or blindness), progressive (e.g., muscular dystrophy), episodic (e.g., epilepsy, asthma), or intermittent disabilities (e.g., multiple sclerosis) that differentially affect functional performance in activities of daily living and in sport. Disability in this chapter reflects those with physical, sensory, or intellectual impairments, and is not inclusive of chronic illness (e.g., cancer, diabetes, heart disease) and should not be confused with disease. Conversely, disease does

Deborah Shapiro, Georgia State University; Ashley Fallaize, BlazeSports America; and Cathy McKay, James Madison University. © Kendall Hunt Publishing Company

not equal disability, as many individuals with disabilities consider themselves to be in good, very good, or excellent health.[5]

Lastly, with regard to disability, we have intentionally used the phrase *people with* or *individuals with* followed by the impairment (e.g., people with a spinal cord injury). This use of *person first* terminology considers the individual first rather than the disability.[8] Words or phrases such as *confined to*, *crippled by*, or *suffers from* are generally not acceptable, and should be avoided when talking, writing, and speaking about disability. Similarly, the term mentally retarded should be replaced with intellectual disability. The choice of words to describe individuals with disabilities can be inclusive and empowering, or can be devaluing, marginalizing, and segregating. Furthermore, language shapes our attitudes and our subsequent behaviors. Person first language should not be considered as politically correct, but instead as a demonstration of respect for individuals with disabilities. The language used to refer to individuals with disabilities ultimately influences attitudes, social policies, laws, and the lives of individuals with and without disabilities.

Sport opportunities for individuals with disabilities tend to be organized around three primary disability groups: individuals who are Deaf, individuals with a physical impairment, and individuals with intellectual disabilities. In some countries, people who are Deaf do not consider deafness a disability and often compete with those without disabilities with minimal to no modifications needed. The focus of this chapter will be on sport for those with physical (inclusive of visual impairment) and intellectual disabilities. The terms *disability sport*, *adapted sport*, *adaptive sport*, and *parasport* are often used interchangeably to refer to sport in which individuals with disabilities participate. Each of these descriptors of sport for individuals with disabilities has its own distinct application.

There are two primary categories of *disability sport*. The first is based off existing able-bodied sport, but with modifications or accommodations to meet the needs of the athletes (e.g., wheelchair basketball, sitting volleyball, aquatics). The second is designed specifically for persons with an impairment (e.g., goalball). Others have defined disability sport inclusive of sport, physical activity, fitness, recreation, or leisure for and including individuals with a disability.[9] Recreational sport organizations tend to use the phrase **adaptive sports**. The word adaptive generally is used to describe behaviors, skills, and functions such as a person's ability to learn, or personal independence. **Adapted Sport** is the preferred terminology when discussing disability sport within a school setting. Adapted sport is consistent with terminology referring to adapted physical education used to describe physical education services for students with a disability outlined in federal legislation such as the Individuals with Disabilities Education Act of 1990.[10] The word adapted refers to modifications (e.g., rules, equipment, facilities) that enable individuals with disabilities to meaningfully participate in physical education or sport. The delivery of sport opportunities for individuals with disabilities are adapted, while the behaviors of individuals are adaptive. Adapted sport can be used to help a participant modify, improve, correct, or enhance age-appropriate adaptive behaviors needed to live independently (such as getting dressed, avoiding dangers, making friends, practicing social skills, and taking personal responsibility).[11] Outside of, and becoming more common in, the United States, **parasport** is used, replacing disability sport, adaptive sport, and adapted sport. Para, meaning parallel, reflects sport by people with physical, visual, and intellectual impairments. Disability sport is also inclusive of Paralympic sport for athletes who compete in the Paralympic Games. Paralympic sports are part of disability sports, but not all disability sports (e.g., rock climbing, kayaking) are Paralympic sports.[12] A para-athlete is a Paralympic athlete only when they compete in the Paralympic games. Throughout this chapter, we will use the term disability sport to refer to recreational and competitive sport for persons with a disability that take place outside of the school setting. We will use the term adapted sport when discussing sport within a K-12 educational context, and parasport when discussing sport specifically for the Paralympic Games.

GROWTH OF THE DISABILITY SPORT MOVEMENT

The disability sport movement, though relatively young, has gained steady momentum in the past 20 years largely due to the increased visibility of sports in the media. The Ching Dynasty in China were some of the first to provide sports and physical activity for individuals with disabilities. Though the importance of physical activity for individuals with disabilities has been noted in early culture, such as the Chinese, there has been a lack of focus specifically on sports for individuals with disabilities. By exploring the history of the disability sport movement, we can better understand the status of disability sport in today's culture, as well as the future direction of the movement. Some of the first coordinated disability sport opportunities arose for Deaf individuals in Germany in 1888, where Sport Clubs for the Deaf were founded in Berlin to connect the Deaf community through playing sports together.[13] As more Sport Clubs for the Deaf were created in different cities over the next 25 years, it became clear that these athletes needed a way to connect to a bigger network of athletes. The Comité International des Sports des Sourds founded the first official disability sporting event in 1924 to connect Deaf athletes, which subsequently became known as the International Silent Games. These first Silent Games joined athletes from nine European nations, and in 1949 the first Winter International Silent Games was founded, which included 33 athletes from five different countries.

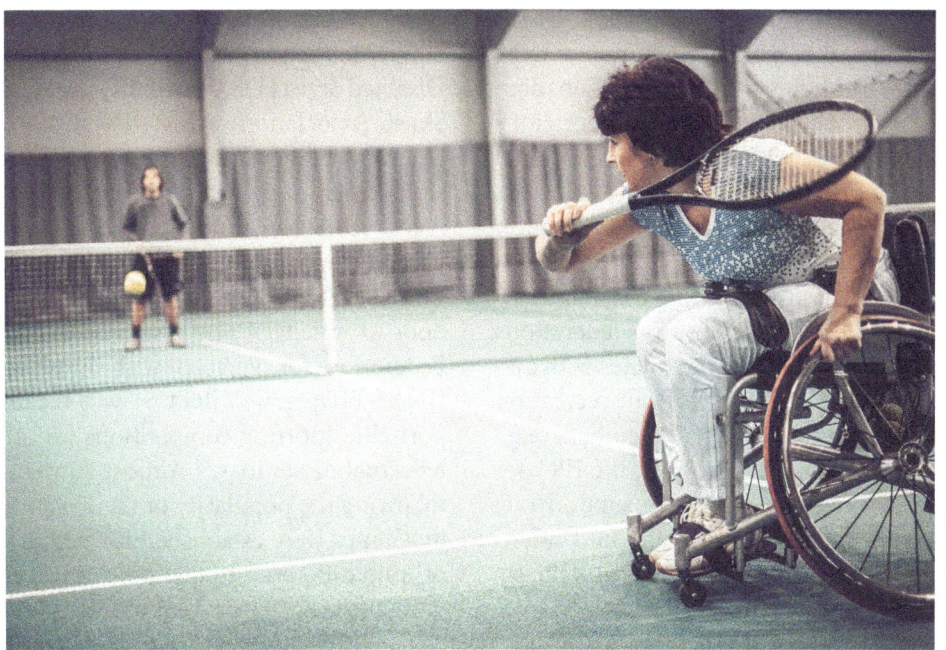

The International Silent Games paved the way for multisport and multiple disability events, and still exists today every four years. After World War II, medical providers encountered a new problem of how to motivate and encourage physical activity for injured servicemen and women to help speed up their rehabilitation. In England, at a hospital called Stoke Mandeville, a neurologist by the name of Sir Ludwig Guttmann came up with a solution.[14] After working with veterans with spinal cord injuries, Guttmann introduced the sport of archery in the rehabilitation process to his patients to increase motivation. This activity quickly became highly successful at the hospital, prompting Guttmann to create the Stoke Mandeville Games in 1948 as a way for his patients to officially compete against their peers, with the competition scheduled the same year as the Olympics. In 1952, the games grew as athletes from rehabilitation programs in the Netherlands began to participate. By 1960 the games had grown so large that they became known as the Paralympic Games—para meaning alongside, as they were run right after the Olympics that year. The first games had over 400 athletes representing 23 countries.[14] Over the next 30 years, the Paralympics slowly grew to include different sports, different disabilities, and an increased number of athletes from even more countries. Some notable additions to the Paralympics were:

- 1975: Included athletes with limb amputations and visual impairments
- 1976: First Winter games were held alongside the Olympic Winter Games
- 1980: Included athletes with cerebral palsy

As the games continued to grow, it was clear that the four organizations helping to put the games together needed to merge into one to streamline the process. The International Coordinating Committee Sports for the Disabled in the World was founded in 1982. By 1986, two more organizations (International Committee of Sports for the Deaf, and International Federations for Persons with an Intellectual Disability) also joined the committee as more of their athletes competed in the games in 1986. On September 22, 1989, the International Paralympic Committee (IPC) was founded to replace the four-organization committee, and serve as the governing body of the Paralympics.[14]

Today, the IPC has over 200 members, which consists of National Paralympic Committees (e.g., U.S. Olympic and Paralympic Committee; Canadian Paralympic Committee), 15 International Federations (IF; e.g., archery, boccia, badminton), International Organizations of Sports for the Disabled (IOSD; e.g., Cerebral Palsy International Sports and Recreation Association, International Blind Sports Federation) recognized by the IPC as representing a specific impairment group, and international sports federations that develop sport opportunities for athletes with disabilities at all levels of competition from recreation to elite but are not eligible to be IPC members (e.g., bobsleigh, bowling, golf).[15] Additionally, the IPC defines as its primary responsibilities "to support our 200 plus members develop Para sport and advocate social inclusion, ensure the successful delivery and organization of the Paralympic Games, and act as the international federation for 10 Para sports."[15] On a national level, each nation has its own National Paralympic Committee that controls selection of and training for athletes, coach education, eligibility, rules, and more. International Federations control the rules and regulations for the sport internationally, such as World Para Alpine Skiing, World Para Powerlifting and World Para Swimming. Lastly, regional organizations are managed across each respective continent, while International Organizations of Sports for the Disabled (like the Cerebral Palsy International Sports and Recreation Association) manage sport and competition for athletes with similar disabilities. While each of these organizations serve a different group of athletes, each plays a crucial role in the current Paralympic Games.

The Paralympic Games are currently held during the summer and winter, immediately following the Olympic Games. To be eligible to compete in the Paralympic Games, an athlete must have one of ten eligible impairments, and that impairment must have a grouping for their sport. Table 10.1, adapted from the classification section of the International Paralympic Committee website,[16] shows which sports are included in the respective summer and winter Paralympic Games, and which disability groups are included in each sport.

The 2016 Rio Paralympic Games saw 4,328 athletes from 160 countries.[17] In contrast, the 2018 winter games held in PyeongChang saw only 567 athletes from just 49 countries.[17] Table 10.2 represents how the Paralympic Games have grown over the last 50+ years.

Along the same time frame that the Paralympic Games were established, other large disability sport organizations were being formed around the world. Similar to the purpose of the Stoke Mandeville games, Disabled Sports USA (formerly the National Amputee Skiers Association) was started in 1967 in the United States by military veterans to help rehabilitate injured servicemen and women returning from Vietnam.[18] A few years later in 1970, the National Center for the Disabled was established from its early origins as a ski school for children with amputations to have outdoor experiences.[19] In 1986, the International Sports Federation for Persons with Intellectual Disability (INAS-FID; now VIRTUS) was established to support elite sporting competitions for athletes with intellectual disabilities.[20] Almost 20 years later in 2006, following the popularity of the X-games, the Extremity Games were established for people with limb loss or limb difference to compete in extreme sports.[21] In 2010, the U.S. Department of Defense Warrior Games were held for the first time. The Warrior Games provide competitive sporting events for wounded, ill, and injured active duty and veteran U.S. military service members.[22] The Invictus Games were subsequently founded in 2013, offering international competition for wounded, ill, and injured service personnel.[23]

While the wide range of organizations introduced thus far in this chapter serve a large population of individuals with physical disabilities, the Special Olympics program (which began around the birth of the Paralympics), serves more individuals with intellectual disabilities nationally and internationally than the other organizations combined. Eunice Kennedy Shriver began what has evolved into the Special Olympics in 1962 by opening a summer camp for individuals with intellectual disabilities.[24] In 1964 the staff, after watching the Paralympic Games, decided to hold their own Special Olympics Summer Games July 20th, 1968 in Chicago. These first Games had over 200 events offered in which athletes with intellectual disabilities could compete. Following the success of these early Games, Special Olympics, Inc. was officially started. Almost 25 years later, following the success of the United States Special Olympics sporting competition for athletes with intellectual disabilities, Special Olympics hosted the first International Special Olympic Games in Louisiana in 1983.[24] Today, Special Olympics serves athletes with developmental disabilities from ages 2-99 by providing 32 individual Olympic style and team sports; programs in health, education, and community building; high quality training; and competition in an inclusive culture through unified sports and the world games every year.

TABLE 10.1 Paralympic sport by impairment group

Sport	Game	Impairment Group Included (*)
Archery	Summer	IMP, A, IPR, H, LD, and A.
Athletics	Summer	All
Badminton	Summer	IMP, A, APR, H, LD, A, LLD, and SS.
Boccia	Summer	IMP, A, IPR, H, LD, and A.
Canoe	Summer	IMP, IPR, and LD.
Cycling	Summer	IMP, A, IPR, H, LD, A, LLD, and VI.
Equestrian	Summer	IMP, A, IPR, H, LD, A, LLD, SS, and Vi.
Football 5-a-side	Summer	VI
Goalball	Summer	VI
Judo	Summer	VI
Powerlifting	Summer	IMP, IPR, LD, LLD, SS, H, A, and AT.
Rowing	Summer	IMP, A, IPR, H, LD, A, and VI.
Shooting Para Sport	Summer	IMP, LD, H, A, AT, and IPR.
Sitting Volleyball	Summer	IMP, A, IPR, H, LD, A, and LLD.
Swimming	Summer	All
Table Tennis	Summer	IMP, AT, IPR, H, LD, A, LLD, SS, and ID.
Taekwondo	Summer	IMP, AT, H, LD, and A.
Triathlon	Summer	IMP, AT, IPR, H, LD, A, and VI.
Wheelchair Basketball	Summer	IMP, AT, IPR, H, LID, A, and LLD.
Wheelchair Fencing	Summer	IMP, AT, IPR, H, LD, A, and LLD.
Wheelchair Rugby	Summer	IMP, AT, IPR, H, LD, and A.
Wheelchair Tennis	Summer	IMP, AT, IPR< H, LD, A, and LLD.
Alpine Skiing	Winter	IMP, LD, H, A, AT, LLD, and VI.
Biathlon	Winter	IMP, LD, H, A, AT, LLD, and VI.
Cross-country skiing	Winter	IMP, LD, H, A, AT, LLD, and VI.
Para Ice Hockey	Winter	IMP, LD, LLD, H, A, AT, and IPR.
Snowboard	Winter	IMP, LD, LLD, H, A, AT, and IPR.
Wheelchair Curling	Winter	IMP, IPR, H, LD, and A.

Note. Adapted from the International Paralympic Committee.[17] Impaired Muscle Power (IMP), Impaired Passive Range of Movement (IPR), Limb Deficiency (LD), Leg Length Difference (LLD), Short Stature (SS), Hypertonia (H), Ataxia (A), Athetosis (AT), Vision Impairment (VI), and Intellectual Impairment (II).

TABLE 10.2 Growth of the paralympic games

Game (season, year, and location)	Athletes (total, women, and men)	# Countries	# Sports	Viewership	Opening Ceremonies Spectatorship
Rome 1960 (Summer)	400+ athletes	23	8		5,000
Tokyo 1964 (Summer)	378	21	9	1st media exposure, 700 media onsite	5,000
Tel Aviv 1968 (Summer)	750	29	10		10,000
Heidelberg 1972 (Summer)	984	43	10		
Ornskoldsvik 1976 (Winter)	198 (161 men and 27 women)	16	2		
Toronto 1976 (Summer)	1,657	40	13	600,000 viewers	24,000
Geilo 1980 (Winter)	299 (229 men and 70 women)	18	4		
Arnhem 1980 (Summer)	1,973	43	13		12,000
Innsbruck 1984 (Winter)	419 (325 men and 94 women)	21	3		
Seoul 1988 (Summer)	3,041 (2,370 men and 671 women)	60	18	2,368 media personnel on grounds	75,000
Tignes-Albertville 1992 (Winter)	365 (228 men and 77 women)	24	3		
Barcelona 1992 (Summer)	2,999 (2,300 men and 699 women)		16	Daily live domestic coverage (millions watched live opening ceremonies on TV)	65,000 (1.5 million attendance)
Lillehammer 1994 (Winter)	469 (379 men and 90 women)	31	5		
Atlanta 1996 (Summer)	3,808 (2,643 men and 1,165 women)	104	19	Paralympics televised in USA: 4 hours of weekend coverage on CBS and 1 hour highlights show. Website: 120,000 hits per day.	388,373
Nagano 1998 (Winter)	562 (440 men and 122 women)	31	5	1,468 media representatives, 7.7 million hits on website	151,376
Sydney 2000 (Summer)	3,879 (2,889 men and 990 women)	123	19	2,300 media personnel, 100 hours of Paralympic sport webcast to 103 countries, website got 300 million hits	1.2 million for all games
Salt Lake City 2002 (Winter)	415 (328 men and 87 women)	36	4	836 media onsite	248,000
Athens 2004 (Summer)	3,808 (2,643 men and 1,165 women)	135	19	1.85 billion watched on TV. 3,103 media onsite. 617 hours were broadcast in 25 countries.	850,000

Torino 2006 (Winter)	474 (375 men and 99 women)	38	5	1,037 media reps, Paralympic Sport TV 40,000 watched from 105 nations.	165,974
Beijing 2008 (Summer)	3,95 (2,568 men and 1,383 women)	146	20	3.8 billion watched	1.82 million tickets
Vancouver 2010 (Winter)	502 (381 men and 121 women)	44	5	1.6 billion 1,200 media reps	230,000
London 2012 (Summer)	4,327 (2,736 men and 1,501 women)	164	20	3.8 billion	2.7 million
Sochi 2014 (Winter)	541 (412 men and 129 women)	45	5	2.1 billion	316,200 tickets
Rio 2016 (Summer)	4,328 (2,657 men and 1,671 women)	159	22	Live coverage from 13 sports.	2.15 million
PyeongChang 2018 (Winter)	563 (430 men and 133 women)	49	7		

Note. Adapted from the International Paralympic Committee.[17]

DISABILITY SPORT PIPELINE

Federal civil rights-based discrimination legislation has guided the development and expansion of opportunities for sport participation for individuals with disabilities within the United States. There are three federal legislations that have guided the access and opportunity for disability sport and adapted sport, the (a) Rehabilitation Act of 1973 Section 504, (b) IDEA, and (c) Americans with Disabilities Act of 1990 (ADA).[10,25,26] Individually and collectively, these laws recognize the inequality and rights of individuals with disabilities to full and equal access to mainstream society including education and sport as a basic human right. Each of these laws will be addressed as they inform sport programming within the community, schools, and Paralympic Games.

A sport continuum framework was developed to provide a variety of options to meet the legal requirements outlined in Section 504, the ADA, and IDEA to provide sport opportunities for individuals with disabilities in the least restrictive (most integrated) setting possible (see figure 10.1).[27] This

Community sporting events.

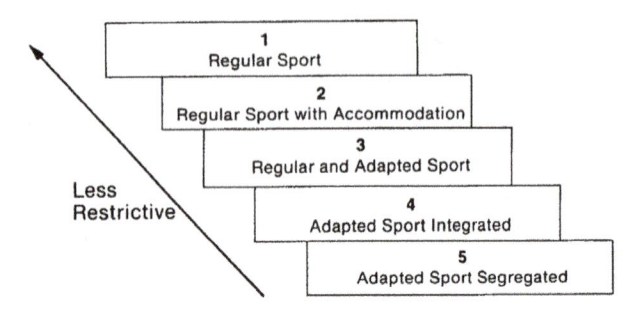

FIGURE 10.1 Sport integration continuum.

Source: Reprinted with permission, from Joseph P. Winnick, 1987, An Integration Continuum for Sport Participation, Adapted Physical Activity Quarterly, vol. 4, issue 3, and pp. 157-161, https://doi.org/10.1123/apaq.4.3.157

continuum of placements initially designed for the school setting, equally applies to community recreation programming as well as the Paralympic Games. We will review how the different levels of the sport continuum have been applied throughout the disability sport pipeline beginning with grass roots community infrastructure through to the Paralympic Games.

Community Disability Sport

Community disability sport organizations are impacted by Section 504 and the ADA. Both Section 504 and Titles II and III of the ADA prohibit discrimination and exclusion of persons with disabilities from participation in or benefits of services, programs, and activities based on disability, and extends to public and private entities (e.g., a state rehabilitation agency, a state university, or community college is public; a nonprofit organization or independently owned business is private), who operate a place of public accommodation.[28] Community programs for individuals with disabilities can be recreational or competitive. At the recreational level, individuals of all ages participate without the commitment often required of a competitive sport. Individuals with disabilities can join a recreational wheelchair tennis team (United States Tennis Association), a beep baseball league (National Beep Baseball Association), participate in rock climbing with friends and/or family without a disability, or participate in Special Olympics recreation and Unified Sport. For example, wheelchair tennis can serve the athletic needs of an individual with a disability at level 5 of the sport continuum, where only athletes with disabilities participate and play against one another using wheelchairs. Wheelchair tennis also can serve the needs of individuals with disabilities at level 3 with doubles tennis where one partner is able-bodied and the other a wheelchair user. The rules are modified to allow the seated player up to two bounces (adapted sport) before returning the ball while the standing player is allowed a single bounce (regular sport).[27] Similarly, beep baseball provides participation opportunities at level 3 as players with sight participate on the team as the pitcher and field spotter, alongside athletes with a visual impairment who are blindfolded for sport participation. Special Olympics Unified Sports also serves individuals with and without an intellectual disability at level 3 in the sport continuum framework, where partners without a disability participate together on a single-day exposure event or across a season or semester. These same opportunities also exist within the community at a competitive level where youth and adults with a physical or intellectual disability can train, travel, and compete against other teams (level 5) from around the country at regional and national competitions such as the National Goalball Championships, National Wheelchair Rugby Championships, or Special Olympic state or national championships. For persons with a physical disability, in some cases, this competitive community participation can lead to the development of skills required for eligibility to earn a collegiate athletic scholarship in wheelchair basketball, or wheelchair track, for example.

K-12 Adapted Sport

The American Association of Adapted Sports Programs (AAASP), established in 1996 as a legacy organization after the Atlanta Paralympic Games,[11] advances the objectives of the Dear Colleague Letter: Students with Disabilities in Extracurricular Athletics (2013) by working in partnership with local, state and national education organizations, including the National Federation of State High School Associations and the National Interscholastic Athletic Administrators Association.[29] The AAASP advances interscholastic athletic opportunities for students with physical disabilities, and offers best practices in education-based athletics in standardized seasons in regular and post season competition in the adapted team sports of wheelchair handball, wheelchair basketball, wheelchair football, and wheelchair track and field. AAASP adapted programming is based on district or regional teams rather than a school-based team, to address the potential limited number of eligible students with a physical disability at a given school. The AAASP model is based on teams that are multidisability (i.e., include students with cerebral palsy, spina bifida, amputations), cross age (any student from grades 1-12) and mix male and female students on the same team. To address the differential in skill level and functional abilities of youth with a physical disability, AAASP developed junior varsity and varsity level teams. The school adapted sports teams are integrated into their school district's extracurricular programming, just as traditional school teams are for the able-bodied student population. The school districts provide the needed resources to support their adapted sports teams, just as they do for their other school teams. This includes a school gym for practices and competitions, adapted sports coaches and a program coordinator plus stipends, uniforms, equipment, and transportation. The AAASP program model brings local opportunity to the school level for students with physical disabilities, the same way disability sports organizations do at the national level (i.e., the National Wheelchair Basketball Association). AAASP has developed inclusive adapted sport policies for participating schools to follow to ensure safe, fair, and equitable statewide competition among the school adapted sports teams. For school districts just starting to develop adapted sport, level 4 could be permitted allowing students without a disability to participate in a wheelchair to ensure enough players to fill a team. The participating school teams of AAASP engage in regular sport (level 1), in that practices and competitions take place in integrated settings such as the public schools, and at the same time and in the same venues for state championships for able-bodied basketball and track and field. Not only are students with a disability participating on their state track and field team (level 1), but their events are also included in team scoring. Similarly for throwing events such as the shotput or discus, a specialized throwing chair provides the accommodation needed (level 2) for a student with a disability to compete meaningfully and safely. Lastly, adapted sport athletes can earn athletic letters just as their peers without a disability. Student athletes who participate in K-12 adapted athletics can be recruited to compete at the collegiate level through NCAA interscholastic sports and potentially advance to a national team for the Paralympic Games.

For students with an intellectual disability, K-12 schools provide opportunities to play on sports teams with students without disabilities as long as the student with an intellectual disability has the requisite skills and does not require modifications that fundamentally alter the sport or adapted sport through partnership with Special Olympics. Special Olympics offers level 5 programming through adapted physical education teachers who often use Special Olympics sport coaching guides in the design and implementation of training programs to prepare students with an intellectual disability for competition against other athletes with an intellectual disability at county, state, national, and Special Olympics World Games competitions.[30] General and adapted physical education programs also offer Special Olympics Unified Sport programs at level 3 on the continuum where approximately equal numbers of athletes with intellectual disabilities and peers without a disability compete together on the same team against other unified teams. Special Olympics Unified Sports include badminton, basketball, bocce, bowling, football, golf, open water swimming, sailing, table tennis, tennis, and volleyball.[30] Unified teams are composed of people of similar age and ability and promote social inclusion through an experience of sport training and competition together. Like the segregated Special Olympics teams, unified sport teams compete at county, state, national, and World Games. Approximately 4,500 K-12 schools also have the designation of a Special Olympics Unified Champion school recognizing their commitment and dedication to Unified Sports.[30]

Collegiate Adapted and Disability Sport

Colleges, like K-12 schools, are required under Section 504 of the Rehabilitation Act and the ADA to offer accessible disability sport for college students with a disability.[25,26] Collegiate programs offer opportunities for college students with a disability to engage in sport through intramural, club sports, and NCAA interscholastic competition. Currently to our knowledge, 29 colleges and universities across the United States offer adapted or disability sport programs at the recreational, club, and interscholastic NCAA levels (see Table 10.3).[31-34]

Colleges and universities are also partnering with Special Olympics for the designation of a Unified Champion school. Over 200 colleges and universities have student-run Special Olympics clubs on campus whose mission is to engage students with an intellectual disability in leadership and provide inclusive sport programming for college students with and without intellectual disabilities. College students without intellectual disabilities participate in Unified Sports and host Special Olympics events on campus and in the community. Many colleges and universities are also offering Special Olympics Unified Sports as intramural leagues. Lastly, NCAA Division III and National Association of Intercollegiate Athletics (NAIA) collegiate student athletes without a disability engage in service-learning opportunities with Special Olympics athletes at existing Special Olympics events on campus and in the community.[30]

Collegiate athletics serve a critical role in the success of the U.S. Olympic and Paralympic teams. Colleges across the United States provide resources for training and competition for student athletes to achieve athletic and academic excellence. The U.S. Olympic and Paralympic Committee (USOPC) established a collegiate partnerships division to enhance the relationship with the NCAA to build and strengthen Olympic and Paralympic sport opportunities for collegiate athletes and facilitate opportunities for student athletes on national Olympic and Paralympic teams.[35] We did our best to identify the level at which various adapted and disability sports were offered in universities in the United States (refer to Table 10.3).[31-34] Many programs do not specify the team/program type of disability sport programming (i.e., intercollegiate, club, or intramural/campus recreation). Apparent in the list is the popularity of wheelchair basketball at both the interscholastic and intramural levels as well as the frequency of schools offering a wide range of adapted intramural, outdoor recreation, and fitness/gym accommodations for students with and without disabilities.

Paralympic Games

Within the United States, the Ted Stevens Olympic and Amateur Sports Act (1998) paved the way for the Olympics and Paralympics to be governed by the same national governing body, the USOPC.[36] The USOPC is responsible for coordinating athletic activity related to international competition including the sports of the Olympic, Paralympic, Pan American, and Parapan American Games. The USOPC is also responsible for promoting and supporting physical fitness and public participation in sports by encouraging developmental programs at the community level. In 2016, the USOPC established partnerships with collegiate sports across the United States to strengthen collegiate contributions to the development of athletes for the Olympic and Paralympic teams.[35] The Olympic and Paralympic Games serve athletes at both level 5 and level 1 in the sport continuum. The Paralympic Games (level 5) are solely for athletes with a disability who qualify for participation based on level of impairment and skill performance. The Olympics serves athletes with a disability at level 1, as, for example, athletes with limb differences have competed in track events and in table tennis in the Olympic Games; athletes who are deaf have competed in volleyball, fencing, and diving in the Olympic Games; and athletes with visual impairments have competed in track and field and archery in the Olympic Games.[37]

CLASSIFICATION

Disability sports present unique challenges that are different from able-bodied sports. In many able-bodied sports, athletes are paired against individuals who have a similar time, same sex, age, or distance. There are some exceptions in sports where classes are used to further classify, such as weightlifting. In parasport, however, one sport can see athletes with multiple levels of abilities. For example, track and field can see athletes with amputations, spinal cord injuries, visual impairments, and other physical disabilities. In many cases, if these athletes were all to compete together, those athletes with less severe mobility impairments would always score higher than counterparts with more severe mobility impairments. One way to level the playing field in disability sport is the process of classification. **Classification**, very simply put, looks at how an athlete moves in daily life and then how they compete in sport to determine which "sport class" would be the most similar for their abilities. Through classification, athletes can be paired against other athletes with abilities similar to their own to enjoy the highest level of competition. Historically, classification first started at the Stoke Mandeville Games after athletes raised the question of whether individuals with higher-level spinal cord injuries (e.g., cervical or upper thoracic levels) should be paired to compete against individuals with lower-level injuries (lower thoracic and lumbar levels).[14]

Classification in disability sport is not a perfect process. It is important to understand the process of classification, the role of classification in disability sports, and what classification looks like for different organizations to analyze the pitfalls and controversies classification can create. There are two philosophical approaches that underly sport classification for individuals with disabilities. In the first approach,

TABLE 10.3 List of colleges/universities with adapted sport programming for students with physical disabilities

School	NCAA	Club Sport	Intramural/Recreational Sport Programming
Arizona State University	Wheelchair basketball (men and women), wheelchair tennis, quad rugby, track and road racing, handcycling, golf		
Auburn University	Wheelchair basketball		Wheelchair tennis, accessible strength and cardio machines, hand cycles
Ball State University		Power soccer	wheelchair basketball
City University of New York	Wheelchair basketball (men and women)		
Edinboro University	Wheelchair basketball (men and women)		Swimming, bowling, exercise programs, snow tubing, target shooting
Grand Valley State University			Wheelchair basketball, wheelchair tennis
Indiana State University-Purdue University Fort Wayne		Wheelchair basketball	Sitting volleyball, rowing, curling
Michigan State University		Boccia, wheelchair slalom, track and field, hand cycling, table tennis	Adapted fitness centers, swimming, goalball, wheelchair tennis, wheelchair basketball, wheelchair floor hockey
Ohio State University			Aquatics, fitness classes, canoeing/kayaking/hiking/backpacking, indoor climbing, personal training
Oregon State University		wheelchair basketball	Wheelchair basketball, track and field, powerlifting, swimming
Penn State University			Wheelchair basketball, adapted soccer, sled hockey, seated volleyball, run, walk and roll races, Wounded Warrior events
Portland State University		Wheelchair basketball	Ski trips, 3v3 wheelchair basketball tournaments, adaptive climbing, swim, goalball and an adapted gym, Fresh Fridays to introduce new inclusive sports or activities
San Diego State University			Adaptive ambulatory track events and wheelchair tennis.
Southern Illinois University			Wheelchair basketball
Southwest Minnesota State	Wheelchair basketball		

(continued)

TABLE 10.3 List of colleges/universities with adapted sport programming for students with physical disabilities *(continued)*

School	NCAA	Club Sport	Intramural/Recreational Sport Programming
Texas A&M			Wheelchair basketball, wheelchair football, wheelchair soccer, beep baseball, sitting volleyball, cross fit
UCLA			Wheelchair basketball, adaptive cycling, adaptive tennis, warm water activities
University of Alabama	Wheelchair basketball (men and women), wheelchair tennis quad rugby, track, road racing, hand cycling		Wheelchair basketball, adapted golf, adapted rowing
University of Arizona	Wheelchair basketball (men and women), quad rugby, tennis, track, and road racing and handcycling		
University of Central Florida			Wheelchair basketball, goalball, swim lessons, student assisted workout program, adaptive rock climbing
University of Central Oklahoma			Military sports program introducing injured soldiers to Paralympic sports, Endeavor Games
University of Nebraska—Omaha	Wheelchair basketball (men)		
University of Florida	Wheelchair basketball		
University of Illinois at Urbana Champaign	Wheelchair basketball (men and women), wheelchair track (men and women)		
University of Missouri	Wheelchair basketball		
University of New Hampshire-Northeast Passage		Sled hockey, quad rugby, power soccer	Archery, court sports, Paralympic boccia, cycling, golf, hiking, Nordic skiing, paddling, water skiing, shooting sports
University of Oregon		Adaptive track team	Adaptive sports club
University of Texas at Arlington	Wheelchair basketball (men and women), wheelchair tennis, cycling, table tennis		Fitness, track and field, swimming, table tennis, boccia
University of Wisconsin at Whitewater	Wheelchair basketball (men and women)		Wheelchair basketball and football, adapted weight room, handcycles
Wright State University			Adapted aquatics, football, soccer, basketball, baseball, kayaking, skiing, climbing, workout buddy

Note. Challenged Athletes Foundation, GRIT: Collegiate Adaptive Sports guide, ACSAA: American Collegiate Society of Adapted Athletics, and National Wheelchair Basketball Association.[32-35]

classification represents the process of integration. All athletes at the top of their physical game, under the same classification system can participate competitively against their peers. This approach does not exclude any athletes. On the flip side, the process of classification could be viewed as segregation, as only athletes with certain disabilities are able to be included in the sport. For example, you must have a qualifying disability and qualifying level of disability to compete in the Paralympics, and since this is not open for everyone, it could be viewed as segregation. By understanding these two philosophical approaches, we are better able to understand the inner workings of the classification process.

To understand classification, we will first look at one of the most prominent examples of classification, the IPC.[16] All Paralympic athletes must undergo classification to compete for their country and on the national circuit. Classification is conducted by a team known as the classification panel. The classification panel normally consists of one medical professional, a physical therapist, and a sport-specific professional who are all trained and certified in classification for a given sport (e.g., boccia, track and field). Classification typically takes one hour per athlete and can be completed at certain sanctioned parasport events. During classification, the athlete is watched to see how they physically compete in the sport, and how they move in activities of daily living. From there, a team of classifiers finalizes and assigns a sport class to the athlete that they will compete in for that sport. It is important to note that sport class can change per event, or even per sport, for athletes. In classification, there are cases where an athlete may consider themselves to be underclassified. This means that they believe the classifiers classified them too high and would place them at a disadvantage in competition. For example, an athlete who has a single leg amputation might be competing against other athletes with minor gait impairment, which would in many cases make the athletes with an amputation less likely to place in competition. In this case, athletes can file a formal appeal to reevaluate their classification. As a lot is at stake in classification, and no two people are physiologically alike, the classification process can be controversial. It is the responsibility of the athlete and coach to understand the classification system as equipment, and support levels (different adapted equipment, use of physical assistance for sport competition) can vary from sport class to sport class based on one's classification. Coaches must identify in early training what sport class an athlete would fall into to better coach them with that level of equipment. For example, in swimming, lower classifications are allowed to perform nontraditional starts on the blocks depending on physical ability.

Classification allows athletes to be the most competitive and ensures that athletes meet the minimum qualifications for participating in a particular sport. Ultimately the classification process for the IPC[16] asks three questions.

1. Does the athlete have an eligible impairment for this sport?
2. Does the athlete's eligible impairment meet the minimum impairment criteria of the sport?
3. Which sport class should the athlete be allocated in based on the extent to which the athlete is able to execute the specific tasks and activities fundamental to the sport?

Question 1 asks if the athletes have an eligible impairment for the sport. There are 10 eligible impairment types recognized by the IPC (see Table 10.4). An athlete must have one of the 10 eligible impairment types to compete. The second question deals with the athlete meeting the minimum criteria for the sport. The Minimum Impairment Criteria "must ensure that an athlete's Eligible Impairment affects the extent to which the athlete is able to execute the specific tasks and activities fundamental to the sport."[16] A good example of this would be goalball. All athletes must meet a Minimum Impairment Criteria of a certain level of vision to be eligible to play. After answering the first two questions, the third question assigns the athlete their sport class. As mentioned before, a sport class is the level at which the athlete competes against others in sport. Some sports have many sport classes (track and field) while others only have one or two (archery).

While the IPC has the most well-known classification system, the IPC system is one of many. Different disability sport groups operate under their own classification systems. For example, Special Olympics has minimum eligibility criteria, and then separates athletes by age, sex, and ability.[38] While other disability sport competitions, like the Dwarf Games, have five different classification levels based on age and specific diagnosis.[39] Other organizations like VIRTUS, which governs para-athletes with an intellectual disability, have different classification levels based simply on diagnosis.[40] School based K-12 adapted sport, as well as recreational and community-based sports seem to follow less rigorous classifications

TABLE 10.4 Eligible impairment types in the paralympic movement

Impairment Type	Description
Impaired Muscle Power	Athletes with Impaired Muscle Power have a health condition that either reduces or eliminates their ability to voluntarily contract their muscles in order to move or to generate force.
Impaired Passive Range of Movement	Athletes with Impaired Passive Range of Movement have a restriction or a lack of passive movement in one or more joints.
Limb Deficiency	Athletes with Limb Deficiency have total or partial absence of bones or joints as a consequence of trauma (e.g., traumatic amputation), illness (e.g., amputation due to bone cancer) or congenital limb deficiency (e.g., dysmelia).
Limb Length Difference	Athletes with Leg Length Difference have a difference in the length of their legs as a result of a disturbance of limb growth, or as a result of trauma.
Short Stature	Athletes with Short Stature have a reduced length in the bones of the upper limbs, lower limbs and/or trunk.
Hypertonia	Athletes with Hypertonia have an increase in muscle tension and a reduced ability of a muscle to stretch caused by damage to the central nervous system.
Ataxia	Athletes with Ataxia have uncoordinated movements caused by damage to the central nervous system.
Athetosis	Athletes with Athetosis have continual slow involuntary movements.
Vision Impairment	Athletes with Vision Impairment have reduced, or no vision caused by damage to the eye structure, optical nerves or optical pathways, or visual cortex of the brain.
Intellectual Impairment	Athletes with an Intellectual Impairment have a restriction in intellectual functioning and adaptive behavior in which affects conceptual, social, and practical adaptive skills required for everyday life. This Impairment must be present before the age of 18.

Note. Adapted from the International Paralympic Committee.[17]

to increase availability of disability sport and allow more athletes to compete. In recent years, there has been talk about switching back to a diagnosis specific classification system that many national governing bodies used before joining with the IPC (such as a classification for all individuals with cerebral palsy). Only time will tell if this movement is adopted. This method of classification may ultimately eliminate some pitfalls in classification, but could also inevitably create new ones.

CHALLENGES TO SPORT PARTICIPATION

The health benefits from participation in sport and physical activity for individuals with disabilities are clearly identified in the research literature and include, but are not limited to, decreased risk of obesity, diabetes, and cardiovascular disease; improvement in health related physical fitness such as strength, flexibility, and cardiovascular endurance; improvements in self-concept, athletic identity and enhanced social relationships; and functional independence for activities of daily living. Yet only 3-7% of individuals with disabilities participate in sport.[7] In addition to lower levels of participation, individuals with disabilities tend to withdraw from sport or physical activity at a higher rate than individuals without disabilities.[41] Scarneo and colleagues share a socioecological model (refer to Figure 10.2) that provides an ideal lens to understand factors influencing disability sport participation of individuals with disabilities across the life span.[42] The socioecological model has multiple levels of factors influencing sport and physical activity participation behaviors including intrapersonal, interpersonal, organizational, environmental, and public policy.[42,43] The levels of the model are interdependent and bidirectional, influencing one another. We will discuss challenges and barriers to participation within these different levels. Understanding these factors is only the first step, as they need to be used as a basis for selecting, designing, and implementing programs and strategies to actively engage individuals with disabilities in sport and physical activity.

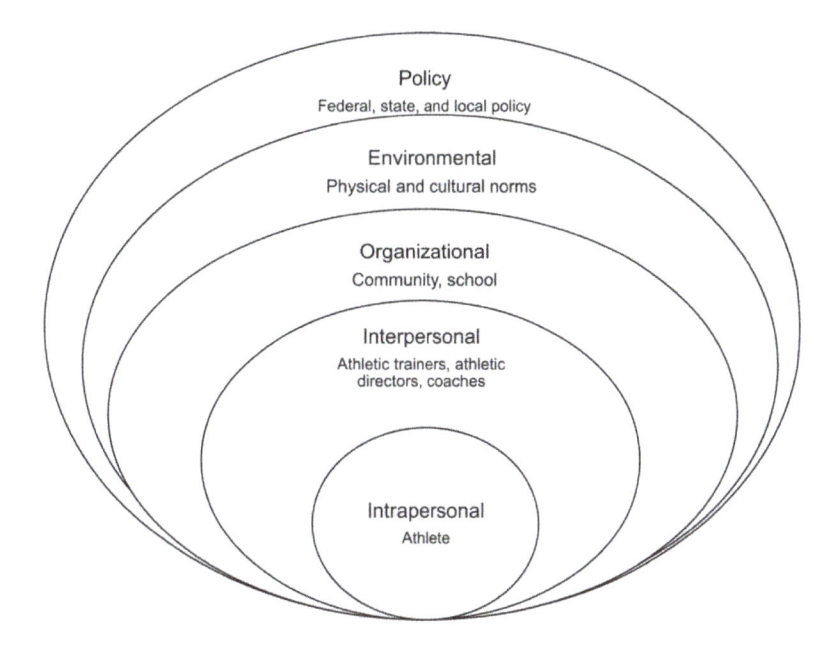

FIGURE 10.2 Levels of socioecological framework.

Source: From *Journal of Athletic Training*, VOL. 54, NO. 4 by Scarneo et al. Copyright © 2019 by Journal of Athletic Training. Reprinted by permission.

Note. Adapted from Scarneo and colleagues.[42]

Intrapersonal Level

Intrapersonal factors are internal to the individual and can be divided between physical and cognitive/psychological characteristics. Disability is a physical barrier to participation for some children and adults. For example, an individual with cerebral palsy may require assistance to work out in a fitness facility. Similarly, a cyclist who is blind would need the help of a sighted pilot to train. Along with the type of disability, severity or level of disability (e.g., paraplegia versus tetraplegia) also acts as a limitation to participation in sport. People with more severe disabilities tend to be less active than people with less severe disabilities. Other physical characteristics acting as barriers to sport participation are impairment related pain, fatigue, energy, and strength. Children and adults with more severe impairments cited these as barriers to sport participation more so than persons with less severe or lower-level spinal cord injuries.[7,41] A third physical factor that has been found to influence activity participation is the wheelchair itself. While the wheelchair provides a means through which individuals with physical disabilities can engage in all activities of daily living, inclusive of sport, individuals with physical disabilities indicate that the weight of many wheelchairs, the lack of sport-specific chairs or the cost of lighter-weight sport chairs, and poor wheelchair fit to the individual are all barriers to participation in sport and physical activity.[7] The challenge of using the wheelchair in the physical environment and the increased pain or fatigue to navigate an environment that lacks accessibility prior to actual sport participation further limit engagement in sport.

Psychological variables include fear, knowledge and skill, motivation and self-perception, and affect/mood/emotion. Fear as a barrier to participation may include that which is associated with the development of tight muscles or joints or of falling. For children, fear of getting hurt was not a significant barrier to participation; however, this is a concern of parents for their child who has a disability illustrating the overlap of the intrapersonal with the interpersonal level as a barrier to participation. Knowledge as a barrier relates to knowing how to find places in which to participate, how to exercise, or the skills needed to play the sports and understand the rules, tactics, and strategy of a sport. One's goal orientation (task/mastery versus performance/ego), feelings of relatedness or connection with others, and perception of competence can influence motivation for sport participation. Individuals with a disability who are task oriented, focused on self-improvement and skill mastery, who feel connected to teammates and peers, and have positive self-concept tend to experience greater enjoyment and intentions to initiate or maintain sport involvement than persons who are performance oriented (i.e., focused on outperforming others and winning) and/or who have lower perceptions of relatedness and physical competence. It is important to consider the personal goals and emotional needs of individual with disabilities to increase likelihood of sport participation. Lastly, related to the psychological intraindividual characteristics, negative mood, depression, anxiety, and embarrassment have been cited as barriers to sport participation.[41]

Individuals with disabilities who experience more intrapersonal barriers tend to have more difficulty overcoming interpersonal, organizational, and environmental barriers than those who experience fewer individual barriers.[7] This is due, in part, to the position of intrapersonal barriers within the model. Intrapersonal factors can be influenced by all other levels within the framework. To increase sport participation, education, intervention, and programming should focus on addressing the individual's knowledge, attitudes, skills, motivations, beliefs, or intentions to engage in sport and may involve strategies to address the role of one's social networks at the interpersonal and organizational levels.[7]

Interpersonal Level

Interpersonal factors have been grouped into three themes: social support, attitudes of others, and social processes (i.e., having a role model).[41] Social support considers formal and informal social networks and relationships with significant others in the individual's life (i.e., teachers, coaches, parents, siblings, peers) that exert influence over participation in sport. Some individuals with disabilities may have the intrapersonal characteristics (e.g., knowledge, motivation, competence, and affect) needed to participate in sport but cannot participate without the physical aide of a personal assistant (e.g., a parent, spouse, or sibling). Dependence on others may be a barrier to participation. Conversely, parents or caregivers who provide sufficient quality of physical support (e.g., transportation, physical assistance) and emotional support facilitate participation in sport for individuals with disabilities.[7] Support from teachers, parents or therapists can impede participation in sport by questioning whether an individual with a disability is capable of participation. In this way, significant others act as a barrier to engaging in sport. Social barriers are often the result of negative attitudes of significant others. Education and contact of teachers and coaches with individuals with disabilities is critical to reducing attitudinal barriers for sport participation generated by individuals without disabilities. Similarly, interventions and programs designed to educate parents of their child's potential and to train parents on how to work with their child with a disability to develop sport related skills have been found to increase the likelihood that children with a visual impairment have the social and emotional support needed to actively participate in sport.[44] Families who are active participants in sport facilitate participation by encouraging and providing opportunities for their child with a disability to be active.

Similarly, friends can be a positive support network to encourage participation and provide opportunities to socialize. Enjoyment and self-competence tend to be high in a peer supportive environment. Conversely, peers, or a lack of friends can act as a barrier to participation in sport for individuals with disabilities. This may be particularly evident in physical education or inclusive sport settings where teasing, bullying, and exclusion of a person with a disability from the team or group due to a perceived lack of skill may be more prevalent, reducing intentions of individuals with disabilities to participate in games and sports with their peers without a disability. Such negative peer attitudes also impact a parent's willingness to support their child's participation for fear of a negative response from their child with a disability to the lack of social support from peers without a disability.[45]

Organizational/Institutional Level

This level considers, for example, the knowledge of people within the organization, the organizational structure, rules, and regulations for operation.

Knowledge of People within the Organization

Staff. People without disabilities are often reluctant to delve into disability sport not because of an unwillingness to do so but because of a lack of knowledge and fear they may do or say the wrong thing. When developing programming for individuals with disabilities, it is important to invite people with disabilities onto the planning committee to understand firsthand the lived experiences and needs of individuals with disabilities and their families. Such insights will ensure that programs are delivered in environments with trained and knowledgeable coaches, in accessible facilities, and that policies for participation are considerate of the health and safety needs of individuals with disabilities. Staff are also encouraged to partner with disability sport organizations and/or universities to acquire the knowledge needed to work with individuals with disabilities.

Coach education. Quality coaching is critical for the development of skills of athletes from the recreation to elite levels. In the mid-1990s approximately 50% of Paralympic athletes reported they coached themselves. Self-coaching is perceived to be a barrier to the growth and development of athletes individually and of disability sport in general. Over the last 10-15 years, however, great strides have been made in coaching training and the coaching career pathway for coaches of athletes with disabilities.[46] The coaching education literature is well developed with regard to training and curriculum needed to support the development of coaches of athletes without disabilities. Coaches of athletes with disabilities need all the same knowledge of the sport and skills of coaches of athletes without disabilities but also have additional needs to understand biomechanical adaptations, equipment adaptations, accessibility issues, promote independence, and provide social support.[47] In fact, most coaches who coach athletes with disabilities are able-bodied, former athletes at the collegiate or national level and were recruited to coach athletes with disabilities when approached by an athlete with a disability who requested their assistance.[46] Coaches of athletes with disabilities tend to lack formal disability sport education. This may reflect a lack of disability content in many coaching education programs. It is harder to recruit coaches for disability sport when coaching education fails to cover content to ensure coaches are competent to meet the diverse needs of athletes with disabilities. It is not surprising, therefore, that traditional able-bodied formal coaching education programs tend to be perceived by disability sport coaches as less effective than a mentorship model in which novice coaches of athletes with disabilities can interact, watch, and communicate with experienced coaches of athletes with disabilities.[47]

Organizational Structure

Organizations tend to spend time and resources in a way that maximizes their return on investment. Decisions regarding programming and finances will favor able-bodied athletes and coaches. This is seen, for example, in the disparity in number of paid coaching positions with more paid coaches for athletes without a disability compared to paid coaching positions for athletes with disabilities. This makes sense as there are more athletes without disabilities competing in sport compared to the number of athletes participating in disability sport. In addition, the number of athletes on an able-bodied team provides a better return on investment for the coach's salary compared to the fewer number of athletes on a disability sport team for the same coaching salary.

Understandably, organizations will focus resources on professional education and certifications for coaches of able-bodied athletes. Often embedded in coach education for able-bodied athletes is the use of an individual module with a focus on inclusion in general rather than on disability sport specific knowledge, biological, physiological, and social effects of an athlete's impairment on sport performance. An emphasis on diversity rather than on disability specific content perpetuates an organizational emphasis on the medical model in coach education rather than a social relational organizational lens for the education of coaches of athletes with disabilities.[47] To develop an infrastructure to support disability sport using the social relational model, organizations need to consider the inter and intrapersonal needs of coaches and athletes with disabilities as well as the environment and their organization and sport's respective policy decisions to support disability sport.

Regulations for operation

Sport managers often consider the application of rules and regulations when guiding a sport for athletes without a disability. These same rules and regulations should be equally applied to disability sport programming. This homogeneous approach to disability sport is also reflected at the national and international levels with the U.S. Olympic and Paralympic movements governed under one organization, the USOPC, and at the Paralympic level where the IPC requires countries interested in hosting an Olympic Games to also bid for and host the Paralympic Games. This merging of able-bodied and disability sports assumes that the determinants of success for able-bodied sport mirrors that of sport for athletes with disabilities.[48] This approach to perceived equality of operational guidelines for athletes with and without disabilities is aligned with the medical model and fails to consider the lived experiences and unique needs of individuals with disabilities in sport. Considerations that regulate program operations unique for individuals with a disability may include costs of insurance to operate programs for individuals with physical disabilities, ADA accessible facilities, need for and cost of transportation for athletes and their sports equipment, lack of private funding and the strong tie that bind programming to grant deliverables, and lack of community support for volunteer recruitment. These programmatic barriers also overlap at the environment and policy levels. Research in collegiate recreation illustrates that marketing, recruitment, and programming decisions to engage college students with and without disabilities in intramural adapted sports are not equally successful as when applied to able-bodied intramural sport.[49] College students with disabilities may lack the sports skills and confidence needed to play due to limited exposure at the community and school level compared with able-bodied college students who may have had ample opportunities at the community and school levels. Disability sport programming at the collegiate level needs to consider the time of day in respect to the availability of paratransit for students commuting to and from campus. Lastly, wheelchairs and additional resources may be required to recruit and train referees for adapted intramural sport.

Environmental/Community Level

The physical environment includes the availability of opportunities, access to facilities, and transportation identified as three of the most identified environmental barriers to sport and physical activity participation for individuals with disabilities. These three barriers individually and collectively overlap to influence the extent to which the environment supports or prevents sport participation for individuals with disabilities. The difficulty of finding programming in which to participate combined with the schedule with which the programs are offered, lack of accessible facilities and equipment, inconvenient location of the facilities (e.g., within a city where one may have to travel too far with traffic, no rural programs, or organizations failing to conduct a needs assessment to find where the population for participation is located or access to transportation), and lack of access to and dissatisfaction with the cost, reliability, and ease of carrying sports equipment when using public transportation are all significant barriers to participation.[7] Coaches should not confuse lack of participation because of environmental barriers with a lack of interest and motivation to participate in sport. Environmental barriers alone may not limit sport participation, but when combined with intra-individual barriers such as impairment related pain, and energy required to access and participate in the program, and interindividual barriers such as lack of an assistant or limited parental support combine to make environmental barriers more insurmountable.

Policy Level

Policies refer to regulatory guidelines developed by organizations or local, state, and national legislation. Ideally, policies should facilitate opportunities and inclusion of individuals with disabilities in sport and physical activity. In addition to federal legislation such as Section 504 of the Rehabilitation Act,[25] IDEA,[10] and the ADA,[26] one way that we see the impact of policy on the opportunity for children and youth with disabilities to participate in physical education and interscholastic school sport is through the passage of the Fitness and Athletic Equity for Students with Disabilities Act.[50] This is an example of the most recent and landmark educational law passed at the state level in Maryland in 2008. The Fitness and Athletic Equity for Students with Disabilities Act was passed in response to a 2006 lawsuit by Tatyana McFadden, to the Howard County School District, for the right to compete in her wheelchair on the same track, at the same time as her teammates.[51] The Fitness and Athletic Equity Act required the boards of education within the state to develop policies and procedures to promote and protect the inclusion of students with disabilities in physical education and athletic programs, try out for and if selected participate in extracurricular or interscholastic sports, ensure reasonable accommodations to include students with a disability, or create allied sports or unified programs specially designed for students with disabilities in compliance with Section 504 of the Rehabilitation Act and Title II of the ADA.[50,51]

In conclusion, it is important to recognize that the scope and magnitude of the challenges/barriers to sport and physical activity participation for individuals with disabilities changes over time and are different for people with different disabilities. The type, level, and severity of one's impairment affect their perceptions of barriers differently as they age or gain more experience participating in sport and skill needed to manage their environment. Coaches and program managers need to consider intraindividual, social, and environmental barriers when developing and making programmatic decisions to serve the needs of individuals with disabilities in sport and physical activity.

PATHWAYS FOR ENGAGEMENT IN DISABILITY SPORT

As the disability sport movement continues to expand and serve an increasing number of individuals with disabilities, there are many ways to engage with disability sport. Depending on a practitioner's background and educational level, both paid and unpaid opportunities exist. This section will explore the different areas in which one can engage in the disability sport movement.

Teacher Education

For students preparing to be general or adapted physical education teachers in K-12 school settings, there is a direct tie to the disability sport movement by assisting students with disabilities to increase physical activity, develop fundamental motor skills, wheelchair skills, wheelchair sport specific skills, and explore potential sport and recreational options. General and adapted physical education teachers often teach students with disabilities alongside students without disabilities in integrated physical education settings. By helping students gain gross motor competency and introducing adapted sports and games into the general physical education curriculum, students with and without disabilities are exposed to sport opportunities that can expand their involvement in school based interscholastic adapted sports or community-based adaptive sport programs. General and adapted physical education teachers can infuse Paralympic School Day[52] into the PE curriculum or as a special event program for the school body to create awareness and understanding of disability sport and athletes with disabilities.[53-55] General and adapted physical education teachers also can serve as a resource to families of children with disabilities looking to access community adaptive sport and recreation programs and recruit eligible students with physical disabilities within their school or district for interscholastic adapted team

Amputee swimmer.

sports. Lastly, physical education teachers with a strong sport background can be eligible to complete classification courses and serve as a sport expert on the classification panel.

Sport Pedagogy

We have talked previously of the need for coaches in the disability sport movement. As the movement grows, more coaches are needed to coach both recreational and elite level disability sports to increase participation and the numbers of athletes moving along the pipeline to the Paralympic Games. Individuals with a background in coaching pedagogy can provide assistance in helping to create coaching and training plans and creating coach education pieces for disability sport organizations. The research shows overwhelmingly that some of the best coaches come from able-bodied coaching with no initial disability sport specific background.[46] Often disability sport coaches, like able-bodied sports coaches, start as volunteers. Many colleges and universities have intramural programs or sanctioned adaptive sports teams on campus where practitioners can complete coaching practicum or service-learning hours. Upon graduation, these volunteer experiences can lead to opportunities for paid coaching positions in disability sports at the community, recreation, and elite level.

Therapeutic Recreation/Community Recreation

There are a small number of personnel currently who work in adaptive or disability sport positions with their local community parks and recreation offices. By increasing the opportunities for individuals to participate in sports at a local level, therapeutic recreation professionals open the door to disability sport to individuals who might have not been aware before or have limited opportunities such as in rural areas. Therapeutic recreation specialists can help grow the disability sport movement by working directly in adaptive sports. The National Council for Therapeutic Recreation Certification (NCTRC) acknowledges a specialty area of adaptive sports.[56] Certified Therapeutic Recreation Specialists (CTRSs) can create adaptive sports programs for their patients as well as add adaptive sports into the therapeutic plan for recovery. Like teachers and sport coaches, CTRSs can also become certified classifiers to work on a classification panel for disability sport competition.

Occupational and Physical Therapy, Athletic Training, Strength and Conditioning

For students with a medical background such as physical therapy and occupational therapy, disability sport organizations are constantly in need of qualified medical personnel to help provide physicals, travel with teams, provide medical services at events, and to spread the word of options and availability of disability sports after injuries to patients. As mentioned early in this chapter, one of the two individuals on the classification panel must have a medical background such as physical therapy. As the disability sport movement grows, one holdup to moving athletes through the pipeline is the constant need for increased numbers of classifiers for competitions.

Athletic trainers and strength and conditioning personnel play a huge role in competitive and elite level disability sports. Athletes need athletic trainers to work with them for prehab and rehab as injuries occur naturally in their training process. There is a huge need also for qualified strength and conditioning personnel to help create training plans to improve athletes' physical conditioning to help increase their level of play in sports. For practitioners interested in personal training for individuals with disabilities, the American College of Sports Medicine partnered with the National Center on Health, Physical Activity and Disability (NCHPAD) to create a Certified Inclusive Fitness Trainer credential,[57] which qualifies individuals with either a bachelors in exercise science (or related field) or a personal training certification, to train individuals with health risks and/or physical limitations (see Table 10.5). The National Strength and Conditioning Association (NSCA) also has articles on their website for strength and conditioning professionals working in exercise programs for individuals with disabilities (see Table 10.6). By helping to increase the physical strength and health of athletes, we can also mitigate risks associated with improper or no training regimen.

Sport Management

On the management side of sports, there are numerous opportunities to engage in the disability sport movement related to sport management with organizations that are for profit and nonprofit. Event management crews for disability sport events include positions for hospitality, event management, media and communications, and finance. Marketing for disability sports is an ever-growing field, as

TABLE 10.5 Professional development resources

Organization	List of Resources	Links to Professional Resources
BlazeSports	Certified Adaptive Recreation and Sport Specialist (CARSS)	http://blazesportsinstitute.org/
	Sport and Coaching videos and podcasts	http://blazesportsinstitute.org/
	Programming, Policy and System Change videos	http://blazesportsinstitute.org/
American Association of Adapted Sports Programs	Rule and Skills handbooks	https://adaptedsports.org/aaasp-resource-center/#aaasp-guides
	YouTube channel videos	www.youtube.com/channel/UCPAyQgrQjLEh6m4iRS9x1Ew/videos
	Coaching adapted sports	https://nfhslearn.com/courses/coaching-adapted-sports
Special Olympics	Introduction to Intellectual Disability	http://learn.specialolympics.org/default.aspx
	Coaching Unified Sport	https://nfhslearn.com/courses/coaching-unified-sports
	Coaching Level 1 Sports Assistant	http://learn.specialolympics.org/default.aspx
	Fit 5	https://resources.specialolympics.org/health/fitness/fit-5
American College of Sports Medicine	Certified Inclusive Fitness Trainer	www.acsm.org/get-stay-certified/get-certified/specialization/cift
NCHPAD	Physical activity and health resources	www.nchpad.org
Canadian Coaches Training	Canada National Coaching Certification Program—Coaching Athletes with a Disability	https://coach.ca/sites/default/files/2020-02/Coaching_Athletes_Disability_update2016.pdf
	Sport for Life—Athletes with a Disability Resources	https://sportforlife.ca/resources/#category_id_104

disability sports gain more visibility and exposure in the United States and across the world. One of the biggest needs of nonprofits for the disability sport movement is fundraising. As fewer athletes compete in these sports compared with able-bodied sports, and historically disability sports have less exposure than able-bodied sports, fundraising is key. Individuals with fundraising backgrounds can help bring money and create more exposure for the needs of equipment, program support, and athlete travel to help increase awareness and availability of disability sports across the globe.

Athlete

Individuals without disabilities can participate in some disability sports as an athlete alongside individuals with disabilities. Athletes with visual impairments seek sighted athletes as teammates for track, and downhill and/or cross-country skiing, for example. Sighted athletes are recruited to train and compete as a sighted guide for competition. In the Special Olympics, athletes without an intellectual disability can participate and compete on Unified Sports teams with ability-matched athletes with an intellectual disability. In many sports, sighted teammates and guides compete in national and international competitions including the Paralympic Games and can earn medals alongside their partners with disabilities.

RESOURCES FOR PROFESSIONAL DEVELOPMENT

There is a growth in the variety of resources available to people interested in pursuing a career working with individuals with disabilities in sport, physical activity, physical education, strength and conditioning, and rehabilitation. Professional development can

TABLE 10.6 Supplemental online resources, webinars, and journals

Organization	Resource	Reference Link
National Federation of State High School Associations	Sports Nutrition	https://nfhslearn.com/courses/sports-nutrition
National Center for Health Physical Activity and disability	Coaching, training, nutrition, fitness	www.nchpad.org
National Strength and Conditioning Association	Article on training considerations for people with disabilities	www.nsca.com/education/articles/ptq/training-considerations-for-people-with-disabilities/
Best Practices for Education Based Adapted Team Sports	American Association of Adapted Sports Programs	https://adaptedsports.org/aaasp-best-practices/
Flaghouse	Adapted Team Sports Kits	www.flaghouse.com/pages/aaasp/
PSYCH/ARMOR	How to talk to someone with a disability	https://psycharmor.org/courses/talk-someone-disability/
PSYCH/ARMOR	Recreational volunteer opportunities with disabled veterans	https://psycharmor.org/courses/recreational-volunteer-opportunities-disabled-veterans/
PSYCH/ARMOR	15 things veterans want you to know	https://psycharmor.org/courses/15-things-veterans-want-you-to-know/
University of Pittsburgh	Essentials of Volunteer training for adaptive sports and recreation	https://propel.shrs.pitt.edu/courses/evotas
Adapted Physical Education National Standards	National Standards Book	https://apens.org/
Sport N Spokes	Magazine	
Palaestra	Practitioner journal	https://js.sagamorepub.com/palaestra
Adapted Physical Activity Quarterly	Research Journal	https://journals.humankinetics.com/view/journals/apaq/apaq-overview.xml
Journal of Physical Education Recreation and Dance	Practitioner Journal	www.shapeamerica.org/publications/journals/joperd/

be obtained through nonprofit organizations, and university programs at the bachelors, masters, and PhD levels. For a complete list of resources, refer to Tables 10.5 and 10.6.

BlazeSports America

Practitioners from all disciplines can pursue certification through the BlazeSports Certified Adaptive Recreation and Sports Specialists (CARSS) certifications.[58] CARSS is offered as an online course with two certification levels. These educational programs are not sport specific but are universal to all adaptive sports and recreation programming, and enhance existing certifications in sport, physical activity, and therapeutic recreation. The CARSS certifications focus on preparing professionals to develop and implement successful adaptive sports and recreation programs for individuals with physical disabilities. BlazeSports also offers online tools and resources including webinars, video and audio podcasts for adaptive sport and physical activity, as well as training tools and resources (refer to Tables 10.5 and 10.6).

American Association of Adapted Sports Programs (AAASP)

Earlier in this chapter we discussed the role of AAASP in the development of education-based interscholastic sport programs for school age students with physical disabilities.[11] To ensure the consistent implementation of wheelchair handball, wheelchair basketball, wheelchair football, and track and field across all partner school districts, AAASP has developed inclusive adapted sport policies, standardized rule books, and coaching guides for all their sports. In addition, AASASP has created guides for wheelchair setup and maintenance, ball shooting, ball handling, and first aid available for free on their website (see Table 10.5 for resource links). AAASP also has published guides related to *Knowing your Rights in Disability and Sport, Best Practices for School Based Adapted Team Sports,* and a *Terminology Guide.* The AAASP YouTube channel includes coaching videos, as well as athlete, parent, and administrator testimonials about the impact and benefits of adapted sport for youth with a physical disability. Lastly, AAASP has partnered with the National Federation of State High School Associations to develop a free course in Coaching Adapted Sports where participants will learn how to create adapted sports teams in one's school or school district and an introduction to the sports, skills, and drills available for coaching youth with a physical disability.

Special Olympics

As mentioned earlier in this chapter, Special Olympics is an international organization that organizes and builds capacity for sport, health, education, and community building focused on individuals with an intellectual disability. On the Special Olympics website[30] is general coaching information on how to become a coach with corresponding videos on the athlete and coach development model, general sport resources, and specific sport resources with rules, fact sheets, coaching guides, quizzes for each sport, and information on Unified Sports. Special Olympics also has a program called the Fit 5 that promotes healthy eating and exercises with corresponding fitness cards and video demonstrations to promote and integrate health related physical fitness into training and conditioning programs for individuals with intellectual disabilities of all ability levels (see Table 10.5).

American College of Sports Medicine (ACSM)/National Center for Heath, Physical Activity and Disability (NCHPAD) Certified Inclusive Fitness Trainer (CIFT)

The ACSM and the NCHPAD collaborated to develop a certified inclusive fitness trainer (CIFT) designation for individuals interested in working with people with health risks and/or physical, sensory, or cognitive impairments.[57] The certification includes content on the ADA policies related to recreation facilities, standards for accessible design, safe adapted exercise techniques and precautions, and programming that promotes effective training. This certificate is directed toward persons interested in working in community and public heath settings, adapted physical education teachers, coaches, gyms and health clubs, and universities where the goal and mission is to improve access to exercise for individuals with disabilities.

National Center on Health Physical Activity and Disability (NCHPAD)

The NCHPAD website is an online resource for information on physical activity, health promotion, and disability. Content on the website is designed to help people with disabilities and chronic health conditions to engage in physical and social activities such as fitness, aquatics, recreational and sport programs, and adapted equipment usage. This website provides individualized information, referral, and consultation services to people with disabilities, families, caregivers, policy makers, community members, health care practitioners, and public health professionals.[59] NCHPAD also conducts national trainings to educate practitioners in community health inclusion.

Canadian Coaching Resources

We also encourage students to review resources from Canada. Sport for Life is a nonprofit organization that brings government, institutions, schools, and sport organizations together to improve programs and services for Canadians with and without a disability.[60] They have free online resources for coaching athletes with a disability inclusive of a *Quality Sport Checklist for Communities and Clubs, Long Term Athlete Development for Athletes with Disabilities,* and a supplement on *Training Athletes with a Physical Disability*. The Canadian National Coaching Certification Program also has a free online resource for coaching athletes with a physical disability (refer to Table 10.4).

Collegiate Academic Programs

Many colleges and universities offer undergraduate minors, certificates, or stand-alone classes in disability sport, which can help practitioners acquire specific knowledge and skills. Students interested in continuing their education can pursue graduate work in areas related to sport pedagogy and coaching, sport psychology, sport administration, and athletic training at a master's degree level. While many master's degree programs do not specifically address disability sport, in all programs there are opportunities for students to explore their interest in disability sport through assignments, internships, directed readings, and course or volunteer research assistantships with faculty in various kinesiology related fields, including physical and occupational therapy, as well as education fields such as exceptional education and special education. Universities with faculty interested in disability sport may be found in kinesiology programs such as physical education teacher education, sport management, exercise psychology, or athletic training, and often have programs with a major or minor related to disability sport or disability studies, or at the very least courses addressing disability and disability sport. Students with an interest in research can pursue their studies through a PhD program, in which the focus is on generating new knowledge about disability sport, coaching, training, conditioning, sport management, injury prevention, prosthetic design, rehabilitation, and so on for individuals with disabilities. Many programs at the master's and especially at the PhD level offer teaching and research assistantships that often cover the tuition expenses, making the pursuit of graduate studies much more affordable and manageable for the 2-4 years it takes to pursue a master's and PhD degree, respectively.

CHAPTER SUMMARY

- There are two primary categories of disability sport. The first is based off existing able-bodied sport but with modifications or accommodations to meet the needs of the athletes. The second is designed specifically for persons with an impairment.
- Exploring the history of the disability sport movement is valuable in being able to understand the status of disability sport in today's culture, as well as the future direction of the movement.
- The International Paralympic Committee (IPC) consists of National Paralympic Committees, International Federations, Regional Organizations, and International Organizations of Sports for the Disabled. The IPC supports the parasport movement, focusing on advocacy, athlete development and support, and the successful delivery and organization of the Paralympic Games.
- There are three federal legislations that have guided the access and opportunity for disability sport and adapted sport, the (a) Rehabilitation Act of 1973 Section 504, (b) IDEA, and (c) Americans with a Disability Act of 1990 (ADA). To meet the legal requirements of these federal legislations, a sport continuum framework was developed to provide sport opportunities for individuals with disabilities in the least restrictive setting possible.
- The disability sport pipeline includes community disability sport, K-12 adapted sport, collegiate adapted and disability sport, and Paralympic sport.
- Classification regulates which athletes are qualified to compete in a sport, and how athletes are grouped, by the severity of activity limitation deriving from the impairment.
- The socioecological model provides a lens through which to understand the factors that influence disability sport participation across the life span. The levels of the model include intrapersonal, interpersonal, organizational, environmental, and public policy.
- There are many ways to engage with disability sport, including teacher education programs, sport pedagogy, therapeutic recreation, occupational and physical therapy, athletic training, strength and conditioning, sport management, and participating as an athlete. In addition, professional development can be obtained through nonprofit organizations, and university programs at the bachelors, masters, and PhD levels.

REFERENCES

1. Goodley, D. (2016). *Disability studies: An interdisciplinary introduction* (2nd ed.). Sage. https://doi.org/10.1080/21640629.2016.1157324
2. World Health Organization. (2001, May 22). *International classification of functioning, disability, and health.* www.who.int/classifications/international-classification-of-functioning-disability-and-health
3. Haslett, D., & Smith, B. (2020). Viewpoints toward disability: Conceptualizing disability in adapted physical education. In J. Haegele, S. R. Hodge & D. R. Shapiro (Eds.), *Routledge Handbook of Adapted Physical Education* (pp. 48–64). Routledge.
4. Townsend, R., Smith, B., & Cushion, C. J. (2016). Disability sports coaching: Towards a critical understanding. *Sports Coaching Review, 4*(2), 80–98. https://doi.org/10.1080/21640629.2016.1157324
5. World Health Organization. (2011). *World report on disability.* www.who.int/disabilities/world_report/2011/report.pdf
6. International Platform on Sport and Development. (n.d.). *Definitions and terminology.* https://www.sportanddev.org/en/learn-more
7. Martin, J. J. (2018). *Handbook of disability sport and exercise psychology.* University Press.
8. Office of Disability Rights. (2006, July 11). *People first language.* DC.gov. https://odr.dc.gov/page/people-first-language
9. DePauw, K. P., & Gavron, S. J. (2005). *Disability and sport* (2nd ed). Human Kinetics.
10. *Individuals with Disabilities Education Act* (IDEA) of 1990, U.S.C., Title 20, §§ 1400 *et seq.*
11. American Association of Adapted Sports Programs. (n.d). *Adapted versus adaptive sport.* www.ghsa.net/sites/default/files/documents/AAASP-Understanding-Disability-Sports-Terminology.pdf
12. Patatas, J., M., De Bosscher, V., & Legg, D. (2018). Understanding disability sport: An analysis of the differences between able-bodied and disability sport from a sport policy perspective. *International Journal of Sport Policy and Politics, 10*(2), 235–254. https://doi.org/10.1080/19406940.2017.1359649
13. Deaflympics. (n.d.). *History.* www.deaflympics.com/icsd/history
14. International Paralympic Committee. (n.d.). *Paralympics history.* www.paralympic.org/ipc/history
15. International Paralympic Committee. (n.d.). *About the international paralympic committee.* www.paralympic.org/ipc/who-we-are
16. International Paralympic Committee. (n.d.). *What is classification.* www.paralympic.org/classification
17. International Paralympic Committee. (n.d.). *Paralympic games.* https://oldwebsite.paralympic.org/paralympic-games/summer
18. Move United. (n.d.). *Early history.* www.moveunitedsport.org/about/our-mission/early-history/
19. National Sports Center for the Disabled. (n.d.). *Our history.* https://nscd.org/about-nscd-adaptive-sports/our-history/
20. VIRTUS: World Intellectual Impairment Sport. (n.d.). *Who we are.* www.virtus.sport/about-us/who-we-are/history-of-virtus
21. Disabled World. (2013, June 13). *Extremity games adaptive sports for athletes with disabilities.* https://www.disabled-world.com/sports/extremity-games.php
22. Department of Defense Warrior Games. (n.d). *About warrior games.* www.dodwarriorgames.com/about/about/
23. Invictus Games Foundation. (n.d.). *Our story.* https://invictusgamesfoundation.org/foundation/story/
24. Special Olympics. (n.d.). *History.* www.specialolympics.org/about/history?locale=en
25. United States Department of Health, Education, and Welfare Office for Civil Rights. (n.d.). *Section 504 of the Rehabilitation act of 1973 Fact sheet: Handicapped persons rights under Federal law.* https://www2.ed.gov/policy/rights/reg/ocr/34cfr104.pdf
26. Americans With Disabilities Act of 1990, 42 U.S.C. § 12101 *et seq.* (1990). www.ada.gov/pubs/adastatute08.htm
27. Winnick, J. P. (1987). An integration continuum for sport participation. *Adapted Physical Activity Quarterly, 4,* 157–161.
28. Mooreman, A. M., & Hums, M. A. (2020). Law and legislation impacting adapted physical education programs. In J. Haegele, S. R. Hodge, & D. R. Shapiro (Eds.), *Routledge Handbook of Adapted Physical Education* (pp. 25–47). Routledge.
29. National Federation of High Schools. (2020, April 14). *California coaches creating opportunities for Para-athletes.* www.nfhs.org/articles/california-coaches-creating-opportunities-for-para-athletes/
30. Special Olympics. (n.d.). *Sports.* www.specialolympics.org/our-work/sports?locale=en
31. Challenged Athletes Foundation. (2019, August). *List of colleges with adaptive sports programs.* www.challengedathletes.org/collegiate-adaptive-sports/
32. GRIT Freedom Chair. (2015, December 14). *Collegiate adaptive sports guide.* www.gogrit.us/news/2015/12/14/the-complete-guide-to-collegiate-adaptive-sports
33. ACSAA: American Collegiate Society of Adapted Athletics. (n.d.). *Resources: Colleges/Universities that offer adapted sports.* www.acsaaorg.org/resources.php
34. NWBA: National Wheelchair Basketball Association. (n.d.). *Find a team.* www.nwba.org/findateam
35. Team USA. (n.d.). *About the U.S. Olympic and Paralympic Committee: Collegiate partnerships.* www.teamusa.org/About-the-USOPC/Collegiate-Partnerships

36. Team USA. (n.d.). *About the U.S. Olympic and Paralympic Committee: History.* www.teamusa.org/about-the-usopc/history
37. Top End Sports. (n.d.). *Disabled olympic participants.* www.topendsports.com/events/summer/athletes/disabled.htm
38. Special Olympics. (n.d.). *Sports essentials: Divisioning.* https://resources.specialolympics.org/sports-essentials/divisioning?locale=en
39. Dwarf Athletic Association of America. (n.d.). *Yes, you can participate!* www.daaa.org/participate.html
40. VIRTUS: World Intellectual Impairment Sport. (n.d.). *About intellectual impairment and classification.* https://www.virtus.sport/applying-for-athlete-eligibility
41. Martin Ginis, K. A., Ma, J. K., Latimer-Cheung, A. E., & Rimmer, J. H. (2016). A systematic review of review articles addressing factors related to physical activity participation among children and adults with physical disabilities. *Health Psychology Review, 10*(4), 478–494. https://doi.org/10.1080/17437199.2016.1198240
42. Scarneo, S. E., Kerr, Z. Y., Kroshus, E., Register-Mihalik, J. K., Hosokawa, Y., Stearns, R. L., DisStefano, L. J., & Casa, D. J. (2019). The socioecological framework: A multifaceted approach to preventing sport-related deaths in high school sports. *Journal of Athletic Training, 54*(4), 356–360. https://doi.org/10.4085/1062-6050-173-18
43. McLeroy, K. R., Bibeau, D., Steckler, A., & Glanz, K. (1988). An ecological perspective on health promotion programs. *Health Education Quarterly, 15*(4), 351–377.
44. Columna, L., Prieto, L., Elias-Revolledo, G., & Haegele, J. A. (2020). The perspectives of parents of youth with disabilities toward physical activity: A systematic review. *Disability and Health Journal, 13*(2). https://doi.org/10.1016/j.dhjo.1029.100851
45. Haegele, J. A., Beuche, J. J., Wilson, W. J., Bradly, E., Zhu, X., & Li, C. (2021). Barriers and facilitators to inclusion in integrated physical education: Adapted physical educators' perspectives. *European Physical Education Review, 27*(2), 297–311. https://doi.org/10.1177/1356336X20944429
46. Bloom G. A. (2020). Paralympic sport coaching. In K. Dieffenhach & M. Thomspon (Eds.). *Coach education essentials: Your guide to developing sport coaches* (pp. 171–184). Human Kinetics.
47. Wareham, Y., Burkett, B., Innes, P., & Lovell, G. P. (2018). Sport coaches' education, training and professional development: The perceptions and preferences of coaches of elite athletes with disability in Australia. *Sport in Society, 21*(1), 1–20. https://doi.org/10.1080/17430437.2018.1487955
48. Peake, R. L. (2019). *Determining international parasport success factors for UK para-athletes* (Publication no. http://shura.shu.ac.uk/25468/) [Doctoral Thesis, Sheffield Hallam University]. Sheffield Hallam University Research Archive. https://doi.org/10.7190/shu-thesis-00265
49. Shapiro, D. R., Pate, J. R., & Cottingham, M. (2020). A multi-institutional review of college campus adapted intramural sports programming for college students with and without a disability. *Recreational Sports Journal, 44*(2), 109–125. https://doi.org/10.1177/2F1558866120952093.
50. Disability Rights Maryland. (2009, June 1). *Fitness and Athletic Equity for Students with Disabilities Act.* www.disabilityrightsmd.org/wp-content/uploads/2010/09/Fitness-and-Athletic-Equity-Law-For-Students-with-Disabilities.pdf
51. The Wrightslaw Way to Special Education Law and Advocacy. (2009, November 11). *Athlete sues for right to complete; state passes athletics equity law.* www.wrightslaw.com/blog/athlete-sues-for-right-to-compete-state-passes-athletics-equity-law/
52. International Paralympic Committee (IPC). (2006). *Paralympic school day manual.* Author.
53. McKay, C. (2013). Paralympic School Day: A disability awareness program. *Palaestra, 27*(4), 14–19.
54. McKay, C., Haegele, J. A., & Block, M. E. (2019). Lessons learned from Paralympic School Day: Reflections from the students. *European Physical Education Review, 25*(3), 745–760. https://doi.org/10.1177/1356336X18768038
55. McKay, C., Block, M. E., & Park, J. Y. (2015). The effect of Paralympic School Day on student attitudes toward inclusion in physical education. *Adapted Physical Activity Quarterly, 32*(4), 331–348. https://doi.org/10.1123/APAQ.2015-0045
56. National Council for Therapeutic Recreation Certification. (n.d.). *Home page.* www.nctrc.org/
57. American College of Sports Medicine. (n.d.). *ACSM/NCHPAD Certified Inclusive Fitness Trainer.* https://www.acsm.org/certification/specialized
58. BlazeSports America. (n.d.). *Certified adapted recreation sports specialist.* http://blazesportsinstitute.org/
59. National Center on Health, Physical Activity, and Disability. (n.d.). *About us.* www.nchpad.org/Aboutus
60. Sport for Life. (n.d.). *What We Do.* https://sportforlife.ca/

CHAPTER 11
SUPPORT SYSTEMS

Bethany L. Hersman, Luis Columna, and Wray Jean Connor

INTRODUCTION

As more individuals with disabilities participate in integrated sports, physical education, fitness centers, and other various physical activity–related contexts, collaborative efforts with supports and support personnel are needed to create a positive and effective experience for everyone involved.[1] The idea behind utilizing support personnel such as paraprofessionals, peers, and parents in activity settings is that practitioners will be collaborating with someone who is more familiar with the individual and their abilities, and is able to help modify movements and activities as needed. These support systems can be employed as a way to support integration with individuals without disabilities and to help the individual to be successful at a level appropriate to their needs.

In this regard, a practitioner cannot assume that support personnel will know what to do in a given situation without appropriate training in a physical education, sport, or physical activity field. In some cases, *support personnel* have not received any guidance on how to work with someone with a disability, so the practitioners may need to do this training on their own in a collaborative setting.[2] For support personnel who have received little to no training, the only references they have are their own experiences, which may or may not have been positive ones, if they have any relevant experience at all. Therefore, training before, during, and after a fitness/therapy program, school year, or sport season must be provided in the settings these individuals will perform.

Comparably, most *practitioners* simply do not receive enough preparation themselves on working with individuals with disabilities and receive little to no training on how to work with support personnel, such as paraprofessionals, within their respective work environments. In some cases, practitioners are simply uncomfortable telling another adult what to do or how they can help, while support personnel may not know how to modify the activities or may not be involved in the activity because they view the time as a break while someone else instructs the individual.[3] We cannot expect them to know what to do without first telling them where we need the actual support.

The unfortunate consequence of this breakdown between practitioners and support systems can lead to role ambiguity between all involved parties if the roles and responsibilities of each professional are not clearly defined. In an integrated physical activity setting, it is important to remember that the practitioner and support personnel are all on the same team, that they are there to support the individual in need, and it is imperative that they work together to help create a positive and appropriate activity environment for all involved.

Bethany L. Hersman, Wright State University; Luis Columna, University of Madison-Wisconsin; and Wray Jean Conner, Adapted Physical Education Teacher. © Kendall Hunt Publishing Company.

Utilizing Support Systems

In movement-related fields, support systems can help to foster and encourage inclusion and integration of individuals with disabilities within various movement settings. Support systems such as paraprofessionals and peer mentors are used commonly in education settings, and are seen in integrated/adapted physical education as well as in classrooms. Within the Individuals with Disabilities Education Act (IDEA), students with disabilities who qualify are to be given supplementary aids and services. These aids and services are also to be provided within extracurricular and nonacademic settings, including school athletics and related services such as physical or occupational therapy.[4] Peer mentors can be successfully incorporated into both physical education and athletics, where students and athletes with disabilities might be integrated. While physical therapy and personal training settings are typically one on one, a support system such as a parent or paraprofessional can help with behavior management, keeping the individual on task, and help with modifying activities as needed. Even in recreational settings, peers, paraprofessionals, and parents/guardians can help individuals with disabilities to exercise and stay active by motivating them and modifying activities as needed.

Benefits and Cautions When Working with Support Systems

Although support individuals can be helpful, there tends to be an overreliance on these individuals to help provide the least restrictive environment for an individual with a disability. Support individuals are usually not adequately prepared to do what is needed in an activity setting to help an individual with a disability to be successful.[5] Not every individual with a disability will need support in physical activity settings, so it is important for the practitioner to first get to know the individual and learn what they are able to do relative to the setting, and then determine if support is needed. Every person and environment is different, but the ultimate goal is to help someone to become independent and reach the goals set for them.

There are numerous benefits to using support systems in physical activity settings, including having: a second person to help; someone who knows the individual and their abilities, likes, and dislikes; someone to help foster inclusion between individuals with and without disabilities; a go between for

Support comes in many forms, including basic life functions like eating.

the teacher, therapists, coaches, and parents; someone to monitor behavior and implement behavioral interventions; a source of motivation, friendship, and encouragment and someone who can modify the activities presented to the individual with a disability. Supports can also provide opportunities for individuals with disabilities that were not previously available, such as receiving personal training at fitness centers or sport opportunities. Support systems can be a valuable source of support when they are given adequate preparation, training, and feedback, and are treated as a member of the special education/service team.

Although support personnel could be an asset to the practitioner, there are also several cautions and things to watch out for that can disrupt the learning experience for the individual with a disability. For example, many times in their aim to support inclusion, support personnel can actually hinder it by overprotecting the individual in physical activity settings and keeping them separated from the rest of the team or class.[6] They might not be doing this on purpose, but in cases where they are consistently separating from the rest of the group, and working one on one with the individual, this is providing a barrier to interaction and integration with others.

In addition, sometimes support personnel may be too helpful and will assist the individual even if it is not needed, completing the task for them or by assuming they cannot complete the task on their own. For example, if an individual is practicing throwing and catching, sometimes they might catch the ball for the individual or throw it back to their partner for them. In addition, when an adult is working closely with an individual with a disability, this can limit the social interaction opportunities because individuals without disabilities may feel intimidated by that adult always being with the individual with the disability, almost as though there is a "parent" hanging around, limiting some types of interactions and incidental learning.[7] Other issues with support personnel proximity to the individual with a disability can be the increased dependence on having someone to do things for them, a loss of personal control and decision making if their decisions are always made for them, a loss of gender identity (e.g., if the paraprofessional helps with toileting and the individual is a different gender), and an interference with the instruction of other athletes or students in integrated settings where the actions of the paraprofessional or other supports can be distracting.[8]

One on one support is not always needed, and it is necessary that the support personnel and the practitioner remember that they are both there to assist with independent learning of the individual with a disability rather than coming in with the attitude that the individual cannot complete the activity/game and doing everything for them. Support personnel are there to modify a task that may be too hard or is not understood by the individual, but sometimes they may do too much, have expectations that are too low, or assume they cannot complete the activity and have them sit on the side to watch.[1] The paraprofessional should remember that not everyone needs help to complete physical activities, and some individuals do not want the support, they want to try things on their own and are able to modify the tasks themselves. This adaptive behavior is essential for these individuals to move beyond support needs. It is important to determine the amount of support each individual will need in the different physical activity environments, and this can happen in the IEP/504 meeting (if applicable), as well as daily in each activity session, as needs could change depending on the tasks and demands being placed on the individual's body.

Communication and Collaboration with Support Systems

There may be time or accessibility barriers to collaborating with a support individual due to the fact that many individuals do not have planning periods or extra time to plan ahead for activity. Many coaches, trainers, and therapists as well as some adapted physical education and physical education teachers work at different school buildings throughout the day, thus making it difficult to find a common time to meet or consult with each other. To avoid those barriers, an open line of communication should be developed through in person and electronic interactions. Be open to thoughts and opinions from support personnel because they may have more experience with the individual, so ask for their opinion and be an active listener who is willing to discuss ideas and options to help all learners to be successful. Part of the training should be about communication-communication between the support personnel and the teacher, the paraprofessional and the student, peer to peer, and others. Best practices for communication and collaboration with support personnel include:

- Keeping an open line of reciprocal communication
- Working to develop a collegial relationship built on trust and respect

- Providing physical activity opportunities for paraprofessionals, peer mentors, and parents to help them learn
- Sharing lesson and activity plans with them ahead of time or involve them in the planning
- Making goals and objectives clear
- Working as a team[9]

Defining Support Personnel

There are many types of support that can be provided to individuals with disabilities in activity settings, but this chapter will discuss three main support systems: paraprofessionals, peer mentors, and parents/guardians. Paraprofessionals have many different names depending on the geographical location and country: paraeducators, education assistants, teacher aides, or learning support assistants, but regardless of the terminology used, the roles and responsibilities are typically the same. For the purposes of this chapter, we will refer to them as paraprofessionals as they can be utilized in education as well as in sport or other physical activity settings. According to the Individuals with Disabilities Education Act[4] (IDEA), a **paraprofessional** is an individual who is appropriately trained and supervised, and helps to assist in the delivery of special education (including physical/adapted physical education) and other related services (such as occupational/physical therapy) for children with disabilities outlined in IDEA. This means that these paraprofessionals are there to work alongside the practitioner, and to help deliver the content in a way that is meaningful and appropriate for that student. A **peer mentor** is defined as a student or peer who assists and supports individuals with disabilities in various settings so they can become successful, learn social skills, and gain independence. **Parents/guardians** can be any person who is responsible for the welfare of a child; for purpose of this chapter the term can include a sibling, grandparent, uncle, and so on. Each of those three different types of support systems/personnel will be discussed further within this chapter, and it is important to remember that these supports can be used in any physical activity or movement based setting as needed. In the next section we will present information regarding the three types of support systems provided in this chapter. For each, we will present information regarding their main characteristics, responsibilities, and training required.

Paraprofessionals

According to the U.S. Bureau of Labor Statistics,[10] in 2021 there was an estimated 1,235,100 paraprofessionals employed in the United States, with a median income of $29,360 per year. The number of paraprofessionals in the schools is projected to increase by about 5% between 2021 and 2031; this increasing number indicates the importance of paraprofessionals, yet they are still one of the most marginalized and underpaid school employee positions.[11] There is a significantly high amount of job turnover and burnout associated with this position, which can be, in part, due to increased reliance on paraprofessionals in integrated settings, added responsibilities with unclear role expectations, and low pay.[11] In some cases, there is an overreliance on paraprofessionals in order to create a least restrictive environment for individuals with disabilities, when the role of the paraprofessional is to supplement the instruction of the practitioner yet they are being asked to deliver instruction, modify activities, manage behaviors, and facilitate learning.[11] Asking paraprofessionals to do more with little to no training can interfere with the delivery of a quality education for school-aged individuals, and the delivery of quality extracurricular or related services if there is an overreliance on an underqualified individual to deliver the instruction.

Currently, new paraprofessionals hired in the United States should have completed at least two years of higher education, or an associate's degree and have to demonstrate knowledge of and the ability to assist in instruction of reading, writing, and math as demonstrated by passing a state sanctioned academic assessment such as the ParaPro assessment provided through Educational Testing Service.[12] The requirements may vary depending on the setting or the type of school employing them, and many schools will require their paraprofessionals to have other certifications or licenses, such as CPR/first aid.[10]

Responsibilities of Paraprofessionals

Paraprofessionals can work in settings outside of education such as sport and recreation, physical therapy, occupational therapy, or fitness centers as needed to support individuals with disabilities in those settings. However, when hiring a paraprofessional, the official job description should include all possible responsibilities and roles of the paraprofessional, including the time period they are expected to be at the school, as well as working with individuals with disabilities and the settings they will be working in. For example, a paraprofessional may be working one-on-one with an individual and they are paid to work with them from the time school starts until the end of the school day. This is in addition to the regular class schedule (including physical education), and might include after school sports, lunch, and various therapies and extracurricular activities as identified in the individual's IEP or other educational plan. Sometimes within the job description, those duties, or clarity in duties, might be left out along with other responsibilities such as help with wheelchair transfers, eating, and toileting.

In a physical activity setting, many times paraprofessionals are asked to support a lesson or sport practice without any clear instructions on what to do, or how to help the individual with a disability in that setting.[13] This is problematic because without clear instruction or training, even though they may have the best intentions, they can cause harm to the individual if they are unfamiliar with how to help them safely complete the activity. If the paraprofessional is expected to help in physical education, sport, or therapy settings, the responsibilities within each of those settings should be included in the job description. It is essential to note that the job description for what a paraprofessional should do in physical activity–related settings should not exceed the official job description the paraprofessional was hired under. Therefore, make sure the setting and activity specific needs are expressed from the before the start of the search for a paraprofessional.[14] As such, collaboration with the special education team or department is important.

Practitioners should ensure that if a paraprofessional will be working within their environment (e.g., gymnasium, fitness center), the expectations are clear for what help is needed before they ever set foot into that environment. If there are tasks or responsibilities that are not in the paraprofessional's skill set, or that they are not confident in carrying them out, the practitioner can do one of two things: 1) if it is an immediate need, then training should occur right away (before the beginning of the school year or sport season); 2) if it is a future task, then training could occur later or that task/responsibility should be eliminated from the job description.[14]

Do not be afraid to delegate tasks and responsibilities to the paraprofessional, in some cases they work with that individual or group of individuals for most of the day and they are familiar with the general needs and abilities of the individuals. Delegation is NOT dumping tasks on the paraprofessional, micromanaging them, a form of punishment, or a way to get back at them for goals not being met. Delegation IS a way to make the most of your time by creating a team and empowering the paraprofessional by maximizing resources and letting them help.[14] In the initial days of working with the paraprofessional, provide them with a list of roles and responsibilities for the setting, let them review the list for knowledge or confidence in providing support in the needed areas, and then make time to discuss any questions they may have or to clarify tasks. See Table 11.1 for a sample list of roles and responsibilities of paraprofessionals in physical activity settings.

TABLE 11.1 Sample roles and responsibilities for paraprofessionals in physical activity settings

Dress appropriate for the activity setting
Help the individual dress for activity when appropriate
Gain a working knowledge of the environment, equipment, and activities
Help with instruction/assist with movements (note: direct instruction is not their role; they are there to help, not provide the primary instruction in the setting)
Modify activities to meet individual needs
Foster independent learning
Support integration and inclusion
Keep the individual focused on the tasks
Behavior management/implement behavior plans
Prompting (verbal, visual demonstrations, physical) and providing learning cues
Transitions from activity to activity, to the locker room, and so on
Aid in assessment (with training)
Safety
Helping others to learn to interact with and respect the individual
Reinforcement and encouragement
Implementing tasks in the IEP, educational plan, or therapy/training plan
Personal care, transfers in and out of wheelchairs and other assistive devices, bathroom breaks
Link to communication between coach, teacher, trainer, parent, therapist
Part of the IEP/educational team
Ask questions if things are unclear

Training Paraprofessionals to Work in Physical Activity Settings

A paraprofessional's contributions are more effective when they have the knowledge, attitude, and willingness to participate within a physical activity setting and to collaborate with the practitioner in that setting.[15] It is not enough to simply tell a paraprofessional what their roles and responsibilities are; they also need to be trained in how to carry out these roles, which will, in turn, help to improve their confidence in helping an individual with a disability to succeed in a physical activity setting. Moreover, as previously mentioned, good lines of communications are imperative. At the beginning of the school year, sport season, or in the initial evaluation for personal training or therapy, take the time to introduce yourself to the paraprofessionals you will be working with and discuss the areas where you can support each other to start building a supportive relationship with them.

When working with a paraprofessional, roles and responsibilities of both the practitioner as well as the paraprofessional should be discussed and clarified from the start so everyone knows what is expected of them. Additionally, the purpose of the activity setting should be introduced with the goals and philosophy for the individuals who the practitioner will be in charge of. When training a paraprofessional to support individuals with disabilities in an activity setting, remember it is a team approach. The practitioner should be comfortable showing the student/client/athlete what to do as well as discussing with the paraprofessional how they can support that individual. When discussing with the paraprofessional how they can help, the approach to the discussion is also of importance—for example, asking for their help versus telling them to do something, showing them versus expecting them to know what to do; this will help to create a partnership between professionals.

In the initial days, orientation to the gym/activity space and facilities, policies, and safety procedures should be reviewed by all staff. Get to know one another, find out why they became a paraprofessional, their experience working with individuals with disabilities specific to that setting, and what related training or experiences they have had (CPR/first aid, behavior management, etc.). Any experience they have had in that setting (specifically related to helping with tasks/activities in that setting) should be discussed along with any negative experiences in sport or physical activity settings to help define the paraprofessional's comfort level.

Once their level of experience and comfort levels have been established, collaboratively discuss what each person's roles and responsibilities are within that specific setting. For example, a paraprofessional for a cross country athlete may be responsible for getting the athlete dressed and to practice on time, helping them to stretch and warm up, and then running with them for their training. Any other needs may be highlighted by the coach and paraprofessional at this time as well. The next step would be to define the job and going over the list of needs together—within the job responsibility list may be things like supervision, delivery/modification of instruction, data collection, activity preparation, attending team meetings, and other health-related/personal tasks such as changing clothes.[14] If physical education, physical therapy, or sport is on their IEP or 504 plan, then the paraprofessional should help to support the individual in those settings.[16] Find out their level of comfort, and ability within each of the needed areas, and this may help to define areas where they will need more or less support and training. For example, in a personal training setting, although the individual with a disability may be one on one with a trainer, the paraprofessional might have a better sense of the abilities and areas of challenge for the individual so they can share that with the trainer and can help to suggest activity modifications for each muscle group assuming they have knowledge and experience in a fitness-based setting such as weight training.

Everyone working with an individual who has an IEP or 504 plan should be familiar with their goals and should have access to these plans. When planning the activity session, remember that each situation and individual is different so no one specific plan will work, but having access to their educational plans (if applicable) is an important first step in determining needs and supports for each individual. If instruction is provided in an integrated setting such as sport or physical education, then the teacher or coach should plan with all learners in mind, and provide the plan ahead of time for the paraprofessional to review and to ask for clarifications if needed. If there are any goals or strategies that should be examined in anticipation of a specific game or activity, those should be discussed ahead of time (i.e., not at the time of implementation) as the paraprofessional may have a grasp on the attention, comprehension, and ability levels of the individual, especially if they work one on one with them every day.

If there are specific behavioral strategies that might work well in a setting, those should also be planned for in advance. For example, with individuals who have autism, they can sometimes become overwhelmed with a lot of noise going on around them, which is common in most physical activity settings. Since many paraprofessionals work one on one with these students for the entire school day, they should be aware of behavioral antecedents that may cause behavior outbursts (e.g., loud noises). They should watch for telltale signs that an individual is starting to become agitated and take the appropriate steps to avoid situations where a behavior plan would need to be enacted. However, the paraprofessional and practitioner should still go over what situations to try to avoid and what behavior management strategies work for this individual in circumstances where they might become upset and act out so if the behavior does occur, a plan is in place. For paraprofessionals who work in classrooms with individuals with disabilities, they may be familiar with specific behavior plans for students who have them and can communicate that ahead of time to help with behavior management. All too often, behavior plans and other classroom teaching strategies such as social stories or visual schedules that work well to manage behavior are not shared with other professionals (e.g., physical education teachers or coaches), so the paraprofessional should be encouraged to share what is used in other settings so that continuity between settings is maintained as much as possible.

Remember that a gym or physical activity setting may be a different setting than what a paraprofessional is used to—it is a bigger space with more distractions, noises, movements, and equipment that they may be unfamiliar with.[17] This means the practitioner will need to help the paraprofessional to become familiar with these aspects through instruction, demonstration, and feedback as the paraprofessional is learning about the setting. A large portion of training should relate to the movements, critical elements of the movements, teaching cues, and how to correct errors in performance. Since paraprofessionals may not be familiar with the movements, the practitioner will need to demonstrate, provide pictures, or videos that will help them understand the movement, and remember that they, and not the paraprofessional, are the lead and are still responsible for the planning, main instruction/delivery, and feedback for all learners.

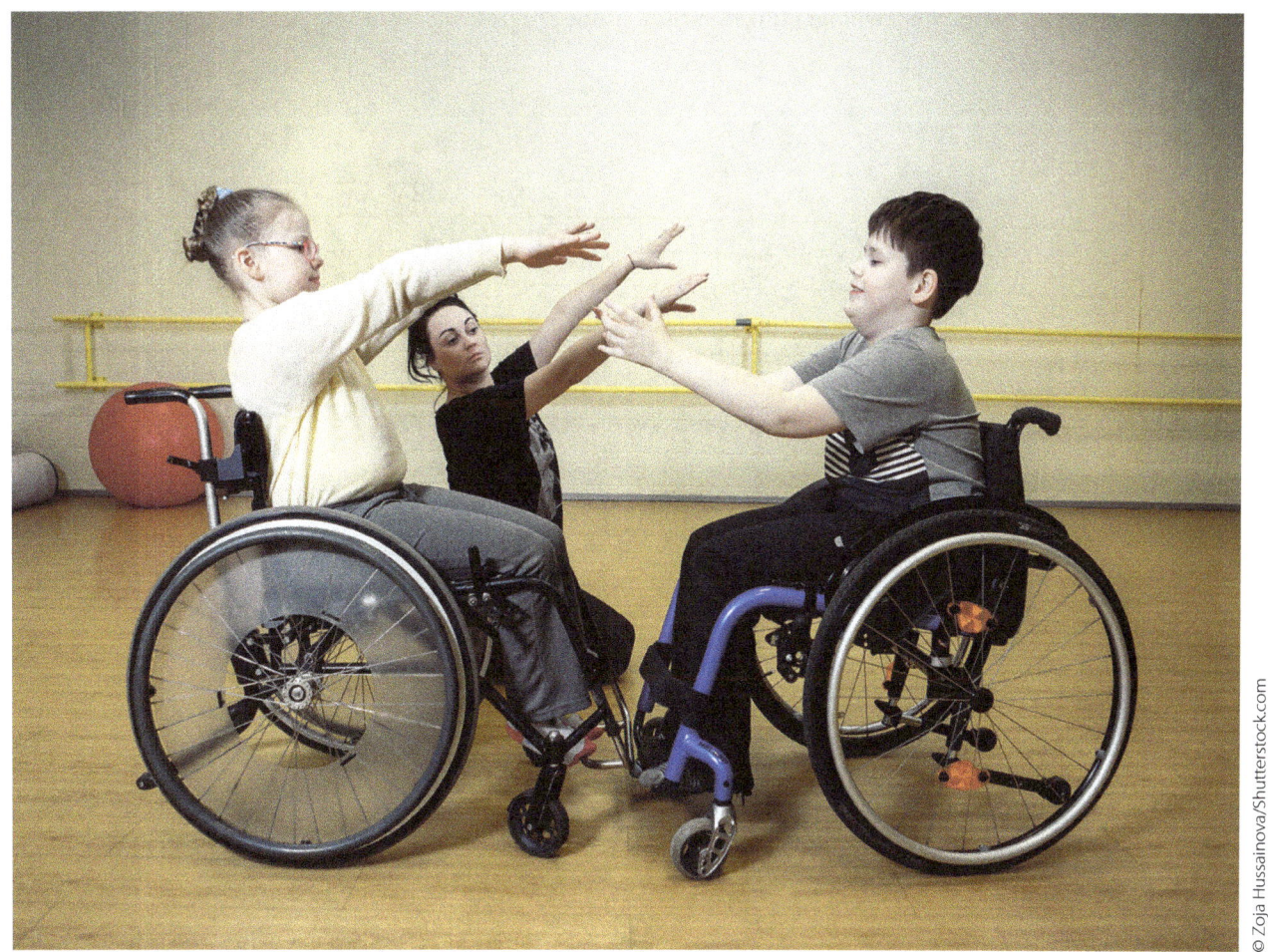

Paraprofessional teaching movement skills.

As the planning stage occurs, activity and movement modifications should be built into the plan and discussed with the paraprofessional ahead of time so they can plan how to identify if modifications are needed as well as how to implement them. Levels of support (e.g., intermittent or as needed, extensive or constant support), and prompting should also be discussed; some individuals with disabilities will need higher levels of prompts such as physical guidance, while others may only need a verbal prompt to complete an activity. It is important to remember that not all levels of support may be needed, and the goal is to help the individual complete tasks and activities independently without help as much as possible.

Lastly, remember that the paraprofessional is learning alongside the individual with a disability, and that you may be asking them to do something that is completely new to them. Make sure to recognize their help and let them know you appreciate them—by doing so, this will lead to them to feeling respected and will help make the partnership more successful.[18] As a result of training and collaboration, paraprofessionals will understand their roles and responsibilities better, they will be utilized more efficiently and effectively, individuals with disabilities will be given more accurate modifications, and there may be an increase in participation as well as an improvement in behaviors and achievement.[5]

Peer Mentors

The growing opportunities for individuals with disabilities to participate in both integrated and adapted physical activity settings correlates to a need for well-trained peer mentors. Through programs such as Special Olympics Unified Sports, various sport organizations, group fitness classes at fitness facilities, and physical and adapted physical education, peers without disabilities are regularly participating alongside individuals with disabilities. Despite these programs and attempts at integration/inclusion, research in physical education classes has shown that many times, individuals with disabilities do not feel as though they are really "included" and a part of the activities going on,[19] and we can also infer the same issues in other integrated venues. This leads us to peer mentoring and the importance of creating a mentoring program that not only trains peers to work with

Peer mentors are essential for both developing social skills and independence.

others who may have disabilities but also teaches them acceptance, communication, and empathy.[20] In integrated activity settings, peer mentors are taught to model the skills, work one on one together, communicate appropriately, and help the individual with a disability gain independence, but this cannot happen without training and constant support from the practitioner. Peer mentors should be prepared in areas such as behavior management (such as what to do when someone has a behavior meltdown), activity modifications, how to use equipment safely, and how to give feedback to others in order to start the mentoring relationship.

In many cases throughout the literature, we see the term "peer tutor" used to describe the interactions that occur between individuals with disabilities and their peers in various integrated settings; however, we prefer "peer mentor" as we feel it more adequately describes the ideal we are trying to portray. For the purposes of this chapter, peer mentors model the skills, lead instruction, and help the individual with a disability gain independence through being a part of a sport-related activity. They are able to gain this independence through repetition and practice, learning to master the skills and knowledge of the rules of sport-related activities important for that setting. Students collaborating together creates an environment for all individual skill levels to be successful.

When and where peer mentors can be utilized

A peer mentor is the biggest asset a teacher, coach, or recreational facility can incorporate into their programs. In the school setting, we call upon peers to serve as mentors to model skills and lead instruction to their classmates. In the athletic setting, team captains take the roles of mentors and set the tone for practices and games for the program. In recreation and leisure sports, mentors can serve as role models for all community activities through these leadership opportunities. A peer mentor can be utilized in any sport or activity that builds socialization through peer relationships. Seeing the value of peer relationships is important to understanding how and when a mentor can be an asset.

With growing opportunities for individuals with disabilities to participate in athletic programs, this corresponds to a need for well-trained peer mentors. Through programs like Unified Sports and physical education, peers are participating in various physical activity opportunities alongside individuals with disabilities, which helps to facilitate acceptance and social inclusion.

Responsibilities of a Mentor

Responsibilities for the peer mentors must be well defined and peer mentors need training for best teaching practices. Mentors collaborate with the practitioner to assist in all facets of the activity. Basic responsibilities of a peer mentor recommended for a high school APE program, youth sports, or recreational program include:

1. Begin each activity with social interactions between peers: Being integrated in a class or athletic setting that provides the least restrictive environment for all individuals helps to build socialization because being a part of a team or a classroom environment in the sports arena can be socially rewarding for all if facilitated appropriately by the practitioner. It is imperative that the peer mentors understand that the conversations should be age appropriate to work on enhancing social skills. Train the mentors on any assistive communication or other devices in advance by utilizing a technology platform that provides video instruction and allows for discussion forum posts. Have the paraprofessional or physical/occupational therapist be proactive with an informational lesson prior to the mentors working with any person that has an assistive device (e.g., wheelchairs, orthotics). Educating the mentors on communication and ambulatory devices helps to eliminate any fears or doubts they may display when socially interacting with an individual. Educating the mentors on how students with disabilities communicate and how they may use assistive devices is key to creating an inclusive social environment.

2. Set Up and Break Down Equipment: Mentors/coaches working alongside individuals with disabilities requires cooperation and organization. Being able to include everyone in the set up and break down of an activity reinforces life skills, examples include: following a set of directions, organizing equipment by colors, placing cones around hazards, and putting on a team jersey. Being involved in the preparation allows all individuals to take an active role in learning cooperation. Working together in sport settings translates to future settings where we can see individuals with disabilities as adults working alongside their peers in the workforce.

3. Demonstrate Skills: Peer mentors serve as leaders. The mentors completing the activity

first through demonstration can motivate individuals with disabilities to try something new by watching a peer do the activity or skill first. Conversely, the individual with a disability can also demonstrate the skill for their mentor because all individuals have abilities and by allowing this reciprocal exchange, it is instilling a sense of "can" in both the person with and without a disability. The mentors are leaders and motivators, but for skill demonstration, you can have a well-balanced model between those with and without disabilities.

4. Model each skill/movement/activity through active participation: Mentors can and should participate in the activities alongside individuals with disabilities. Participation from all ability levels unifies every activity and person and helps each person to learn patience and leadership skills as everyone is learning together. The mentor must also be aware of safety during participation and know how to modify activities if needed, since the activity should be adapted to include all individuals as active participants rather than having someone sit on the sideline because they are unable to complete the activities. Similar to the paraprofessional, the mentor should not dominate the activity and allow for everyone to be a participant. Mentors must be aware of surroundings and be advised about not being that person who jumps in front of someone to field every ball, or the person who has to take every shot, but instead letting everyone have a chance. The lessons learned through sport carry over into daily life with socialization into adulthood and understanding there are different ability levels of people who can successfully participate not only in sport but also in society.

5. Complete lessons and training prior to activities: Providing lessons or plans on the sport or fitness related activity prior to the day it is implemented helps mentors with content knowledge ahead of time rather than just on the day you plan to do the activities. The mentor must feel comfortable performing the skill and have knowledge of game rules, so the practitioner should plan ahead of time to prepare them to model these skills and activities. Having educational videos, articles, and graphics available for mentors to review prior to an activity will help the flow of the sport-related activity.

Peer mentors need training on individuals with disabilities to help them understand how to be a better mentor. Utilizing a family member, prior coach, or

Support can come in various forms and setting to ensure all are able to participate.

paraprofessional to gain knowledge of how to communicate, mobility hurdles, or strengths in advance of the activity can provide insight on the best way to maximize participation.

Sample Activities for Peer Mentors

1. FlipGrid Introductions: Utilizing the technology of FlipGrid® connects individuals prior to an activity (see https://info.flipgrid.com for more information on how to create). Each person can create a video that answers basic questions in a prompt: What is your name, What is one cool thing you did this summer? What is your favorite sport? Every person can see how each individual communicates and place a face with a name.
2. ABC Workout (see Table 11.2): This type of workout can be used to learn names and create a smaller group for individuals who are transitioning into a new environment. Provide a template to all students with the 26 letters and squares that they can fill in gifs of them performing an exercise. This activity can progress to the student with a disability being the model for the gifs that are added to the workout sheet and by the end of the year they can have their own ABC workout of them that they can take home and do on their own or with their families.

Assignment Directions: Create an ABC workout for your peers. For each letter of the alphabet, assign an exercise and a goal for each. During the activity, you can practice spelling different words using the exercises associated with each letter (like your name).

Exercise Types: Create exercises that cross the center line of the body, work different muscle groups in the body, develop core strength, or build cardio. Create exercises that can be done in a smaller space of the gym. You are the model for the exercise. Make a gif for each exercise utilizing an app that is available on your electronic device. Examples: bicycle crunches, lunges, squats.

Mentor Application Process

How would you select a mentor in a physical education, sport-related, or recreational setting? The mentors are working with modeling and participating alongside individuals with disabilities for a large portion of time in a school, recreation facility, or summer camp setting so it is important that there is a systematic approach to finding the motivated mentor. The selection process must be valid and include deadlines with a start and end date. A peer can serve as a role model in negative and positive ways, so it is important that the selection process is thorough. Providing a diverse set of questions for open-ended written responses allows for a broader selection process for all mentor applicants. Creating a Google form allows the applicants' responses to be recorded anonymously and with point values awarded for some of the questions accommodates a fair process. Having a greater number of mentors than needed is a good problem to have in case a mentor misses a day of school or practice. This is especially helpful when working with

TABLE 11.2 *ABC Workout*

Mentors: Create a gif for each exercise **Directions:** Select a workout based on your name or any other word with your peers.			
A 20 Jumping Jacks	**B** 10 Jump Squats	**C** 20 Squats	**D** 10 Frankenstein Kicks
E 10 Squats	**F** 20 Mountain Climbers	**G** 20 Arm Circles	**H** 20 Side Lunges
I 20 Bicycle Crunches	**J** 10 Lunges	**K** 20 High Knees	**L** 10 Jump Squats
M 10 Push-Ups	**N** 20 Supermans	**O** 10 Burpees	**P** 10 Frankenstein Kicks
Q 20 Sit-Ups	**R** 20 Crunches	**S** 10 Inch Worms	**T** 1 Minute Wall Sit
U 20 Swimmers	**V** 20 Alt Superman	**W** 20 Calf Raises	**X** 20 Mountain Climbers
Y 10 Lunges	**Z** 20 Windmills	**LEVELS** Beg—Reach Goals Int—Try More Reps Adv—Add Weights	

individuals with autism because they tend to need routine and working with the same person helps to maintain that routine, so having two or three people they are comfortable working with will alleviate that issue if one happens to be absent.

In the application, you can create a point system for questions 3, 4, and 7 (see the following list) to help narrow the selection process. For questions 3 and 4 it asks about family members with disabilities. Family members of individuals with disabilities can add insight and help train peer mentors, and having prior experience interacting with individuals with disabilities can be helpful. For question 7, the selection process can narrow by taking the applicants with future career paths in special education, physical therapy, or speech therapy and award them a point for career related interest. Many mentors will leave the class or sport program and discover that the mentoring experience led them to a future career path by working alongside the professionals already in the career field.

Sample application questions for the selection of mentors

1. Why do you want to be a peer mentor for the APE/sport program? Answer in 4 or more sentences.
2. What is inclusion and why is it important to you?
3. Do you have a sibling that has a disability?
4. Do you have a family member that has a disability?
5. List 3 ways you would try to provide motivation for a peer who does not want to participate in a sport or fitness related activity.
6. List 3 strengths you have that would be valuable as a peer mentor.
7. What is your future career path beyond high school?

Implementing the program

Mentors will leave a well-run peer mentoring program with more empathy, compassion, and understanding of individuals with disabilities. Implementing a program that is well organized and beneficial for all who are involved takes energy and a lot of support as well as planning ahead of time. Mentors who are engaged in an activity alongside their peers leave the experience with the impression that was echoed throughout: "You will learn more from the individual than you could ever teach them." Having more opportunity for young people to be involved in a mentoring program in the APE or sport setting translates to friendships and more understanding of individuals with a disability which can continue to be developed and maintained in adulthood.

The peer mentor experience may only be one class or one sport, but the connection that is made between students with and without disabilities can have a lifelong effect on everyone involved. Peer mentors will learn just as much if not more from individuals with disabilities than the other way around. In order to expand the mentoring experience into other venues, a practitioner can continue to provide peer mentors with resources to be part of other experiences in the community to make a difference for individuals with disabilities.

Volunteering opportunities

1. Special Olympics—www.specialolympics.org/get-involved/volunteer
2. Coaching Unified Sports—https://nfhslearn.com/courses/coaching-unified-sports
3. Volunteer Match—www.volunteermatch.org/search/opp433267.jsp
4. Down Syndrome Sports of America—www.dssasports.org/

Parents and/or Guardians

Why parents? IDEA mandates that parents and/or guardians be included as part of the educational process of their children with disabilities, in fact, parents are to be included as part of the multidisciplinary team outlined on the IEP or 504 plan. Despite this mandate, parents are often mere spectators in this process.[21] It has been documented that when parents are included and involved in their children's education, children tend to do better academically[22] and this has also been noted in physical activity settings.[23] In fact, parental involvement has a stronger effect on their child's academic performance than parental income or education level.[24] Even though parents may or may not have an educational background regarding their child's disabilities, parents know their children and their tendencies best. They can provide input about likes and dislikes of their children and their families, and can provide insight into family activities and sports, which is valuable information when developing the child's educational, exercise, or therapy plan. Throughout the rest of this section, we will refer to parents and guardians as "parents," but note we are referring to anyone who has guardianship of the individual.

When and Where Parents Can be Utilized

Parents can be great assets in terms of practicing the skills their children learned at school or in recreation/sports by performing those skills at home. As previously mentioned, and stipulated by IDEA, parents are part of their children's multidisciplinary team. Therefore, they should be part of the development of their children's IEP, and they are key players in the decision making for their children. That includes providing information regarding the activities to be included in their child's education. Unfortunately, research studies highlight the fact that not all families are familiar with the educational services their children receive.[25–27] Therefore, a strong communication between teachers, parents, and coaches must exist. We will expand on the importance of communication in a later section.

Parents can also be of great assistance when developing and running school activities. For example, when organizing a field day, parents can assist teachers in the organization and even provide ideas on how to better include their children. During this process, both teachers and parents should discuss the types of activities that will be taking place as well as modifications that can be made to each activity or station to help all children to be successful. By utilizing this approach, parents may feel welcome and may feel they are part of the education team. Teachers can ask parents for their opinion in terms of the content and sequencing of activities. Teachers can even build upon parental expertise in terms of their child's likes and dislikes. Researchers have also demonstrated the effectiveness of using parents as teachers for their children to assist in the improvement of fundamental motor skills[28,29] and aquatic skills.[30] In those studies, physical activity professionals, such as physical education teachers, provided parents with teaching tips and strategies for parents to practice the activities with their children at home.

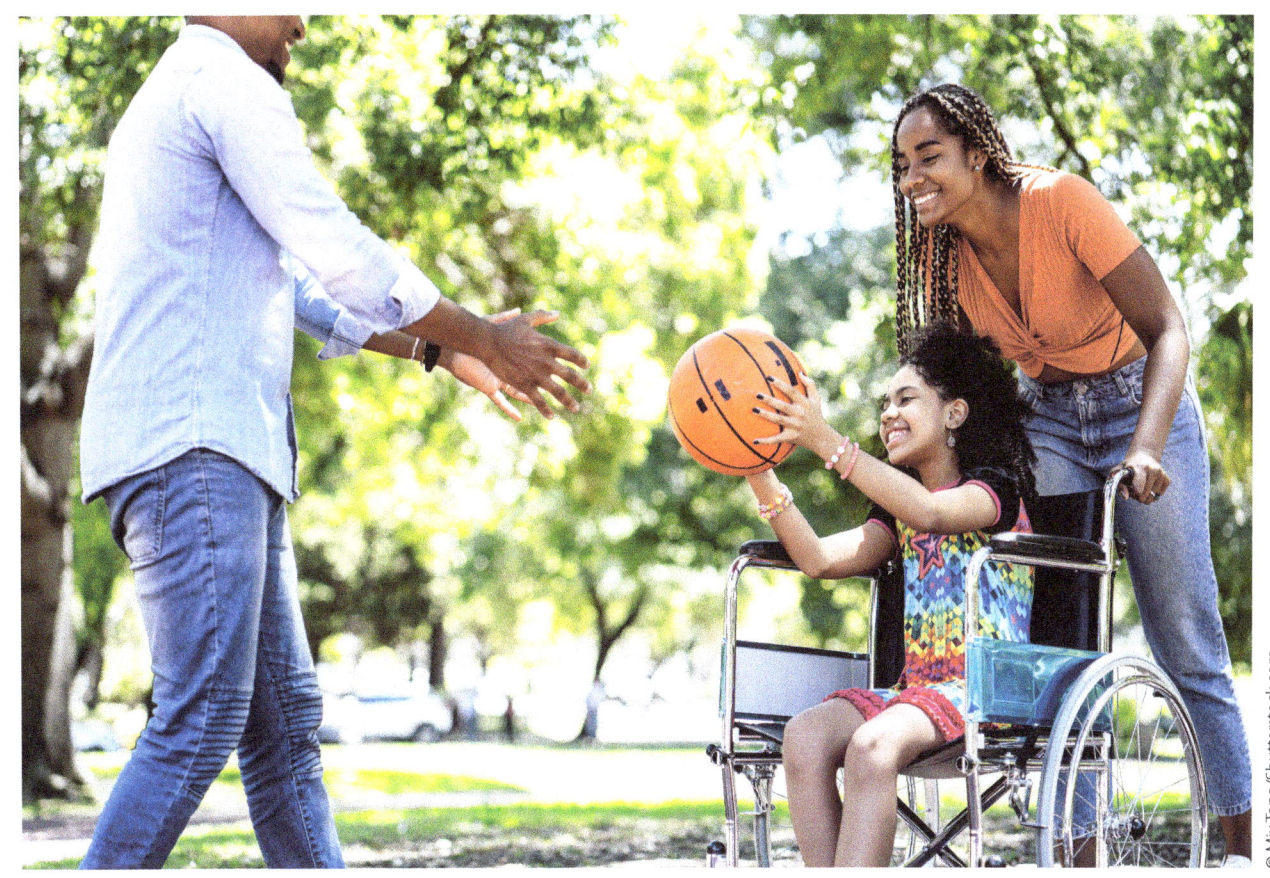

Advantages of Utilizing Parents

By including parents into their child's education, this is beneficial not only for the teacher but also for the child and the parent. For starters, parents can assist and expand on the skills learned at school and other activity based settings to their home environment. Also, as we have previously indicated, parents can provide practitioners with pertinent information that can assist them when delivering their instruction or services. However, one of the most important advantages of including parents is that this practice can empower them to try to better teach and advocate for their children. When parents are able to do that, their children will be better equipped to participate in physical activities within different settings. Moreover, parents will have the skills to collaborate, support, and expand the content taught by practitioners to their children. When practitioners work with parents, one of the key components should be providing them with essential information that will result in parental acquisition of teaching and advocacy skills.[28]

Communication with Parents

Practitioners are typically taught in their undergraduate programs how to implement and make accommodations in terms of games and activities specific to their work setting. However, what is not typically taught to future practitioners is how to effectively communicate and collaborate with parents, particularly with diverse families.[31,32] Therefore, it is critical for practitioners to welcome parents, and establish direct and ongoing lines of communication with them. Beyond the mandates required by law, practitioners should find ways to communicate on a regular and consistent basis with families. This communication can take several forms including, but not limited to, verbal communication, written notification, and the use of technology (e.g., Facebook, text messaging). Is important to note that each of these forms of communication has advantages and disadvantages. For example, while Facebook has become extremely popular among parents of children with disabilities, and many are part of Facebook groups, it is important to remember that

© Jaren Jai Wicklund/Shutterstock.com

not all parents have access to or are proficient with this platform. Therefore, teachers must identify the preferred method of communication parents typically utilize or prefer.

Best Practices for Training Parents

There is no simple recipe to work efficiently with parents. However, from an educational or a physical activity point of view, the first step is to get to know the individual and their families. Families of individuals with disabilities face multiple barriers in accessing community resources. These barriers include lack of program availability, financial constraints, the individual's disability, lack of program information, and a need for disability awareness in the community.[33]

Once you have a clear understanding of perceived or existing barriers, do not assume that they lack the knowledge on how you can better work with their children. Build upon their expertise and ask them simple questions such as, "What do you like to do in your free time as a family?" or "What community resources do you have available to you?" Be careful when asking simple questions on how you can better support the parents because sometimes parents are unaware of the support they need, or types of support available for their children. Many parents tend to be overwhelmed with their children's education to a point that physical activity, including physical education, is placed on the back burner.

Researchers have indicated that when parents are taught appropriate skills versus only given general information, the outcomes tend to be greater.[27,34] That is, instead of only providing basic information about the importance of physical activity and nutrition, it will be more beneficial teaching them how to engage in physical activity together or how to prepare a healthy meal. School nights are excellent venues to teach skills to multiple families all together in the same setting (e.g., school gymnasium), becoming more effective than setting separate individual meetings with each family. However, it is important to note that those individual meetings are also important to create a bond between the practitioner and the family. Furthermore, because of technology, teachers can create short videos of ideas on how to play games and activities at home or as a family. Similarly, via text messages, e-mails, or social media pages, practitioners can share ideas with parents about games, social events, and teaching/coaching tips.

Sample Program for Training Parents

An example of a program that teaches parents how to play and enhance physical activity participation for their children who have disabilities is Fit Families, created by Dr. Luis Columna and housed at the University of Wisconsin-Madison. In this section we will briefly discuss the original program designed for children with visual impairments (VI) and then, we will present a description of a second program designed for children with autism spectrum disorder (ASD) and their parents. As part of the Fit Families program, parents are taught to meet the physical activity needs of their children. The purpose of the program for children with VI was to enhance the quality of life of the children and their families by promoting activity and maximizing the physical activity opportunities of the families.[28,35] This was made possible through a series of workshops covering information related to (a) orientation and mobility, (b) physical activity and motor development, (c) aquatics, and (d) sports.[35] As part of this program, specialists from the fields of adapted physical education, orientation and mobility, and special education provided parents with the skills to teach a variety of games and activities to their children along with how to use the related equipment. At the culmination of each workshop, families received a variety of free equipment (e.g., beep balls, soccer balls) pertinent to each of the workshops.

Building on the success obtained from the VI program, Columna and his team designed a similar program for children with ASD. Because the needs of children with VI tend to be different than the needs of children with ASD, the content and structure of the workshops was modified to fit the needs of the families. Therefore, Columna and his team provided five workshops covering the topics of (a) sensory integration, (b) communication, (c) aquatics, (d) physical activity, and (e) sports. The sensory integration and communication workshops were added because these are some of the hallmark characteristics of autism. Physical activity and sports were selected because children with ASD tend to have minimal participation and opportunities in these areas.[36] A workshop in aquatics was selected because drowning is the number one cause of death among children with ASD.[37] Like the VI program, parents received physical education equipment and lesson plans for them to practice the activities at home.

Fit Families training

As part of Fit Families, each workshop is divided into two sections. For the first part, the parents attend the workshops (e.g., sensory integration, physical activity) where parents learn about each of the topics and about different games to promote fundamental motor skills and physical activity.[38] Also, during this session, parents receive the related equipment and activity booklets, and they are taught how to use them. All booklets focus on addressing locomotor skills such as run, gallop, skip, hop, slide, and horizontal jump. Ball control activities such as overhand and underhand throw, catch, kick, dribble, and one and two hand strike are also included. Figure 11.8 is an example of the games/activities included in each of the booklets (Please note: the QR code in the figure has been deactivated, but the games and activities can be recorded and attached to a QR code.). In this example, parents learn how to introduce and modify a dribbling game for their child. Each "lesson plan" includes the equipment the participants will need from the equipment they were provided and the formation (e.g., set up of the activity). Also, the task(s) the parent and the child need to perform are also included. There is also a section that includes modifications on how to make the activities easier or more challenging for the children. An aspect that it is well received by parents is the addition of QR codes with a video demonstration on how to play each game. While parents are attending the workshops, their children are participating with undergraduate students in various physical activities related to what the parents are learning in the workshops.

The second part of each training session is where parents have an opportunity to practice newly acquired skills with their children. While parents are interacting and practicing some of the games with their children, undergraduate students and staff members support them and provide feedback on the interactions between the parent and the child (i.e., how they play each of the games and on the feedback provided by parents to the child).

Practitioners can use the framework presented earlier and share physical activity ideas and equipment use with parents. For example, teachers can share short videos of the games they are planning to play during a given week. Ideally, they can also share the equipment they will be using with the parents so they can practice the activities together

Treasure Hunt

Equipment: 1 Basketball or 1 Playground ball. Several small objects in the "treasure chest." **Preparation:** Start and end point using a hallway or outdoor space. The "treasure chest" can be a bucket, a kitchen bowl, or any other object around the house. Place 5-6 toys in the chest for the child to retrieve.	**Skill:** Dribbling

Formation: The child will start at the start line, and wait until the parent says "Go" for the activity to start.

What the parent will do:	What the child will do:
The parent will set up pathway for student to dribble. Parent will make sure the child is maintaining a dribble, and only picking up the dribble when picking up the "treasure."	The child will start at the beginning, and dribble the pathway all the way to the end to collect the "treasure." Collecting only one piece of the "treasure" with hand, and bring it all the way to the start.

Modifications:

Too easy? Add zigzags to pathway. Use a smaller playground ball. Can Time Child

Too difficult? Keep the pathway in a straight line. Allow the child to throw the object back to the beginning, so they do not have to carry the object as well as dribble.

http://uqr.to/ajhr

FIGURE 11.8 Example physical activity for families to participate in together.

Source: Luis Columna

Note: QR Code is currently inactive.

with their children at home. To accomplish this, the practitioner can create a loaner system in which parents who may need a certain piece of equipment can borrow and return it afterward, especially if adapted equipment is needed as it can sometimes be pricey or difficult to obtain. Another alternative is sharing ideas of games and activities that require minimal to no equipment such as body weight exercises and activities. The overall idea here is that we need to begin providing training to parents and extend the physical education curriculum, sport activities, and physical activity opportunities to their home environments, and programs such as Fit Families are an excellent way to provide this training and support.

CHAPTER SUMMARY

- Support personnel can work with practitioners in a variety of settings, including, but not limited to, physical/occupational therapy, physical/adapted physical education, sports, and fitness centers/community programs.
- Many times, practitioners expect that support personnel know what to do in physical activity settings when, in fact, they do not.
- Paraeducators typically work with individuals with disabilities in educational settings and be adequately prepared and trained to work in physical activity settings before they start working in those settings.
- Peer mentors are an integral part to promoting integration and more importantly, inclusion of individuals with disabilities in sports,

fitness/physical activities, and physical education, but they too must be prepared ahead of implementing a mentoring program.
- Parents can help their children to practice the activities learned in physical activity settings and can help them to learn to generalize the skills and activities to settings outside the school or gym environment.
- With paraeducators, peers, and parents, it is important that all responsibilities are laid out ahead of time and discussed to clarify any unclear movements or activities that will be done during the activity session.
- Paraeducators, peers, and parents can all be assets to any practitioner but the key is communication and collaboration among one another. Mutual respect and open lines of communication will help to strengthen any program.

REFERENCES

1. Bryan, R. R., McCubbin, J. A., & van der Mars, H. (2013). The ambiguous role of the paraeducator in the general physical education environment. *Adapted Physical Activity Quarterly, 29*, 164–183.
2. Morrison, H. J., & Gleddie, D. (2019). Playing on the same team: Collaboration between teachers and educational assistants for inclusive physical education. *Journal of Physical Education, Recreation, and Dance, 90*(8), 34–41.
3. French, N. K., & Gerlach, K. (1999). Paraeducators: Who are they and what do they do? *Teaching Exceptional Children, 32*(1), 65–69.
4. Individuals with Disabilities Education Improvement Act of 2004, *Public Law No. 108 446*, 118 Stat. 2647 (2004).
5. Giangreco, M. F., Edelman, S. W., & Broer, S. M. (2003). Schoolwide planning to improve paraeducator supports. *Exceptional Children, 70*, 63–79.
6. Goodwin, D. L., Rossow-Kimball, B., & Connolly, M. (2021). Students' experiences of paraeducator support in inclusive physical education: Helping or hindering? *Sport, Education and Society*, Advance Online Publication. www.doi.org/10.1080/13573322.2021.1931835
7. Haegele, J. Sato, T., Zhu, X., & Kirk, T. N. (2019). Paraeducator support in integrated physical education as reflected by adults with visual impairments. *Adapted Physical Activity Quarterly, 36*, 91–108.
8. Giangreco, M. F., Edelman, S. W., Luiselli, T. E., & MacFarland, S. Z. (1997). Helping or hovering? Effects of instructional assistant proximity on students with disabilities. *Exceptional Children, 64*, 7–18.
9. Lee, S., & Haegele, J. (2016). Tips for effectively utilizing paraprofessionals in physical education. *Journal of Physical Education, Recreation, and Dance, 87*(1), 46–48.
10. U.S. Bureau of Labor Statistics (2022). *Teacher assistants.* https://www.bls.gov/ooh/education-training-and-library/teacher-assistants.htm
11. Giangreco, M. F., Suter, J. C., & Doyle, M. B. (2010). Paraprofessionals in inclusive schools: A review of recent research. *Journal of Educational and Psychological Consultation, 20*, 41–57.
12. Educational Testing Service. (2021). *ETS ParaPro.* www.ets.org/parapro/.
13. Geslak, D. (2019). Paraeducators: Valuable front-line insights for physical educators. *Palaestra, 33*(4), 53–57.
14. French, N. K. (2003). *Managing paraeducators in your school: How to hire, train, and supervise non-certified staff.* Corwin Press.
15. Haycock, D., & Smith, A. (2011). To assist or not to assist? A study of teachers' views of the roles of learning support assistants in the provision of inclusive physical education in England. *International Journal of Inclusive Education, 15*, 835–849.
16. Davis, R. W., Kotecki, J. E., Harvey, M. W., & Oliver, A. (2007). Responsibilities and training needs of paraeducators in physical education. *Adapted Physical Activity Quarterly, 24*, 70–83.
17. Piletic, C., Davis, R., & Aschemeier, A. (2005). Paraeducators in physical education. *Journal of Physical Education, Recreation, and Dance, 76*(5), 47–55.
18. Lytle, R., Lieberman, L., & Aiello, R. (2007). Motivating paraeducators to be actively involved in physical education programs. *Journal of Physical Education, Recreation, and Dance, 78*(4), 26–50.
19. Haegele, J. A., & Zhu, X. (2017). Experiences of individuals with visual impairments in integrated physical education: A retrospective study. *Research Quarterly for Exercise and Sport, 88*, 425–435.
20. Ginis, K. A. M., Nigg, C. R., & Smith, A. L. (2013). Peer-delivered physical activity interventions: an overlooked opportunity for physical activity promotion. *Translational Behavioral Medicine, 3*(4), 434–443.
21. Burke, M. M. (2013). Improving parental involvement: Training special education advocates. *Journal of Disability Policy Studies, 23*(4), 225–234.
22. Flores de Apodaca, R., Gentling, D. G., Steinhaus, J. K., & Rosenberg, E. A. (2015). Parental involvement as a mediator of academic performance among special

education middle school students. *School Community Journal, 25*(2), 35–54.
23. Siebert, E. A., Hamm, J., & Yun, J. (2017). Parental influence on physical activity of children with disabilities. *International Journal of Disability, Development and Education, 64*(4), 378–390.
24. Henderson, A. T., & Mapp, K. L. (2002). A new wave of evidence: The impact of school, family, and community connections on student achievement. *Annual Synthesis*. https://sedl.org/connections/resources/evidence.pdf
25. An, J., & Goodwin, D. (2007). Physical education for students with spina bifida: Mothers' perspectives. *Adapted Physical Activity Quarterly, 24,* 38–58.
26. Columna, L., Pyfer, J., Senne, T., Velez, L., Bridenthrall, N., & Canabal, M. Y. (2008). Parental expectations of adapted physical educators: A Hispanic perspective. *Adapted Physical Activity Quarterly, 25*(3), 228–246.
27. Columna, L., Felizola, G., Prieto, L., Myers, B., Streete, D., & Lightburn, A. (2020). The experiences of Hispanic families of children with autism spectrum disorder regarding physical activity. *Research in Developmental Disabilities, 107,* 103785.
28. Columna, L., Streete, D. A., Hodge, S. R., Dillon, S. R., Myers, B., Norris, M. L., Barreira, T. V., & Heffernan, K. S. (2018). Parents' beliefs about physical activity for their children with visual impairments. *Adapted Physical Activity Quarterly, 35*(4), 361–380.
29. Sayers, L. K., Cowden, J. E., & Sherrill, C. (2002). Parents' perceptions of motor interventions for infants and toddlers with Down syndrome. *Adapted Physical Activity Quarterly, 19,* 199–219.
30. Prupas, A., Harvey, W. J., & Benjamin, J. (2006). Early intervention aquatics: A program for children with autism and their families. *Journal of Physical Education, Recreation, and Dance, 77*(2), 46–51.
31. Chaapel, H., Columna, L., Lytle, R., & Bailey, J. (2013). Parental expectations about adapted physical education services. *The Journal of Special Education, 47*(3), 186–196.
32. Columna, L., Senne, T. A., & Lytle, R. (2009). Communicating with Hispanic parents of children with and without disabilities. *Journal of Physical Education, Recreation & Dance, 80*(4), 48–54.
33. Columna, L., Prieto, L., Elias-Revolledo, G., & Haegele, J. A. (2020). The perspectives of parents of youth with disabilities toward physical activity: A systematic review. *Disability and health journal, 13*(2), 100851.
34. O'Connor, T. M., Jago, R., & Baranowski, T. (2009). Engaging parents to increase youth physical activity: A systematic review. *American Journal of Preventive Medicine, 37*(2), 141–149.
35. Columna, L. (2017). Syracuse university fit families program: Physical activity program for families of children with visual impairments. *Palaestra, 31*(1), 32–39.
36. McCoy, S. M., & Morgan, K. (2020). Obesity, physical activity, and sedentary behaviors in adolescents with autism spectrum disorder compared with typically developing peers. *Autism, 24*(2), 387–399.
37. Lepore, M., Columna, L., & Friedlander-Litzner, L. (2015). *Assessments and activities for teaching swimming*. Human Kinetics.
38. Davis, T., Columna, L., Abdo, A. L., Russo, N., Toole, K., & Norris, M. L. (2017). Sensory motor activities training for families of children with autism spectrum disorders. *Palaestra, 31*(4), 35–40.

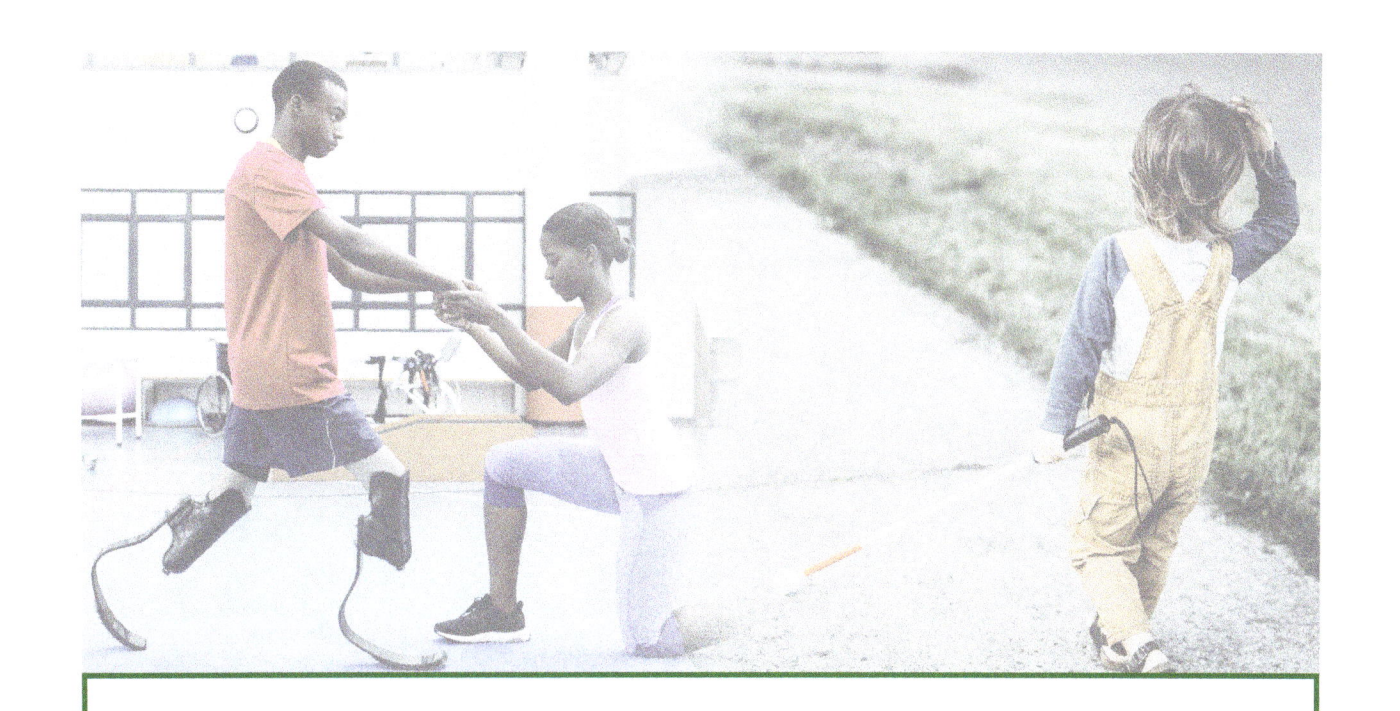

PART 2
DISABILITIES

CHAPTER 12
ADULT ONSET AND LIFESTYLE DISEASES AND DISABILITIES

Karen Wonders and Bethany L. Hersman

This chapter presents the use of exercise and lifestyle changes to manage chronic disease or disability. The first section gives an overview of general physical activity guidelines for a healthy population, as well as characteristics that mark diseases where these guidelines are not met. Whether you are working with a healthy individual, or one with a chronic disease or disability, exercise and medical history must be collected before designing any type of exercise program. Data regarding aerobic capacity, muscular strength and endurance, flexibility, neuromuscular ability, and functional limitations must be collected. This information will guide the exercise prescription and programming, identify any potential risks associated with training, or determine whether a multidisciplinary health care team is warranted.

GENERAL PHYSICAL ACTIVITY GUIDELINES

The conviction that good health is obtained through physical activity and proper nutrition predates historical Greek philosophy and medicine. Hippocrates (460–370 B.C.) is credited as saying, "If we could give every individual the right amount of nourishment and exercise, not too little and not too much, we would have found the safest way to health." Present-day research has allowed for this statement to come full circle, as now we have guidelines to define precisely what the "right amount of exercise is." The World Health Organization (WHO) recommends that children and adolescents aged 5 to 17 years get at least an average of 60 minutes per day of moderate-to-vigorous–intensity aerobic activity. Adults should strive for between 150 and 300 minutes of moderate-intensity aerobic physical activity (or at least 75–150 minutes of vigorous-intensity aerobic physical activity) over the course of 1 week. In addition, adults should do muscle-strengthening activities on 2 or more days/week for additional health benefits.[1]

RISKS OF PHYSICAL INACTIVITY

It is estimated that 92% of adolescents and more than 95% of adults do not meet the current guidelines for physical activity.[2] Overwhelming evidence links reductions in physical activity to numerous health conditions, including an increased risk for high blood pressure, type 2 diabetes, coronary heart disease, cancer, anxiety, and depression. In fact, the Centers for Disease Control (CDC) defines physical inactivity as an actual cause of several chronic conditions such as heart disease and diabetes. Overall, physical inactivity is the fourth leading cause of death in the world, taking more than 5 million lives each year. Thus, physical inactivity has a major health effect worldwide. Any decrease in sedentary behavior may therefore improve health sustainability.[3,4]

METABOLIC DISEASES

During the metabolic process, energy is produced from carbohydrates, fats, and proteins. When abnormal chemical reactions in your body disrupt the normal metabolic process, metabolic diseases result.

Karen Wonders and Bethany L. Hersman, Wright State University. © Kendall Hunt Publishing Company.

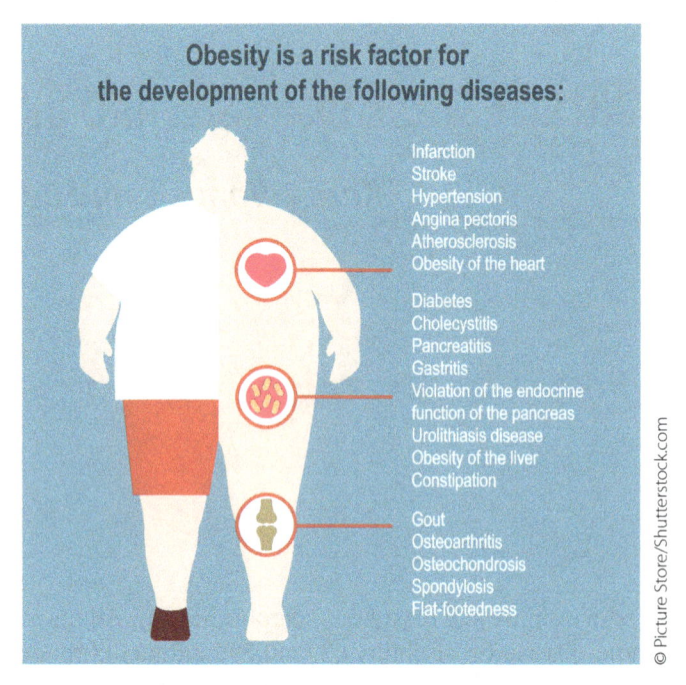

Disease risk increases due to obesity.

Metabolic diseases are a cluster of cardiometabolic risk factors associated with multiple chronic diseases, including cancer and cardiovascular disease. They are characterized by abdominal obesity, and can take on many forms, including:

- A missing enzyme or vitamin that is necessary for a chemical reaction to take place,
- A disease in the liver, endocrine glands, pancreas, or other organs involved in metabolism,
- Nutritional deficiencies, and
- Abnormal chemical reactions that hinder the metabolic processes.

Metabolic diseases include chronic diseases, such as hyperlipidemia, diabetes, and obesity. These can result from genetics, hormone/enzyme deficiency, and improper nutrition. In 2012, more than one-third of all U.S. adults met the criteria for metabolic disease, with the highest prevalence among non-Hispanic black adults and those with low socioeconomic status. Prevalence of metabolic disease increases rapidly with age, suggesting that efforts to increase education and awareness strategies to increase physical activity and proper nutrition should begin early such as in physical and health education classes in school.[5]

Hyperlipidemia

Lipids include fats, fatty acids, cholesterol, and triglycerides. They play a vital role in the storage of biochemical energy, structure of cell membranes, and regulation of metabolism. Because lipids are hydrophobic, cholesterol must be transported throughout the body by combining with lipoproteins. Two types of lipoproteins are **low-density lipoproteins (LDL)**, which is the principal carrier of cholesterol, and **high-density lipoprotein (HDL)**, which is involved in the reverse transport of cholesterol (i.e., from the peripheral tissues back to the liver).

The lipoprotein metabolic pathways can be altered through various environmental, genetic, and pathologic factors, including gender, age, body fat, nutrition status, cigarette smoking, certain medication, genetic disposition, and physical activity levels.[6] When these factors combine to yield elevated blood triglyceride and cholesterol levels in the body, hyperlipidemia results. Table 12.1 presents normal and elevated levels of triglycerides and cholesterol.

Management and Medications

The management of hyperlipidemia begins with dietary modifications, exercise, and weight loss as an initial treatment for the first 6 weeks after diagnosis. Following this, pharmacological therapy is the primary treatment modality. Even with pharmacological treatment, daily exercise is recommended for all individuals, due to research that shows a decrease in plasma triglycerides and increase in glucose tolerance (a contributing factor to hyperlipidemia). The most common lipid-lowering medication is statin

TABLE 12.1 Cholesterol and triglyceride levels

	Triglycerides (mg/dl)	Total Cholesterol (mg/dl)	LDL (mg/dl)	HDL (mg/dl)
Normal	<150	<200	<100	<40 for men, <50 for women
Borderline high	150–199	200–239	200–239	
High	200–499	>240	>240	>60
Very high	>500			

therapy, which inhibits liver enzymes involved in lipid transport. Statins are generally well tolerated, and at their maximal doses reduce LDL cholesterol by 20% to 60%, while increasing HDL by 6% to 10%. The primary side effect from statin use is muscular discomfort, which tends to be exacerbated by eccentric exercise because the muscle lengthens as it contracts (for example, the downward motion of a squat or lowering weights for a shoulder press).[7]

Effects of Exercise

Hyperlipidemia alone does not alter the exercise response, unless it has contributed to cardiovascular disease and exercise is limited by angina (chest pain). On the other hand, regular participation in exercise results in beneficial changes to lipid concentrations for both healthy individuals and those with hyperlipidemia.[8] These changes include:

- Lower triglyceride levels
- Decreased LDL concentrations
- Higher HDL levels
- Increased lipoprotein enzyme activity
- Improved glycemic control

Exercise testing should be performed to determine functional capacity and appropriate intensity range for aerobic training. If comorbidities are present, exercise testing should follow the published recommendations for that particular disorder in question. It is important to note that medications may limit exercise performance through muscle damage. Further, hyperlipidemia alone can lead to cardiac and arterial insufficiency, intravascular sludging, and ischemia (restricted blood flow to the affected area).[8]

Recommendations for Exercise Programming

For the reasons outlined earlier, exercise prescription should take into account any lipid-lowering medications the participant is taking. The primary goal for exercise training is to expend calories, as research indicates favorable lipid changes following aerobic training. Specifically, HDL concentrations increase in exercise regimens expending 1,200 to 1,500 kcals/week, and triglyceride levels were found to decrease after 2 weeks of aerobic exercise in men with hypertriglyceridemia. Resistance training and flexibility exercises are recommended as an addition to aerobic training. According to the American College of Sports Medicine, blood lipid changes are best measured with an exercise program that is:

- Performed at 40% to 80% of maximal functional capacity (moderate intensity),
- Performed at least 5 days/week, for 20 to 60 min/session,
- Incorporates resistance training that is 60% to 80% of 1RM, 2 to 4 sets of 8 to 12 reps, 2 to 3 days/week.[9]

Diabetes

Diabetes is a chronic metabolic disease characterized by insulin deficiency that results in hyperglycemia. Diabetes is diagnosed following a fasting blood glucose level of >125 mg/dl, a glucose level of >200 mg/dl with hyperglycemic symptoms, or a 2 hours glucose of >200 mg/dl during an oral glucose tolerance test. Individuals with diabetes are at an increased risk of developing retinopathy, nephropathy, neuropathy, ischemia, heart attack, and stroke.[10]

While several distinct forms of diabetes exist, this chapter will focus on Type 1 and Type 2 diabetes mellitus. Individuals with **Type 1 diabetes** have a marked reduction in insulin-secreting beta cells of the pancreas, resulting in insulin deficiency. As such, exogenous insulin, or insulin not produced by the body, must be supplied by injection or insulin pump. Insulin allows glucose to enter the cells of insulin-sensitive tissue. An insulin pump is a small computerized device that delivers insulin through a catheter.

Medication is usually only able to manage chronic diseases, not cure them.

It is set to deliver basal insulin at a slow rate under resting conditions, and a large bolus dose at mealtimes. The cause of Type 1 diabetes is unclear, although it is thought to involve an autoimmune response triggered by viruses or toxins. Most Type 1 diabetes diagnoses occur before the age of 30.[10]

Type 2 diabetes affects approximately 90% to 95% of the 20.8 million people with diabetes. It is characterized by hyperglycemia regardless of the individual's insulin status. In short, individuals have a relative insulin deficiency with either high, low, or normal insulin levels. With insulin resistance, glucose does not readily enter the insulin sensitive tissues (i.e., muscle and adipose tissue), resulting in an increase in blood glucose levels.[11] In an attempt to maintain normal blood glucose concentration, the increase in blood glucose levels causes the pancreas to secrete more insulin.

The underlying cause of Type 2 diabetes is unclear, but most individuals are overweight or obese at onset, linking obesity as a clear significant contributor to insulin resistance. In addition, Type 2 diabetes is associated with old age, physical inactivity, family history, race, and/or ethnicity. The ethnic groups most commonly affected include African Americans, Hispanic-Latino Americans, American Indians, and Alaskan Natives.[10]

Management and Medications

Diabetes management is dependent on the type of diabetes, blood glucose status, and the presence and severity of any related complications. The ultimate goal is to safely normalize blood glucose levels. This is primarily accomplished through insulin or oral agents, an individualized nutrition plan, and participation in an exercise program. Medication also tends to include aspirin, antihypertensives, and lipid-lowering agents, since mortality and morbidity in diabetes are largely related to cardiovascular disease. The most significant effect of some oral agents used in the treatment of Type 2 diabetes, namely glucosidase inhibitors, meglitinides, and secretagogues, can produce hypoglycemia during or after exercise. Therefore, the timing of food intake; medication; and blood glucose levels before, during, and after exercise are necessary. Blood glucose levels should be checked during any exercise session lasting longer than 60 minutes, to ensure that they have not dropped to dangerously low levels.[12]

Recommendations for Exercise Programming

Exercise testing recommendations are dependent upon age, type and duration of diabetes, and presence of diabetic complications. In general, protocols for populations at risk for coronary artery disease are recommended for individuals with Type 1 diabetes and who are over the age of 30 and/or have had Type 1 diabetes longer than 15 years. In addition, these protocols are recommended in individuals with Type 2 diabetes who are over the age of 35, those who have one or more risk factors for coronary artery disease, or who have any microvascular or neurological diabetic complications.[9]

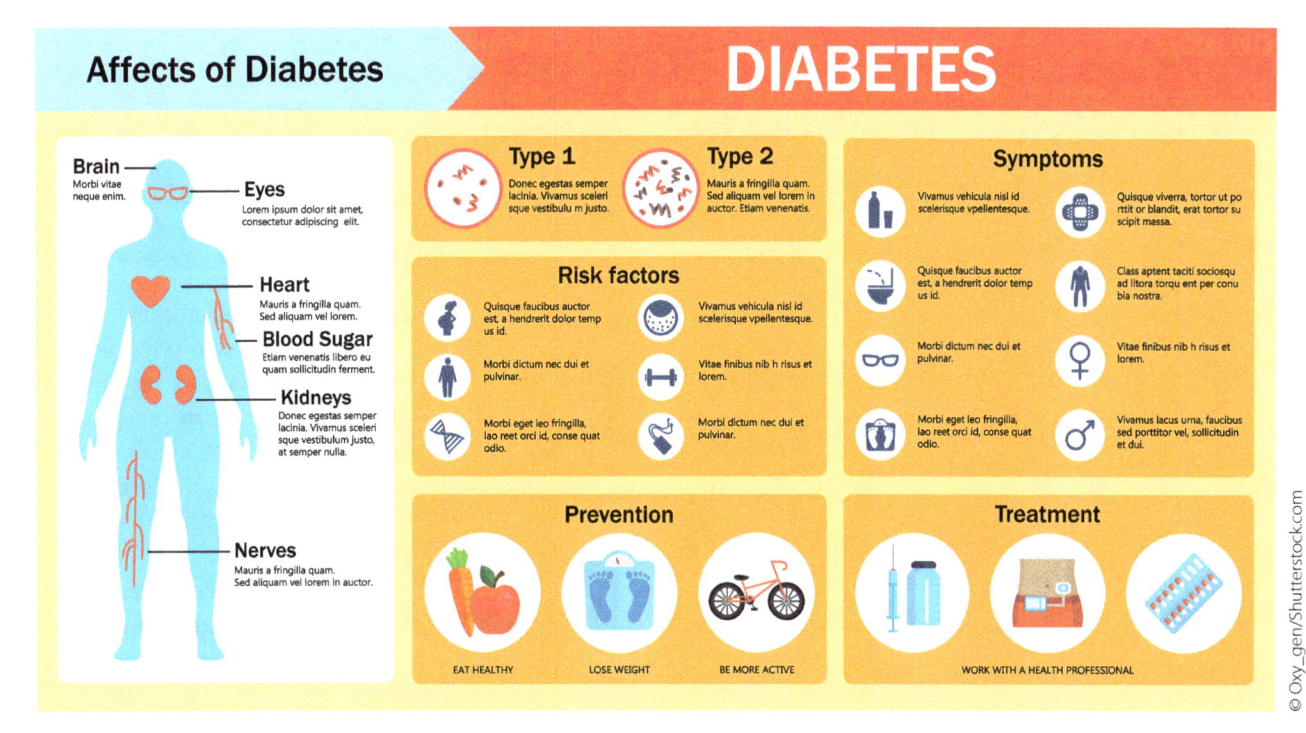

Understanding diabetes and what affects it.

The primary objectives of exercise testing in a diabetic population are to identify the presence and severity of coronary artery disease and determine appropriate intensity for aerobic exercise testing, which is usually done by an exercise physiologist or a nurse. Because of the high risk of underlying cardiovascular and neurological complications, methods of exercise testing are conservative. A cycle aerobic test protocol is ideal for individuals with poor circulation or peripheral neuropathy. Endpoints for such test include serious dysrhythmias, ST-segment elevation or depression, ischemic threshold, and/or significant T-wave change. In addition, any blood pressure change (SBP >250 mmHg or DBP >115 mmHg) or onset of peripheral pain.[9]

Following exercise testing, the exercise program must be individualized according to the individual's medication, presence and extent of diabetic complications, and desired outcomes of the exercise program. In general, aerobic exercise should be completed between 4 and 7 times/week for 20 to 60 min/session at an intensity of 50% to 80% of VO_{2max}. Resistance training should include low-resistance/high-repetition exercises. Individuals with controlled diabetes can perform high resistance exercises. Flexibility training should be performed to increase range of motion 2 to 3 times/week. In addition, because of the high prevalence of neurological complications observed with the diabetic population, neuromuscular exercises (yoga/balance) should be performed each week to improve coordination and balance.[9,12]

Exercise Considerations

Exercise is contraindicated in a diabetic population under the following conditions.

- Illness or infection is present.
- Blood glucose levels are above 250 mg/dl and ketones are present.
- Blood glucose levels are less than 70 mg/dl.
- Active renal hemorrhage is present.

In addition, a source of carbohydrate should be readily available during exercise. The individual should be encouraged to consume adequate fluids before, during, and after exercise. Finally, individuals should be encouraged to practice proper foot care by wearing proper shoes, cotton socks, and inspecting feet after exercise to watch for blisters or sores as these issues tend not to heal well due to impaired wound healing from a lack of circulation at the site of the injury, especially in the extremities. These issues with reduced circulation in the extremities can lead to eventual infection and possible amputation if not treated and taken care of.[9,12]

Obesity

The excessive accumulation of body fat can lead to the conditions of overweight and **obesity**. Body mass index (BMI) is used as a screening tool for overweight and obesity, and is calculated by dividing a person's body weight in kilograms by the square of height in meters. A high BMI is indicative of overweight or obesity. The following values are used as indices in this determination[13]:

- BMI of 18.5 or less: underweight
- BMI of 18.5 to <25: healthy weight
- BMI of 25.0 to <30: overweight
- BMI > 30.0: obese

Obesity, in particular, is a serious chronic disease that is becoming increasingly more common in the United States. It is associated with numerous life-threatening comorbidities, including insulin resistance, type 2 diabetes, dyslipidemia, hypertension, stroke, cancer, and cardiovascular disease. In the United States, it was estimated that 40.0% of adults aged 20 to 39 years, 44.8% of adults aged 40 to 59 years, and 42.8% of adults aged 60 and older are obese.[14] Rates are notably higher in Hispanic and non-Hispanic black women, and in those without a college education. Similarly, both men and women in the highest income group have the lowest rates of obesity.[15] Despite a two-decade trend of obesity rates increasing, levels have appeared to stabilize since 2006.

Among children and adolescents in the United States, it was estimated that 13.4% of children ages 2 to 5, 20.3% ages 6 to 11, and 21.2% ages 12 to 19 were considered obese in 2017–2018, representing about 14.4 million youth in total.[13] With regard to socioeconomic status, as the education level of the head of household increased, obesity rates declined, and prevalence of obesity was reported at 18.9%, 19.9%, and 10.9% among youth in the lowest, middle, and highest income groups, respectively. Obesity rates were also higher among non-Hispanic black (24.2%) and Hispanic (25.6%) youth as compared to their non-Hispanic white (16.1%) and non-Hispanic Asian counterparts (8.7%).[16] It is important to note that although these numbers have fluctuated over the years in some ethnic groups, the trend shows an increasing rate of obesity among youth since 1963.[17]

Research suggests that a sedentary lifestyle, energy imbalance (the consumption of excess total calories of a diet high in fat and refined sugar), or both are the primary cause(s) of obesity. When the body experiences a period of energy imbalance over an extended period of time, it can induce a physiological response that includes increased fasting insulin and insulin response to glucose, increased adrenocortical hormones, and increased cholesterol synthesis and excretion, as well as decreases in insulin sensitivity, growth hormone, and hormone-sensitive lipase.[18] All of these are associated with obesity.

The distribution of body fat may contribute more to disease than total body fat alone. Individuals with android obesity (upper body fat distribution) have higher rates of coronary artery disease, hyperlipidemia, and diabetes.[15] A technique used to assess body fat distribution is the waist–hip ratio. For this assessment, the minimal waist circumference is measured (at or above the umbilicus) and divided by the circumference of the hips at the widest gluteus level.[9] Standards for the waist–hip ratio are listed in Table 12.2.

TABLE 12.2 Standards for Waist–Hip Ratio

<0.776	Lower body fat distribution for men and women
>0.913	Upper body fat distribution for men
>0.861	Upper body fat distribution for women

Management and Medications

The primary objective of obesity management is the reduction of body fat weight with the preservation of lean body weight. As such, the most common accepted intervention for the treatment of obesity is behavior change that focuses on diet and physical activity. This is the most successful in those individuals who are only slightly or moderately obese, have a sincere desire to lose weight, became overweight as an adult, and do not have a history of weight cycling (losing weight by dieting, gaining the weight back, then dieting again, and so on). Motivational strategies, such as goal setting, help improve the individual's readiness for change.[9]

Pharmacological agents approved by the Food and Drug Administration (FDA), such as orlistat, lorcaserin, and liraglutide, work by reducing fat absorption, stimulating the central nervous system, and suppressing appetite. Of note, many of these pharmacological agents can cause an increase in exercise blood pressure and/or possible cardiovascular risks. Therefore, blood pressure must be continually monitored during exercise.[9]

The surgical treatment of obesity, including laparoscopic gastric banding and the Roux-en-Y gastric bypass procedure, have been found to reduce excess body weight by an average of 50% to 60%. However, these are considered appropriate only for those who are **morbidly obese** (BMI > 40).

Effects of Exercise Training

Physical activity is thought to be the most important factor in weight loss because of the increase in energy expenditure. This often leads to a concurrent positive behavior change in caloric intake. Additional benefits of exercise training include the preservation of lean body mass, improved insulin sensitivity, favorable changes in lipid profiles, and reduced blood pressure. Of note is the finding that exercise promotes the loss of regional fat, particularly in the abdominal area, leading to an overall reduction in comorbidities. Finally, exercise training has profound effects on glucose metabolism, including decreased fasting insulin and glucose levels, decreased insulin resistance, and increased glucose tolerance.[9]

Recommendations for Exercise Programming

Before beginning an exercise program, any comorbidities, orthopedic limitations, and medications should be taken into consideration. Exercise can increase the level of stress on the joints, thereby negatively impacting gait and/or increasing the risk of osteoarthritis. If the individual has been cleared for exercise, standard exercise testing protocols may be appropriate. However, individuals who are obese tend to present with a lower functional capacity. Therefore, low-level protocols are often warranted.

The exercise program for individuals who are obese should ideally optimize energy expenditure while minimizing the potential for injury. It may be more tolerable for the individual to engage in two or more short exercise sessions each day, rather than one longer session. Multiple exercise sessions a day results in an elevated energy expenditure for recovery, sustaining for a longer period of time than a single session, and also decreases the risk of heat intolerance.

The American College of Sports Medicine recommends aerobic exercise that is non–weight bearing (e.g., swimming, rowing, or biking) daily or at least five sessions per week. Initial intensity and duration should be low (40%–60% VO_{2max}, 30–60 min/day). Progression should focus on increasing duration first, followed by increasing intensity later. Resistance training can be incorporated into the program, as it leads to a preservation of lean body mass. However, aerobic activity has a greater potential to decrease body fat and increase energy expenditure, and should be the primary focus of the exercise program. Finally, functional movements designed to increase the ease of performing activities of daily living, increasing vocational potential, and increasing self-confidence should be included.[9]

CARDIOVASCULAR AND PULMONARY DISEASE

Cardiovascular diseases (CVDs) are a group of diseases and disorders that affect the heart and blood vessels. They include **coronary heart disease** (disease of the blood vessels supplying the heart muscle), **cerebrovascular disease** (disease of the blood vessels supplying the brain), **rheumatic heart disease** (damage to the heart muscle and heart valves from rheumatic fever), **congenital heart disease** (malformations of the heart structure existing at birth), **peripheral arterial disease** (disease of the blood vessels supplying the arms and legs), and **deep vein thrombosis** and **pulmonary embolism** (blood clots in the leg veins, which can dislodge and move to the heart and lungs).[19] CVDs are the number one cause of death globally, killing an estimated 17.9 million people each year. Of these deaths, 85% are due to heart attack and stroke.[20]

Most of the risk factors for CVD are modifiable behavior risk factors, including an unhealthy diet, physical inactivity, smoking, and excessive alcohol consumption. In addition, increased blood pressure, diabetes, hyperlipidemia, overweight, and obesity are also risk factors. Finally, family history and gender/age (male > 55 and female > 65) are nonmodifiable risk factors for CVD. This chapter will focus on two of the most common forms of CVD—hypertension and myocardial infarction. We will also explore chronic obstructive pulmonary disease (COPD), a progressive lung disease that is typically associated with CVD.[20]

Hypertension

Blood pressure is determined by the amount of resistance to blood flow in the walls of the arteries. It is measured as systolic blood pressure (SBP, the amount of pressure present during contraction) and diastolic blood pressure (DBP; the amount of pressure present during relaxation). Normal blood pressure is defined as SBP < 120 mmHg and DBP < 80 mmHg. **Hypertension** is elevated blood pressure. The classification of blood pressure for adults, as recommended by the American Heart Association, is presented in Table 12.3.[21]

TABLE 12.3 Blood Pressure Classifications

BLOOD PRESSURE CATEGORY	SYSTOLIC mm Hg (upper number)	and/or	DIASTOLIC mm Hg (lower number)
NORMAL	LESS THAN 120	And	LESS THAN 80
ELEVATED	120 – 129	and	LESS THAN 80
HIGH BLOOD PRESSURE (HYPERTENSION) STAGE 1	130 – 139	or	80 – 89
HIGH BLOOD PRESSURE (HYPERTENSION) STAGE 2	140 OR HIGHER	or	90 OR HIGHER
HYPERTENSIVE CRISIS (consult your doctor immediately)	HIGHER THAN 180	and/or	HIGHER THAN 120

Source: American Heart Association (AHA)

There are two forms of hypertension: **essential hypertension**, whereby there is no identifiable cause of hypertension, and the disease develops gradually over many years; and **secondary hypertension**, which is attributed to an underlying condition. This type of hypertension tends to appear very suddenly and can cause higher blood pressure readings than essential hypertension.[22] Often, the causes of secondary hypertension are linked to sleep apnea, kidney disease, thyroid and adrenal gland problems, decongestants, and illegal drugs, including cocaine and amphetamines.[23]

Uncontrolled high blood pressure increases the risk of CVD, including heart attack and stroke. It can also increase the risk of aneurysm, heart failure, kidney disease, metabolic syndrome, memory loss, dementia, and damage blood vessels in the eyes. It is estimated that 37% of U.S. adults have prehypertension, and nearly one-third of adults have hypertension.[23] Unfortunately, recent public health data indicates that the prevalence of hypertension is on the rise. Risk factors for hypertension include:

- Age: Women over the age of 65 and men over the age of 55
- Family history: first degree relative
- Race: Hypertension is more common in African Americans
- Overweight or obesity: increases the pressure on arterial walls
- Sedentary lifestyle: contributes to a higher resting heart rate and increases risk of obesity
- Tobacco use: acute increase in blood pressure, as well as damage to arterial walls
- Diet high in sodium: causes fluid retention, which increases blood pressure
- High alcohol consumption: more than one drink/day for women, 2 drinks/day for men
- Stress: acute increase in blood pressure, as well as unhealthy stress-related habits (overeating, tobacco or alcohol use, etc.).
- Chronic conditions: kidney disease, diabetes, sleep apnea
- Too little potassium in diet: potassium helps to balance sodium in the body, lack of potassium causes sodium to build up in the blood.

Management and Medications

Most people with hypertension do not have any signs or symptoms, even at blood pressures of dangerously high levels. Some people might have headaches, nose bleeds, or shortness of breath, but these symptoms are not specific and typically do not occur until blood pressure is so high that it becomes life threatening.[24] The ultimate goal of antihypertensive therapy is to control blood pressure while reducing related morbidity and mortality in the least intrusive means possible. Lifestyle modifications are generally recommended for all levels of hypertension, and include the following.

- Weight management, or reduction
- Eat a diet rich in fruits and vegetables. Reduce saturated fat and cholesterol intake.
- Increase potassium intake to 4.7 g/day
- Reduce sodium intake to 1.5 g/day
- Smoking cessation
- Limit alcohol intake to no more than two drinks/day for men and one drink/day for women
- Perform aerobic physical activity at least 30 min/day, most days each week.

Drug therapy is often initiated in combination with lifestyle modifications when hypertension is severe (at least Stage 1) and/or other cardiovascular disease or risk factors are present. Diuretics are often used in combination therapy for individuals with uncomplicated disease. In individuals with high-risk conditions, including heart failure, myocardial infarction, coronary artery disease, diabetes, chronic kidney disease, and stroke, other antihypertensive medications are warranted, either alone or in combination

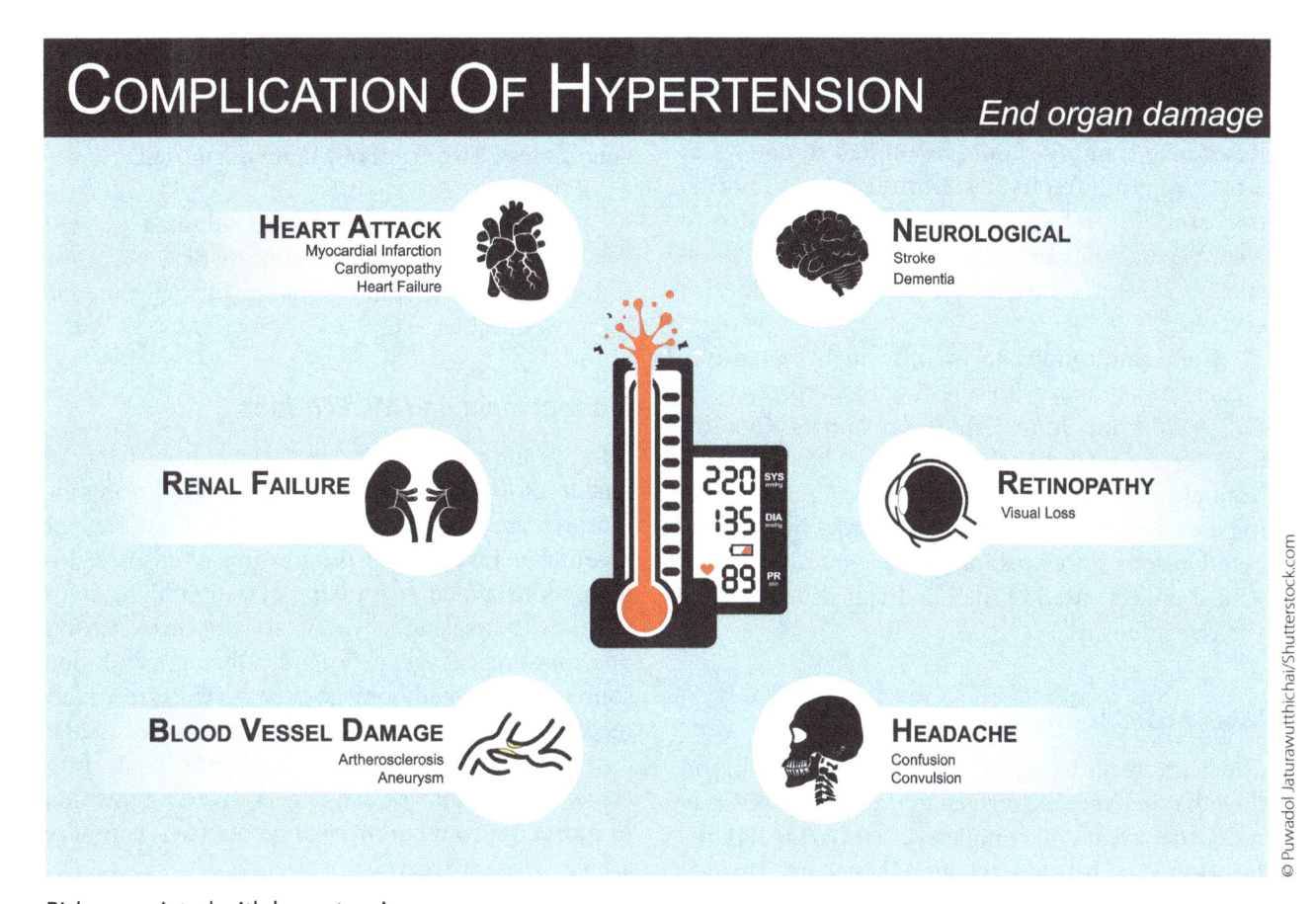

COMPLICATION OF HYPERTENSION
End organ damage

- **Heart Attack**: Myocardial Infarction, Cardiomyopathy, Heart Failure
- **Neurological**: Stroke, Dementia
- **Renal Failure**
- **Retinopathy**: Visual Loss
- **Blood Vessel Damage**: Artherosclerosis, Aneurysm
- **Headache**: Confusion, Convulsion

Risks associated with hypertension.

with diuretics.[23] These drugs include beta-blockers, angiotensin-converting enzyme (ACE) inhibitors, aldosterone antagonists, and angiotensin receptor blockers (ARBs). Worth noting is that beta-blockers reduce the heart rate response to submaximal and maximal exercise by 30 beats-per-minute (bpm), and may also reduce exercise capacity. They also attenuate the magnitude of SBP increase during exercise. Finally, research indicates that beta-blockers may also delay the signs of myocardial ischemia and increase exercise tolerance in individuals with exertional angina.[24]

Vasodilators, ACE inhibitors, and angiotensin receptor blockers do not typically affect heart rate response to exercise. However, individuals may be subject to hypotensive episodes following exercise. As such, adequate cool-down is required.[24]

Effects of Exercise

The American College of Sports Medicine recommends regular aerobic exercise as a preventative strategy to reduce the incidence of hypertension.[9] Research indicates that aerobic training may elicit an average of 5 to 7 mmHg reduction in both SBP and DBP in individuals with hypertension. Hypertensive individuals who are physically active have lower mortality rates than their sedentary counterparts. Exercise appears to reduce blood pressure by decreasing the plasma norepinephrine levels, increasing circulating vasodilators, and altering kidney function.[22]

Recommendations for Exercise Programming

Standard exercise testing protocols may be suitable for individuals with hypertension.[9] It is recommended that the individual take their usual antihypertensive medications, and that the exercise testing be performed at the same time of day as when the individual intends to exercise, because the significant reduction in exercise heart rate may dissipate over time. Electrocardiogram (ECG) monitoring may be warranted before starting a vigorous exercise program, particularly in those with known cardiovascular disease or symptoms indicative of cardiovascular disease.[22]

The goals of an exercise program should be blood pressure control, improve cardiovascular disease risk factors, and increase ventilatory threshold and peak work capacity.[25]

Aerobic exercise training should include large muscle group activities performed at 40% to 70%

VO_{2max} (or RPE of 11–13/20 for individuals on beta-blockers), at least 30 min/session, 4–7 days/week. Resistance training should be limited to one set of 8 to 12 reps at 60% to 80% 1RM. It is worth noting that exercise performed at the intensity of 40% to 70% VO_{2max} appears to lower resting blood pressure to a greater extent than higher intensities of exercise.[9,22]

Contraindications to exercise in hypertensives include individuals with a resting blood pressure of SBP > 200 mmHg or DBP > 115 mmHg. In addition, certain types of calcium channel blocker medications and vasodilators may cause postexercise hypotension, and should be monitored. Finally, since beta-blockers lower resting and exercise heart rate, RPE should be used in these individuals to monitor exercise intensity.[25]

Myocardial Infarction

The heart needs oxygen to survive. When the blood flow that delivers the oxygen to the heart is severely reduced or cut off completely, a **myocardial infarction** (i.e., heart attack, or MI) occurs. This often occurs when coronary arteries that supply the myocardium with blood become narrowed from a buildup of plaque (composed of cholesterol, fat, and other substances) through a process called atherosclerosis.[26] If plaque inside a coronary artery breaks off, a blood clot forms around it which can narrow the blood flow through the artery to the myocardium. If the myocardium is starved for oxygen and nutrients for a period of time, ischemia results. This leads to irreversible tissue death, called necrosis.[25]

Myocardial infarctions are characterized by the following indicators.[26]

- Severe, prolonged chest pressure or pain. Often pain is accompanied by sweating and nausea and will radiate to the arm, neck, or back.
- Increased serum levels of cardiac enzyme.
- ECG changes that are indicative of myocardial necrosis.

Approximately every 40 seconds, someone in the United States has an MI, totaling to more than 1.5 million Americans each year. Of these, approximately one-third will die.[27,28] After an acute MI, the risk of further cardiovascular morbidity and mortality is largely determined by the extent to which the left ventricle is damaged, the degree of residual myocardial ischemia, and the individual's level of cardiovascular fitness. Two types of MI are diagnosed.

- Subendocardial infarction—limited to the inner-half of the myocardium, or
- Transmural infarction—involving the full ventricular wall

Management and Medications

Lifestyle and palliative management, or improving the quality of life for individuals facing life-threatening illnesses, are often the first line of defense to stall, or potentially reverse, the progression of disease. Interventions aimed at smoking cessation, lipid modification, increasing physical activity, hypertensive pharmacological agents, weight reduction, and food sources that provide omega-3 fatty acids are widely recommended to decrease risk of cardiovascular morbidity and mortality. Finally, individuals with moderate or high risk can expect to see a reduction in mortality from coronary angioplasty or coronary artery bypass surgery.[29]

Effects of Exercise

Exercise is beneficial in individuals with MIs, as it leads to an increase in VO_{2max}, improves ventilatory threshold and heart rate variability, increases HDL cholesterol, and provides relief of anginal symptoms. Further, individuals may experience increased vagal tone and decreased blood platelet adhesiveness.[30]

Because individuals with a history of MI are typically on one or more medications, these will need to be taken into consideration during exercise along with any accompanying side effects.[31] Accordingly, individuals on beta-blockers will experience a decrease in resting and exercise heart rate, and need to be monitored using the RPE scale.[30] Further, central nervous system-active drugs also have attenuating effects on heart rate and blood pressure during exercise. Postexercise hypotension can result without an adequate cool-down.[29]

Recommendations for Exercise

It is generally recommended that individuals with previous MIs perform low level exercise testing with a protocol that focuses on the individual's ability to perform lower-extremity exercises. If the individual is unable to perform treadmill or cycle ergometer exercise, they may instead be evaluated with an upper-body arm ergometry assessment, or pharmacologic stress testing.[30] The exercise test should begin at a low intensity level and increase gradually in 2 or 3-minute stages, with hemodynamic measures being made at each stage. Ideally, increments in workload should increase so that time to volitional fatigue occurs in approximately 10 to 12 min.[30]

The exercise program should consist of large muscle group, rhythmic exercise (e.g., walking, cycle ergometry, stair climbing), and whole-body strength training, using both limbs. Aerobic exercise should be performed at 40% to 80% of the individual's VO_{2max} at least 3 days/week for 20 to 60 min/session. It is important that the individual include 5 to 10 min of warm-up and cool-down activities. The goal of the aerobic exercise program is to increase aerobic capacity, while decreasing blood pressure and heart rate response to submaximal exercise. Strength training should be 30% to 40% 1RM for the upper body and 50% to 60% 1RM for lower body exercises, 2 to 3 days/week, 2 to 4 sets of 12 to 15 reps. Exercises should be designed to increase the ability of the individual to perform activities of daily living and increase muscular strength and endurance.[9,30]

Chronic Obstructive Pulmonary Disease (COPD)

COPD is a chronic, progressive inflammatory lung disease marked by irreversible airway obstruction. Typically, this is brought about by chronic bronchitis or emphysema (or both). COPD is characterized by difficulty breathing, wheezing, cough, and sputum production.[31] The primary cause of COPD is cigarette smoking, accounting for an estimated 80% of cases. Other causes include allergies, asthma, poor nutrition, or exposure to irritating gases through environmental and occupational pollutants. At present, COPD is the fourth leading cause of death in the United States, and most commonly affects white males over the age of 60. Approximately 24 million Americans currently have COPD.[32]

The effects of COPD result in an impairment of ventilation and gas exchange. This leads to shortness of breath and other compensatory responses throughout the body. These impairments include the following.[31]

- Decrease in airway size and lung volume decrease caused by increased airway resistance and obstruction.
- Reduced lung elasticity.
- Increased work of breathing necessary to overcome air flow obstruction.
- Ventilatory muscle weakness, fatigue, and inefficiency due to increased dead space ventilation.
- Chronic bronchitis leading to an impairment in pulmonary gas exchange.
- Increased risk of cardiovascular disease and deconditioning due to reduced physical activity.
- Anxiety and depression related to their symptoms and limited abilities to perform activities of daily living.

Management and Medications

The primary goal of COPD management is to reduce breathlessness. Secondary objectives include increasing exercise capacity, slowing disease progression, improving quality of life, and prolonging survival.[33] Common medications include the following.

- Methylxanthines, which have potent bronchodilator action. Side effects include tachycardia, cardiac dysrhythmias, central nervous system stimulation, and risk of seizure.
- Selective beta-adrenoceptor agonists, which relax bronchial smooth muscle and cause bronchodilation. Side effects include a reduction in peripheral vascular resistance, heart palpitations, and tachycardia.
- Thiazide diuretics, which are often prescribed to reduce fluid retention. This could lead to intravascular volume depletion and hypotension during exercise.
- Glucocorticoids, which reduce inflammation and improve pulmonary function. Side effects include osteoporosis, muscle atrophy, and myopathy.[34]

Result of Exercise Training

Because of the level of deconditioning many individuals with COPD experience, exercise training is an integral component of clinical management. Any amount of physical activity can lead to favorable improvements in oxygen utilization and work capacity in individuals with COPD, as well as an overall cardiovascular reconditioning, improved ventilation, desensitization to breathlessness, and general improvements in fitness parameters (flexibility, body composition, muscular strength, and balance).[35]

During exercise, individuals with COPD often experience impeded exhalation, incomplete lung emptying, and air trapping, all of which can cause hyperinflation. Hyperinflation is marked by reduced lung elasticity and airway resistance.[36] During exercise, this can result in a reduced inspiratory capacity and tidal volume, and is directly linked to breathlessness. Further, in individuals with emphysema (one of the diseases under the umbrella of COPD), destruction in the alveolar-capillary membrane reduces breathing efficiency and may result in hypoxemia (low level of oxygen in the blood). Individuals who smoke also have increases in carboxyhemoglobin, which impairs blood oxygen transport.[37] All of these have the potential to compromise circulation during exercise and limit exercise capacity.

Recommendations for Exercise

COPD often is accompanied with cardiovascular disease. Therefore, prior to the development of the exercise program, exercise testing is necessary in order to determine exercise capacity, as well as the presence of exercise-induced hypoxemia, hypertension, and/or myocardial dysrhythmias or ischemia.[38] Maximal exercise testing will most accurately define individual limitations, and is safe to perform with appropriate monitoring. Treadmill testing best relates to activities of daily living and would be well tolerated by individuals who do not have advanced peripheral neuropathy (condition that results from damage to the nerves outside the brain and spinal cord). The cycle ergometer provides the best means of controlling work load and would be appropriate for those with balance or foot problems.[37,38] The overall goal of the cardiovascular test would be to gradually increase workload every three minutes at a rate of 5, 10, 15, or 20 Watts/min, until exhaustion is reached (ideally within 8–12 minutes of exercise).[38] Watts are indicative of power output, where power is work divided by time.

The exercise program should include large muscle activities that are enjoyable to the individual at a comfortable workload of 11–13/20 RPE. Be sure to monitor for breathlessness throughout the session. Shorter intermittent exercise sessions may be necessary, so the individual may complete 1 to 2 sessions each day 3 to 5 days/week. It is important to emphasize progression of exercise duration rather than intensity, especially initially. Strength training should be performed at a low resistance and high number of repetitions 2 to 3 days/week. Finally, flexibility and neuromuscular exercises should be performed at least 3 days/week in order to improve range of motion, gait, balance, and breathing efficiency.[9,38]

Example of COPD treatment.

COGNITIVE/PSYCHOLOGICAL DISORDERS

Cognitive and psychological disorders are a broad group of mental health disorders that primarily affect learning, problem solving, memory, and perception. While they include a number of disorders, including anxiety, obsessive-compulsive disorder, depression, post-traumatic stress disorder, personality disorders, eating disorders, and psychotic disorders, this chapter will focus on Alzheimer's disease and anxiety disorders.[39]

Cognitive disorders can have a variety of causes. Some result from hormonal imbalances during pregnancy or genetic predisposition. Others are the result of brain trauma, stroke, and even cardiac issues. Finally, environmental causes, including improper nutrition during vulnerable stages of development (particularly infancy), can impact cognitive development. They often begin subtly but progress until they significantly impact the individual's quality of life.[40]

Some of the more common signs and symptoms of a cognitive disorder include confusion, loss of short-term or long-term memory, impaired judgment, and poor motor coordination. While cognitive problems manifest in a variety of different ways, often times they develop in stages with the symptoms increasing in severity as the disease progresses.[40] More than 16 million people in the United States are currently living with cognitive impairment.[39]

Alzheimer's Disease

Alzheimer's disease (AD) is a chronic progressive (eventually fatal) brain disorder. At present, 5.1 million Americans suffer from AD, and it is the seventh leading cause of death in the United States. The highest prevalence of Alzheimer's is found in those who are 85 years or older, although after the age of 65 the percentage of those affected doubles with every decade of life.[41] AD is progressive and degenerative, and there is no known cure.[41] It is believed that AD begins in the entorhinal cortex of the brain and spreads to the hippocampus, which is the area responsible for memory formation. Short-term memory begins to deteriorate as the hippocampal neurons degenerate. From here, AD progresses to the cerebral cortex of the brain, where language and ability to reason are impacted.[42]

A diagnosis of AD is confirmed at autopsy.[41] Hallmarks include findings of amyloid plaques, neurofibrillary tangles, and synaptic and neuronal cell death. Prior to death, probable AD is confirmed when dementia is clinically significant and confirmed by neuropsychological tests and unusual memory loss. In addition, other symptoms include language deterioration, judgment problems, paranoia, agitation, and eventual inability of the individual to carry out activities of daily living.[42] A pattern of symptom progression has been established and used to develop a Phase Model to help understand AD. In this model, AD is divided into three phases.[41]

- Phase I: Short-term memory loss and forgetfulness, accompanied by anxiety associated with forgetting.
- Phase II: Confusion and intellectual impairment, difficulty concentrating, problems with short-term memory and orientation.
- Phase III: Increased delusions, agitation, loss of basic abilities, incontinence.

Management and Medications

For the most part, treatment for AD is limited. The primary goal of medical intervention is to improve memory and cognition and delay the progression of the disease. Five pharmaceutical agents are currently approved by the FDA for the treatment of AD. They include acetylcholinesterase inhibitors donepezil, rivastigmine, galantamine, N-methyl-D-aspartate receptor antagonist memantine, and tacrine. In addition, the antioxidants vitamin E and selegiline have been found to slow the progression of AD. Finally, other drugs have been used to help control depression, agitation, aggression, agitation, and sleep disturbances.[43]

Result of Exercise Training

The benefits associated with AD and exercise vary considerably, based on the age at onset, comorbidities, phase of disease, and health status. In a limited number of clinical studies, exercise has improved physical fitness and mood, led to a slower decline in mental status, and resulted in significant cognitive improvement and decreased depression.[44]

Recommendations for Exercise

Because of the impact of AD on mental capacity, typical exercise tests may be difficult or even impossible to complete, especially during the mid- to late stages of the disease.[45] This is because increased agitation and impaired cognition impede the ability of the individual to tolerate extended exercise sessions. Therefore, it is recommended that the individual try several practice sessions prior to the actual exercise test. If the individual becomes agitated or confused, the test should be terminated immediately and rescheduled for a different day. Finally, it is recommended that all testing be conducted in the morning, as individuals with AD tend to function better during the early hours of the morning.[44,45]

Exercise training should be completed at a low intensity and focus on helping the individual to perform typical activities of daily living. Simple repetitive exercises (e.g., walking, riding a stationary bike) will be easier for the individual to perform and are recommended. In the early stages of the disease, exercise is important to establish a regular routine for the individual. Consistency is key, as is patience and enjoyment. Constant supervision is necessary to ensure safety, and verbal encouragement will help maintain interest. Finally, it is suggested to break exercise bouts into 10 minute intervals to keep the individual active throughout the day.[45]

Aerobic exercise training should emphasize enjoyment and maintaining function. Select exercises that have a low risk of falls should be utilized, such as chair aerobic exercises. Strength training can be completed with therabands to strengthen postural muscles. Use 10 to 12 repetitions as tolerated. Finally, flexibility training on postural muscle groups may be performed. Because this population tends to have difficulty getting down or up from the floor, focus on exercises that can be done on a raised platform or chair.[44,45]

Anxiety Disorders

Stress is defined as a condition or feeling experienced when a person perceives that the demands of a situation exceed their personal and social resources. Excess stress can be detrimental to our health, relationships, and quality of life. Physiological hallmarks of stress include activation of the sympathetic nervous system and activation of the hypothalamic–pituitary–adrenal (HPA) axis, an area of the brain critical for memory, cognition, and emotion—all of which are altered by stressful stimulation.[46]

Perceived stress can elicit extreme worry or apprehension, and can occur frequently and without any real threat. This is termed **anxiety**, a condition that encompasses a variety of disorders including phobias, obsessive-compulsive disorder, post-traumatic stress disorder, panic disorder, and generalized anxiety disorder.[47]

Management and Medications

Typically, psychotherapy, behavioral therapy, pharmacological intervention, or a combination of the three are used in the management of stress and anxiety disorders. Pharmacological drugs can be used to correct chemical imbalances in the brain and self-examination is also often used in an attempt to train the person to control stress and anxiety. Typically, drug treatments initially use less potent and less habit-forming medications with a gradual increase to stronger, more potent drugs, in an effort to prevent drug abuse or habit-forming medications. It is important to note that some medications have side effects that can significantly impair an individual's desire to be physically active. In addition, some drugs induce dizziness and inhibit motor function, both of which can impact exercise response. Finally, aerobic exercise has been used as a predominant modality for the management of stress and anxiety disorders.[48]

Results of Exercise Training

Clinical tests indicate that approximately 20 to 30 min of moderate-to-intense exercise training can significantly reduce the symptoms related to stress and anxiety. It is important, however, to avoid overtraining, which is characterized by a decrease in performance, as well as heightened levels of anxiety, depression,

Anxiety has a high risk of causing other chronic illnesses.

and fatigue. In extreme cases of overtraining, abnormal endocrine function can occur, which results in generalized immunosuppression (inability for the body's immune system to fight disease).[49]

Recommendations for Exercise

Individuals with stress or anxiety disorders must be evaluated for neuromuscular function, as a number of medications can impact perception, alertness, and coordination. Otherwise, cardiovascular, muscular strength/endurance, body composition, and flexibility can be evaluated in the normal fashion.[49]

For the exercise program, aerobic exercise training should be performed 3 to 5 days/week for 20 to 30 min at a time, at an intensity of 50% to 85% of their VO_{2max}. Strength training should be performed a minimum of 2 days/week, with at least one set of 8 to 12 reps per exercise, at a resistance level of 60% to 85% of their max. Finally, static stretching for all major upper and lower body muscles should follow each exercise session. Individual should stretch to a point of mild discomfort and hold for 15 to 30 seconds.[50]

ORTHOPEDIC DISEASES AND DISABILITIES

It is estimated that one in two U.S. citizens are affected by an orthopedic condition. **Orthopedic** conditions affect the musculoskeletal system, including the muscles, bones, nerves, joints, ligaments, tendons, and other connective tissues. General orthopedic problems may be acute in nature, including bone fractures or joint dislocations, while other conditions may be chronic, such as osteoporosis, osteomyelitis, or tendinitis. The symptoms of orthopedic disease or disabilities vary according to the specific condition or body part, and may include deformities or unusual appearance of a joint, joint pain or swelling, limited range of motion, numbness or tingling, or infection.[51]

In general, trauma is a common cause for many acute orthopedic conditions. Degenerative conditions or overuse can wear on joints over time, leading to chronic orthopedic conditions. Risk factors include aging, overweight and obesity, smoking, and using improper body mechanics to perform activities. Without proper treatment and adequate recovery, orthopedic conditions can lead to chronic problems.[51] This chapter will look specifically at the orthopedic conditions of low-back pain, osteoporosis, joint replacements, and arthritis.

Low-Back Pain

Affecting between 58% and 70% of the population, one of the most widely experienced health-related problems in the world is low-back pain. **Low-back pain** is defined as pain and/or discomfort localized below the costal margin and above the inferior gluteal folds, with or without accompanying leg pain. The most common form of low-back pain is nonspecific, which is not attributed to a known specific pathology, such as infection or fracture. This type of low-back pain generally occurs suddenly and results from a major trauma. Consequences from low-back pain include reduced health-related quality of life, loss of work, increased health care utilization, and disability.[52]

Management and Medications

The most common medication given to individuals who suffer from low-back pain include nonsteroidal anti-inflammatory medications (NSAIDs), such as aspirin, ibuprofen, or indomethacin. Nonnarcotic analgesics, including acetaminophen or tramadol, are also administered either alone or in combination with the NSAIDs. These medications should have no effect on the individual's exercise capacity.[52] In severe cases, muscle relaxants, opiates, and oral steroids are used for short term management of acute back pain. Muscle relaxants can cause drowsiness, but the others should not impact exercise response.[52,53]

Response to Exercise Training

A number of investigations have shown that exercise is significantly more effective than resting for lower-back pain. However, in spite of this, many people with lower-back pain tend to have inappropriate fears and misconceptions surrounding exercise causing further pain or reinjury. The degree to which individuals with low-back pain engage in an exercise program is greatly impacted by these beliefs. It is important to understand that for most individuals with low-back pain, no specific treatment is necessary, and at most, minor modification of heavy activities and support devices such as a weight belt when lifting may be warranted. Therefore, an early return to normal activities should be encouraged, and exercise strongly recommended.[54]

Recommendations for Exercise

Most individuals with low-back pain should be able to perform all standard exercise tests. However, they may be limited in performance due to an actual or anticipated increase in pain. Therefore, the practitioner should allow for adequate practice time on different modalities to select the most appropriate one prior to testing.[54] Otherwise, exercise guidelines are similar to that established by ACSM for apparently healthy populations, with appropriate adjustments made as needed. Programs should be designed to increase exercise tolerance and prevent deconditioning, as well as minimize stress to the lower back. If pain is present, hip and back exercises should be delayed. Intensity should be low, and duration should be graded and gradual in progression.[55]

Osteoporosis

The bone in our bodies is living tissue that is constantly being broken down and replaced. After the age of 35, bone-forming cells decline in activity. As such, all individuals incur a small reduction in bone mass each year thereafter. The term **osteopenia** refers to low bone mass, which is observed in nearly all elderly men and women in industrialized countries across the world. Once low bone mass becomes severe enough to result in fractures from minimal trauma, it is clinically defined as **osteoporosis**. Specifically, osteoporosis is a condition in which the bones become weak and brittle.[56]

The WHO standards for diagnosing osteoporosis are based on bone mineral density levels at the hip and spine as measured by central dual-energy X-ray absorptiometry that are more than 2.5 standard deviations below the "young normal" adult value. It is estimated that 34 million U.S. citizens have a low bone mass, with an additional 10 million having osteoporosis. While osteoporosis can occur in both genders and at all ages, it primarily affects postmenopausal women aged 50 to 75 years. This is due to estrogen deficiency, which alters bone resorption and formation rates. The most common risk factors for osteoporosis include female gender, estrogen deficiency, loss of lean body mass, chronic physical inactivity, old age, Caucasian, Asian, or Hispanic/Latino race, family history, smoking, alcohol consumption (more than 3 drinks/day), vitamin D insufficiency, and excessive intake of protein, sodium, caffeine, and vitamin A.[56] In addition, the medications phenytoin, carbamazepine, and primidone can increase an individual's risk for developing osteoporosis, as will gastric bypass surgery.

Compression fractures of the vertebrae are common in older individuals with osteoporosis. It is possible for several to accumulate before they are detected. When multiple vertebral fractures accumulate, it can lead to thoracic kyphosis and several associated functional limitations leading to increased risk of falls and shift in the center of gravity.[57]

Management and Medications

At present, there is no cure for osteoporosis. However, it is possible to successfully manage this disease. The National Osteoporosis Foundation recommends the following to maximize bone health and prevent osteoporosis.[57]

- Obtain the recommended amounts of calcium and vitamin D each day.
- Engage in regular weight-bearing exercise training.
- Avoid tobacco use and excessive alcohol intake.
- Have a bone mineral density exam and take medication as recommended.

Upon diagnosis, the primary form of treatment is the use of medications to slow bone resorption and/or increase bone formation. Physical therapy may be used to treat back pain and increase trunk muscle, hip and knee extensor, and ankle strength, as well as improve balance. Bracing the torso may be needed to prevent worsening of kyphosis.[58]

Response to Exercise Training

Exercise has been shown to slow the age-related decline in bone mass, and delay the point at which clinically significant osteoporosis is diagnosed. Specifically, regular weight-bearing, aerobic exercise and strength training have been shown to have a positive effect on bone mineral density in postmenopausal women. Further, walking has been found to effectively impact hip bone mineral density. However, in individuals with osteoporosis, exercise training may be limited due to fractures or possible coexisting conditions, such as osteoporosis. Therefore, the primary goals of an exercise program are to improve balance, muscular strength, and mobility in order to avoid falls, noting that orthopedic limitations may slow progress.[59]

Recommendations for Exercise

The standard exercise testing protocols used for older individuals who are at risk for coronary artery disease are generally appropriate for those with osteoporosis, unless severe kyphosis is present. In situations with kyphosis, treadmill exercise is deemed unsafe, because of the shift in center of gravity that occurs, which may affect balance. Cycle ergometry is a safer alternative, provided it does not result in compression of the anterior aspect of the spine.[60]

Because individuals with osteoporosis are more likely to be deconditioned, low-intensity exercise is recommended. Exercises that are focused on improving balance and modification of activities of daily living, as well as improving muscular strength for the upper and lower body and trunk muscles are recommended, but they should avoid trunk flexion to prevent compression fractures. Finally, individuals with multiple fractures, severe back pain, or extremely low bone mass should avoid weight-bearing exercises altogether, and opt for water-based or chair exercises.[60]

Arthritis

Arthritis is defined by the CDC as inflammation or swelling in one or more joints within the body.[61] Overall, the CDC has reported that there are approximately 54.4 million adults (22.7% of the population) diagnosed with arthritis by a doctor, with women having higher reported occurrences of arthritis (23.5%) compared to men (18.1%).[61] As we age, the likelihood of experiencing arthritis also increases; however, individuals who are physically active may have a lower likelihood of experiencing arthritis versus those who do not achieve the recommended levels of physical activity. Although there are several different types of arthritis, including osteoarthritis (OA), rheumatoid arthritis (RA), childhood arthritis, fibromyalgia, gout, and lupus, this chapter will cover OA and RA since they are the most common forms of arthritis seen in adults and can have a limiting effect on physical activity, sport, and exercise.

Osteoarthritis is the most common form of arthritis and is typically a result of either a biomechanical failure in cartilage within a joint or due to repetitive wear and tear in a joint.[61] This type of arthritis is typically asymmetrical (not affecting both sides of the body) and tends to occur in the larger joints of the body, such as the hip, knee, and shoulder, which can lead to a need for possible joint replacement surgery depending on the severity. It is estimated that about 32.5 million adults in the United States suffer from OA, and risk factors include overuse/repetitive stress on a joint, increased age, obesity, gender (OA affects more females), and genetics.[61]

RA is an autoimmune disorder typically affecting the smaller joints such as the hands and ankles, and affects these joints symmetrically (on both sides of the body).[17] With RA, the immune system starts to attack healthy cells in the body, which, in turn, causes swelling of the joints, causing chronic pain, issues with balance/stabilization, and eventual joint deformity.[61] For individuals with RA, there may be times where symptoms flare up, and other times where the symptoms go away. Typical symptoms include pain/stiffness/tenderness in more than one joint and on both sides of the body, fatigue, fever, and weakness. Risk factors for RA are age, gender (affecting more women than men), genetics, smoking, obesity, certain early life exposures to things like second hand smoke, and being a female who has never given birth.[62]

Management and Medications

There is no current cure for either RA or OA, although in more advanced stages of OA, individuals may have replacement surgery in the affected joint. Treatment typically consists of a combination of medications such as painkillers (Tylenol or in more severe cases, prescription strength opioids) and NSAIDs to help reduce inflammation, physical/occupational therapy, and sometimes surgery to fuse, repair, or replace the joint.[63] In addition, some interventions such as injecting steroids, platelet rich plasma, or stem cells have also shown to decrease symptoms of OA.[64] For individuals with RA, additional medications such as corticosteroids (used to reduce inflammation and suppresses the immune system), disease-modifying antirheumatic drugs (help slow the immune system down to keep from attacking the joints), and biologic response modifiers (used to target protein molecules involved in the immune response) may also be prescribed by a doctor.[63] Arthritis is also managed through exercise, weight loss, and use of assistive devices such as canes or walkers.

Response to Exercise Training

Regular physical activity is encouraged for individuals with RA and OA as it can decrease the pain and improve movement and functioning in the affected joints. In addition, maintaining a healthy weight can help reduce symptoms experienced and can actually limit the progression of arthritis. Adults with arthritis should aim to achieve at least 150 minutes of moderate physical activity a week, which can be broken up into smaller bouts of exercise throughout the week.[61] For those adults who engage in regular physical activity, this can help to improve their quality of life and help them to perform better in activities of daily living, at work, and at home.

Recommendations for Exercise

As individuals with arthritis age, the focus of exercise should center on pain-free participation in physical activity/sport. For individuals with mild cases of arthritis, exercise plans can follow the ACSM guidelines for adults. Weight-bearing activities can be done as long as they do not increase pain in the affected joints. Typically non–weight-bearing or low-impact exercises such as biking, swimming, and water aerobics are suggested for individuals who experience more severe joint pain due to arthritis. Walking should be limited to activities of daily living in individuals who have joint damage, as higher intensity weight-bearing exercises can speed up the progression of the damage.[65] In the case of weakened grip for individuals with RA, supports such as wrist straps or grips may be used to help when lifting weights. Individuals with arthritis may be afraid of exercising due to joint pain, and therefore may experience weight gain, muscle atrophy, and movement limitations. As such, practitioners should encourage exercise at any level that is pain-free to help them to maintain their ability to move, and exercises should be individualized to meet the needs and abilities of the individual. When designing an exercise program, plan to start with lighter weights and allow their body to become accustomed to the activity so they can see how their body will tolerate the exercises. Strengthening the muscles around the affected joint(s) as well as core strengthening exercises should be added to work on stabilization and balance as these are often impaired in individuals with arthritis.[65]

Joint Replacement

Joint replacement surgery is considered one of the most cost-effective and common among treatments for end-stage joint diseases such as OA.[66] In the United States, the rate of total hip and knee **arthroplasty** (replacement) has steadily increased as the population continues to age and experiences injuries or other health conditions such as obesity or arthritis. According to the American Academy of Orthopaedic Surgeons (AAOS) 2020 Annual Report, the most common types of joint replacement are total knee replacement, with 995,410 completed from 2012–2019 (53% of all joint replacements) and total hip replacement with 625,097 completed during the same time frame (33.3% of all joint replacements).[67] Additionally, the AAOS also reported that most of the joint replacements were completed on females (58.8%), and the average age for total hip and total knee replacements were 66 and 66.9 years old, respectively.[67] Given these data, coupled with the increasing trend of people having joint replacement surgery, exercise and weight management are important considerations for individuals who have had joints replaced, as obesity does also play a part in people having to have a revision of their joint replacement in later years.

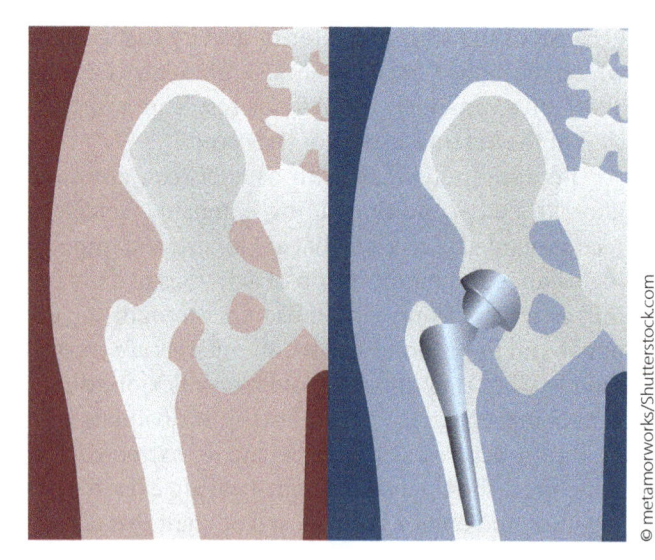

Comparing a normal joint with a replaced joint.

Management and Medications

Immediately following surgery, individuals will be prescribed medications such as Percocet or Vicodin to manage pain. It is important that pain medication is taken on time, to allow the individual to stay ahead of the pain and rest comfortably. As time progresses, they may take ibuprofen as needed. Some individuals who are at risk of blood clots may also be wearing compression socks or devices to help maintain blood flow throughout the affected area. There is also a chance of infection in the area, so individuals may take antibiotics prior to, and sometimes following surgery. In the early days following surgery, they will be asked to get up and move around and to start using that joint as per doctor recommendations with the help of mobility devices such as walkers or canes. These individuals will need to learn how to use these devices and how to get around their living quarters, including getting in and out of the bathtub, going up and down steps, and getting in and out of bed; these are all things the physical or occupational therapist can teach them, so they are able to be mobile at home. As they begin to heal, they will start physical therapy to work on improving functionality, strength, and range of motion. After the doctor has cleared them to exercise, an exercise plan should be developed to help develop and progressively increase the strength of the muscles around the joint.

Response to Exercise Training

Exercise before and after joint replacement surgery is recommended, as it can help to strengthen the muscles surrounding the affected joint. Prior to surgery, exercises should focus on stretching, strengthening, and endurance. They should be done three to four times a week for about 30 and 60 minutes each session. Exercises should not cause significant pain or discomfort, so should be done as tolerated and as directed by the surgeon prior to and following surgery. Warming up with stretching to a tolerable discomfort (but not pain), and endurance activities such as walking on the treadmill, exercise bike, elliptical, or swimming will help to strengthen the muscles and can be done for a few minutes up to an hour depending on the exercise and whether or not the individual is experiencing pain.

Recommendations for Exercise

Following a total knee or hip replacement, individuals will typically go through physical therapy sessions at home, and then at a physical therapy clinic once the individual is more functional and able to move around better. Individuals are encouraged to do their home therapy exercises several times a day in the early stages postoperation. Due to the fact that their muscles may have atrophied and have experienced trauma from surgery, adherence to the physical therapy and occupational therapy protocol is important as is maintaining recommended levels of physical activity after rehabilitation is complete. Following release from physical/occupational therapy, the individual should continue to focus on activities that improve strength and range of motion in order to regain functionality.

Initially after surgery, exercises will be less about improving strength and more about increasing blood flow through the affected area and targeting range of motion. Gradually, exercises can include low weight or body weight only exercises, but the individual should consult with their surgeon and/or physical therapist to get started on exercises that will not damage the affected area or the joint implant. Typically most individuals are able to regain full function and will be able to exercise without pain, but it is important to first determine where the limitations or strength deficits are and then to target those areas in an exercise plan. Closed chain exercises (e.g., body weight squat going down ¼ of the way with both feet planted on the ground) are recommended for individuals who have had hip or knee replacement surgery to help improve strength and functionality in the lower extremities.[68]

IMMUNOLOGICAL AND HEMATOLOGICAL DISORDERS

Immunohematology encompasses a broad array of clinical disorders in which immune reactions are involved in the pathogenesis of hematologic diseases. Diseases of the blood affect millions of Americans each year, and include a variety of symptoms.[69] This chapter will focus specifically on cancer and chronic fatigue syndrome.

Chronic Fatigue Syndrome

Chronic fatigue syndrome (CFS) is a complex condition that lacks any definitive diagnostic criteria. Therefore, it is defined only by its symptoms, which include persistent, debilitating fatigue that is not relieved by rest, frequent sore throats, painful lymph nodes, low-grade fever, and difficulty concentrating. The cause of CFS is unknown, but possible causes may include viral infection, immunological dysfunction, hypotension, psychological stress, or nutritional deficiency. Approximately 500,000 people in the United States experience CFS, and it disproportionally impacts well-educated Caucasian women.[70]

Management and Medications

Treatment for chronic fatigue syndrome is largely focused at reducing symptoms since the etiology of the disease is largely unknown. As such, medications vary according to the symptoms present, and may include analgesic, antidepressant, immunosuppressive, gastrointestinal, and endocrine agents; stimulants; muscle relaxants; and/or sleep aids.[71]

Response to Exercise Training

Individuals with chronic fatigue syndrome tend to limit their exercise because of fear (either real or perceived) that their fatigue will worsen after physical activity. As such, these individuals tend to be deconditioned and have mild reductions in VO_{2max} and ventilatory threshold as compared to those without CFS or other disabilities.[72]

Recommendations for Exercise Training

Little is known about the clinical impact of exercise training in individuals with CFS, so exercise recommendations are difficult to make. The goal of exercise programming should be to prevent further deconditioning. Because of the possibility of exacerbating the fatigue, exercise intensity should be very low, and utilize a familiar activity (e.g., walking). Strength training should focus on strength preservation so that the individual can continue performing activities of daily living. Flexibility can be performed to help preserve normal range of motion. Finally, progression should focus on increasing duration prior to increasing intensity.[72]

Cancer

In normal tissues, the rate of new cell growth and old cell death are kept in delicate balance. Normal cells have different rates of growth and division. For example, once a nerve cell matures, it does not grow anymore and cell division stops. However, epithelial cells on the skin grow and divide rapidly, replacing epithelial cells that have been lost. **Cancer**, on the other hand, occurs when cells in the body lose their normal mechanisms of control, resulting in an uncontrolled division of cells in the body. These abnormal cells form a mass of tissue, called a tumor, and have the ability to form new blood vessels through a process called angiogenesis. This allows the tumor to become self-sufficient and spread throughout the body.[73]

From a histological standpoint, there are thousands of different cancer types. Typically, cancer is named for the organs or tissues they originate from. Cancer that originates in the breast is called breast cancer. Cancer that originates in the lung is called lung cancer. Tumors are classified according to the type of tissue in which the cancer cells begin to develop. There are five major tumor classifications: carcinoma, lymphoma, leukemia, myeloma, and sarcoma (see Table 12.4).[74]

Specific signs and symptoms of cancer are listed here.[75]

- Unexplained weight loss
- Fever
- Fatigue
- Pain
- Skin changes
- Change in bowel or bladder function
- Sores that do not heal
- Unusual bleeding or discharge
- Lump
- Change in moles (color, size)
- Cough that does not go away

It is also important to note that some types of early cancer may not have symptoms. This is why regular screenings are so important.

After cancer has been diagnosed, the tumor is staged. The **cancer staging system** is a standardized way to describe the extent to which a cancer has spread. Staging is typically based on a compilation of an individual's physical examination, imaging, and measurements taken after surgical removal of a tumor. There are four primary stages of cancer ranging from stage 0 (noninvasive) to stage IV (advanced). Additionally, solid tumors are generally grouped according to the **TNM classification system**. *T* refers to the size of the tumor, *N* is a measure of the degree of lymph node involvement, and *M* describes the presence or absence of distant metastasis. A basic summary of tumor staging is presented in Table 12.5.[76]

TABLE 12.4 Tumor Classifications

Classification	Description	Example
Carcinoma	Cancers that originate in the tissue that lines organs and tubes	Breast, prostate, lung, pancreas, colon cancers
Lymphoma	Cancer that originates in the lymphatic tissue	Hodgkin's lymphoma; non-Hodgkin's lymphoma
Leukemia	Cancer that originates in the blood	Acute lymphocytic leukemia, chronic lymphocytic leukemia, acute myeloid leukemia, chronic myeloid leukemia
Myeloma	Cancer that originates in the bone marrow	Multiple myeloma
Sarcoma	Cancer that originates in the connective or supportive tissue	Bone, cartilage, fat, nerve

TABLE 12.5 Summary of Tumor Staging

Stage	Description
Stage 0	Cancer limited to surface cells
Stage I	Cancer limited to tissue of origin
Stage II	Limited local spread of cancerous cells
Stage III	Extensive local and regional spread
Stage IV	Distant metastasis

Medication and Management

The current armaments for treating cancer include surgery; chemotherapy; irradiation; and biological, hormonal, and targeted therapies. Treating cancer, for the most part, is based on an understanding of cellular kinetics and the growth of tumor cells. Cancer cells involve DNA mutations that often occur during DNA replication. In the normal cell cycle, checkpoints facilitate DNA repair; however, tumor cells lose their checkpoint integrity and escape DNA repair. The resulting mutations impact the regulatory mechanisms that restrict normal cell proliferation. **Chemotherapeutic agents**, for example, interrupt the cell cycle to prevent cell proliferation and typically are most effective when cells are actively dividing. Chemotherapy can be delivered intravenously or prescribed orally. Treatment is individualized according to type and duration. Using a combination of agents rather than just one provides a synergistic cell kill with the potential that less drug-resistant cells remain.[77] The negative of systemic chemotherapeutic agents is that normal cells, as well as malignant cells, are disrupted, leading to many side and untoward effects and often long-term morbidities, which refer to complications or issues that result from cancer treatment such as heart failure. Treatment-related morbidities impact functional ability and quality of life. Many comorbidities are encountered by cancer survivors, including nausea, vomiting, hair loss, fatigue, constipation/diarrhea, bone marrow suppression, cardiovascular dysfunction, muscle weakness, pain, mucositis, sleep disturbances, and peripheral neuropathy.

Surgery is the oldest form of cancer treatment. Most people with cancer will have some type of surgery. The side effects of surgery include pain, limited range of motion depending on the location of the surgery, fatigue, and changes in body image. Radiation uses high-energy particles or waves, such as x-rays, gamma rays, electron beams, or protons to destroy or damage cancer cells. Radiation works by damaging the genetic material of the cell, making it impossible for the cell to grow and divide. Cells going through mitosis, or division, are affected by radiation. Often, damage to normal tissue is limited to the area being treated, and most normal cells recover and function properly after radiation treatment. Frequent side effects include fatigue, pain, mouth sores, hair loss, taste changes, esophagitis, dry mouth, cardiovascular dysfunction, pulmonary changes, reproductive changes, lymphedema, skin changes, and damages to bone health.[78]

Effects of Exercise Training

Exercise is safe and effective both during and after most types of cancer treatment, and should therefore be included as an integral part of an individual's cancer care plan. More than two decades of research support a link between a physically active lifestyle and positive physiological and psychological changes in cancer survivors. These include improvements in $VO_{2\,max}$, which, in turn, improve heart and lung function and promote a healthy blood pressure, blood volume, and gas exchange. In addition, improvements in quality of life, muscular strength and endurance, fatigue reduction, anxiety, depression, body image, immune function and emotional well-being have been reported. Specific benefits as they relate to the aforementioned toxicities are presented in Table 12.6.[79]

Recommendations for Exercise Training

There are a number of recommendations for physical activity, based largely on observational epidemiologic research linking exercise and cancer risk.[80] The most current recommendations for prevention and survival come from the World Cancer Research Fund, American Institute for Cancer Research, American Cancer Society, and American College of Sports Medicine. More research has been provided discussing benefits of exercise with a risk reduction in cancer diagnosis. Little research, however, has been done on the benefits of exercise with cancer survivorship, so current recommendations reflect prevention guidelines with some treatment- and disease-specific modifications. Both guidelines include moderate physical activity (such as a brisk walk) for at least 30 minutes every day, as well as strength training and stretching of major muscle groups a minimum of 2 days each

TABLE 12.6 Benefits of Exercise Training

Adverse Effect of Cancer Treatment	Description	Physiological Effect of Exercise
Muscular Degeneration	Cancer treatments can damage the integrity of muscle tissue by decreasing protein synthesis. The release of hormones that cause muscle cell growth and development are blunted.	Exercise increases the integrity of muscle tissue and protein synthesis, stimulates the release of numerous hormones that increase muscle cell growth and development, and improves metabolism.
Cardiotoxicity	Cancer treatments can lead to left ventricular dysfunction, reduced ejection fraction, diminished contractility, reduced cardiac output, decreased nutrient and oxygen delivery to tissues.	Exercise can improve cardiovascular efficiency by: • Strengthening the myocardium • Increasing cardiac output and stroke volume • Decreasing resting heart rate and lowering exercise heart rate.
Pulmonary toxicity	Cancer treatments can cause a disruption in the structural integrity of the airways.	Exercise can improve ventilation and transport of oxygen from the environment to the cellular level.
Fatigue	Cancer treatments cause persistent, whole-body exhaustion that interferes with daily functioning.	Exercise has been shown to decrease fatigue and anxiety, and improve quality of life.
Pain	Pain can be caused by damage to tissue and nerves from the original tumor by the cancer itself or its related treatment.	Pain thresholds and pain tolerance levels have been reported to increase both during and following exercise. In addition, intensity ratings of pain appear to decrease following exercise.
Neuropathy	Damage to the peripheral nervous system caused by chemotherapy is referred to as chemotherapy-induced peripheral neuropathy, and produce pain symptoms that are often described as burning, sudden violent stabbing, or electric shocklike sensations and are often accompanied by pins-and-needles sensations and itching.	Several studies report improvements in muscular strength following moderate resistance exercise programs in individuals with hereditary motor and sensory neuropathies.
Immune Dysfunction	White blood cells have the ability to destroy foreign cells, including cancer cells in the body. Certain cancer treatments may cause a decrease in the body's white blood cell count, making it harder to fight off infection.	Chronic exercise training at a moderate intensity is associated with improved immune function through increases the amount of white blood cells and therefore strengthens the immune system.
Endocrine changes	The majority of endocrine changes are tumor-specific and treatment-specific. Reproductive function, thyroid health, and bone health are often adversely affected.	During exercise, extracellular substrates are mobilized that augment the effects of the endocrine system.
Gastrointestinal dysfunction	Cancer treatments can often result in disruption to the gastrointestinal system, causing constipation, malabsorption, diarrhea.	Exercise can improve gastric emptying and lower the relative risk of colon cancer. Overtime, regular physical activity can strengthen the digestive tract, making muscles more efficient.
Weight loss	Some people may experience weight loss both before diagnosis and as an effect of chemotherapy and radiation treatments. Factors that contribute to weight loss during treatment include loss of appetite, early satiety (feeling full), altered sense of taste and smell, difficulty chewing and swallowing, nausea, vomiting, diarrhea, and compromised nutrient intake	Exercise training has been suggested as a promising measure to prevent cachexia (muscle wasting) and restore muscular strength and endurance.

TABLE 12.7 Guidelines for Exercise Programming

	Aerobic Training	Strength Training	Flexibility Training
Frequency	3–5 days/wk	2–3 days/wk	2–7 days/wk
Intensity	40%–60% HRR*	40%–60% HRR*	Stretch to the point of mild discomfort
Duration	20–60 min/session	1–3 sets, 8–12 reps per exercise	10–30 seconds per stretch
Mode	Walking, cycling, cross trainers, swimming	Free weights, machines, resistance bands, resistance balls	Static stretching

week. Based on available data, Table 12.7 presents some general guidelines a cancer exercise instructor may follow when designing an exercise program.[81]

Initially, intensity will depend on the person's functional status and exercise history prior to cancer diagnosis. Typically, individuals who were previously active may continue their exercise regimen, although intensity may need to be decreased during treatment. Progression should consist of increases in frequency and duration rather than intensity.[81]

CHAPTER SUMMARY

Exercise is a powerful tool that can help an individual who is battling chronic disease to manage symptoms and possibly improve disease severity. In summary, the following recommendations will help guide exercise programming for individuals with chronic disease.

- *Hyperlipidemia:* Focus on expending calories through aerobic exercise performed at 40% to 80% maximal functional capacity at least 5 days/week, 20 to 60 min/session. Resistance training may be incorporated at 60% to 80% of 1RM, 2 to 4 sets of 8 to 12 reps, 2 to 3 days/week.
- *Diabetes:* Exercise testing recommendations are dependent upon age, type and duration of diabetes, and presence of diabetic complications. Aerobic exercise should be completed 4 to 7 times/week for 20 to 60 min/session at an intensity of 50 to 80% of VO_{2max}. Resistance training should include low-resistance/high-repetition exercises.
- *Obesity:* Physical activity is thought to be the most important factor in weight loss because of the increase in energy expenditure. Prior to programming, take into consideration any comorbidities, orthopedic limitations, and medications. Non–weight-bearing activity should be performed daily, or at least 5 sessions per week, at an initial intensity of 40% to 60% VO_{2max}, for 30 to 60 min/day. Increase exercise duration before increasing intensity, and focus on functional movements to ease performance of activities of daily living.
- *Hypertension:* The goals of an exercise program for an individual with hypertension should be blood pressure control, improve cardiovascular disease risk factors, and increase ventilatory threshold and peak work capacity. Aerobic exercise training should include large muscle group activities performed at 40% to 70% VO_{2max} (or RPE of 11–13/20 for individuals on beta-blockers), at least 30 min/session, 4 to 7 days/week. Resistance training should be limited to one set of 8 to 12 reps at 60% to 80% 1RM.
- *Myocardial infarction:* Individuals with MIs should perform aerobic exercises that involves large muscle group, rhythmic exercises and whole-body strength training, using both limbs. Aerobic exercise should be performed at 40% to 80% of the individuals VO_{2max} at least three days/week for 20 to 60 min/session, and include a warm-up and cool-down.
- *Chronic obstructive pulmonary disease:* The exercise program should include large muscle

activities that are enjoyable to the individual at a comfortable workload of 11–13/20 RPE. Breathlessness should be monitored and it may be necessary for shorter, intermittent exercise sessions to be completed throughout the day, 3 to 5 days/week. Strength training should be performed at a low resistance and high number of repetitions 2 to 3 days/week. Flexibility and neuromuscular exercises should be performed at least 3 days/week in order to improve range of motion, gait, balance, and breathing efficiency.

- *Alzheimer's disease:* Exercise training should be completed at a low intensity and focus on helping the individual to perform typical activities of daily living. Simple repetitive exercises will be easier for the individual to perform and are recommended. In the early stages of the disease, exercise is important to establish a regular routine for the individual. Constant supervision is necessary to ensure safety.
- *Anxiety disorders:* Individuals with stress or anxiety disorders must be evaluated for neuromuscular function, as a number of medications can impact perception, alertness, and coordination. Aerobic exercise training should be performed 3 to 5 days/week for 20 to 30 min at a time, at an intensity of 50%–85% of their VO_{2max}. Strength training should be performed a minimum of 2 days/week, with at least one set of 8 to 12 reps per exercise, at a resistance level of 60% to 85% of their max.
- *Low-back pain:* Most individuals with low-back pain should be able to perform all standard exercises. Therefore, exercise guidelines are similar to that established by ACSM for apparently healthy populations, with appropriate adjustments made as needed. Programs should be designed to increase exercise tolerance and prevent deconditioning, as well as minimize stress to the lower back.
- *Osteoporosis:* Regular weight-bearing, aerobic exercise and strength training have been shown to have a positive effect on bone mineral density in postmenopausal women. Individuals with osteoporosis are more likely to be deconditioned, so low-intensity exercise is recommended, with focus on improving balance and modification of activities of daily living, as well as improving muscular strength for the upper and lower body and trunk muscles.
- *Arthritis:* Exercise should focus on pain-free movements. Non–weight-bearing and low-impact exercises are suggested for individuals who experience more severe joint pain. Exercises should be individualized to meet the needs and abilities of the individual.
- *Joint replacement:* Exercise is recommended both before and after joint replacement surgery to help to strengthen the muscles surrounding the affected joint. Prior to surgery, exercises should focus on stretching, strengthening, and endurance. Exercises may be performed three to four times a week for about 30 to 60 minutes each session, as tolerated.
- *Chronic fatigue syndrome:* The goal of exercise programming should be to prevent deconditioning. Because of the possibility of exacerbating fatigue, exercise intensity should be very low and utilize a familiar activity. Strength training should focus on strength preservation and activities of daily living.
- *Cancer:* Most individuals who battle cancer can safely perform moderate physical activity for at least 30 minutes every day at an intensity of 40% to 60% HRR, as well as strength training and stretching of major muscle groups a minimum of 2 days each week.

WEB RESOURCES

Metabolic Diseases

National Cholesterol Education Program. www.nhlbinih.gov/about/ncep/index.htm
Independent Drug Information Service (iDiS). www.rxfacts.org
American Diabetes Association. www.diabetes.org/home.jsp
National Diabetes Information Clearinghouse (NDIC). http://diabetes.niddk.nih.gov/
National Heart, Lung, and Blood Institute. www.nhlbi.nih.gov

Cardiovascular and Pulmonary Disease

American Heart Association. www.americanheart.org
American Association of Cardiovascular and Pulmonary Rehabilitation. www.aacvpr.org
American College of Cardiology. www.acc.org
American College of Sports Medicine. www.acsm.org
American Lung Association. https://www.lung.org/

Cognitive/Psychological Disorders

Alzheimer's Association. www.alz.org/

National Association of Social Workers. www.helpstart-shere.org/Default.aspx?PageID=1238

National Center on Physical Activity and Disability. www.ncpad.org

National Institute on Aging. National Institutes of Health. www.nia.nih.gov/alzheimers

American Psychological Association. www.apa.org

Orthopedic Diseases and Disabilities

American Academy of Spine Physicians. www.spine-physicians.org

American Association of Neurological Surgeons. www.aans.org

Congress of Neurological Surgeons. www.neurosurgeon.org

North American Spine Society. www.spine.org

International Osteoporosis Foundation. www.iofbonehealth.org

International Society for Clinical Densitometry. www.iscd.org

National Osteoporosis Foundation. www.nof.org

American Academy of Orthopedic Surgeons. https://www.aaos.org/

Immunological and Hematological Disorders

Centers for Disease Control: Chronic Fatigue Syndrome. www.cdc.gov/cfs

CFIDS Association of America.

IACFS/ME International Association for CFFs/ME. www.iacfsme.org/

Maple Tree Cancer Alliance. https://www.mapletreecanceralliance.org/

Breast Cancer Watch. http://breeastcancer.evidence-watch.com

National Cancer Institute. www.cancer.gov

BOOKS AND PRINTED MATERIALS

Moore, G. E., Durstine, J. L, & Painter, P. L. (2016). *ACSM's exercise management for persons with chronic diseases and disabilities* (4th ed.). Human Kinetics.

REFERENCES

1. World Health Organization. (2021, February 3). *Physical activity*. https://www.who.int/news-room/fact-sheets/detail/physical-activity
2. Troiano, R. P., Berrigan, D., Dodd, K. W., Mâsse, L. C., Tilert, T., & McDowell, M. (2008). Physical activity in the United States measured by accelerometer. *Medicine and Science in Sports and Exercise, 40*(1), 181–188.
3. Hahn, R. A., Teutsch, S. M., Rothenberg, R. B., & Marks, J. S. (1990). Excess deaths from nine chronic diseases in the United States. *Journal of the American Medical Association, 264*, 2654–2659.
4. Lee, I. M., Shiroma, E. J., Lobelo, F., Puska, P., Blair, S. N., & Katzmarzyk, P. T. (2012). Effect of physical inactivity on major non-communicable diseases worldwide: An analysis of burden of disease and life expectancy. *The Lancet, 380*(9838), 219–229.
5. Rothschild, J., Hoddy, K. K., Jambazian, P., & Varady, K. A. (2014). Time-restricted feeding and risk of metabolic disease: A review of human and animal studies. *Nutrition Reviews, 72*(5), 308–318. https://doi.org/10.1111/nure.12104
6. Karr, S. (2017). Epidemiology and management of hyperlipidemia. *American Journal of Managed Care, 23*(9). S139-S148.
7. Wakatsuki, A. (2006). Hyperlipidemia. *Nihon Rinsho 64*(4), 375–380. Japanese.
8. He, N., & Ye, H. (2020). Exercise and hyperlipidemia. *Advances in Experimental Medicine and Biology, 1228*, 79–90. https://doi.org/10.1007/978-981-15-1792-1_5.
9. American College of Sports Medicine. (2021). *The American College of Sports Medicine*. https://www.acsm.org/
10. Karaa, A., & Goldstein, A. (2015). The spectrum of clinical presentation, diagnosis, and management of mitochondrial forms of diabetes. *Pediatric Diabetes, 16*(1), 1–9. https://doi.org/10.1111/pedi.12223.
11. Bell, T. N. (1994). Diabetes insipidus. *Critical Care Nursing Clinics of North America, 6*(4), 675–685.
12. Galassetti, P., & Riddell, M. C. (2013). Exercise and type 1 diabetes (T1DM). *Comprehensive Physiology, 3*(3), 1309–1336. https://doi.org/10.1002/cphy.c110040.
13. Centers for Disease Control and Prevention. (2021, April 5). *Childhood obesity facts*. https://www.cdc.gov/obesity/data/childhood.html.
14. Conway, B., & Rene, A. (2004). Obesity as a disease: No lightweight matter. *Obesity Reviews, 5*(3), 145–151. https://doi.org/10.1111/j.1467-789X.2004.00144.x.
15. Volaco, A., Cavalcanti, A. M., Filho, R. P., & Précoma, D. B. (2018). Socioeconomic status: The missing link between obesity and diabetes mellitus? *Current Diabetes Reviews, 14*(4), 321–326. https://doi.org/10.2174/1573399813666170621123227. PMID: 28637406.

16. Fryar C. D., Carroll, M. D., & Afful, J. (2020). *Prevalence of overweight, obesity, and severe obesity among children and adolescents aged 2–19 years: United States, 1963–1965 through 2017–2018*. https://www.cdc.gov/nchs/data/hestat/obesity-child-17-18/obesity-child.htm#table3.
17. Wing, C. (2012). *ACSM/NCHPAD resources for the inclusive fitness trainer*. American College of Sports Medicine.
18. De Lorenzo, A., Romano, L., Di Renzo, L., Di Lorenzo, N., Cenname, G., & Gualtieri, P. (2020). Obesity: A preventable, treatable, but relapsing disease. *Nutrition, 71*, 110615. https://doi.org/10.1016/j.nut.2019.110615.
19. Rabe, K. F., Hurst, J. R., & Suissa, S. (2018). Cardiovascular disease and COPD: Dangerous liaisons? *European Respiratory Review, 27(149)*, 180057. https://doi.org/10.1183/16000617.0057-2018.
20. So, J. Y., Zhao, H., Voelker, H., Reed, R. M., Sin, D., Marchetti, N., & Criner, G. J. (2018). Seasonal and regional variations in chronic obstructive pulmonary disease exacerbation rates in adults without cardiovascular risk factors. *Annals of the American Thoracic Society, 15(11)*, 1296–1303. https://doi.org/10.1513/AnnalsATS.201801-070OC.
21. Elliott, W. J. (2007). Systemic hypertension. *Current Problems in Cardiology, 32(4)*, 201–259. https://doi.org/10.1016/j.cpcardiol.2007.01.002.
22. Ruivo, J. A., & Alcântara, P. (2012). Hipertensão arterial e exercício físico [Hypertension and exercise]. *Revista Portuguesa de Cardiologia, 31(2)*, 151–158. Portuguese. https://doi.org10.1016/j.repc.2011.12.012.
23. Oliveras, A., & de la Sierra, A. (2014). Resistant hypertension: Patient characteristics, risk factors, comorbidities and outcomes. *Journal of Human Hypertension, 28(4)*, 213–217. https://doi.org/10.1038/jhh.2013.77.
24. Axon, R. N., Turner, M., & Buckley, R. (2015). An update on inpatient hypertension management. *Current Cardiology Reports, 17(11)*, 94. https://doi.org/10.1007/s11886-015-0648-y.
25. Boutcher, Y. N., & Boutcher, S. H. (2017). Exercise intensity and hypertension: What's new? *Journal of Human Hypertension, 31(3)*, 157–164. https://doi.org/10.1038/jhh.2016.62.
26. Pollard, T. J. (2000). The acute myocardial infarction. *Primary Care, 27(3)*, 631–649. https://doi.org/10.1016/s0095-4543(05)70167-6.
27. Lu, L., Liu, M., Sun, R., Zheng, Y., & Zhang, P. (2015). Myocardial infarction: Symptoms and treatments. *Cell Biochemistry and Biophysics, 72(3)*, 865–867. https://doi.org/10.1007/s12013-015-0553-4.
28. Yeh, R. W., Sidney, S., Chandra, M., Sorel, M., Selby, J. V., & Go, A. S. (2010). Population trends in the incidence and outcomes of acute myocardial infarction. *New England Journal of Medicine, 362(23)*, 2155–2165. https://doi.org/10.1056/NEJMoa0908610.
29. Tibaut, M., Mekis, D., & Petrovic, D. (2017). Pathophysiology of myocardial infarction and acute management strategies. *Cardiovascular and Hematological Agents in Medicinal Chemistry, 14(3)*, 150–159. https://doi.org/10.2174/1871525714666161216100553.
30. Moraes-Silva, I. C., Rodrigues, B., Coelho-Junior, H. J., Feriani, D. J., & Irigoyen, M. C. (2017). Myocardial infarction and exercise training: Evidence from basic science. *Advances in Experimental Medicine and Biology, 999*, 139–153. https://doi.org/10.1007/978-981-10-4307-9_9.
31. Labaki, W. W. & Rosenberg, S. R. (2020). Chronic obstructive pulmonary disease. *Annals of Internal Medicine, 173(3)*, ITC17–ITC32. https://doi.org/10.7326/AITC202008040.
32. Hattab, Y., Alhassan, S., Balaan, M., Lega, M., & Singh, A. C. (2016). Chronic obstructive pulmonary disease. *Critical Care Nursing Quarterly, 39(2)*, 124–130. https://doi.org/10.1097/CNQ.0000000000000105.
33. Duffy, S. P., & Criner, G. J. (2019). Chronic obstructive pulmonary disease: Evaluation and management. *Medical Clinics of North America, 103(3)*, 453–461. https://doi.org/10.1016/j.mcna.2018.12.005.
34. Ritchie, A. I., & Wedzicha, J. A. (2020). Definition, causes, pathogenesis, and consequences of chronic obstructive pulmonary disease exacerbations. *Clinics in Chest Medicine, 41(3)*, 421–438. https://doi.org/10.1016/j.ccm.2020.06.007.
35. Sorathia, L. (2019). Palliative care in chronic obstructive pulmonary disease. *Medical Clinics of North America, 103(3)*, 517–526. https://doi.org/10.1016/j.mcna.2018.12.010.
36. Gloeckl, R., Schneeberger, T., Jarosch, I., & Kenn, K. (2018). Pulmonary rehabilitation and exercise training in chronic obstructive pulmonary disease. *Deutsches Arzteblatt International, 115(8)*, 117–123. https://doi.org/10.3238/arztebl.2018.0117.
37. Fiorentino, G., Esquinas, A. M., & Annunziata, A. (2020). Exercise and chronic obstructive pulmonary disease (COPD). *Advances in Experimental Medicine and Biology, 1228*, 355–368. https://doi.org/10.1007/978-981-15-1792-1_24.
38. Paneroni, M., Simonelli, C., Vitacca, M., & Ambrosino, N. (2017). Aerobic exercise training in very severe chronic obstructive pulmonary disease: A systematic review and meta-analysis. *American Journal of Physical Medicine and Rehabilitation, 96(8)*, 541–548. https://doi.org/10.1097/PHM.0000000000000667.
39. McWhirter, L., Ritchie, C., Stone, J., & Carson, A. (2020). Functional cognitive disorders: A systematic review. *Lancet Psychiatry, 7(2)*, 191–207. https://doi.org/10.1016/S2215-0366(19)30405-5.
40. Claire, G. (2019). Administration des médicaments et troubles cognitifs: de l'écrasement au consentement? [Medication administration and cognitive disorders: from crushing to consent?]. *Revue de l'Infirmiere*,

68(253), 41-43. French. https://doi.org/10.1016/j.revinf.2019.07.003.
41. Soria Lopez, J. A., González, H. M., & Léger, G. C. (2019). Alzheimer's disease. *Handbook of Clinical Neurology, 167*, 231-255. https://doi.org/10.1016/B978-0-12-804766-8.00013-3.
42. Mantzavinos, V., & Alexiou, A. (2017). Biomarkers for Alzheimer's disease diagnosis. *Current Alzheimer Research, 14*(11), 1149-1154. https://doi.org/10.2174/1567205014666170203125942. PMID: 28164766.
43. Briggs, R., Kennelly, S. P., & O'Neill, D. (2016). Drug treatments in Alzheimer's disease. *Clinical Medicine (London), 16*(3), 247-253. https://doi.org/10.7861/clinmedicine.16-3-247.
44. Cass, S. P. (2017). Alzheimer's disease and exercise: A literature review. *Current Sports Medicine Reports, 16*(1), 19-22. https://doi.org/10.1249/JSR.0000000000000332.
45. Deslandes, A., Moraes, H., Ferreira, C., Veiga, H., Silveira, H., Mouta, R., Pompeu, F. A., Coutinho, E. S., & Laks, J. (2009). Exercise and mental health: Many reasons to move. *Neuropsychobiology, 59*(4), 191-198. https://doi.org/10.1159/000223730.
46. Love, A. S., & Love, R. (2019). Anxiety disorders in primary care settings. *Nursing Clinics of North America, 54*(4), 473-493. https://doi.org/10.1016/j.cnur.2019.07.002.
47. Maron, E., & Nutt, D. (2017). Biological markers of generalized anxiety disorder. *Dialogues in Clinical Neuroscience, 19*(2), 147-158. https://doi.org/10.31887/DCNS.2017.19.2/dnutt.
48. Bandelow, B., Reitt, M., Röver, C., Michaelis, S., Görlich, Y., & Wedekind, D. (2015). Efficacy of treatments for anxiety disorders: A meta-analysis. *International Clinical Psychopharmacology, 30*(4), 183-192. https://doi.org/10.1097/YIC.0000000000000078.
49. Ströhle, A. (2009). Physical activity, exercise, depression and anxiety disorders. *Journal of Neural Transmission, 116*(6), 777-784. https://doi.org/10.1007/s00702-008-0092-x.
50. Carek, P. J., Laibstain, S. E., & Carek, S. M. (2011). Exercise for the treatment of depression and anxiety. *International Journal of Psychiatry in Medicine, 41*(1), 15-28. https://doi.org/10.2190/PM.41.1.c.
51. Holder, M., Henniger, M., & Rehart, S. (2013). Orthopädische Rheumatologie [Orthopedic rheumatology]. *Z Orthop Unfall, 151*(4), 407-421; quiz 422-3. German. https://doi.org/10.1055/s-0032-1328721.
52. Maher, C., Underwood, M., & Buchbinder, R. (2017). Non-specific low back pain. *Lancet, 389*(10070), 736-747. https://doi.org/10.1016/S0140-6736(16)30970-9.
53. Delitto, A., George, S. Z., Van Dillen, L., Whitman, J. M., Sowa, G., Shekelle, P., Denninger, T. R., & Godges, J. J. (2012). Orthopaedic section of the American Physical Therapy Association. Low back pain. *Journal of Orthopaedic Sports Physical Therapy, 42*(4), A1-A57. https://doi.org/10.2519/jospt.2012.42.4.A1.
54. Wewege, M. A., Booth, J., & Parmenter, B. J. (2018). Aerobic vs. resistance exercise for chronic non-specific low back pain: A systematic review and meta-analysis. *Journal of Back and Musculoskeletal Rehabilitation, 31*(5), 889-899. https://doi.org/10.3233/BMR-170920.
55. Owen, P. J., Miller, C. T., Mundell, N. L., Verswijveren, S. J. J. M., Tagliaferri, S. D., Brisby, H., Bowe, S. J., & Belavy, D. L. (2020). Which specific modes of exercise training are most effective for treating low back pain? Network meta-analysis. *British Journal of Sports Medicine, 54*(21), 1279-1287. https://doi.org/10.1136/bjsports-2019-100886.
56. Armas, L. A., & Recker, R. R. (2012). Pathophysiology of osteoporosis: New mechanistic insights. *Endocrinology and Metabolism Clinics of North America, 41*(3), 475-486. https://doi.org/10.1016/j.ecl.2012.04.006.
57. Srivastava, M., & Deal, C. (2002). Osteoporosis in elderly: Prevention and treatment. *Clinics in Geriatric Medicine, 18*(3), 529-555. https://doi.org/10.1016/s0749-0690(02)00022-8.
58. Baccaro, L. F., Conde, D. M., Costa-Paiva, L., & Pinto-Neto, A. M. (2015). The epidemiology and management of postmenopausal osteoporosis: a viewpoint from Brazil. *Clinical Interventions in Aging, 10*, 583-591. https://doi.org/10.2147/CIA.S54614.
59. Fritz, R., Edwards, L., & Jacob, R. (2021). Osteoporosis in adult patients with intellectual and developmental disabilities: Special considerations for diagnosis, prevention, and management. *Southern Medical Journal, 114*(4), 246-251. https://doi.org/10.14423/SMJ.0000000000001231.
60. Watanabe, K., Kamijo, Y., Yanagi, M., Ishibashi, Y., Harada, T., & Kohzuki, M. (2021). Home-based exercise and bone mineral density in peritoneal dialysis patients: A randomized pilot study. *BMC Nephrology, 22*(1), 98. https://doi.org/10.1186/s12882-021-02289-y.
61. Centers for Disease Control and Prevention. (2019, February 20). *Arthritis.* https://www.cdc.gov/arthritis/index.htm.
62. Centers for Disease Control and Prevention. (2020, July 27). *Rheumatoid arthritis.* https://www.cdc.gov/arthritis/basics/rheumatoid-arthritis.html.
63. Mayo Foundation for Medical Education and Research. (2019, July 19). *Arthritis.* https://www.mayoclinic.org/diseases-conditions/arthritis/diagnosis-treatment/drc-20350777.
64. Charlesworth, J., Fitzpatrick, J., Perera, N. K., & Orchard, J. (2019). Osteoarthritis-A systematic review of long-term safety implications for osteoarthritis of the knee. *BMC Musculoskeletal Disorders, 20*, 1-12.
65. Moore, G. E., Durstine, J. L., & Painter, P. L. (Eds.). (2016). *ACSM's exercise management for persons with chronic diseases and disabilities.* Human Kinetics.
66. Snell, D. L., Hipango, J., Sinnott, K. A., Dunn, J. A., Rothwell, A., Hsieh, C. J., DeJong, G., & Hooper, G.

(2018). Rehabilitation after total joint replacement: A scoping study. *Disability and Rehabilitation, 40,* 1718–1731.
67. American Academy of Orthopaedic Surgeons. (2020). *The seventh annual report of the AJRR on hip and knee arthroplasty.* www.aaos.org/AJRRannualreport.
68. Traistaru, M. R., Kamal, D., Kamal, K. C., Alexandru, D. O., & Radu, M. (2020). Complex rehabilitation in patients with knee arthroplasty. *Health, Sports, & Rehabilitation Medicine, 21,* 140–149.
69. Reid, M. E., & Denomme, G. A. (2011). DNA-based methods in the immunohematology reference laboratory. *Transfusion and Apheresis Science, 44*(1), 65–72. https://doi.org/10.1016/j.transci.2010.12.011.
70. Yancey, J. R., & Thomas, S. M. (2012). Chronic fatigue syndrome: Diagnosis and treatment. *American Family Physician, 86*(8), 741–746.
71. Castro-Marrero, J., Sáez-Francàs, N., Santillo, D., & Alegre, J. (2017). Treatment and management of chronic fatigue syndrome/myalgic encephalomyelitis: All roads lead to Rome. *British Journal of Pharmacology, 174(5),* 345–369. https://doi.org/10.1111/bph.13702.
72. Larun, L., Brurberg, K. G., Odgaard-Jensen, J., & Price, J. R. (2017). Exercise therapy for chronic fatigue syndrome. *Cochrane Database of Systematic Reviews,* 4(4), CD003200. https://doi.org/10.1002/14651858.CD003200.pub7.
73. Hausman, D. M. (2019). What is cancer? *Perspectives in Biology and Medicine, 62*(4), 778–784. https://doi.org/10.1353/pbm.2019.0046.
74. Wang, J. J., Lei, K. F., & Han, F. (2018). Tumor microenvironment: Recent advances in various cancer treatments. *European Review for Medical and Pharmacological Sciences, 22*(12), 3855–3864. https://doi.org/10.26355/eurrev_201806_15270.
75. Lauby-Secretan, B., Dossus, L., Marant-Micallef, C., & His, M. (2019). Obésité et cancer [Obesity and Cancer]. *Bulletin du Cancer,106*(7-8), 635–646. French. https://doi.org/10.1016/j.bulcan.2019.04.008.
76. Amin, M. B., Greene, F. L., Edge, S. B., Compton, C. C., Gershenwald, J. E., Brookland, R. K., Meyer, L., Gress, D. M., Byrd, D. R., & Winchester, D. P. (2017). The Eighth Edition AJCC Cancer Staging Manual: Continuing to build a bridge from a population-based to a more "personalized" approach to cancer staging. *CA: A Cancer Journal for Clinicians, 67*(2), 93–99. https://doi.org/10.3322/caac.21388.
77. Yates, P. (2017). Symptom management and palliative care for patients with cancer. *Nursing Clinics of North America, 52*(1), 179–191. https://doi.org/10.1016/j.cnur.2016.10.006.
78. Deng, G. (2019). Integrative medicine therapies for pain management in cancer patients. *The Cancer Journal, 25*(5), 343–348. https://doi.org/10.1097/PPO.0000000000000399.
79. Christensen, J. F., Simonsen, C., & Hojman, P. (2018). Exercise training in cancer control and treatment. *Comprehensive Physiology, 9(1),* 165–205. https://doi.org/10.1002/cphy.c180016.
80. Schwartz, A. L., de Heer, H. D., & Bea, J. W. (2017). Initiating exercise interventions to promote wellness in cancer patients and survivors. *Oncology (Williston Park), 31*(10), 711–717.
81. Campbell, K. L., Winters-Stone, K. M., Wiskemann, J., May, A. M., Schwartz, A. L., Courneya, K. S., Zucker, D. S., Matthews, C. E., Ligibel, J. A., Gerber, L. H., Morris, G. S., Patel, A. V., Hue, T. F., Perna, F. M., & Schmitz, K. H. (2019). Exercise guidelines for cancer survivors: Consensus statement from international multidisciplinary roundtable. *Medicine and Science in Sports and Exercise, 51*(11), 2375–2390. https://doi.org/10.1249/MSS.0000000000002116.

CHAPTER 13
INTELLECTUAL DISABILITIES

Kevin Casebolt and Bethany L. Hersman

INTELLECTUAL DISABILITY: TERMINOLOGY AND DEFINITIONS

In order to define intellectual disability, it is first important to understand that the accepted terminology for this disability has gone through changes to what is considered appropriate terminology today: *intellectual disability*. In the past, and even still today, we see the term "mental retardation" used, many times because people are unaware of what the proper terminology is or that it has changed. The term was at one point in time a medical category used to describe individuals with intellectual disabilities, but over time evolved into a slang term used by society to degrade or make fun of people. This term is outdated and is considered offensive and degrading to those with intellectual disabilities, so much so that in 2010 President Obama signed Public Law 111-256 (Rosa's Law) into effect.[1] This law replaced "mental retardation" and "mentally retarded" with "intellectual disability" in federal legislation such as the Rehabilitation Act, the Individuals with Disabilities Education Act, and the Elementary and Secondary Education Act. Being familiar with and using proper and accepted terminology for all disabilities is important, especially in sport or movement-based settings where many individuals who may work with these individuals do not have the proper knowledge of or background in disability-related studies and legislation.

Definition and Diagnosis

To fully understand how we define intellectual disability, we must first discuss intelligence. Defining intelligence will help encompass the various capacities that we are referring to and will make it easier to identify where within these areas an individual with an intellectual disability may experience differences. **Intelligence** is the general mental capacity that involves reasoning, planning, solving problems, thinking abstractly, comprehending complex ideas, learning efficiently, and learning from experience.[2] There are several authoritative bodies (e.g., The International Classification of Diseases [ICD], American Psychiatric Association's *Diagnostic and Statistical Manual of Mental Disorders, V [DSM-5]*)[3] that are accepted by the medical and educational community for diagnosing intellectual disabilities. For consistency and clarity of the use of language, in this chapter, we will honor the definition of intellectual disability set forth by the *DSM-5*. The *DSM-5* defines intellectual disabilities as neurodevelopmental disorders that begin in childhood and are characterized by intellectual difficulties as well as difficulties in conceptual, social, and practical areas of living. The *DSM-5* established diagnosis of an intellectual disability refers to an individual that has an IQ score of below 70 or two standard deviations below the mean of 100 in the population. However, while IQ is one component of

Kevin Casebolt, East Stroudsburg University; and Bethany L. Hersman, Wright State University. © Kendall Hunt Publishing Company.

an intellectual disability, it is not the only criterion that must be satisfied. They must also demonstrate significant deficits in the functional areas described below. The *DSM-5* requires the satisfaction of three criteria for its diagnosis:

1. Deficits in intellectual functioning that have been previously defined as such areas as reasoning, planning, solving problems, thinking abstractly, comprehending complex ideas, learning efficiently, and learning from experience.[2]
2. Deficits in adaptive functioning that significantly hamper conforming to developmental and sociocultural standards for the individual's independence and ability to meet their social responsibility.
3. The onset of these deficits occurs during childhood.[4]

Although the onset of deficits occurs during childhood, an individual is not clinically diagnosed until they reach the age of developmental maturity, or age 22. The primary difference between the diagnosis of intellectual disability between *DSM-IV* and 5 is that the *DSM-5* criteria place more emphasis on adaptive functioning and the performance of usual life skills, allowing for a more comprehensive definition of intellectual disability than was reported in *DSM-IV*. The *DSM-5* also places more emphasis on how an individual functions in the social, cognitive, and physical domains that are important to understand in physical activity settings.

Breaking this definition down into component parts and phrases within the definition will aid in understanding the meaning of the entire term. Within this definition, the phrase **intellectual functioning** generally refers to mental capacity, or one's aptitude to learn, problem solve, and think critically. Generally, an **Intelligence Quotient (IQ) test** (e.g., Wechsler Adult Intelligence Scale, Stanford-Binet Intelligence Scale, and Woodcock Johnson III Tests of Cognitive Disabilities) is used to measure intellectual functioning. Individuals with a threshold of an IQ score of 70 or lower are deemed to have a limitation in intellectual functioning. Another important construct to understand within this definition is **adaptive behavior**. The American Association on Intellectual and Developmental Disabilities (AAIDD) defines adaptive behavior as the collection of conceptual, social, and practical skills that are learned and performed by people in their daily lives[2]. Conceptual skills refer to fundamental educational aptitudes such as understanding language and literacy, basic use of numbers, understanding how to tell time, basic skills in money management, and self-direction. Social skills involve proper conduct in social situations, social responsibility, and the ability to follow rules. Practical skills involve personal hygiene and personal self-care, health care, the ability to travel independently, the ability to develop and follow a schedule or routine, and understanding the use of a telephone.[3]

PATHOPHYSIOLOGY AND PSYCHOPHYSIOLOGY

It is best to use caution when considering the use of labels or classification systems to identify groups of people as this may trigger a negative reaction from the classified group. However, to aid in the understanding of the description of functional limitations of intellectual disability, it is helpful for practitioners to understand how they may offer educational, behavioral, and social support by understanding the extent of the deficits in functioning levels and abilities of this group of individuals. The *DSM-5* refers to the terms "mild," "moderate," "severe," and "profound" when attempting to classify or understand the differences in the intellectual capacity of individuals identified with intellectual disabilities, which will be discussed in the following sections.[4]

Mild Intellectual Disability

Individuals classified as mild to moderate intellectual disability comprise a majority (85%)[5] of individuals with intellectual disabilities and this classification is most closely associated with being slower in the areas of conceptual development and daily social skills. Educationally, this group can achieve academic success (IQ range from 50–55 to 70–75). They are mostly self-sufficient and have the capacity to learn practical life skills that allow them to function independently and with minimal levels of support.

Moderate Intellectual Disability

Individuals classified as having moderate intellectual disability comprise a small number (10%)[5] and their IQ ranges from 35 to 55. These individuals typically need more support with understanding the use of appropriate social cues, social judgment, and social decisions. They can take care of themselves but may require extended support and instruction to do so. They can gain independent employment, but may be qualified for positions that involve limited conceptual or social skills.

Severe Intellectual Disability

Individuals classified as having a severe intellectual disability comprise 3% to 4% of the population and have major delays in development (IQ range 20–40) such as very limited in communication skills; conceptual skills such as reading and writing; social skills that include interpersonal skills and the ability to obey rules and laws; and practical occupational skills.[5] Individuals with severe intellectual disabilities often require supervision and may live in a group home for this reason.

Profound Intellectual Disability

Individuals classified as having a profound intellectual disability comprise 1% to 2%[4] of the population and require 24-hour care and supervision (IQ below 20). Individuals with profound intellectual disabilities depend entirely on others for all aspects of their daily care and their communication skills are quite limited.

Evaluation of Severity and Support

When working with individuals who display varying degrees of functional limitation as noted earlier, it is also important to recognize the degree of support required to assist individuals with intellectual disabilities. The levels of support needed for individuals with intellectual disabilities can more accurately be described as a fluid continuum rather than distinct categories. As such, the AAIDD attempted to identify a model that would adequately describe the appropriate amount of support needed for individuals with intellectual disabilities with the development of the Supports Intensity Scale.[6] This scale provides normative data on support needs in 49 life activities grouped into six components: home living, community living, lifelong learning, employment, health and safety, and social. This system aims to evaluate a person's strengths and abilities, not just their limitations categorizing their functioning level on one of four levels of support needed to function well within their environment.[7] The first level, intermittent support, is defined as support on an "as-needed" basis and is typically offered during times of transition, uncertainty, or stress. Individuals previously diagnosed as "mild" level of impairment typically require this level of support. Physical activity practitioners might select activities that stimulate language development and problem-solving skills for individuals with intellectual disabilities at this level. Limited support, the second level, is typically the level needed for individuals with moderate intellectual disability and allows that, with additional training, individuals with intellectual disabilities can improve upon their adaptive behaviors and can increase their conceptual, social, and practical skills. Practitioners may want to concentrate on concepts of team play, strategy, and rules for individuals with intellectual disabilities at this level. Third, extensive supports are more intensive and typical of individuals associated with severe intellectual disability and typically require daily support of such tasks. The practitioner may concentrate on socially including students with intellectual disabilities into integrated settings at this level. Lastly, pervasive support is typically associated with profound intellectual disability and requires lifelong support. At this level, the practitioner should concentrate on sensorimotor programs that develop the senses.[6]

PREVALENCE

In 2019–2020, the National Center for Education Statistics reported that states served 441,744 children aged 3 to 21 with services under the auspices of the Individuals with Disabilities Education Act, Part B[8] as having an intellectual disability, or 6.1% of the total student enrollment.[9] This figure is relatively low because most individuals with intellectual disabilities do not need special education services, so they are not included in those statistics. The prevalence of adults with intellectual disabilities has ranged from .05% to .08%.[10] Individuals with intellectual disabilities are typically diagnosed by the time they reach 22 years of age. The age of diagnosis also typically depends on the specific cause of the disability with individuals that have a more severe disability typically being diagnosed earlier in life.[11] Males are more likely than females to be diagnosed with an intellectual disability with a rate of .78% in males to .63% in females.[12] The reason for the higher rate of prevalence of males versus females diagnosed with intellectual disability may be explained by the nature of the cause of the disability, such as fragile X syndrome, which will be explained in more detail later in the chapter.[13] Black non-Hispanic children are twice as likely and Hispanic children are approximately one and a half times as likely as white children to be diagnosed with intellectual disability. However, black non-Hispanic children and Hispanic children scored dramatically higher when they were raised in white homes suggesting social and cultural environments as the reason for this test score difference.[14] Language differences and poverty likely contribute to these differences based on cognitive testing and there is evidence that testing bias may also contribute to rates of diagnosis of individuals with intellectual disabilities.[15] Additionally, poverty has been one of the most consistent socioeconomic status (SES) markers for explaining the significant disparity of individuals being diagnosed with intellectual disabilities. Children below 200% of the federal poverty level (FPL) were diagnosed at a rate of 1.03% while those above 200% of the FPL were diagnosed at a rate of 0.5%.[12] Statistically, data has presented that the association between low SES and poverty level is markedly stronger for individuals with mild intellectual disability than it is for individuals with more severe intellectual disability.[16]

KNOWN CAUSES AND TYPES

Disorders that cause intellectual disabilities are typically classified according to the gestational time period that they occur—prenatally (before childbirth), perinatally (around the time of birth from 5 months prior, to one month afterward), or postnatally (after childbirth). During the first couple weeks of pregnancy, or prenatally, any one of more than 750 genetic disorders associated with intellectual disabilities could occur. Specifically, these are single-gene disorders, when a certain gene is known to cause the disability; chromosomal disorders, abnormal conditions of the chromosomes; and multifactorial inheritance, when multiple genetic factors are involved in conjunction with environmental factors that may cause the disorder.[17] Genetic causes, including Down syndrome, which is the largest genetic cause, and Fragile X syndrome, the largest inherited cause of intellectual disability, account for 45% of all intellectual disabilities.[18]

Prenatal causes of intellectual disabilities include advanced maternal age, maternal Black race, low maternal education, alcohol, drugs, and toxins.[19] Perinatal causes of intellectual disability include abnormal labor and delivery, anoxia (absence of oxygen) at birth, metabolic disorders, and nutritional disorders. Postnatal causes of intellectual disability include traumatic brain injury, infections, seizure disorders, and malnutrition.[7]

Down Syndrome

Down syndrome, the most common chromosomal condition of individuals diagnosed with intellectual disability, has a prevalence rate in the United States of one in 700 babies, or about 6,000 born each year.[19] There are three types of Down syndrome; the most common is trisomy 21 that accounts for 95% of the population of individuals with Down syndrome. Other types include translocation, and mosaicism, which are less common.[19] Individuals with Down syndrome have an increased risk of developing congenital heart defects, respiratory and hearing problems, Alzheimer's disease, childhood leukemia, and thyroid conditions. Their physical traits may consist of low muscle tone, small stature, an upward slant of the eyes, and a single

Child with Down syndrome.

deep crease across the center of their palm. Individuals with Down syndrome also tend to have hypermobile joints and tend to have increased rates of obesity along with lower muscle tone, so it is important to be careful when stretching or putting extra pressure on the joints without sufficient support. Individuals with Down syndrome may have some of these characteristics to varying degrees or none at all. The life expectancy of individuals with Down syndrome has increased from age 25 in 1983 to 60 in 2021.[19]

Fetal Alcohol Syndrome

Fetal alcohol syndrome (FASD) in a child results from alcohol exposure during a mother's pregnancy that can cause brain damage and growth problems, the severity of which varies individually. Fetal alcohol syndrome is the largest environmental cause of intellectual disability. Physical defects may include small eyes, a thin upper lip, an upturned nose, deformities in the joints, limbs, and fingers; slow physical growth before and after birth, small head circumference and brain size; and heart defects.[20,21] FASD is categorized as a neurodevelopmental disorder[22] (NDD) and can also include brain and central nervous system problems such as poor coordination and balance, poor memory, trouble with attention and processing information, difficulty with reasoning and problem solving, poor judgment skills, and rapidly changing moods. It may also manifest itself socially and behaviorally for children with FASD with difficulty in school, trouble getting along with others, poor social skills, trouble changing from one task to another, problems staying on task, poor concept of time, and difficulty with working toward a goal.[21] A physician may diagnose fetal alcohol syndrome by monitoring the timing and amount of alcohol consumption during pregnancy and watching the child for the first few months after birth to determine risk factors and to look for signs and symptoms of FASD. Physiological diagnosis involves monitoring the child's brain development. Diagnosis may also manifest itself with learning and language difficulties.[20]

Fragile X Syndrome

Fragile X syndrome (FXS) is the most common inherited cause of intellectual disability and is a genetic disorder caused by changes in a gene called fragile X mental retardation 1 (FMR1) that impairs normal brain development. FXS affects approximately 1 in 7,000 males and 1 in 11,000 females.[23] Similar to attention-deficit disorder, attention-deficit/hyperactivity disorder and autism, a child diagnosed with FXS might experience developmental delays such as talking out

Craniofacial features associated with fetal alcohol syndrome

Facial features of FAS

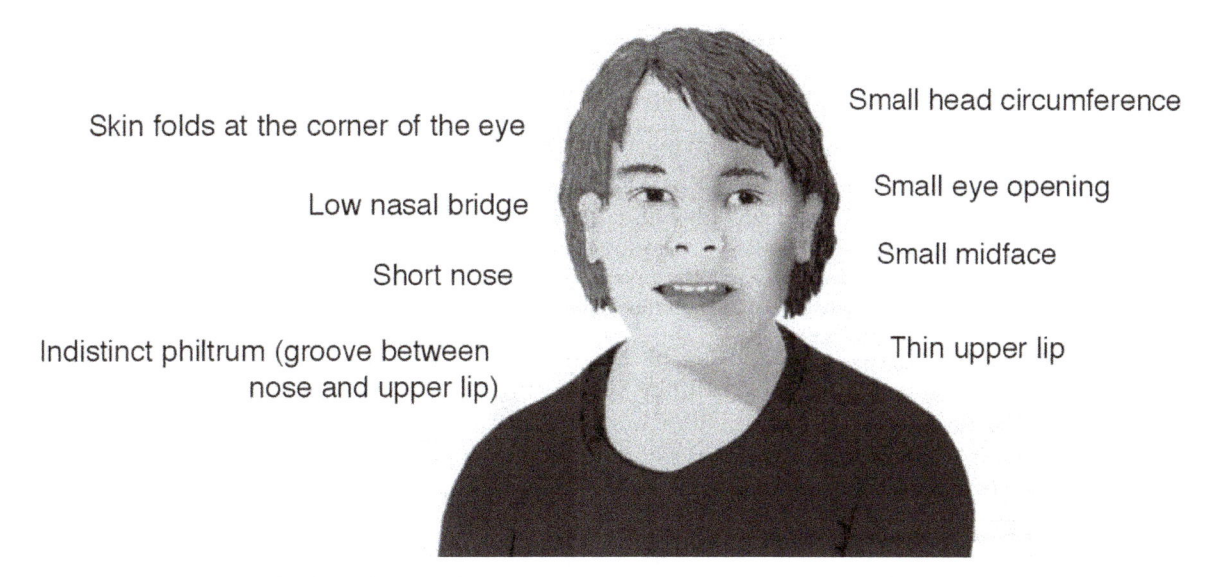

- Skin folds at the corner of the eye
- Low nasal bridge
- Short nose
- Indistinct philtrum (groove between nose and upper lip)
- Small head circumference
- Small eye opening
- Small midface
- Thin upper lip

Facial features of child with fetal alcohol syndrome.
Source: NIH/National Institute on Alcohol Abuse and Alcoholism

FRAGILE X SYNDROME

Broad forehead
Elongated face
Large prominent ears
Strabismus (crossed eyes)
Highly arched palette

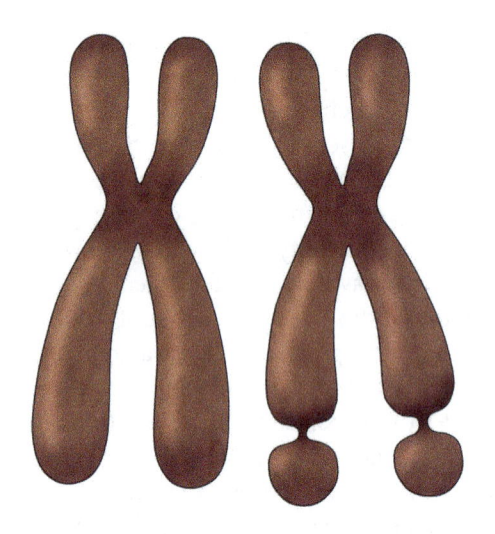

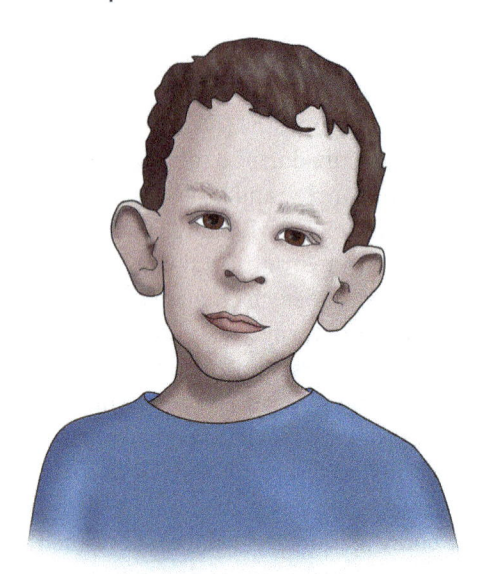

Hyperextensible Joints
Hand calluses
Pectus Excavatum
   (indentation of chest)
Mitral valve prolapse
Enlarged testicles
Hypotonia (low muscle tone)
Soft, fleshy skin
Flat feet
Seizures in 10%

FIGURE 13.1
Source: Science History Images / Alamy Stock Phot

of turn; difficulty learning new skills, and social and behavioral problems such as not making clear eye contact, anxiety, inattentiveness, hand flapping, and hyperactivity. In fact, individuals diagnosed with FXS are frequently diagnosed with autism spectrum disorder as well. Diagnosis is typically secured from a candidate via a DNA blood test from a qualified physician or genetic counselor.[24] See Figure 13.1 for a picture of the facial features of someone with FXS.

INTELLECTUAL DISABILITY AND MOVEMENT

Individuals with intellectual disabilities maintain similar physical and motor movements as their peers without intellectual disabilities.[25] However, they do tend to experience developmental motor delays that are often connected to their cognitive functioning such as limited attention span and comprehension capability. In general, the more severe the intellectual disability, the greater the delay they experience in achieving various developmental milestones. For example, a child with FXS might have developmental delays such as trouble sitting or walking or sensory-motor integration deficits that may result in delayed development of balance, poor coordination, motor planning deficits, and tactile defensiveness (a heightened sensitivity to touch).[26]

In terms of the health-related components of fitness, children with intellectual disabilities typically score lower on such measures as cardiovascular fitness,[26] strength, endurance, and flexibility as well as skill-related components of fitness, such as agility, balance, running speed, and reaction time, than their peers without intellectual disabilities.[27] Additionally, they have been reported to have lower maximal heart rates, lower rate of muscular development, and greater body fat than individuals without intellectual disabilities.[28] Results of empirical physical and motor assessment of individuals with intellectual disabilities may be limited due to their lack of motivation to participate in testing or their lack of understanding of the motor task they are asked to perform.[26,29] This lack of motivation, and ability to process information, has also been reported as a difference in the development of their performance on motor tasks such as stability, gross agility, locomotor movement, and ball control.[30] There seems to be a relationship between the classification of individuals with intellectual disabilities and the development of their motor abilities, where the more severe the classification, the more significant the developmental delay tends to be.[26] In general, the performance of males with intellectual disabilities on fitness testing (e.g., cardiovascular endurance, muscular strength, and endurance) generally exceeds that of females.[27] The discrepancy of differences in fitness levels is larger as the classification of disability becomes more severe.[27] However, females tend to perform better than males on tests of balance and flexibility, and individuals with Down syndrome tend to perform better on flexibility tests than individuals with other types of intellectual disability.[30] Individuals with Down syndrome also tend to perform higher than individuals with other types of intellectual disability in rhythmic movements (e.g., skipping, marching, and dancing).[32]

PREVENTION AND MANAGEMENT OF INTELLECTUAL DISABILITY

Management of intellectual disability begins with prevention and education that informs expecting mothers about the inherent risks of alcohol consumption and taking drugs during pregnancy. Expectant mothers can visit with their primary care physician about effective counseling that would include abstention from alcohol and drugs and other informed choices during their pregnancy. In addition, they may seek further counseling about their newborn baby that may include potential signs and symptoms to look for, behavioral therapy, cognitive therapy, and educational support for the individual and their family, in addition to sensorimotor programming. The goal of therapeutic intervention is to minimize the modifiable symptoms and secondary health conditions of the disability and to improve the quality of life of the individual with an intellectual disability through early intervention.

The goal of behavioral therapy is to encourage positive behaviors in the individual with an intellectual disability while discouraging undesirable behaviors. Positive reinforcement and mild punishments such as the use of "time-outs" are forms of behavioral therapy. Understanding what may trigger emotional outbursts and either avoiding or redirecting the behavior are other forms of behavioral therapy that may be successful in physical activity settings. Cognitive therapy is built upon the premise of connecting an individual's behavior, emotions, and cognitions and seeks to correct negative behaviors by adjusting that negative behavior and associated stress into a more positive outcome. Educational support may come in the form of special education in the classroom and adapted physical education during physical education and seeks to provide individuals with intellectual disabilities with academic modifications while they are in school to promote success as well as transitional planning to promote self-sufficiency and independence once they graduate.[33] Lastly, infants and children with intellectual disabilities tend to benefit from sensorimotor programming. Early models of sensorimotor programming have been used to manage the disability through activities that promote the improvement of body awareness, prelocomotion movement skills, object manipulation skills, and to develop improved posture and locomotion patterns.[34]

SPECIFIC BENEFITS OF PHYSICAL ACTIVITY AND EXERCISE

In a previous section of the chapter, various deficit areas in the health-related and skill-related components of fitness were identified for individuals with intellectual disabilities.[27] Recent research supports that individuals with intellectual disabilities tend to lead sedentary lifestyles and do not typically exercise with the frequency and intensity as is recommended by the World Health Organization (WHO).[35,36] Similarly, individuals with intellectual disabilities typically do not participate in physical activity as much as their same-age peers without disabilities.[37] Not only do individuals with intellectual disabilities tend to be less fit and more overweight than their peers without disabilities, but they are also more likely to experience symptoms of anxiety and depression.[38-40]

Children with Intellectual Disabilities

Children with disabilities get about half of their physical activity during physical education class.[41] Within the context of physical education, it has been suggested that children with intellectual disabilities experience improvements in both physical and psychosocial health, with the larger improvements being in the realm of physical health improvement. Physical education has a significant impact on the improvement of the physical wellness and psychosocial health of children with intellectual disabilities after they perform such activities as resistance

Example of a child with disabilities participating in physiotherapy.

training, aerobic training, balance/core stability training, and activities that center on playing a sport such as basketball, soccer, throwing balls, judo, and table tennis.[42]

Adults with Intellectual Disabilities

The creation of a physical activity plan that includes regular exercise and health-related components of fitness such as cardiovascular endurance exercises, muscular strength, and endurance, and flexibility should be the focus for adults with intellectual disabilities, although it would also be beneficial for children. When designing a physical activity program for aerobic fitness, a practitioner should include activities that involve 30 to 60 minutes per session of cardiorespiratory endurance at moderate intensity, 5 days per week. In addition to aerobic fitness, resistance training for each muscle group should be included 2 to 3 days per week and one to four sets of 10 to 15 repetitions per muscle group allowing for a slow progression. Flexibility training should also be included 2 to 3 days per week that involves holding each stretch for 10 to 30 seconds repeating each stretch two to four times that targets the shoulder girdle, chest, neck, trunk, lower back, hips, posterior and anterior legs, and ankles. Lastly, a neuromotor program should be included 2 to 3 days per week for 20 to 30 minutes each day that includes exercises involving agility, balance, coordination, and gait.[43] This type of program will not only improve the health-related areas of physical wellness but also skill-related areas of physical wellness such as agility, power, reaction time, and speed.[44] It is important to remember that individuals with Down syndrome are at higher risk of being born with congenital heart disease. It has been suggested that participation in a structured physical activity program can result in increased aerobic capacity and muscular strength and endurance and may help to reduce the risk of heart disease for those with Down Syndrome as well as all individuals with intellectual disabilities.[45]

CONTRAINDICATIONS FOR MOTOR MOVEMENT

While the previous section outlined the benefits of physical activity for individuals with intellectual disabilities, it is also important to understand the types of movements that are not recommended for individuals with intellectual disabilities. Contrary indications for movements, or simply contraindications, are exactly that. These are movements that are not recommended because they may predispose people to exacerbate a preexisting condition that they have due to being diagnosed with an intellectual disability and the accompanying characteristics of that disability. In particular, this concern resides with individuals with intellectual disabilities who have also been diagnosed with atlantoaxial instability, hypermobile joints, and obesity. Specific types of movements that are contraindicated for these three conditions are outlined in the following sections.

Atlantoaxial Instability

Atlantoaxial instability is a condition that impacts approximately 17% of the population of people with Down syndrome[34] and is characterized by relaxed joints between the first two cervical vertebrae that may potentially allow the vertebrae to slip out of alignment easily. As such, movements that require forceful bending of the neck, such as gymnastics, diving, the butterfly stroke in swimming, heading a soccer ball, or other such sports, are not recommended, as they may dislocate the atlas causing damage to the spinal cord.[34]

Hypermobile Joints

Joint hypermobility, the ability of a joint to move beyond its normal range of motion,[47] may occur in individuals with intellectual disabilities, particularly many people with Down syndrome. Individuals with Down syndrome are prone to have underdeveloped muscle tone that may make them candidates for hypermobile joints.[34] Additionally, individuals with hypermobile joints should be restricted from activities that could result in hyperflexion, or flexion beyond the typical range of motion, and hyperextension activities, or those activities that may forcefully extend a limb or joint beyond its normal range of motion.[46] Similar to atlantoaxial instability, activities such as dancing, swimming, yoga, or gymnastics that place the joints at risk for hyperextension or hyperflexion and should be avoided.

Obesity

It has been previously mentioned that individuals with intellectual disabilities, in general, tend to lead an inactive and sedentary lifestyle. The lack of movement associated with a sedentary lifestyle places individuals with intellectual disabilities at risk for becoming overweight, or even obese. The Center for Disease Control (CDC) defines obesity as weight that is higher than what is considered a healthy weight for a given height.[48] Activities performed should emphasize the use of large muscle groups in low-impact aerobic activities; intensity should be deemphasized, and duration should be stressed.[49] High-impact activities may cause discomfort to the low back or various joint areas[50] of individuals who are obese due to the excess weight they are carrying and are not recommended. Lastly, obesity is also associated with reduced postural control and stability that could hinder their ability to adapt to changes in terrain while performing simple movements such as walking.[51] Therefore, activities that involve a high amount of balance and control should be closely monitored as these individuals are more prone to injuries as a result of falls due to their unstable static and dynamic balance.

MODIFICATIONS FOR INDIVIDUALS WITH INTELLECTUAL DISABILITIES

Due to a tendency for individuals with intellectual disabilities to be more sedentary,[35,36] encouraging participation in physical education, sports, aquatics, and fitness-based activities as a part of a regular routine can help to avoid or reduce many of the secondary health issues facing some individuals. Individuals with intellectual disabilities are able to participate in many activities and sports without modifications; however, depending on their existing strength, muscle tone, and other health conditions, they may need to have activities modified to fit their needs and abilities.

Equipment and Activity Modifications

Assessing to determine present level of performance, baseline fitness levels, and movement abilities is essential to determine the appropriate modifications for individuals with intellectual disabilities. Before beginning any exercise program, sport, or school year, always consult the individual's educational plan and

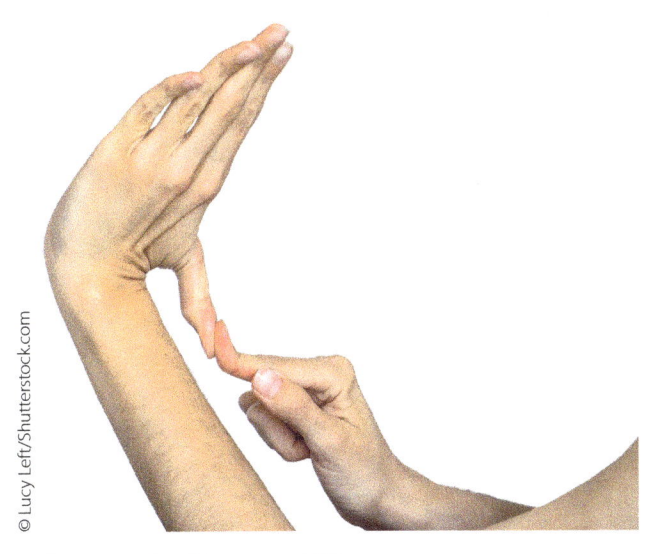

An example of hypermobility.

medical records to learn more about their comorbidities and medical history. The following modifications can be implemented in various settings, but keep in mind that not all modifications will be necessary, and may be tailored to meet the unique needs of each individual. Based on individual characteristics of individuals with intellectual disabilities, such as lower IQ, difficulty thinking abstractly, obesity, and hypermobile joints, the following are suggested modifications that can be made in various physical activity environments.

- Modify rules for a game or activity so they are easier to understand.
- Break complex movements down into smaller parts or steps.
- Make open skills (e.g., hitting a pitched ball) into closed skills (e.g., hitting a ball off a tee) when first learning and practicing the skill to help slow it down.
- Use pictures or other visuals to help aid with understanding of skills or tasks that may be hard to remember.
- If a setting is new to them, allow time to explore and learn where things are, take them through the setting and show them the equipment and facilities.
- Don't assume they know or understand how to do something—ask them to demonstrate or tell you what you want them to do to check for understanding.
- Allow extra time to complete tasks or activities.
- Alter implements used in sports.
  - Lighter weight or broader rackets, bats, and other handheld items.
  - Use larger, brighter, softer, slower moving balls (e.g., beach balls instead of volleyballs).
- Set concrete boundaries that are easy to see (use cones or other items to delineate playing area).
- Reduce the size of the playing field.
- Using larger targets or goals, allow them to stand closer to targets and gradually have them move back.
- For those with atlantoaxial instability, avoid exercises that put pressure on the head and neck (e.g., certain gymnastic skills, heading a soccer ball, diving).
- Avoid strength training to exhaustion and high impact activities; due to joint instability and hypermobility, individuals tend to tire easier, which may increase the risk of injury.
- Start slow and low when strength training—use body-weight or lightweight exercises and have them perform the movements slowly. As they gain strength and are able to successfully perform the activities, you can add more weight and increase the intensity.
- Starting with shorter and more frequent training sessions can help to maintain their attention and avoid injury.
- Flexibility activities should be closely monitored due to hypermobility in the joints.
- Some individuals with intellectual disabilities have a lower max HR (about 8%–20% less than those without disabilities), so it is important to monitor heart rate during cardiovascular activities.
- Individuals with intellectual disabilities have a lower metabolic rate, which makes it easier for them to gain weight, so engage them in activities that build muscle to help speed up the metabolism.
- Be aware of exercises that put a lot of pressure on the joints (e.g., running on the treadmill) because they can be painful or may cause injury, so opt for low impact exercises like swimming or using an exercise bike.
- Include functional exercises that they will engage in on a daily basis at home, work or school such as bending, lifting, walking, and balancing exercises.
- Select activities that are appropriate to the individual's chronological age (e.g., if working with an adult, pick activities that are relevant for adults to do rather than playing tag games).
- Design tasks and activities that are appropriate for the individual's cognitive level so that they can comprehend what is being asked of them.
- Use rewards, reinforcement, and other motivational techniques to encourage participation.
- Give more frequent breaks as they may tire more easily than others.[52-54]

Assessment Modifications

For individuals with intellectual disabilities, most physical activity assessments reside in the areas of physical fitness and in task analyses. In movement-based settings, there are several different types of physical fitness assessments that can be used depending on individual needs and abilities. The Brockport Physical Fitness test[55] is a modified version of the FITNESSGRAM Physical Fitness test and has adapted fitness

TABLE 13.1 Sample Task Analysis Checklist for a Bicep Curl

Check when done	Activity	Picture
	Pick up appropriate size weight	
	Start with arms at side, feet shoulder width apart	
	Slowly bend arm at elbow to bring weight up to body and lower weight to starting position	
	Complete 10 in a row	

standards specific to individuals with intellectual disabilities. This test is appropriate for individuals between the ages of 10 to 17 years old. It can also be used for individuals who are older than 17; however, the standards may not apply to them as the test has not been standardized for that age group (adults).

Task analyses also work well with individuals who have intellectual disabilities because a skill, activity, or workout session can be broken down into smaller, more manageable steps that make it easier for an individual to understand and remember.[52] A task analysis can be done for an individual skill, such as what is listed in Table 13.1, or for an entire workout session, combining activities to create a workout. The individual may need to be taught the steps for each skill/workout session as well as to practice the steps to help create a routine they are familiar and comfortable with repeating, with the goal of learning the steps and being able to complete them independently.

CONSIDERATIONS AND RECOMMENDATIONS FOR PRACTITIONERS

It is always a good idea to be knowledgeable of each person's medical background and to determine a baseline level of fitness, level of communication, and movement abilities before starting a program with individuals who have intellectual disabilities to ensure safe participation. Collaboration and communication between practitioners who work with individuals with intellectual disabilities will help to create a well-rounded approach to improving the overall health and physical activity levels of these individuals. The value of each practitioner involved in the care, education, and training of intellectual disabilities cannot go without mention because movement and function is a team approach. Practitioners will need to present the activities in ways that are appropriate to the level of knowledge, ability, understanding, and experience of each individual. Once a baseline ability level is determined, the practitioner can develop the program or plan to enhance areas where the individual(s) may be delayed or those that the individual wishes to develop.

Practitioners should also prepare individuals with intellectual disabilities for activities that generalize to the community around them, such as how to use a fitness center and pick exercises, choose equipment, exercise safely, and who to ask if they need help. In addition, finding out if they participate in a sport team or organization and then practicing the skills and sport specific needs can help them to transfer the knowledge and skills learned in a physical education or therapy session into their sports. When presenting activities to someone with an intellectual disability, using visuals such as demonstrations or pictures/videos of certain exercises or skills can be helpful to support what it is you want them to do, especially if they do not understand your explanation. For example, in multielement skills such as batting a pitched ball, a picture of each component of the skill can aid in understanding of the elements and the order in which they should be completed.

Communication Strategies

Breaking activities or skills into smaller blocks of information can be helpful; in this case the practitioner would be taking larger more complex skills or activities and piecing them into smaller, more manageable concepts. For example, if the goal of a basketball activity is to receive a pass, dribble the ball down the court, and then shoot the ball into the basket, the practitioner could first teach how to catch a ball (it could be any type of ball that is easy for them to catch). Then, they could teach dribbling after they are successful with catching. Following their success in both skills, then combine catching and dribbling down the court, and so on. This is known as behavior chaining, and is frequently utilized in behavior modification plans.[56] Behavior chains can also be used when teaching new skills that have many different discrete movements, such as lifting weights or using exercise machines. See Obrusnikova et al. (2019, 2020, and 2021)[57–59] for studies implementing fitness programs using chaining and prompts for adults with intellectual disabilities. Broken into steps, the progression would look like this.

1. Learn to catch a ball (catching may also require chaining for the different parts of catching, dribbling, and shooting first)
2. Learn to dribble a ball while maintaining a stationary position
3. Learn to dribble in motion
4. Catch a ball and dribble down to the end of the court
5. Learn to shoot a ball
6. Combine catching, dribbling, and shooting into the basket

When presenting activities, it is important to use the individual's preferred mode of communication and to communicate at a level they can understand, while not patronizing them or treating them as though they are a child (if they are an adult). If an individual uses sign language or a Picture Exchange Communication System (PECS) to communicate, the practitioner should do their best to learn important activity-related signs and/or how to use the PECS in their setting to effectively communicate with the individual. Some individuals with intellectual disabilities may have difficulty expressing their feelings. It is important for the practitioner to learn how each person expresses anger, frustration, or sadness and to watch their nonverbal expressions and body language in case they need to intervene or redirect behavior.[53]

When presenting information, delivering instructions and demonstrations concisely can help individuals with intellectual disabilities maintain their attention and focus on the task and may keep them from experiencing information overload. This can also help them remember what they are supposed to do. Additionally, individuals with intellectual disabilities may not be able to generalize information from one day to the next or one sport to another. The practitioner should be aware of this and may need to repeat or further explain directions as necessary.[53]

Behavior Management Strategies

Using behavior modification strategies can help to increase motivation, participation, and success in movement settings.[56] Presenting the individual with a choice of activity or equipment to start with can help with motivation as they are being given choices to pick what THEY want to use or do. This also allows them to have a sense of independence so they can take charge of their exercise routine, for example. In addition, exploring ways to encourage and reinforce movement and positive behaviors (such as following directions or cooperating with a teammate) can help to keep them motivated throughout the duration of the activity and engaging in the desired activities. Similarly, utilizing a token economy or reward system can help to motivate and encourage activity participation.

Teaching and maintaining routines and schedules can help to manage the behavior of individuals with intellectual disabilities by making it easier for them to transition from one activity to the next since they know what is expected of them from the time they enter the physical activity setting to the time they leave. Many individuals with intellectual disabilities have deficits in adaptive behavior and they are not able to successfully deviate from their routines, and may, consequently, display negative or unacceptable behaviors if they are asked deviate from a routine. Keeping with their routine on a daily basis will help them maintain consistency and predictability making it easier for them to engage in the activities.[52]

Lastly, engaging in activity within an environment that is free from distractions will help individuals with intellectual disabilities to maintain positive and task-oriented behavior by helping them concentrate on the task at hand. Understandably, this can be difficult in activity and movement settings such as sport, fitness centers, and physical education classes. Prompting the individual to keep their back to others while engaging in physical activity while they complete their exercises may encourage focus and attention on the task at hand.

SPORT ORGANIZATIONS FOR INDIVIDUALS WITH INTELLECTUAL DISABILITIES

Individuals with intellectual disabilities can be fully integrated and included into sporting and physical activity opportunities within the school and the community successfully. There are likely many different inclusive/integrated programs, organizations, and events within the community, and practitioners in a physical activity–related field may be asked to find appropriate sport or physical activity opportunities for individuals with intellectual disabilities. The following is a list of sport organizations that exist for individuals with intellectual disabilities. Practitioners are encouraged to look within their community/state/country for other organizations such as camps, recreation facilities, and other sporting opportunities because there are some that include all individuals with disabilities and do not specialize in only intellectual disabilities.

Special Olympics

The Special Olympics was officially founded in 1968, with Eunice Kennedy Shriver as the driving force behind this organization. The first Special Olympics games were held that year at Soldier Field in Chicago, Illinois and included about 1000 athletes.[60] Today, Special Olympics has grown as a national and international organization, supporting more than 5 million athletes in 170 countries.[60] The mission of the Special Olympics is:

> To provide year-round sports training and athletic competition in a variety of Olympic-type sports for children and adults with intellectual disabilities, giving them continuing opportunities to develop physical fitness, demonstrate courage, experience joy and participate in a sharing of gifts, skills and friendship with their families, other Special Olympics athletes and the community. (para 1)

Within the organization are various programs and opportunities for individuals with intellectual disabilities who are 8 years old and older. Special Olympics also created a Young Athletes Program for children between the ages of 2 and 7 who can practice and learn many of the skills and activities that are a part of Special Olympics events for when they are old enough to participate. In addition, the Motor Activity Training Program was developed for those individuals who may have more severe intellectual disabilities and/or limited levels of functioning and who are not able to participate in the other Special Olympics sports.[61] There are currently 36 winter and summer sports under the Special Olympics umbrella, and in order to qualify, an athlete must have an intellectual disability (e.g., Down syndrome, Fragile X syndrome, or other disabilities that may cause or that an individual may have in conjunction with an intellectual disability). Each of the sports is also coached by a certified volunteer coach who is able to utilize the many sport skill coaching resources available for free on the Special Olympics website (the link is listed in the Web Resources section).

Special Olympics also has a Healthy Athletes Program aimed at providing free medical screenings for the athletes since many of them do not receive the health screening exams that they should such as dentistry, physical therapy, health/physical exams, eye screenings, and more. In addition to health screenings, Special Olympics provides information for health care workers with the information they need to comfortably provide the many medical services to individuals with intellectual disabilities.

There is also a fitness training component to the Special Olympics. The aim of the fitness training component is to improve the fitness of the athletes and to help teach them about living a healthy lifestyle. This includes, but is not limited to, engaging in regular physical activity, eating 5 fruits and vegetables a day, and drinking 5 bottles of water each day.[62] During the 2020 pandemic, the Special Olympics also developed a program called School of Strength, which is an online exercise training program targeted specially toward individuals with intellectual disabilities with activities that are safe and appropriate for individuals of varying abilities. Coaching for the Special Olympics has different opportunities as does being a trainer for the School of Strength program.

Each program has its own certification/training process for coaches and fitness/personal trainers. Please review the Special Olympics website for more information on helping someone to become an athlete and to find a local team or if a practitioner is interested in becoming a trainer or coach.

Special Olympics Unified Sports

In addition to the sports that are only for athletes with intellectual disabilities, Special Olympics also has a Unified Sport program for athletes with and without intellectual disabilities to participate together on the same team. This program is guided by the principle that by participating and practicing together, the athletes will learn from one another and develop friendships, thus promoting social inclusion. On the Unified Sports teams, athletes of similar ages and ability are paired together to keep the competitions fun and challenging for all who participate. Unified Sports teams are created for 11 different sports, including basketball, football, golf, and sailing, among others. See the Unified Sports website link listed in the Web Resources section for more information.[63]

Special Olympics held in the UK.

Paralympics

Athletes with intellectual disabilities are also able to participate in the Paralympic games as long as they fulfill certain criteria and meet qualifying standards. Athletes with intellectual disabilities have been included since the 1996 Paralympic Games; each potential athlete has to go through classification in order to be determined eligible for participation (see Chapter 10 for more information about classification in sports). The International Paralympic Committee defines intellectual disability as "a restriction in intellectual functioning and adaptive behaviour in which affects conceptual, social and practical adaptive skills required for everyday life," which fulfills the World Health Organization of intellectual disability.[64] Since this disability is sometimes considered "invisible," it is hard to classify at times and can be easier for people to try to impersonate people with intellectual disabilities in order to be deemed eligible. Paralympic sports for athletes with intellectual disabilities include swimming, athletics (track and field), and table tennis.

Little League/Senior Challenger Division

Challenger baseball was created for any individual who may have a physical or intellectual disability; little league athletes who participate must be between the ages of 4 and 18 (or 22 if they are still in high school), while the senior league athletes can be anywhere from ages 15 and up. The games can be held on traditional or synthetic baseball fields depending on the availability and accessibility of fields and the unique needs of the athletes. Games last one or two innings providing everyone with an opportunity to bat and play defense. Individuals who have more limitations are allowed to have a "buddy" who helps them to bat, run the bases, or field the ball for the purpose of keeping them safe while they are playing. Batting can be modified to hit a slow-pitched ball or a ball off a tee if necessary.[65]

TOPSoccer

The Outreach Program for Soccer, or TOPSoccer, is a soccer program that has been created for individuals with intellectual, emotional, or physical disabilities that allows individuals of all playing abilities to enjoy the game. In TOPSoccer programs, coaches provide practice and training activities to work on the development of skills for each athlete. The composition of team members within these programs may vary. Games can be small-sided (e.g., 3 on 3) full field (11 on 11), unified (athletes with and without disabilities playing together), indoor, outdoor, in a camp format, skilled practice only, or a mixture of any of the aforementioned styles of play. The TOPSoccer website also includes coaching resources that have activities for athletes with a variety of disabilities.[66]

Example of a boy with down syndrome playing TOPSoccer.

CHAPTER SUMMARY

- *Intellectual disability* is the accepted term over the term "mental retardation."
- Intellectual disability is defined as a neurodevelopmental disorder that originates in childhood and is characterized by intellectual difficulties along with difficulties in conceptual, social, and practical areas of living.
- IQ must be at 70 or below to be diagnosed with an intellectual disability.
- Intellectual disabilities are classified as either mild, moderate, severe, or profound in severity.
- Individuals may need different levels of support: intermittent, limited, extensive, or pervasive depending on individual needs in each activity.
- There are several types of intellectual disabilities, including Down syndrome, fragile X syndrome, and fetal alcohol syndrome.
- Individuals with intellectual disabilities experience developmental motor delays and lower fitness levels.
- Behavior and cognitive therapies are utilized to help individuals with intellectual disabilities to manage their behaviors in various settings.
- Contraindications for physical activity exist for those with atlantoaxial instability, hypermobile joints, and obesity.
- Modifications to sport, exercise, and physical education settings can help encourage safe and age/developmentally appropriate participation.
- Appropriate assessment modifications include using the Brockport Physical Fitness Test and task analyses.
- Knowledge of medical conditions is important to help design appropriate activities.
- Modify communication to meet the needs and abilities of the individual.
- Behavior modification strategies are useful to help increase motivation, participation, and compliance with activities.
- Sport organizations for individuals with intellectual disabilities include Special Olympics, Challenger Baseball, and TOPSoccer.
- Individuals with intellectual disabilities are able to participate in the Paralympic events of swimming, track and field, and table tennis.

WEB RESOURCES

American Association on Intellectual and Developmental Disabilities www.aaidd.org/
ARC https://thearc.org/
Challenger Baseball www.littleleague.org/play-little-league/challenger/
Eunice Kennedy Shriver National Institute of Child Health and Human Development www.nichd.nih.gov/
National Down Syndrome Society www.ndss.org/
National Fragile X Syndrome Foundation https://fragilex.org/
FASD United http://fasdunited.org/
Special Olympics www.specialolympics.org/
Special Olympics Coaching Resources www.specialolympics.org/our-work/sports/sports-offered?locale=en
Special Olympics: Unified Sport www.specialolympics.org/our-work/sports/unified-sports
TOPSoccer www.usyouthsoccer.org/programs/topsoccer/
U.S. Organizations for People with Intellectual Disabilities www.clearhelper.org/resources/cwa/sites/orgs/id/us/

BOOKS AND PRINTED MATERIALS

Bryze, K. (2020). *Occupational therapy for adults with intellectual disabilities.* Slack Books.
Connolly, B. H. & Montgomery, P. (2020). *Therapeutic exercises for children with developmental disabilities.* Slack Books.
Matson, J. L. (2019). *Handbook of intellectual disabilities.* Springer Link.
Prasher, V. P., & Janicki, M. P. (2019). *Physical health of adults with intellectual and developmental disabilities.* Springer Link.
Stein, D. (2016). *Supporting positive behavior in children and teens with Down syndrome.* Woodbine House.
Wehmeyer, M. L., Brown, I., Percy, M., & Fung, W. L. (2017). *A comprehensive guide to intellectual and developmental disabilities* (2nd ed.). Brookes Publishing.
Winders, P. C. (2014). *Gross motor skills for children with down syndrome.* Woodbine house.
Winnick., J. P., & Short, F. X. (2014). *The Brockport physical fitness test manual.* (2nd ed.). Human Kinetics.

REFERENCES

1. Office of the Federal Register. (n.d.). Rosa's law. https://www.federalregister.gov/documents/2017/07/11/2017-14343/rosas-law
2. AAIDD (American Association on Intellectual Developmental Disabilities). (2010). *Intellectual disability: Definition, classification, and systems of supports*. AAIDD.
3. American Association of Intellectual and Developmental Disabilities. (2021, February 5). Definition of intellectual disability. http://www.aaidd.org/intellectual-disability/definition
4. American Psychiatric Association. (2013). *Diagnostic and statistical manual of mental disorders* (5th ed.). Author.
5. Sattler, J. M. (2002). *Assessment of children: Behavioral and clinical applications* (4th ed.). Jerome M. Sattler Publisher.
6. Thompson, J. R., Bryant, B. R., Campbell, E. M. Craig, E. M., Hughes, C. M., Rotholz, D. A., Schalock, R. L., Silverman, W. P., Tasse', M. J., & Wehmeyer, M. L. (2004). *Supports intensity scale: User's manual*. American Association on Mental Retardation.
7. Luckasson, R., Borthwick-Duffy, S., Buntinx, W. H. E., Coulter, D. L., Craig, E. M. (P.), Reeve, A., Schalock, R. L., Snell, M. E., Spitalnik, D. M., Spreat, S., Tassé, M. J., & The AAMR AD HOC Committee on Terminology and Classification. (2002). *Mental retardation: Definition, classification, and systems of supports* (10th ed.). American Association on Mental Retardation.
8. Individuals with Disabilities Education Improvement Act of 2004, *Public Law No. 108-446,* 118 Stat. 2647 (2004).
9. National Center for Education Statistics (NCES). (2019). Digest of education statistics, 2018. https://nces.ed.gov/fastfacts/display.asp?id=64
10. National Academy of Sciences. (2015). Clinical characteristics of intellectual disabilities. https://www.ncbi.nlm.nih.gov/books/NBK332877
11. McKenzie, K., Milton, M., Smith, G., & Oullette-Kuntz, H. (2016). Systematic review of the prevalence and incidence of intellectual disabilities: Current trends and issues. *Current Developmental Disorders Reports, 3*, 104–115.
12. Boyle, C. A., Boulet, S., Schieve, L. A., Cohen, R. A., Blumberg, S. J., Yeargin-Allsopp, M., Visser, S., Kogan, M. D (2011). Trends in the prevalence of developmental disabilities in U.S. children 1997-2008. *Pediatrics, 127*(6), 1034–1042.
13. Durkin, M. S., Schupf, N., Stein, Z. A., & Susser, M. W. (2007). *Public health and preventive medicine* (15th ed.) (R. Wallace, Ed., pp. 1173–1184). Appleton & Lange.
14. Bhasin, T. K., Brocksen, S., Avchen, R. N., & Braun, K. V. N. (2006). Prevalence of four developmental disabilities among children aged 8 years: Metropolitan Atlanta Developmental Disabilities Surveillance Program, 1996 and 2000. *Morbidity and Mortality Weekly Report, 55*(SS01), 1–9.
15. Jencks, C., & Phillips, M., (1998). *The Black-white test score gap*. The Brookings Institution.
16. Drews, C. D., Yeargin-Allsopp, M., Decouflé, P., & Murphy, C. C. (1995). Variation in the influence of selected sociodemographic risk factors for mental retardation. *American Journal of Public Health, 85*(3), 329–334.
17. Harris, J. C. (2006). *Intellectual disability: Understanding its development, causes, classification, evaluation, and treatment*. Oxford University Press.
18. Batshaw, M. L., Roizen, N., & Lotrecchiano, G. R. (2013). *Children with disabilities* (7th ed.). Brookes Publishing.
19. Huang, J., Zhu, T., Qu, Y., & Mu, D. (2016). Prenatal, perinatal and neonatal risk factors for intellectual disability: A systemic review and meta-analysis. *PLoS ONE, 11*(4), e0153655. https://doi.org/10.1371/journal.pone.0153655
20. National Down syndrome Society. (2021). About Down syndrome: Down syndrome facts. www.ndss.org/about-down-syndrome/down-syndrome-facts/
21. Mayo Clinic. (2021). Patient care and health information. Diseases and conditions. Fetal alcohol syndrome. www.mayoclinic.org/diseases-conditions/fetal-alcohol-syndrome/symptoms-causes/syc-20352901
22. Pei, J., Reid-Westoby, C., Siddiqua, A., Elshamy, Y., Rorem, D., Bennett, T., Birken, C., Coplan, R., Duku, E., Ferro, M.A., Forer, B., Georgiades, S., Gorter, J.W., Guhn, M., Maguire, J., Manson, H., Santos, R., Brownell, M., & Janus, M. (2020). Teacher-reported prevalence of FASD in kindergarten in Canada: Association with child development and problems at home. *Journal of Autism and Developmental Disorders, 51,* 433–443. https://doi.org/10.1007/s10803-020-04545-w
23. Hunter, J., Rivero-Arias, O., Angelov, A., Kim, E., Fotheringham, I., & Leal, J. (2014). Epidemiology of fragile X syndrome : A systematic review and meta-analysis. *American Journal of Medical Genetics, 164A*(7). 1648–1658.
24. Center for Disease Control and Prevention (CDC). (2020). National center on birth defects and developmental disabilities. Fragile X syndrome. www.cdc.gov/ncbddd/fxs/facts.html
25. Pitetti, K. H., Millar, A. L., & Fernhall, B. (2000). Reliability of a peak performance treadmill test for children and adolescents with and without mental

retardation. *Adapted Physical Activity Quarterly, 17,* 322–332.
26. Hagerman, R. (1989). Behaviour and treatment of the fragile X syndrome. In Davies, K. E. (eds.). *The fragile X syndrome.* Oxford University Press.
27. Pitetti, K., Yarmer, D. A., & Fernhall, B. (2001). Cardiovascular fitness and body composition of youth with and without mental retardation. *Adapted Physical Activity Quarterly, 18,* 127–141.
28. Skowronski, W., Horvat, M., Nocera, J., Roswal, G., & Croce, R. (2009). Eurofit special: European Fitness battery score variation among individuals with intellectual disabilities. *Adapted Physical Activity Quarterly, 26,* 54–67.
29. Fernhall, B. (1992). Physical fitness and exercise training of individuals with mental retardation. *Medicine and Science in Sports and Exercise, 25*(4), 442–450.
30. Fernhall, B., & Tymeson, G. T. (1987). Graded exercise testing of mentally retarded adults: A study of feasibility. *Archives of Physical Medicine and Rehabilitation, 68,* 363–365.
31. Horvat, M., & Croce, R. (1995). Physical rehabilitation of individuals with mental retardation: Physical fitness and information processing. *Critical Reviews in Physical and Rehabilitation Medicine, 7*(3), 233–252.
32. Stratford, B., & Ching, E. (1983). Rhythm and time in the perception of Down syndrome children. *Journal of Mental Deficiency Research, 27,* 23–38.
33. Lumen. (2021). *Etiology and treatment for intellectual development disorders.* https://courses.lumenlearning.com/wm-abnormalpsych/chapter/etiology-and-treatment-for-intellectual-developmental-disorders
34. Sherrill, C. (1993). *Adapted physical activity, recreation, and sport: Crossdisciplinary and lifespan.* WCB/McGraw-Hill publishers.
35. Wouters, M., Evenhuis, H. M., & Hilgenkamp, T. I. M. (2019). Physical activity levels of children and adolescents with moderate to severe intellectual disability. *Journal of Applied Research in Intellectual Disabilities, 32,* 131–142. https://doi.org/10.1111/jar.12515
36. Einarsson, I. T., Johannsson, E., Daly, D., & Arngrimsson, S. A. (2016). Physical activity during school and after school among youth with and without intellectual disability. *Research in Developmental Disabilities, 56,* 60–70. https://doi.org/10.1016/j.ridd.2016.05.016
37. Horvat, M., & Franklin, C. (2001). The effects of the environment on physical activity patterns of children with mental retardation. *Research Quarterly for Exercise and Sport, 72*(2), 189–195. https://doi.org/10.1080/02701367.2001.10608949
38. Oppewal, A., Hilgenkamp, T. I. M., van Wijck, R., & Evenhuis, H. M. (2013). Cadriorespiratory fitness in individuals with intellectual disabilities: A review. *Research in Developmental Disabilities, 34,* 3301–3316. https://doi.org/10.1016/j.ridd.2013.07.005
39. Maïano, C. (2013). Prevalence and risk factors of overweight and obesity among children and adolescents with intellectual disabilities. *Obesity Reviews, 12,* 189–197. https://doi.org/10.1111/j.1467-789X.2010.00744.x
40. Emerson, E., & Hatton, C. (2007). Mental health of children and adolescents with intellectual disabilities in Britain. *The British Journal of Psychiatry, 191,* 493–499. https://doi.org/10.1192/bjp.bp.107.038729
41. Queralt, A., Vicente-Ortiz, A., & Molina-Garcia, J. (2016). The physical activity patters of adolescents with intellectual disabilities: a descriptive study. *Disability Health Journal, 9,* 341–345. https://doi.org/10.1016/j.dhjo.2015.09.005
42. Kapsal, N., J., Dicke, T., Morin, A. J. S., Vasconsellos, D., Maiano, C., Lee, J., & Lonsdale, C. (2019). Effects of physical activity on the physical and psychosocial health of youth with intellectual disabilities: A systematic review and meta-analysis. *Journal of Physical Activity and Health, 16,* 1187–1195.
43. Duplanty, A., Vingren, J., & Keller, J. (2014). Exercise training recommendations working with individuals with intellectual disabilities. *Strength and Conditioning Journal, 36*(2), 29–31.
44. Jeng, S.-C., Chang, C.-W., Liu, W.-Y., Hou, Y.-J., & Lin., Y.-H. (2017). Exercise training on skill-related physical fitness in adolescents with intellectual disability: A systematic review and meta-analysis. *Disability Health Journal, 10*(2), 198–206.
45. Collins, K., & Staples K. (2017). The role of physical activity in improving physical fitness in children with intellectual and developmental disabilities. *Research in Developmental Disabilities, 69,* 49–60. https://doi.org/10.1016/j.ridd.2017.07.020
46. Mayo Clinic. (2021). Joint hypermobility: What causes lose joints? www.mayoclinic.org/hypermobility/expert-answers/faq-20058285
47. Antony, R. A. (1986). Atlantoaxial instability: Why the sudden concern? *Adapted Physical Activity Quarterly, 3,* 320–328.
48. Center for Disease Control and Prevention. (2021). Defining overweight & obesity. www.cdc.gov/obesity/adult/defining.html
49. Short, F., McCubbin, J., & Frey, G. (1999). Cardiorespiratory endurance and body composition. In J. Winnick & F. Shorts (Eds.), *The Brockport physical fitness training guide.* Human Kinetics.
50. Forhan, M., & Gill, S. V. (2013). Obesity, functional mobility, and quality of life. *Best Practice & Research Clinical Endocrinology & Metabolism, 27,* 129–137.
51. Hruby, A., & Hu, F. B. (2015). The epidemiology of obesity: A big picture. *Pharmacoeconomics, 33*(7), 673–689. https://doi.org/10.1007/s40273-014-0243-x
52. Winnick, J. P., & Porretta, D. L. (Eds.). (2017). *Adapted physical education and sport* (6th ed.). Human Kinetics.

53. Wing, C. (Ed.). (2012). *Inclusive fitness trainer*. American College of Sports Medicine.
54. Hodge, S. R., Lieberman, L. J., & Murata, N. M. (2012). *Essentials of teaching adapted physical education: Diversity, culture, and inclusion*. Holcomb Hathaway.
55. Winnick, J. P. & Short, F. X. (2014). *Brockport physical fitness test manual: A health-related assessment for youngsters with disabilities* (2nd ed.). Human Kinetics.
56. Cooper, J. O., Heron, T. E., & Heward, W. L. (2020). *Applied behavior analysis* (3rd ed.). Pearson.
57. Obrusnikova, I., Novak, H. M., & Cavalier, A. R. (2019). The effect of systematic prompting on the acquisition of five muscle-strengthening exercises by adults with mild intellectual disabilities. *Adapted Physical Activity Quarterly, 36*, 447–471.
58. Obrusnikova, I., Cavalier, A. R., Novak, H. M., & Blair, A. E. (2020). The effect of systematic prompting on the acquisition of two muscle-strengthening exercises by adults with moderate intellectual disabilities. *Journal of Behavioral Education, 29*, 584–605.
59. Obrusnikova, I., Cavalier, A. R., Suminski, R. R., Blair, A. E., Firkin, C. J., & Steinbrecher, A. M. (2021). A resistance training intervention for adults with intellectual disability in the community: A pilot randomized clinical trial. *Adapted Physical Activity Quarterly, 38*, 546–568.
60. Joseph P. Kennedy Foundation. (2021). *Special Olympics*. https://www.specialolympics.org/
61. Special Olympics. (2021). *Motor activity training program*. https://www.specialolympics.org/our-work/sports/motor-activity-training-program
62. Special Olympics. (2021). *Inclusive health: Fitness*. https://www.specialolympics.org/our-work/inclusive-health/fitness?locale=en
63. Special Olympics. (2021). *Unified sports*. https://www.specialolympics.org/our-work/sports/unified-sports?locale=en
64. International Paralympic Committee. (n.d.). *Classification*. https://www.paralympic.org/classification
65. Little League. (2021). *Little league challenger*. https://www.littleleague.org/play-little-league/challenger/
66. U.S. Youth Soccer. (2021). *TOPSoccer*. https://www.usyouthsoccer.org/topsoccer/

CHAPTER 14
AUTISM SPECTRUM DISORDER

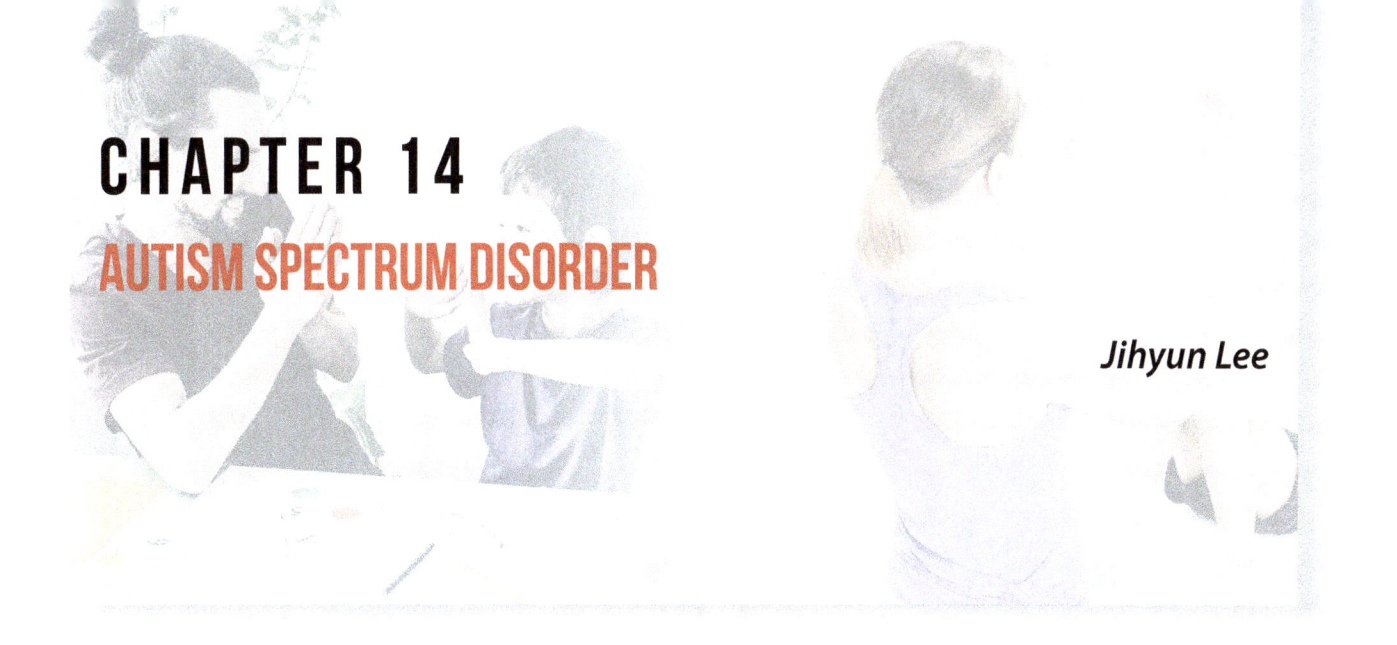

Jihyun Lee

DEFINING AUTISM

Autism spectrum disorder (ASD) is a neurodevelopmental disorder that is manifested by distinctive social, communication, and behavior characteristics. According to the fifth edition of the *Diagnostic and Statistical Manual of Mental Disorders* (*DSM-5*), individuals who have this disorder show delays in social communication and social interaction, as well as restricted, repeated, and stereotyped patterns of behaviors, interests, or activities.[1] The name "autism" stems from the Greek word "autos," which means "self," and it was first used by Eugen Bleuler in 1908 to describe his patients with schizophrenia. The term "spectrum" represents its wide variation in the mode and severity of symptoms that individuals with this disorder experience and manifest.[2]

Dr. Stephen Shore, a person on the autism spectrum, reflects on the great diversity within ASD with his famous quote, "If you've met one individual with autism, you've met one individual with autism."[3] Moreover, individuals on the higher-functioning end of the spectrum show above-average verbal skills and cognitive performance, but individuals on the lower-functioning end are likely to use alternative means for communicating instead of speech and may also have an intellectual disability as well as many sensory and behavioral issues. In addition to its heterogeneity, this disorder is not visible, unlike a physical disability. Most importantly, symptoms may appear unexpectedly during certain times, in certain settings, and in different contexts. Since these symptoms and severities exist on a wide spectrum, people who are accustomed to interacting with individuals without disabilities are often frustrated because they do not understand why an individual with ASD behaves in a certain way. Therefore, understanding this disorder will help practitioners such as educators and therapists provide quality services to their students and clients with ASD.

PREVALENCE AND CURRENT STATISTICS

According to the latest report from the Autism and Developmental Disabilities Monitoring Network funded by the Centers for Disease Control and Prevention, approximately 1 in 54 or 1.85% of 8-year-old children in the United States were diagnosed with ASD in 2016.[4] The prevalence of ASD has shown a steady increase over the last two decades based on the estimated percentages of ASD from previous reports: 1 in 69 in 2012, 1 in 88 in 2008, and 1 in 150 in 2000.[5] This marked increase in the prevalence of ASD in children might be due to ongoing revisions of the DSM, which now recognizes more children who have ASD symptoms. Additional reasons may include more widespread availability of early intervention services for children with ASD, as well as an increased public awareness of ASD, meaning parents and professionals are now more likely to notice or recognize it in children.[6]

There are no marked increases in terms of certain racial, ethnic, and socioeconomic groups; however, the number of Hispanic children identified with ASD is still lower compared to white or black children.[4] A strong male bias has been observed, as ASD diagnoses are four times more likely to be recognized for

Jihyun Lee, San Jose State University. © Kendall Hunt Publishing Company.

Autism heart.

boys than for girls. Although this male dominance of ASD has been under active investigation for some time, one plausible explanation is that relatively higher levels of visible and typical social behaviors in girls may mask key ASD symptoms, which makes the diagnosis more difficult.[7]

Since there is no medical test such as a blood test to identify ASD, diagnosing this disorder relies on screening tools that observe the behaviors and development milestones of the child. Diagnoses of ASD have been established by standard criteria stated in the *DSM-5*.[1] The DSM has been the standard reference that experts use to identify mental and behavioral disorders including ASD and has been revised multiple times in accordance with accumulated research evidence. For example, the DSM-4-TR included a category called "pervasive developmental disorders (PDD) and was used to include separate diagnoses of five conditions that share similar characteristics: autistic disorder (autism), Asperger's disorder, childhood disintegrative disorder, Rett's disorder, and pervasive developmental disorder—not otherwise specified (PDD-NOS). The diagnostic criteria for the five disorders are shown in Figure 14.1. In the *DSM-5*, a new term "ASD" replaced PDD and unified four of the five conditions of the PDD. Rett's disorder was removed from the *DSM-5* because of its known genetic causes, since, according to the American Psychiatric Association, the DSM is a behavior-based tool, and is not about etiology. Thus, including Rett's disorder was deemed inappropriate in this case due to the known causes.[8] In addition, the *DSM-5* allow the simultaneous diagnosis of attention deficit/hyperactivity disorder (ADHD) and ASD because of a significant comorbidity of ADHD in ASD.[9,10] This also provides an important implication for physical activity programs as sedentary lifestyles and obesity have been frequently reported in ADHD and ASD populations.[11,13]

In addition to the *DSM-5*, various assessment tools are available to identify the severity of ASD symptoms and delays in particular domains. Some examples of these tools are the Autism Diagnostic Observation Schedule—Second Edition (ADOS-2), Autism Diagnosis Interview—Revised (ADI-R), Childhood Autism Rating Scale (CARS), and Gilliam Autism Rating Scale—Second Edition (GARS-2).

ETIOLOGY

Although a clear cause of ASD has not yet been identified, a great body of research has shown potential risk factors for those diagnosed with it. It is important to note that no evidence has been obtained to show connections between vaccines and ASD to date, while some people believe certain vaccines can cause ASD due to falsified data provided by one particular study. This false belief about vaccines being a

Diagnostic Criteria for 299.00 Autistic Disorders

A. A total of six (or more) items from (1), (2), and (3), with at least two from (1), and one each from (2) and (3):
   1. qualitative impairment in social interaction, as manifested by at least two of the following:
      a. marked impairment in the use of multiple nonverbal behaviors such as eye-to-eye gaze, facial expression, body postures, and gestures to regulate social interaction
      b. failure to develop peer relationships appropriate to developmental level
      c. a lack of spontaneous seeking to share enjoyment, interests, or achievements with other people (e.g., by a lack of showing, bringing, or pointing out objects of interest)
      d. lack of social or emotional reciprocity
   2. qualitative impairments in communication as manifested by at least one of the following:
      a. delay in, or total lack of, the development of spoken language (not accompanied by an attempt to compensate through alternative modes of communication such as gesture or mime)
      b. in individuals with adequate speech, marked impairment in the ability to initiate or sustain a conversation with others
      c. stereotyped and repetitive use of language or idiosyncratic language
      d. lack of varied, spontaneous make-believe play or social imitative play appropriate to developmental level
   3. restricted repetitive and stereotyped patterns of behavior, interests, and activities, as manifested by at least one of the following:
      a. encompassing preoccupation with one or more stereotyped and restricted patterns of interest that is abnormal either in intensity or focus
      b. apparently inflexible adherence to specific, nonfunctional routines or rituals
      c. stereotyped and repetitive motor manners (e.g., hand or finger flapping or twisting, or complex whole-body movements)
      d. persistent preoccupation with parts of objects
B. Delays or abnormal functioning in at least one of the following areas, with onset prior to age 3 years: (1) social interaction, (2) language as used in social communication, or (3) symbolic or imaginative play.
C. The disturbance is not better accounted for by Rett Disorder or Childhood Disintegrative Disorder.

Diagnostic Criteria for 299.80 Asperger's Disorder

A. Qualitative impairment in social interaction, as manifested by at least two of the following:
   a. marked impairment in the use of multiple nonverbal behaviors such as eye-to eye gaze, facial expression, body postures, and gestures to regulate social interaction
   b. failure to develop peer relationships appropriate to developmental level
   c. a lack of spontaneous seeking to share enjoyment, interests, or achievements with other people (e.g., by a lack of showing, bringing, or pointing out objects of interest to other people)
   d. lack of social or emotional reciprocity
   2. Restricted repetitive and stereotyped patterns of behavior, interests, and activities, as manifested by at least one of the following:
   3. encompassing preoccupation with one or more stereotyped and restricted patterns of interest that is abnormal either in intensity of focus
   4. apparently inflexible adherence to specific, nonfunctional routines or rituals
   5. stereotyped and repetitive motor mannerisms (e.g., hand or finger flapping or twisting, or complex whole body movements)
   6. persistent preoccupation with parts of objects
B. The disturbance causes clinically significant impairment in social, occupational, or other important areas of functioning.
C. There is no clinically significant general delay in language (e.g., single words used by age 2 years, communicative phrases used by age 3 years).
D. There is no clinically significant delay in cognitive development or in the development of age-appropriate self-help skills, adaptive behavior (other than in social interaction), and curiosity about the environment in childhood.

Criteria are not met for another specific Pervasive Developmental Disorder or Schizophrenia.

(Continued)

299.80 Pervasive Developmental Disorder—Not Otherwise Specified
(Including Atypical Autism)

This category should be used when there is a severe and pervasive impairment in the development of reciprocal social interaction associated with impairment in either verbal or nonverbal communication skills or with the presence of stereotyped behavior, interests, and activities, but the criteria are not met for a specific Pervasive Developmental Disorder, Schizophrenia, Schizotypal Personality Disorder, or Avoidant Personality Disorder. For example, this category includes "atypical autism"—presentations that do not meet the criteria for Autistic Disorder because of late

age at onset, atypical symptomatology, or subthreshold symptomatology, or all of these

Diagnostic Criteria for 299.80 Rett Disorder

A. All of the following:
   1. Apparently normal prenatal and perinatal development
   2. Apparently normal psychomotor development through the first 5 months after birth
   3. Normal head circumference at birth
B. Onset of all of the following after the period of normal development:
   1. Deceleration of head growth between ages 5 and 48 months
   2. Loss of previously acquired purposeful hand skills between 5 and 30 months with the subsequent development of stereotyped hand movements (e.g., hand-wringing or hand washing)
   3. Loss of social engagement early in the course (although often social interaction develops later)
   4. Appearance of poorly coordinated gait or trunk movements
   5. Severely impaired expressive and receptive language development with severe psychomotor retardation

Diagnostic Criteria for 299.10 Childhood Disintegrative Disorder

A. Apparently normal development for at least the first 2 years after birth as manifested by the presence of age-appropriate verbal and nonverbal communication, social relationships, play, and adaptive behavior.
B. Clinically significant loss of previously acquired skills (before age 10 years) in at least two of the following areas:
   1. Expressive or receptive language
   2. Social skills or adaptive behavior
   3. Bowel or bladder control
   4. Play
   5. Motor skills

C. Abnormalities of functioning in at least two of the following areas:
   1. qualitative impairment in social interaction (e.g., impairment in nonverbal behaviors, failure to develop peer relationships, lack of social or emotional reciprocity)
   2. qualitative impairments in communication (e.g., delay or lack of spoken language, inability to initiate or sustain a conversation, stereotyped and repetitive use of language, lack of varied make-believe play)
   3. restricted, repetitive, and stereotyped patterns of behavior, interest, and activities, including motor stereotypes and mannerisms
D. The disturbance is not better accounted for by another specific Pervasive Developmental Disorder or by Schizophrenia.

FIGURE 14.1 Diagnostic criteria used in the diagnostic and statistical manual of mental disorders, 4th edition-text revision (adopted from the centers for disease control and prevention's autism case training: a developmental-behavioral pediatrics curriculum. Retrieved from www.cdc.gov/ncbddd/actearly/autism/case-modules/pdf/diagnosis/DSM-IV-TR-Diagnostic-Criteria-for-Pervasive-Development-Disorders.pdf).

Source: From "Physical Activity into Socialization: A Movement-based Social Skills Program for Children with Autism Spectrum Disorder," by Jihyun Lee and Kristina K. Vargo, *Journal of Physical Education, Recreation & Dance*, Vol. 88, No. 4, pp. 7-13. Copyright © 2017

potential cause of ASD began with a study conducted by Wakefield et al. (1998),[14] which created a link between the measles, mumps, and rubella (MMR) vaccine and the onset of ASD-related symptoms. The study reported that symptoms of ASD first appeared in patients who had received an MMR vaccine one month prior, which was based on a self-referred cohort of only 8 children without control subjects. Fortunately, the article was retracted by the journal and numerous large-scale studies have since identified no association between the MMR vaccine and ASD. However, this study by Wakefield et al. greatly contributed to parental fears toward vaccines.[15]

To date, research evidence indicates that both environmental and genetic factors contribute to the development of ASD,[16] as twin and sibling studies reported higher chances of ASD. For example, if one twin in a set of identical twins has ASD, there is a 36%–95% chance that the other twin will also have ASD. In fraternal twins, the chance of the other twin being affected decreases to 0–30%.[17-19] In addition, if a family already has a child with ASD, the possibility of having another child with ASD increases. For example, families with two or more siblings with ASD have a twice higher risk of having ASD at age 3 than children with only one sibling with ASD.[20]

Researchers also have argued that shared genetic structures between certain disorders and ASD exist. For example, fragile X syndrome is a genetic condition often associated with ASD because of the many overlapping symptoms. Fragile X syndrome accounts for about 2–3% of all ASD cases; however, unlike ASD, it can be diagnosed by a DNA blood test.[21] In fact, individuals with ASD have a high risk of psychiatric comorbidity and other developmental and medical conditions other than fragile X syndrome, including attention-deficit/hyperactivity disorder, anxiety disorder, sensory processing disorder, bipolar disorder, gastrointestinal disorder, intellectual disabilities including Down syndrome, learning disorder, language disorder, obsessive compulsive disorder, schizophrenia, and seizure disorders.[22,23]

When it comes to environmental factors, events before and during birth or prenatal risk factors are considered, such as advanced parental age, maternal physical and mental health, and medications taken during pregnancy.[24] For example, parents with psychiatric disorders such as schizophrenia or mothers taking valproate during pregnancy, which is used to treat epilepsy and other neuropsychological disorders, have an increased risk of having a child with ASD.[25,26]

INTERVENTION AND TREATMENT OPTIONS

Children can be diagnosed with ASD when they are as young as 18 months of age, as some early signs of ASD include not meeting developmental milestones, such as not playing "pretend" games or not making eye contact.[27] ASD affects many overall aspects of a child's development, so obtaining intervention services at an early age is important.

As the causes of ASD have never been clearly identified, there is no existing treatment to cure ASD. However, many intervention options are available to help relieve ASD-related symptoms, in order to maximize a child's development so that they can participate in various activities in the household, at school, or at a community level, which is the ultimate goal of any intervention or treatment. Because individuals with ASD are frequently codiagnosed with other psychiatric and developmental disorders or other medical conditions, multiple treatments or intervention approaches might be needed to support everyday functions while managing symptoms from other coexisting conditions.

Since managing inappropriate behaviors and developing age-appropriate social communication skills are often the main focus of behavior interventions for individuals with ASD, such intervention approaches have been evaluated through research studies. Some examples of supportive approaches that are known to be effective are social stories, behavioral skills training such as ABA and TEACCH, and various assistive technologies.

Social stories use short stories that describe an individualized social situation.[28] A social story includes social concepts or social skills for the reader, who can then learn cues in social contexts and appropriate responses, such as where and when a given situation takes place, who is involved, what is occurring, and why.[29] Although studies have reported that social stories that teach social skills lead to more interactions for individuals with ASD, it is recommended that this intervention method be used in combination with other strategies for better results.[30]

Behavioral skills training such as applied behavior analysis (ABA) has been widely applied to the ASD population. ABA uses systematic observations and measurements of target behaviors in order to teach socially important behaviors to individuals, with the goal of enhancing their quality of life.[31] ABA helps practitioners understand the underlying functions of certain behaviors and support positive behaviors while modifying challenging behaviors based

Individuals with Autism may struggle with recognizing and expressing emotions.

on systematic behavior intervention strategies. Many intervention studies using ABA have been conducted that focus on various areas of development for individuals with ASD. These include language and social skills, life skills, and challenging behaviors including self-injurious behaviors and stereotypic behaviors.[32]

The TEACCH® Autism Program is an evidence-based clinical, training, and research program[33] designed to meet the unique learning needs of individuals with ASD. TEACCH (Training and Education of Autistic and Related Communication-handicapped Children) uses a structured teaching method that provides visual information to promote executive functions and meaningful engagement for learners with ASD. The following five elements of structured teaching build on one another, respectively: visual structure of materials, routines and visual strategies, work systems, schedules, and physical structures. For more detailed information, visit the TEACCH website (https://teacch.com).

Finally, technology has been actively incorporated in many interventions, as more and more evidence has surfaced regarding the effectiveness of different types of technologies used to develop the social, language, cognitive, and psychomotor domains of individuals with ASD. Examples of current technologies are devices primarily used for communication such as augmentative and alternative communication (AAC) devices, interactive robots for social skills, and computer-assisted technologies. Computer-assisted technologies include augmented reality, virtual reality, and exergaming, which have all been applied to support language skills, social interaction, cognitive skills, and movement learning for individuals with ASD. Many of these are based on the rationale that individuals with ASD prefer to use technologies such as computers to communicate. Furthermore, technology-related interventions such as interactive robots[34] provide consistent and safe learning environments for learners with ASD and can help with selective sensory stimuli for individuals with ASD at different learning stages or severities.

Medications might also be used as interventions for individuals with ASD, particularly those who have other conditions such as anxiety, depression, sleep difficulties, and concentration issues,[35,36] but these also result in side effects.[37] Thus, for individuals with ASD incorporating physical activity into the daily routine is imperative because physical activity can promote well-being and lower levels of anxiety and depressive symptoms in general[38,39] and can decrease sleep-related problems in those with ASD.[40] Special diets and dietary supplements have also been suggested for individuals with ASD, although there is no clear correlation between dietary approaches and ASD symptoms. For example, some individuals with ASD use Cannabidiol or CBD to help with ASD-associated symptoms, although the long-term effects and interactions with other medications and coexisting conditions requires more research.[41]

Other supplemental therapies and approaches should also be recognized, such as speech therapy, recreational therapy, occupational therapy, physical therapy, play therapy, music therapy, aquatic therapy, and horse therapy. Treatment decisions are made on an individual basis, as there is a wide range of symptoms, needs, and preferences among individuals with ASD.

HOW ASD AFFECTS THE BODY AND MIND

Development during childhood is a complex process, as constant interactions can occur in psychomotor, social, emotional, and cognitive domains.[42,43] Thus, social communication skills and behavioral characteristics affect the overall psychosocial wellbeing of individuals with ASD, as well as how they interact with others in various settings. Although this section explains the social communication and behavior characteristics of individuals with ASD and its potential effects separately, it is important to understand how one aspect of development may significantly affect larger areas of development for individuals with ASD.

Social Communication Characteristics

Social communication characteristics and competence can vary among individuals with ASD, depending on the person's intellectual, social, and emotional capabilities. Additionally, both verbal and nonverbal areas of communication need to be considered. Some commonly addressed social communication challenges are failure to read or misreading nonverbal interactions (e.g., gestures) and facial expressions; a lack of social-emotional reciprocity (e.g., conversation skills, sharing of emotions); speaking in fragmented sentences; a lack of eye contact; and relationship development (e.g., interest in peers, imaginative play).[1,27] One frequently addressed hypothesis in terms of social communication challenges for those with ASD is a lack of Theory of Mind, which refers to the ability to comprehend thoughts and feelings that others intend.[44] This hypothesis suggests that those with ASD have difficulty putting themselves in the mind of another person, which affects that individual's ability to interact with others in ways that are generally considered socially appropriate for particular contexts. Some examples of a lack of Theory of Mind may include not understanding personal space boundaries, responding inappropriately to conversations/interactions, and being unable to read or exchange nonverbal cues. Empathetic communication requires cognitive-communication skills based on Theory of Mind. Knowing how to effectively communicate empathy is important to build relationships and thus promote quality of life as individuals get older. It is unsurprising that many individuals with ASD have challenges participating in group games and sports, which are social contexts that require Theory of Mind. Physical activity programs contain various social contexts and thus, can provide individuals with ASD with the opportunity to practice social skills. Thus, considerations can be made when designing physical activity programs to include components for participants with ASD to repeatedly simulate social interactions and practice empathetic communication skills.

Behavior Characteristics

Another ASD diagnostic category is repetitive, restricted, and stereotyped patterns of behaviors, interests, or activities. For example, stereotypic behaviors (i.e., stimming), an overdependence on routines, and being highly sensitive to changes in an environment are common in individuals with ASD. In order to explain the behavioral characteristics of ASD, there are many common sensory issues that individuals with this disorder may experience, which need to be addressed first. Approximately 90% of individuals with ASD are known to experience various sensory issues.[45] The *DSM-5* states that hyper- or hyposensitivity to sensory stimuli and unusual sensory interests in environments are common in individuals with ASD.[1] Thus, these individuals may show unusual responses to sensory stimuli such as touch, smell, sound, sight, and taste. A more visible example of this is a child with ASD covering their ears during physical education in a gymnasium; this means that the child might be sensitive to noise and is trying to block auditory stimuli. Conversely, when more sensory input is needed, a child with ASD is likely to be engaged in sensory-seeking behavior (i.e., stimming) to create any needed sensory stimuli. Interestingly, hypersensitivity may link to hyposensitivity, as when someone is completely occupied by a particular stimulus, they can fail to attend to another stimuli. Thus, individuals with ASD may easily become distracted (i.e., short attention span) and may not respond to certain stimuli. In addition, very selective or detailed visual attention characterized as '"seeing the trees, but not the forest"' represents visual perceptual processing in ASD, as well as altered or delayed auditory processing, both of which are frequently found in individuals with ASD.[46,47]

Examples of fidget toys.

Stereotyped or repetitive motor movements concerning the use of objects or speech[1] are behaviors addressed in ASD diagnostic criteria. A behavior is considered stereotypic when it is repetitive, does not appear to serve a functional purpose, and appears to be inappropriate for the context.[48] Stereotypic behaviors encompass a wide range of fine motor and gross motor bodily movements, as well as behaviors with or without objects such as hand flapping, body spinning and rocking, lining up toys, flipping objects, and verbal and nonverbal behaviors such as echolalia (i.e., repetition or echoing of verbal utterances) and idiosyncratic phrases.[1,48,49] Stereotypic behavior is often regarded as socially inappropriate, stigmatizing, and even dangerous to the self or to others.[48–50] This behavior can interfere with psychosocial functioning, which can not only hinder learning and applying new skills but can also be disruptive to others in a setting.[50,51] Thus, stereotypic behavior in individuals with ASD is often addressed as one of the most challenging aspects.

Other challenging behaviors include aggression, self-injury, destructiveness, disruptions, and noncompliance, which are frequently reported in learning contexts.[50–52] Challenging behaviors may fulfill specific sensory and social needs such as getting attention, tangible needs such as getting a desired item, and communicating what one wants or does not want.[52] In the latter case, these behaviors are attributed to limited communication skills, meaning the individual has a hard time expressing himself or herself appropriately when he or she cannot explain what he/she feels or wants. For example, an individual with ASD is likely to engage in challenging behaviors when experiencing sensory deprivation or sensory overload. Additionally, an individual with ASD who does not use speech for communicating may feel frustration when communicating and/or may not yet have communication skills to express his or her feelings and experiences in an appropriate way.

Lastly, a preference for sameness and inflexible adherence to routines are common in individuals with ASD and may result in anxiety and aggression when expected patterns are broken (or when unexpected events occur). For instance, an individual with ASD may get upset or become anxious when they are asked to perform a new activity or if a routine is suddenly changed.

Specific Issues with Movement

The core characteristics of ASD lie within the areas of social communication and behavior, which affect how an individual interacts with others, learns new skills, and performs tasks in various contexts including physical activity. Many physical activity contexts require social interactions such as physical education

Individuals with Autism often suffer from sensory overstimulation.

or community-based sports programs. In addition, learning movement skills involves multisensory experiences, which often require the learners to process complex steps. Although delays in movement skills are not one of the diagnostic criteria for ASD, studies have reported that children with ASD tend to experience difficulties developing certain motor skills at specific ages.[53,54] A recent study surveying 16,705 parents of children with ASD showed that more than 85% reported their children's motor impairments.[55] Even at early ages, infants and toddlers with ASD can show signs of motor delays such as delayed onset of walking, poor rhythm, gait, balance, and posture.[56,57]

Motor delays and motor processing issues are apparent in both fine and gross motor areas.[56–58] Children with ASD often have significant delays in fundamental motor skills and motor abilities that are essential to building age-appropriate movement skills for physical education or community-based sports programs.[53] Delayed fine motor skills, bilateral coordination and balance, as well as visual perceptual processing issues in individuals with ASD significantly affect many movement tasks such as throwing and catching.[58–60] Sensory processing difficulties common in individuals with ASD may contribute to overloaded attentional capacities and delays when performing dual motor tasks. As a result, individuals with ASD may experience disrupted attention or may have difficulty processing information when performing tasks that require multiple movement concepts.[61]

Such fundamental motor skill delays can limit a child's choices when participating in physical activities, and can lead to sedentary activities in addition to social challenges that can further interfere with physical activity.[62] As children grow, certain levels of social-communicative behaviors are expected in contexts where social interactions occur, including participating in diverse physical activity settings such as physical education and youth sport programs.[63] Thus, delays in social-communicative behaviors can result in the unwillingness of a child with ASD to participate in group-based physical activities or team sports. This usually occurs because of a lack of understanding of rules or expectations, or simply because there is a lack of interest in social interactions with others. Also, both social communication and behavior characteristics may lead a child to experience exclusion or denial from other children in a physical activity setting. As a result, children and youth with ASD may have fewer opportunities to participate in physical activities when compared with their counterparts. Fewer opportunities to participate in daily physical activities and practice various movement skills may deteriorate movement skills even further. Evidence exists that children with ASD can experience exclusion, isolation and bullying in various physical activity contexts due to their behaviors, their social characteristics, as well as their low motor skills.[64] They also may tend to have low self-esteem and confidence when it comes to physical activities, which can not only negatively affect their motivation to participate but can stunt their actual motor skills.[65]

SPECIFIC BENEFITS OF PHYSICAL ACTIVITY AND EXERCISE

As physical activity is beneficial for all individuals, those with ASD can also benefit from regular participation in physical activity. Physical activity is an ideal supplemental approach to other therapies because of its cost-effectiveness and potential secondary benefits, such as maintaining and increasing physical and mental health. Increased fitness outcomes such as strength, cardiovascular function, and flexibility in individuals with ASD have been well documented.[66,67] In addition, motor skill intervention studies have reported that children and youth with ASD can learn movement skills through various types of physical activities.[66-68] Improved motor skills and fitness through various physical activities can increase opportunities for individuals with ASD to participate in many community-based leisure activities. This can, in turn, improve social inclusion and social communication skills. Increased fitness is not only helpful for performing different physical activities but also improves daily activities including job performance, which contributes to an increased quality of life. For individuals with ASD, physical activities can provide multisensory experiences, which is why music and rhythm-based movement programs, aquatics, and horseback riding have been found to be helpful.[68]

Physical activity interventions can be specially designed for individuals with ASD in order to increase various skills and support many areas of development. First, physical activities can provide age-appropriate naturalistic opportunities for physically active social interactions. Individuals with ASD can engage in these activities and develop better social and communication skills.[63,68] Furthermore, interventions have shown that physical activities can help individuals with ASD develop appropriate play skills, positive social interactions and engagements, speech/communication skills, turn taking, adaptive behaviors, and social functioning.[68] Physical activity also seems to encourage individuals with ASD to have better self-regulation and attention, which helps them become more motivated to learn with more focus during learning time. As such, short bouts of physical activity may be implemented to increase academic engagement and decrease off-task behaviors in academic settings.[66,69]

Enhanced sensory regulations including decreased stereotypic behaviors have also been observed in physical activity interventions for individuals with ASD.[66,70-72] The mechanism responsible for this behavior change has not yet been clearly identified, although researchers suggest several explanations such as neurological effects (i.e., changes within the serotonergic, dopaminergic, and GABA neurotransmitter systems due to exercise),[73,74] fatigue effects,[75] exercises that meet the sensory needs of individuals,[76] and increased executive functioning and attention when engaging in motor tasks that require cognitive skills to coordinate movements.[77] Certain intensities and durations of physical activities that can decrease stereotypic behaviors and increase positive outcomes have been investigated; however, individual characteristics such as sensory needs, preference, and goals of the intervention should be carefully considered when using physical activity as part of an intervention or program.

Lastly, although this is not a diagnostic category, sleep problems in ASD have been reported in numerous studies. Sleep deprivation can affect a person's overall functioning and quality of life, and ASD studies concerning sleep have shown that physical activity has positive effects on sleep, including its efficiency, quality, and duration.[78,79]

SUGGESTED MODIFICATIONS FOR PHYSICAL ACTIVITY

Many individuals with ASD can participate in various types of physical activities without major difficulties, when they do not have physical disabilities or sensory disabilities (hard of hearing, visual impairments, etc.). However, given the characteristics of ASD, certain modifications are highly recommended to help individuals learn more effectively and experience more success and enjoyment when participating in various physical activities such as sports programs and physical education. These modifications are created in accordance with the core characteristics of ASD, including social communication and repeated and restricted behaviors, interests, or activities.

Strategies for Effective Communication

Effective communication helps individuals follow directions, minimize miscommunication and frustrations, learn better, and experience more success in physical activity settings. To facilitate effective communication, practitioners should use various communication strategies and mix and match what works for each individual.

Verbal Communication

When giving verbal directions, the use of short and precise phrases allows an individual with ASD to process the information well. Considering that individuals with ASD may lack Theory of Mind (comprehending others' intent), physical activity practitioners need to avoid using analogies, double meanings, and sarcasm when working with learners with ASD. Additionally, certain words can trigger negative reactions in individuals with ASD. For example, 'no' or 'don't' words may incite tantrums in a child with ASD. Thus, practitioners need to make sure to communicate positively when giving directions and setting rules in physical activity contexts. Also, allowing extra processing time can be effective, as some individuals with ASD may need more time to process auditory information.

Visual Communication

Although not all individuals with ASD are visual learners, many studies have reported that the use of visual aids such as task cards and videos along with other prompts can increase understanding and lead to better communication.[80,81] Visual prompts such as pictorial task cards and videos can be created and used based on what the learner can understand best. Regardless of whether the learner has already used certain symbols, the learner's preferred modality can be used along with visual prompts. One effective system that utilizes visual cues when teaching language to individuals with ASD and facilitates communication is the picture exchange communication system (PECS). The PECS is an example of augmentative and alternative communication systems and is produced by Pyramid Educational Consultants (https://pecsusa.com/pecs/) that uses pictures or icons instead of words.[80,82] The PECS assists individuals with ASD in initiating requests, responding to questions, making choices, communicating in sentences and commenting about their environment.[82] Many visual systems models such as the PECS can help create task cards and picture-based instructions that are associated with specific physical activity tasks.

Video modeling is defined as the demonstration of behavior presented via video, in order to change existing behaviors or teach new ones.[83] Thus, the learner who views the model on the screen is taught to imitate the observed responses. Video modeling is useful because the same models and the same responses can be viewed as many times as necessary, which means repeated practices are possible. This ensures that auditory and visual consistency from videos are likely to enable learners with ASD to feel a high level of comfort due to the predictability of the learning environment. Also, video models allow practitioners to provide additional prompts and reinforcers directly while the individuals are attending to the video-based instruction, which may help practitioners better manage integrated physical activity programs. When using video modeling, the learner needs to use responses learned from the video in similar contexts even when the video is not present, to ensure that the targeted skill has been learned.

Communication Devices

Although physical cue cards and task cards can be created to facilitate communication and learning, electronic communication devices or AAC devices can also be used, especially for individuals with ASD who do not use speech for communication in physical activity settings. These devices display icons that represent certain needs and actions. Then, the user touches the icons to make the device communicate the meaning of the icon. Electronic communication devices come from a variety of manufacturers, and commercially available tablets such as iPads and smart phones allow individuals with ASD to download and use various communication apps. Also, more and more apps have been developed that are designed to encourage individuals with ASD to follow certain gross motor tasks and increase physical activity levels (e.g., Exercise Buddy®).

Encouragement of Communication

Physical activity settings can provide individuals with ASD opportunities to practice age-appropriate and natural social communication skills.[63,68] In particular, many tasks in movement settings are interactive in nature, such as passing a ball to another person or exchanging verbal and nonverbal cues during game situations. Thus, it is important to allow individuals with ASD to practice social communication skills in natural ways by asking questions that require short answers and prompting correct responses.

It is important that practitioners avoid making any assumptions toward individuals with ASD who are not able to use speech to communicate. Not using speech for communication does not always mean the person cannot understand verbal directions well. People who do not use speech can have excellent receptive language skills (understanding what they are told). On the other hand, when a person with ASD uses verbal communication, this does not mean they have good communication skills. Thus, understanding a person's level of receptive language and expressive language skills is important in order to communicate. In addition, collaboration with other professionals such as classroom teachers, speech therapists, and ABA therapists is important, as similar social communication skills can be learned and practiced across multiple settings.

Behavior Management Strategies

Behavior management strategies are emphasized when it comes to behaviors of individuals with ASD, especially when their functions can be understood based on principles of behavior. ABA provides useful tools for therapists, teachers, and parents to understand the functions of a behavior (to escape from an undesired situation, to get attention, etc.) that needs to be intervened when designing a behavior management plan based on data. Focusing on preventive strategies rather than reactive strategies is another important thing to consider, because it is difficult to intervene once challenging behaviors occur. One basic preventative strategy that can be used is setting clear behavior expectations and sharing them frequently (e.g., use them as part of a routine, post rules on a wall) in a consistent manner and in a clear and firm voice. To help reinforce desirable behaviors, it is also helpful to provide models to follow, such as desirable words, phrases, and behaviors to practice, and then immediately following up with positive comments, praise, or other appropriate rewards. Cognitive behavior therapy (CBT) is a frequently addressed psychotherapeutic strategy when it comes to regulating emotion and minimizing anxiety in the ASD population.[84,85] CBT targets the underlying cognitions and behaviors that maintain the individuals' thoughts and emotions. Thus, CBT helps the individual to see the associations between his or her thoughts, actions, and feelings, and to learn to develop coping strategies. A growing body of research shows the effectiveness of CBT on developing the ability to modify arousal and emotional states so that the individual can respond more appropriately to anxiety or any other negative feelings that come with the incorporation of physical activity in their routines.[86,87]

Use of Routines and Clear Structures

Creating clear routines and tasks in physical activity settings and using them consistently is an important way to facilitate task-oriented behaviors while minimizing behavior issues. When provided with a consistent and clear routine, learners with ASD can anticipate what is coming next and will know how to appropriately respond. Previewing activities for the day should be part of a learner's daily routine, and practitioners can provide brief introductions to overall tasks in a sequential order. Practitioners can accommodate learners with ASD and promote self-monitoring skills by using easily removable adhesives (e.g., Velcro) along with laminated pictures or text of the activities to be completed. This type of activity board may involve a time card next to each task to show the corresponding time required so that the learner can self-monitor their time. After each activity is completed, the learner can remove the task card to confirm that the activity has been finished and it is time to move onto the next activity. Alternatively, electronic devices with apps that serve a similar function can be used, and these types of activity routines enable settings to be more structured.

Physical aspects of spatial structure in physical activity settings can create boundaries and visual markers for activity tasks. This method can be achieved by placing cones or labels around the perimeter of an activity area such as a gymnasium. This way, the learner can have a concrete understanding of the expectations of the practitioner with regard to moving around the space. The use of matching colors and shapes to provide visual cues is another example of a physical structure that helps individuals' motor planning. For example, using the same-colored bat, ball, and batting tee for a striking task or matching-colored targets and balls for a throwing task can give the learner additional visual cues, to show them that all striking equipment should stay together in the activity area, or that the blue ball needs to hit the blue target (see Figure 14.2). It is important to note that these structured elements may not be learned automatically and practitioners need to teach learners about structured environments prior to working within them.

FIGURE 14.2 Examples of the use of matching colors and shapes to provide more visual cues and structured movement tasks.
Source: Jihyun Lee

Understanding Sensory Challenges

For individuals with ASD who have sensory issues, physical activity contexts can pose many challenges because of considerable stimuli existing in these settings.[79] If a learner with ASD tends to have a hard time processing multiple sensory inputs, the coexistence of multiple stimuli within an activity setting. For example, the sound and sight of the ball bouncing around and people moving, various colors and shapes of equipment, and the smell of sweat from people exercising can cause a sense of overstimulation (i.e., sensory overload). Using a separate room for one-on-one instruction, having the learner face a wall in one corner of a gym, or using noise-blocking headphones may reduce sensory inputs and help the individual with ASD deal with overflowing sensory stimuli that might be painful or distracting.

Experts explain some possible reasons for challenging behaviors in learners with ASD within physical education settings, while providing several recommendations for teachers who want to manage and prevent those behaviors. Sensory overload, aversive or overfocused sensory inputs, and different functions (e.g., to escape from unwanted demand or to communicate and express a need or desire) are addressed as potential causes of challenging behaviors that may frequently occur during physical education as well as other activity settings.[88]

Understanding Social Challenges

Some individuals with ASD engage in challenging behaviors and have difficultly regulating emotions when they lose a game or when a game does not go in a direction they expected. This might be due to the delays in social communication skills that prevent individuals with ASD from communicating their emotions in socially acceptable ways. Again, this is partly due to a lack of Theory of Mind, which causes them to misunderstand the objectives of a game or situation. Or they are simply not ready to experience an unexpected situation like losing a game, which may give them a high level of anxiety.

Providing individuals with ASD with sufficient practice opportunities (e.g., role-play and cooperative games) to lose games can help them develop coping strategies when they actually lose in games. Fun, risk-free or low-risk games can be implemented using a structure that gives everyone an equal chance to lose in a sequential way (make sure not to select the individual with ASD as the first person to lose), or one that gives both the losing and winning people some kind of prize. In these situations, social stories can be used to teach individuals with ASD various scenarios of losing and winning, along with desirable responses to those situations.

Considering Comorbidities

There are some concurrent health conditions that an individual with ASD can experience such as cerebral palsy or sensory processing disorder, which can pose challenges when performing and learning motor tasks. Some individuals with ASD may also experience higher touch sensitivity (tactile defensiveness), which should be noticed in physical activity contexts where frequent touches can occur such as physical assistance from practitioners. In this case, the person with ASD may withdraw himself or herself from the activity or show challenging behaviors such as self-injury or aggression toward others. Thus, the practitioner in the movement setting should identify whether or not the individual with ASD has hypersensitivity to touch, and should also ask for permission before touching a body part of that individual. Also, a good strategy is to minimize touch by using a floatation device or a pool noodle, thereby ensuring the least amount of physical touch possible during swim instruction, for instance.

Understanding Motor Planning Issues

Because of motor planning, processing difficulties, and preference of sameness in learners with ASD, activities that are too complicated or "open" (the performer needs to control changing external factors) are challenging. Examples of open activities are receiving a pass from another player during a basketball game and kicking a soccer ball toward the goal where a goalkeeper is guarding. Since these activities require spontaneity, instant predication, and adaptability, closed activities such as walking, jogging, cycling, horseback riding, and swimming are widely enjoyed by individuals with ASD.[62] During these "closed" activities, the performer can reproduce the same patterns of movement over and over again and not worry about external factors that are hard to anticipate, such as opponents or rapidly changing game situations. Most open movement tasks can be modified into closed movement tasks; for example, rather than having the learner attempt to hit a pitched ball, the practitioner can place a ball on a batting tee to eliminate the uncertainty and unpredictable nature of hitting a ball out of the air. Thus, individuals with ASD can benefit from learning closed movement activities first, before being introduced to open movement tasks in physical activity programs or therapeutic programs.

Activities that require one to follow a set pace such as group exercise classes or fast-paced activities like team-based sports are examples of activities that change too rapidly without enough processing time for a person with ASD. Conversely, activities in smaller segments with clear directions can help learners with ASD process appropriate amounts of information at a time. Use of visual aids such as pictures and videos with behavioral approaches such as ABA and TEACCH would also help learners with ASD perform movement tasks effectively. In physical and occupational therapy settings as well as in fitness-based settings with personal trainers, the changing up of tasks and activities can cause stress or anxiety in many individuals with autism, so following a routine and schedule of activities each session as well as having visual schedules prepared ahead of time can help the session to run more smoothly.

Considerations for Practitioners

Help participants develop self-determination through goal setting, choice making, decision making, and self-advocating in physical activity settings. Examples of some skills that can be taught and practiced in physical activity settings that may lead to enhanced self-determination among participants with ASD would be problem-solving games,[89] self-monitoring,[90] and self-regulation skills.[91] Better self-determination is linked to positive school and adult outcomes such as higher quality of life and life satisfaction.[92] Practicing these skills to promote self-determination should be carefully considered when designing a physical activity program.

Find potential rewards that are effective and are based on the individual's interests and preferences. Preference assessments are helpful in identifying preferred items or activities that can be potentially used as rewards.[93] Also, preferred items and topics can be useful for designing lessons or creating materials based on the individual's interests (e.g., a jungle theme-based lesson or a reward board in an airplane design), which may act as natural rewards and increase motivation for better engagement. The practitioner may find that the individual has a strong preference toward certain activities and equipment. For example, a sensory ball may provide them with activating their preferred senses whether it is through texture or sound of the ball. Use of activities and equipment that match sensory needs and preferences of the individual may help him or her keep motivated, stay on task, learn better, and aid in processing the sensory information. Figure 14.3 shows some examples of sensory equipment that can be used in physical activity programs.

Try new technologies. More and more computer-assisted or device-based activities are being developed such as exergaming and virtual-reality games. Although such approaches are relatively new and evidence of their effectiveness has not been robust, exergaming may inform future research regarding whether computer-assisted approaches are beneficial for clients/students who want to increase their physical activity and learn new motor skills.

Remember that all individuals with ASD are unique. The strategies introduced in this chapter may not be effective for all learners with ASD, and a strategy that that worked well today may not work well tomorrow. Thus, it is important for practitioners to be patient when planned strategies, or activities do not work well. Equipping as many tools as possible allows practitioners to try alternative approaches or combine multiple approaches when one thing does not work.

Collaborating with and gathering information from the family and other experts is an effective strategy. Members of a team can share what worked well so that effective and consistent strategies can be applied across different learning settings. In particular, family members can tell practitioners what the individual can already do well and communicate their interests. In turn, practitioners can encourage family members to help the individual practice similar tasks at home to become familiar with movements and relevant cues. Moreover, practitioners can create social stories before lessons and have the family go over the story with the client. Previewing an activity, a setting, and the expectations surrounding it can help the client reduce their anxiety before they are expected to perform a task.

Work toward generalization. **Generalization** refers to the use of newly acquired behaviors (motor or sport skills) in nontrained environments.[31] Since individuals with ASD prefer sameness, providing consistencies (prompts, equipment, routines, etc.) is one of the general instructional recommendations that can meet this need. Individuals with ASD may have difficulty generalizing and applying skills learned in one environment to other environments.[94] This means that individuals with ASD tend to struggle when demonstrating newly learned skills in different settings, using different equipment, with different people, or at different times of day. Thus, once the individual feels comfortable with the current equipment, people, cues,

FIGURE 14.3 Examples of sensory equipment that can be used in physical activity programs to accommodate sensory needs of individuals with ASD.

Source: Jihyun Lee

and setting, it helps to gradually change these elements (one at a time) so that the individual can expand his or her comfort zone in order to become more flexible and tolerant.

Closely supervise. Some individuals with ASD lack fear and engage in unpredictable behaviors that are potentially dangerous. In addition to lack of fear, it is common for individuals with ASD to exhibit wandering behavior or elopement, which is leaving a safe, supervised area and/or a responsible caregiver.[95,96] Thus, practitioners should always prepare for potentially dangerous situations, such as swimmers jumping right into the water without permission or an entry signal from the program leader, or going into the middle of a pool or lake without supervision. In fact, accidental drowning incidents in children under 15 with ASD are surprisingly frequent.[97] Overall, precautions need to be taken when working with individuals with ASD in physical activity settings. Teaching them to follow safety rules and to ask for help is required and recommended as part of any activity.

Known Sports and Physical Activity Opportunities

Individual sports or recreational activities such as swimming, running, horseback riding, and bowling are generally popular among individuals with ASD. In particular, many swimming and horseback riding programs are available and are even specially designed for learners with ASD. Though many individuals with ASD may have challenges when participating in team-based sports such as basketball and soccer, with increased awareness, more and more sports programs can use strategies to accommodate learners with ASD. Autism Speaks, the largest ASD organization in the United States that advocates for individuals with ASD and their families, suggests various organizations that provide physical activity opportunities for individuals with ASD[89] such as Challenger Baseball (www.bcchallenger.org), TOPSoccer (www.usyouthsoccer.org/programs/topsoccer/), Special Olympics (www.specialolympics.org), YMCA (www.ymca.net), and the Pop Warner Challenger Division Football (www.popwarner.com/Default.aspx?tabid=1476179). These organizations provide community-based programs that are safe and offer structured learning experiences for children and youth with disabilities including ASD. For more information, visit the Autism Speaks website.[98]

RELEVANT WEBSITES OR ORGANIZATIONS TO LEARN ABOUT ASD FURTHER

With the increase of ASD populations, there has been an active debate in the ASD community over identity-first ("an autistic person") versus person-first ("a person with autism") language. The general recommendation within academia and professional fields is the use of person-first language as the most respectful way to refer to individuals with ASD. However, many individuals in the ASD community express a preference for identity-first language, such as "I'm autistic," because they believe that ASD is a part of their identity and personality.[99] Those who support identity-first language point out that separating the diagnosis from the person may sound as if ASD is a disease or an illness that needs to be fixed, which could increase the stigma surrounding ASD. Nevertheless, the ongoing terminology debate should be recognized and continuously encouraged to improve the public awareness of ASD, create discussion and improve the self-advocacy of individuals with ASD and their families. To learn more about this discussion and other principles surrounding the disability rights movement for individuals with ASD, visit the Autistic Self Advocacy Network (https://autisticadvocacy.org).

There are many other organizations that support the ASD community by supporting research activities, advocating for systems changes, and educating family members, professionals, educators, and friends. The Autism Science Foundation https://autismsciencefoundation.org provides funding opportunities for researchers to conduct ASD-related research, to discover the possible causes of ASD and to provide evidence-based treatment options. The Organization for Autism Research (OAR) https://researchautism.org aims to support applied community-focused research that can inform practices to improve the daily lives of individuals with ASD. ACSM (www.acsm.org) is an autism exercise specialist continuing education course that helps fitness specialists equip more strategies for assessment and instruction in order to implement effective exercise programs for individuals with ASD.

There are several books that can help people understand ASD, particularly through the lens of actual individuals with ASD. For example, Dr. Temple Grandin is one of the most well-known individuals with ASD, whose life has been documented in many books, films, and lectures. Her books *The Way I See It* and *The Autistic Brain: Thinking Across the Spectrum* have been able to provide others with experiences and perspectives of a person with ASD.

CHAPTER SUMMARY

- Individuals with ASD show diverse characteristics related to social communication and restricted, repeated, and stereotyped patterns of behaviors, interests, or activities. These can all affect how an individual functions and learns in various physical activity settings.
- ASD is a spectrum disorder, meaning that wide variations exist in terms of severity of symptoms. Its highly heterogeneous nature requires individualized approaches when working with individuals with ASD.
- Many individuals with ASD experience sensory issues such as hyposensitivity and hypersensitivity to certain sensory inputs, and physical activity environments often interact with the sensory characteristics of individuals with ASD.
- Physical activity can provide many benefits to individuals with ASD, such as increased mental and physical health, enhanced sensory regulations, better on-task time management, and decreased stereotypic behaviors.
- Children and youth with ASD can learn movement skills through various physical activities that can, in turn, provide more opportunities to develop age-appropriate social skills and social interactions with similarly aged peers.
- Many strategies can be implemented for learners with ASD in physical activity settings in order to help them communicate effectively and engage in various tasks with higher success.
- Many recreational, educational, and therapeutic physical activity options are available for individuals with ASD. Thus, physical activity service providers should individualize approaches and use effective strategies to enable individuals with ASD to experience enjoyable and successful physical activities.

REFERENCES

1. American Psychiatric Association. (2013). *Diagnostic and statistical manual of mental disorders* (5th ed.). Author.
2. National Institute of Mental Health. (n.d.). *Autism spectrum disorder*. www.nimh.nih.gov/health/topics/autism-spectrum-disorders-asd/index.shtml
3. DeCourcy, R. (2018). The autism spectrum at a glance. *Forensic Scholars Today, 4*(3), 1–3.
4. Maenner, M. J., Shaw, K. A., Baio, J., Daniels, J., Warren, Z., Kurzius-Spencer, M., Zahorodny, W., Rosenberg, C. R., White, T., Durkin, M. S., Imm, P., Nikolaou, L., Yeargin-Allsopp, M., Lee, L.-C., Harrington, R., Lopez, M., Fitzgerald, R. T., Hewitt, A., Pettygrove, S., Constantino, J. N., Vehorn, A., Shenouda, J., Hall-Lande, J., Van Naarden Braun, K., & Dowling, N. F. (2020). Prevalence of autism spectrum disorder among children aged 8 years–Autism and developmental disabilities monitoring network, 11 Sites, United States, 2016. *MMWR Surveillance Summaries, 69*(No. SS-4), 1–12. http://dx.doi.org/10.15585/mmwr.ss6904a1external icon.
5. Centers for Disease Control and Prevention. (n.d.). *Autism spectrum disorder (ASD): Data & statistics*. www.cdc.gov/ncbddd/autism/data.html
6. Hyman, S. L., Levy, S. E., Myers, S. M., & Council on Children with Disabilities, Section on Developmental and Behavioral Pediatrics. (2020). Identification, evaluation, and management of children with autism spectrum disorder. *Pediatrics, 145*(1), e20193447. https://doi.org/10.1542/peds.2019-3447
7. Werling, D. M., & Geschwind, D. H. (2013). Sex differences in autism spectrum disorders. *Current Opinion in Neurology, 26*(2), 146–153. https://doi.org/10.1097/WCO.0b013e32835ee548
8. Deacon, B. (2013). The biomedical model of mental disorder: A critical analysis of its validity, utility, and effects on psychotherapy research. *Clinical Psychology Review, 33*, 846-861.
9. Antshel, K. M., Zhang-James, Y., Wagner, K. E., Ledesma, A., & Faraone, S. V. (2016). An update on the comorbidity of ADHD and ASD: a focus on clinical management. *Expert Review of Neurotherapeutics, 16*(3), 279–293. https://doi.org/10.1586/14737175.2016.1146591
10. Zablotsky, B., Bramlett, M. D., & Blumberg, S. J. (2020). The co-occurrence of autism spectrum disorder in children with ADHD. *Journal of Attention Disorders, 24*(1), 94–103. https://doi.org/10.1177/1087054717713638
11. Curtin, C., Bandini, L. G., Perrin, E. C. Tybor, D. J., & Must, A. (2005). Prevalence of overweight in children and adolescents with attention deficit hyperactivity disorder and autism spectrum disorders: A chart review. *BMC Pediatrics, 5*, 48. https://doi.org/10.1186/1471-2431-5-48
12. Hill, A. P., Zuckerman, K. E., & Fombonne, E. (2015). Obesity and autism. *Pediatrics, 136*(6), 1051–1061. https://doi.org/10.1542/peds.2015-1437

13. McCoy, S. M., Jakicic, J. M., & Gibbs, B. B. (2016). Comparison of obesity, physical activity, and sedentary behaviors between adolescents with autism spectrum disorders and without. *Journal of Autism and Developmental Disorders, 46*, 2317–2326. https://doi.org/10.1007/s10803-016-2762-0
14. Wakefield, A. J., Murch, S. H., Anthony, A., Linnell, J., Casson, D. M., Malik, M., Berelowitz, M., Dhillon, A. P., Thomson, M. A., Harvey, P., Valentine, A., Davies, S. E., & Walker-Smith, J. A. (1998). Ileal-lymphoid-nodular hyperplasia, non-specific colitis, and pervasive developmental disorder in children. *Lancet (London, England), 351*(9103), 637–641. https://doi.org/10.1016/s0140-6736(97)11096-0 (Retraction published Lancet. 2010 Feb 6;375(9713):445)
15. Gerber, J. S., & Offit, P. A. (2009). Vaccines and autism: A tale of shifting hypotheses. *Clinical Infectious Diseases, 48*(4), 456–461. https://doi.org/10.1086/596476
16. Huquet, G., Ey, E., & Bourgeron, T. (2013). The genetic landscapes of autism spectrum disorders. *Annual Review of Genomics and Human Genetics, 14*, 191–213. https://doi.org/10.1146/annurev-genom-091212-153431
17. Bailey, A., Le Couteur, A., Gottesman, I., Bolton, P., Simonoff, E., Yuzda, E., & Rutter, M. (1995). Autism as a strongly genetic disorder: evidence from a British twin study. *Psychological Medicine, 25*(1), 63–77. https://doi.org/10.1017/s0033291700028099
18. Hallmayer, J., Cleveland, S., Torres, A., Phillips, J., Cohen, B., Torigoe, T., Miller, J., Fedele, A., Collins, J., Smith, K., Lotspeich, L., Croen, L. A., Ozonoff, S., Lajonchere, C., Grether, J. K., & Risch, N. (2011). Genetic heritability and shared environmental factors among twin pairs with autism. *Archives of General Psychiatry, 68*(11), 1095–1102. https://doi.org/10.1001/archgenpsychiatry.2011.76
19. Rosenberg, R. E., Law, J. K., Yenokyan, G., McGready, J., Kaufmann, W. E., & Law, P. A. (2009). Characteristics and concordance of autism spectrum disorders among 277 twin pairs. *Archives Pediatrics and Adolescent Medicine, 163*(10), 907–914. https://doi.org/10.1001/archpediatrics.2009.98
20. McDonald, N. M., Senturk, D., Scheffler, A., Brian, J. A., Carver, L. J., Charman, T., Chawarska, K., Curtin, S., Hertz-Picciotto, I., Jones, E., Klin, A., Landa, R., Messinger, D. S., Ozonoff, S., Stone, W. L., Tager-Flusberg, H., Webb, S. J., Young, G., Zwaigenbaum, L., & Jeste, S. S. (2020). Developmental trajectories of infants with multiplex family risk for autism: A baby siblings research consortium study. *JAMA Neurology, 77*(1), 73–81. https://doi.org/10.1001/jamaneurol.2019.3341
21. Fragile X Clinical & Research Consortium. (2014). *Consensus of the fragile X clinical & research consortium on clinical practices. Autism spectrum disorder in fragile X syndrome.* https://fragilex.org/wp-content/uploads/2012/08/Autism-Spectrum-Disorder-in-Fragile-X-Syndrome-2014-Nov.pdf
22. Kushki, A., Anagnostou, E., Hammill, C., Kushki, A., Anagnostou, E., Hammill, C., Duez, P., Brian, J., Iaboni, A., Schachar, R., Crosbie, J., Arnold, P., & Lerch, J. P. (2019). Examining overlap and homogeneity in ASD, ADHD, and OCD: A data-driven, diagnosis-agnostic approach. *Translational Psychiatry, 9*, 318. https://doi.org/10.1038/s41398-019-0631-2
23. Simonoff, E., Pickles, A., Charman, T., Chandler, S., Loucas, T., & Baird, G. (2008). Psychiatric disorders in children with autism spectrum disorders: prevalence, comorbidity, and associated factors in a population-derived sample. *Journal of the American Academy of Child and Adolescent Psychiatry, 47*(8), 921–929. https://doi.org/10.1097/CHI.0b013e318179964f
24. Karimi, P., Kamali, E., Mousavi, S. M., & Karahmadi, M. (2017). Environmental factors influencing the risk of autism. *Journal of research in medical sciences: the official journal of Isfahan University of Medical Sciences, 22*, 27. https://doi.org/10.4103/1735-1995.200272
25. Christensen, J., Grønborg, T. K., Sørensen, M. J., Schendel, D., Parner, E. T., Pedersen, L. H., & Vestergaard, M. (2013). Prenatal valproate exposure and risk of autism spectrum disorders and childhood autism. *JAMA, 309*(16), https://doi.org/10.1001/jama.2013.2270
26. Jokiranta, E., Brown, A. S., Heinimaa, M., Cheslack-Postava, K., Suominen, A., & Sourander, A. (2013). Parental psychiatric disorders and autism spectrum disorders. *Psychiatry Research, 207*(3), 203–211. https://doi.org/10.1016/j.psychres.2013.01.005
27. Centers for Disease Control and Prevention. (n.d.). *Autism spectrum disorder (ASD): Signs and symptoms.* www.cdc.gov/ncbddd/autism/signs.html
28. Gray, C. A. (1998). *Social stories and comic strip conversations with students with Asperger syndrome and high-functioning autism.* In E. Schopler, G. B. Mesibov, & L. J. Kunce (Eds.), *Current issues in autism. Asperger syndrome or high-functioning autism?* (pp. 167–198). Plenum Press. https://doi.org/10.1007/978-1-4615-5369-4_9
29. Karal, M. A., & Wolfe, P. S. (2018). Social story effectiveness on social interaction for students with autism: A review of the literature. *Education and Training in Autism and Developmental Disabilities, 53*(1), 44–58.
30. Qi, C. H., Barton, E. E., Collier, M., Lin, Y.-L., & Montoya, C. (2018). A systematic review of effects of social stories interventions for individuals with autism spectrum disorder. *Focus on Autism and Other Developmental Disabilities, 33*(1), 25–34. https://doi.org/10.1177/1088357615613516
31. Cooper, J. O., Heron, T. E., & Heward, W. L. (2007). *Applied behavior analysis* (2nd ed.). Pearson.
32. Matson, J. L., Turygin, N. C., Beighley, J., Rieske, R., Tureck, K., & Matson, M. L. (2012). Applied behavior analysis in autism spectrum disorders: Recent developments, strengths, and pitfalls. *Research in Autism Spectrum Disorders, 6*(1), 144–150.

33. Autism Speaks. (n.d.). TEACCH: What is TEACCH? www.autismspeaks.org/teacch-0
34. Sartorato, F., Przybylowski, L., & Sarko, D. K. (2017). Improving therapeutic outcomes in autism spectrum disorders: Enhancing social communication and sensory processing through the use of interactive robots. *Journal of Psychiatric Research, 90*, 1–11. https://doi.org/10.1016/j.jpsychires.2017.02.004
35. Frazier, T. W., Shattuck, P. T., Narendorf, S. C., Cooper, B. P., Wagner, M., & Spitznagel, E. L. (2011). Prevalence and correlates of psychotropic medication use in adolescents with an autism spectrum disorder with and without caregiver-reported attention-deficit/hyperactivity disorder. *Journal of Child and Adolescent Psychopharmacology, 21*(6), 571–579. https://doi.org/10.1089/cap.2011.0057
36. Howes, O. D., Rogdaki, M., Findon, J. L., Wichers, R. H., Charman, T., King, B. H., Loth, E., McAlonan, G. M., McCracken, J. T., Parr, J. R., Povey, C., Santosh, P., Wallace, S., Simonoff, E., & Murphy, D. G. (2018). Autism spectrum disorder: Consensus guidelines on assessment, treatment and research from the British Association for Psychopharmacology. *Journal of Psychopharmacology, 32*(1), 3–29. https://doi.org/10.1177/0269881117741766
37. Siegel, M., & Beaulieu, A. A. (2012). Psychotropic medications in children with autism spectrum disorders: a systematic review and synthesis for evidence-based practice. *Journal of Autism and Developmental Disorders, 42*(8), 1592–1605. https://doi.org/10.1007/s10803-011-1399-2
38. Dale, L., Vanderloo, L., Moore, S. A., & Faulkner, G. (2019). Physical activity and depression, anxiety, and self-esteem in children and youth: An umbrella systematic review. *Mental Health and Physical Activity, 16*, 66–79.
39. McMahon, E. M., Corcoran, P., O'Regan, G., Keeley, H., Cannon, M., Carli, V., Wasserman, C., Hadlaczky, G., Sarchiapone, M., Apter, A., Balazs, J., Balint, M., Bobes, J., Brunner, R., Cozman, D., Haring, C., Iosue, M., Kaess, M., Kahn, J. P., Nemes, B., Podlogar, T., Poštuvan, V., Sβiz, P., Sisask, M., Tubiana, A., Värnik, P., Hoven, C. W., & Wasserman, D. (2017). Physical activity in European adolescents and associations with anxiety, depression and well-being. *European Child and Adolescent Psychiatry, 26*(1), 111–122. https://doi.org/10.1007/s00787-016-0875-9
40. Wachob, D., & Lorenzi, D. G. (2015). Brief report: Influence of physical activity on sleep quality in children with autism. *Journal of Autism and Developmental Disorders, 45*, 2641–2646. https://doi.org/10.1007/s10803-015-2424-7
41. Poleg, S., Golubchik, P., Offen, D., & Weizman, A. (2019). Cannabidiol as a suggested candidate for treatment of autism spectrum disorder. *Progress in Neuro-Psychopharmacology & Biological Psychiatry, 89*, 90–96. https://doi.org/10.1016/j.pnpbp.2018.08.030
42. Gibson, E. (1988). Exploratory behavior in the development of perceiving, acting, and the acquiring of knowledge. *Annual Review of Psychology, 39*(1), 1–42. https://doi.org/10.1146/annurev.ps.39.020188.000245
43. Thelen, E. (1995). Motor development: A new synthesis. *American Physiologist, 50*, 2, 79–95. https://doi.org/10.1037//0003-066x.50.2.79
44. Bauminger-Zviely, N., Eden, S., Zancanaro, M., Weiss, P. L., & Gal, E. (2013). Increasing social engagement in children with high-functioning autism spectrum disorder using collaborative technologies in the school environment. *Autism, 17*(3), 317–339. https://doi.org/10.1177/1362361312472989
45. Leekam, S. R., Nieto, C., Libby, S. J., Wing, L., & Gould, J. (2007). Describing the sensory abnormalities of children and adults with autism. *Journal of Autism and Developmental Disorders, 37*(5), 894–910. https://doi.org/10.1007/s10803-006-0218-7
46. Marco, E. J., Hinkley, L. B. N., Hill, S. S., & Nagarajan, S. S. (2011). Sensory processing in autism: A review of neurophysiologic findings. *Pediatric Research, 69*, 48–54. https://doi.org/10.1203/PDR.0b013e3182130c54
47. Robertson, C. E., Thomas, C., Kravitz, D. J., Wallace, G. L., Baron-Cohen, S., Martin, A., & Baker, C. I. (2014). Global motion perception deficits in autism are reflected as early as primary visual cortex. *Brain: A Journal of Neurology, 137*(9), 2588–2599. https://doi.org/10.1093/brain/awu189
48. Dhossche, D. M., Wing, L., Ohta, M., & Neumärker, K.-J. (2006). *Catatonia in autism spectrum disorders*. London: Elsevier.
49. Cunningham, A. B., & Schreibman, L. (2008). Stereotypy in autism: The importance of function. *Research in Autism Spectrum Disorders, 2*, 469–479. https://doi.org/10.1016/j.rasd.2007.09.006
50. Honey, E., Leekam, S., Turner, M., & McConachie, M. (2007). Repetitive behavior and play in typically developing children and children with autism spectrum disorders. *Journal of Autism Developmental Disabilities, 37*, 1107–1115. https://doi.org/10.1007/s10803-006-0253-4
51. Baghdadli, A., Pascal, C., Grisi, S., & Aussiloux, C. (2003). Risk factors for self-injurious behaviors among 222 young children with autistic disorders. *Journal of Intellectual Disability Research, 47*, 622–627. https://doi.org/10.1046/j.1365-2788.2003.00507.x
52. Emerson, E. (2001). *Challenging behavior: Analysis and intervention in people with severe intellectual disabilities* (2nd ed.). Cambridge, UK: Cambridge University Press.
53. Green, D., Charman, T., Pickles, A., Chandler, S., Loucas, T., Simonoff, E., & Baird, G. (2009). Impairment in movement skills of children with autistic spectrum disorders. *Developmental Medicine and Child Neurology, 51*(4), 311–316. https://doi.org/10.1111/j.1469-8749.2008.03242.x

54. Staples, K. L., & Reid, G. (2010). Fundamental movement skills and autism spectrum disorders. *Journal of Autism and Developmental Disorders, 40*, 209–217. https://doi.org/10.1007/s10803-009-0854-9
55. Bhat A. N. (2020). Is motor impairment in autism spectrum disorder distinct from developmental coordination disorder? A report from the SPARK study. *Physical therapy, 100*(4), 633–644. https://doi.org/10.1093/ptj/pzz190
56. Bhat, A. N., Landa, R. J., & Galloway, J. C. (2011). Current perspectives on motor functioning in infants, children, and adults with autism spectrum disorders, *Physical Therapy, 91*(7), 1116–1129. https://doi.org/10.2522/ptj.20100294
57. Provost, B., Lopez, B. R., & Heimerl, S. (2007). A comparison of motor delays in young children: Autism spectrum disorder, developmental delay, and developmental concerns. *Journal of Autism and Developmental Disorders, 37*(2), 321–328. https://doi.org/10.1007/s10803-006-0170-6
58. Lloyd, M., MacDonald, M., & Lord, C. (2013). Motor skills of toddlers with autism spectrum disorders. *Autism, 17*(2), 133–146. https://doi.org/10.1177/1362361311402230
59. Ament, K., Mejia, A., Buhlman, R., Erklin, S., Caffo, B., Mostofsky, S., & Wodka, E. (2015). Evidence for specificity of motor impairments in catching and balance in children with autism. *Journal of Autism and Developmental Disorders, 45*(3), 742–751. https://doi.org/10.1007/s10803-014-2229-0
60. Fulceri, F., Grossi, E., Contaldo, A., Narzisi, A., Apicella, F., Parrini, I., Tancredi, R., Calderoni, S., & Muratori, F. (2019). Motor skills as moderators of core symptoms in autism spectrum disorders: Preliminary data from an exploratory analysis with artificial neural networks. *Frontiers in Psychology, 9*, 2683. https://doi.org/10.3389/fpsyg.2018.02683
61. Van der Hallen, R., Manning, C., Evers, K., & Wagemans, J. (2019). Global motion perception in autism spectrum disorder: A meta-analysis. *Journal of Autism and Developmental Disorders, 49*, 4901–4918. https://doi.org/10.1007/s10803-019-04194-8
62. Srinivasan, S. M., Pescatello, L. S., & Bhat, A. N. (2014). Current perspectives on physical activity and exercise recommendations for children and adolescents with autism spectrum disorders. *Physical Therapy, 94*(6), 875–889. https://doi.org/10.2522/ptj.20130157
63. Lee, J., & Vargo, K. K. (2017). Physical activity into socialization: A movement-based social skills program for children with autism spectrum disorder. *Journal of Physical Education, Recreation and Dance, 88*(4), 7–13. https://doi.org/10.1080/07303084.2016.1270788
64. Healy, S., Msetfi, R., & Gallagher, S. (2013). "Happy and a bit nervous": The experiences of children with autism in physical education. *British Journal of Learning Disabilities. 41*, 222–228. http://doi.org/10.1111/bld.12053
65. Arnell, S., Jerlinder, K., & Lundqvist, L. O. (2018). Perceptions of physical activity participation among adolescents with autism spectrum disorders: A conceptual model of conditional participation. *Journal Autism and Developmental Disorders, 48*, 1792–1802. https://doi.org/10.1007/s10803-017-3436-2
66. Lang, R., Koegel, L. K., Ashbaugh, K., Regester, A., Ence, W., & Smith, W. (2010). Physical exercise and individuals with autism spectrum disorders. *Research in Autism Spectrum Disorders, 4*(4), 565–576. http://doi.org/10.1016/j.rasd.2010.01.006
67. Sorensen, C., & Zarrett, N. (2014). Benefits of physical activity for adolescents with autism spectrum disorders: A comprehensive review. *Review Journal of Autism and Developmental Disorders, 1*, 344–353. https://doi.org/10.1007/s40489-014-0027-4
68. Colombo-Dougovito, A., & Lee, J. (2020). Social skill outcomes following physical activity-based interventions for individuals on the autism spectrum: A scoping review spanning young childhood through young adulthood. *Adapted Physical Activity Quarterly.* Ahead of Print (December, 2020). https://doi.org/10.1123/apaq.2019-0080
69. Nicholson, H., Kehle, T., Bray, M., & van Heest, J. (2011). The effects of antecedent physical activity on the academic engagement of children with autism spectrum disorder. *Psychology in the Schools, 48*, 198–213. http://doi.org/10.1002/pits.20537
70. Bremer, E., Crozier, M., & Lloyd, M. (2016). A systematic review of the behavioral outcomes following exercise interventions for children and youth with autism spectrum disorder. *Autism, 20*(8), 1–17. http://doi.org/10.1177/1362361315616002
71. Dillon, S. R., Adams, D., Goudy, L., Bittner, M., & McNamara, S. (2017). Evaluating exercise as evidence-based practice for individuals with autism spectrum disorder. *Frontiers in Public Health, 4*(290), 1–9. http://doi.org/10.3389/fpubh.2016.00290
72. Tarr, C. W., Rineer-Hershey, A., & Larwin, K. (2020). The effects of physical exercise on stereotypic behaviors in autism: Small-n meta-analyses. *Focus on Autism and Other Developmental Disabilities, 35*(1), 26–35. https://doi.org/10.1177/1088357619881220
73. Ma, Q. (2008). Beneficial effects of moderate voluntary physical exercise and its biological mechanisms on brain health. *Neuroscience Bulletin, 24*, 265–270.
74. Petzinger, G. M., Holschneider, D. P., Fisher, B. E., McEwen, S., Kintz, N., Halliday, M., Toy, W., Walsh, J. W., Beeler, J., & Jakowec, M. W. (2015). The effects of exercise on dopamine neurotransmission in Parkinson's disease: Targeting neuroplasticity to modulate basal ganglia circuitry. *Brain Plasticity, 1*(1), 29–39. https://doi.org/10.3233/bpl-150021
75. Neely, L., Rispoli, M., Gerow, S., & Ninci, J. (2015). Effects of antecedent exercise on academic engagement and stereotypy during instruction. *Behavior Modification, 39*, 98–116. https://doi.org/10.1177/0145445514552891

76. Morrison, H., Roscoe, E. M., & Atwell, A. (2011). An evaluation of antecedent exercise on behavior maintained by automatic reinforcement using a three-component multiple schedule. *Journal of Applied Behavior Analysis, 44*, 523–541. https://doi.org/10.1901/jaba.2011.44-523
77. Bremer, E., Graham, J. D., Heisz, J. J., & Cairney, J. (2020). Effect of acute exercise on prefrontal oxygenation and inhibitory control among male children with autism spectrum disorder: An exploratory study. *Frontiers in Behavioral Neuroscience, 14*, 84. https://doi.org/10.3389/fnbeh.2020.00084
78. Brand, S., Jossen, S., Holsboer-Trachsler, E., Pühse, U., & Gerber, M. (2015). Impact of aerobic exercise on sleep and motor skills in children with autism spectrum disorders–a pilot study. *Neuropsychiatric Disease and Treatment, 11*, 1911–1920. https://doi.org/10.2147/NDT.S85650
79. Tse, C., Lee, H. P., Chan, K., Edgar, V. B., Wilkinson-Smith, A., & Lai, W. (2019). Examining the impact of physical activity on sleep quality and executive functions in children with autism spectrum disorder: A randomized controlled trial. *Autism, 23*(7), 1699–1710. https://doi.org/10.1177/1362361318823910
80. Charlop-Christy, M. H., Carpenter, M., Le, L., LeBlanc, L. A., & Kellet, K. (2002). Using the picture exchange communication system (PECS) with children with autism: Assessment of PECS acquisition, speech, social-communicative behavior, and problem behavior. *Journal of Applied Behavior Analysis, 35*(3), 213–231. https://doi.org/10.1901/jaba.2002.35-213
81. Sancho, K., Sidener, T., Reeve, S., & Sidener, D. (2010). Two variations of video modeling interventions for teaching play skills to children with autism. *Education and Treatment of Children, 33*(3), 421–442.
82. Frost, L. A., & Bondy, A. S. (2002). *PECS: The picture exchange communication system training manual* (2nd ed.). Pyramid Educational Products Inc.
83. Dowrick, P. W. (1991). *Practical guide to using video in the behavioral sciences*. Wiley Interscience.
84. Anderson, S., & Morris, J. (2006). Cognitive behavior therapy for people with Asperger syndrome. *Behavioral and Cognitive Psychotherapy, 34*(3), 293–303. https://doi.org/10.1017/S1352465805002651
85. Attwood, T. (2004). Cognitive behavior therapy for children and adults with Asperger's Syndrome. *Behaviour Change, 21*, 147–161. https://doi.org/10.1375/bech.21.3.147.55995
86. Lang, R., Regester, A., Lauderdale, S., Ashbaugh, K., & Haring, A. (2010). Treatment of anxiety in autism spectrum disorders using cognitive behavior therapy: A systematic review. *Developmental Neurorehabilitation, 13*(1), 53–63. https://doi.org/10.3109/17518420903236288
87. Weston, L., Hodgekins, J., & Langdon, P. E. (2016). Effectiveness of cognitive behavioral therapy with people who have autistic spectrum disorders: A systematic review and meta-analysis. *Clinical Psychology Review, 49*, 41–54. https://doi.org/10.1016/j.cpr.2016.08.001
88. Lee, J., & Haegele, J. A. (2016). Understanding challenging behaviors of students with autism spectrum disorder in physical education. *Journal of Physical Education, Recreation and Dance, 87*(7), 27–30.
89. Lee, D., Frey, G., Cheng, A., & Shih, P. C. (2018). Puzzle walk: A gamified mobile app to increase physical activity in adults with autism spectrum disorder. *10th International Conference on Virtual Worlds and Games for Serious Applications (VS-Games)*, 1–4. https://doi.org/10.1109/VS-Games.2018.8493439
90. Todd, T., & Reid, G. (2006). Increasing physical activity in individuals with autism. *Focus on Autism and Other Developmental Disabilities, 21*(3), 167–176. https://doi.org/10.1177/10883576060210030501
91. Todd, T., Reid, G., & Butler-Kisber, L. (2010). Cycling for students with ASD: self-regulation promotes sustained physical activity. *Adapted Physical Activity Quarterly, 27*(3), 226–241. https://doi.org/10.1123/apaq.27.3.226
92. Chou, Y.-C., Wehmeyer, M. L., Palmer, S. B., & Lee, J. (2017). Comparisons of self-determination among students with autism, intellectual disability, and learning disabilities: A multivariate analysis. *Focus on Autism and Other Developmental Disabilities, 32*(2), 124–132. https://doi.org/10.1177/1088357615625059
93. Tullis, C. A., Cannella-Malone, H. I., Basbigill, A. R., Yeager, A. R., Fleming, C. V., Payne, D. O., & Wu, P. (2011). Review of the choice and preference assessment literature for individuals with severe to profound disabilities. *Education and Training in Autism and Developmental Disabilities, 46*, 576–595.
94. Krasny, L., Williams, B. J., Provencal, S., & Ozonoff, S. (2003). Social skills interventions for the autism spectrum: essential ingredients and a model curriculum. *Child and Adolescent Psychiatric Clinics of North America, 12*(1), 107–122. https://doi.org/10.1016/s1056-4993(02)00051-2
95. Centers for Disease Control and Prevention. (n.d.). *Safety and child with disabilities. Disability and safety: Information on wandering (elopement)*. www.cdc.gov/ncbddd/disabilityandsafety/wandering.html
96. Anderson, C., Law, J. K., Daniels, A., Rice, C., Mandell, D. S., Hagopian, L., & Law, P. A. (2012). Occurrence and family impact of elopement in children with autism spectrum disorders. *Pediatrics, 130*(5), 870–877. https://doi.org/10.1542/peds.2012-0762
97. Guan, J., & Li, G. (2017). Characteristics of unintentional drowning deaths in children with autism spectrum disorder. *Injury Epidemiology, 4*, 32. https://doi.org/10.1186/s40621-017-0129-4
98. Autism Speaks. (n.d.). *Recreation*. www.autismspeaks.org/activites-children-autism
99. Kenny, L., Hattersley, C., Molins, B., Buckley, C., Povey, C., & Pellicano, E. (2016). Which terms should be used to describe autism? Perspectives from the UK autism community. *Autism, 20*(4), 442–462. https://doi.org/10.1177/1362361315588200

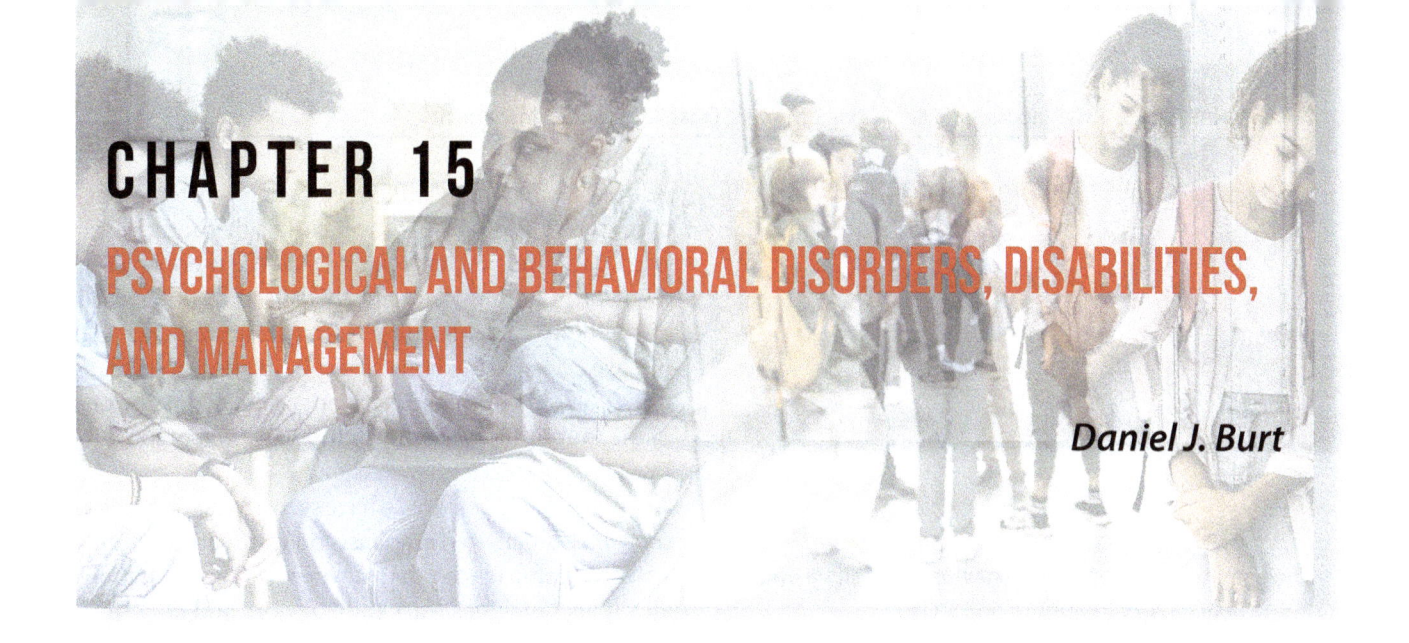

CHAPTER 15
PSYCHOLOGICAL AND BEHAVIORAL DISORDERS, DISABILITIES, AND MANAGEMENT

Daniel J. Burt

INTRODUCTION TO PSYCHOLOGICAL AND BEHAVIORAL ISSUES

Many of the psychological and behavioral disorders discussed in this chapter fall into the category of Neurodevelopmental Disorders within the fifth edition of the *Diagnostic and Statistics Manual of Mental Disorders* (*DSM-5*); however, the term is broad and tends to cover a number of disabilities and disorders, like intellectual disabilities and autism, found elsewhere in this book. Disabilities and disorders that tend to relate to behavior, especially if they do not cohabitate with an intellectual disability, are often undiagnosed, and usually the individuals are treated punitively in a form of behavioral correction. This stems from a societal perspective with deep roots in specific religious beliefs on work ethics that leave little room to create an understanding on the importance of set tasks and instead create an expectation on the idea of mere compliance. Many individuals growing up are familiar with the phrase, "because I said so" when simply asking why a task needs to be performed, never learning the importance of specific tasks, behaviors, or even expectations.[1] In discussing behavior, it is required to break down the concepts of behavior into the before, during, and after to fully understand how a behavior might have occurred and the reception of the behavior afterward to see how long-term behaviors might be developed or avoided. Often, this is done by observing and recording not just the behavior but the situational factors and actions surrounding the behavior. This is broken into what is known as A-B-C (antecedent–behavior–consequence) data collection, where the practitioner records all three of these as they relate to one another, helping them to look for patterns that emerge. **Antecedent** refers to the events, actions, and different circumstances that occur before a behavior. **Behavior** refers to the behavior that occurs and denotes the specific physical, emotional, and communication actions that transpire. **Consequence** refers to the action or response that happens after the behavior. This includes how the environment and individuals in it change based on the behavior itself that may or may not encourage the behavior to occur again.[2]

The history of psychology and disabilities was referenced in Chapter 1 and does not reflect well on most of the religious, scientific, and medical communities throughout time. However, there are noteworthy moments through history that need to be mentioned as they marched us toward our current acceptance and somewhat support of mental illness and disabilities. While there are a number of disorders, diseases, and disabilities that would fall under the categories below, they have been broken down into three groups: mental illnesses, emotional disturbances (EDs) and behavioral disorders, and learning disabilities.

Daniel J. Burt, Texas A&M University-Kingsville. © Kendall Hunt Publishing.

The change from negative behaviors to positive ones is at the heart of psychological research.

Mental Illness

Mental illness has an interesting and complex history and also ebbs and flows in how it is treated in various cultures because it resulted in various behavioral outcomes. How those behaviors were accepted in a culture may alter the acceptance of mental illness in a society. Unfortunately, it has also been used as a way to limit and control individuals, especially in places like the United States, where it affected educational access and even reproductive rights. Note the following causes did not replace each other, but all occurred off and on and are overlapping throughout history. Mental illness has been attributed to a number of things over the ages. Probably the first major belief as to the cause of mental illness, and the one guiding most of history, were *Supernatural* causes that were believed to be related to astrological signs, demonic possession, and sin. Examples seem to be present in cave art showing surgical drilling for head injuries to allow evil spirits out as far back as 6500 BC. The imbalance of Yin and Yang as positive and negative forces found in the body have been discussed in 2700 BC. While the field of medicine was developing, even witches were blamed for mental illness between the 13th and 16th centuries, with the Malleus Maleficarum, a guide to witch hunting, detailing these issues caused by witches. In a bit of a plot twist, two men, Johann Weyer and Reginald Scot, wrote that many individuals had mental issues due to disease and not demonic possession and that they were not witches. Unfortunately, the Inquisition banned their writing as heretical. As forms of ancient medicine and various practices of "science" took over the past few millennia, *Somatogenic* ideas also took hold and assumed mental illness to be related to physical or materially related issues. This led to the assumption that it was genetic, brain damage, or an imbalance of some bodily function like increased yellow bile. Egyptian and Greek beliefs written on papyri from 1900 BC show beliefs that the body developed odd fluids on its own and that the uterus had its own spirit, animus, and attached itself to other parts of the body causing discomfort and hysteria. In 400 BC, we even see the famed Hippocrates try to categorize problems in the body as an excess or loss of one of the four humors (bodily fluids): phlegm, blood, yellow bile, and black bile.

The past 150 years or so have seen a focus on the *Psychogenic*, which is an emphasis on traumatic or highly stressful experiences that have occurred. Additionally, it also includes learned behaviors and cognitive/distorted perceptions. Unfortunately, many of these ideas are linked with asylums and mental hospitals, which have associations with poor care and abuse, and are even a main part of the horror fiction genre today. While some of the more famous institutions, like St. Mary of Bethlehem in London (known as Bedlam), took patients who were mentally ill in the 16th and 17th centuries, most of these were related to restricting the individuals from being in and around the public, institutionalizing them without consent. As mentioned in Chapter 1, this eventually led to some perspective changes in that more humane treatment would be needed, and objecting/protesting started to occur in the 1700s. Several physicians during this time focused on "moral treatment" and advocated for rooms that did not include restraints or chains, with clean air and light, and the ability to have time outside. While part of these made their way to the United States, labor was also attached to the beliefs of helping individuals feel human. Overcrowding led to state hospitals being developed and created new opportunities away from private control. Germ theory in the late 1800s led to vaccines and an idea for mental hygiene, where general health improvement, and absence of disease, led to mental health improvement. As the 1800s led to the 1900s, Sigmund Freud led the charge to focus on a psychogenic explanation as the premier thought, which led to a psychoanalytic approach. While psychoanalysis is not the predominant theory or approach today, it led to many of the current therapeutic approaches and the growth of the professional therapy field, creating accountability for therapists and professional counselors. Somatogenic approaches can be seen in the last century through the use of restraints, lobotomies, and electroconvulsive shock therapy that continued into the 1970s. While some use of electroconvulsive shock therapy is used today, most examples of somatogenic treatment can be seen in the heavy uses of pharmaceutical options.[3]

Emotional Disturbances and Behavioral Disorders

In terms of Attention-Deficit Hyperactivity Disorder (ADHD), the first reference in some form might be a poem printed in a 1902 volume of the esteemed British medical journal *The Lancet* called "The Story of Fidgety Philip" and about how the individual in the poem wiggles, giggles, swinging their arms and legs, then tilting their chair up and down.[5]

- By 1955, the FDA approved the drug Ritalin as a treatment for depression and fatigue, but it wasn't approved until 1961 for children who were defined as "hyperkinetic."
- Emotional Disturbance as a term was first introduced in the 1960s by Eli Bower.[4] This term was used to encompass anxiety, bipolar, conduct, eating, psychotic, and obsessive-compulsive disorders (OCDs).
- In 1980, the term Hyperkinetic Impulse Disorder was replaced by Attention-Deficit Disorder (ADD), which was then changed to Attention-Deficit Hyperactivity Disorder in 1987 when the DSM was revised.
- The 1980s and 1990s saw a rise in celebrities and public figures discussing and raising awareness on everything from emotional and behavioral issues to learning disabilities.
- In 1997, IDEA was revised to allow ADHD to qualify in special considerations under the "Other Health Impairment" criteria.
- In 2007, researchers at the Medical Investigation of Neurodevelopment Disorders Institute, known as the MIND Institute, founded at the University of California, Davis, were able to recognize the differences in electrical brain patterns for those who have ADHD, which showed that there were biological explanations for attention issues.

Learning Disabilities

Learning Disabilities had some form of recognition but little understanding in the 1800s. Adolf Kussmaul, a German neurologist, coined the term "word blindness" in 1877 to describe individuals who could not read various words or texts even though their intelligence, vision, and ability to speak were fine.

- Dr. Rudolf Berlin coined the term "dyslexia" to denote these reading issues in 1887. The first academic paper on reading issues in children, called the *Study of Reading*, was published in 1905 and was an observational on reading inhibition.
- Dyslexia did not become a common term used in medical and academic circles until the 1930s.

The 1960s and 1970s saw a real change in the recognition of learning disabilities and their categorizations.

- The term "learning disability" was first used at an educational conference in 1963 by Dr. Samuel Kirk, also known as the father of learning disabilities.
- The 1960s also saw the first public school programs created to address a growing recognition of learning disabilities; these were developed by Syracuse University and Dr. William Cruickshank.
- A year later, the Association for Children with Learning Disabilities (ACLD) was developed in the United States and a chapter in each of states was created, the name was later changed to the Learning Disability Association of America (known now as LDA).
- Congress passed the Children with Specific Learning Disabilities Act in 1969 to create support for students with learning disabilities.
- This was absorbed into the Education of all Handicapped Children Act of 1970, later reauthorized as IDEA. The National Center for Learning Disabilities was founded privately by parents of children with learning disabilities to create resources for other parents.
- By 1985, Texas was the first state to require school districts to provide dyslexia screening and create specific instructional interventions if signs of dyslexia are present and multiple states followed suit over time.
- In 1996, the National Institute of Mental Health discovered that neurologically, there were regions of the brain that work differently for individuals with specific learning disabilities.
- This will be later confirmed in 2002 by researchers at Yale University showing that fMRI technology demonstrated brains of individuals with specific learning disabilities, like dyslexia, react differently than those of their peers when performing tasks like reading. University College London researchers were able to brain image individuals with dyscalculia and show that they activate differently during work on mathematics.

Old testing center for those deemed incapable of learning.

- *DSM-5* expands the definition for the specific learning disability. Post 2015, the world has seen an increase in the LDA partnering with governmental organizations to reduce potential environmental factors causing learning disabilities.
- The Environmental Protection Agency (EPA), Walgreens, The Home Depot, and Lowes commit to removing products that contain or are known to have chemicals (flooring, lumber, chemical treatments, and paint) that slow or reduce brain development.[5]

Common Qualifiers of Disorders

Behavioral issues stem from a variety of things, especially from our reactions to our environment and challenges to expectations. As noted in Chapter 3, especially when it is harder to identify disabilities and disorders, there are some parameters that must be viewed to consider behavioral issues for legal protection under the laws of ADA and IDEA.

Length of Time

This looks at behavior that might have been going on for some time, and a pattern may or may not have emerged if tracked. However, the expected occurrence on what might be considered extreme behavior, for example, physical attacks, screaming, verbal abuse, breaking of things around an individual, is usually going to happen very few times in their life. However, outside an incidence of crisis, for example, a death of a family member or parental divorce, this is a behavior that consistently occurs regardless of the inconvenience of the stimuli and antecedent. The behavior's continued reoccurrence allows for it to be considered medically and psychologically chronic. An example could be a young child's physical and/or emotional outbursts occurring frequently and suddenly just a few days after their parent's divorce compared to a child who does not seem to have a home or school complications but regularly engages in severe behavior for months or even years.

Marked Degree

Behavior that is overly extreme or severe response in a mismatched way to the stimuli (e.g., reacting to being told no to something), allows for a behavior to be further suspect for the potential presence of a disability. A physical attack, or a verbal tirade, in response to not liking or wanting something may raise a cause for concern. However, a major difference in understanding those who have extreme behavior responses due to a disability from those who have learned behavior is what happens when the individual gets what they are wanting. Typically, someone using a "tantrum" as leverage to gain something will stop as a form of reward to continue to get what they want in the future. Often, those with behavior issues could get what they want but would still be struggling to reign in the emotional response due to uncontrolled emotional regulation or impulsiveness. Marked degree considers the severity, or magnitude, as well as the length and frequency of one's responding behavior.

IDEA: It Inhibits Your Education

Unfortunately, the need for "compliance" in our current form of education has led to a complication in diagnosing individuals with behavior-related disabilities if they have decent grades or are successfully completing IEP set objectives. Behavioral issues are hard to separate from a conflict between individual's expectations with their surroundings, the limited education or training on behavior for teachers and administrators, as well as people's personal beliefs or values. These beliefs and training often dictating their response to behavioral expectations and compliance (e.g., religion), it becomes hard for behavioral issues to be addressed as part of the IEP. In fact, unless aggressive or combative behavior occurs in a school setting, many behavioral issues are not truly addressed. Even more complicated is that antecedents are not discovered to help limit the issues or frequency of behaviors. While schools do try to avoid this when looking at whether grades are satisfactory, it should be noted that the Supreme Court in *Endrew F. v. Douglas County School District* (2017) has noted that grades alone should not be a consideration on aid and support provided through a student's IEP, and it represents a "de minimis" approach. While a student is not promised the best of anything under IDEA, specific and appropriate support to increase student success to their potential should be offered, including if this student is making successful and/or average grades.

Common Tendencies

Numerous behavioral tendencies can be associated with psychological disorders and EDs as well as behavior from learning disabilities. The few mentioned below are common and meant to serve as illustrations for understanding how the tendencies may impact life and school for an individual.

Hyperactivity

The concept of **hyperactivity** relates to a condition of abnormal or extreme motor activity and disruptive behavior. It often occurs constantly and in social situations where it is not appropriate. It is very common for individuals who are struggling with hyperactivity to show motor excess in constantly moving or having their feet or hands tapping or twitching. They may struggle to stay in a normal seated position and instead may be seen moving their core body in different positions every few seconds.[6] They may have visual and auditory stimulation issues that cause them to make their hands drum loudly or clap at times or make consistent and odd sounds with their mouth that are out of place and may lead to the feeling that they annoy others. It isn't uncommon that hyperactivity also seems to cause excessive talking and social interaction. This means they may miss social cues and talk to individuals without end and may not even let the other person engage in conversation with them. Additional complications can be seen in the inability to complete tasks, being unable to wait a turn, participating in risky behavior without thought of the outcomes, and consistently interrupting others in separate conversations. Individuals often know these behaviors may irritate others and creates increased anxiety and depression in those exhibiting them when in social situations.[7]

Task Refusal

While it is not recommended to focus on mere compliance in dealing with behavior, it is situationally an issue at times. There has to be a recognition that some tasks must be handled, this often is seen when safety becomes an issue or eventually schoolwork needs to be completed. An example could be an instance in which an individual physically and/or verbally refuses to follow an instruction or complete a task. This could be simply and repeatedly saying no, this could also result in them being verbally aggressive in saying no or just tossing items from a table to the floor as an action of meaning "no." This can be seen when they refuse instructions and redirections and when they are potentially being disruptive in general as a response to the request being made of them.

Transition Issues

Transition is defined as a shift from one state of being or moving from one task to another. Individuals with behavior or psychological disturbances may struggle with a change from one task or expectation to another. This could be for a variety of reasons. It may be that things are changing often and the person is feeling uncomfortable, or it could be they are doing something they like to do and do not want to move on to something else even if they know that the change or the need to switch tasks is going to occur. This can also happen merely from being in a task or situation of comfort and being asked to try something new or are put into what they feel is an uncomfortable situation. An example could be a student being asked to move on from their computer class to their next class, which is math. However, due to how much they enjoy computers, or potentially hate math, they begin to react with maladaptive behavior.

High Distractibility Versus Inattention

A highly referenced tendency, especially with those who have ADHD, is high distractibility and inattention. While similar, they are not the same thing. **High distractibility** is usually a lapse in one's ability to concentrate on a stimulus or task due to immediately refocusing on a new or meaningful stimuli. This might be a conversation that is interrupted when an individual notices a cat that looks like theirs or an idea based on a word someone says, causing them to focus solely on a side story that occurred last week. **Inattentiveness** is the inability to direct and sustain attention, not because there are other stimuli occurring, but because the individual cannot maintain focus on the current stimuli regardless. Thereby, they usually are only able to spend a limited amount of time on an item or project.

Cognitive Distortions

A concept that is common in individuals struggling with psychological and behavioral issues is a negative **mindset** or established set of values or attitudes that are a frame of view in which we filter our experiences. These can create negative view points in which we intentionally or unintentionally perceive the world around us and behave in response to these skewed viewpoints, commonly known as **cognitive distortions**. While the number of recognized cognitive distortions is quite a lot, there are some common view points that appear often. Examples include:

- *polarized thinking*, assuming everything is black-or-white and that everything only falls into extreme categories of either/or, where the world does not have gray areas;
- *mind reading*, assuming we know what someone was thinking or their intentions when they said something or engaged in a behavior and often ignore social context clues;
- *emotional reasoning*, where we assume our emotional feelings are fact, for example, if we feel like a failure that must mean it is true;
- *heaven's reward fallacy*, that we assume we are suffering and need to suffer because our benefits and rewards are delayed for it; and
- *labeling*, that an individual will assign judgment to oneself and others based on a single negative incident. Instead of taking the time to identify that a mistake was made, a label is created and inflated based on one mistake.

It needs to be clear that cognitive distortions are symptoms of psychological issues and should not be mistaken for, or replace, a diagnosis like depression or bipolar disorder.

Causes of Psychological and Behavioral Issues

In both psychological and behavioral issues, and specifically maladaptive behavior, it can be hard to identify causes without extensive time with the participant in a therapy setting. Our behavior, and our ideas on acceptable behavior, are shaped for a number of reasons. It can be chemical and electrical issues in the brain, it can be learned from individuals who have served as role models, or it can develop as a response to actions or events around us or expectations placed on the society we grew up in. However, it is worth noting that many of these issues are driven by one simple fact, and that is **expectations versus reality**. What individuals expect to happen and then what actually occurs may not be the same and serves to provide a dissonance in our perceived, and usually preferred, version of reality. This continued friction often leads to frustration, but most individuals tend to adapt around it in their behavior to continue with their plans at the time. Some are not able to adapt, and this may lead to complications in acceptable behavioral responses.

Congenital

Most congenital issues are related to biological and physiological functions within the brain and are considered to have a potentially strong genetic relationship between one or both parents. It must be clear though that there does not have to be a hereditary link for a biological development in behavioral or psychological disorders. The most common cause in a congenital development tends to be an alteration in the development and function of **neurotransmitters**. Neurotransmitters are chemicals that allow various neurons to communicate with each other throughout the body. An example of this can be seen with dopamine, which is believed to be tied to the reward-inducing sections of the brain, creating positive responses when more dopamine is available.

Environmental Dissonance

Our broader environment may play an extreme role in how we react with and handle our behavior. This can be developed from role models, or adapting to the expectations around our social and family environments. *Family* can play a major role in creating expectations. At times, this can be just because individuals experience their first reaction, stimuli, and

Even a simple visit to a doctor or other professional can be a struggle when a child cannot contain hyperactive behavior.

feedback to what is at home. The most common issues that tend to cause dissonance in behavior is when there is a complication already in the home, which can be related to divorce, physical abuse, and toxic parental behaviors, and research also seems to indicate that when these complications are present alongside a psychological or behavioral disability, results are far more severe. *School* plays a larger role than many realize due to the amount of time in our formative years that we are present at school. With many children spending 6–8 hours a day and 5 days a week in school, developing and shaping behavior there matters. Additionally, research supports that school represents one of our strongest connections to social development, regardless if a parent wants it to be or not.[39] However, schools often continue to insist that children must engage in compliance and that children's behavior issues are due to them not being used to stricter, often choosing the term "structured," environments. As we have seen above, most state education agencies denote the need for teaching behaviors at school as part of health components.[39] Without developing consistent plans to handle behavior to begin with, proper training on behavioral understanding, and certainly knowledge of behavioral disabilities, schools can often be a hinderance in social and behavioral development. This most often occurs due to inconsistent expectations on students from class to class, lack of acknowledgment, and lack of respect of individual feelings and needs or underdevelopment of behavioral plans or reinforcement. Often, poor models exist, where students are expected to behave in certain ways, but instructors and administrators do not explain the purpose of expected behavior, they merely use their structurally built-in power to create compliance. *Society or Culture* also plays a role in creating expectations, especially when they are rooted in the home and then supported outside the home in a community. Even more complex, this is often the key area for creation of value, which is what individuals hold in high regard as things that cannot be deviated from. These foundational beliefs can come in many forms, they can be based on beliefs and/or religion, they can be due to being raised in a certain ethnic culture, and they can also occur by regional values in an area in which one grows up. Typically, this comes into conflict because the values learned and held may be different, in minority to, or even in conflict to, those beliefs surrounding them now in their current situation. Furthermore, values held by people often tend to create forms of bias and prejudiced behavior, even unintentionally, if not reflected on and adjusted for. Added to that, some societal or cultural groups also create expectations and take pride in being in the minority, reward increasing the conflict, and maladapted behavior becomes celebrated as some form of rebellion. The most common issue though is that expectations to behave one way are at conflict with or different than the location or area one is at and the unknown or lack of ability to meet the expectation may result in behavioral issues; this is often seen when children come to school for the first time when they have been used to being at home.

Developed Apathy

While there are some congenital reasons apathy may develop in individuals, the most common one is usually due to consistent correction because of failure to meet expectations. **Apathy** is described as a lack of interest, enthusiasm, and/or concern and is often seen through diminished motivation and reduced goal-directed behavior as well as declining emotional responsiveness.[8] This can be due to the individual having expectations of their own that they are not meeting. An example could be that they expect that they will excel at a physical task and they find they are not able to (especially in competitive environments such as sports). This can also be due to the expectations that others place on them and that they are failing to meet, and over time, they begin to feel a lack of interest or enthusiasm for the task or purpose of the task. An example may be an individual failing to perform a free throw correctly several times, and constantly receiving negative feedback; over time, this continues to contribute to declining motivation and emotional responsiveness. Severe apathy can lead to complications in even trying to modify behavior since many management strategies in the end require the participant to choose to engage. This may require the individual to develop a willingness to participate through consistent positive reinforcement and engaging actions before being able to consider behavioral management and shaping techniques, overall focusing first on developing an individual's self-worth and self-confidence.

UNDERSTANDING SPECIFIC DISORDERS AND DISABILITIES

This chapter covers a large collection of disorders and disabilities all of which relate to psychology in one form or another. Specifically, this chapter addresses the behaviors that are resultant of the relevant

Feeling overwhelmed is often the first sign to engage in self-care to avoid feelings of anxiety and depression.

diseases and disorders mentioned below. As noted previously, these can be caused by a large variety of factors and may be congenital or adventitious, and individuals may only struggle with one of these or multiple diagnoses at the same time. The key point is that the disorders themselves are vast and it is recommended that a practitioner never assume about what little they know on it regarding their client/student/patient/athlete. Additionally, the lack of awareness and individual beliefs from clients, practitioners, medical staff, and school staff can also leave many issues unidentified and unresolved.

Anxiety

While often referred to as a single diagnosis, anxiety disorders refer to a vast group of illnesses that surround General Anxiety Disorder (GAD), OCD, Post-Traumatic Stress Disorder (PTSD), Panic Disorders, Social Anxiety, and various phobias. It needs to be stressed that anxiety and its various components do affect people differently, both psychologically and physiologically, and it is recommended to not treat all people who have anxiety the same way. This includes a practitioner with anxiety; while empathy is important, there should not be an assumption that it is relatable to the same traits or outcomes. Why bring this up? Currently, it is estimated that around 19% of adults in the United States have had some form of anxiety in the past year.[10] It is also considered one of the most untreated and undiagnosed disorders among health conditions.[11] When an individual is having an acute bout of anxiety, they may physiologically feel the effects of the body entering flight-or-fight mode and experience one or multiple of the following: tachycardia, muscle tension or weakness, nausea, increased blood pressure, perspiration, chest pain, dizziness, or shortness of breath. Most treatments use therapy methods listed later in this chapter and can include Cognitive Behavioral Therapy (CBT) or similar awareness methods. While physical exercise is recommended to improve neurotransmitters, pharmaceuticals tend to be the primary initial response, especially since response to exercise interventions take time for overall benefits.

Depression/Major Depressive Disorder/ Persistent Depressive Disorder

A point of clarification needs to be made when discussing depression at large, which is that depression will be experienced by everyone at some point. This requires a distinction between the depression people are expected to feel when extremely traumatic things happen in life, like the loss of a job or a loved one and the development of clinical depression. However, when this becomes a chronic condition and interferes with life activities for an extended period of time or a medical issue has occurred from a car accident or a psychological dissonance from a decrease in neurotransmitters, for example, it becomes clinical depression. This is when it is classified as **Major Depressive Disorder (MDD),** and it is one of the leading causes of disability in the United States and the world.[11] It is also considered one of the overall global burdens of disease, with women affected more than men worldwide.[9] It is believed that one in five adults suffers from MDD, and potentially 16% of adults in the United States will exhibit the symptoms listed in *DSM-5*: significant weight loss or gain, fatigue or loss of energy, feeling guilt or worthlessness, inability to think or concentrate, altering sleep patterns, motor agitation, and/or continued thoughts on death or suicide. To qualify, an individual must have five of the symptoms listed in the *DSM-5* that last consistently for 2 weeks or more.

While previously called dysthymia in previous DSM editions, **Persistent Depressive Disorder (PDD)** is considered a chronic depression that has less severe mood points but has a continued feeling of lower mood and energy. It is often characterized by a low appetite, sleep disturbances, and being consistently tired. This can result in feeling very irritable, experiencing increased anxiety and stress, and/or having a lack of pleasure and enjoyment in most things or for very long. While the symptoms are less severe than MDD, most recommendations for prevention and management are the same.

Emotional Disturbance

The term **Emotional Disturbance** is complicated to clearly defining ages, qualifications and diagnoses in what qualifies under this disorder. While it is a categorization under IDEA, it is very broad and leads to some confusion on what management tools can be used under emotional disturbance. Somtimes this allows sometimes allows schools to acknowledge a disability, but not utilize appropriate resources since there is less federal guidance. Therefore, IDEA defines it under the following broad criteria: (1) inability to learn that is not explained by intellectual, sensory, or health factors; (2) inability to maintain satisfactory relationships with peers and teachers; (3) having inappropriate types of behavior or feelings under normal circumstances; (4) a general pervasive mood of feeling unhappy or depressed; (5) a predisposition to develop physical symptoms or fears related to personal, home, or school issues.[12] Causes can range from factors that are related to diet, stress, home and family issues, heredity, and undefined brain disorders.[13] The most common tendencies looked at to determine if there is a potential for qualifying under ED are severe hyperactivity, aggression, withdrawals (socially), immaturity (inappropriate social skills), and noted learning difficulties. This may also lead to increased anxiety, motor excess, mood swings, and distorted thinking. **Distorted thinking** refers to the concept of cognitive distortions, which are habitual ways of thinking that recreate negative, inaccurate, and biased thoughts, as mentioned above. While a multitude of disabilities or psychological maladaptive behaviors might fall under the umbrella term ED, most educational considerations tend to place the following under this diagnosis:

- anxiety disorders
- bipolar disorder
- conduct disorders
- eating disorders
- OCD
- psychotic disorders.[13]

Bipolar Disorder

Known as a manic-depressive illness, individuals with bipolar disorder experience manic emotional shifts for days or weeks where a mood, energy, or behavior might change drastically. This is usually so extreme that they are unable to engage in their daily living activities, which interferes with home, work, or family life. It is often marked by extreme moments of euphoria, compulsivity, and hyperactivity to severe emotions of helplessness, anxiety, and exhaustion. It is very common for individuals to experience disruption of sleep, energy, and behavioral changes during these manic episodes. In some cases, they may even behave irrationally and engage in dangerous activities through impulsive choices. This can be very confusing from an outsider's perspective because the moments that are good and not manic in nature seem to be normalized, but since this can change without warning, it becomes risky to assume an individual will remain that way. While some therapies are beneficial and highly recommended to help identify the issues or triggers that might lead to a manic episode, truly pharmaceutical drug therapy is the chief option to balance the phases as much as possible. One change in the *DSM-5* from previous editions is that minors often are now classified not under bipolar but under **Disruptive Mood Dysregulation Disorder (DMDD)**. As a distinction, DMDD is noted as a childhood condition that results in anger, consistent irritability, and common and intense outbursts, but, unlike bipolar disorder, there are no manic phases and psychotic symptoms are rare.[14,15]

Schizophrenia

Schizophrenia is a disorder that falls under ED and a schizophrenic is diagnosed as a person who interprets reality abnormally. This can result in a collection of disordered thinking, delusions, and hallucinations that create altered behavior so prevalent that it interferes with daily activities and function. While a direct cause of schizophrenia is not known or understood, it is believed that some combination of genetics, environment, along with brain chemistry and/or structure deviation may intersect to cause it to develop.[17] This can result in complications with disorganized thinking and cognitive focus. It is common for them to hear voices, struggle with incoherent speech, interact with delusions, and suppress their emotional responses. There is no cure for schizophrenia, merely management of symptoms, and it is a chronic illness. In some cases, it can become progressively more debilitating, especially in terms of cognitive organization. Additionally, individuals with schizophrenia also struggle with sleep complications and are commonly diagnosed with Excessive Daytime Sleepiness (EDS), which interferes with remaining alert and awake during the day, leading to further complications in cognitive function.[16,17]

Schizophrenia symptoms.

Behavioral outcomes that can result from schizophrenia are social isolation, compulsive behavior, hostility/agitation, and potential self-harm. Mood developments can also occur and change, with feelings moving between depression, detachment, apathy, anger, anxiety, and manic mood changes. Finally, speech can alter to become rapid and frenzied or it may become unorganized and incoherent. They may develop **circumstantial speech**, where unwarranted and highly unrelated/inappropriate details are part of speech, and this can even be evident in their writing.[18]

Obsessive-Compulsive Disorder (OCD)

Overall, **OCD** is a chronic and consistent irrepressible desire or fixation that involves engages in obsessive thoughts and/or compulsive behaviors. Often, they are fixations that require the individual to perform an action or activity over and over again. Many of these behaviors or thoughts may be unwanted, but to not perform or engage in them creates anxiety, to the point it is physiologically or psychologically distressing. This compulsion is usually strong enough that it might interrupt a person's daily life activities, forcing them to interrupt the activities until the compulsion is met. Examples of categories of OCD behavior include the following:

- *Contamination/Cleaning*: This involves a deep fear of germs contaminating hands, or locations, things that are touched and therefore fanatically cleaning them repeatedly to get rid of the germs.
- *Checking*: usually to reassure oneself; for example (1) repeatedly checking that the doors are locked or that the stove is turned off or (2) checking on emotions, an example could be asking a friend again and again inside a short time frame if they are angry at you, even if there is no rationale for them to be so.
- *Symmetry and Arranging* is a fixation on the position and arrangement of objects because the objects are uncomfortable to the point of being psychologically upsetting.
- *Intrusive Thoughts, Rumination, or Reassurance* are the feelings of anxiety psychologically and feelings of negative thoughts or mindset tied to specific items. This can relate to people, location, or an item. Individuals may have such strong responses that they will make sure to avoid these things to prevent the physiological or psychological response.
- *Hoarding* is a condition that involves excessively acquiring items and either creating clutter out of specific items being hoarded or generally collecting a multitude of things.[18]

Attention-Deficit/Hyperactivity Disorder

While children as a whole may struggle with being able to maintain their attention for long periods of time, and also adults if it is something they are not interested in, the intensity and continued effects of this with other symptoms over a long period of time might be indicative of ADHD. By far, it is the most common neurodevelopmental disorder among children, and they do not grow out of it (which unfortunately often is said will happen when they become more mature).

Common tendencies may include

- fidgeting or moving around a lot,
- impulsive or risky behavior and inability to resist temptation,
- inability to wait or take turns,
- struggling with adapting to or working with others,
- often losing things or unable to keep up with a list,
- continuous talking, and
- making clumsy movements or easy mistakes on tasks.[19]

Currently, there are three categories for ADHD: First is **Inattentive Presentation** where a person may struggle to finish a task and usually is easily distracted and forgets to complete daily routines or easy tasks. Second, **Hyperactive-Impulsive Presentation** is where individuals seemingly talk continuously and fidget often throughout the day. People who tend to exhibit this often feel extremely twitchy, are impulsive, and experience constant interruptions. Individuals often tend to experience higher rates of injury due to impulsive behavior. Last is **Combined Presentation**, which represents an individual who would exhibit both of the previous presentation types. Therefore, they may struggle with the inability to hold attention while also exhibiting hyperactivity. It is extremely common for those with ADHD to be diagnosed with anxiety, sleep disturbances, depression, as well as learning disturbances. Causes of ADHD are broad in their categorization, but research correlated to the disability tends to connect it to genetics, environmental complications, fetal alcohol syndrome, and premature birth.[19] Diagnosing is usually complicated to a degree because there is no such thing as a standard singular test for ADHD. Usually, multiple tests are required to rule out sensory information, learning disabilities specifically, and the diagnosis items mentioned above.[20]

Oppositional Defiant Disorder

Occasionally, individuals may exhibit, or develop, a pattern of anger, defiance, irritability and outright arguing or physical aggression, usually toward adults or authority figures. This can even create issues of vindictiveness, where actions of maliciousness, taunting, and revenge can be developed if it is left unaddressed. This can usually be seen clearly in a frequency of at least four specific behaviors out of

- refusing tasks/or complying with requests,
- losing one's temper,
- arguing with adults or authority figures,
- blaming others for their mistakes,
- being spiteful and saying hateful things, and
- easily annoyed or irritated over how specific things have to be done.[20]

As an individual becomes older, this may become more severe and will be labeled as a Conduct Disorder. Oppositional defiant disorder (ODD) is typically associated and coexists with other disabilities, such as ADHD, depression, or autism. Under IDEA, an ODD diagnosis is not grounds for eligibility itself, but it can be included in conjunction with another disability for eligibility. Most of the known causes of ODD seem to be related to genetics, where neurobiological issues have affected the way the brain functions or can be related to the environment where parenting or authority figures have inadvertently exacerbated an issue or even created it through inconsistent discipline, abuse, or neglect. ODD is often characterized into mild (where symptoms seem to only appear in one setting), moderate (where symptoms can be seen in two separate settings), or severe (where symptoms occur in three or more settings).[21] When the above behaviors appear and multiple appropriate behavior strategies/plans have been enacted and failed to progress toward positive behavior, it might be time to consider this as a diagnosis. Treatment will usually involve a multitude of behavioral and emotional awareness therapy sessions, parent and teacher training, and additional social skills training.[22]

Learning Disabilities

A person who is diagnosed with a learning disability is typically an individual with average or above average intelligence, but they have a specific disorder that inhibits their learning capability, usually through a specific sensory feedback problem that affects academic learning. According to the *DSM-5*, a learning disability is still considered a neurodevelopmental disorder, and it is common that they may perform academically fine in some "areas" and it feels sudden that they are not performing well in other areas depending on the specific learning disability. Unfortunately, early intervention can be hard to diagnose depending on the disability until an individual starts formal education. Individuals who have learning disabilities often go undetected since they can easily accomplish early education expectations, but content requiring more study time eventually becomes harder to keep up with.[23,24] The following are the more common learning disabilities, what they affect, and related complications that may come with them:

- **Dyslexia** refers to difficulty in reading and usually additional issues in regard to writing, spelling words, and speaking and pronunciation.

- **Dyscalculia** refers to difficulty in math and is usually demonstrated by an individual having trouble doing math problems, understanding time, or using money.

- **Dysgraphia** refers to difficulty with writing, and clear problems with handwriting, spelling, and organizing ideas.

- **Dyspraxia (Sensory Integration Disorder)** is a difficulty with fine motor skills. Common problems with hand–eye coordination, balance, and manual dexterity are usually present.

- **Dysphasia/Aphasia** refers to difficulty with language. Related complications in understanding spoken language and poor reading comprehension have been connected.

- **Auditory Processing Disorder** refers to difficulty in hearing differences between sounds. Problems with reading, comprehension, and language are present.

- **Visual Processing Disorder** refers to a difficulty interpreting visual information and relates to problems with reading, math, maps, charts, symbols, and pictures.

Learning disorders are often a result of family history and also prenatal and neonatal risks, like poor growth, premature birth, and alcohol/drug use during pregnancy. Additionally, exposure to psychological and physical trauma may be related to increased learning disabilities. Environmental exposures to toxins and poor water quality have also been associated with an increased probability of learning disabilities.[25]

APPROACHES TO MANAGING PSYCHOLOGICAL/BEHAVIORAL ISSUES

Various approaches have been developed on managing individuals and behavior; just as the various causes of behavior can differ, the approaches can diverge to better meet unique behavior needs. This concept is important so that individuals are not treated from the assumption of universal behavior control, although this is very common in homes and schools. The concept of reaching compliance of behavior in the fastest way possible is often the consideration of parents, teachers, and administrators. Often, this has led to a focus on quick solutions to gain compliance and to an assumption that a pharmaceutical resolution found in the biogenic approach is best. Instead, behavior management should be tailored to the type of maladaptive behavior and the rationale for the behavioral antecedent. Keep in mind, multiple approaches could be used at one time to address behavioral issues.

Humanistic Approach

The humanistic approach is grounded in the concepts of self-actualization theory under Abraham Maslow's Hierarchy of Needs. It focuses on basic human needs climbing up to becoming psychological essentials. It contains five categories: physiological needs (shelter, food, etc.), safety (employment, healthcare, etc.), belongingness (to a group, connectedness, friends, and family), self-esteem (respect, status, recognition), and self-actualization. Self-actualization is an emphasis on truly attempting to be the best one can potentially be. While many will be very supportive of the first two categories of the hierarchy, the third is often a societal struggle and the fourth and fifth are problematic in developing if not intentionally worked on. This requires taking the time to move beyond compliance expectation to the development of "why" a certain behavior or reaction should occur. This becomes about understanding and fostering an emerging individualistic mindset that begins to understand what their potential is and striving to achieve it. This means understanding and working through maladaptive behavior and creating adaptive interactions with others. This is essential as a component for physical movement and individuals with disabilities, as many drop their physical movement over time due to believing they are not capable.

Ecological Approach

The premise of the ecological approach is that maladaptive behavior occurs due to disruptions in an individual's environment or social structures. Essentially, some trait of the individual reacts to an environmental stimulus, and the environment further reacts to the individual, and this irritates the individual more. It denotes that the environment itself is also responsible for the maladaptive behavior now occurring in the individual, many of these instances are due to social interactions. An example could be a student who is not wanting to participate with the class in an activity and is telling their teacher no, but the teacher forces them to participate by calling on them, and the student reacts with anger and begins to yell at the teacher. An important aspect of this approach is to understand and be able to define a behavior to the location or environment that it might only occur in. This is essential for understanding the antecedents of the behavior. In school settings, a Functional Behavior Assessment (FBA) becomes key in using assessments to determine "why" a behavior is caused in certain environments and how it might be continuing to be agitated, as well as mitigated. Additional information that assists in looking at ecological issues to behavior is knowing if there are behavior expectations and how those are clearly being explained to individuals in that specific setting. Often changes and understanding behavioral expectations leads into developing interventions to meet both initial complications, and additional behavioral conflicts as friction occurs between the individual and the environment.

Biogenic Approach

This approach focuses on the neurophysiological dysfunction issues and relevant signs and symptoms. Specifically, the idea is to isolate identified behavioral traits (e.g., hyperactivity, impulsiveness, extreme emotions, etc.). It may also note motor or academic issues that arise, like problems in balance or gait, as well as learning comprehension issues or speech. Biogenics focuses often on the potential physiological causes of one's behavior and the relationship to the central nervous system. This leads to a more medical-oriented approach in solutions. Pharmaceutical management of many of the issues plays a large role and is often used to try to minimize short attention spans, hyperactivity, impulsiveness, mood, etc. It is worth mentioning that in terms of school-aged children, increasingly the volume of mitigating medication is being prescribed more than ever before.[26] While medication may help in more extreme circumstances, it does nothing to develop adaptations of behavior or assist in controlling reactions to antecedents that can be found in appropriate therapy and behavioral interventions. It is also worth noting that schools have no legal authority, or right, to consider or impose pharmaceutical treatments over individuals. It is beyond their scope and should remain between the medical professional and guardians. It should have no bearing on determining if a person is legally qualified under ADA, Section 504, and IDEA.

Antidepressants are often used to alleviate depression, but they also have been used to help control ritualist and self-harming behaviors. They are frequently used in those with ADHD and/or OCD diagnoses for curbing many impulsive behaviors but are also noted for increased side effects of anxiety, sleepiness, decreased mental acuity, sleep disturbance, etc. Practitioners working with individuals on these medications should be aware of the specific medication an individual may be taking and the ramifications it could have on motor movement or learning skills.

Stimulants are extremely common in individuals diagnosed with ADHD. While it may seem unusual to treat a person who struggles with impulsiveness, hyperactivity, and distractibility with a stimulant, this works due to it increasing the number of neurotransmitters available (dopamine, serotonin, and norepinephrine), thereby increasing the capability of memory, attention, and cognition for the individual. Common drugs found on the market are Ritalin, Focalin, and Concerta (drugs may be short or long acting based on design). Practitioners should be aware of two major issues that occur with stimulants. The first is that developing the dose and timing the dosing correctly can take time to figure out between the individual, their guardians, and the medical provider. This can take days, weeks, or even months as there is usually a balancing of side effects across different drugs, age, weight, metabolism, and dosage. The second consideration is that some individuals tend to experience an effect called "rebounding" that occurs after taking a stimulant. An example might be taking the stimulant in the morning and it helps with attention and impulsivity throughout much of the day, but when it wears off, the individual experiences a rush and increased impulsivity issues and lack of focus due to it all coming back at once. If rebounding is an issue, it is one of the several things that takes a lot of work to balance when trying to time medications. Individuals who start stimulants young also tend to grow out of their dosages at different rates and may require an adjusted dosage on a regular basis. In addition to the issues of finding a fitting dose, side effects may be increased anxiety, weight loss, suppressed appetite, irritability, and disruptive sleep.

Neuroleptics, also known as tranquilizers, are often used to control extreme hyperactive, aggressive, and self-injury inclinations. These drugs are widely used in individuals with disabilities to alter mood, perception, and behaviors. Additionally, they are used to control psychotic behavior (e.g., schizophrenia) that results in the potential for delusions, hallucinations, extreme agitation, and combativeness. It is worth mentioning that if an individual is on neuroleptics, it should not imply that it is for an extreme issue, they can be categorially placed in major or minor categories, with dosages ranging extensively, as well as the variety of their treatment uses. Minor neuroleptics are often used to treat mild anxiety and tension. Major neuroleptics, which are considered antipsychotics, are used to treat major psychological issues. Side effects of using neuroleptics tend to be fatigue, decreased mental acuity, lethargy, and vertigo.

Psychodynamic Approach

Instead of a single theory behind an approach, this approach utilizes multiple theories to provide intervention options. The idea is to focus on the psychological dysfunction that is currently occurring. Its emphasis is on the socioemotional functions occurring and learning to work with the individual but not accepting their maladaptive behavior. This requires a close self-reflection process to understand their own emotions and how those emotions react with others. This is usually identified through individual interviews and observations utilizing psychoanalysis (reviewing the interaction of conscious and unconscious elements in the mind) and followed up with psychotherapy (therapy based on based on regular personal interaction to help a person change behavior). It should be noted this is more common in areas that interact with psychiatry, such as hospital settings, and unfortunately it is not near as common in schools or other areas where untreated psychological issues may result in complex anxiety and depression forming. Considerations about this approach to keep in mind are that it is extremely expensive and time consuming and provides interventions that are really long-term therapy plans. This may not demonstrate how to deal with a situation where someone engages in task refusal in a time-sensitive and group setting (like a classroom).

Psychoeducational Approach

This approach considers that the maladaptive behavior occurring is due to conflict resulting from, or coping with, the surrounding environment. This approach draws attention to the fact that the behavior, and any related educational lapse, can be corrected through a balance of the students' needs from a cognitive and psychosocial need. This can be done by preparing an individual's expectations and understanding of transitions from one location to another, whether from home to school, or a quiet home setting to a busy social setting. Especially in younger children, they may not realize why they have differing behavior in diverse locations, which requires creating awareness of the various emotions that may develop due to this. Unlike the psychodynamic approach, which tends to take a longer view of creating solutions in general transitions, the psychoeducational approach tends to be more applied and focuses on the current situation in front of the individual. Instead of trying to explain an issue and why a behavior occurs, it instead focuses on the individual's self-esteem and their interaction with peers and authority, especially since anxiety in these situations may relate to many of the behaviors. It filters those interactions and emotions to identify how the individual feels and then how to control or adapt those emotions. A common example would be CBT where the individual is allowed to recognize their own emotions and triggers and then the behavior symptoms are reduced by training themselves or others to intervene with breathing techniques, taking time to be calm and process emotions, and provide reinforcements. However, this approach also allows for a reduction of potential triggers by acknowledging them and allowing techniques to naturally reduce potential behavioral anxiety through modeling, clear expectations on behavior, and developing positive intrinsic rewards.

SPECIFIC ISSUES WITH MOTOR MOVEMENT

Movement is affected for many mental illnesses and behavior disorders, but the exact causes are not always known, nor is every person affected the same way. Our understanding of the brain and neuroscience is extremely finite and since the disorders and disabilities being discussed are dealing with the brain, there is a relationship of some form. An example could be seen in a study that demonstrated 28% of individuals with schizophrenia showed dyskinesia, an impairment, or abnormal voluntary movement.[27] In individuals with ADHD, a marked decline in fine motor skills may be prevalent.[28] In clients with bipolar disorder, concerns exist over motor skills declining not just because of the disorder but also from the drugs commonly used, and skills like force scaling (the ability to adjust the needed exertion of force on an object) could be affected.[29] Those with learning disabilities commonly experience a struggle in both gross and fine motor skills. Gross motor skills may be directly tied to inhibitions of learning, but fine motor skills tend to be a struggle for unknown reasons or task avoidance like writing, and occupational therapy is often recommended if diagnosed at an early age.

SPECIFIC MODALITIES
Applied Behavior Analysis Therapy

The idea behind applied behavior analysis therapy (ABA) is to focus on understanding and improving behavior. ABA is considered a scientific approach to addressing environmental variables that influence critical, socially significant behavior. Additionally, it uses data collected from observations to target specific behaviors by developing objective description, measurement options, and experimentation to create relationships between interventions and behavior improvements. ABA puts heavy emphasis on specific items, with antecedents, stimulus, behavior and behavior response class (classification of behavior occurring), environments, and consequences. These items are classified together and used to create an intervention plan for positive behavior change, oftentimes challenging and compelling a specific behavior to teach management and mitigation techniques.[40] An example could be a young child in a sport who tends to display anger when they perceive a child on the opposing team looking at, or believe they are "staring" at, them and cannot be

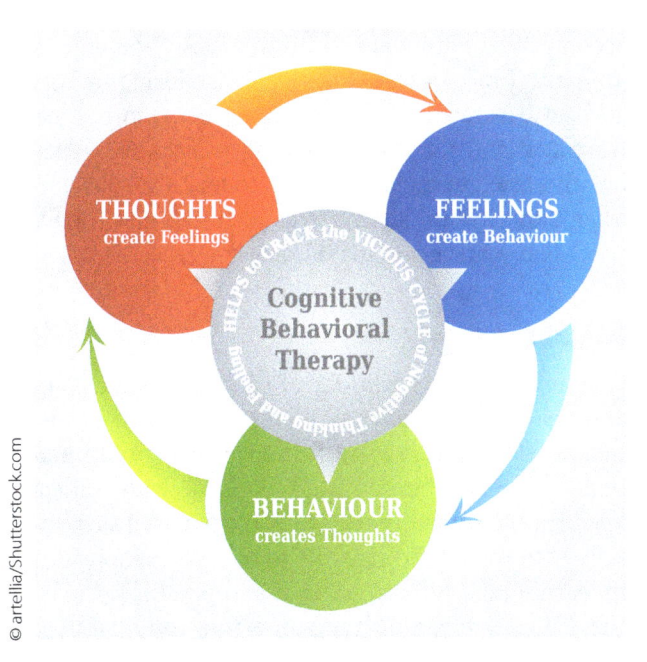

CBT Cycle.

convinced otherwise. An ABA therapist acknowledges that the child feels this way, and that it doesn't matter if the staring is actually occurring or not. Instead they might intentionally stare, or have a peer stare, causing behavioral irritation, and begin to have the child identify and work on controlling their emotional and physical responses to the perceived staring. This will eventually allow the child to learn to focus on the actual sports through management techniques.

Cognitive Behavior Therapy

CBT specifically looks into psychosocial issues and interventions to improve ways of thinking and mindsets. This is done by spending time in therapy situations that address emotions, negative ways of thinking, and engaging in unhealthy behaviors. It emphasizes changing an individual thinking pattern to help with coping in transitions, anxiety-oriented situations, interpersonal conflict, and mitigating cognitive distortions. CBT emphasizes the progress that is developed by the individual under the guidance of a therapist. At the heart of the therapy, the individual does much of the recognition and application. While not always called CBT, it serves as the basis or adjacent modality to other known therapies. An example could be seen in dialectic behavior therapy used for borderline personality disorders, prolonged exposure used for PTSD.

Trauma-Informed Care Approach

Trauma-Informed Care (TIC) is the recognition that trauma can have long-lasting effects, especially emotionally, psychologically, and neurologically, and this can lead to complications in social, behavioral, and biological issues. It should not be surprising that with a strong psychosocial component, and a poor historic view of psychological healthcare, many with behavioral maladaptive complications have experienced trauma caused by or in response to their behavior maladaptation. This approach takes the idea that the practitioner is not just the expert in a therapy situation, but they are also a partner, they work WITH the individual through the recovery processes. There are three major elements to a TIC approach: (1) realizing the prevalence of trauma; (2) recognizing how trauma affects all in a school, program, employment; and (3) putting this knowledge into active practice. This concept of recognizing the causes of harm and reducing further harm is done through five guiding principles.

Safety is ensured by developing a situation where trauma risks feel reduced by creating an area for emotional and physical safety. *Trustworthiness* is created through clear boundaries and expectations so that treatment and services are not surprises or unknown when used. *Choices* help create enablement by allowing the client to participate in having options for treatment, like choosing between two exercises that will accomplish the same motor therapy goals. *Collaboration* puts emphasis on the coworking relationship between the practitioner and the client that uses empathy and intuition between the two to move forward. *Empowerment* allows clients to build on existing strengths, having them recognize what they have accomplished toward their goals and continue to shape their progressive momentum. This assists in creating resilience and more importantly hope that physical and behavioral goal attainment is possible.[30]

Teaching Personal and Social Responsibility Model

Designed by Dr. Don Hellison in 1995, Teaching Personal and Social Responsibility (TPSR) is an ethical-oriented theory model in which individuals are viewed as accountable for fulfilling their civic duty, and the actions of an individual must benefit the whole community in which they are involved (e.g., classroom, job, etc.). This is accomplished by giving them increasing amounts of responsibility and by carefully shifting a significant portion of decision-making responsibilities to them. Additionally, the practitioner allows the client to take more responsibility for their actions and continuing to teach them to be concerned about the rights, feelings, and needs of others. In this model, creating effort and self-direction become critical for being able to respect others' feelings and rights. This creates an informal progression of levels or goals designed by the TPSR model that may help practitioners and clients become aware of their behaviors and to focus their efforts as they move toward desired outcomes. In this model, there are five levels of responsibility: (1) *Respect*, recognizing one's own behavior and respecting the feelings and rights of others; (2) *Participation and Effort*, whereby clients are encouraged to explore the connection between effort and outcomes, accept challenges, and arrive at a personal definition of success; (3) *Self-Direction*, where clients assume increased responsibility for their work and actions; they are able to work more independently on tasks. Clients also learn to identify their own specific needs and interests, set their own personal goals, and create related tasks for achieving them. Additionally, they also learn to develop measurement and evaluation of their progress; (4) *Caring and Helping*, the client develops interpersonal skills and learns to reach beyond themselves to show support, concern, and compassion to others without expectation of anything in return; (5) *Integration Beyond the Learning Environment* means that a change of context or setting does not reduce the tools and skills learned in the responsibility model.[31]

Social Stories

The use of social stories was created by Carol Gray in the 1990s for individuals with Autism Spectrum Disorder. However, they have been shown to be beneficial with individuals who struggle with behavioral or psychological issues as they pertain to work with others or in social situations. Social stories are created narratives to assist in increasing appropriate social behaviors. These social stories are usually designed to be visual and may differ for each social situation provided. They often give specific step-by-step information for that social circumstance. Most social stories are written in a child's voice and from their limited perspective. There are five primary components of a social story: (1) *Descriptive*, which answers the question of where it is, who it's occurring with, and why it's happening; (2) *Perspective*, which includes opinions, feelings, and ideas related to the social situation; (3) *Directive*, a social story also tends to include a potential range of responses for a particular situation; (4) *Affirmative*, this part of the social story includes statements that enhance the importance of the story's message to reassure the client. (5) *Co-operative*, this part of the social story includes statements to assist in providing meaning to the social situation being illustrated. A short example of this could be seen in the following although usually accompanied with colorful illustrations: "Sometimes, Tom and I race each other. I don't like losing to Tom and get frustrated when he wins. When I lose, I feel frustrated and sometimes get angry, I can take deep breaths, listen to music, or count to ten. I can also talk to an adult if I am still frustrated. Sometimes friends win when we race and that is okay."[32]

Social Autopsies

Championed by Richard Lavoie during the late 1980s and 1990s, a social autopsy serves to help a client dissect or take apart an identified error in a social situation. While also heavily used for those with Autism Spectrum Disorder, they have also been used successfully with those who struggle in social situations due to learning disabilities, ADHD, and psychological issues. There are various types of errors you might use social autopsies for. The goal typically is to assist the client to better understand a specific social situation and additionally assist the client to respond more effectively when similar situations are encountered. Social autopsies tend to promote the client to choose alternative solutions to correct those social errors in the future. There are four common steps for the solution identification: (1) identifying the error, (2) determining who was harmed by the error, (3) deciding how to correct the error, and (4) developing a plan so the error doesn't happen again.[33] Social autopsies are typically categorized by the severity of the social situation, similar to the following: *Simple Social Errors*, like forgetting someone's name; *Significant Social Errors*, like upsetting someone or ignoring their feelings; *Errors with Significant Consequences*, screaming at someone who disagreed with us or following someone we like instead of talking to them; and *Meltdowns or Extreme Behavioral Issues*, when a social situation results in screaming or throwing items because their expectations of the situation are not being met.[34]

BENEFITS AND CONSIDERATIONS OF PHYSICAL ACTIVITY AND EXERCISE

While exercise is not curative, it does contain a number of benefits across multiple levels. Notably, exercise is beneficial in avoiding chronic diseases like diabetes, cancer, and high blood pressure, many of which end up being the primary cause of death for those struggling with mental illness. However, additional benefits include increased neurotransmitters so that there is an elevated feeling of elation. While these are temporary, continued exercises, specifically with aerobic exercise, allow for reduction of symptoms in depression and anxiety, which commonly affect most individuals with the disorders and disabilities mentioned in this chapter. Notably, the chances for relapse or complications, as related to exercise, are almost nonexistent when compared to medication. In research on anxiety specifically, some studies have shown it to be more beneficial than CBT.

LEARNED HELPLESSNESS AND OTHER PSYCHOSOCIAL CONTRIBUTIONS

Unfortunately, interactions throughout life and with the rest of society tend to leave their mark, and for some clients this becomes overwhelming in how they are able to handle them. **Learned helplessness** is when an individual experiences continued negative and stressful situations that they eventually believe they are not able to control anything that results in or from negative circumstances. This usually means they begin to miss the positive and potential opportunities that present themselves. Authors who have written on the topic have noted that eventually people stop trying and apathy develops, and this occurs not only in humans but also in animals.[11] Often, this results in driving behaviors and conversations for the benefit of attention and sympathy. It stems from, and also leads to, depression, anxiety, and PTSD. This also displays in forms of low self-esteem, decreased motivation, and a belief that all attempts at making changes in life will result in continuously poor outcomes. There is also a strong correlation between addiction and learned helplessness, and they often tend to quickly cycle each other, compounding and intensifying issues with each other. Recommendations for solving learned helplessness include engaging in professional therapy, creating positive journalism and affirmations, also walking through positive self-talk.[35]

Psychosocial Contributions are items that intensify mental health issues, increasing their development and/or risk for them. Common issues or risks can be seen in a variety of ways that prevent people from addressing pending mental health issues. Primarily among them is the idea that they can delay assistance and that people need to learn to merely compartmentalize or adapt without the professional help to know how to do so safely.[36] With the increased focus on mental illness, some individuals dismiss looking into potential risks, instead thinking "everyone has mental health issues" and that it is less concerning than it really is. It is often explained away as lack of motivation due to fatigue in a complex and busy society. Lack of access to healthcare, specifically mental healthcare, is a major issue in many countries, including wealthier countries. Some cultures continue to struggle with the ideas of mental illness and the need for psychological help. In other cases, it is treated as resolvable by finding medication as a way to "solve" the problem.

Understanding the Effects of Medications on Motor Movement

It would be hard to list all medications and details that may be taken with the large number of disorders and disabilities that would be under many of these categories. Additionally, numerous drugs exist on the market and more continue to be added every year, so broad categories have been used to better address common concerns that fit into classification categories. Drugs that would fall into these categories may also have more than one use and may be used to do things like regulate hypotension for example. A primary consideration is to be aware of how medication affects the individual and the peak times of its use and to work to perfect timing for optimal exercise performance when possible.

- *Antianxiety*: Depending on the drug used, side effects like fatigue, headaches, dizziness and impaired coordination could all prevent having the energy to complete regular exercise.
- *Antidepressants*: These are used to alter the levels of neurotransmitters, often norepinephrine or serotonin. Depending on the drug, they could cause a range of effects on exercise by increasing dehydration, increasing heart rate, altering blood pressure and blood sugar, increased sweating, fatigue, and weight gain.
- *Mood Stabilizers*: These are used to pharmaceutically treat a number of the above-mentioned disorders, but they are commonly used to treat bipolar disorders; an example is Lithium as a first-line mood stabilizer. Additional medications may be provided for specific manic phases. Motor movement may be problematic with adverse side effects due to creating tremors, nausea, weakness, and twitching. Other complications could arise in a recreational or therapeutic setting due to confusion and decreasing memory.
- *Antipsychotics*: These are also used with mood stabilizers for bipolar disorder and treating schizophrenia. They are known for dyskinesia, restlessness, sedation, weight gain, fatigue, and increasing the risk of diabetes.

Stimulants: These are commonly seen in treating ADHD; they may increase the risk of high blood pressure, suppressing appetite, sleep disruptions, increased body temperature, increased heart rate, and potential irritability and hallucinations.

Non-Stimulants: These are commonly seen in Clonidine and Guanfacine frequently in treating ADHD as a way to slow down hyperactivity and impulsiveness but often leave the individual feeling tired. They are known for potentially causing nausea, dizziness, fatigue, and mood swings. Especially as the drug begins to wear off, *rebounding*, where the tendencies being controlled come back even stronger, may occur.

Electroconvulsive Therapy: This is quite uncommon but used when severe MDD might be a problem. Modern use is considered significantly safer and not at all similar to the abusive historic use. The idea being that the electronic current flows through the brain and resets the neurotransmitters. It has been considered successful in most cases, but short-term issues can relate to muscle contractions (effects from the electricity) and short-term memory loss affecting learning new movements.

Understanding Behavior Shaping and Modification

Behavior Shaping reviews the consequences and outcomes of a behavior. Specifically, a behavior is typically reinforced with some form of feedback to limit or encourage a type of behavior.[37] **Behavior Modification** is where specific goals for a client are set to be encouraged and achieved through behavioral techniques. These ideas take place through the following theoretical steps: observational learning, contingency management, and operant conditioning. **Observational Learning** is where behavior is learned though observing and copying another. **Contingency Management** refers to clarifying the relationship between a behavior and the consequences/events following the behavior. Last, **Operant Conditioning** happens where the person's behavior may be controlled due to controlling the consequences following a behavior, including encouraging and discouraging the behavior.[37] Operant conditioning can entail multiple components, layers of contingency management, and methods of consequence control. The list below encompasses many of the ideas and methods used by parents, teachers, and therapists for controlling behavior, but there are many more options to consider.

- *Stimulus*: This is viewed as an object or event that produces a response from an individual.
- *Reinforcement*: This is a form of stimulus that is given after a specific behavior as a consequence, typically used to increase the chance of the behavior occurring again.
- *Punishment*: This refers to when a consequence is used to decrease a specific behavior from reoccurring, especially in the future.
- *Intrinsic Reinforcer*: This refers to when the activity or item being used is able to reinforce itself because it is desired. This can often be seen when children play together and agree to rules for the enjoyment of playing itself or socialization.
- *Tangible Reinforcer*: This refers to when an item that can be held or eaten is given after a preferred behavior as a reinforcer. This is used often so an individual has something of immediate value, like receiving a candy after exhibiting good behavior.
- *Extinction (Planned Ignoring)*: This is a consequence used to control behavior by withholding a reinforcement of some kind after a specific behavior. This is often used as a strategy when an individual does not acknowledge a negative behavior, because that behavior is being done for attention-seeking reasons in the first place.
- *Prompting*: This is based on the concept of cueing, it is used to remind individuals of specific behavior they are to be engaged in. It acts like a specific stimulus for a designated behavior.
- *Social Reinforcer:* This refers to presenting a reinforcement that can be recognized socially by others at the current moment, such as verbally being given praise through physical contact like handshakes or high-fives, and proximity by an authority figure showing support.
- *Public Posting*: This refers to when an individual displays someone's name or performance in a way to recognize how they are behaving, as a reward or punishment. However, it is worth noting that using public posting as a form of punishment is considered an inappropriate use of it, and with individuals with behavior disorders, this may result in additional conflict or outbursts.

- *Token Economy System:* This is a form of reinforcement that involves receiving a token reward, like a coin or sticker, which they can then turn in to receive a delayed tangible item, benefit, or activity. This is often seen in coffee shops that have punch card rewards or kids who save stickers to eventually reach enough to get a reward.
- *Premack Principle:* This refers to when a preferred activity or behavior is used as a consequence/reinforcer to a less preferred activity. Coaches of young children use this often to allow a scrimmage game, preferred by athletes, after doing continuous drill work, less preferred by athletes due to repetition.
- *Differential Reinforcement:* When dealing with a group of individuals, the authority figure (teacher, coach, therapist) may treat individuals in their care differently and by clear, but separate, rules for each of them. This is to increase or decrease the behaviors for individuals differently based on their unique needs and understanding. Rules for behavioral conduct governing those with individuals for disability may have this type of reinforcement occur compared to the rest of class.

BEHAVIORAL INTERVENTION PLAN

A Behavior Intervention Plan (BIP) is an individualized plan for positive behavior and is used to help the student be successful in educational settings under IDEA. It is designed to note any change or alteration in curriculum, support systems or interventions to be added, and environmental needs. This is specifically designed after completion of an FBA. The FBA is designed to be a single assessment or multiple assessments, sometimes through observation and other times through formal assessments, to review the behavior issues surrounding an individual, as well as antecedents, consequences, and the environments that might make a behavior occur. This is then matched with interventions or prevention strategies that will allow for a reduction in negative behaviors. Interestingly enough, a BIP does not have to be done due to a child having a 504 or IDEA designation, they can be used by others outside disabilities to assist with creating a management strategy to improve behavior. However, they are often most seen when a student has an IEP and is used in conjunction with the IEP team.[38]

Example of a Functional Behavior Assessment (FBA)

Random Educational Consultation

Examplesville Independent School District

355 W 3rd St

Examplesville. STATE 12345

Phone: 597-465-8836

FUNCTIONAL BEHAVIOR ASSESSMENT (FBA)

NAME: James Lastname   **SCHOOL**: Every Elementary

DOB: 11/27/13   **GRADE**: K

PARENTS: Mr. and Mrs. Lastname   **DATE OF REPORT**: 1/15/2018

EXAMINER(S): Random Person, LSSP   **CURRENT ELIGBILITY:** OHI

Reason for Evaluation

James currently receives Special Education services as a student with an Other Health Impairment due to Attention-Deficit/Hyperactivity Disorder (ADHD). He is currently receiving support in the mainstream classroom. James has a paraprofessional assigned to support him in the classroom.

FIGURE 15.7 FBA Final

(*Continued*)

The ARD committee requested a Functional Behavioral Assessment (FBA) to be completed due to concerns regarding his behavior in the classroom. At the time of the request, James has been having significant behavioral issues in the classroom. He has been aggressive with peers and staff, hitting and kicking them. In addition, he has refused to comply with staff directions and has been verbally aggressive toward them.

Sources of Data:
Review of Records
Motivation Assessment Scale-Second Edition (MAS-II)
Behavior Assessment for Children System-Third Edition (BASC-3)
Teacher Functional Behavior Assessment Questionnaire
Classroom Observation
Parent Interview

Review of Records

James was evaluated in May of 2018, by Dr. Dave Nobody, Clinical Psychologist. At the time of the evaluation, James was attending a daycare program at Sunshine Daycare. James was having issues at the daycare, hitting the teacher, refusing to follow directions and throwing tantrums. A review of the Behavior Assessment System for Children-3rd Edition (BASC-3) indicated Mr. and Mrs. Lastname rated the following subscales in the Clinically Significant range: Aggression and Depression. The daycare teacher rated the following subscales in the Clinically Significant range: Hyperactivity, Aggression, Depression, and Withdrawal. Based on the data collected, Dr. Nobody diagnosed James with Attention-Deficit/Hyperactivity Disorder (ADHD) and Oppositional Defiant Disorder (ODD).

A Full and Individual Evaluation was completed in October of 2019 by Examplesville ISD. James was administered the Woodcock-Johnson IV Tests of Cognitive Abilities (WJ-IV-C). He received an overall General Intellectual Ability score of 108, which was in the Average range. The results were:

Oral Vocabulary-109-Average
Number Series-115-Above Average
Verbal Attention-115-Above Average
Letter-Pattern Matching-95-Average
Phonological Processing-98-Average
Story Recall-92-Average
Visualization-130-Well Above Average

James was administered the Woodcock-Johnson-IV Tests of Achievement (WJ-IV-A). The results were:

Basic Reading-97-Average
Reading Comprehension-93-Average
Written Expression-114-Average
Math Problem Solving-103-Average
Math Calculation-100-Average

The results of the evaluation report indicated James met criteria as a student with an Other Health Impairment due to Attention-Deficit/Hyperactivity Disorder (ADHD).

James' current program is in the mainstream classroom with a paraprofessional assigned to him. A review of discipline records from October 10th to November 20th indicated there were eleven incidents including inappropriate behaviors, class disruption, harassment, and hurting students.

A review of his current Annual ARD noted the following classroom accommodations were in place:1 to 2 step direction, check for understanding, clearly defined/consistent limits, cooling-off period, frequent breaks, frequent reminder of the rules, paraprofessional support, preferential seating / proximity control and reduced assignments (as needed).

Behavior Assessment System for Children-Third Edition (BASC-3)

Updated data was gathered from the Behavior Assessment System 3rd Edition, to assist in identifying target behaviors reported from parent and teachers.

Parent BASC-3

A review of the parent BASC-3 indicated the following subscales were in the Clinically Significant range: Aggression, Anxiety, Depression, and Withdrawal. The following items were identified as critical:
- Almost Always loses control when angry
- Often hits children

Some targeted behaviors included:
- Often hits children
- Often clings to parent in strange surroundings
- Almost Always isolates self from others
- Almost Always interrupts others when they are speaking
- Sometimes cannot wait his turn
- Sometimes teases others

Teacher BASC-3

A review of the teacher BASC-3 indicated the following subscales were in the Clinically Significant range: Hyperactivity, Aggression, and Withdrawal. The following items were identified as critical:
- Almost Always loses control when angry
- Often threatens to hurt others
- Almost Always hits other children
- Almost Always bullies others
- Often eats things that are not food

Some targeted behaviors included:
- Almost Always annoys others on purpose
- Almost Always loses temper too easily
- Almost Always hits other children
- Almost Always has trouble keeping hands or feet to self
- Almost Always bullies others
- Often disrupts the play of other children
- Often threatens to hurt others

Teacher Questionnaire

Ms. Teacher, classroom teacher, completed the Teacher FBA questionnaire form. She listed the following behaviors as concerns: hitting, profanity, and running away. For hitting, Ms. Teacher indicated there was no specific time of the day that this occurs. She did report that the behavior does occur when James is asked to complete work or if he feels threatened. Prior to hitting, she reported he becomes upset and will yell at her. The following strategies have been attempted: giving him what he desires, offering him a walk with his shadow, giving time to draw instead of his assignment or in between work. The following reinforcers have been effective: letting him draw and asking him, "Would your mom like what you are doing?" An effective consequence for the hitting is sending home a report of his behavior and reminding him to not hit staff the way he did before. Ms. Teacher feels getting his way is what is driving this behavior.

The use of profanity, can occur at any time of the day. James will typically start arguing with her and when he does not get what he wants, he begins to use inappropriate language. When he does this, Ms. Teacher tries to explain to him that those are not kind words and offers him a break to cool off in the classroom library. She

(Continued)

indicated some effective strategies have been to tell James that his parent will be notified and remind him that he will lose his treat if he continues to use those words. He has started to respond better to the behavior chart which is tied to a reward at home. She feels his need to have things his way is what is driving his behavior.

The third behavior, running from staff, occurs throughout the day. This behavior typically occurs when the class is working or transitioning from one subject to another. Some strategies that have been implemented include having him go cool off in the front office as well as allow him to draw and take his work to the front office. He has shown a desire to get all his checks on his behavior chart and this has been effective on some days. She feels his anger about not getting his way is what is driving this behavior.

Parent Interview

Mrs. Lastname, parent, participated in a parent interview. She indicated James is the youngest of three children. James began displaying behavior issues as a toddler. When he was three, he had issues with aggression at his daycare and was no longer able to attend. The Lastnames attempted to place him in the pre-school program in Othertown, but after a short period of time, the transfer request was revoked and he was not allowed to attend. Mrs. Lastname indicated James began play therapy at the age of 3 and continues to receive it at this time.

At home, Mrs. Lastname indicated James follows a structured schedule. When he gets home from school, they check his folder, he completes any homework he has and then he can play Legos, jump on the trampoline or play video games. Recently, if he meets his goal at school, they have been going to get ice cream as a reward. At home, he does have some anger issues, but they do not escalate to the level that the school has experienced. She did indicate he does struggle with transitions and when he gets upset, he will yell, ball his fists up, throw and hit things. She indicated they address this by first offering him choices in lieu of demands and they use timers to signal to him when they are transitioning to something else at home. When James has an outburst, she makes it a point to process with him what happened and discuss how he can make better choices. Mrs. Lastname reported James has started taking Karate and he has been doing well. His first interaction with the instructor resulted in him having to serve a timeout. While he was upset and refused to rejoin the group that day, James returned the next day and he has done well. She did report James has normal conflicts with his older brother. She explained that they typically have an issue about once a week at home.

Mrs. Lastname indicated James has been talking about school more. She will ask him how his day was and he is more open about his friends at school. He will talk about his classmates and one that he has a crush on. James plays well with others outside of school and will interact with his older sibling's friends when they come to the house. James also enjoys talking to the other kids at Karate. She feels James does display anxiety when he is presented with a new, unfamiliar situation. She cited his first day at Karate as an example. She also indicated James gets anxious at PE because he feels that others will laugh at him. In the past, James has had anxiety regarding attending school which manifested itself by him wetting the bed. This issue has for the most part gone away, but there have been times that he has not gone to the bathroom and had accidents at home. She reported while she felt James displayed some depressive characteristics in the past, she feels he is having more "happy" moments and does not currently see those characteristics. She explained that in the past, he would make comments like "I want die."

Mrs. Lastname indicated James has a good relationship with his family. He is close to his siblings and as a family they travel, enjoy hobbies and play video games together. In the past, they had significant difficulty taking James out to restaurants and other public places. While at times he does have some difficulty, his behavior in the community has improved. At home, he enjoys watching cartoons and playing video games like Minecraft.

Classroom Observation

James was observed on 1/17/2018 in his classroom. He was seated at his desk while his peers were on the carpet. James was playing with objects at his table and the paraprofessional attempted to verbally redirect him. James ignored her and asked to go to the restroom. He returned quickly and his classroom teacher attempted to get him to join the class. She prompted him twice, and he did not respond. The paraprofessional asked James to get his book out. He ignored her and continued to play with the items at his desk. The teacher came over and brought him his book. After a few minutes of James continuing to play, the teacher came over and asked him to stop and helped him get on task. James was on task for the reminder of the class time (12 minutes). He followed along and answered the teacher's questions appropriately. At one point, he noticed the observer and waved. He worked on the assignment and engaged in conversation with the paraprofessional while he completed the task. The class began to prepare to go to PE.

James listened to the teacher and lined up for PE. The class took a bathroom break and James sat and waited for his peers to finish. He had a hard time sitting still and was redirected several times to remain in his area. The class walked to PE and lined up. They began exercising and he followed along. James had an issue with his sock and was fixing it when he was prompted to do the exercises. He explained what he was doing and when he finished fixing his sock, he continued to do the exercises. While he was redirected several times for talking to his peers around him, James was not the only one redirected for this behavior. He complied with the redirection and participated in the activities at PE with minimal issues. He was observed to be appropriate and on task from the entire class period.

James transitioned back to the classroom. Once inside, he took out his paper toy and began playing with it. He had a hard time transitioning in from PE to the classroom activity. It took 7 minutes for him to sit and get ready to work. He sat down and began working on the task. He asked the teacher for help and she came over and worked with him. He became a little frustrated, but received verbal praise from both the teacher and the paraprofessional. Once he was done, he called the teacher over to show her what he did. The class was prompted to put their books away and move to the carpet. James had no interest in joining the group and he began moving and jumping around the classroom. He refused to listen to the teacher or the paraprofessional. The teacher informed him that she was going to move his clip down. James became upset and ran to block the teacher from moving his clip. He yelled at her and the paraprofessional. James hit the teacher and ran over to kick the paraprofessional. He continued to yell and hit them and did not listen to any of their prompts to stop hitting and calm down. James continued to escalate, punching and kicking them. He jumped up on the table and began running and jumping from table to table. He refused to listen to them. At this point, he was restrained for approximately 2 minutes until he informed them he was calm. Once they released him, he began hitting them again and jumped on the table. He began running and jumping from table to table and was restrained again. After being released, the examiner suggested they go to the nurse and check out his scab that had fallen off. He eventually agreed and met the examiner at the front office. Once there, he appeared calm and asked the examiner if he would like to play Tic Tac Toe. At this time, he was no longer upset and interacted with the examiner appropriately. James saw the nurse and was polite and allowed her to clean his arm and put a band aid on it.

After visiting the nurse, James met with the examiner and while playing Tic Tac Toe talked about school and his behavior. He told the examiner that he enjoyed doing centers but does not like when he does not get to play. He started drawing a picture and told the examiner it was Slender Man. When asked how he knew about Slender Man, he told the examiner his brother shows it to him on You Tube. James informed the examiner that he played Minecraft, Fortnite and Super Mario Brothers. He explained he likes to build with Legos and watches PJ Masks on TV. James explained that when he gets angry, he feels hot and just wants to hit. He talked about getting angry at his teacher and when asked if he realized that it was wrong to hit adults, he replied "Yes". He agreed that when they returned to class, James would apologize for hitting the staff. Once in the room, he apologized for hitting and began working on the class assignments. He continued to work until it was time for lunch. James wanted to finish what he was doing, so he was the last in line. Once in the lunch room, James got his tray and sat down. He interacted with several girls seated around him and ate his lunch without any issues. The paraprofessional was seated in close proximity.

The class returned from lunch and they started working on an activity. James became frustrated at first, but the teacher came over and provided support. He responded to her and was rewarded with having his clip moved up. He continued to work on the project without any issues. Once it was time to clean up, James cleaned up his area and went and got out his paper toys to play with. He asked the teacher if he could have some paper to draw with and she provided it to him. He interacted with several of his peers before returning to his area

(Continued)

and drawing break. He went to sharpen his pencil and the teacher helped him out. James thanked the teacher for her help and turned the light off for her so the class could watch a video on the carpet. While the rest of the class engaged in the movement activity, James continued to draw. Once he was done, he showed the examiner his character and told him it was a monster from SlenderMan. James joined his peers on the carpet for the math activity, but needed a movement break before he sat down to work on his math assignment. With the examiner seated with him, James completed his assignment quickly and was allowed to go to one of the math centers. As he was playing with some of the math manipulatives, he was observed helping another peer with his math assignment. Eventually, James settled on the cylinder center and played there for the remainder of center time. The teacher informed the examiner that he typically chooses that center and does not switch to anything else. The teacher called him over to do some work with a group. At first he refused, but when he was informed that he would be able to earn a clip move he complied. While he required several prompts to focus, James participated and completed all the tasks in the group. He finished the activity and returned to playing with the cylinders. The class was asked to clean up so they could go out to recess. James required several prompts and with the paraprofessionals assistance, he cleaned up his station and lined up.

The class went out to the playground. James had no issues going out to the playground. He asked the examiner to play tag, but was okay when told the examiner had to sit and watch the class. James played with the other students on the playscape. He did not have any problems and seemed to enjoy interacting with them. They would chase each other up and down the playscape and he did not require any redirection. However, once it was time to come in from recess, James refused to get off the playscape and was the last one off. After several attempts form the paraprofessional to get him off the playscape, James complied, but started digging in the dirt. The paraprofessional made numerous attempts to verbally redirect him back to the building, but he ignored her. The class went in without him and the paraprofessional remained with James. After about five minutes, the examiner went over and talked with James. He praised him on how he had gotten his clip moved up and discussed how it would be a shame if it had to get moved because he chose to stay outside. James thought about it for approximately a minute and then followed the examiner and the paraprofessional back into the building. At this time, the class was in the computer class. He entered the room and went to his computer. James was engaged in the activity on the computer for the entire time and transitioned back to his classroom without any issues.

Motivation Assessment Scale-Second Edition (MAS-II)

The Motivation Assessment Scale-Second Edition (MAS-II) is a rating scale that assesses functions of problem behavior in individuals with developmental disabilities through informant responses. It includes 16 questions and is comprised of four subscales that each represents a possible function of the behavior: attention, escape, sensory, and tangible. Each question has six response options (0 = never, 1 = almost never, 2 = seldom, 3 = half the time, 4 = usually, 5 = almost always, and 6 = always). Scores are calculated by summing the item ratings within a particular subscale/function and calculating the mean rating for that subscale. High scores for one or more of the subscales suggest that those functions may be maintaining the individual's problem behavior.

The Behavior description included hitting the teacher and running away from staff. The setting description is whole group instruction. A review of the results indicated the Escape, Attention and Tangible scores were all equal identifying there are multiple functions to James' behavior.

Summary

A review of the data gathered within this FBA, indicated there appears to be two different antecedents to the two behaviors. In regards to his running and not following directions, the antecedent appears to be transitioning to a new task and the function appears to be an inability to self-regulate his behavior to begin the new task. While most of James' peers can transition to the new task and are ready to learn, James has a hard time self-regulating, leading to off task behaviors and non-compliance. In regards to hitting and using appropriate words, the antecedent appears to be being told "No" or being presented with a negative consequence and the function appears to a loss of emotional regulation. In these moments, James is told "No' or his behavior is corrected in a manner he perceives as a threat he becomes angry, leading to his inability to regulate this emotion and resulting in him yelling, hitting and kicking.

Recommendations

1. James would benefit from movement breaks that are strategically planned out to help give him time to regulate his behavior and be ready to learn. This may be accomplished by having him complete a "task" in the classroom, such as "take something" to the office, go get some water, and/or use the restroom. By giving him these breaks, once he returns to the classroom, James should be in better control to begin the new task.
2. To get James in the mindset to be compliant, have James complete minor tasks that require compliance. For example, asking him to sharpen a pencil, help you pass out papers, follow you to his seat and then ask him to get started on his assignment. This series of compliant task, helps to get him in the mindset to follow directions.
3. Reinforce compliant behaviors and do not focus on the behaviors you are trying to eliminate. If you set up his reinforcer system to focus on listening to staff, completing tasks, instead of focusing on his non-compliant or verbal aggression, it allows you to reward the positive behaviors.
4. Students with Oppositional Defiant Disorder (ODD) tend to respond with "No' regardless of what the request is. It is recommended you offer James two choices consisting of two tasks you would like him to do. Giving him this "perceived control" allows him to feel as if he is making the choice, while you are having him complete one of two things you want.
5. When correcting James behavior, how you word it is key to avoid having him react with anger. Focusing on the positive things going for him and how you would be sad he would lose something may be more effective than leading with "You have lost……..." James appears to lose control quickly and if you lead with consequences, he is unlikely to hear the positive things he could earn.
6. Avoid using ultimatums and angry or confrontational tones with James. This may lead to him reacting to the challenge with anger and aggression.
7. James needs to be taught replacement behaviors to express his anger by staff trained in behavioral support. While there are strategies to help limit his anger, when he is angry, he needs to be shown that there are more appropriate responses. James can be taught "new tools' to use through social skills training and/or counseling. It is key that these "new tools" be taught when he is calm and he needs to be given a chance to practice them and understand why it is important to use them.
8. When James becomes angry, the staff needs to prompt James to use his replacement behaviors and reward him when he does.
9. Staff should use an interest inventory to help develop a behavior chart. The chart should consist of the desired behaviors and not the inappropriate behaviors. It is important his reinforcers be meaningful to him. Offering him high interest reinforcers to earn, will increase buy in to the behavior chart.
10. The behavior chart should provide immediate reinforcement and a larger more meaningful delayed reinforcer. For example, his immediate reinforcer may be a stamp or sticker and the delayed reinforcer may be an opportunity to draw for 15 minutes, extra recess with the paraprofessional or another high interest activity. It is recommended the student has two opportunities to earn a delayed reinforcer. This can be done at lunch and right before the end of the day.
11. As staff begins to work with James is changing his behavior, when James is angry and upset, he needs to be allowed to go to a designated area where trained staff can work to deescalate him away from the mainstream classroom. This allows the staff to remove the "energy" from the room as well as shield James from his peers witnessing his behavior. Once James is in control of his behavior, staff should compete a debrief with him and review the positive things he did as well as address the inappropriate behaviors and discuss how to respond the next time. Once this occurs, James can return to his mainstream classroom and resume academic activities.
12. It is important for staff to understand that behavior may escalate as you put a plan into place before it gets better. It is recommended the staff give the plan at least six weeks to determine if his behavior is changing and if he has begun using his replacement behaviors.
13. By using a daily reinforcement sheet, staff can collect data and should meet at least once a week to review James' progress to determine if they are seeing changes.

Random Person, M.A.
Licensed Specialist in School Psychology

CHAPTER 15: Psychological and Behavioral Disorders, Disabilities, and Management

Example of a Behavior Intervention Plan (BIP)

Behavior Intervention Plan

Student Name: Suzy   Action Team Members: Teacher, Counselor, Parent, Admin   Date of Meeting:

COMPETING BEHAVIOR PATHWAY

		Desired Replacement (Long Term Objective) Work on task, raise hand or ask to work with teacher or peers, socialize at breaks	**Reinforcing Consequences for Desired Replacement** Suzy will experience academic success and enjoy positive interaction with adults and peers	
Combined for webinar to say: Independent work time with peers nearby.				
Setting Event When certain friends or peers are present	**Triggering Antecedent** Suzy is asked to work independently	**Problem Behavior** Suzy interrupts, talks out, and jokes	**Maintaining Consequences** Peers laugh or respond, teacher attention	**Function** To get attention
		Alternative Replacement Behavior (Short-term Replacement) Work with peer or earn peer interaction by completing parts of assignments		

INTERVENTION STRATEGIES

2.1 Setting Event Strategies	2.2 Antecedent Strategies	2.3 Teaching Strategies	2.4 Consequence Strategies to Reinforce Appropriate Behavior
Arrange seating so Suzy's work area is free of distraction, and set up for working with a peer	Teacher will clarify expectations for independent work and provide pre-corrects	Teacher will clarify each step of working independently, and focus on role playing and providing feedback for Suzy in using strategies to ask to work with peers or get help from the teacher	Respond immediately when Suzy uses desired social skills, provide praise for working quietly

CONSEQUENCE STRATEGIES
(Response strategies &/or environmental manipulations that make consequences for problem behavior ineffective)

Use planned ignoring for identified problem behavior (interrupting, talking out, joking). Provide praise to other students exhibiting desired behavior. Provide quick, simple corrective feedback, then walk away.

FIGURE 15.8 BIP Final

Source: https://dese.mo.gov/media/pdf/fba-bip-part-3-bip-process-sample-suzy

IMPLEMENTATION PLAN
Person responsible for training school personnel how to implement each part of the BIP: _School counselor_

Deadline for completing the training: _Within 2 weeks of plan development_

Tasks to Complete & Resources Needed	Person Responsible for Implementing	Person Responsible for Training	Timeline
Arrange classroom seating to minimize distraction	Classroom Teacher	N/A	By end of week 1
Meet with Suzy to clarify expectations for independent work time, and provide Suzy with a checklist of steps for working independently	Classroom Teacher	N/A	Beginning of week 2
Direct instruction and role playing of expected behaviors during independent work time, providing practice and feedback	Counselor, Classroom Teacher	Counselor	Beginning of week 2
Increase use of behavior specific feedback and provide recognition when Suzy uses expected behavior Develop and provide a system for working with peers	Classroom Teacher	N/A	Begin week 1
Use planned ignoring and provide increased positive feedback to peers performing expected behavior	Classroom Teacher	N/A	Begin week 1

MONITORING & EVALUATION PLAN

Behavioral Objective (specific, observable, measurable)	Procedures for Data Collection	Person Responsible & Timeline	Review Date:	Evaluation Decision • Monitor • Modify • Discontinue
Suzy will complete small parts of independent tasks and check work with a peer 3 out of 5 days each week	Daily checklist outlining independent tasks assigned, amount completed and opportunities for peer interaction	Classroom teacher and student, if applicable Daily during reading, writing, and math	Every 3 weeks *List dates when intervention begins	

(Continued)

CHAPTER 15: Psychological and Behavioral Disorders, Disabilities, and Management

Data to be Collected	Procedures for Data Collection	Person Responsible	Timeline
Is Plan Being Implemented? (Fidelity of Implementation)	BIP Fidelity Monitoring Form	Classroom Teacher Building Principal	Self-report weekly Monitor every 2 weeks
Is Plan Making a Difference? Student View Teacher View			

GENERALIZATION & MAINTENANCE

Generalization Strategies	Person Responsible & Timeline
Other teachers and staff will provide additional feedback and positive recognition to Suzy consistent with the teacher's feedback in schoolwide and non-classroom areas (PE, music, cafeteria, playground)	Counselor will communicate to other teachers and staff Within 2 weeks

Maintenance Strategies	Person Responsible & Timeline
Suzy will earn recognition with each reporting period (extra note from teacher on behavior success, certificate of self-monitoring)	Classroom teacher (every 9 weeks)
Suzy may choose 2 peers for lunch with administrator in conference room at each reporting period	Administrator (every 9 weeks)
Suzy may be selected to act as a mentor to younger students in reading	Admin, Classroom Teacher, 1st Grade Teacher (after the first successful reporting period)

Notes:

FIGURE 15.8 (*Continued*)

REFERENCES

1. Dix, T., Stewart, A. D., Gershoff, E. T., & Day, W. H. (2007). Autonomy and children's reactions to being controlled: Evidence that both compliance and defiance may be positive markers in early development. *Child Development, 78*(4), 1204–1221.
2. Pratt, C., & Dubie, M. (2000). Observing behavior using A-B-C data. *Indiana Resource Center for Autism.* https://www.iidc.indiana.edu/irca/articles/observing-behavior-using-a-b-c-data.html
3. Farreras, I. G. (2022). History of mental illness. In R. Biswas-Diener & E. Diener (Eds.), *Noba textbook series: Psychology.* DEF publishers. http://noba.to/65w3s7ex
4. Farley, C. (2012). History of emotional disturbances. *Elementary Emotional Disturbance.* https://elementaryemotionaldisturbance.weebly.com/history-of-emotional-disturbance.html#:~:text=The%20term%20%E2%80%9Cemotional%20disturbance%E2%80%9D%20was,severe%20emotional%20and%20behavioral%20problems
5. Moin, A. (2021). A history of learning disabilities and ADHD. *Understood.* https://www.understood.org/en/articles/history-of-learning-disabilities-and-adhd
6. National Institute of Mental Health. (2022). Attention-deficit/hyperactivity disorder. https://www.nimh.nih.gov/health/topics/attention-deficit-hyperactivity-disorder-adhd
7. National Health Services. (2022). Attention deficit hyperactivity disorder (ADHD) symptoms. https://www.nhs.uk/conditions/attention-deficit-hyperactivity-disorder-adhd/symptoms/
8. Miller, D., Robert, P., Ereshefsky, L., Adler, L., Bateman, D., Cummings, J., DeKosky, S. T., Fischer, C. E., Husain, M., Ismail, Z., Jaeger, J., Lerner, A. J., Li, A., Lyketsos, C. G., Manera, V., Mintzer, J., Moebius, H. J., Mortby, M., Meulien, D., Pollentier, S., … Lanctôt, K. L. (2021). Diagnostic criteria for apathy in neurocognitive disorders. *Alzheimer's & Dementia, 17*(12), 1892–1904.
9. World Health Organization. (2021). Depression. https://www.who.int/news-room/fact-sheets/detail/depression#:~:text=Depression%20is%20a%20leading%20cause,%2C%20moderate%2C%20and%20severe%20depression
10. National Institute of Mental Health. (2019). Any Anxiety Disorder. *https://www.nimh.nih.gov/health/statistics/any-anxiety-disorder#:~:text=Prevalence%20of%20Any%20Anxiety%20Disorder%20Among%20Adults,-Based%20on%20diagnostic&text=An%20estimated%2031.1%25%20of%20U.S.,some%20time%20in%20their%20lives*
11. Moore, G., Durstine, J., and Painter, P. (2016) *ACSM's exercise management for persons with chronic diseases and disabilities* (4th ed). Human Kinetics.
12. Montana DPHHS. (2021). *Emotional disturbance.* https://dphhs.mt.gov/schoolhealth/chronichealth/developmentaldisabilities/emotionaldisturbance#:~:text=IDEA%20definition%3A,%2C%20sensory%2C%20or%20health%20factors
13. Division for Emotion Behavioral and Health. (2020). *Behavior disorders: Definitions, characteristics & related information.* https://debh.exceptionalchildren.org/behavior-disorders-definitions-characteristics-related-information
14. Kansas State Department of Education. (2020). *Fact Sheet: Emotional disturbance.* https://www.ksde.org/Portals/0/ECSETS/FactSheets/FactSheet-SpEd-ED.pdf
15. National Institute of Mental Health. (2019). *Disruptive mood dysregulation disorder.* https://www.nimh.nih.gov/health/topics/disruptive-mood-dysregulation-disorder-dmdd/disruptive-mood-dysregulation-disorder#:~:text=Disruptive%20mood%20dysregulation%20disorder%20(DMDD,impairment%20that%20requires%20clinical%20attention.
16. World Health Organization. (2021). *Depression.* https://www.who.int/news-room/fact-sheets/detail/depression#:~:text=Depression%20is%20a%20leading%20cause,%2C%20moderate%2C%20and%20severe%20depression
17. Sharma, P., Dikshit, R., Shah, N., Karia, S., & De Sousa, A. (2016). Excessive daytime sleepiness in schizophrenia: A naturalistic clinical study. *Journal of Clinical Diagnosis Research, 10*(10), VC06–VC08. https://doi.org/10.7860/JCDR/2016/21272.8627
18. Mayo Clinic. (2021). *Schizophrenia.* https://www.mayoclinic.org/diseases-conditions/schizophrenia/symptoms-causes/syc-20354443
19. National Health Services. (2022). *Symptoms—obsessive compulsive disorder (OCD).* https://www.nhs.uk/mental-health/conditions/obsessive-compulsive-disorder-ocd/symptoms/
20. Centers for Disease Control and Prevention. (2022). *What is ADHD?* https://www.cdc.gov/ncbddd/adhd/facts.html
21. Semel Institute for Neuroscience and Human Behavior. (2022). *ODD & conduct disorder.* https://www.semel.ucla.edu/adhdandmood/odd-conduct-disorder
22. Mayo Clinic. (2021). *Oppositional defiant disorder (ODD).* https://www.mayoclinic.org/diseases-conditions/oppositional-defiant-disorder/symptoms-causes/syc-20375831

23. Anna Courtad, C., & Bakken, J. P. (2011). History of learning disabilities. In A. F. Rotatori, F. E. Obiakor, & J. P. Bakken (Eds.), *History of special education (Advances in Special Education*, Vol. 21, Chap. 4, pp. 61–87). Emerald Group Publishing Limitedhttps://doi.org/10.1108/S0270-4013(2011)0000021007
24. International Dyslexia Association. (2018). *DSM-5 changes in diagnostic criteria for specific learning disabilities (SLD)1: What are the implications?* https://dyslexiaida.org/dsm-5-changes-in-diagnostic-criteria-for-specific-learning-disabilities-sld1-what-are-the-implications/
25. Mayo Clinic. (2022). *Learning disorders: Know the signs, how to help.* https://www.mayoclinic.org/healthy-lifestyle/childrens-health/in-depth/learning-disorders/art-20046105
26. Hales, C., Kit, B., Gu, Q., & Ogden, C. (2018). Trends in prescription medication use among children and adolescents—United States, 1999–2014. *Journal of American Medical Association, 319*(19), 2009–2020. https://doi.org/10.1001/jama.2018.5690
27. Whitty, P., Owoeye, O., & Waddington, J. (2009). Neurological signs and involuntary movements in schizophrenia: Intrinsic to and informative on systems pathobiology. *Schizophrenia Bulletin, 35*(2), 415–424. https://doi.org/10.1093/schbul/sbn126
28. Mokobane, M., Pillay, B., & Meyer, A. (2019). Fine motor deficits and attention deficit hyperactivity disorder in primary school children. *South African Journal of Psychiatry, 22*(25), 1232. https://doi.org/10.4102/sajpsychiatry.v25i0.1232
29. Lohr, J., & Caligiuri, M. (2006). Abnormalities in motor physiology in bipolar disorder. *The Journal of Neuropsychiatry and Clinical Neurosciences, 18*(3), 342–349. https://neuro.psychiatryonline.org/doi/10.1176/jnp.2006.18.3.342#:~:text=We%20found%20that%20approximately%2060,having%20abnormalities%20on%20either%20measure
30. Integrative Life Care. (2021). *The 5 principles of trauma-informed care.* https://integrativelifecenter.com/the-5-principles-of-trauma-informed-care/
31. Wuest, D. (2020). Disciplining students by promoting responsibility. *PE Central.* https://www.pecentral.org/climate/january99article.html
32. LLA Therapy. (2017). *The 5 essential elements of an incredibly effective social story.* https://llatherapy.org/the-5-essential-elements-of-an-incredibly-effective-social-story/
33. OCALI. (2021). *Social autopsy.* https://www.ocali.org/project/resource_gallery_of_interventions/page/social_autopsy
34. Autism Classroom Resources. (2020). *Social autopsies: What are they and why you need them.* https://autismclassroomresources.com/social-autopsy/
35. *Psychology Today.* (2020). Learned helplessness. https://www.psychologytoday.com/us/basics/learned-helplessness
36. Sirey, J. (2008). The impact of psychosocial factors on experience of illness and mental health service use. *American Journal of Geriatric Psychiatry, 16*(9), 703–705. https://doi.org/10.1097/JGP.0b013e318182550b
37. WebMD. (2022). What is Operant Conditioning. https://www.webmd.com/mental-health/what-is-operant-conditioning
38. Family Matters. (2022, February). *Behavior intervention plans (BIPs) fact sheet.* Michigan Department of Education Office of Special Education. https://www.michigan.gov/-/media/Project/Websites/mde/specialeducation/familymatters/FM1/BIP_FactSheet.pdf?rev=6dc5853e921640a0b15200d6facadfd8#:~:text=A%20behavior%20intervention%20plan%20(BIP,-improve%20or%20replace%20the%20behavior
39. Social and Character Development Research Consortium. (2010). *Efficacy of schoolwide programs to promote social and character development and reduce problem behavior in elementary school children (NCER 2011–2001).* National Center for Education Research, Institute of Education Sciences, U.S. Department of Education.
40. Forgan, J., & Richey, M. (2012). *Raising boys with ADHD: Secrets for parenting healthy, happy sons* (1st ed.). Routledge.

CHAPTER 16
VISUAL IMPAIRMENTS

T.N. Kirk and Justin A. Haegele

DEFINING VISUAL IMPAIRMENT

The American Foundation for the Blind (AFB) considers **visual impairment** to be an umbrella term that refers to "a range of visual function from low vision through total blindness" that is not correctable using even the strongest prescription eyeglasses and interferes with tasks of daily life.[1] However, terms like visual impairment and blindness may be defined differently by various organizations. Though exact thresholds of what constitutes visual impairment varies, visual acuity and visual field are the two criteria that most often make up this definition. **Visual acuity** refers to crispness or clarity of vision. Typical, or 20/20, vision refers to what a person with average vision can see on a standard eye chart from a distance of 20 feet away. In contrast, 20/200 vision means that the individual can see at 20 feet away what someone with average vision can see from 200 feet away. **Visual field** refers to the area that can be seen when the eye is focused on a fixed point. An average visual field is about 120 degrees horizontally. Meeting the criteria for either reduced visual acuity or visual field, but not necessarily both, is enough to be considered to have a visual impairment.

Under the larger umbrella of visual impairment, quality of vision can be further described using terms like "low vision," "legal blindness," and "total blindness," and others, which refer to the degree of impairment. In the United States, the least impactful degree of visual impairment, often termed low vision, is associated with visual acuity that is 20/70 or worse.

Legal blindness refers to visual impairment with either visual acuity of 20/200 or less, or a visual field of 20 degrees or less in the better eye with best possible correction. Many individuals who meet the criteria for legal blindness have some usable vision, and only some read braille or use mobility devices such as the long white cane or guide dogs. Finally, individuals who have no light perception in either eye are considered to have total blindness.

Within the context of sport, individuals with visual impairments are given classification levels that correspond with their degree of impairment. For example, the Paralympic Games use the International Blind Sport Federation classifications that range from B3 (i.e., least impairment) to B1 (i.e., most impairment). Under this system, athletes in the B3 class have a visual acuity above 20/600 up to 20/200, and/or a visual field of between 5 and 20 degrees in the better eye. Athletes in the B2 class have visual acuity ranging from the ability to recognize the shape of a hand up to 20/600, and/or a visual field of less than 5 degrees. Lastly, athletes in the B1 class are unable to recognize the shape of a hand at any distance and includes those with minimal to no light perception. While the International Blind Sport Federation classifications and the Paralympic games do not include athletes with low vision, the United States Association of Blind Athletes (USABA) recognizes the B4 class that includes athletes whose visual acuities fall between 20/200 and 20/70 and whose visual fields are greater than 20 degrees.[2]

T. Nicole Kirk, University of Georgia; and Justin A. Haegele, Old Dominion University. © Kendall Hunt Publishing Company.

PREVALENCE AND KNOWN CAUSES

According to the World Health Organization (WHO), about 285 million people are estimated to have low vision (246 million people) and legal blindness (39 million people) worldwide.[3] Visual impairment is closely associated with aging, as 65% of those with visual impairments are aged 50 or older. Prevalence of visual impairment varies across countries, and about 90% of individuals with visual impairments reside in lower-income regions.[3] It is further estimated that among the world population about 80% of visual impairments are preventable. For example, in low- to middle-income countries, acquired visual impairment remains high because of the increased health threats such as inadequate access to clean water, malnutrition, and lack of comprehensive medical care to treat emerging vision issues. It is estimated that about 2.3% of Americans of all ages have a visual impairment, including an estimated 585,000 children.[4]

There are many causes of visual impairment. Loss of vision is closely associated with older adulthood, but visual impairment may also occur before birth (**congenital**) or may be acquired later in life (**adventitious**). Some causes of visual impairments become more impactful over time (**progressive**), while others do not change (**stable**). Different causes of visual impairment may be associated with a specific set of symptoms and level of visual impairment. Among children, the most common causes of visual impairment are congenital cataracts, albinism, retinopathy of prematurity, optic atrophy, and optic nerve hypoplasia.[5] Among adults—especially older populations—common causes of visual impairment include glaucoma, cataracts, macular degeneration, and diabetic retinopathy. See Table 16.1 for a description of common causes of visual impairments.

VISUAL IMPAIRMENT AND MOTOR MOVEMENT

Prior to discussing strategies to help enhance experiences in movement-related contexts, we must first gain an understanding of how individuals with visual impairments may experience different movement-related concepts. As such, the following subsections provide an overview of research focused on individuals with visual impairments with regard to (a) fundamental motor skills, (b) orientation and mobility training, (c) school-based physical education, and (d) physical activity and exercise. This overview is in no way exhaustive, but rather intended to provide general content that should inform practice.

Fundamental Motor Skills

Throughout early childhood, children with visual impairments tend to have less developed fine and gross motor skills as compared with their sighted peers.[6–8] Because sight is the most predominant of the senses, infants with visual impairments are less able to use visual information to interact with their environments, mimic movement patterns of those around them, and engage in other forms of incidental learning.[9] For example, since early vision is generally goal-oriented, infants with visual impairments may not be motivated to crawl toward a toy or a loved one in their environment. In addition to lack of visual stimuli, infants and toddlers with visual impairments may have less opportunity to practice motor skills like crawling and walking due to lack of opportunity and overprotection from family members who do not want them to get hurt in an environment they cannot see. While children with visual impairments may improve locomotor skills like walking, galloping, and running later in childhood, differences in object control skills—especially receptive skills like hitting a ball with a bat or racket or catching a ball—tend to persist.[10] Some research suggests that participation in sports and physical activity can improve these skills among youth with visual impairments.[9,11] As such, Brian[7] suggests, and we agree, that practitioners need to move past deficit-based approaches where children with visual impairments are "protected" from injury by being removed from physical activity, which can delay motor skill learning. Rather, children with visual impairments need to enjoy safe and developmentally appropriate activities where they can be "risky" in their movements while being supported to enhance motor skills.

Postural Control

Like fine and gross motor skills, individuals with visual impairments may also experience reduced postural control. Postural control "represents neuromotor processes/mechanisms which facilitate goal-directed movement control and coordination" (p. 18).[12] This concept is encompassing of common terms like balance or stability, and includes all goal-directed movements. Pennell[12] noted that individuals with visual impairments are certainly capable of having proficient postural control; however, differences between individuals with and without visual impairments have been noted in early life and may be related to overprotective practices or other restrictions in activities that may reduce opportunities to practice

TABLE 16.1 Common causes of visual impairment and characteristics

Common Causes of Visual Impairment	Characteristics
Albinism	- Lack of tissue pigment, often affects skin and eye color - Abnormal optic nerve development - Decreased visual acuity - Photophobia (sensitivity to light) - Nystagmus (involuntary eye movements) - Central scotomas (a blind or partially blind area in the visual field) - Strabismus (the inability of one or both eyes to focus at the same time)
Cataracts	- Opacity of the lens that restricts the passage of light - Reduced acuity, blurred vision, poor color vision, photophobia, and sometimes nystagmus. - Visual ability fluctuates according to light
Cortical Visual Impairment	- Damage to the visual cortex of the brain, not to the eye itself - Often the eye can see, but nerve communication between the eye and brain is affected - Usable acuity and field vary - Visual processing can take a great deal of effort
Diabetic Retinopathy	- Common among individuals with diabetes mellitus - Bleeding in the retina causes blurred vision and floating spots in visual field
Glaucoma	- Increased pressure in the eye - Vision loss may be gradual, sudden, or present at birth. - Photophobia
Macular Degeneration	- Central vision loss - Photophobia - Poor color vision - Peripheral vision is unaffected
Optic Nerve Hypoplasia	- Underdevelopment of optic nerve in utero - Nystagmus - Can occur in one or both eyes
Retinitis Pigmentosa	- Progressive peripheral vision loss (tunnel vision) - Decreased acuity and depth perception - Spotty vision because of retinal scarring - Photophobia
Retinoblastoma	- Malignancy of the retina in early childhood (cancer of the eye) - Usually requires enucleation (removal of the eye) - Can occur in one or both eyes
Retinopathy of Prematurity	- Occurs in some infants who are born prematurely - Ranges from reduced acuity to total blindness
Rubella (German Measles)	- Occurs in utero - Complications may cause limited vision - Co-occurring disabilities are likely

postural control. It is important to note, therefore, that there may not be an automatic connection between visual impairment and postural control, but rather the lack of opportunities to engage in physical or motor activities, likely due to the perceptions of service providers or parents toward the capabilities of those with visual impairments, restricting the development of postural control. This supports assertions made in the prior section, that children with visual impairments need to be permitted to engage in safe physical activities so that they can develop these critical movement-related concepts.

Orientation and Mobility Training

One area that is critical for developing locomotor and independent travel skills among individuals with visual impairments of all ages is orientation and mobility training. Orientation and mobility training is used to develop effective and safe travel skills among individuals with visual impairments. Though orientation and mobility includes many skills, travel cane skills are among the most important for many individuals with visual impairments, particularly those who with less usable vision (i.e., persons with B1 and B2 vision classifications). The travel cane is a long, thin stick that is typically swept or tapped along the ground in front of the user to identify the path of travel and obstacles along the path. It is important to note that although individuals with more usable vision (i.e., those with B3 and B4 level vision) may not use travel canes, they often learn other orientation and mobility skills to travel, such as visual scanning techniques that work with their vision capabilities to safely navigate the environment. In youth populations, orientation and mobility training often takes place in school settings, while community-based training centers for the blind provide such training for older individuals. While practitioners in physical education, exercise, and/or recreation should not consider orientation and mobility training to be an area for them to work directly within, collaboration with certified orientation and mobility professionals may be fruitful when considering and implementing programs for individuals with visual impairments.

Physical Education

Physical education is the only content area in schools where individuals, including those with visual impairments, engage in material specifically designed to develop motor skills and health-enhancing behaviors. Within the United States, legislation such as the Individuals with Disabilities Education Act (IDEA)[13] acknowledges the significant role of physical education for health and skill acquisition. In fact, IDEA mandates that all youth with qualifying disabilities receive physical education services. Despite the promise that physical education has in contributing to the lives of individuals with visual impairments, it is not clear that this promise is being met. Unfortunately, studies show that many individuals with visual impairments recall primarily negative experiences in school physical education.[14] For example, instances of bullying or ostracization by peers, removal from class activities, and lowered expectations from teachers and peers alike are commonplace.[14,15] These types of experiences are critical to informing individuals' understandings of their abilities and can lead youth to choose to abstain from physical education activities and in-school and out of school physical activities (e.g., sports, exercise, and unstructured play). Withdrawal from physical activity among youth often persists into inactivity in adulthood.[16]

Physical Activity and Exercise

Regular engagement in physical activity has been identified as a modifiable lifestyle choice that can help reduce the possibility of developing physiological and psychological issues during childhood.[17,18] Given the favorable health-related outcomes of physical activity, international guidelines have been published that

For many individuals with visual impairment, developing cane skills is an important part of orientation and mobility.

provide recommendations for children (i.e., at least 60 minutes of daily moderate-to-vigorous–intensity physical activity [MVPA]). Unfortunately, youth with visual impairments are often reported to be physically inactive and unlikely to meet expected MVPA recommendations.[19,20] Because of their relative inactivity, youth with visual impairments appear to be at risk for developing a number of health-related issues, such as obesity and psychological distress. Recommendations to increase physical activity engagement among youth include enhancing school-based physical education programs as well as implementing targeted activities that can be successfully completed with siblings or friends outside the school context.

Engagement in MVPA has also been associated with physical and psychological health benefits among adults with visual impairments. Although adults with visual impairments tend to report low levels of health-related quality of life,[21] physical activity engagement has been identified as a means of improving this psychological outcome.[22] While many factors are likely to contribute to physical inactivity among adults with visual impairments, understanding motivation to be active may be key to increasing physical activity engagement. According to Kirk and colleagues,[23] "understanding the motivational factors that underpin physical activity engagement or abstinence is essential to understanding and promotion of physical activity for all populations, including those with visual impairments" (p. 112). What this means for practitioners, briefly, is that for individuals to undertake a behavior, they should feel confident that they are capable of success, they should perceive it as meaningful or useful, and they should feel supported by others to pursue it.[24-27] As such, practitioners should take care to design and implement sport and physical activity opportunities with these concepts in mind.[27]

CONTRAINDICATIONS OF MOVEMENT

Generally speaking, there are few contraindications that should preclude individuals with visual impairments from engaging in exercise, sport, or physical activities. However, some individuals who have visual impairments are at an increased risk of a serious eye injury called retinal detachment. The retina is the light-sensitive layer of tissue that lines the inside of the eye that may become detached—that is, lifted or pulled from its normal position—through direct trauma to the eye or the head.[28] If left untreated, a retinal detachment can lead to permanent vision loss.

As such, high-risk activities for individuals who are at risk for retinal detachment include any sports where fast-paced moving projectiles are involved (e.g., basketball, baseball, softball, soccer) or during heavy lifting or weight training activities that require physically moving more than the individual's body weight.[28]

A second risk among individuals with certain types of visual impairment, such as glaucoma and diabetic retinopathy, is increased intraocular pressure, or very high pressure within the eye itself. When pressure within the eye becomes too high because of fluid buildup, it can damage blood vessels and nerves, leading to permanent vision loss. High-risk activities for individuals who have high intraocular pressure include inversion activities like certain yoga and gymnastics techniques, swimming and diving in deep water, and weightlifting activities. It is important to note that not all individuals with visual impairments are at a high-risk for detached retinas or increased intraocular pressure. Additionally, practitioners need to realize that individuals may be concerned about engaging in physical activity or exercises that require a lot of balancing or forward bending movements requiring postural control, like a bent-over barbell row. Therefore, practitioners must seek out this information about their students or clients whenever possible and help them practice these movements with minimal weight at first to help them develop the control and confidence needed for such movements. Retinal detachment, intraocular pressure, and other contraindications or coexisting conditions are not reasons to reduce or limit engagement in physical activity, exercise, and sport. Rather, individuals with visual impairments should continue to engage in activities with modifications when needed.

CONSIDERATIONS FOR PRACTITIONERS

Many recommendations for practitioners working with individuals with visual impairments have been presented in published literature, spanning considerations pertaining to activity contexts, teaching strategies, activity modifications, and fitness modifications. This section of the chapter will provide a thorough representation of these recommendations. Perhaps the most critical recommendation for providing appropriate and meaningful opportunities is open and ongoing *communication* between the individuals and the practitioners. Often, individuals with visual impairments are the foremost experts about themselves and their learning needs. Therefore, we strongly encourage active and equal status dialogue between practitioners and individuals prior to, during, and after any physical activity, sport, or exercise opportunity. Because of the critical importance of listening to the needs and recommendations of individuals with visual impairments, active and reciprocal communication between practitioners and individuals with visual impairments is a common thread embedded in every recommendation presented herein. With that, it is important for practitioners to position themselves as an expert in physical activity, recreation, physical education, or exercise, but to also respect each individual's own expertise in their personal experiences and abilities to coconstruct the best learning environment <u>for the individual</u>.

Interactional Considerations

When first beginning to work with individuals with visual impairments, there are a few interactional considerations that practitioners should keep in mind that are outside of their typical behavior when interacting with other individuals. For example, when speaking to persons with visual impairments, practitioners should use the same tone of voice and pace of speaking as they normally would, and should speak directly to the individual, rather than relaying messages through coaches or paraprofessionals who might be assisting them. Practitioners need not worry about using terms like "see," "look," or "watch," as most individuals with visual impairments use such terms in their everyday language. However, there are some specific considerations that are helpful when interacting with individuals who have significant visual impairments. In the following, readers can find useful interactional tips for instructing and assisting leaners with visual impairments in physical activity, sport, or exercise contexts.

- When you begin a new interaction, identify yourself by name. This way, the individual with a visual impairment does not have to guess who is speaking to them.
- If you are addressing individuals within a larger group, it is helpful to identify them by name to avoid confusion. Remember that certain cues, such as pointing, may not be sufficient.
- When leaving a conversation, it may be helpful to let individuals with minimal to no light perception know that you have left the conversation so that they may continue to be aware of their surroundings.
- If possible, give individuals an opportunity to orient themselves by exploring the space and equipment you will be using.
- Offer assistance, but allow the individual to decide whether help is needed and in what way it will be most helpful. Do not assume that help is needed because you, the practitioner, think it is needed.
- Respect individuals' bodily autonomy and independence by receiving their permission before touching their bodies or belongings. This includes touching or moving mobility devices like canes. Limit physical touch to when it is necessary, rather than relying on touching or moving bodies of individuals with visual impairments because it is convenient.
- Use anchoring when you leave an individual alone, especially in a large or unfamiliar space. **Anchoring** means positioning the individual in contact with a wall, chair, or other stationary object and informing them of their surroundings.
- Keep directions as clear as possible, using left or right according to the way in which the individual is facing.
- Remember to be verbal. Hand gestures, including those that are combined with directional phrases like "over there," are generally meaningless to people who are unable to see them.

Activity Contexts

The contexts in which sports, exercise, and physical activity opportunities are provided can have important implications for how individuals experience those activities. Individuals may engage in opportunities in a variety of settings, including those that are designed specifically for and used by persons with visual impairments (e.g., self-contained or adapted sport programs), or those that are designed for individuals with and without visual impairments to engage in activities together (e.g., integrated programs). Readers are encouraged review Chapter 2 of this text for an extended conversation about self-contained versus integrated contexts.

The conversation about activity contexts is an important one for individuals with visual impairments, particularly among school-based activities. Prior to the 1980s, many students with visual impairments in the United States engaged in physical education and sport opportunities in self-contained contexts, such as residential schools for the blind. The introduction of educational legislation like the Individuals with Disabilities Education Act, as well as the inclusion movement, influenced a shift from self-contained settings to integrated, general physical education and sport contexts.[29] This has resulted in more students with visual impairments being enrolled in integrated physical education and sport over the past few decades. Today, most youth with visual impairments are enrolled in integrated schools that offer mostly integrated sport and physical education experiences. Meanwhile, enrollment in physical education and sport programs at residential schools has declined with the make-up of these schools largely transitioned from students with visual impairments to students with multiple disabilities, fundamentally changing the types of opportunities offered at these schools.[30]

Most sport and physical activity opportunities that are available to students with visual impairments take place in integrated, and often school-based, settings.[31] Within integrated settings, those with visual impairments tend not to be active participants and are often relegated to the sidelines.[32] As such, there are questions about whether these opportunities can deliver meaningful benefits for youth with visual impairments.[15,31] When considering opportunities for sport, exercise, or physical education for individuals with visual impairments, it is important for practitioners to consider the reasons why a specific context is being considered. Generally speaking, when activity contexts are selected based on the individual's preferences to be in settings with (or without) peers without visual impairments or are selected based on identifiable and assessable benefits for the individual, then practitioners are likely making well informed decisions. However, practitioners should exercise caution when making decisions for activity contexts based solely on their own philosophical orientations, where their opinions trump data or the opinions of individuals themselves, which is a behavior that appears to be a rampant decision-making concern in this area of research and practice.

Pedagogical Strategies

Sport, exercise, and physical activity are typified by complex skills and movements that can be inherently challenging for individuals with visual impairments to observe and replicate. As such, a number of pedagogical strategies have been developed that make observation and demonstrations accessible for those with little or no vision. These include (a) verbal instruction, (b) tactile modeling, (c) physical guidance, and (d) tactile mapping/boards. It is important to note that these pedagogical strategies may be used in isolation, or in combination with one another. Further, and to reiterate a point mentioned earlier, practitioners should ***never*** implement these approaches, particularly those that include physical touch, without first consulting with the person with a visual impairment whom they are instructing. It is never acceptable for a practitioner to touch a person with a visual impairment without thoroughly discussing the activity, and obtaining consent to use that pedagogical strategy first.

Verbal Instruction

Verbal instruction is intuitive; it includes practitioners thoroughly describing aspects of a movement that the individual must do to execute the movement appropriately and successfully. According to Lieberman and colleagues,[33] verbal instruction is most useful for simple skills that do not include complex or multifaceted components, or for movements in which the individual is familiar with. When using verbal instruction, practitioners should be mindful to include language that is both precise (i.e., it clearly and accurately describes the movement) and consistent (i.e., it uses the same cues repeatedly). Of the pedagogical strategies described in this section, verbal instruction is the most likely to be implemented in combination with others, as verbal information is seldom enough for individuals with visual impairments when attempting to learn new and complex movement patterns.

Tactile Modeling and Physical Guidance

Tactile modeling and physical guidance are considered ***modeling*** techniques that are commonly implemented when working with individuals with visual impairments. Modeling techniques help individuals to develop a mental picture of how a skill or activity is performed, which helps them reproduce the skill. Tactile modeling, also known as hand-under-hand instruction, is a technique where individuals touch and explore a movement by touching a model's (i.e., the instructor's) body while the model demonstrates the movement.[34] This strategy is generally used for persons with more significant visual impairments. Advocates of tactile modeling suggest that this technique can help clarify misunderstandings of movements more comprehensively than other pedagogical strategies (e.g., verbal instruction) and it allows individuals to control their own learning pace.

Physical guidance, or hand-over-hand instruction, is a second modeling technique that is commonly used for individuals with visual impairments. Physical guidance is reciprocal to tactile modeling in that the individual's body is being physically moved (or, guided) by the practitioner's, rather than the individual touching the model. According to O'Connell and colleagues,[34] physical guidance is typically used to help individuals to understand the rhythm and motion of a movement. As noted previously, constant dialogue between the practitioner and individual is critical while implementing strategies that include touch, such as tactile modeling and physical guidance, to ensure that strategies are used in both meaningful and consensual ways.[16] As such, we suggest that practitioners actively document conversations to note preferences with touch related strategies.

Tactile Mapping

For individuals with visual impairments, the ability to understand the spatial layout of the playing area of a sport or the physical layout of an exercise facility is an important pedagogical consideration.[35] One technique that is used to help individuals with visual impairments understand the layout of physical spaces is tactile mapping. **Tactile mapping** consists of a hard surface (e.g., a clipboard) that utilizes raised lines and/or symbols to indicate where landmarks are located, such as boundaries, obstacles, equipment, participants, goals, or targets. When using tactile maps, practitioners must describe and explain the instructional area using the board while the individual explores the area physically. This combination allows the individual to understand the playing area while also navigating the area to grasp the scale of the full area in comparison to the map. Generally, tactile maps should be utilized prior to instruction or practice within the physical space. By exploring the tactile map and the physical space prior to any instruction, the individual can gain a sense of the layout and player positions (if applicable) prior to activities.

Activity Modifications

When activities are sufficiently modified to meet their needs, individuals with visual impairments can participate in many types of sports and physical activities. To understand and develop appropriate modifications, practitioners must first consult with the individual about their personal needs. Remember that individuals with visual impairments are often the most expert on their own strengths and needs, so it is important that practitioners engage individuals as equal partners, rather than making assumptions about what supports and modifications might benefit them.

Practitioners can modify elements of sports or physical activities in order to enhance engagement for individuals, including rules and regulations, equipment, and boundaries. Within each activity, these

TABLE 16.2. Activity modifications

Modification Type	Example
Equipment Modifications	• Using a larger ball • Using a bright or high contrast ball • Using a softer ball • Deflate a ball to slow it down • Use balloons or scarves that are light and will stay in the air longer • Add sound sources • Add a beeper or bells to the ball • Lower or make goals larger • Tie a plastic bag around a ball to make noise
Rule Modifications	• Give offensive player more space between himself and defender • Bounce passes or rolling the ball only during basketball • Forgive technicalities • Allow more bounces • Assign player roles • Everyone must touch the ball before scoring • Give everyone a turn before changing possession
Boundary Modifications	• Increase or decrease playing area • Rope under tape to give rise to boundaries • Caution tape or flag-rope to mark off playing area • Sound sources behind goals or other target areas • Bright tape or high contract colors on floor to make boundaries • Larger cones to mark area.

Note: Adapted from Haegele & Mescall.[36]

elements can be modified in many simple and creative ways to ensure active participation. Table 16.2 displays examples of each of these types of modifications that are derived from prior work from Haegele and Mescall.[36] A modification may be as simple as a rule change for someone who is completely blind that allows them to walk to a net and feel it before striking a volleyball, or as complex as engaging in a modified version of a sport with new rules.

Fitness or Exercise Specific Modifications

In addition to organized sports, individuals with visual impairments participate in an array of unstructured fitness and exercise activities. Research indicates that walking, running, recreational cycling, swimming, and fitness center–based activities are among the most popular physical activities among adults with visual impairments.[37] While such forms of physical activity may be made fully accessible to individuals with visual impairments, it is important to note that barriers such as inaccessible environments, equipment, and instruction can have a negative impact on physical activity engagement among this group.[25] Therefore, it is important to talk with the student or client with a visual impairment to determine what accommodations and modifications will help them to access both the physical space in which they are exercising, as well as the techniques that comprise the activities of the workout.

In the following subsections, we will describe modifications to several of the most popular fitness activities among adults with visual impairments,[37] including walking, running, cycling, and swimming. Depending on the individual, it may be important to introduce several different modifications (e.g., tethered running and guidewire running) so that each person can decide how the activity works best for them. In addition to these specific fitness or exercise activity modifications, practitioners should also help individuals with navigating the locations or physical spaces in which the activities take place. Engaging individuals in conversations about where fitness or exercise activities can take place is one strategy to enhance the likelihood that they will spend their leisure time engaged in some of these activities.

Walking

The most common sport mentioned among active adults with visual impairments is walking.[37] This is not surprising, as walking is generally considered to be among the most commonly selected leisure-time activities, and requires little to no modification. One consideration, however, is in how one might track the amount that they walk. While activity trackers like pedometers usually provide information on step counts visually, talking pedometers have been designed that provide auditory as well as visual feedback that is most suitable for those with visual impairments.[38]

In the past decade, technology in activity monitors has improved and now many trackers and apps

Runners with visual impairments may use a guide runner and tether for races or running for fitness.

(e.g., Fitbit) that measure steps, workouts, and more have become accessible for users with visual impairments via screen readers and other assistive technology.[39] The Fitbit Zip model was one particular model that tested favorably for accuracy for youth with visual impairments,[40] making it one that could provide an appropriate method for assessing walking (i.e., steps) for individuals with visual impairments. However, the Zip model has recently been replaced with the Inspire model, which has yet to be tested for this population.

Running

Running is a fundamental movement skill that is incorporated into a variety of sports and activities. In addition, running is among the most common leisure-time exercises for adults with visual impairments.[37] Benefits of running as a leisure-time exercise include decreased risk of cardiovascular disease, increased longevity, and enhanced self-esteem and life satisfaction.[41] To help encourage running, practitioners should be aware of modifications that can help provide those with visual impairments the option to engage in running for exercise. Recommendations vary across visual impairment levels and include options for running in guided and independent conditions. Practitioners are encouraged to offer a variety of running modifications, to allow individuals to select the modifications that best fit their needs. Please see Table 16.3 for an overview on these various running modifications.

Cycling

Cycling is a popular recreational activity that is also a Paralympic sport for individuals with visual impairments (this is discussed later in the chapter). While individuals with low vision may elect to ride a standard bicycle, individuals with visual impairments may experience difficulties such as light–dark transitions, crossing intersections without traffic lights, and other bicycle and car traffic when cycling.[42] For those with more significant visual impairments, tandem bicycles are likely the most common selection. Tandem bicycles are designed to be ridden by two individuals who sit one behind the other, with a pilot in the front chair, and a stoker in the back chair. In addition, there are a variety of other types of bicycles that can make recreational cycling accessible for individuals with visual impairments. For example, side-by-side bikes, where two bikers sit and ride next to each other, provide an option where individuals can cycle with minimal balance and communication issues.

TABLE 16.3 Running modifications

Modification	Description
Independent Running	Runners with low vision run independently on tracks with bold, thick white lines.
Guide Wire	A guide wire is a fixed rope or wire that is pulled tightly across a running area. A rope loop or handle is held by the runner to ensure they do not get rope burn. The runner holds the loop or handle and runs independently for time.
Sighted Guide with Tether	A sighted guide is a sighted running partner who runs alongside the athlete. The runner grasps a tether (i.e., a short string) to allow the runner a full range of motion of the arms.
Sighted Guide's Shirt	Runners with low vision run behind a guide who is wearing a brightly colored shirt. This must be done in areas that are not overly crowded.
Sighted Guide with Sound Source	Runners run next to a guide who has a sound implement (e.g., a bell).
Sound Source from a Distance	Runners sprint toward a sound source, such as a clap or bell, that is in a fixed position

Swimming

Like walking, running, and cycling, swimming is also identified as a popular fitness activity among adults with visual impairments.[37] A variety of different methods can be used for individuals with visual impairments to engage in lap swimming. For example, many swimmers with visual impairments use the side of the pool or lane lines to help guide them to swim in a straight line. In addition, swimmers can keep track of how many strokes it takes to swim from one side of the pool to the other, and then count their strokes while swimming to have an idea of where they are in the pool. In addition to behaviors that swimmers can adopt, there are also several assistive devices that may be used to help swimmers with visual impairments. For example, a sighted coach may tap a swimmer on the shoulder with a *tapper*, a long pole with a soft material at the end or a foam noodle, when they are about 8 feet from the wall as a signal to turn. If a sighted coach is unavailable, a swimmer may elect to set up a sprinkler to break the water at the same position in order to signal to swimmers that they are approaching the wall. Finally, swimmers with visual

A stoker with a visual impairment (rear) and a sighted pilot (front) ride a tandem road bike.

impairments may elect to swim with spotters, swimmers who are in parallel lanes who communicate position or emergencies to the swimmer.

SPORTS AND SPORT ORGANIZATIONS FOR INDIVIDUALS WITH VISUAL IMPAIRMENTS

There are numerous forms of physical activity—including sports, exercise, and recreation—available for individuals with visual impairments across the life span. As mentioned earlier, individuals with visual impairments participate in physical activities designed for sighted populations using modifications and accommodations to suit their needs. In addition to these activities, there exist a number of sports and activities specifically designed or modified for those with visual impairments. Individuals with visual impairments may choose to participate in sports and activities specific to the population because they present an opportunity to socialize and compete with others with visual impairments at levels of competition ranging from recreational to elite. The following passage describes many common sports and activities for visual impairment populations but is by no means exhaustive.

Team Sports

Goalball

Goalball is a sport for the blind played at all skill levels, including recreational clubs for youth and adults, scholastic competitions contested by schools for the blind, intercollegiate club competitions, and elite-level competitions at the Paralympic Games. Originally developed by Hans Lorenzen and Sepp Reindle as a rehabilitative sport for veterans who acquired visual impairments in World War II, goalball has the unique distinction of being the only Paralympic event that was designed specifically for a disability population and is not a modified version of an Olympic sport. The object of the game is to score by rolling ("throwing") a rubber ball with bells inside into the opposing team's goal. While some club-level teams allow sighted individuals to compete, all athletes at the elite level must meet the criteria for B1, B2, or B3 classification. At all levels, all competitors must wear black out eyeshades to create a fair game for players of any level of vision. Globally, goalball is governed by the International Blind Sports Federation (IBSA); the United States Association of Blind Athletes

In the sport of goalball, players use their bodies to block shots on goal.

(USABA) organizes programming for the sport in the United States.

Five-a-Side Football

Five-a-Side football, sometimes called "blind soccer," is a small-sided version of soccer designed for players with visual impairments. Five-a-Side football is played by four outfield players who have visual impairments using a ball that contains pellets that make a rattling sound when kicked. In addition to the outfield players, each team has a goalkeeper, who may be sighted, have low vision, or be legally blind. The movement of the outfield players is guided by verbal cues given by two coaches and the goalkeeper, who help keep the players organized in attack, midfield, and defense. In addition to the modified ball, other differences from full-sided soccer include slight differences in rulesets, reduced match duration (two 25-minute halves), field dimensions (40 m by 20 m), and one-meter high boards along the sidelines to keep the ball from going out of play. At the elite level, the IBSA holds World Championships in both the B1 and combined B2–B3 divisions, while the Paralympic Games holds a competition in the B1 division only. Currently, elite competitions are open to men only, but the women's game is beginning to develop across the globe. In the United States, five-a-side football is just beginning to develop, mostly at youth and recreational levels. To date, there is no U.S. men's or women's national five-a-side soccer team, while countries like Brazil and Argentina are among the most decorated in international play.

Beep Baseball

Beep baseball is a version of traditional baseball modified for individuals with visual impairments. Like traditional baseball, the object of beep baseball is to score more runs than the opposing team by hitting a ball and successfully running bases. However, in beep baseball, there are differences in the ball, the bases, and the rules of the game. The ball is 16-inches in diameter and emits a continuous beeping sound to help batters and fielders alike to track it. Runs are scored when the batter touches one of two buzzing, 1.5-meter-tall foam bases located just outside the first and third baselines before an opposing field player locates the ball and picks it up. Teams are typically co-ed, and all players except for the pitcher and catcher have visual impairments and wear eyeshades during play. Unlike traditional baseball, the beep baseball pitcher and catcher play for the same team as the batter. Beep baseball is played in recreational, scholastic, and competitive settings, the latter of which culminates in the United States with the Beep Baseball World Series, which is governed by the National Beep Baseball Association (NBBA). Outside of the United States, beep baseball is still early in its development, though teams have formed in Asia and Europe. Beep tee ball and beep kickball are popular recreational variants of the sport.

Blind Hockey

Blind hockey, or adaptive hockey, is a newer sport for individuals with visual impairments adapted from ice hockey. Blind hockey follows IBSA and Paralympic Games classifications to determine player eligibility and all players on blind hockey teams have a visual impairment. Equipment modifications include the use of a larger, audible puck and shorter goal nets (3 feet), and full protective face masks are required for all players. The largest rule modification from traditional hockey is that teams must complete at least one pass in the attacking zone before scoring to allow goalies and defenders (B1 and B2 players, respectively) to better track the puck during the action. Elite-level competition is still emerging in the sport. The International Blind Ice Hockey Federation (IBIHF) was founded in Canada in 2015, and Canada and the United States are the only countries to develop national teams in the sport to date. The eventual goal of the IBIHF is to introduce blind hockey world championships and to apply for inclusion in the Winter Paralympic Games.[43]

Individual Sports and Activities

Blind Tennis

Blind tennis, also called Visually Impaired Tennis, was created in Japan by Miyoshi Takei in 1984.[44] Blind tennis includes singles and doubles rules and uses an audible ball, usually outfitted with rattles or bells. Player classifications follow those used by IBSA and USABA, and court dimensions, markings and gameplay rules vary by classification level. For example, B1 players use eyeshades, play on a smaller court with tactile markers and a lower net. B2–B4 players play on a standard tennis court and are not required to wear eyeshades. The number of bounces a player may take before returning the ball is determined by their classification, wherein those with less vision are allowed more bounces—up to three at the B1 level—while those with more vision may take fewer bounces. In all classes, play begins with a verbal interaction wherein the server asks "ready," the receiver replies "ready," and the server shouts "play" prior to serving the ball. Recreational matches may be played between individuals with different classifications, even sighted people may play with and against athletes with visual impairments. In national and international competitions, players typically compete against others within their classification.

Judo and Wrestling

Though judo and wrestling are two different sports with different objects and rulesets, both utilize takedowns or throws, grappling maneuvers, and pins during gameplay. Both sports have enjoyed popularity among individuals with visual impairments because the close contact necessitated by grappling sports means that they may be played with very few modifications. Further, the individual nature of grappling sports allows for lifelong participation, especially in the case of judo, since clubs and dojos are available in many communities.

Judo is a Japanese grappling-based martial art and sport. As a sport, judo is popular worldwide and is contested at all levels, including the Olympic and Paralympic Games. The Paralympic judo competition is held only for athletes in visual impairment categories ranging from B1 to B3. Judo players wear heavy jackets called judogi (or gi) that are built to withstand the gripping and pulling associated with performing the sport's hallmark throws. Judo matches are won by throwing, pinning, or outscoring one's opponent. In teen and adult divisions, matches may also be won by applying a number of submission holds, such as strangles or armlocks. At all levels and ages, strikes are not permitted in judo competition. Paralympic judo follows the same general ruleset as Olympic judo, with one notable exception: players in visual impairment divisions must maintain a constant grip on their opponent's judogi jacket with at least one hand. Judo players in all visual impairment classifications compete together in a single division and eyeshades are not worn during matches. At the recreational levels, it is commonplace for judo players with visual impairments to train and compete with sighted opponents.

A judo player with a visual impairment throws her opponent in a match.

Typically, sighted players adopt the gripping rules of Paralympic judo when they compete against opponents with visual impairments.

Like judo, wrestling is a grappling-based sport that prohibits strikes in competition and its object is usually to control or outscore one's opponent using takedowns and pins. While wrestling is not contested at the Paralympic Games, it is a popular sport among youth with visual impairment who may compete on scholastic wrestling teams at schools for the blind or in public or private schools. Wrestlers with visual impairments may compete against other wrestlers within any visual impairment classification or against sighted opponents. A contact rule, similar to the gripping rule found in judo, is usually employed when at least one of the competitors in a match has a visual impairment, and eyeshades are not typically worn in the sport.

Track and Field

Running—including track events, distance races, and triathlon—is popular as a competitive sport and a lifelong activity for individuals with visual impairments. Those with visual impairments compete in running events at recreational, scholastic, and elite levels, including the Paralympic Games. Many runners in B1 and B2 classifications elect to run with guide runners. Techniques for guide running are presented earlier in the chapter. In some competitions, sprint events may be completed by runners with visual impairments without a guide runner using a guidewire system. In such events, sprint lanes are demarcated with an inflexible guidewire between them. Runners with less vision may choose to use a tether that slides along the guidewire to provide tactile cues that keep them in their lane, while runners with more vision may use the guidewires as an additional visual cue without holding onto a tether. In field events such as the long jump, triple jump, and discus, individuals with visual impairments typically use strategies like counting their steps prior to taking off for a jump. They may also use a sighted caller to provide verbal prompts to help the athlete orient themselves to perform the event.

Swimming

Swimming is another popular recreational and competitive activity among individuals with visual impairments. Like track and field, swimming is a contested sport among athletes with visual impairments at the Paralympic Games. In addition to counting strokes, swimmers with visual impairments may use lane markers and sound sources at the end of the pool to help them orient themselves as they move across the pool. In competitive settings, swimmers at the B2 and B1 level may use a tapper—that is, a sighted sport guide who uses a long foam pole to tap the swimmer on the head or shoulder to indicate an upcoming turn.

Cycling

Cycling is another popular recreation and competitive activity among individuals with visual impairments.[45] At the Paralympic Games, athletes with visual impairments compete in track, road, and triathlon races. In races, athletes with visual impairments ride tandem bikes with a sighted rider who is responsible for steering and navigation. This partnership between a rider who is visually impaired, called a stoker, and a sighted partner, called a pilot, is also common in recreational settings among individuals with visual impairments, especially those in B1 or B2 classifications. Riders at the B3 or B4 levels may choose to use a pilot, but often ride independently.

CHAPTER SUMMARY

- Visual impairment is an umbrella term that refers to "a range of visual function from low vision through total blindness" that is not correctable using even the strongest prescription eyeglasses and interferes with tasks of daily life.[1]
- The considerations offered in this chapter are intended to help practitioners to think further about specific characteristics, modifications, and adaptations that might be helpful when interacting and working with individuals with visual impairments.
- Readers should acknowledge, though, that no recommendation provided within this chapter is suitable for all individuals with visual impairments, and all individuals will not need, enjoy or appreciate each and every one of these recommendations.
- Each individual with a visual impairment has their own needs, and those needs must be understood and respected by practitioner. This sentiment is reflected throughout the chapter, where the common thread across each of the recommendations provided is that practitioners must engage in consistent and equal status conversations with individuals to understand their wants, needs, goals, and preferences.
- It is only through active engagement with individuals with visual impairments that practitioners can ensure that they are providing the best possible experience for the population in which they are serving.

WEB RESOURCES

American Blind Skiing Foundation www.absf.org/
American Printing House for the Blind Physical Education Content https://sites.aph.org/physical-education/
Blind Judo Foundation www.blindjudofoundation.org/wp/
International Blind Golf Association https://internationalblindgolf.com/
International Blind Sports Federation www.ibsasport.org/
National Beep Baseball Association www.nbba.org/
See Now Vision Simulator https://simulator.seenow.org/
United States Association of Blind Athletes www.usaba.org/
Vision Aware Sports and Exercise Content https://visionaware.org/everyday-living/recreation-and-leisure/sports-and-exercise/

BOOKS AND PRINTED MATERIALS

Haegele, J.A. (2021). *Movement and visual impairment: Research across disciplines.* Routledge

Lieberman, L.J., Ponchillia, P.E., & Ponchillia, S.V. (2013). *Physical education and sports for people with visual impairments and deaf-blindness: Foundations of instruction.* AFB Press.

Liebs, A. (2013). *The encyclopedia of sports and recreation for people with visual impairments.* Information Age Publishing.

REFERENCES

1. American Foundation for the Blind. (2020, October). *Key definitions of statistical terms.* www.afb.org/research-and-initiatives/statistics/key-definitions-statistical-terms
2. United States Association of Blind Athletes. (n.d.). *Visual classifications.* www.usaba.org/membership/visual-classifications/#:~:text=USABA%20Recognized%20Low%20Vision%20Classification,the%20best%20practical%20eye%20correction
3. World Health Organization. (2014, August). *Visual impairment and blindness.* World Health Organization. https://web.archive.org/web/20150512062236/ www.who.int/mediacentre/factsheets/fs282/en/
4. Erickson, W., Lee, C., & von Schrader, S. (2021). *Disability statistics from the 2018 American Community Survey (ACS). Ithaca, NY: Cornell University Yang-Tan Institute (YTI).* Cornell University Disability Statistics. www.disabilitystatistics.org
5. Bruce, S. M. (2004). Visual impairment across the life span. In Fisher, C. B., & Lerner, R. M. (Eds.), *Encyclopedia of applied developmental science* (pp. 1126–1130). Sage Publications.
6. Atkinson, J., Anker, S., Nardini, M., Braddick, O., Hughes, C., Rae, S., Wattam-Bell, J., & Atkinson, S. (2002). Infant vision screening predicts failures on motor and cognitive tests up to school age. *Strabismus, 10*(3), 187–198.
7. Brian, A. (2021). Motor skill development. In J. A. Haegele (Ed.), *Movement and Visual Impairment: Research across Disciplines* (pp. 4–16). Routledge.
8. Prechtl, H. F., Cioni, G., Einspieler, C., Bos, A. F., & Ferrari, F. (2001). Role of vision on early motor development: lessons from the blind. *Developmental Medicine & Child Neurology, 43*(3), 198–201.
9. Houwen, S., Visscher, C., Hartman, E., & Lemmink, K. A. (2007). Gross motor skills and sports participation of children with visual impairments. *Research Quarterly for Exercise and Sport, 78*(2), 16–23.
10. Haegele, J. A., Brian, A., & Goodway, J. (2015). Fundamental motor skills and school-aged individuals with visual impairments: A review. *Review Journal of Autism and Developmental Disorders, 2*(3), 320–327.
11. Brian, A., Bostick, L., Starrett, A., Klavina, A., Taunton, S., Pennell, A., Stribing, A., Gilbert, E., & Lieberman, L. J. (2020). The effects of ecologically-valid intervention strategies on the locomotor skills of children with visual impairments. *Adapted Physical Activity Quarterly, 37*(2), 177–192.
12. Pennell, A. (2021). Postural control and balance. In J. A. Haegele (Ed.), *Movement and visual impairment: Research across Disciplines* (pp. 17–31). Routledge.
13. Individuals with Disabilities Education Act. (2004). Pub. L. No/ 108-446. Sec. 602, 118 Stat 2557.
14. Haegele, J. A., & Zhu, X. (2021). School-based physical education. In J.A. Haegele (Ed.), *Movement and Visual Impairment: Research across Disciplines* (pp. 47–59). Routledge.
15. Haegele, J. A., & Kirk, T. N. (2018). Experiences in physical education: Exploring the intersection of visual impairment and maleness. *Adapted Physical Activity Quarterly, 35*(2), 196–213.
16. Yessick, A. B., & Haegele, J. A. (2019). "Missed opportunities": Adults with visual impairments' reflections on the impact of physical education on current physical activity. *British Journal of Visual Impairment, 37*(1), 40–49.
17. Centers for Disease Control and Prevention. (2016). *How much physical activity do children need?* www.cdc.gov/physicalactivity/basics/index.htm?CDC_AA_refVal=https%3A%2F%2Fwww.cdc.gov%2Fphysicalactivity%2Fbasics%2Fchildren%2Findex.htm
18. Zhu, X., Haegele, J. A., & Healy, S. (2019). Movement and mental health: Behavioral correlates of anxiety and depression among children of 6-17 years old in the U.S. *Mental Health & Physical Activity, 16*, 60–65. https://www.doi.org/10.1016/j.mhpa.2019.04.002
19. Haegele, J. A., Aigner, C., & Healy, S. (2019). Prevalence of meeting physical activity, screen-time, and sleep guidelines among children and adolescents with and without visual impairments in the United States. *Adapted Physical Activity Quarterly, 36*(3), 399–405. https://www.doi.org/10.1123/apaq.2018-0130
20. Haegele, J. A., Zhu, X., & Kirk, T. N. (2021). Physical activity among children with visual impairments, siblings, and parents: Exploring familial factors. *Maternal & Child Health Journal, 25*(3), 471–478. https://www.doi.org/10.1007/s10995-020-03080-5
21. Park, Y., Shin, J., Yang, S., Yim, H., Kim, H., & Park, Y. H. (2015). The relationship between visual impairment and health-related quality of life in Korean adults: The Korea national health and nutrition examination survey (2008-2012). *Plos One, 10*(7), e0132779.
22. Haegele, J. A., & Zhu, X. (2021). Physical activity, self-efficacy, and health-related quality of life among adults with visual impairments. *Disability & Rehabilitation, 43*(4), 530–536. https://www.doi.org/10.1080/09638288.2019.1631397
23. Kirk, T. N., Haegele, J. A., & Zhu, X. (2021). Barriers, expectancy-value beliefs, and physical activity engagement among adults with visual impairments. *Adapted Physical Activity Quarterly, 38*(2), 286–306.
24. Kirk, T.N., & Haegele, J.A. (2021). Expectancy-value beliefs, identity, and physical activity among adults with visual impairments. *Disability & Rehabilitation, 43*(4), 516–524. doi:10.1080/09638288.2019.1631395

25. Kirk, T. N., Haegele, J. A., & Zhu, X. (2021). Development and validation of a barriers to physical activity scale for adults with visual impairments. *Journal of Developmental and Physical Disabilities*, 1–14.
26. Haegele, J. A., Kirk, T. N., & Zhu, X. (2018). Self-efficacy and physical activity among adults with visual impairments. *Disability & Health Journal, 11*(1), 324–329.
27. Kirk, T. N. (2021). *Motivational psychology.* In J.A. Haegele (Ed.), *Movement and Visual Impairment: Research across Disciplines* (pp.98-114). Routledge.
28. Pennington, C., & Webb, L. (2020). Enhancing physical education for students with vision impairment and preventing retinal detachment. *Journal of Physical Education, Recreation, & Dance, 91*(3), 53–54.
29. Haegele, J. A., & Sutherland, S. (2015). The perspectives of students with disabilities toward physical education: A review of qualitative inquiry. *Quest, 67*(3), 255–273.
30. Haegele, J. A., & Lieberman, L. J. (2016). The current experiences of physical education teachers at schools for blind students in the United States. *Journal of Visual Impairment & Blindness, 110*(5), 323–334.
31. Haegele, J. A. (2019). Inclusion illusion: Questioning the inclusiveness of integrated physical education. *Quest, 71*(4), 389–397.
32. Haegele, J. A., Hodge, S. R., Zhu, X., Holland, S. K., & Wilson, W. J. (2020). Understanding the inclusiveness of integrated physical education from the perspectives of adults with visual impairments. *Adapted Physical Activity Quarterly, 37*(2), 141–159.
33. Lieberman, L. J., Ponchillia, P., & Ponchillia, S. (2013). *Physical education and sports for people with visual impairments and deaf blindness: Foundations for instruction.* AFB Press.
34. O'Connell, M., Lieberman, L. J., & Petersen, S. (2006). The use of tactile modeling and physical guidance as instructional strategies in physical activity for children who are blind. *Journal of Visual Impairment & Blindness, 100*(8), 471–477.
35. Renshaw, R., & Zimmerman, G. (2007). Using a tactile map with a 5-year-old child in a large-scale outdoor environment. *RE:view, 39*(3), 113–121.
36. Haegele, J. A. & Mescall, M. (2013). Inclusive physical education. *Division of Visual Impairment Quarterly, 58*(3), 7–16.
37. Jaarsma, E. A., Dekker, R., Koopmans, S. A., Dijkstra, P. U., & Geertzen, J. H. (2014). Barriers to and facilitators of sports participation in people with visual impairments. *Adapted Physical Activity Quarterly, 31*(3), 240–264.
38. Haegele, J.A., & Porretta, D.L. (2015). Validation of a talking pedometer for adolescents with visual impairments in free-living settings. *Journal of Visual Impairment & Blindness, 109*(3), 219–223.
39. Preece, A., & Reuschel, W. (2014). Mobile connected health devices: The future of health technology? *AFB Access World Magazine, 15*(11), Retrieved from www.afb.org/afbpress/pub.asp?DocID=aw151toc&All#aw151107
40. Haegele, J. A., Brian, A., & Wolf, D. (2017). Accuracy of the Fitbit Zip for measuring steps for adolescents with visual impairments. *Adapted Physical Activity Quarterly, 34*, 195–200.
41. Holland, K., Haegele, J.A., & Zhu, X. (2020). "My eyes have nothing to do with how my legs move": Individuals with visual impairments' experiences with learning to run. *Adapted Physical Activity Quarterly, 37*, 253–269.
42. Jelija, B., Heutink, J., de Waard, D., Brookhuis, K. A., & Melis-Dankers, B. J. M. (2019). Cycling difficulties of visually impaired people. *British Journal of Visual Impairment, 37*(2), 124–139. doi:10.1177/0264619619830443
43. International Blind Ice Hockey Federation (n.d.). *International blind ice hockey federation (IBIHF).* Canadian Blind Hockey. Retrieved January, 6 2021 from https://canadianblindhockey.com/international-blind-ice-hockey-federation/
44. Battarel, O. (2017, June). *History of blind tennis.* Metro Blind Sport. www.metroblindsport.org/sports/tennis/history-blind-tennis/#:~:text=Blind%20tennis%20was%20created%20in,tried%20to%20adapt%20this%20sport.&text=So%20in%202007%20Takei%20embarked,one%20day%20a%20Paralympic%20sport
45. Lieberman, L. J. (2002). Fitness for individuals who are visually impaired or deafblind. *RE:view, 34*(1), 13–23.

CHAPTER 17
DEAFNESS AND DEAF PEOPLE IN SPORT, PHYSICAL ACTIVITY, AND PHYSICAL EDUCATION

Anthony J. Maher

CONCEPTUALIZING AND DEFINING HEARING IMPAIRMENT AND DEAFNESS

Much has been said and written about definitions and conceptualizations of hearing impairment, hearing loss, and deafness. As a rule, it is crucial to use the terminology preferred by the person or people you are talking to or about. Disability is an integral part of identity; thus, people with disabilities should have ownership over its meaning and usage to ensure that the power to decide resides with those who have lived and embodied, in this instance, deafness. This is especially important when people without disabilities interact and develop relationships with young people and adults with disabilities in sport, physical activity, and physical education settings. This section will critically discuss concepts of hearing impairment and deafness so that you can learn, and therefore make more informed decisions, about the language you use when talking to and about hearing impaired and/or Deaf people. I also hope that this chapter supports you to critical reflect on your own beliefs and values about impairment, disability, and deafness so that you can draw to the surfaces how your ways of thinking may influence how you talk about and act toward Deaf people now and in the future. The onus should be on hearing people to learn about deafness so that they can more appropriately support Deaf people through practice.

Historically and still today deafness is considered a biomedical deficit; a defunct human sense in need of treatment and cure. This purview of deafness is rooted in a medical model understanding of disability that casts the individual and their impairment as the problem that needs to be fixed and normalized, typically through medical intervention.[1] Linguistically, this is tied to the words typically used to describe "people or persons with a hearing impairment." While this terminology places the person before the impairment, it nonetheless implies that this sensory difference is an impairment that the person "has" when compared to hearing individuals. It is cast as an individual possession rather than an integral part of identity. Thus, the issues and problems that arise "because of" the impairment, as Deaf people interact with others in myriad contexts and situations, is for them to deal with and solve. Of course, attempts are being and continue to be made by the hearing majority to "fit" Deaf people into a hearing and speaking world. The use of cochlear implantation and a focus on speech therapy and oralism so that Deaf children can lip read and speak are two examples of deafness being pathologized and attempts being made to assimilate Deaf people into social and cultural norms.[2] A social model understanding of deafness, on the other hand, casts established social and organizational policies, practices, and attitudes as the problem, in need of radical change, rather than medical interventions.[3] In sport, physical activity, and physical education contexts, this is tied to philosophies underpinning equality, equal opportunities, and integration. This could be done by (re)considering the curriculum, assessment, and pedagogical strategies used in school physical education

Anthony J. Maher, Leeds Beckett University, UK. © Kendall Hunt Publishing Company.

Deaf art.

departments to support the learning of Deaf children and those with disabilities.[4] Indeed, many of the established pedagogical strategies in physical education, or coaching practices in sport, were developed by hearing people for hearing people on the assumption that "one size fits all" and, thus, would need to be significantly changed to be appropriate for Deaf people. For instance, teachers and coaches need to more effectively use nonverbal cues and be much more aware of where they position themselves when they demonstrate a technique or activity than is typically the case. The "Strategies" section of this chapter provides many more examples like this to help you support Deaf people in sport, physical activity and physical education.

Many within the Deaf community, however, have shunned the medical and social model understanding of deafness by, instead, embracing a cultural linguistic model. Here, deafness is considered a distinct linguistic identity,[5,6] based mainly on shared lived, embodied experiences of deafness, and collective values, beliefs, and behaviors that bind them together as a Deaf community.[7] For members of the Deaf community, deafness is neither an impairment nor disability; rather, it refers to a group of people who form part of a sociolinguistic minority with a collective, shared sense of themselves as people. Here, you may have noticed that I have (intentionally) used a capital "D" when referring to Deaf people and the Deaf community as it aligns with the work of critical Deaf studies scholars.[8] According to Friedner and Helmreich,[9] the move from "deaf" to "Deaf" marked a challenge and ultimate rejection of deafness as impairment, and an affirmation of Deaf culture and Deaf identity. Hopefully, by now, you are beginning to appreciate the complexity and nuance of the language you use when talking about and to Deaf people. Most Deaf people are very open to discussions about terminology, and they are not easily offended if you happen to use the "wrong" terminology. It is crucial to remember, though, that Deaf people should be the ones determining the language that is used, and that hearing people should be committed to "listening" across difference to learn about Deaf people.[10] This will enable you to make more informed decisions and be a more inclusive practitioner.

PREVALENCE AND KNOWN CAUSES

Despite Deaf people themselves advocating for social-cultural-linguistic understandings and considerations of deafness, governments and associated organizations collect statistical data based on biomedical definitions of deafness and hearing loss. On that basis, according to the National Institute on Deafness and Other Communication Disorders (NIDCD),[11] approximately 2 to 3 out of every 1,000 children in the United States are born with hearing loss in one or both ears. Of these, over 90% are born to hearing parents despite research suggesting that deafness can be inherited. Standard hearing examinations carried out in the United States have found that over 30 million young people and adults, aged 12 years or older, experience hearing loss. Generally, age is a strong predictor of hearing loss. For instance, approximately 2 percent of adults aged 45 to 54 have disabling hearing loss, a rate that increases to 8.5 percent for adults aged 55 to 64. Nearly 25 percent of those aged 65 to 74 and 50 percent of those who are 75 and older also experience disabling hearing loss.[11] On the other side of the Atlantic Ocean, in the United Kingdom (UK), 12 million of its nearly 67 million population experience deafness.[12] More than 40 percent of people over 50 years old have hearing loss, rising to more than 70 percent of people over the age of 70. By 2035 it is estimated that that will rise to approximately 14.2 million adults across the UK. At present, there are at least 50,000 children in the UK who are deaf. While the figures differ from country-to-country, the World Health Organization (WHO) estimates that there are 466 million people in the world with disabling hearing loss, or 6 percent of the global population.[13]

Of these, 432 million, or 93 percent, are adults (190 million women compared to 242 million men). According to the most recent data, roughly one-third of people over 65 years experience disabling hearing loss.[13] The World Health Organization projects that the prevalence of hearing loss is likely to increase over coming years, to 630 million by 2030 and over 900 million by 2050 because of aging populations.[13]

Deafness can be congenital; however, there are many causes of hearing loss in adults especially, which helps to explain why it is much more prevalent in later life. The American Speech, Language, and Hearing Association suggests the following causes.[14]

1. **Otosclerosis**, which is a disease affecting the middle of the ear. It limits movement of the small bones in the middle ear. This is a type of hearing loss that gets gradually worse over time. It becomes increasingly more difficult to hear low, deep sounds and whispers, and often results in the person speaking quietly because their own voice sounds loud to them. Otosclerosis can be treated with surgery.
2. **Ménière's disease**. The cause of Ménière's disease is unknown, but it affects the inner ear. Typically, it starts in people between 30 and 50 years old. Dizziness, ringing in the ear, and hypersensitivity to loud sounds are common. Ménière's disease may cause hearing loss to come and go, but over time some hearing loss becomes permanent.

Anatomy of the Ear

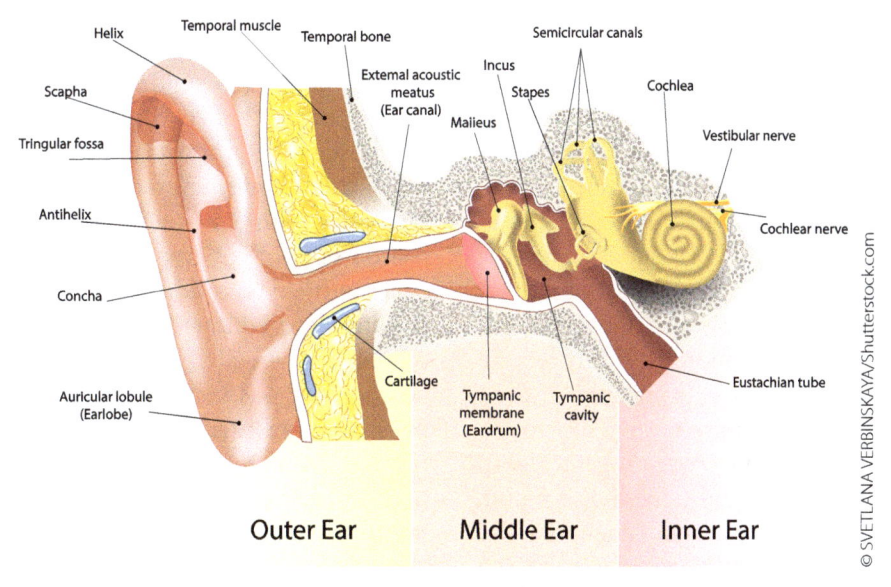

Hearing loss is often dependent on the parts of the ear that are affected.

3. **Autoimmune inner ear disease.** This type of hearing loss can happen rapidly, often without warning when the body's immune system attacks cells in the inner ear, thinking the cells are a virus or bacteria. This autoimmune disorder can be treated medically to minimize hearing loss, if action is taken quickly and can happen in isolation or in conjunction with other autoimmune disorders such as rheumatoid arthritis.
4. **Very loud noise.** Loud noise can cause permanent hearing loss. Noise-induced hearing loss is painless and usually happens slowly, over time. Noisy working environments, particularly those where appropriate safety measures are not taken, are one cause.
5. **Acoustic neuroma.** A tumor that causes hearing loss. It can also cause ringing in your ear and feeling like your ears are full. Acoustic neuroma can also be treated medically.
6. **Physical head injury.** A traumatic brain injury can damage the ear and result in hearing loss.
7. **Presbycusis.** This is a sensorineural hearing loss that can happen slowly as you get older. As a result, speech may sound muffled.

DEAFNESS AND MOTOR MOVEMENT

Most research about the motor movement of Deaf people centers around Deaf children and young people. Accordingly, there is an expansive body of literature suggesting that Deaf children, from as early as 3 years of age, are likely to experience delays in balance and motor development, among other things. More specifically, studies have suggested that when compared to their same aged hearing peers, Deaf children have poorer balance[15,16] and demonstrate lag when it comes to motor development.[17] Indeed, it is important to note that balance disorders can negatively affect motor skills such as sensory integration,[18] general dynamic coordination, and eye coordination.[15,19] Moreover, research has found that Deaf children often use irregular and shorter steps,[20] slower gait speed,[21] and are more likely to require support when walking.[20] When compared to their hearing peers, Deaf children are more likely to experience dizziness and to fall over. Together with balance issues, Gheysen and colleagues[22] also found, through using the Movement Assessment Battery for Children (MABC), that Deaf children scored worse than their hearing peers on all scales including manual dexterity and ball skills. Regardless of the purpose of engaging in sport, physical activity, or physical education, the consequences of poor balance on motor movement are obvious. Indeed, postural control and balance are crucial for performing the skilled bodily movements often promoted, used, and valued in physical activity contexts. Simple and complex gross and fine motor movements require a person to maintain their center of gravity over the base of support[23] so that they can throw and catch balls, and swing bats, racquets, and clubs. Thus, physical education teachers, for instance, will need to be cognizant of this, and plan their curriculum, assessment strategies, and pedagogical approach accordingly. For instance, when judging movement in physical education, whether that be through informal or formal assessment procedures, it may be inappropriate to use standardized methods and criteria that have been developed based on normative movement abilities. Rather, teacher expectations, judgments, and learning goals should be tailored to the movement competencies of the Deaf student rather than being compared to hearing peers.

Much of the research that endeavors to explain poor balance and delayed motor development among Deaf children and young people is, inevitable, biomedical in nature. Rine and colleagues,[17] for instance, suggest that, because the labyrinth and the cochlea are inextricably linked, both anatomically and developmentally, a related vestibular deficit is a potential finding when a hearing mechanism is impaired. This is supported by research conducted by others who argue that damage to the vestibular afferent fibers, vestibular, cerebellar, or central nervous system impairment are possible explanation for the balance deficit among Deaf children.[18,24] To this list, Gheysen and colleagues[22] offer what may be considered more psychosociocultural reasons, such as a lack of verbal representation of motor skills, and emotional issues associated with parental behaviors, such as overprotection of Deaf children. Others cast light on differences in the type of education, such as whether Deaf children are educated in specialist self-contained schools or integrated schools, as well as the age that hearing loss was identified and the associated commencement of intervention.[25,26] In this respect, much research has noted the importance of early identification of hearing loss and appropriate intervention to improve balance, minimize motor development lag and ensure a better health-related quality of life.[23]

Physical Activity Among Deaf People

There are no specific physical activity recommendations for Deaf children or adults. Instead, a one size fits all approach is often used. For example, The World Health Organization[13] recommends that all children, including those with disabilities, engage in at least 60 minutes of moderate-to-vigorous–intensity physical activity (MVPA) each day. A review by Jung and colleagues[27] suggested that barriers can differ depending on "type" of disability. Both Lobenius-Palmér et al.[28] and Ng et al.[29] used accelerometers to measure how physically active Deaf children and young people in Sweden and Finland were, finding that participants engaged in 110 and 118 min/day of MVPA, respectively. In China, Li et al.[30] found that Deaf children and young people spent 25 min/day participating in MVPA based on a self-report questionnaire. When it comes to comparing the physical activity participation levels and tendencies of Deaf young people and their hearing peers, the results are mixed. For instance, studies have found that Deaf young people spend less time being physically active during the day than their hearing age-peers.[28,30,31] However, Ng et al.[29] reported that young Deaf people participated more in MVPA and light PA (LPA) per day than other young people, whereas Williams et al.[32] found no significant difference existed in the MVPA level between these two groups. Unfortunately, the research about the engagement of Deaf adults in physical activity is extremely scarce. From the limited research currently available, it has been reported that Deaf women and men performed an average of 5,667 and 6,548 steps per day, which is notably below the 10,000 steps per day recommendation for adults.[33] In this respect, however, it is crucial to note that most people do not achieve the recommendation of 10,000 steps per day.[34] Interestingly, research suggests that Deaf adults are generally more physically active than people with other types of disability.[35]

The U.S. Department of Health and Human Services[36] suggests that developing a physically active lifestyle at an early age may decrease the chances of developing health-related problems in later life. Indeed, regular participation in physical activity has physical, psychological, and social benefits.[13] For instance, being physically active can improve cardiovascular and musculoskeletal health,[37] and is linked to reduced mortality and contributes toward the prevention of hypertension, stroke, diabetes, and some cancers.[38] Further benefits include reduction in anxiety and stress,[39] increased self-esteem,[40] and a positive impact on cognitive functioning, with a lower risk of neurocognitive disorders developing.[41] Participation in physical activity is also associated with building friendships and enhancing social skills,[42,43] which are especially important for children and young people with disabilities,[44] including those experiencing deafness, who often find themselves on the periphery of social groupings because of, among other things, barriers to communication.

Despite the notable benefits of being physically active, there are numerous barriers preventing Deaf children and young people from achieving physical activity recommendations. A review of research identified 12 factors influencing the physical activity tendencies of Deaf children and young people, which they categorized as "personal," "parental," "environmental," and "instructional."[45] In relation to "personal," gender, age, socioeconomic status, and type of deafness were all linked to engagement in physical activity.[45] For instance, Li et al. (2018),[30] Lobenius-Palmér (2018),[28] and Martin et al. (2013)[46] all found that Deaf boys were more physically active than Deaf girls, while Engel-Yeger and Hamed-Daher (2013)[31] reported a positive association between age and higher levels and intensity of physical activity. Interestingly, socioeconomic status and "severity" of deafness were not found to relate to MVPA.[32] When it comes to parental factors, Ellis et al. (2013) examined the relationship between parents' hearing status, values toward their child being physically fit and participating in sport, and the physical activity participation tendencies of their child. This research found a positive relationship between these parental factors and their Deaf children's engagement in physical activity. In short, Deaf children that had at least one Deaf parent who valued sport and physical activity were most physically active because their shared experiences of deafness meant that parents understood the support required to engage in physical activity contexts.

Tsai and Fung[48] found that inaccessible information about how to be physically active, and the places and times to engage in organized physical activity were significant barriers. Time of year was reported as another environmental factor linked to the MVPA of Deaf children, with physical activity highest in winter months (Sit et al.,[50]). Interestingly, hardly any of the research currently available has explored the influence of "instruction" on the physical activity participation of Deaf children and young people. Lieberman and colleagues[49] were among a few researchers to buck this trend when they examined the effect of peer tutoring on the MVPA time of eight Deaf students in integrated elementary physical education classes. Their research found that after 11–14 sessions of peer tutoring intervention, Deaf students increased their MVPA from 22 percent to 41.5 percent. This paucity of research is concerning given claims by Overton et al.[50] that teacher pedagogies, which includes instruction, are crucial for ensuring that children with disabilities have meaningful experiences in physical education. In this respect, Maher[7] emphasized the importance of physical education teachers, and this could be extended to include sport coaches, personal trainers, and physical and occupational therapists, challenging "phonocentrism" in their practices to ensure that Deaf people have more inclusive and meaningful experiences of sport, physical activity, and physical education. Therefore, before I discuss some of the ways practitioners can challenge phonocentrism, the next section will briefly unpack the concept.

Phonocentricism

Phonocentricism is a term initially coined by Derrida[51] to refer to the dominance of sound and the spoken word in the course of human social history. According to Bauman,[52] listening and speaking are integral to the concept of Self because of their cultural role in human interaction and relationship formation. Indeed, from the moment (most) children learn to speak and hear, they use linguistic frameworks to construct meaning about themselves, others, their environments, and the objects they interact with. The significance of this is illustrated by Batton et al.[53]

> A key aspect of development for every child, whether deaf or hearing, is the ability to interact socially. Social interactions and friendships in childhood are associated with a wide range of factors related to psychological well-being and can be considered protective factors against life stressors and developmental challenges, such as those faced by deaf children. (p. 285)

It is cultural bias toward hearing and speech that results in phonocentrism and, in turn, Deaf people experiencing what Fernandes and Myers[54] consider **symbolic forms of violence** as nonhearing (and in some cases speaking) people in a hearing-centric world. It is the domination of **audism**—that is,

Tablet sign.

hearing and speaking—that results in the oppression and subordination of Deaf people through, for instance, societal failure to recognize, promote, celebrate, and elevate the linguistic status of sign language and other modes of nonverbal communication used by Deaf people. Thus, according to Maher,[7] it is crucial that practitioners advocate for and actively commit to disrupting phonocentric practices by critically reflecting on and (re)considering their modes of communication when interacting with Deaf people. More specifically, I advocate for what Sparkes[55] terms an **intersensorial approach**, which recognizes and utilizes the ways in which the senses are connected and work together as people make sense of and construct meaning about environments and their relationships with others. In this respect, it is noteworthy that some members of Deaf communities refer to themselves as "people of the eye."[2] Like most (besides, of course, some of those who experience visual impairment), Deaf people are ocular-centric beings[56] in that sight is the main sense that shapes how they interpret experiences of everyday life, including sport, physical activity, and physical education. Thus, the recommendations that follow are tied to how the senses of sight and touch should be central to instructional decisions when working with Deaf people as part of a multisensory approach that can contribute to disrupting phonocentricism.

Strategies for Supporting Deaf People in Sport, Physical Activity, and Physical Education

Interestingly, sport, physical activity and physical education practices have done more than most to embrace what I term elsewhere "visual pedagogies"[7] (p. 2) and consequently—albeit unintentionally—contributed toward disrupting phonocentricism. For example, the use of demonstrations, whereby the practitioner performs a bodily action to "show" their students, players, or clients the "correct" or "desirable" movement technique or pattern are widely used and considered crucial for developing an understanding of tasks.[57] It is important to note, in this respect, that most demonstrations are traditionally tied to phonocentricism in that they are performed by sighted people for sighted people. For instance, it is common for these demonstrations to be complemented by verbal instruction, which may not be particularly useful for some Deaf people.[50] Moreover, according to Maher,[7] demonstrations are often performed too quickly, only once, and little attempt is made by the practitioner to draw the observer's eyes to the important aspects of the modeled skill or pattern. This can be confusing for some Deaf people who may not know what part of the body they should be observing and trying to replicate. Thus, when using demonstrations, it is crucial that practitioners try to slow down the movement, breaking it down into phases or stages, and draw the observer's eyes to key areas of focus by pointing to body parts. It is also useful to repeat the demonstration as many times as necessary, perhaps even changing the demonstration if it is not understood. This will be useful when working with Deaf people specifically, but also young people in general, especially those who have trouble processing information.[4] In short, always ensure that the person has a clear understanding of what they are expected to do. According to Shultz et al.[58] it is a good idea to ask Deaf people and their hearing peers to demonstrate the skill or activity to ensure comprehension and give feedback before moving on.

For demonstrating specifically and working with Deaf people more generally, you need to carefully consider where you are positioned. Obviously, even the richest and most considered demonstrations are only useful if Deaf people can see them. It probably goes without saying but performing a demonstration with your back to a Deaf person may be of limited value; unless, of course, it is the back of your body you want them to observe. If the Deaf person can lip read, it is crucial that they can always see your mouth.[58] For personal trainers, working one-on-one with clients, this may be quite easy. However, for physical education teachers or coaches working with a large group of people, in a much more frenetic environment and during dynamic activities such as basketball, this will be much more challenging. Here, there may be multiple bodies, in a comparatively small space, that are moving in different directions and at different speeds. Therefore, as a physical education teacher or coach, it is crucial that you carefully consider your position and keep moving too, especially if you want to provide instruction, feedback, or enforce the rules of the game.[58] In this respect, preservice teachers in research by Maher[7] found it useful to use brightly colored bibs or flags as visual cues to gain the attention of those who could not hear them during team game activities. For this, they tried to position themselves in the eyeline of the participants before waving the brightly colored flag to gain their attention before giving them instruction. This is something that could be used with students or athletes because it works for both Deaf and hearing individuals. Reich and Lavay[59] remind us of the importance of facing the student or participant, and making eye contact while speaking when working with Deaf people who can hear some sound. If you speak while looking down at your notes, or while holding your clipboard up to your face, the sound waves will deflect, making your voice difficult or impossible to understand.

While the demonstration and modeling of skills and activities are vital for Deaf people and therefore will support their participation in sport, physical activity and physical education, other visual pedagogical tools such as videos, posters, smart boards, and electronic tablet devices can be used to convey instructional information,[58] provide feedback,[60] and develop fundamental motor skills.[61] In this respect, prospective physical education teachers in research conducted by Maher[7] engaged in pedagogical experimentation using story boards and speech-to-text smart phone applications to interact with and relay instructional information and feedback to peers who were wearing noise-cancelling ear defenders. The ethics of "simulating" impairment aside (see Maher et al.[62] and Leo & Goodwin[63] for a critique), prospective teachers in Maher's[7] research generally found the story boards and speech-to-text applications beneficial modes of nonverbal communication. It is important to note, however, that the development of story boards and other forms of picture exchange needs careful consideration. They need to be part of practitioner planning. When it came to text-to-speech applications, users have noted issues with the accuracy of interpretations, especially for those with "regional accents" and when colloquiums are evident.[7] Therefore, it is crucial that the practitioner speaks clearly and slowly into the device, and spends time utilizing the application to become familiar with it. It is important to note here that Cawthon[64] has argued that such devices are no substitute for the use of more formal, structured, and nuanced body signaling such as sign language, which they claim to be the most effective form of communication for increasing comprehension among Deaf individuals. This is supported by Shultz et al.[58] who encouraged all of those working with Deaf people in sport, physical activity, and physical education contexts to learn at least the basics of sign language to supplement and complement other modes of communication.

Sign language.

It is not uncommon for Deaf people to be supported by an interpreter in sport, physical activity, and physical education contexts. Therefore, it is important to consider the interactional dynamics involved in communicating with a Deaf person and interpreter. At first, it can be quite confusing to understand who you should look at and talk to during these interactions. In short, the interpreter is there to facilitate communication between the practitioner and the Deaf person.[65] Lest we forget, however, that interpreters are also human beings rather than auxiliary devices. Hence, while most of the talking and eye contact should be directed toward the Deaf person, it is perfectly appropriate, even desirable, to consider the interpreter as an integral part of a collective conversation. The best interpreters not only use accurate and effective language skills to support Deaf people to communicate, but, like you the practitioner, should also understand Deaf cultural norms and the Deaf community.[58] It is extremely useful to meet with the Deaf person and interpreter prior to any sessions or lessons to clarify communication content and interactional cues. This can also help you to learn about the etiquette of this mode of communication and to clarify the role of the interpreter in the context you are interacting in. While one size does not fit all because Deaf people, like all people, have different communication preferences, Lieberman[66] offers some useful information about working with interpreters. For instance, practitioners should meet with the interpreter before the first lesson or coaching session to clarify content terminology and instructional cues. Moreover, it is important that communication etiquette is established and agreed upon by the Deaf person, interpreter and practitioner so that, for example, the coach looks at the Deaf person (rather than the interpreter) when they are talking to them.

Given the corporeality of sport, physical activity, and physical education, where the bodies of participants are at the center of experience, it may be useful where appropriate to use touch for instructional and general communication purposes. For example, touching the shoulder or arm of a Deaf person to gain attention, correct technique and indicate directions of travel are all established practices when it comes to working with Deaf people. This haptic and more tactile approach, which according to Sparkes[55] is often neglected by academics and practitioners, can contribute toward disrupting phonocentric orientations.[7,54] It is important to highlight, however, the notable ethical issues associated with using touch techniques for instructional purposes. First, there is an inherent power imbalance between a hearing practitioner and Deaf participant. The power imbalance becomes even sharper when transferred to school contexts whereby a hearing adult teacher is teaching a Deaf child. Therefore, it is crucial that all decisions about whether touch should be used, how it should be used, and who can initiate should reside with the Deaf person. According to Maher,[7] it is important that hearing people avoid enacting what Bourdieu[67] refers to as symbolic violence by never initiating touch, especially when working with Deaf children, who may not expect or consent to it. Indeed, discussions about touch as an instructional tool for children and young people must be situated with the contested terrain of child welfare and more specific thinking about pedagogies or care. For this, I draw your attention to Piper's edited book: *Touch in Sports Coaching and Physical Education: Fear, Risk, and Moral Panic*.[68] This text features critical discussion about the so-called moral panic that has resulted in some calling for "hands-off" and "no-touch" when working with children and young people in sport and physical education. As I and others have stated previously, I have concerns that the fear of intergenerational touch and its avoidance in sport, physical activity, and physical education settings has major pedagogical consequences for all learners,[7,69] especially in relation to the development of integrated and inclusive movement settings.

ORGANIZATIONS THAT SUPPORT DEAF PEOPLE

Before ending this chapter, I wanted to remind those either working or aspiring to work in sport, physical activity, and physical education that it is important that they continue to learn more about Deaf culture, Deaf identity, and the excellent work being done to support and advocate for Deaf people. Therefore, this final section provides a brief overview and offers the e-mail addresses of a few of the many organizations that support Deaf people. For instance, the National Association of the Deaf (NAD) (visit www.nad.org/) is a civil rights organization of, by, and for Deaf people. The NAD's advocacy works covers early intervention, education, health care, employment, and youth leadership, among others, as part of its commitment to improving the lives of all Deaf and hard of hearing Americans. The National Black Deaf Advocates (NBDA) (visit www.nbda.org/) was formed to center the experiences and amplify the voices of black Deaf people in America. The NBDA is a growing organization that has been at the forefront of advocacy efforts for civil rights and equal access to education, employment, and social services on behalf of black Deaf and hard of hearing people. While both organizations represent and advocate for Deaf children, the American Society for Deaf Children (https://deafchildren.org/) focuses on empowering families of Deaf children so that they can access language-rich contexts and settings through mentoring, resources, and collaboration with other key stakeholders. When it comes to Deaf people in sport, I recommend that you learn more about USA Deaf Sports (USADSF) by visiting their website (www.usdeafsports.org/about/history/). USADSF develop and regulate the rules of affiliate sports organizations, facilitate the participation of elite Deaf athletes in international competition, such as the Deaflympics (https://deaflympics.com/), and are actively involved in promoting equity in sport.

REFERENCES

1. Barnes, C., Mercer, G., & Shakespeare, T. (1999). *Exploring disability: A sociological introduction*. Polity Press.
2. Friedner, M., & Block, P. (2017). Deaf Studies meets Autistic Studies. *The Senses and Society*, 12(3), 282–300.
3. Kim, E., Byrne, B., & Parish, S. (2018). Deaf people and economic well-being: Findings from the life opportunities survey. *Disability & Society*, 33(3), 374–391.
4. Vickerman, P., & Maher, A. J. (2018). *Teaching physical education to children with special educational needs and disabilities* (2nd ed.), Routledge.
5. Conama, J. (2004). Diverse needs of the Deaf community. *Journal of the Irish College of General Practitioners*, 21(10), 16–17.
6. Hodge, S., Lieberman, L., & Murata, N. (2012). *Essentials of teaching physical education: Culture, diversity, and inclusion*. Holcomb Hathaway.
7. Maher, A. J. (2020). Disrupting phonocentricism for teaching Deaf pupils: Prospective physical education teachers' learning about visual pedagogies and non-verbal communication. *Physical Education and Sport Pedagogy*. https://doi.org/10.1080/17408989.2020.1806996
8. Padden, C., & Humphries., T. (1988). *Deaf in America*. Harvard University Press.
9. Friedner, M., & Helmreich, S. (2012). Sound Studies meets Deaf Studies. *The Senses and Society*, 7(1), 72–86.
10. Goggin, G. (2009). Disability and the ethics of listening. *Continuum: Journal of Media and Cultural Studies*, 23(4), 489–502.
11. National Institute on Deafness and Other Communication Disorders (NIDCD, May 04). (2021). *Quick statistics about hearing impairment*. www.nidcd.nih.gov/health/statistics/quick-statistics-hearing
12. Royal National Institute for Deaf People (RNID). (2021, May 02). Facts and figures. https://rnid.org.uk/about-us/research-and-policy/facts-and-figures/
13. World Health Organization. (2020, May 4). Fact Sheet on Physical Activity. http://www.who.int/mediacentre/factsheets/fs385/en/
14. World Health Organization. (2018). *Prevention of blindness and deafness: Estimates*. www.who.int/pbd/deafness/estimates/en/
15. American Speech, Language, and Hearing Association. (2021, September 27). Types of hearing loss. www.asha.org/public/hearing/Types-of-Hearing-Loss/
16. De Kegel, A., Dhooge, I., Cambier, D., Baetens, T., Palmans, T., & Van Waelvelde, H. (2011). Test–retest reliability of the assessment of postural stability in typically developing children and in hearing impaired children. *Gait & Posture*, 33(4), 679–685.
17. Majlesi, M., Farahpour, N., Azadian, E., & Amini, M. (2014). The effect of interventional proprioceptive training on static balance and gait in deaf children. *Research in Developmental Disabilities*, 35(12), 3562–3567.
18. Rine, R., Cornwall, G., Can, K., Locascio, C., O'Hare, T., Robinson, E., Rice, M. (2000). Evidence of progressive delay of motor development in children with sensorineural hearing loss and concurrent vestibular dysfunction. *Perceptual and Motor Skills*, 90(3), 1101–1112.
19. Jafari, Z., & Asad Malayeri, S. (2011). The effect of saccular function on static balance ability of profound hearing-impaired children. *International Journal of Pediatric Otorhinolaryngology*, 75(7), 919–924.
20. De Sousa, A., De Franca Barros, J., & De Sousa Neto, B. (2012). Postural control in children with typical development and children with profound hearing loss. *International Journal of General Medicine*, 5, 433–439.
21. Melo, R., Silva, P., Tassitano, R., Macky, C., & Silva, L. (2012). Balance and gait evaluation: Comparative study between deaf and hearing students, *Revista Paulista de Pediatria*, 30(3), 385–391.
22. Simonsick, L., Ferrucci, L., & Lin, F. (2013). Hearing loss and gait speed among older adults in the United States, *Gait Posture*, 38(1), 25–29.

23. Gheysen, F., Loots, G., & Van Waelvelde, H. (2008). Motor development of deaf children with and without cochlear implants. *Journal of Deaf Studies and Deaf Education, 13*(2), 215–224.
24. Rajendran, V., Roy, F., & Jeevanantham, D. (2012). Postural control, motor skills, and health-related quality of life in children with hearing impairment: A systematic review, *European Archives of Otorhinolaryngology, 269*(4), 1063–1071.
25. Rajendran, V., & Roy, F. (2011). An overview of motor skill performance and balance in hearing impaired children. *Italian Journal of Pediatrics, 37*(1), 33–37.
26. Lieberman, L., Volding, L., & Winnick, J. (2004). Comparing motor development of deaf children of deaf parents and deaf children of hearing parents. *American Annals of the Deaf, 149*(3), 281–289.
27. Horn, D., Pisoni, D., & Miyamoto, R. (2006). Divergence of fine and gross motor skills in prelingually deaf children: Implications for cochlear implantation. *The Laryngoscope, 116*(8), 1500–1506.
28. Jung, J., Leung, W., Schram, B., & Yun, J. (2018). Meta-analysis of physical activity levels in youth with and without disabilities. *Adapted Physical Activity Quarterly, 35*(4), 381–402.
29. Lobenius-Palmér, K., Sjqvist, B., Hurtig-Wennlof, A., & Lundqvist, L. (2018). Accelerometer-assessed physical activity and sedentary time in youth with disabilities. *Adapted Physical Activity Quarterly, 35*(1), 1–19.
30. Ng, K., Rintala, P., Husu, P., Villberg, J., Vasankari, T., & Kokko, S. (2019). Device-based physical activity levels among Finnish adolescents with functional limitations. *Disability and Health Journal, 12*(1), 114–120.
31. Li, C., Haegele, J., & Wu, L. (2018). Comparing physical activity and sedentary behavior levels between deaf and hearing adolescents. *Disability and Health Journal, 12*(3), 514–518.
32. Engel-Yeger, B., & Hamed-Daher, S. (2013). Comparing participation in out of school activities between children with visual impairments, children with hearing impairments, and typical peers. *Research in Developmental Disabilities, 34*(10), 3124–3132.
33. Williams, G., Aggio, D., Stubbs, B., Pardhan, S., Gardner, B., & Smith, L. (2017). Physical activity levels in children with sensory problems: Cross-sectional analyses from the millennium cohort study. *Disability and Health Journal, 11*(1), 58–61.
34. Tudor-Locke, C., & Bassett, D. (2004). How many steps/day are enough? Preliminary pedometer indices for public health. *Sports Medicine, 34*(1), 1–8.
35. Colley, R., Garriguet, D., Janssen, I., Craig, C., Clarke, J., & Tremblay, M. (2011). Physical activity of Canadian adults: Accelerometer results from the 2007 to 2009 Canadian Health Measures Survey. *Health Reports, 22*(1), 7–14.
36. Marmeleira, J., Laranjo, L., Bravo, J., & Menezes, D. (2019). Physical activity patterns in adults who are Deaf. *European Journal of Adapted Physical Activity, 12*(1). https://doi.org/10.5507/euj.2019.002
37. United States Department of Health and Human Services. (2021, May 04). *Physical activity*. www.healthypeople.gov/2020/topics-objectives/topic/physical-activity
38. Burgeson, C., Wechsler, H., Brener, N., Young, J., & Spain, C. (2001). Physical education and activity: Results from the School Health Policies and Programs Study. *Journal of School Health, 71*(7), 279–293.
39. Lee, P., Macfarlane, D., Lam, T., & Stewart, S. (2011). Validity of the International Physical Activity Questionnaire short form (IPAQ-E): A systematic review. *International Journal of Behavioral Nutrition and Physical Activity, 8*(115). https://doi.org/10.1186/1479-5868-8-115
40. Bloemen, M., Backx, F., Takken, T., Wittink, H., Benner, J., Mollema, J., & Groot, J. (2015). Factors associated with physical activity in children and adolescents with a physical disability: A systematic review. *Developmental Medicine and Child Neurology, 57*(2), 137–148.
41. Biddle, S., & Asare, M. (2011). Physical activity and mental health in children and adolescents: A review of reviews. *British Journal of Sports Medicine, 45*(11), 886–895.
42. Marmeleira, J. (2013). An examination of the mechanisms underlying the effects of physical activity on brain and cognition. *European Review of Aging and Physical Activity, 10*(2), 83–94.
43. Howie, L., Lukacs, S., Pastor, P., Reuben, C., & Mendola, P. (2010). Participation in activities outside of school hours in relation to problem behavior and social skills in middle childhood. *Journal of School Health, 80*(3), 119–125.
44. Su, J., Wu, Z., & Su, Y. (2018). Physical exercise predicts social competence and general well-being in Chinese children 10 to 15 years old: A preliminary study. *Child Indicators Research, 11*(2), 1935–1949.
45. Shields, N., & Synnot, A. (2016). Perceived barriers and facilitators to participation in physical activity for children with disability: A qualitative study. *BMC Pediatrics, 16*(9). https://doi.org/10.1186/s12887-016-0544-7.
46. Xu, W., Li., C., & Wang, L. (2020). Physical activity of children and adolescents with hearing impairments: A systematic review. *International Journal of Environmental Research and Public Health, 17*(12). https://doi.org/10.3390/ijerph17124575.
47. Martin, J., Shapiro, D., & Prokesova, E. (2013). Predictors of physical activity among Czech and American children with hearing impairment. *European Journal of Adapted Physical Activity, 6*(2), 38–47.

48. Ellis, M., Lieberman, L., & Dummer, G. (2013). Parent Influences on Physical Activity Participation and Physical Fitness of Deaf Children. *Journal of Deaf Studies and Deaf Education, 19*(2), 270–281.
49. Tsai, E., & Fung, L. (2005). Perceived constraints to leisure time physical activity participation of students with hearing impairment. *Therapeutic Recreation Journal, 39*(3), 192–206.
50. Lieberman, L., Dunn, J., van der Mars, H., & McCubbin, J. (2000). Peers tutors' effects on activity levels of Deaf students in inclusive elementary physical education. *Adapted Physical Activity Quarterly, 17*, 20–39.
51. Overton, H., Wrench, A., & Garrett, R. (2017). Pedagogies for inclusion of junior primary students with disabilities in PE. *Physical Education and Sport Pedagogy, 22*(4), 414–426.
52. Derrida, J. (1976). *Of Grammatology*. Johns Hopkins University Press.
53. Bauman, H. (2008). Listening to phonocentrism with deaf eyes: Derrida's mute philosophy of (sign) language. *Essays in Philosophy, 9*(1), 41–54.
54. Batten, G., Oakes, P., & Alexander, T. (2013). Factors associated with social interactions between Deaf children and their hearing peers: A systematic literature review. *Journal of Deaf Studies and Deaf Education, 19*(3), 285–301.
55. Fernandes, J., & Myers, S. (2010). Inclusive Deaf Studies: Barriers and pathways. *Journal of Deaf Studies and Deaf Education, 15*(1), 17–29.
56. Sparkes, A. (2017). Researching the senses in physical culture: Charting the territory and locating an emerging field. In A. Sparkes (Ed.), *Seeking the senses in physical culture: Sensuous scholarship in action* (pp. 1–24). Routledge.
57. Macpherson, F. (2009). *The senses: Classic and contemporary philosophical perspectives*. Oxford University Press.
58. Tinning, R. (2011). *Pedagogy and human movement: Theory, practice, research*. Routledge.
59. Schultz, J., Lieberman, L., Ellis, M., & Hilgenbrinck, L. (2013). Ensuring the success of Deaf students in inclusive physical education. *Journal of Physical Education, Recreation & Dance, 84*(5), 51–56.
60. Reich, L., & Lavay, B. (2009). Physical education and sport adaptations for students who are hard of hearing. *Journal of Physical Education, Recreation & Dance, 80*(3), 38–42, 49.
61. O'Loughlin, J., Chróinín, D., & O'Grady, D. (2013). Digital video: The impact on children's learning experiences in primary physical education. *European Physical Education Review, 19*(2), 165–182.
62. Haynes, J., & J. Miller. (2015). Preparing pre-service primary school teachers to assess fundamental motor skills: Two skills and two approaches. *Physical Education and Sport Pedagogy, 20*(4), 397–408.
63. Maher, A. J., Haegele, J., & Sparkes, A. (2021) "It's better than going into it blind": Reflections by people with visual impairments regarding the use of simulation for pedagogical purposes, *Sport, Education, and Society*. Advance online publication. https://doi.org/10.1080/13573322.2021.1897562.
64. Leo, J., & Goodwin, D. (2016). Simulating others' realities: Insiders reflect on disability simulations. *Adapted Physical Activity Quarterly, 33*(2), 156–175.
65. Cawthon, S. (2001). Teaching strategies in inclusive classrooms with Deaf students. *Journal of Deaf Studies and Deaf Education, 6*(3), 212–225.
66. Best, C., Lieberman, L., & Arndt, K. (2002). Effective use of interpreters in general physical education. *Journal of Physical Education, Recreation & Dance, 73*(8), 45–50.
67. Lieberman, L. (2011). Hard-of-hearing, deaf, or deaf-blind. In D. Porretta & J. Winnick (Eds.), *Adapted physical education and sport* (5th ed., pp. 253–269). Human Kinetics.
68. Bourdieu, P. (1991). *Language and symbolic power*. Harvard University Press.
69. Piper, H. (Ed.). (2015). *Touch in sports coaching and physical education: Fear, risk, and moral panic*. Routledge.
70. Öhman, M., & Quennerstedt, A. (2017). Questioning the no-touch discourse in physical education from a children's rights perspective. *Sport, Education and Society, 22*(3), 305–320.

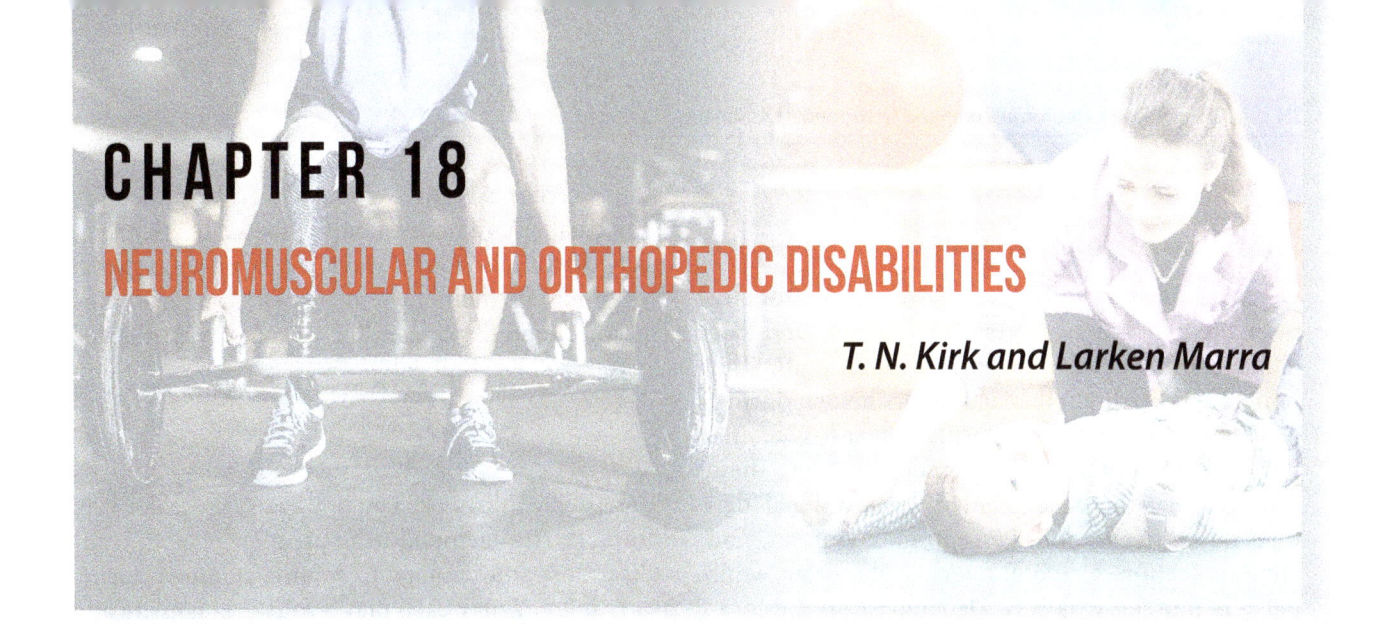

CHAPTER 18
NEUROMUSCULAR AND ORTHOPEDIC DISABILITIES

T. N. Kirk and Larken Marra

INTRODUCTION

The term **neuromuscular** refers to the interaction between nerves and muscles in the body. In this chapter, neuromuscular disabilities are impairments that impact nerve signals between the brain and muscles throughout the body. Individuals with neuromuscular disabilities often experience movement differences that impact daily life. While orthopedic disabilities include many types of impairment, the term **orthopedic** simply refers to an impact on bones and muscles throughout the body. This chapter presents several common neuromuscular and orthopedic disabilities, their known causes, influence on the body and mind, and recommendations to help practitioners guide individuals with neuromuscular and orthopedic disabilities in sport, exercise, and physical activity contexts.

GENERAL RECOMMENDATIONS FOR PRACTITIONERS

All persons with disabilities, even those who share a diagnosis, have individual strengths, interests, and needs. Therefore, it is difficult to make sweeping recommendations for all those with neuromotor or orthopedic disabilities across all physical activity settings. However, the following general recommendations may be a good starting point for developing meaningful activity programs. Perhaps the most important way to ensure that physical activity programming is appropriate for each person is to engage in ongoing communication throughout the process of working together. Individuals with disabilities tend to be the foremost experts on themselves and the impact of their impairment on tasks of daily life. Therefore, the practitioner should foster an open dialog in which the participant feels safe to communicate what they want and need before, during, and after sessions. For youth populations, it can also be beneficial to ask family members or guardians for information that the child cannot adequately communicate themselves, such as medical and therapeutic recommendations, changes to their treatment plans, and current information on their functional status.

Practitioners must also consider safety and accessibility for each individual when approaching the physical activity space, equipment, and tasks. In fitness and physical education settings, pathways should be kept clear and open for those who use wheelchairs and other mobility devices, and equipment should be placed in areas that are accessible. When choosing outdoor activity environments, practitioners should ensure that the path to the area they have selected is accessible, as well as the area itself. Equipment chosen should reflect the needs of the individual. If the practitioner is providing modified equipment, they should be certain that it is ready when needed and that it is safe and appropriate for them to use. If it is provided by the individual, be sure that they bring it to the session and that the practitioner knows how to use, or support its use. Specific physical activity recommendations for each population are presented throughout the chapter.

T. Nicole Kirk, University of Georgia; and Larken Marra, University of Michigan. © Kendall Hunt Publishing Company.

CEREBRAL PALSY

Definition of Cerebral Palsy

Cerebral palsy is an umbrella term for a group of permanent disorders of movement that occur due to damage to the developing fetal or infant brain. This nonprogressive brain damage occurs before, during, or shortly after birth and displays as a loss or impairment of voluntary muscle coordination. These disorders can be accompanied by additional disturbances of sensation, perception, cognition, and communication. Cerebral refers to the brain while palsy is muscle weakness. Depending on the location and severity of the injury to the brain, symptoms of cerebral palsy can vary widely from mild to severe. Regardless of severity, most individuals with cerebral palsy have some degree of abnormal reflex development, which contributes to the difficulty coordinating and integrating basic movement patterns.[1] Common differences in reflex development among individuals with cerebral palsy include increased muscle response (e.g., involuntary flexing of muscles that causes tightness in muscles such as the biceps and quadriceps), decreased protective reflexes (e.g., slow or absent reflexes to loss of balance or changes in head posture), and primitive reflexes (i.e., reflexes that are present at or shortly after birth) that do not fade in accordance with typical developmental stages of infancy and early childhood. Due to the movement limitations associated with cerebral palsy, it is not uncommon to see secondary medical complications among this population, including abnormal bone growth, joint misalignment, or contractures.

Prevalence and Current Statistics

Cerebral palsy is the most common childhood onset neurological disability and accounts for 2 to 3 in 1,000 live births in the United States. There are generally three neuromotor classifications including spastic, athetoid (dyskinetic), and ataxic cerebral palsy. The most common is spastic cerebral palsy, which accounts for 75% of all cases.[2] Symptoms of spastic cerebral palsy include hyperactive reflexes that lead to tight, contracted muscles, especially in the arms and legs. Athetoid and ataxic cerebral palsy classifications account for 15% to 20% and 5% to 10% of the population with cerebral palsy, respectively. Individuals with athetoid cerebral palsy can have difficulty controlling muscle movements due to inconsistent signals from the brain to the muscles. Ataxic cerebral palsy is characterized by difficulties with balance and understanding spatial relations. Finally, some individuals show a mix of neuromotor symptoms in their movements, such as combined spasticity and dyskinesis; this is sometimes referred to as mixed cerebral palsy.

Etiology and Known Causes

The true etiology of cerebral palsy is unknown; however, risk factors during pregnancy, birth complications, and damage to brain structures during early infancy may each play a role. Prematurity and low birth weight are two of the largest risk factors of cerebral palsy, and premature babies are five times more likely to have cerebral palsy than a full-term baby. Other risk factors include birth complications like anoxia (lack of oxygen to the brain), meningitis (inflammation of brain or spinal cord), brain hemorrhage, or brain injury during infancy. In general, medical professionals and researchers believe that cerebral palsy is a result of numerous causal pathways as opposed to one singular factor.[3] Unlike disabilities such as Down syndrome or Spina bifida, that may be diagnosed before birth with amniocentesis, diagnosis of cerebral palsy is based on clinical findings of delayed developmental milestones and neuroimaging. Because the etiology of cerebral palsy is unknown, preventative care during pregnancy is limited. However, treatments that reduce pregnancy complications, and that help prevent preterm delivery, may reduce the likelihood of cerebral palsy.[4]

Pathophysiology and Psychophysiology

Cerebral palsy has an extensive classification system, which is due, in large part, to the heterogeneity of the disability. This means that individuals with similar classifications may display very different movement patterns because the structure and function of individual bodies differ. Cerebral palsy classification systems are largely based on the observable symptoms and may categorize individuals by neuromotor characteristics, affected body parts (i.e., topographical; Figures 18.1 and 18.2), or ease of mobility and tasks of daily living (i.e., functional; Table 18.1). See Table 18.1 for more information on classifications. Finally, the Paralympic games employ a type of functional classification wherein athletes with different disability diagnoses, but similar functional status may be grouped together in competitive events.[5]

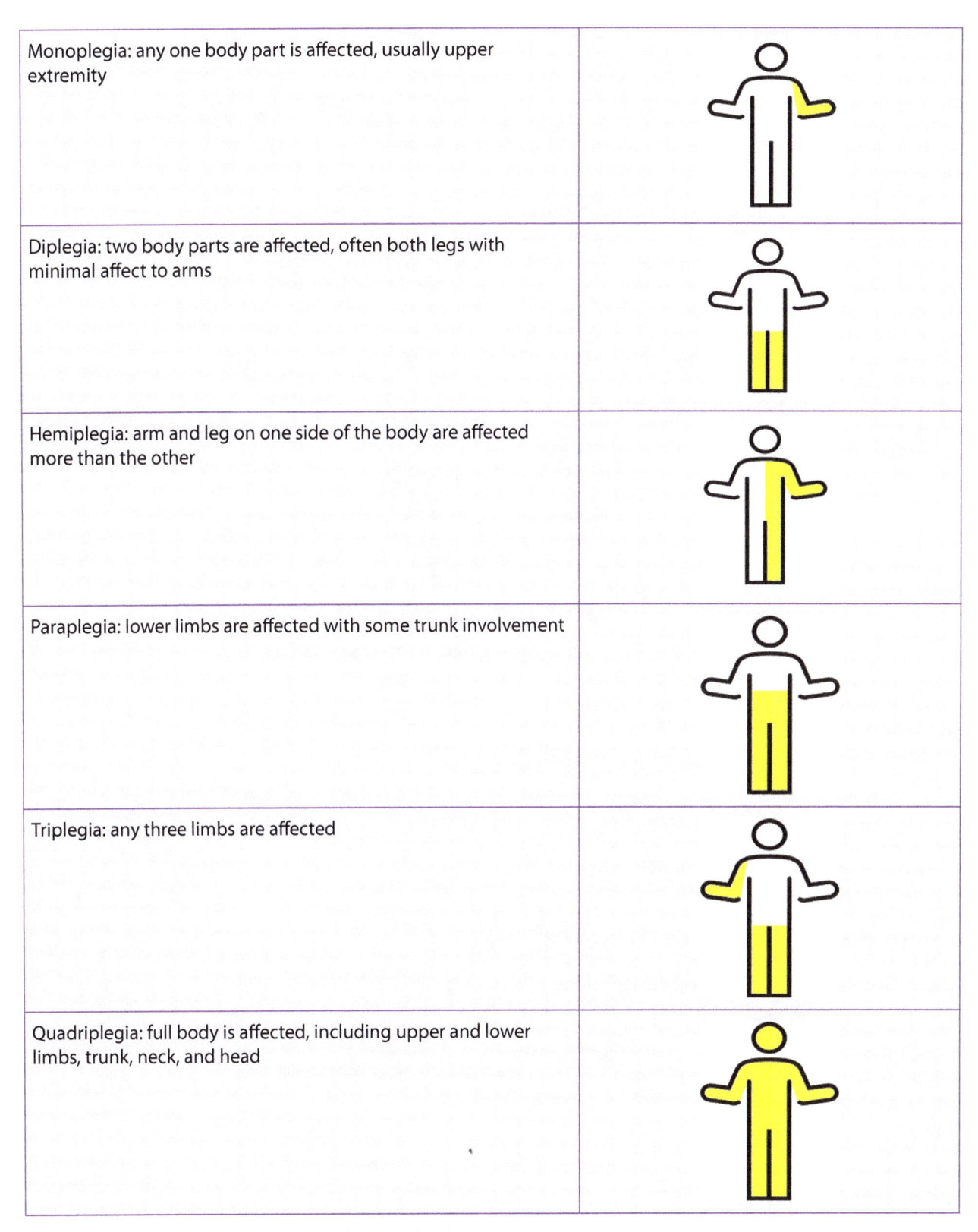

Monoplegia: any one body part is affected, usually upper extremity	
Diplegia: two body parts are affected, often both legs with minimal affect to arms	
Hemiplegia: arm and leg on one side of the body are affected more than the other	
Paraplegia: lower limbs are affected with some trunk involvement	
Triplegia: any three limbs are affected	
Quadriplegia: full body is affected, including upper and lower limbs, trunk, neck, and head	

FIGURE 18.1 Topographical classification of cerebral palsy.
Source: T. N. Kirk and Larken Marra

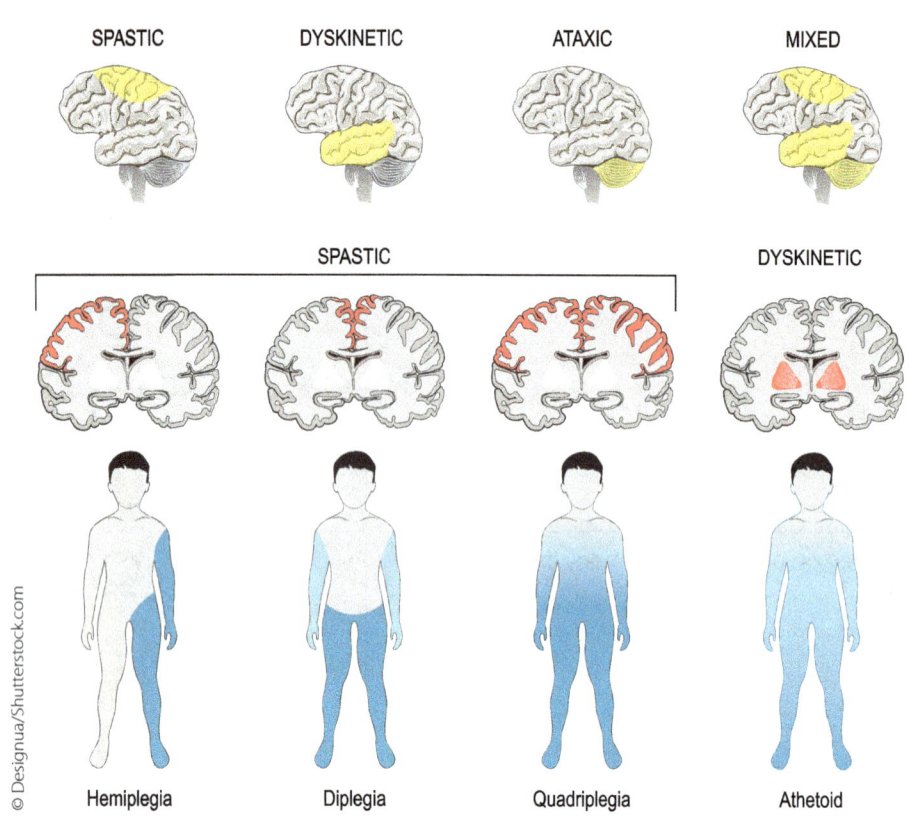

FIGURE 18.2 Examples of neuromotor representations of cerebral palsy and accompanying topography.

TABLE 18.1 Gross Motor Function Classification System (GMFCS) for Cerebral Palsy

Level 1	Can walk at home, school, outdoors, and in the community. Ability to climb stairs without use of a railing. Able to perform gross motor skills, but speed, balance, and coordination may be limited.
Level 2	Can walk in most settings and climb stairs with railing. May have difficulty walking long distances or balancing on uneven surfaces or inclines. May require physical assistance for long distances. May only have minimal ability to perform gross motor tasks.
Level 3	Use of hand-held mobility devices in most indoor settings. May climb stairs with railing and supervision or assistance. May use powered mobility for long distances and self-propel for shorter distances.
Level 4	Use of powered or physically assisted mobility in most settings. May walk very short distances in the home, but in school or community usually transported in manual or powered wheelchairs.
Level 5	Transported in a manual, physically assisted wheelchair in all settings. Limited in ability to maintain antigravity head and trunk positions and control arm and leg movements.

Source: Palisano et al. (1997)[41]

Specific Issues with Motor Movement

Specific neuromotor differences among individuals with cerebral palsy are largely related to the areas of the brain that have been affected. Spastic cerebral palsy is caused by damage to the motor cortex of the brain that results in hypertonia, or an increase in muscle tone, and hyperactive stretch reflex, an involuntary and consistent contraction that occurs when affected muscles are stretched. Individuals with spasticity often appear to be very rigid and tight and may have a lower range of motion in the impacted body parts. Muscle tightness may be exacerbated when the individual is frightened or excited. Spasticity in the lower extremities can be seen mainly in the hip flexors as the thighs and knees pull inward to midline. This low range of motion results in a walking pattern with a narrow base of support, sometimes called a scissor gait, that can make locomotor activities such as running and jumping more difficult.

Athetoid, or dyskinetic, cerebral palsy is caused by damage to the basal ganglia, which results in a flood of conflicting motor impulses to the muscles. An individual with athetosis may experience fluctuations between hypertonicity and hypotonicity (i.e., tight and lax muscles), which cause movements to appear writhing, uncoordinated, or involuntary. Often, times individuals with athetosis will have difficulty with head control, which can impact activities of daily living and physical activity. In particular, lack of head control can make tasks that involve visual tracking more difficult. Therefore, individuals with athetosis may have difficulty tracking objects like balls or pucks, responding quickly to others' movements during sports and tag games, or accurately hitting a target.

Ataxia, the least common neuromotor type of cerebral palsy, is caused by damage to the cerebellum, the area of the brain that controls balance and assists in "fine-tuning" movements. Individuals with ataxia have low muscle tone and often walk with an unsteady gait, a wide base of support with arms at guard (i.e., arms held at chest level with flexed elbows), or with mobility devices like walkers.[4] Individuals with ataxia may also experience involuntary eye movements called nystagmus that impact visual tracking and can further interfere with balance. Individuals with ataxia may have trouble performing motor skills that emphasize dynamic balance such as running, jumping, or hopping.[6]

Management and Treatment of Cerebral Palsy

It is important to remember that cerebral palsy is not a disease and therefore cannot be "cured." However, there are many surgical and nonsurgical ways to manage symptoms of cerebral palsy. Therapeutic approaches like physical and occupational therapy, especially when begun early in life (i.e., before 2 years of age), help increase neuroplasticity in the developing brain and afford opportunities for the child to explore their environment and develop efficient individual motor patterns.[7] Ongoing physical therapy helps maintain established functional capacity well into adulthood. Physical therapists may suggest flexible braces called ankle–foot orthoses (AFO) or ankle–knee orthoses (AKO) that are worn to support weak joints and musculature and to help with ambulation. Occupational therapists work with individuals with cerebral palsy to develop the strength and fine motor skills needed to engage in a wide range of

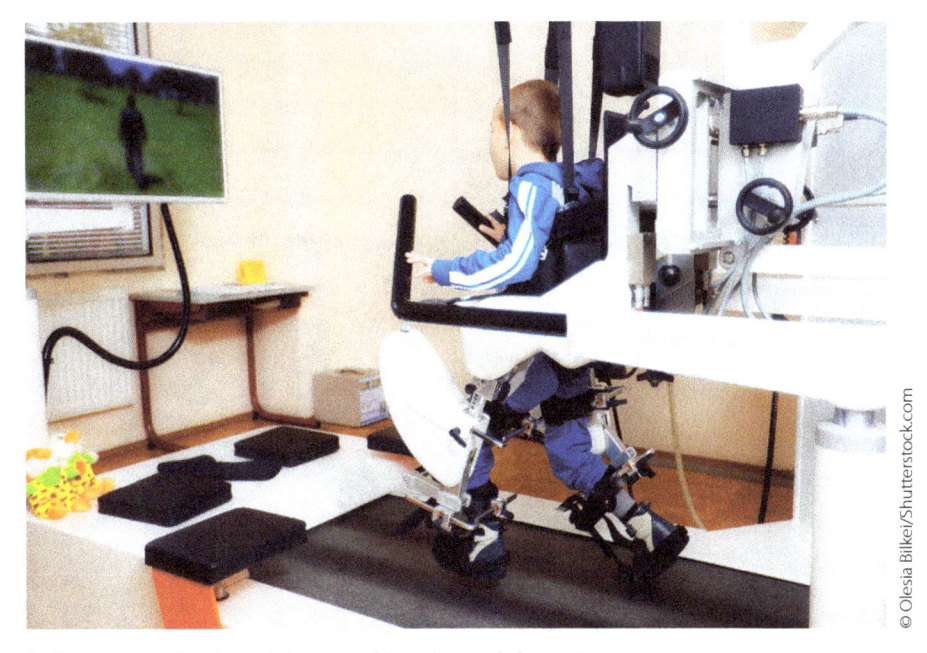

Robot-assisted gait training used by physical therapists.

tasks of daily living. Physical and occupational therapists often work together to create a holistic approach to habilitation that focuses on goals tailored to each individual.

Medications to help prevent or lessen the occurrence of seizures and control spasticity are often the first step in treatment plans before surgical treatments are discussed. Surgical management can include minimally invasive procedures like the placement of a baclofen pump in the abdomen that connects directly to the nerves in the spine and helps to control spasticity. Additionally, botulinum toxin, more commonly known as Botox, may be injected into muscles with high spasticity (i.e., hamstrings, gastrocnemius, adductors, etc.) to help decrease muscle contractions in that area.[8] More invasive procedures like tendon release surgery are used to increase range of motion and improve movement efficiency by cutting the tight tendon (oftentimes the Achilles tendon) horizontally, manually lengthening it, and then reattaching it. Dorsal rhizotomy, a highly invasive spinal surgery, may be employed to decrease spasticity, particularly in the legs. The procedure involves identifying and cutting the nerve most responsible for spasticity of a muscle.[4] Regardless of which method is used to help manage motoric differences associated with cerebral palsy, it is best to supplement these methods with regular adapted physical activity.

Specific Benefits of Physical Activity

The benefits of physical activity and exercise for individuals with cerebral palsy, traumatic brain injury, and stroke are not unlike the benefits for those without disabilities; however, there are benefits specific to these populations. First, physical activity and exercise can help decrease the effects of spasticity and increase range of motion, especially when combined with dynamic and static stretching. Physical activity and exercise also support quality of life and independence among individuals with cerebral palsy by increasing neuromotor control, movement fluidity and balance, and muscular strength and endurance. While cerebral palsy is considered a nonprogressive, childhood-onset disability, there are signs of accelerated aging among this population that may be partially mitigated through physical activity engagement.[9]

Contraindications for Motor Movement

When working with individuals with spasticity, it is important to remember not to force limbs or joints to move. Instead, work within the individual's functional range of motion during activities and aim to gradually increase range of motion using slow passive and active static stretches. For individuals with athetosis who may have difficulty with head control, it is necessary to maintain their head in an upright and neutral position for them to successfully

Modifications based around individual abilities can help increase participation.

coordinate their movements. Depending on the topographic representation of the individual, they may also require assistance with both gross and fine motor activities.

Suggested Modifications for Sports, Physical Activity, and Physical Education

Modifications to sports, physical activity, and physical education for individuals with cerebral palsy are based largely around individual abilities and the activity itself. Because falls and fatigue are common among individuals with cerebral palsy, providing individuals—especially children—with soft surfaces will help alleviate some of the discomfort of falling and will provide a comfortable space for the individual to regain their footing. Similarly, providing a place for individuals to rest when fatigued is an easy modification to the space that allows for the person to collect themselves before returning to the activity at hand. Modifications to equipment or tasks are common and can include things such as increased size of object for manipulation; hand over hand assistance with object control; powered mobility; manual, auditory, or visual cues; more time for task completion; and others based on individual ability.

Recommendations for Practitioners in Physical Activity Settings

To support motor function among individuals with cerebral palsy, practitioners should incorporate physical activity skills with high carryover to tasks of daily living. Examples could be efficient gait, efficient gait, bending, twisting, carrying, and manipulating objects; and maneuvering around spatial obstacles, varying inclines, and ground material. Developing these skills will improve strength and cardiovascular endurance, which often align with individual functional goals. Include movements that cross the midline, fine motor skill activities, and encourage the use of more affected and less affected limbs. Stability and balance practices can help decrease the severity and occurrence of falls and safe fall training can help mitigate fall-related injury. Isokinetic exercises like weight bearing through the shoulders, hips, and ankles can also assist with balance and stability by strengthening the supporting musculature. Concentric and eccentric weight training are advantageous for this population, but isometric exercises involving static resistance may be unsuitable for individuals with cerebral palsy because they can increase the tone of an already tight muscle. Finally, practitioners should engage in open communication with the individual to ensure that activities are enjoyable, safe, and reflect their interests.

Sport and Physical Activity Opportunities and Organizations

Physical activity opportunities for individuals with cerebral palsy include therapeutic approaches, recreational activities, and competitive sports. Many individuals with cerebral palsy participate in sports and physical activities alongside their nondisabled peers with few modifications. In adapted sport contexts, persons with cerebral palsy compete in the Paralympic Games under various classifications in sports such as archery, badminton, boccia, cycling, swimming, track and field, and wheelchair sports. The Cerebral Palsy International Sports and Recreation Association (CPISRA) governs recreational, developmental, and elite activities including boccia, seven-a-side football (soccer), and race running. It also sponsors recreational outdoor camps for youth and adults with cerebral palsy and their families. Other organizations provide opportunities for physical activity for some individuals with cerebral palsy, including the International Wheelchair Sports Association, BlazeSports America, Move United, and more.

In addition to these activities, some individuals with cerebral palsy may be well-suited to power chair sports like power soccer and hockey. Both power soccer and power hockey are sports designed for users of power wheelchairs for whom other adapted sports are not suitable. Power soccer is played on a regulation basketball court using a 13-inch soccer ball. Each team consists of four players, three outfield players and a goalkeeper, who dribble, pass, and score goals by manipulating the ball with the guard on the front of their chairs.[10] Like power soccer, power hockey (or power chair hockey) uses a basketball court as the field of play and utilizes a ball instead of a puck as in traditional hockey. Players use lightweight plastic hockey sticks that may be held or affixed to their chairs to move the ball, pass, and shoot. Though neither power soccer nor power hockey are currently part of the Paralympic sports program, both have held world championships since at least the early 2000s.

TRAUMATIC BRAIN INJURY

Definition of Traumatic Brain Injury

Traumatic brain injury refers to an alteration of brain function due to an injury to the brain, such as a blow to the head or a penetrating head injury. Initially, this injury may result in altered or diminished states of consciousness and ongoing changes or impairments in physical, cognitive, behavioral, social, or emotional functioning. Not all blows to the head result in a traumatic brain injury, and the severity of such injuries ranges from mild (i.e., a brief change in mental status) to severe (i.e., an extended period of unconsciousness or memory loss after injury). Traumatic brain injuries are sometimes classified as either closed, in which the brain has ricocheted off of the inside of the skull, or open, in which the brain has been penetrated by an object.[11] While some traumatic brain injuries are related to temporary or sustained disability, the majority are mild, including concussions.

Prevalence and Current Statistics

The Centers for Disease Control (CDC) stated that from 2006 to 2014 the number of traumatic brain injury–related hospital visits and deaths in the United States increased by 53%. In 2014, 2.53 million traumatic brain injury-related emergency room visits occurred with 288,000 hospitalizations and 56,800 deaths. Often, traumatic brain injuries lead to some degree of permanent disability. Males are about 1.5 times more likely to sustain a traumatic brain injury than are females, particularly during adolescence or early adulthood.[12]

Etiology and Known Causes

There are multiple causes for traumatic brain injury, but falls, intentional self-harm, and motor vehicle crashes are most common. Other known causes include trauma to the head as a result of sport or recreational accidents, child abuse, or violent assaults. The mechanisms that cause injury to the brain include intense forces to the body that cause the brain to ricochet into the skull, direct blows to the skull, and penetrating or blast injuries to the brain, such as those experienced by military personnel. In addition to the initial impact to the brain, secondary injury can occur because of swelling in the brain, death to nerve tissues in the brain, insufficient oxygen to the brain, and other complications.[13]

Pathophysiology and Psychophysiology

The severity of a traumatic brain injury is typically measured using various instruments and techniques, depending on the type of impact being examined. For example, cognitive functioning can be measured using the Ranchos Los Amigos Scale, while neuroimaging can help measure the visible damage to brain structures.[11] Because there is a great deal of variance in the location, severity, and potential for recovery associated with traumatic brain injuries, the physical and cognitive functional effects vary greatly across persons. The damage and impact of an open brain injury is often more limited to the area of the brain in which the trauma occurred and the functions related to it. Conversely, severe closed brain injuries may result in more pervasive physical and cognitive impact from secondary injury (i.e., subsequent damage to the brain caused by swelling or cell death). However, some common physical changes in individuals with traumatic brain injuries include muscle spasticity and weakness, seizures, and problems coordinating body movements. Cognitively, individuals may experience changes to their personalities, increased impulsivity, difficulty with executive function (i.e., planning and problem solving), and memory loss. Individuals with traumatic brain injuries may also experience emotional changes (e.g., mood swings, anxiety, and depression), especially shortly after the injury has occurred. If these issues persist, individuals may benefit from psychological and pharmacological (e.g., medication) supports.[14]

Specific Issues with Motor Movement

Depending on the severity and mechanism of the traumatic brain injury, some individuals may experience spasticity and/or weakness in muscles innervated by the area of the brain that sustained the injury. In more severe cases, individuals may experience general limitations in mobility that require the use of a wheelchair or other mobility devices, but this is less common among those with mild and moderate traumatic brain injury. Often, individuals with traumatic brain injuries experience difficulty with planning and sequencing movements, lack of coordination, headaches, or sensory impairments including vision and/or hearing complications.

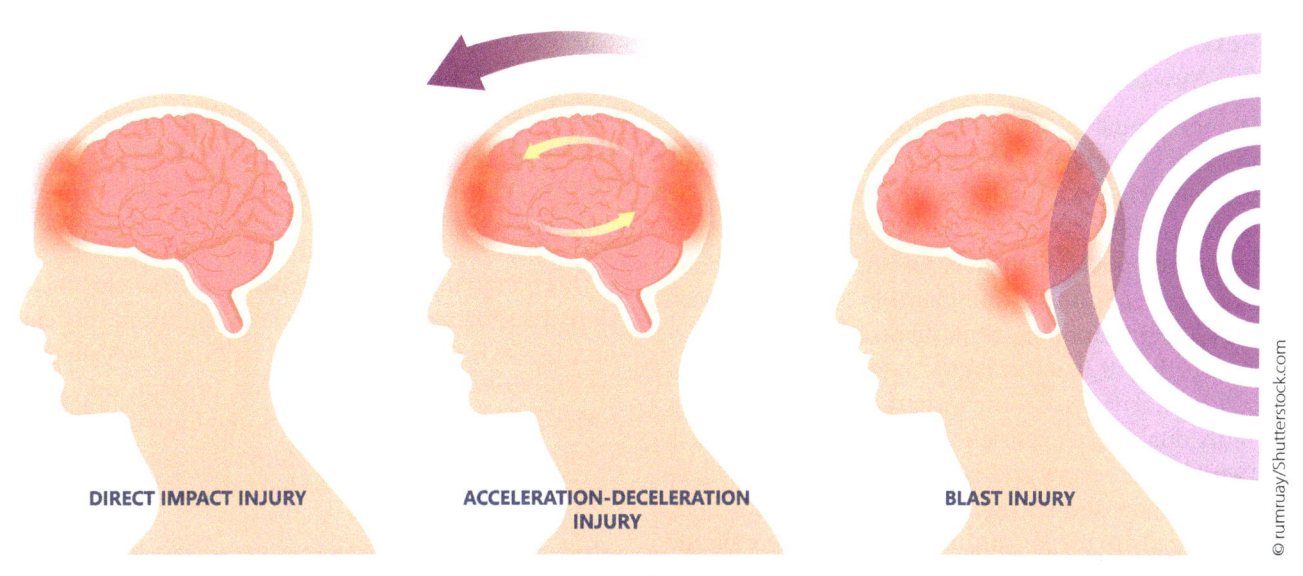

DIRECT IMPACT INJURY   ACCELERATION-DECELERATION INJURY   BLAST INJURY

Impact to the head can cause traumatic brain injury, including concussion.

Improving motor control and movement is a typical goal of acute and long-term rehabilitation programs aimed at optimizing recovery and outcomes for individuals with traumatic brain injury.

Management and Treatment of Traumatic Brain Injury

The intention of initial injury management for traumatic brain injury is to preserve as much nerve tissue as possible. This approach, called neuroprotection, further aims to prevent additional brain damage as a result of high blood pressure in the brain and atypical neural activity like seizures. In the longer term, however, traumatic brain injury is primarily managed through rehabilitation. The duration and frequency of rehabilitation depends largely on the severity of the injury and the speed at which improvements are being made. The goal of rehabilitation is to increase functional independence and neurocognitive abilities using age-appropriate activities of daily living.[15] Beyond rehabilitation, physicians can prescribe medications to help alleviate symptoms of secondary conditions associated with traumatic brain injury including seizures, muscle spasticity, and psychological conditions like anxiety and depression.

Specific Benefits of Physical Activity

In general, the benefits of physical activity for individuals with traumatic brain injury are similar to those for individuals without disabilities. For specific benefits for those with neuromuscular disabilities, refer to the cerebral palsy section of this chapter. Additionally, individuals with traumatic brain injury often show some functional improvement after injury in association with continued physical activity.

Contraindications for Motor Movement

Because traumatic brain injury is a form of brain damage, additional compact forces through contact activities like football, wrestling, and hockey are not generally favorable for this population. However, proper modifications and adaptations that limit the potential for further contact injuries can increase inclusion and opportunities for this group. While few motoric contraindications to exercise exist for those with traumatic brain injury, it is important to consider the cognitive needs of these individuals when designing programs or lessons involving skill instruction.

Suggested Modifications for Sports, Physical Activity, and Physical Education

Equipment and activity modifications are similar to those for individuals with cerebral palsy. Further modifications to support those with executive function and memory issues associated with traumatic brain injury may benefit from instructional strategies that break the activity into smaller, more manageable parts that allow for more attention and time-on-task. Visual prompts that include activity instructions or other information, such as task cards or picture schedules, may also be of use for individuals with traumatic brain injury.

Recommendations for Practitioners in Physical Activity Settings

Recommendations for practitioners who work with persons with traumatic brain injury are highly individualized but may be similar to those for individuals with cerebral palsy. Decreasing the speed of play, providing accessible equipment for improved manipulation, and considering the interests of the individual are all critical for long-term success in physical activity. Further, it is important to consider potential instructional needs of those with traumatic brain injury. Individuals may experience decreases in short term (working) memory and long-term memory recall, so practitioners should use consistent reminders, cues, or prompts to assist with recall. Practitioners should also prepare by breaking activities into smaller components or steps that match the individual's processing speed, focusing first on the most important parts of a skill/activity and filling in additional details over the course of subsequent sessions. Interspersing familiar and new tasks into shorter bursts throughout the session may also help participants work within their attention spans to avoid mental fatigue.

Executive function, or one's ability to organize incoming stimuli and regulate behavior in response, may be affected in those with a frontal lobe traumatic brain injury. Regulating the environment for minimal distractions while incorporating the previously mentioned strategies will help manage impulsivity. Finally, individuals who have experienced a traumatic brain injury may experience social, emotional, or behavioral impairments that are important to keep in mind when teaching new skills or when working in a large group setting. Some individuals with traumatic brain injury may display lack of motivation due to poor self-esteem; they may experience mood swings, or self-centeredness, perseveration (i.e., getting "stuck" on an idea or activity and unable to transition to something else), or even depression; and some individuals may respond inappropriately to contextual situations, or have difficulty relating to others. Therefore, it is important to include activities that allow for initial success, while minimizing situations that spotlight individual performances.

Sport and Physical Activity Opportunities and Organizations

Much like individuals with cerebral palsy, many individuals with traumatic brain injuries participate in sports and physical activities with individuals without traumatic brain injuries or other disabilities with few modifications. In sports contexts, athletes with traumatic brain injuries are often grouped according to functional classifications, rather than by diagnosis. For example, elite athletes with traumatic brain injuries who meet the classification standards for hypertonia, ataxia, and athetosis may compete in the Paralympic Games under various classifications in sports such as archery, badminton, boccia, cycling, swimming, track and field, and wheelchair sports. Other organizations that provide opportunities for physical activity for some individuals with traumatic brain injuries include BlazeSports America, the Challenged Athletes Foundation, Move United, and more.

STROKE

Definition of Stroke

Also called cerebrovascular accidents, **strokes** are damage to the brain caused by temporary disruption of blood circulation to the brain. Following a stroke, the brain may incur serious damage that influences the control of essential body functions. Similar to cerebral palsy and traumatic brain injury, individuals who have had strokes may experience changes to motor ability, sensation, perception, and communication. The impact of stroke ranges from minimal to significant, depending on the type and severity of stroke.[16]

Prevalence and Current Statistics

The American Heart Association Heart Disease and Stroke Statistics report that each year approximately 795,000 U.S. citizens experience a stroke, making stroke the fifth leading cause of death or disability in the United States, and second worldwide. The majority (87%) of strokes are ischemic, meaning that they are caused by a blocked artery. More than half of those who have strokes survive the event, but about 90% of individuals will experience a lasting functional impact. Women and older adults are at the highest risk for a stroke; however, perinatal (occurring at ≤28 days of life including in utero) stroke is a growing area of concern among medical professionals.[17] The prevalence of perinatal stroke is 1 in every 3,500 live births in the United States. Between 20% and 40% of infants who have strokes will not survive, and those who do are likely to exhibit lifelong disabilities, such as cerebral palsy, epilepsy, sensory impairments, and intellectual disability.[18]

Ischemic stroke   Hemorrhagic stroke

Blocked blood vessel   Ruptured blood vessel

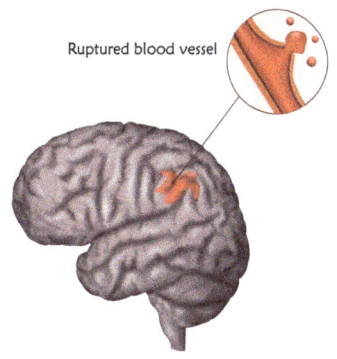

Ischemic and hemorrhagic strokes.

Etiology and Known Causes

While there are many factors that contribute to the development of stroke, risk among adults is often associated with lifestyle-related factors include hypertension, obesity, diabetes mellitus, smoking, diet, and sedentary lifestyle. Childhood and adolescent strokes are typically the result of underlying medical issues like congenital heart defects, migraines, head or neck trauma, or exposure to certain infections. Finally, perinatal strokes are often related to diseases that cause blood clots, such as thromboembolism. There are many types of stroke, but they are generally categorized as either hemorrhagic or ischemic. Hemorrhagic strokes, the more serious type, occur when an artery within the brain ruptures and bleeding develops in and around the brain. The more common type, ischemic strokes, refer to lack of sufficient blood flow to the brain due to a blocked artery, typically caused by a progressive narrowing of the artery or an embolism lodging into smaller vessels.[16]

Pathophysiology and Psychophysiology

While the effect of a stroke on the body and mind varies across individuals, persons who have had a stroke may experience vision loss, paralysis in certain parts of the body, seizures, muscle weakness, apraxia, difficulties toileting, walking, and/or completing tasks of daily living. Cognitive changes related to receptive language comprehension, speech, executive function, attention, and dementia are not uncommon. Some individuals may have difficulty with proprioception and movement on one side of the body. Psychological symptoms include depression, loss of self-esteem, impulsivity, and inappropriate emotional response.[19]

Specific Issues with Motor Movement

Depending on the location and severity of the damage to the brain, many of the symptoms of stroke can be similar to those of both cerebral palsy and traumatic brain injury. Generally, individuals may experience decreased gross and fine motor control following strokes. Partial or total paralysis on one side of the body may impact many aspects of motor activities, such as ambulation, reacting to stimuli, manipulating objects using the affected side, and movements that require crossing the midline. Changes in muscle tone, including both spasticity and weakness of skeletal muscles can also impact movement.[17] Cognitive and emotional changes, such as those related to language comprehension, reasoning, attention, and motivation may further reduce opportunities for physical activity engagement.

Management and Treatment of Strokes

Successful management of strokes is closely related to response time, wherein strokes that are recognized and treated early often have better outcomes. Therefore, using guides to identify stroke symptoms, such as FAST (i.e., facial droop, arm weakness, speech difficulty, and time to call emergency services) is recommended. Intravenous drugs must be administered within a few hours of the clinical signs of a stroke to mitigate some of the damage sustained. Depending on the severity of the stroke and accompanying tissue damage, management can include either anticoagulants or antiplatelet therapy to address problems with clots and bleeding.[16] After the initial treatment, intensive and ongoing physical rehabilitation therapy are usually necessary to improve individual functioning and prevent secondary conditions associated with moderate and severe strokes. Similar to traumatic brain injury, acute rehabilitation is critical, as the likelihood of regaining prestroke abilities is highest soon after stabilization.[20] Many people who have had a stroke will likely continue to experience changes in motor and cognitive deficits and issues with communication and may benefit from ongoing rehabilitation such as physical, speech, and occupational therapies.

Specific Benefits of Physical Activity

In general, the benefits of physical activity for individuals who have had a stroke are similar to those for individuals without disabilities. For specific benefits for those with neuromuscular disabilities, refer to the cerebral palsy section of this chapter. In addition to the benefits described therein, individuals who have experienced strokes often show some functional improvement in motor function after injury in association with continued physical activity.[21] Physical activity programs that include walking for cardiorespiratory exercise have shown particular promise in improving balance and mobility.[22]

Contraindications for Motor Movement

Individuals who have suffered a stroke may have similar contraindications to physical activity and exercise as those with cerebral palsy and traumatic brain injury. Symptoms such as spasticity, asymmetrical weakness, behavior changes, balance difficulties, and memory recall may have a direct or indirect impact on movement. Further, as stroke is closely associated with older adults, other health concerns among this subgroup may confer their own contraindications.

Suggested Modifications for Sports, Physical Activity, and Physical Education

Many modifications from the cerebral palsy and traumatic brain injury sections may be suitable for use among individuals who have had strokes. Additionally, the use of wrist or ankle cuffs to assist with coordination of movements and object manipulation may be helpful. Cuffs can be outfitted with apparatus like hooks for holding weights, Velcro for catching objects, straps for holding equipment like tennis rackets, and increased surface area for striking and kicking activities.

Recommendations for Practitioners in Physical Activity Settings

Prior to beginning any physical activity training, it is important to be sure that the individual is acting under the advice of their doctor and is cleared to participate. Many of the recommendations for working with individuals with cerebral palsy and traumatic brain injury are applicable to this population. In addition to those, specific planning and accommodations may be needed for individuals who have hemiplegic paralysis as a result of stroke. Practitioners may use strategies such as hand-over-hand assistance and balance support for activities involving the affected side of the body. These supports may be faded gradually as the individual regains strength and function over time. Activities in which weight goes above the head (either in a seated or supine position) should be monitored very carefully, especially during early stages of rehabilitation as strength, pronation, and fine motor manipulation may be affected by stroke. Finally, practitioners should be mindful of co-occurring disabilities or conditions, particularly among older adults who have experienced a stroke.

Sport and Physical Activity Opportunities and Organizations

Many of the physical activity and sports opportunities available to those with cerebral palsy or traumatic brain injuries are also available to individuals who have had a stroke. For example, elite athletes who have had strokes may meet the classification requirements for hypertonia, ataxia, or athetosis may be eligible to compete in certain events at the Paralympic Games. Further, many recreational and developmental sports organizations that are open to those with cerebral palsy and traumatic brain injuries are also available to those who have had strokes. For more information, please refer to the cerebral palsy and traumatic brain injury sections, as well as the resource list at the end of the chapter.

MUSCULAR DYSTROPHY

Definition of Muscular Dystrophy

Muscular dystrophy is a group of genetic disorders characterized by progressive muscle weakness that impacts mobility over time. Various types of muscular dystrophy are caused by different gene mutations, therefore, age of onset, affected body systems, and degree of mobility impairment vary. While many variants of muscular dystrophy are linked with minor functional impairments, the progression of others, such as Duchenne, can cause significant muscle loss, including loss of cardiovascular and respiratory muscles. Certain types of muscular dystrophy tend to occur early in life while others have a much later onset.

Prevalence and Current Statistics

Because muscular dystrophy is actually a group of disorders with specific genetic causes and ages of onset, it is difficult to measure the prevalence of muscular dystrophy overall. Duchenne muscular dystrophy, the most common type of childhood-onset muscular dystrophy, is estimated to occur in approximately one in 5,000 males.[23] Typically, children with Duchenne muscular dystrophy develop symptoms by the age of five.[24] Another common type of muscular dystrophy, myotonic muscular dystrophy, is thought to affect about one in 8,000 people, mainly adults.[25] Rarer types of muscular dystrophy such as Emery–Dreifuss, limb-girdle, and distal types are each estimated to affect fewer than one in 100,000 people.

Etiology and Known Causes

All types of muscular dystrophy are caused by mutations to genes, and the vast majority of these genetic differences are inherited from one or both biological parents. However, the exact pattern of inheritance and gene involvement vary across muscular dystrophy types. Duchenne and the similar but less impactful Becker types of muscular dystrophy are both caused by mutations to the X chromosomes. Because biological males typically have only one X chromosome, they are much more likely to develop an X-linked condition than are females. As such, male children are much more likely than female children to have Duchenne or Becker muscular dystrophy. Other types of muscular dystrophy are inherited through autosomal dominant or autosomal recessive patterns of inheritance and occur with similar prevalence across biological sexes.

Pathophysiology and Impact on Movement

All types of muscular dystrophies are characterized by changes to the structure of muscles, including the skeletal muscles that allow for movement. In cases of

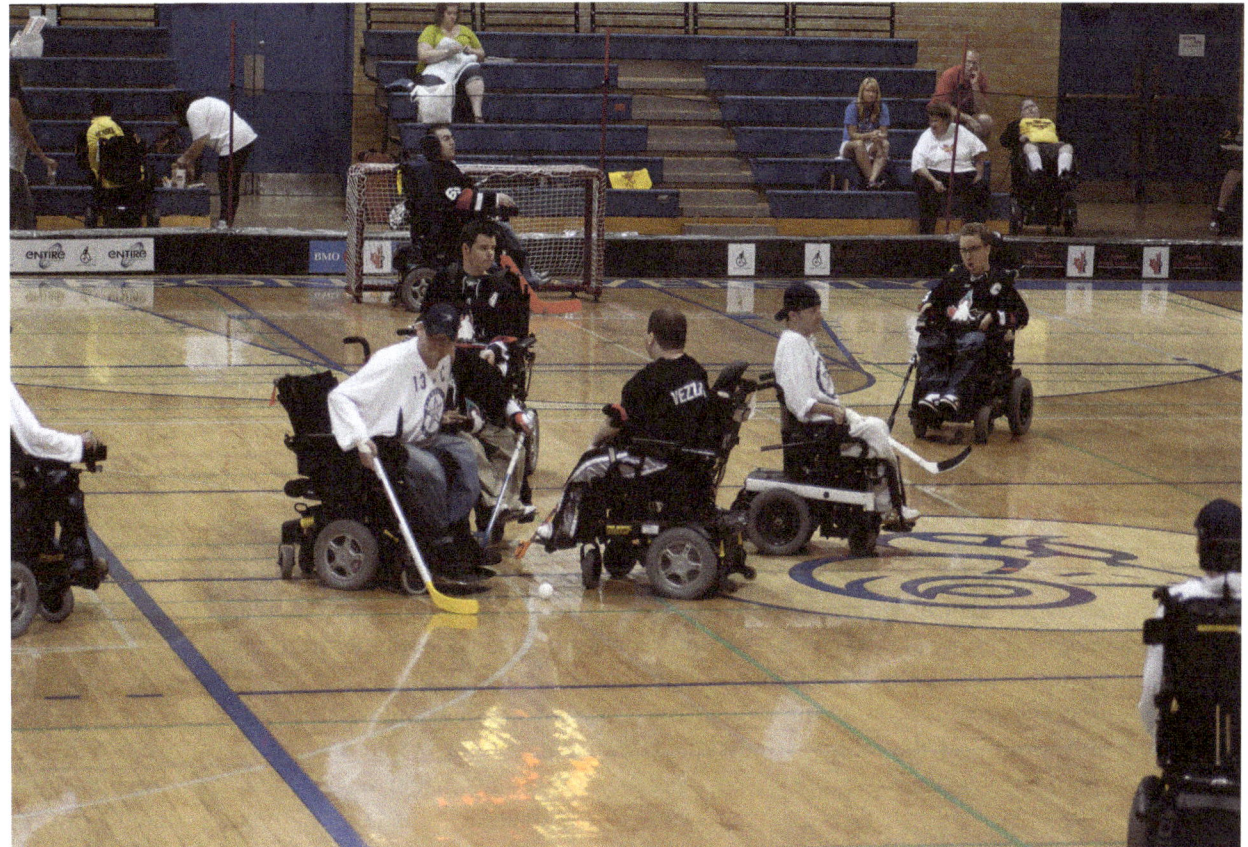

Athletes with neuromuscular disabilities play power hockey.

muscular dystrophy, genetic mutations change the instructions for building muscle proteins, which results in loss of muscle tissue. Symptoms of Duchenne muscular dystrophy, the most common and most severe childhood-onset type, tend to appear in toddler-aged children and include weakness first in the upper legs and hips that then spreads to the arms. Early movement differences in children with Duchenne muscular dystrophy include a waddling gait, difficulty moving from sitting to standing, difficulty climbing stairs, weakened breathing patterns, and changes to spinal posture. Some children also have difficulty with locomotor activities like running and jumping because of weaker muscles in the hips and thighs. Though muscle loss is ongoing during this time, arm and leg muscles may look larger and more developed in appearance because of the presence of excessive fat and connective tissues around skeletal muscles, a phenomenon known as pseudohypertrophy.

As children with Duchenne muscular dystrophy age, muscle deterioration often impacts muscles associated with breathing, including the diaphragm, and they may begin to have difficulty with activities of daily life like swallowing and coughing to relieve congestion in the chest. By adolescence, many children with Duchenne muscular dystrophy may begin to use manual wheelchairs or power wheelchairs. Throughout this time, careful medical care is needed to manage the progression of their conditions, especially with regard to cardiorespiratory weakness. The life expectancy for persons with Duchenne muscular dystrophy has risen in recent years, with many adults now living into their 30s and even 40s. Closely related to the Duchenne type, persons with Becker muscular dystrophy show less severe symptoms and may continue to be able to walk and move into their 30s. Individuals with Becker muscular dystrophy are less likely to experience severe reduction in cardiac capacity than those with the Duchenne type.

Myotonic muscular dystrophy is the most common type of muscular dystrophy in adults. Individuals with the myotonic type have skeletal muscular weakness that is common to most types of muscular dystrophy, but also experience myotonia, or prolonged muscle spasms after exertion. Myotonic muscular dystrophy also affects the nervous system and the heart, may cause cataracts in the eyes, and is associated with insulin resistance. Many individuals with myotonic muscular dystrophy use pacemakers to help regulate their heart rhythms and may also use ankle–foot orthotics to aid in walking because of muscle weakness in the lower legs and feet.

Individuals with limb-girdle muscular dystrophy tend to first show symptoms during adolescence or early adulthood. Initial signs include weakness in either the hips or shoulders, and some people with limb-girdle muscular dystrophy quickly experience difficulty climbing stairs, standing up, lifting objects, or raising their arms overhead. Though either the upper or lower body tends to be impacted at the onset, both areas will eventually become involved over time. There is a high degree of variability among mobility restriction associated with limb-girdle muscular dystrophy; some individuals may maintain their ability to walk, while others may use wheelchairs for ambulation.

Management and Treatment of Muscular Dystrophy

Treatment of muscular dystrophy varies depending on type, severity, and age of onset. Medications are often used to manage the symptoms and progression of muscular dystrophy. Corticosteroids may be prescribed to help preserve muscle strength and delay the deterioration of muscle tissue. People with muscular dystrophy may wear orthotic devices on their limbs or trunks to support weaker muscles or to slow the occurrence of joint contractures (i.e., joints that become stiff and immobile over time). Many people with muscular dystrophy use mobility devices including canes, walkers, and wheelchairs. Breathing assistance, such as ventilators, may be used by some individuals with severe muscle loss that impacts respiration. Because muscular dystrophy is progressive, many individuals will use different treatments, orthotics, and devices across their life spans.

Specific Benefits of Physical Activity

There is relatively little research about the safety and benefit of physical activity for individuals with muscular dystrophy; however, some studies have shown that carefully executed physical activity programs can be useful for supporting muscular function and joint mobility among individuals with muscular dystrophy.[26] Activities that increase muscular strength, muscular endurance, and support cardiovascular wellness may be particularly beneficial. Aerobic activities like stationary or hand cycling and walking may be suitable for some individuals. Light intensity resistance training with exercise bands, hand weights, and cable machines may help maintain muscle strength and endurance. Swimming and water aerobics may be used to increase muscular endurance and mobility while placing minimal stress on fragile muscle tissues. However, it is important to note that physical activity undertaken by individuals with muscular dystrophy be approached gradually and under the advice of the individual's healthcare providers, as there may be a greater potential for damage due to muscle overuse among this group.

Contraindications for Movement

While physical activity and exercise can be beneficial for individuals with muscular dystrophy, it is important to note the general risks associated with physical exertion for this group. Physical activity risks for individuals with muscular dystrophy include environmental safety, potential muscle damage, and cardiorespiratory stress. First, because individuals with muscular dystrophy tend to have weakness in the muscles of the lower body, weight-bearing ballistic activities like running and jumping should be carefully monitored. In particular, environmental conditions like uneven and downhill terrain may increase the risk of falls and injury because of the demands on the hips, knees, and ankles. Second, it is important to avoid muscular overexertion that may damage fragile cells in affected muscle groups of persons with muscular dystrophy. Finally, many types of muscular dystrophy have a direct impact on the function of cardiac and respiratory muscles. As is the case with muscular exertion, cardiorespiratory activity should be carefully monitored to avoid stress and long-term damage.[27]

Suggested Modifications for Sports, Physical Activity, and Physical Education

Due to the highly individualized nature of the symptoms and progression of muscular dystrophy across individuals, it is difficult to make wholesale recommendations suitable for all persons with the condition. In general, activities for individuals with muscular dystrophy should focus on maintaining mobility, ambulation, and muscular strength and endurance rather than on optimizing athletic performance or health-related fitness. For example, a trainer working with an adult with muscular dystrophy will likely develop a gentler program built on activities featuring lower intensity and mobility than they would an aspiring athlete. Within the context of physical education, modifications to game play that emphasize cooperative activities and progressive self-improvement may be chosen over competitive activities that rely on speed, strength, and athleticism for success. Individuals who are in later stages of muscular dystrophy are likely to benefit from highly modified or alternative activities that focus on mobility and breathing. Activities such as assisted stretching, yoga, and breathing exercises may be performed in and out of wheelchairs as needed for each individual.

Recommendations for Practitioners in Physical Activity Settings

When preparing for participants with muscular dystrophy, it is important that practitioners develop an individualized, responsive approach, rather than attempting to make individuals with muscular dystrophy fit their needs into a "one size fits all" program. Because muscular dystrophy affects individuals differently, activities or exercises that are suitable for one person with muscular dystrophy may be wholly inappropriate for another. Therefore, it is important to plan with each individual in mind. Because muscular dystrophy is progressive, modifications and supports for each person will change over time. As such, practitioners should be responsive and quick to make new modifications as needed. Finally, research indicates that persons with muscular dystrophy tend to report lower health-related quality of life as compared with peers without disabilities.[28] Practitioners should aim to create a psychologically supportive climate that provides ample opportunities for success and fosters positive interactions that increase social support.

Sport and Physical Activity Opportunities

Sports and physical activity opportunities for persons with muscular dystrophy vary greatly depending on the type and stage of impairment. Individuals who are in the earlier stages of muscular dystrophy or who have a type of the condition that is less impactful are often able to participate in unmodified or minimally modified sports and physical activity. For example, some individuals with muscular dystrophy compete in elite-level events at the Paralympic games as part of the Impaired Muscle Power athlete class. Examples of Paralympic events for athletes with muscular dystrophy include track and field events (called "athletics"), boccia, swimming, archery, table tennis, wheelchair rugby, and wheelchair basketball.

As individuals with muscular dystrophy lose mobility and strength, physical activity engagement may begin to shift toward the therapeutic, including the mobility, aerobic, resistance, and aquatic opportunities described earlier. In addition to these activities, some individuals with muscular dystrophy may be well-suited to power chair sports like power soccer and hockey. More information about both sports may be found in the cerebral palsy section of this chapter.

DWARFISM

Definition of Dwarfism

Little People of America, an advocacy group for individuals with dwarfism, defines **dwarfism** as "a medical or genetic condition that usually results in an adult height of 4'10" or shorter," although it is noted that occasionally persons with dwarfism are slightly taller.[28] Individuals who have dwarfism may be short in stature with proportionate limbs, torso, and heads (known as proportionate dwarfism), or may be short in stature with longer torsos and shorter limbs (known as disproportionate dwarfism). In addition to "person with dwarfism," the dwarfism community also considers "little person" or "person of short stature" to be preferred terminology.

Prevalence and Current Statistics

Because there are over 300 causes of dwarfism, it is difficult to measure its overall prevalence.[29] However, the incidence of several common medical causes of dwarfism have been estimated. Achondroplasia, the condition that accounts for over 90% of disproportionate dwarfism,[30] is estimated to occur in between .36 and .60 per 10,000 live births in the Unites States.[31] Globally, at least 250,000 people have achondroplasia.[32]

Etiology and Known Causes

As previously stated, there are hundreds of medical causes of short stature. Some conditions related to dwarfism may be inherited from one or both parents, while others occur spontaneously. Achondroplasia, a genetic difference that may be inherited or spontaneously developed, accounts for the vast majority of cases of disproportionate dwarfism. Individuals with achondroplasia have shorter than average limbs because of a gene that impedes the development of cartilage into bone during development, particularly in the long bones, including those in the arms and legs. Other causes of disproportionate dwarfism include spondyloepiphyseal dysplasia congenita, which impacts development of the spinal bones,[33] and diastrophic dysplasia. While there are many underlying causes of proportionate dwarfism, they are most often linked to medical conditions related to lower than typical production of human growth hormone before birth or during childhood.[34]

Pathophysiology and Psychophysiology

Dwarfism may present in various ways related to the underlying medical cause. For example, individuals with disproportionate dwarfism may experience orthopedic complications in their legs and/or spine. Knee instability among individuals with achondroplasia is not uncommon and may result in pain and eventually osteoarthritis if not treated.[35] Spinal differences are important considerations among individuals with disproportionate dwarfism that may cause pain or numbness and impact movement. Spinal curvature issues like scoliosis or lordosis may cause pain and movement issues. More seriously, spinal stenosis—a condition in which the opening of the spinal column is too small for the spinal cord—may cause pain, muscle weakness, and numbness if not treated surgically. Finally, some individuals with dwarfism may have hydrocephalus (i.e., a buildup of fluid in and around the brain), a condition that is usually treated surgically.

Motor Movement among Individuals with Dwarfism

The benefits of physical activity for persons of short stature are the same as those for persons of average height including decreased risk of heart disease, stroke, and obesity, and improved psychological well-being. Likewise, there are few contraindications regarding physical activity for this group. However, individuals with disproportionate dwarfism who experience some of the joint problems described earlier should be careful when participating in activities that might cause strain or dislocation of affected joints. In particular, individuals with skeletal dysplasia should use caution when participating in activities that place strain or pressure on the spine, such as headstands and inversions, heading a soccer ball, long-distance running, and certain contact sports.

Management and Treatment of Dwarfism

Treatment of conditions related to dwarfism vary depending on the affected systems of the body. Certain spinal and orthopedic symptoms may be treated using orthotics, while others may be addressed surgically. For example, individuals with hydrocephalus (i.e., a buildup of fluid in and around the brain) may have surgery to place a shunt to drain spinal fluid from the brain, and those with spinal stenosis may undergo procedures to decompress the spinal cord or to widen the spinal canal. Some individuals may have their legs straightened surgically to help mitigate arthritis in lower limb joints. Mobility exercises may be prescribed to improve joint range of motion as needed. Treatments for proportionate dwarfism often center around increasing height using human growth hormone during childhood and adolescence.

Contraindications for Movement

While many people with dwarfism have no contraindications for movement, some movements could be approached with caution. For example, ballistic movements (e.g., jumping, leaping, and tumbling) may not be appropriate for individuals of short stature who have joint instability or arthritis. Those who have neck or spinal issues, including spinal stenosis or a shunt, should be cautious when approaching activities or sports that require inverting or putting excess pressure on the cervical spine, such as gymnastics movement and even certain yoga poses. Though it is important for practitioners to be mindful of the possibility of such contraindications, their presence and impact vary greatly across individuals with dwarfism. Therefore, it is critical to learn about each person's needs and movement constraints.

Suggested Modifications for Sports, Physical Activity, and Physical Education

Many individuals with dwarfism can successfully participate in physical activity with minimal modification. However, providing smaller pieces of equipment or adjusting dimensions of playing space may make gameplay easier for individuals with dwarfism. For example, while some persons of short stature may elect to use standard height basketball hoops, volleyball and badminton nets, it may be appropriate to lower such equipment, particularly for youth or novice participants. Bicycles and tricycles may be fitted to individuals of short stature by lowering seats or adding height to the pedals using blocks. Similarly, individuals with dwarfism may benefit from equipment designed to help them access physical spaces in which physical activity programs are located, such as step ladders or boxes to reach taller gym equipment. In instances in which fitness machines cannot be sized to accommodate persons of short stature, practitioners may instead design activities using free weights, resistance bands, or body weight exercises, depending on each client's goals and fitness.

Recommendations for Practitioners in Physical Activity Settings

In general, few programming modifications are needed for individuals with dwarfism. The Dwarf Sports Association of the United Kingdom (DSAUK) recommends that individuals with dwarfism should become involved in physical activity and sport, particularly activities that strengthen muscles and joints around the hip, knee, and ankle.[36] However, practitioners should use caution when planning for individuals with spinal issues and may need to avoid activities like gymnastics, long jump, and high jump. Depending on the needs of the individual, equipment may need to be modified in order to be accessible. When planning sports and activities in which participants have individualized equipment (e.g., baseball gloves or hockey sticks), it is important to provide appropriately sized equipment for all participants, including those with smaller bodies.

Sport and Physical Activity Opportunities and Organizations

Founded in 1985, the Dwarf Athletic Association of America (DAAA) holds organized sport competitions for individuals with dwarfism. The DAAA holds regional and national competitions in many sports including badminton, basketball, boccia, flag football, floor hockey, curling, powerlifting, table tennis, track and field, soccer, swimming, and volleyball. Divisions vary by sport, but often include separate juniors, open, and master's divisions. Internationally, persons of short stature can compete at the World Dwarf Games and at the Paralympic Games. Paralympic events for athletes of short stature include swimming, athletics (i.e., track and field), equestrian, wheelchair tennis, table tennis, and powerlifting.

AMPUTATION AND LIMB DIFFERENCE

Definition of Amputation and Limb Difference

The terms amputation and limb difference cover a wide array of congenital and acquired causes of differences in the appearance and function of arms, hands, legs, or feet. Limb differences may be categorized as acquired or congenital, and refer to the body part or parts affected (i.e., lower or upper limb), or the degree to which limbs are affected (i.e., below or above the knee, at the hip, etc.). One common example of congenital limb difference is phocomelia, a medical condition that results in various structural differences of the limbs, hips, and digits. Individuals with phocomelia may have shortened or absent long bones in the limbs such that their hand or foot may be attached at the shoulder or hip.

Prevalence and Current Statistics

In the United States, an estimated 1.6 million individuals have had an amputation involving all or part of a limb.[37] Amputations of the leg, either above or below the knee, are more common than upper limb amputations. Most amputations are acquired, while congenital amputations affecting upper and lower limbs account for account for 2 and 4 out of 10,000 births, respectively.[38]

Etiology and Known Causes

Acquired amputations have many causes. Currently, the most common reason for lower limb amputations is a vascular disease called peripheral artery disease, which is a narrowing of arteries that restricts blood flow and leads to infection. Diabetes, smoking, high blood pressure, and obesity are all risk factors associated with developing peripheral artery disease.[39] Other causes of acquired amputations include cancer or tumors, infections such as meningitis, exposure, and traumatic injury, such as car accidents, serious burns, or as a result of combat-related injury.[37] Though many causes of congenital amputation remain unknown, one common cause is amniotic band syndrome, in which fibrous bands of amniotic tissue constrict the limbs and digits of the fetus as it develops, sometimes leading to structural changes and amputations. Many other known causes of congenital amputation are related to various adverse events during pregnancy, such as infection, consumption of drugs like thalidomide, radiation, and harmful chemical exposure.[38]

Pathophysiology and Psychophysiology

The physiological impact of amputation varies greatly between individuals. For example, persons with lower body amputations only are likely to experience differences related to ambulation and may use prostheses, crutches, wheelchairs, or a combination of mobility devices for daily living. As individuals learn to use prostheses, they may be at a greater risk for injury due to falls. Ambulation among individuals with only upper body amputations is generally unaffected; however, this group may work with rehabilitation professionals such as physical and occupational therapists to develop suitable adaptations for tasks of daily living that most people complete using their hands. For example, persons with upper body amputations may develop individualized modifications for tasks like dressing, cooking, eating, driving, and manipulating objects. Similarly, individuals with amputations involving multiple limbs are likely to use some combination of upper body and lower body adaptations that is specific to their strengths and needs.

Depending on circumstances surrounding their amputations, individuals may also experience psychological effects of limb loss. Depression, post-traumatic stress disorder, and body image problems are not uncommon following limb loss, particularly among individuals whose amputations have been the result of traumatic injury.[40] Individuals who have acquired amputations because of illness may experience physical implications beyond the amputation itself. For example, individuals with amputations due to diabetes may also have additional symptoms such as visual impairment, nerve damage, and cardiovascular disease that could affect their overall mobility. Finally, physical pain at the amputation site, between the amputation and the prosthesis, and phantom pain—that is, the sensation of pain, pressure, or even itching in the missing limb—are not uncommon among individuals with amputations.

Specific Issues with Motor Movement

As discussed earlier in this section, there are many potential changes to mobility for individuals who have amputations, and they often vary over time. For example, an individual who has recently acquired a lower limb amputation may need to be fitted for a prosthesis or mobility device and then engage in physical therapy to learn to ambulate effectively. Over time, the individual is likely to experience physical changes to their amputation site (e.g., bone movement or development of excess scar tissue) that can necessitate additional surgeries, new prostheses, and additional rehabilitation. Each time this process is undertaken may mean months using a wheelchair or crutches while preparing for and recovering from surgery, and while new prostheses are fitted. This can be particularly true among children with amputations, as their mobility device needs are likely to change as they grow and age. Finally, persons with vascular and nerve damage in their limbs should take particular care to avoid injury to the affected body parts during physical activity.

Specific Benefits of Physical Activity

For individuals whose amputations are not related to vascular disease, the benefits of physical activity are largely the same as those for individuals without disabilities. Namely, sufficient physical activity reduces the risk of developing cardiovascular disease, high blood pressure, and obesity. For individuals with amputations related to vascular disease, physical activity can be part of a treatment plan intended to slow the progression of the disorder.

Contraindications for Motor Movement

Among individuals who use prostheses, especially prosthetic lower limbs, it is important to check the amputation site regularly for indications of skin irritation and infection, such as open sores or abrasions. Persons with nerve damage and loss of sensation should be particularly careful to monitor their amputation sites, as they may not be able to feel that an injury has occurred. All individuals with amputations should avoid overuse injuries to both affected and unaffected limbs.

Suggested Modifications for Sports, Physical Activity, and Physical Education

As with many disabilities, modifications are often individual and wide-ranging. For individuals with amputations, modifications may be related to the age, type of amputation, time since acquisition of the amputation, use of prostheses, additional medical concerns, and the context of the activity. In fitness settings, individuals with upper limb amputations may benefit from specially designed or modified devices to help them utilize strength equipment for upper body exercises. Conversely, individuals who use wheelchairs or forearm crutches may benefit from using hand cycles to increase their upper body strength and endurance. In physical education, participants with amputations may create modified versions of skills that suit their individual needs, such as catching a basketball between their hand and their trunk, or exploring modified locomotor skills that reflect how their bodies move. For example, in a session situated around running activities, individuals who are learning to use lower body prostheses may benefit from tasks with reduced distances, longer time expectations, and fewer pivots.

Recommendations for Practitioners in Physical Activity Settings

When developing physical activity programs for persons with amputations, information about the area of amputation, mobility devices used, time since acquired amputation, related medical conditions, and physical activity goals should all be used to inform the practitioner about how they can best serve each individual. When working with youth populations, practitioners should also communicate with parents and guardians or other service providers to learn information that the child may not know. For example, a child's in-school physical therapist can provide insights on wheelchair skills or balance development for walking with a lower limb prosthesis that the child cannot. In all populations, it is helpful to know about each individual's experience and comfort level using their mobility devices in order to set appropriate training goals. For example, individuals who are learning to balance and walk using their first prosthetic device will likely engage in very different physical activities than those who have used a device for years and are interested in pursuing sports or high-level fitness goals.

An athlete with a lower limb amputation competes in climbing championship.

Sport and Physical Activity Opportunities and Organizations

Physical activity opportunities for individuals with amputations vary greatly and may be therapeutic, recreational, fitness, or elite in focus. At the elite level, individuals with amputations are well-represented at the Paralympic Games in events such as track and field, sitting volleyball, sled hockey, archery, wheelchair basketball, fencing, equestrian, swimming, and many others. Many of these sports and activities are also available to individuals with amputations at recreational or developmental levels through organizations such as Move United, Blaze Sports, the Orthotic and Prosthetic Activities Foundation, and the Wheelchair Sports Federation.

CHAPTER SUMMARY

- Practitioners should communicate with individuals with disabilities to design meaningful and appropriate physical activities.
- Individuals with cerebral palsy may benefit from physical activities that develop balance and coordination, but do not overstimulate hypertonic muscles.
- Individuals with traumatic brain injuries may benefit from straightforward instructions and visual reminders in physical activity and exercise settings.
- The physical activity needs of individuals who have had strokes vary depending on age and physical impact of the stroke. Often, the goal is to maintain or regain physical function.
- The physical activity goals for individuals with muscular dystrophy, especially the Duchenne type, will likely center around preserving mobility and muscular function.
- Most individuals with dwarfism can participate in physical activity with few modifications. Precautions should be taken to minimize joint and connective tissue stress during activity.
- The physical activity needs of individuals who have experienced amputations vary depending on the age of the individual, affected body parts, and related medical conditions.

WEB RESOURCES FOR SPORT, EXERCISE, AND PHYSICAL EDUCATION

CEREBRAL PALSY

Cerebral Palsy Foundation: www.cerebralpalsy.org/
Cerebral Palsy International Sports and Recreation Association: https://cpisra.org/
Cerebral Palsy Sport: www.cpsport.org/

TRAUMATIC BRAIN INJURY

Brain Injury Association of America: www.biausa.org/

STROKE

American Stroke Association: www.stroke.org/en

MUSCULAR DYSTROPHY

Muscular Dystrophy Association: www.mda.org/

DWARFISM

Dwarf Athletic Association of America: www.daaa.org/disabled-sports-organizations.html
International Dwarf Sports Federation: http://internationaldwarfsportsfederation.com/world-dwarf-games/
Dwarf Athletic Association of America: www.daaa.org/disabled-sports-organizations.html
Little People of America: www.lpaonline.org/

AMPUTATIONS

International Wheelchair & Amputee Sports: www.iwasf.com/iwasf

GENERAL SPORTS AND PHYSICAL ACTIVITY RESOURCES

BlazeSports America: https://blazesports.org/
Challenged Athletes Foundation: www.challengedathletes.org/
International Power Chair Hockey: http://powerchairhockey.org/
Move United: www.moveunitedsport.org/
National Center on Health Physical Activity and Disability: http://nchpad.org

Orthopedic and Prosthetic Activities Foundation: www.opaffirstclinics.org/
Power Soccer USA: www.powersoccerusa.org/
Wheelchair Sports Federation: wheelchairsportsfederation.org
World T.E.A.M. Sports: https://worldteamsports.org/

REFERENCES

1. Korzeniewski, S. J., Slaughter, J., Lenski, M., Haak, P., & Paneth, N. (2018). The complex aetiology of cerebral palsy. *Nature Reviews Neurology, 14*(9), 528–543. https://doi.org/10.1038/s41582-018-0043-6
2. Wimalasundera, N., & Stevenson, V. L. (2016). Cerebral palsy. *Practical Neurology, 16*(3), 184–194. https://doi.org/10.1136/practneurol-2015-001184
3. Reddihough, D. S., & Collins, K. J. (2003). The epidemiology and causes of cerebral palsy. *Australian Journal of Physiotherapy, 49*(1), 7–12.
4. Graham, H. K., Rosenbaum, P., Paneth, N., Dan, B., Lin, J.-P., Damiano, D. L., Becher, J. G., Gaebler-Spira, D., Colver, A., Reddihough, D. S., Crompton, K. E., & Lieber, R. L. (2016). Cerebral palsy. *Nature Reviews Disease Primers, 2*(1), 15082. https://doi.org/10.1038/nrdp.2015.82
5. International Paralympic Committee. (n.d.). https://www.paralympic.org/classification
6. Winnick, J., & Porretta, D. L. (2016). *Adapted physical education and sport* (6th ed.). Human Kinetics.
7. Piek, J. P., & Carman, R. (1994). Developmental profiles of spontaneous movements in infants. *Early Human Development, 39*(2), 109–126. https://doi.org/10.1016/03783782(94)90160-0
8. Aisen, M. L., Kerkovich, D., Mast, J., Mulroy, S., Wren, T. A., Kay, R. M., & Rethlefsen, S. A. (2011). Cerebral palsy: Clinical care and neurological rehabilitation. *The Lancet Neurology, 10*(9), 844–852. https://doi.org/10.1016/S1474-4422(11)70176-4
9. Haak, P., Lenski, M., Hidecker, M. J. C., Li, M., & Paneth, N. (2009). Cerebral palsy and aging. *Developmental Medicine & Child Neurology, 51*, 16–23. https://doi.org/10.1111/j.1469-8749.2009.03428.x
10. Sack, M. L. (January 19, 2018). *What is power soccer and some unique rules?* United States Power Soccer Association. https://www.powersoccerusa.org/post/what-is-power-soccer-and-some-unique-rules
11. Capizzi, A., Woo, J., & Verduzco-Gutierrez, M. (2020). Traumatic brain injury. *Medical Clinics of North America, 104*(2), 213–238. https://doi.org/10.1016/j.mcna.2019.11.001
12. Centers for Disease Control and Prevention. (March 11, 2019). *Traumatic brain injury and concussion.* https://www.cdc.gov/traumaticbraininjury/get_the_facts.html
13. Park, E., Bell, J. D., & Baker, A. J. (2008). Traumatic brain injury: Can the consequences be stopped?. *CMAJ, 178*(9), 1163–1170. http://doi.org.10.1503/cmaj.080282
14. Hawryluk, G. W., & Manley, G. T. (2015). Classification of traumatic brain injury: Past, present, and future. *Handbook of Clinical Neurology, 127*, 15–21. https://doi.org/10.1016/B978-0-444-52892-6.00002-7
15. Popernack, M. L., Gray, N., & Reuter-Rice, K. (2015). Moderate-to-Severe traumatic brain injury in children: Complications and rehabilitation strategies. *Journal of Pediatric Health Care, 29*(3), e1–e7. https://doi.org/10.1016/j.pedhc.2014.09.003
16. Ekker, M. S., Boot, E. M., Singhal, A. B., Tan, K. S., Debette, S., Tuladhar, A. M., & de Leeuw, F.-E. (2018). Epidemiology, aetiology, and management of ischaemic stroke in young adults. *The Lancet Neurology, 17*(9), 790–801. https://doi.org/10.1016/S1474-4422(18)30233-3
17. Virani, S. S., Alonso, A., Benjamin, E. J., Bittencourt, M. S., Callaway, C. W., Carson, A. P., Chamberlain, A. M., Chang, A. R., Cheng, S., Delling, F. N., Djousse, L., Elkind, M. S. V., Ferguson, J. F., Fornage, M., Khan, S. S., Kissela, B. M., Knutson, K. L., Kwan, T. W., Lackland, D. T., Lewis, T. T., Lichtman, J. H., Longenecker, C. T., Loop, M. S., Lutsey, P. L., Martin, S. S., Matsushita, K., Moran, A. E., Mussolino, M. E., Perak, A. M., Rosamond, W. D., Roth, G. A., Sampson, U. K. A., Satou, G. M., Schroeder, E. B., Shah, S. H., Shay, C. M., Spartano, N. L., Stokes, A., Tirschwell, D. L., VanWagner, L. B., Tsao, C. W., & On behalf of the American Heart Association Council on Epidemiology and Prevention Statistics Committee and Stroke Statistics Subcommittee. (2020). Heart disease and stroke statistics—2020 update: A report from the American Heart Association. *Circulation, 141*(9). https://doi.org/10.1161/CIR.0000000000000757
18. Roach, E. S., Golomb, M. R., Adams, R., Biller, J., Daniels, S., deVeber, G., Ferriero, D., Jones, B. V., Kirkham, F. J., Scott, R. M., & Smith, E. R. (2008). Management of stroke in infants and children: A scientific statement from a Special Writing Group of the American Heart Association Stroke Council and the Council on Cardiovascular Disease in the Young. *Stroke, 39*(9), 2644–2691.
19. Levin, M. F., Kleim, J. A., & Wolf, S. L. (2009). What do motor "recovery" and "compensation" mean in patients following stroke?. *Neurorehabilitation and Neural Repair, 23*(4), 313–319. https://doi.org.10.1177/1545968308328727
20. Foley, N., McClure, J. A., Meyer, M., Salter, K., Bureau, Y., & Teasell, R. (2012). Inpatient rehabilitation following stroke: Amount of therapy received and associations with functional recovery. *Disability and Rehabilitation, 34*(25), 2132–2138. https://doi.org/10.3109/09638288.2012.676145

21. Vahlberg, B., Cederholm, T., Lindmark, B., Zetterberg, L., & Hellström, K. (2017). Short-term and long-term effects of a progressive resistance and balance exercise program in individuals with chronic stroke: A randomized controlled trial. *Disability and Rehabilitation, 39*(16), 1615–1622. https://doi.org.0.1080/09638288.2016.1206631
22. Saunders, D. H., Sanderson, M., Hayes, S., Johnson, L., Kramer, S., Carter, D. D., Jarvis, H., Brazzelli, M., & Mead, G. E. (2020). Physical fitness training for stroke patients. *Cochrane Database of Systematic Reviews,* (3). https://doi.org.10.1002/14651858.CD003316.pub7
23. Stark, A. E. (2015). Determinants of the incidence of Duchenne muscular dystrophy. *Annals of Translational Medicine, 3*(19), 1–3. http://dx.doi.org/10.3978/j.issn.2305-5839.2015.10.45
24. Ciafaloni, E., Kumar, A., Liu, K., Pandya, S., Westfield, C., Fox, D. J., Caspers Conway, K.M., Cunniff, C., Mathews, K., West, N., Romitti, P. A., & McDermott, M. P. (2016). Age at onset of first signs or symptoms predicts age at loss of ambulation in Duchenne and Becker muscular dystrophy: Data from the MD STAR net. *Journal of Pediatric Rehabilitation Medicine, 9*(1), 5–11. https://doi.org.10.3233/PRM-160361
25. Suominen, T., Bachinski, L. L., Auvinen, S., Hackman, P., Baggerly, K. A., Angelini, C., Peltonen, L., Krahe, R., & Udd, B. (2011). Population frequency of myotonic dystrophy: Higher than expected frequency of myotonic dystrophy type 2 (DM2) mutation in Finland. *European Journal of Human Genetics, 19*(7), 776–782. https://doi.org.10.1038/ejhg.2011.23
26. Alemdaroğlu, I., Karaduman, A., Yilmaz, Ö. T., & Topaloğlu, H. (2015). Different types of upper extremity exercise training in Duchenne muscular dystrophy: Effects on functional performance, strength, endurance, and ambulation. *Muscle & Nerve, 51*(5), 697–705. https://doi.org.10.1002/mus.24451
27. Grange, R. W., & Call, J. A. (2007). Recommendations to define exercise prescription for Duchenne muscular dystrophy. *Exercise and Sport Sciences Reviews, 35*(1), 12–17. https://doi.org.10.1249/01.jes.0000240020.84630.9d
28. Grootenhuis, M. A., De Boone, J., & Van der Kooi, A. J. (2007). Living with muscular dystrophy: Health related quality of life consequences for children and adults. *Health and Quality of Life Outcomes, 5*(1), 1–8. https://doi.org.10.1186/1477-7525-5-31
29. Little People of America. (2020). *Frequently asked questions.* https://www.lpaonline.org/faq-#Definition
30. Vajo, Z., Francomano, C. A., & Wilkin, D. J. (2000). The molecular and genetic basis of fibroblast growth factor receptor 3 disorders: The achondroplasia family of skeletal dysplasias, Muenke craniosynostosis, and Crouzon syndrome with acanthosis nigricans. *Endocrine Reviews, 21*(1), 23–39. https://doi.org.10.1210/edrv.21.1.0387
31. Waller, D. K., Correa, A., Vo, T. M., Wang, Y., Hobbs, C., Langlois, P. H., Pearson, K., Romitti, P. A., Shaw G. M., & Hecht, J. T. (2008). The population-based prevalence of achondroplasia and thanatophoric dysplasia in selected regions of the US. *American Journal of Medical Genetics Part A, 146*(18), 2385–2389. https://doi.org.10.1002/ajmg.a.32485
32. Ireland, P. J., Pacey, V., Zankl, A., Edwards, P., Johnston, L. M., & Savarirayan, R. (2014). Optimal management of complications associated with achondroplasia. *The Application of Clinical Genetics, 7*(1), 117–125. https://doi.org.10.2147/TACG.S51485
33. National Center for Advancing Translational Sciences. (January 11, 2012). *Spondyloepiphyseal dysplasia congenita.* https://rarediseases.info.nih.gov/diseases/4987/disease#ref_3443
34. Argente, J., & Pérez-Jurado, L. A. (2018). Genetic causes of proportionate short stature. *Best Practice & Research Clinical Endocrinology & Metabolism, 32*(4), 499–522. https://doi.org.10.1016/j.beem.2018.05.012
35. Pauli, R. M. (2019). Achondroplasia: A comprehensive clinical review. *Orphanet Journal of Rare Diseases, 14*(1), 1–49. https://doi.org/10.1186/s13023-018-0972-6
36. Dwarf Sports Association United Kingdom. (n.d.). Research and insight. https://www.dsauk.org/resources/research-and-insight/#the-activity-trap
37. Ziegler-Graham, K., MacKenzie, E. J., Ephraim, P. L., Travison, T. G., & Brookmeyer, R. (2008). Estimating the prevalence of limb loss in the United States: 2005 to 2050. *Archives of Physical Medicine and Rehabilitation, 89*(3), 422–429. https://doi.org.10.1016/j.apmr.2007.11.005
38. Centers for Disease Control and Prevention. (October 26, 2020). *Facts about upper and lower limb reduction defects.* https://www.cdc.gov/ncbddd/birthdefects/ul-limbreductiondefects.html
39. American Heart Association. (October 31, 2016). *About peripheral artery disease (PAD).* https://www.heart.org/en/health-topics/peripheral-artery-disease/about-peripheral-artery-disease-pad
40. Fukunishi, I., Sasaki, K., Chishima, Y., Anze, M., & Saijo, M. (1996). Emotional disturbances in trauma patients during the rehabilitation phase: Studies of posttraumatic stress disorder and alexithymia. *General hospital psychiatry, 18*(2), 121–127. https://doi.org/10.1016/0163-8343(95)00121-2
41. Palisano, R., Rosenbaum, P., Walter, S., Russell, D., Wood, E., & Galuppi, B. (1997). Development and reliability of a system to classify gross motor function in children with cerebral palsy. *Developmental Medicine & Child Neurology, 39*(4), 214–223.

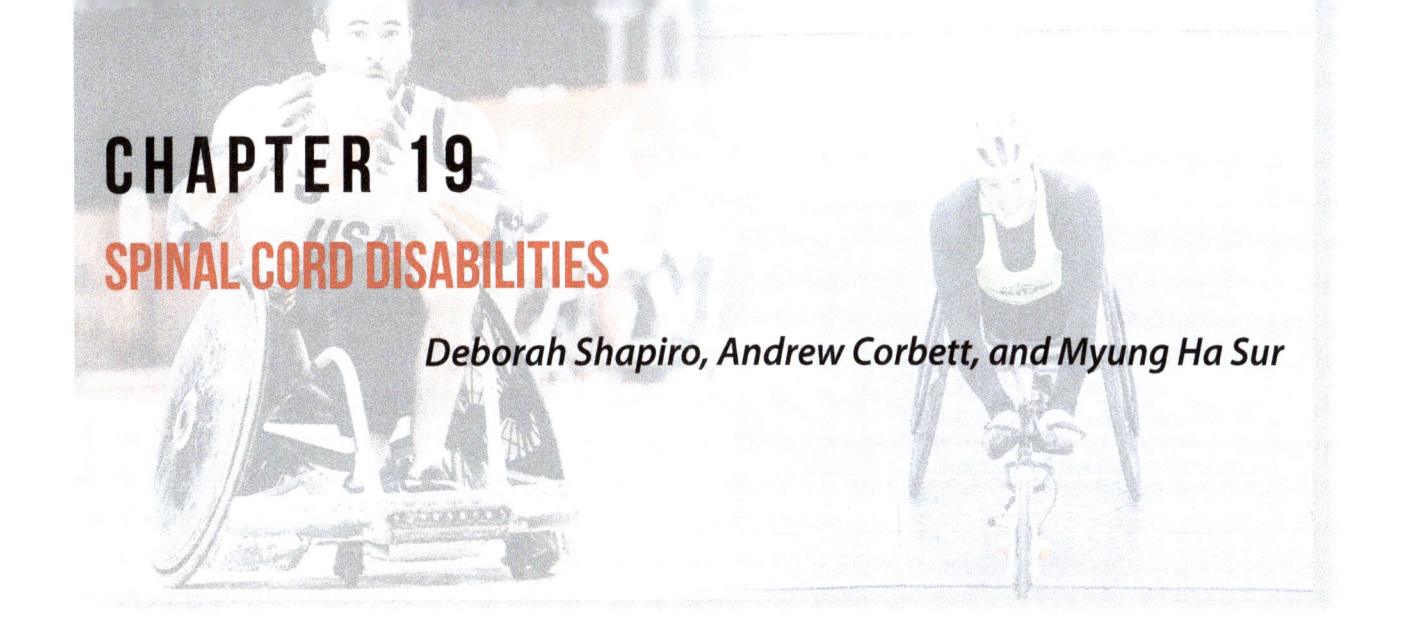

CHAPTER 19
SPINAL CORD DISABILITIES

Deborah Shapiro, Andrew Corbett, and Myung Ha Sur

When one hears about someone experiencing a spinal cord injury, the first thing that often comes to mind is paralysis of the muscles used for walking. However, there are a wide range of spinal cord disabilities all of which influence functional performance in physical activity, sport, and physical education in similar yet unique ways. These disabilities include spinal cord injury (SCI), spina bifida, kyphosis, lordosis, scoliosis, spondylosis and spondylolisthesis, traverse myelitis, and Guillain–Barre syndrome. We will discuss each of these beginning with SCI.

DEFINING SCI

An **SCI** is damage to the spinal cord that results in a loss of function such as mobility or feeling. The **spinal cord** is cylindrical in shape and extends from the base of the skull to about two-thirds down the vertebral column. An SCI is different from other back injuries such as ruptured disks or pinched nerves where damage to the spinal cord may not occur. Additionally, someone can "break their back or neck" and not sustain an SCI if only the bones around it are damaged. This is due to the structure of the spinal cord and vertebral column where broken bones may not damage the nearby nerves. For reference, Figure 19.1 illustrates a portion of the spinal cord while Figure 19.2 shows the vertebral column.

Anatomy of the Spinal Cord

The spinal cord is part of the central nervous system. The **spinal column**, also known as the backbone, is made up of vertebra and membrane. The function of the spinal cord is to act as the main source of communication between the brain and the body by carrying messages that allow us to move and feel sensation. Neurons carry messages that leave through holes in the vertebrae to and from the spinal cord. Spinal nerve routes branch off the spinal cord in pairs, one going to each side of the body. Each nerve has a specific job for movement and feeling and tells the muscles when and how to move. When an SCI occurs, sensation or movement may be interrupted temporarily or permanently and might result in a loss of function or paralysis.[1] **Level of injury** refers to where the spinal cord is functioning or the neurological level of injury. The level of injury designation is a letter followed by a number that corresponds to the spinal nerves. Injury to the spinal cord in the **cervical** region (C1-7) results in loss of function in arms and legs and is called tetraplegia. Functionally, individuals with a cervical spinal injury will have difficulty to varying degrees with grip function (finger and wrist flexion and extension) needed to push a wheelchair, use an arm ergometer, or grasp a ball, muscles of the abdomen and back needed to support the trunk to maintain upright posture while sitting, and limited to no lower limb function. **Thoracic** (T1-12) level injury is associated with loss of function affecting the

Deborah Shapiro and Andrew Corbett, Georgia State University; Myung Ha Sur, University of South Carolina.
© Kendall Hunt Publishing Company.

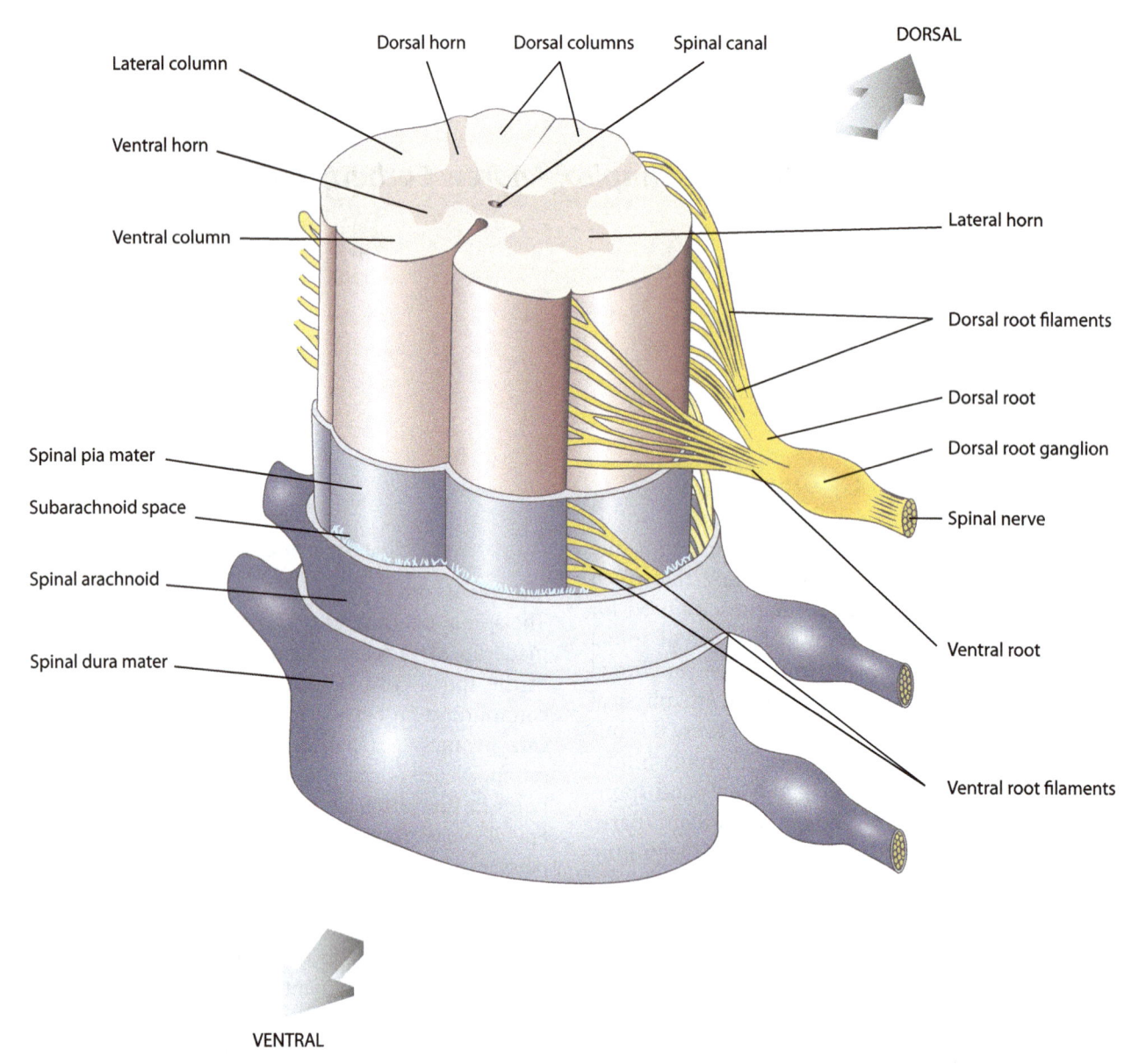

FIGURE 19.1 Image of the spinal cord.

trunk and legs and is called paraplegia. Individuals with a thoracic level injury will have full function of all muscle above the level of the injury. These individuals may, depending on the level of the injury in the thoracic region, have difficulty with abdominal muscle function and lower limb function. **Lumbar** (L1-5) and **sacral** (S1-5) SCI result in loss in functioning in hips and legs and is also called paraplegia.[2] Individuals with lumbar and sacral level injuries have all upper extremity and back muscle function, good abdominal and spinal flexion, normal stability, but some impairment of lower limb function. The higher up on the spinal cord the injury occurs, the greater the loss of function the person experiences.

Medical Classifications

The accepted standard for classifying spinal cord injuries is a **neurological classification system**. Rather than looking at which vertebrae are damaged, the neurological classification looks at the lowest segment of the spinal cord with normal function. Based on the impairment due to the SCI, injuries will be categorized as either tetraplegia or paraplegia, and damage to the spinal cord is categorized as either complete or incomplete. **Tetraplegia** refers to impairment or loss of function in the arms and typically the trunk and legs including the four extremities. Quadriplegia, similarly, refers to impairment of all four limbs. The word "Tetra" is

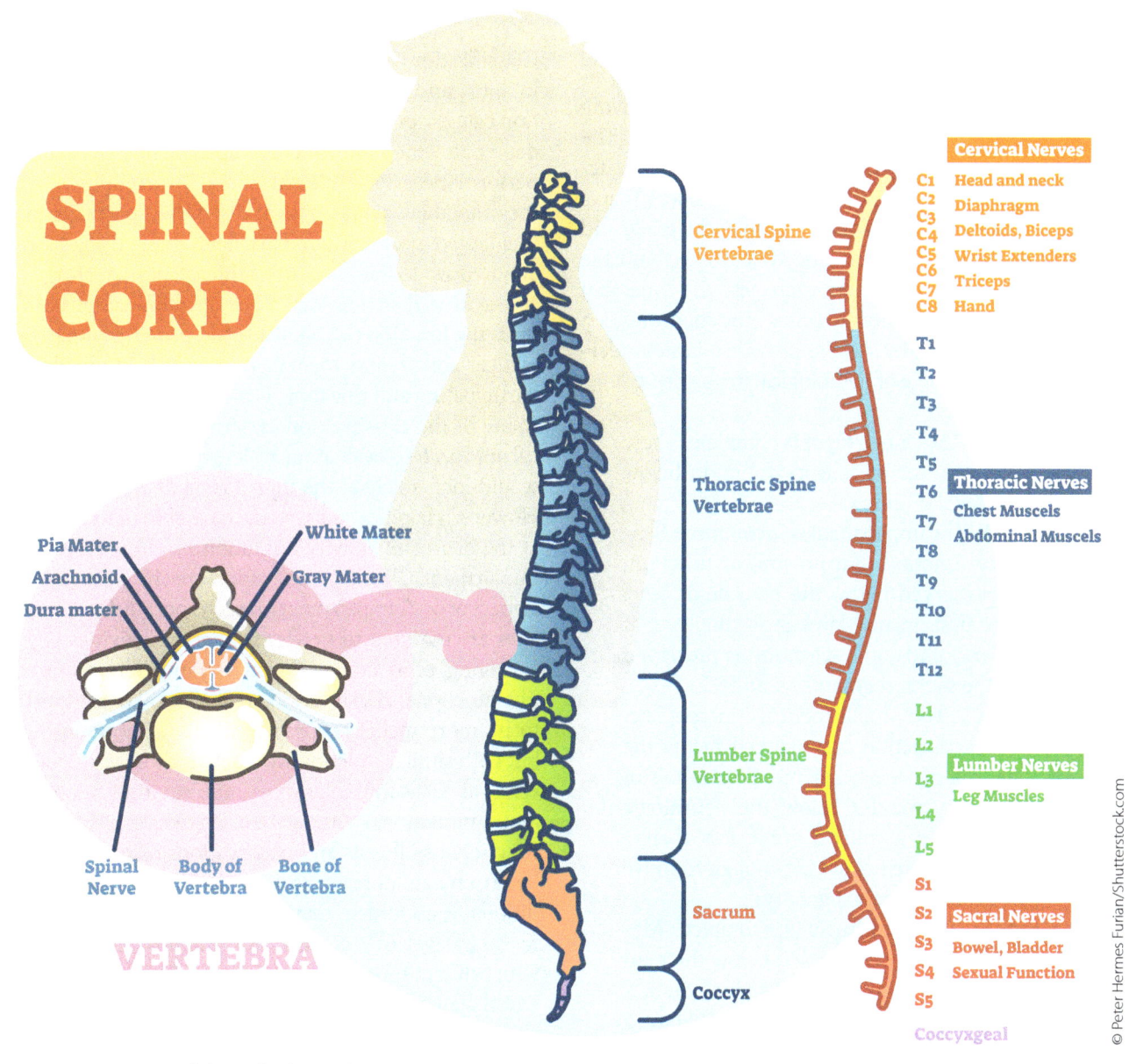

FIGURE 19.2 Image of the spinal vertebrae.

Greek for four and "Plegia" in Greek means paralysis. The word tetraplegia therefore comes from the Greek meaning paralysis in all four limbs. Comparably, "Quadri" means four in Latin and adds the Greek word for paralysis combining two different languages—Quadriplegia. Tetraplegia is the preferred term to quadriplegia in the UK for example, but within the United States quadriplegia and tetraplegia are used interchangeably.[3] Individuals with this level of impairment will sometimes be referred to colloquially as "quads." **Paraplegia** refers to injury below the cervical level where arm function is spared but trunk and leg function may or may not be impaired depending on the level of injury. Individuals with this level of impairment will sometimes be referred to colloquially as "paras." A **complete SCI** means the spinal cord is completely severed and there is no motor (movement) or sensory function (feeling of temperature, pain) below the level of injury. Persons with a complete SCI use power or manual wheelchairs for activities of daily living An **incomplete SCI** refers to an SCI that has some motor or sensory function and control below the level of injury. Incomplete quads may have motor and sensory function to allow them to walk independently, but these individuals tend to be more functional when using a wheelchair for activities of daily living.

The **American Spinal Injury Association Impairment Scale (ASIA)** is a designation used in grading the degree of impairment. The ASIA scale has five classification levels. The grades range from A to E with A having the highest level of impairment and E the lowest. The results of this scale help the rehabilitation team set functional goals based on neurological level of injury that is determined. The process of determining the grade and the development of the grading system is beyond the scope of this chapter; to learn more, visit the American Spinal Injury Association website.[4] The following is a summary of the ASIA scale to provide a basic understanding of the range of neurological impairment.

> **Grade A:** The impairment is complete. There is no motor or sensory function below the level of injury.
> **Grade B:** The impairment is incomplete. Sensory function, but not motor function, is preserved below the neurologic level (the first normal level above the level of injury) and some sensation is preserved in the sacral segments S4 and S5.
> **Grade C:** The impairment is incomplete. Motor function is preserved below the neurologic level, but more than half of the key muscles below the neurologic level have a muscle grade less than 3 (i.e., they are not strong enough to move voluntarily against gravity).
> **Grade D:** The impairment is incomplete. Motor function is preserved below the neurologic level, and at least half of the key muscles below the neurologic level have a muscle grade of 3 or more (i.e., the joints can be moved voluntarily against gravity).
> **Grade E:** The individual's functions are normal. All motor and sensory functions are unhindered.

An important factor when working with individuals with an SCI is that everyone's function is unique even if the cause and location of the injury is the same. For example, John and Jack both sustained their injury from a fall and have an SCI at the C7 level and have the same ASIA designation; however, John has less impairment of function of his legs while Jack has almost no leg function. The medical classification is only part of the story when it comes to working with these individuals. It is important to consider the individual's abilities and functioning rather than solely looking at their medical classification.

Sport Classifications

Classification determines who is eligible to compete in sport and it groups eligible athletes into competition categories referred to as sport classes based on the degree to which the athlete's impairment affects sport performance. Sport classification is a complex topic for individuals with physical disabilities participating in adaptive sports. There have been many discussions about how to best classify athletes participating in sports as well as how well a classification system captures the function (i.e., skill, fitness, power, endurance, tactical ability, and mental focus) of the individuals participating and this topic is not without controversy. Many of the classification systems started as a medical approach to evaluating athletes where the classifier would look solely at the injury level of an individual. However, classification systems have shifted to looking at the degree of activity limitation resulting from the impairment. Classification is sport specific because the impact of one's impairment on each sport differs as athletes are required to perform different activities (e.g., springing, propelling a wheelchair) in different sports. The functional classification system has allowed sports to be more inclusive for individuals without an SCI but with similar functioning (such as those with polio, cerebral palsy, muscular dystrophy, multiple sclerosis, and amputations). Often these systems make use of functional skill tests and observations of gameplay to determine an athlete's class for their given sport. Additionally, an athlete may not classify for a sport due to their level of function. For example, individuals with full arm function would not be able to classify for wheelchair rugby as they may be considered to have less than the minimal functional impairment required for participation. For questions about sport classifications, it is worth finding each sport's governing body to read further on their classification system. The International Paralympic Committee also publishes a guide to Paralympic classification, which includes sports for athletes with other disabilities as well as SCI.[5]

PREVALENCE AND CURRENT STATISTICS

Each year in the United States there are about 17,900 new spinal cord injuries and it is estimated that about 296,000 individuals with spinal cord injuries live in the United States. The average age at the time of injury is currently 43 years and the majority (78%) of new SCI cases are male. To learn more and see more statistics regarding spinal cord injuries visit the National SCI Statistical Center website.[6]

ETIOLOGY

SCI can occur from any situation that causes the spinal cord to be compressed, severely rotated, flex or extended, or inflicts direct damage to the spinal cord. Thus, the causes for SCI are varied and unique though they can be organized into broad categories. As of 2020, most cases of SCI stem from vehicle crashes followed by falls as the second leading cause. Other common causes are acts of violence, which are primarily gunshot wounds, and sport activities.

PATHOPHYSIOLOGY/PSYCHOPHYSIOLOGY

Following SCI, individuals will experience altered physiological functioning and unique health concerns, which are important for practitioners to be aware of. We will first discuss health conditions secondary to SCI and then specific concerns that can affect physical activity for this population.

Secondary Health Conditions

Pressure Sores and Skin Integrity

One of the main concerns for individuals with spinal cord injuries is skin integrity and **pressure sores**, also known as decubitus ulcers. The primary purpose of the skin is to protect the body and help control body temperature. After injury, the skin still protects the body, but there may be changes in some of the other functions. Individuals may experience limited or absent feeling in certain areas of the body and may not be able to tell if pain is present or if an injury such as a burn, bruise, or cut has occurred due to loss of or impairment in sensation in areas below the level of the injury. Additionally, limited or absent body movement decreases blood flow to the skin, which makes it more likely to break down, and can lead to pressure or skin sores.

Skin sores can develop due to pressure, friction, moisture, burns, or accidents. Because of absent or limited sensation, this can happen without the individual knowing it. Sores can easily become infected, leading to greater complications, and healing can be difficult and cause future health issues. Listed here are the main types of skin problems, causes, and preventative measures.

Pressure Sores

These are the biggest cause of skin breakdown and are likely to occur in areas without much padding between the skin and bones such as heels, elbows, hips, and base of the spine. Some causes are: sitting or lying in one position for long periods, wearing clothes or shoes that are too tight, using a wheelchair that is the wrong size, and sitting on unpadded surfaces. Prevention includes doing regular weight shifts (also known as wheelchair push-ups), wearing properly fitting clothes and shoes, using a fitted wheelchair, and checking skin for red spots.

Shearing

Shearing is a gravity force pushing down on an individual's body with resistance between the individual and a chair or bed.[7] Shearing can occur from slumping in a wheelchair, sliding the body over a surface using a gait belt or sliding board when doing a transfer (moving into or out of a wheelchair), and sitting in bed too long.

Friction

Friction occurs when the skin is rubbed hard across another surface or repeatedly rubs a surface. Friction usually comes with shear as friction contributes to the development of shearing by keeping the skin in place against a support surface while the rest of the individual's body moves, when incorrectly performing transfers, for example.[7] Pressure redistribution and repositioning are strategies to reduce shearing and friction, proper posture when sitting to avoid sliding or dragging movements downward/forward, increasing contact area with support surfaces, using lower friction support covers, and management of skin moisture to avoid becoming too damp.[8]

Accidents

Accidents can come from bumps, bruises, cuts, or burns that injure the skin, and due to decreased sensation, the individual may not even know that an injury occurred. Some examples of common accidents include bumping feet when moving around in a wheelchair, contact with hot surfaces, and spilling hot drinks.

Moisture

Moisture is wetness on the skin, which can soften the skin and make it more likely to break down and become a sore. Some causes of moisture include urine on the skin from wetting accidents, leaking catheters, or poor hygiene, stool that stays on the skin, sweat from overheating or infections with fever, or water. Cooling the body can be accomplished by reducing the number of covers, frequent repositioning to allow skin that has been in contact with surfaces to be exposed to the air to cool, use of a fan, wearing breathable cotton clothing, barrier creams or sprays to protect most skin from damage, manage incontinence and use absorbent underpads as long as they don't interfere with pressure redistribution.[8]

Complications Related to Pathophysiology

Hypotension

Individuals with spinal cord injuries may have lowered resting blood pressure. Individuals with lower thoracic or lumbar injuries have normal resting blood pressure while those with cervical and high thoracic injuries tend to have low baseline blood pressure. Related to low blood pressure is orthostatic hypotension, which is a drop in blood pressure when taking an upright posture. Symptoms of **hypotension** include dizziness, loss of consciousness, blurred vision, tunnel vision, loss of coloration, auditory deficits, nonspecific weakness, and lethargy. These symptoms might be worse in the morning or after a heavy meal while physical exertion, alcohol intake, hot environments, or dehydration may bring about symptoms of orthostatic hypotension. Symptoms are less likely to occur for individuals with incomplete injuries or injuries below T6. Be aware of symptoms and take precautions including but not exclusive to: reduce prolonged periods of sitting by assuming a recumbent or semirecumbent position, drink water and ensure adequate salt intake, avoid alcohol and caffeine, use compression bandages or support stockings to restrict blood pooling in the legs.[9]

Thermoregulation

Following an SCI, the body cannot control temperature very well and it sometimes does not know whether to sweat or shiver causing the body to become too hot or too cold. When working with this population, it is important to recognize the signs of overheating and low body temperature, what to do if it occurs, and preventative measures to take. Some signs of overheating include headache, flushed face, dizziness, appearing tired or weak, elevated body temperature, upset stomach, cramps, and thirst. If overheating occurs, have the individual drink cool fluids, sponge their body with cool water, remove any heavy clothing or blankets, stay in a cool place, and if their temperature is over 100 degrees Fahrenheit, call their doctor. Some important preventative measures are: staying in a cool, shady spot if outdoors in the heat; to avoid being in direct sun or very hot weather for extended periods of time; drink plenty of water; use a water spray bottle to keep cool; wear lightweight clothing; and avoid very active exercise in hot weather if possible. On the other hand, there are situations where body temperature gets too low. Signs of low body temperature are shivering above the level of injury, body temperature below 97.6, and pale or white hands, fingers, toes, lips, and face. If body temperature is too low, try moving to a warmer place, cover up with blankets, dress in layers, drink warm liquids, and keep skin dry to avoid the risk of or onset of hypothermia.

Autonomic Dysreflexia

As a result of an SCI, nerve signals from parts of the body below the level of the injury are blocked from reaching the brain, which can cause a condition called **autonomic dysreflexia** to occur. This reflex causes blood vessels below the injury level to tighten and causes the blood pressure to rise. Since signals cannot get past the SCI to the brain, blood pressure can continue to rise and high, uncontrolled blood pressure can cause stroke, heart attack, or death. For practitioners working with athletes with spinal cord injuries, it is important to be able to recognize the signs and causes of autonomic dysreflexia. Potential causes of autonomic dysreflexia include full bladder, full bowel, bladder infections, skin pressure or skin sores, tight-fitting clothing, and ingrown toenails. Full bladders are the top cause of dysreflexia. Some signs of autonomic dysreflexia are a severe headache, high blood pressure, sweating, goosebumps, or red blotches above the level of injury, and a stuffy nose. This condition is unique to individuals with injuries above the T6 level.

For practitioners, it is important to know about autonomic dysreflexia and how it affects each individual since it might occur during sport and exercise. It is an especially important topic for athletes competing and is also known as "boosting" when done intentionally. Boosting is when athletes intentionally induce autonomic dysreflexia to enhance performance. The intent is to increase blood pressure and increase blood flow to muscles. The increased blood flow carries additional oxygen to the muscles to allow the body to train and perform longer, harder, and faster, thereby enhancing performance. Intentionally triggering autonomic dysreflexia is banned in competition due to health concerns for the athletes.

Specific Issues with Motor Movement

A major concern for individuals with spinal cord injuries is pain and overuse injuries. Most individuals with spinal cord injuries rely on their upper extremities for mobility and activities of daily life and upper-extremity pain can decrease an individual's quality of life. Common pain diagnoses are neuropathic pain and musculoskeletal pain.

Neuropathic pain is complex and often chronic. The pain may be caused by damaged, dysfunctional, or injured nerve fibers, which send incorrect signals that can change nerve function around the site of the injury. Common neuropathic pain symptoms include shooting and burning pain and tingling and numbness. **Musculoskeletal pain** affects muscles, ligaments, tendons, and bones, and has many different causes. Tissues can be damaged by wear and tear of daily activities, trauma to an area, poor posture, repetitive movements, overuse, and prolonged immobilization. The following are common sources of pain for individuals with spinal cord injuries.

Shoulder

The shoulder is the most common source of pain for individuals with spinal cord injuries. Muscle imbalance (i.e., when muscles on one side of the body are larger, smaller, stronger, or weaker than the muscles on the other side) caused by overuse (usually of anterior muscle groups) is thought to lead to abnormal biomechanics that can cause injury. Older individuals and women are more likely to develop shoulder issues. Individuals with SCI who engage in greater levels of physical activity tend to have less evidence of injury.

Elbow

Issues at the elbow tend to result from strained muscles and tendons or nerve impingement and most of the pain is related to conditions such as tendonitis and bursitis. A primary cause for this pain is the propulsive stroke of wheelchair users either in everyday or athletic settings.

Wrist

For individuals with pain at the wrist, carpal tunnel syndrome is a common diagnosis, which is caused by compression of the median nerve. This is a direct relationship between an individual's weight and wheelchair propulsion biomechanics and damage to the median nerve.

There are additional musculoskeletal system changes as a result of an SCI, the most common of which are (a) muscle atrophy, (b) contractures, (c) osteoporosis, and (d) changes in body composition. Muscle atrophy refers to the loss or shrinkage of muscles. This can occur because damage to the nerves cannot trigger muscle contractions (denervation atrophy; more common in individuals with a complete SCI) or from not using the muscles enough (disuse atrophy) more common in individuals with an incomplete SCI.[10,11] Loss of movement in a joint can lead to shortening of muscles, ligaments, and tendons causing contractures. Spasticity can lead to difficulty with functional ability and contribute to the development of contractures. Osteoporosis can occur due to a lack of weight-bearing activities causing a thinning and loss of bone mass.[9] Lastly, weight loss due to decreased bone and muscle mass and increased propensity to increase fat percentage often due to changes in diet and reduced physical activity can lead to the development of obesity and diabetes.[11]

Management of Spinal Cord Injuries

As with most conditions for any population, prevention is preferable to treatment. For individuals with an SCI, an exercise program that maintains joint range of motion and prevents muscle imbalances will help with prevention. Additionally, ergonomic work and home setups can reduce strain along with proper wheelchair setup and good seating and positioning.

If complications arise, early treatment of pain can reduce future symptoms and complications. Compared to individuals without spinal cord injuries, the most unique factor is the use of extremities. For many with an SCI, it is impossible to rest an extremity. For example, resting a shoulder for paraplegics may mean going from complete independence to complete dependence. When treating injuries and pain, exercise is usually the first step. Depending on the condition, accompanying stretching with strengthening can help. Low-impact exercise equipment such as ergometers can be beneficial. Exercise to strengthen the weak/atrophied muscles, and stretch any spastic muscles should help to address any muscular imbalances that may exist (e.g., anterior and posterior muscle groups used for pushing a wheelchair, muscles on the left or right side of the body in individuals with incomplete SCI, flexors and extensor muscle groups for individuals with incomplete SCI or paraplegia). Finally, it is important to ensure proper shoulder mechanics and position to protect against wear and tear as well as impingement. In addition to exercise, it is important to modify activities to limit stress on the joints. This includes modifying transfer techniques and wheelchair propulsion techniques to reduce joint strain.

Benefits of Physical Activity and Exercise

Regular exercise and sport participation can have many benefits for individuals with spinal cord injuries and should be encouraged for this population. Conditions such as cardiovascular disease, hyperlipidemia, insulin resistance, musculoskeletal decline, and visceral obesity are commonly reported for individuals with SCI as they age, and the onset of these conditions also tend to occur earlier in life for individuals with SCI compared to those without. Exercise can help to treat and prevent the onset of these conditions, which highlights the importance to select exercise and physical activities that reduce health risks while also not increasing risks of injury. Outside of the physical benefits of physical activity, exercise, and sport participation, individuals experience other benefits impacting their social and emotional wellbeing. Individuals have reported expanded social networks, improved senses of freedom and success, improved self-image, and feelings of normalcy.[12] Additionally, regular participation in sport and recreational activity has been shown to have positive associations with quality of life, life satisfaction, community reintegration, mood, and employment among those with SCI.[13]

Risks associated with exercise are similar for both individuals with and without SCI. However, complications such as overuse will be greater for individuals with SCI and such complications will compromise daily activities to a greater extent than for those without SCI. Exercises and activities should be selected that are appropriate for an individual's level of function and ability to perform safely.

Modifications for Sports, Physical Activity, and Physical Education

Wheelchair Setup and Padding

The first concern for setup and participation in physical activity, exercise, and sports is the safety of the participants. When setting up, ensure that participants are using properly fitted equipment and they have good posture and positioning. Before beginning an activity, check for areas where skin may rub against surfaces or be at risk for breakdown. The use of things such as foam can be used to pad off surfaces and doing so will protect against skin issues. After physical activity, it is prudent to check the participant's skin to be aware of whether any breakdowns occurred.

Adapted Equipment

When preparing for events, if individuals with a certain level of injury or function are the target population, bring adapted equipment appropriate for those individuals. For example, grasping cuffs such as those from Active Hands® (see Figure 19.3) might be necessary for exercise for individuals with limited hand function. Other examples of adapted equipment include but are not limited to throwing chairs for field events, wheelchairs for track events and road racing, sit skis for winter sports, surfboards, adapted rifle scopes for hunters and shooters, adapted fishing equipment, modified golf carts, accessible beach wheelchairs, adapted weight lifting equipment with more varied weight ranges, gripping cuffs, wheelchair training rollers, and wheelchair resistance bands and movable seats in fitness systems to allow room for a wheelchair.

Practitioners should be flexible making modifications or preparing for physical activity, and be ready for the unexpected. Some adapted equipment will work, while other pieces will not work as you expect and some will only seem to work for some participants. Plan to be flexible and try to include participants in the setup and problem-solving process because there is a chance they have experienced something similar in the past and have a solution or

FIGURE 19.3 Example of General Purpose Gripping Aid.
Source: Copyright © 2022 by Active Hands. Reprinted by permission.

have an idea that might work for them. Also, if something is not working as expected or is going poorly, do not be afraid to switch it up and try something else. If you notice that something is not right, the participant has probably noticed as well, so having an open line of communication between you and the individual is extremely important.

Instructional Strategies

Within a school setting, many students with an SCI may need some physical modifications and/or accommodations, while others may need scheduling, testing, classroom, and/or program accommodations. Schools and recreational/sports facilities should consider the following when planning for individuals with an SCI.

Physical accommodations
- Building accessibility (ramps inside and outside).
- Elevators in multilevel buildings.
- Doorways wide enough to accommodate a wheelchair.
- Accessible general areas (gym, cafeteria, auditorium).
- Accessible bathrooms with grab bars and stall doors that open outward.
- Classrooms and weight rooms with enough space to accommodate a student's wheelchair turning space.
- Accessible lockers.
- Fire and emergency evacuation plans.
- Private area for catheterization and other personal care.

Program accommodations
- Assistance/peer partner for help with setup of equipment.
- Training of staff about the disability and health considerations.
- Adapted equipment needs.
- Breaks for rest, hydration, and personal care.
- Time of day of programming to consider ambient temperature (indoors and outdoors).
- When going outside for physical education classes or to access a recreation center's outdoor facilities, consider the surface individuals will travel across in order to reach accessible facilities (e.g., navigating a wheelchair through the grass to get to a hard surface/court for sport participation) or going around to the back of a building to access a wheelchair ramp.

Instruction
- Modify techniques to utilize stronger muscle groups or function (i.e., hold and throw a chest pass using knuckles/outside of hands if hand function is limited).
- Experiment with different techniques to find the best possible option for each participant (i.e., throwing backward or to the side may be better than chest pass, or pushing a wheelchair with the forearms when finger and grip strength is limited to grasp a wheelchair tire for propulsion).

Recommendations for Practitioners

It is prudent to learn more about injury levels, nerve innervation, health considerations, and population-specific concerns; however, it takes time to learn, especially with more and more information and research emerging about SCI. Do not let this deter you from starting to get involved with working with this population. Some of the most important lessons for working with individuals with SCI are about interpersonal interactions that you can start learning right now.

Person First Terminology

One of the most important pieces to working with this population is to be inclusive and use inclusive language. Individuals with SCI are more than their injury. Their injury is a part of their life, but it is not their life. See beyond the injury and look at the individual in front of you. As for inclusive language, these are individuals with an SCI or with a disability and not an injured or disabled person. Likewise, if they use a wheelchair, say "they use a wheelchair" instead of "they're in a wheelchair," "confined to a chair," or "wheelchair bound." Do not define the person by their injury or equipment they use.

Providing Assistance

Do not automatically assume someone needs help, it is better to ask if they need your help with anything than assuming they do. As illustrated in this section, everyone will have unique characteristics and conditions. Do not assume because you have seen an individual with a similar injury that another will present the same. Everyone will be different so be prepared to adapt based on the unique needs of the individuals you work with.

Inquiring about the Disability

It is also important to be sensitive about the injury. Depending on the situation, it is not rude to ask about an individual's level of injury and may be necessary to determine if an activity is appropriate. However, refrain from asking about the cause of injury. This can be a very sensitive subject. Some individuals may openly talk about their injury while others may never be comfortable talking about their experience.

SPINA BIFIDA

Defining Spina Bifida

Spina bifida is a congenital birth defect of a person's spine. Within the first month of pregnancy, the neural tube forms becoming the brain, spinal cord, and structures around the cord. The failure of the neural tube to close causes the backbone that protects the spinal cord to not form or close resulting in possible damage to the spinal cord and nerves.[14] The incomplete neural tube closure (called a neural tube defect) can occur anywhere along the formation of the brain and spine. There are three types of Spina bifida depending on the size and location in the opening of the spine and whether part of the spinal cord and nerves are affected. The three types of spina bifida are occulta, meningocele, and myelomeningocele (See Figure 19.4).

Occulta

Spina bifida occulta is the mildest form of spina bifida. The spinal column does not close entirely, but the spinal fluid and spinal nerves do not come out into the open area remaining in its usual place. Since there is no apparent damage to the spinal cord in persons with spina bifida occulta, people generally experience few if any changes in movement function

or sensation. An individual with spina bifida occulta may not be aware that they have this diagnosis as there may be no observable changes in the skin, opening, or sack on the back with the exception of a possible dimple over the area of the spinal cord or a tuft of hair.[14,15] Spina bifida occulta is often detected only through a screening such as X-ray, MRI, or CT scan of the spine.

Meningocele

The meninge is a protective covering around the spinal cord. In **spina bifida meningocele**, the protective covering pushes through the opening in the vertebrae into a sac called the meningocele. Spina bifida meningocele occurs when a pouch of cerebral spinal fluid (liquid that cushions the brain and spine) pokes through the open spine. Since the spinal cord remains intact and no nerves are included in the sac, there is often no nerve damage and therefore may be minor symptoms of movement or sensory impairment or none at all.[15]

Myelomeningocele (MM)

Spina bifida myelomeningocele (MM) is the most common and severe form of spina bifida. The pouch on the back protruding through the open spinal cord contains a portion of the spinal cord, **cerebrospinal fluid**, and spinal nerves. The sac may be covered with skin or may expose tissues and nerves. The displacement of the nerves into this sac results in moderate to severe disabilities such as problems in functional abilities like walking, toileting, and sensation (loss of feeling in the legs and feet), and inability to move the legs.[14,15] When people refer to spina bifida, they usually are referencing spina bifida MM.

Prevalence and Etiology

Spina bifida occurs during the first three to four few weeks of pregnancy before a women knows she is pregnant.[15] Spina bifida is often identified before or at birth with occasional diagnosis of spina bifida occulta in adulthood. During pregnancy, screening such as blood tests or amniocentesis for fetal proteins or ultrasounds check for spina bifida and other congenital birth impairments. About 1,427 babies are born with spina bifida each year, or 1 in every 2,758 births.[14,16] Hispanic women tend to have the highest rates of having a child with spina bifida with 3.8 per 10,000 live births, followed by Caucasian women at 3.09 per 10,000 live births, and Black or African American women with approximately 2.73 per 10,000 live births.[17]

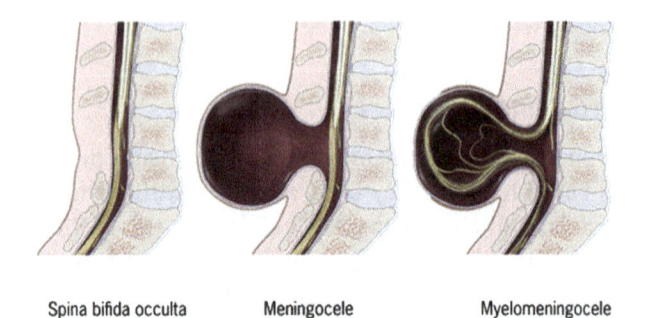

FIGURE 19.4 Types of spina bifida.
From: https://www.cdc.gov/ncbddd/spinabifida/facts.html
Source: Centers for Disease Control and Prevention

The exact cause of spina bifida is unknown. Scientists suspect that multiple factors (i.e., genetics and environment) are involved. The development of spina bifida may be due in part to a lack of folic acid in the mother's diet. Folic acid is a nutrient found in green leafy foods. However, typical diets usually do not contain enough folic acid. Women of childbearing age are recommended to take folic acid supplements daily prior to conception and during the first few months of pregnancy in addition to prenatal vitamins to address any additional vitamin deficiencies such as zinc and selenium that may contribute to spina bifida.[15] Other recommendations to minimize the risk of spina bifida include controlling diabetes or obesity, avoiding overheating the body using hot tubs or saunas, and treating fever with doctor approved medications.[14]

Pathophysiology/Psychophysiology

Spina bifida occulta and meningocele may have no or minor symptoms, with myelomeningocele associated with moderate to severe loss of sensation, motor movement, and related symptoms. Spina bifida MM is associated with conditions related to the brain and nervous system including Chiari (or Arnold–Chiari) malformation, hydrocephalus, and tethered cord syndrome. We will briefly describe each condition starting with its structural characteristics and common symptoms. The impact of these conditions on movement will be discussed in the following section.

Chiari Malformation

Chiari malformation is a condition in which the brain stem and cerebellum are displaced downward below an opening in the skull called the foramen magnum into the spinal canal interfering with the normal flow of cerebrospinal fluid that protects the brain and spinal cord. Pressure on the cerebellum and brain stem may affect functions controlled by these areas and block circulation of cerebrospinal fluid and signals transmitted from the brain to the body. Of the four types of Chiari malformation, type II is associated with spina bifida MM and is specifically referred to as Arnold–Chiari malformation. Symptoms of Chiari malformation may include headaches, neck pain, hearing or balance problems, muscle weakness or numbness, dizziness, difficulty breathing, and swallowing.[18]

Hydrocephalus

Hydrocephalus is a chronic, neurological condition caused by a buildup of cerebrospinal fluid around within the ventricles of the brain (see Figure 19.5). The cerebrospinal fluid protects the brain and spinal cord. Too much fluid buildup in the brain causes increased pressure and may lead to brain damage. Hydrocephalus occurs in 80-90% of children with myelomeningocele.[18] Signs of hydrocephalus may include rapid head growth, full or tense soft spot on the back of the head, unusual irritability, repeated vomiting, crossed eyes, an inability to look up, or difficulty

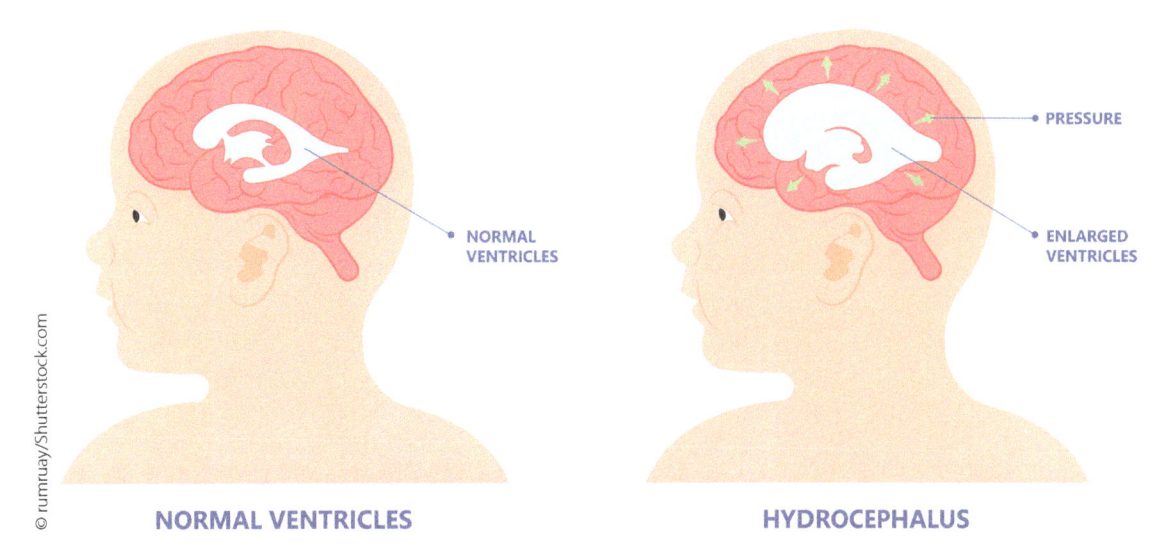

FIGURE 19.5 Picture of hydrocehpalus.
https://kidshealth.org/EN/images/illustrations/hydrocephalus_a_enIL.jpg

swallowing. A head ultrasound, CT scan or MRI is used to diagnose the buildup of fluid in the brain.[19]

Tethered Spinal Cord

The spinal cord usually hangs loose in the spinal canal moving freely to allow bending, stretching, and growth to occur. With a **tethered cord,** the spinal cord attaches to the surrounding tissues of the spinal canal. As the person grows, the spinal cord stretches, damaging the spinal cord from both a lack of blood flow to the spinal nerves and the stretching itself. Tethering can occur before or after birth and usually is seen in the lumbar level of the spine.[20] Individuals with a tethered cord may experience symptoms such as back pain, scoliosis, leg and foot weakness, and changes in bowel and bladder control.

Management and Treatment of Spina Bifida

The management and treatment of spina bifida is ongoing as needs change while children develop and grow into adults. Treatment of spina bifida can begin in utero and continue throughout life involving support from medical specialists including neurosurgeons, urologists, orthopedists, physical and occupational therapists, nurses, dietitians, and teachers. Spina bifida cannot be cured. Management and treatment may be surgical or rehabilitative to lessen the impact of impairment on function and improve quality of life of individuals with spina bifida.

Surgery

Myelomeningocele and meningocele require surgical treatment that can be conducted in utero to close the opening in the fetus' spinal cord or shortly after birth to return the spinal cord and nerves to the spinal canal and remove the sac to prevent further damage or infection such as meningitis, and to maximize function.

Chiari Malformation

Symptoms that do not interfere with activities of daily living are monitored by a physician. Surgery is available to ease symptoms or stop the progression of the damage to the central nervous system. Children with spina bifida MM usually require surgery to reposition the brain stem and cerebellum to a more normal alignment.

Hydrocephalus

Hydrocephalus can be treated surgically by implanting a **shunt**, which is a hollow tube, under the skin either in the edge of the soft spot in the head, above or behind the ear, or the back of the head. The shunt can drain fluid from the brain to one of three locations in the body (see Figure 19.6 for an example), the abdomen (ventriculoperitoneal, VP shunt), a vein (ventriculoatrial, VA shunt) or the gall bladder (ventriculo-gall bladder shunt). Shunts have valves and work by controlling the direction and amount of fluid that is drained. The shunts tend to work automatically when

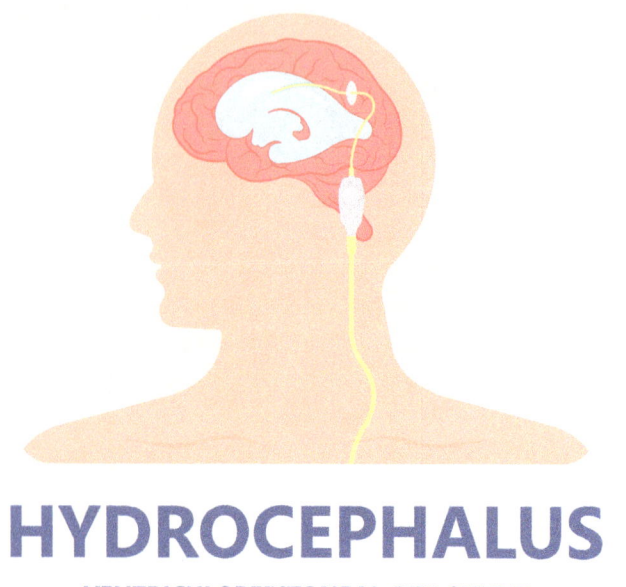

FIGURE 19.6 Shunt.

fluid pressure in the head becomes too high, protecting the brain from too much pressure.[19,21] Individuals with hydrocephalus should be followed by a doctor and issues with hydrocephalus treated throughout life to prevent brain injury.[14] Additional surgeries may be needed to change the shunt as the child grows or if the shunt becomes blocked or infected. Signs of shunt problems may include headache, seizures, change in intellect, school performance, or personality, back pain at the spina bifida closure site, worsening arm or leg function, increasing scoliosis, worsening speech, or changes in bowel and bladder function.[14,22] Problems with the shunt may look similar to those of Chiari malformation or spinal cord tethering.

Tethered Spinal Cord

Almost all children with spina bifida MM have tethering of the spinal cord. Surgery to untether the spinal cord may be done after determining if the symptoms presented are not due to a problem with the shunt and is performed when there are signs of back and leg pain, muscle function loss, deterioration in gait, and/or sensory deterioration.[20]

Therapeutic Rehabilitation

Physical therapy will focus on gross motor movements and mobility and positioning using a wheelchair, walker, or assistive devices along with muscular strength and transfers.[15] Children with spina bifida should be encouraged to ambulate with braces to stimulate the growth of bone and circulation in lower limbs unless the total loss of motor function is the case. An occupational therapist will focus on fine motor movements and activities of daily living such as feeding, dressing, and eating.[15]

Specific Issues with Motor Movement

For persons with MM, there is weakness in the areas that the damaged nerves control such as muscles to the abdomen, legs, bowel, and bladder. The loss or weakness of function is common in the lower limbs as the malformation of the neural tube tends to be in the lumbar vertebrae. Therefore, lower limbs are the primarily impacted body parts that may show loss or weakness of motor function due to loss of sensation, muscle contracture, bone deformity, hip dislocation, and rigid joints. Some children with spina bifida may experience cerebellar dysfunction, including lack of coordination in movement, poor fine motor function, tremors, and uncontrolled and repetitive movements in the eyes.

Based on the severity of the impacted limbs, the mode of mobility varies. An individual with meningocele may walk freely without any assistive devices, or a child with myelomeningocele may need to use a wheelchair to engage in exercise or sports programs. Each individual with spina bifida needs an individual assessment of motor function to determine the appropriate programming.

The loss of sensation on the impacted body parts can pose an increased risk of injury and related infection. Children and adults with spina bifida experience the same sensory impairments (limitations in feeling some of their body) as described previously for persons with SCI. These sensory impairments affect the ability to feel cuts, bruises, and dry skin leading to skin breakdown. Individuals who use a wheelchair for activities of daily living and sport or physical activity tend to sit in one position for long periods of time increasing the risk for pressure sores that result from skin damage caused by prolonged pressure. If people with spina bifida or spinal cord injuries experience swelling in the feet or legs during physical activity or sport, checking the skin for breakdowns in the area of swelling and elevating the legs can help reduce any further complications. Compression stockings may be helpful to minimize swelling. Along with checking the skin regularly for redness, persons with spina bifida and SCI can protect the skin by avoiding hot bath water, hot dishes, hot car seats, and metal seat belt clasps as they may cause burns; wearing properly fitted shoes; and applying sunscreen and limiting sun exposure.

Associated Conditions with Spina Bifida

There are several health considerations that occur in conjunction with neural tube issues. While not everyone with spina bifida has these conditions, as a practitioner, it is important to be aware of their potential impact on the way individuals with spina bifida learn and engage in sport and physical activity.

Perceptual Motor Delays

Children with spina bifida, particularly those with hydrocephalus, demonstrate delays in hand-eye coordination and fundamental motor skills. Such impairments can impact one's ability to move as well as academically with reading and writing.[23]

Learning and Attention

Like all people with or without a disability, there is a broad range of scores on IQ tests by individuals with spina bifida ranging from exceptional to learning difficulties. Children with myelomeningocele commonly show difficulty paying attention, experience perceptual difficulties, and may have behavioral problems, impaired memory, and difficulty in problem-solving. School-age children with spina bifida may receive special education services under the diagnosis of an orthopedic impairment under the Individuals with Disabilities Education Act (IDEA) or modifications or accommodations provided through a 504 plan under the Rehabilitation Act.[23] Additionally, students with spina bifida may be educated in the general education and physical education setting or in a self-contained special education and adapted physical education class depending on the degree to which their impairment impacts their educational performance and the least restrictive environment in which students can best meet their individual academic goals and state and national academic and physical education standards.

Obesity

Individuals with spina bifida tend to be overweight. The major reason is the reduced energy expenditure from the loss of large muscle groups (i.e., legs), reduced aerobic capacity, lower functional ambulation, and lower muscular strength often leading toward a more sedentary lifestyle.

Latex Allergy

Individuals with spina bifida are at high risk for latex or rubber allergy. A latex allergy means a person is allergic to proteins in natural rubber latex. After birth, several surgical treatments such as removing the sac or implanting a shunt and catheterization for bowel and bladder control and regulation can cause a cumulative effect that increases the latex sensitivity.[24] A latex allergy can be progressive that may start with mild irritation and progress to become more serious leading to **anaphylaxis**. Allergic symptoms include itching, skin redness or rash, sneezing, runny nose, cough, or shortness of breath, but sometimes severe allergic reactions can be life-threatening. The most common cause of latex allergy comes through touching latex products. Practitioners working with individuals with spina bifida are advised to avoid the use of materials containing natural rubber latex such as balloons, balls, swim goggles, and racket handles. Practitioners should check if any of their equipment is made of latex and find alternative equipment made with silicone, plastic, nitrile, or vinyl when necessary. Spalding, Rawlings, and Wilson all make basketballs, footballs, soccer balls, and baseballs that are latex free. Sport equipment companies like GOPHER Sports also have playground markers, cones, rubber balls, tennis balls, and baseball bases that are latex free. Facilities may need to create latex-free zones to minimize exposure to products made of natural rubber latex. Airborne exposure to latex occurs largely in operating rooms as the latex examination/surgical gloves release latex particles into the air that can be inhaled. Exposure to airborne latex antigens can trigger an allergic reaction and anaphylactic reactions in sensitive individuals. Some people with latex allergies also may present with allergies to fruits and vegetables like bananas, chestnuts, kiwi, avocado, and tomato.[15,24]

Epilepsy and Seizures

Seizures or epilepsy may develop in children with spina bifida due to the effects of hydrocephalus. Seizures also may develop due to trauma and brain injury. For example, the tension in the brain created by tethering of the spinal cord may lead to the development of seizures. Medications are typically used to manage seizures.[15]

Orthopedic Impairment

The spine, hips, legs, and feet in children with spina bifida often do not develop or work as they do in individuals without disabilities. This is because the nerves that normally tell the body parts how and when to function are not formed or properly connected to the bones and muscles of the lower body. In most cases there is no or minimal impairment in the arms or upper chest. The lack of usage and stimulation of the impacted limbs prevent the growth of the lower body. The loss of motor function and **contracture** (shortening or hardening of the muscles, tendons, and other tissue leading to deformity and rigidity of the joints) and muscle imbalances (i.e., some muscle groups stronger than others) may cause hip dislocation, scoliosis, kyphosis, and osteoporosis.[14] Bone deformity and postural deviations can prevent individuals with spina bifida from participating in activities without proper adaptation. The risk of fractures of weak limbs due to osteoporosis is increased in persons with spina bifida. For people with poor sensation, a sign of fracture may be redness and swelling of the limb without pain. Strengthening exercises, therapeutic intervention, and adapted equipment can help individuals with spina bifida to become more independent.

Visual Impairment

Some children with spina bifida, specifically those with hydrocephalus, may develop strabismus (wandering eye) due to an imbalance of the muscles that move the eye. In this case, the weaker eye may stop sending visual messages to the brain. With the help of an ophthalmologist, eye patches, eye exercises, or surgery to correct the eye muscles may help strengthen the alignment of the eyes.[15]

Bowel and Bladder

Most individuals with myelomeningocele also have a loss or difficulty of bladder control, needing the use of a catheter to regularly drain their bladder. Bowel functions are addressed through bowel programs including nutrition and stool softeners. Incomplete bowel or bladder discharge can cause urinary tract and other blood infections.[15]

Social/Emotional Functioning

Physical impairments caused by spina bifida can impact a person's emotional and social development. Families, teachers, coaches, and therapists should encourage children to be independent and to participate in activities with their peers without disabilities to the maximum extent possible. Depression can occur in individuals with spina bifida at a higher incidence rate due in part to their chronic health care needs and concerns.[15] School counselors or psychologists can help provide strategies for students and families to address the impact of depression and to enhance social and emotional functioning of individuals with spina bifida.

Contraindications for Motor Movement

Practitioners should complete an assessment with input from the individual or their family/caregivers of the person's functional abilities before participation in physical activity and sport takes place. While spina bifida itself is nonprogressive, precautions and contraindications should be considered due to the association with Chiari malformation, tethered cord, and shunts related to hydrocephalus that can change over time. The following precautions and contraindications should be considered. Pain is a key indicator of tolerance. When one experiences pain, movement should be modified, avoided, or stopped until one experiences no pain when engaging in physical activity or sport. Individuals should consult with a physician before continuing involvement in sport and physical activity if there is the appearance or worsening of pain or neurologic systems or a breakdown in skin integrity. For individuals with a shunt, it is generally recommended to avoid activities such as extreme flexion, extension, or rotation of the neck that could put undue stress or burden on the neck region that could damage the shunt.

Benefits of Physical Activity and Exercise

Regular physical activity is important for persons with spina bifida. People with spina bifida may engage in active play with friends, roll or walk, participate in community programs, complete exercises recommended by a physical therapist or personal trainer, and participate in individual and team sport activities in both inclusive and in programs or teams comprised solely of persons with physical disabilities. Yet, the research shows that people with spina bifida tend to engage in less physical activity than their peers without disabilities, have higher body mass index (BMI), reduced aerobic capacity, lower functional ambulation, and lower muscular strength compared to people without spina bifida.[25] Appropriately designed adapted physical education, activity, and exercise for individuals with spina bifida is critical to offset and ameliorate the loss of strength or fitness. Otherwise, that may lead to less independence and function in completing activities of daily living. Increasing physical activity in individuals with spina bifida has been found to promote function and endurance, prevent obesity, decrease difficulty with activity, improve constipation, resist infection, reduce risk of secondary health risks (e.g., diabetes and high blood pressure), improve mood, reduce stress, facilitate positive perceptions of athletic competence, athletic identity, physical competence, and improve overall perceptions of quality of life.[24] Individuals with spina bifida are encouraged to engage in physical activity following the U.S. national guidelines for individuals without a disability. Specific information about frequency, duration, intensity, time, and type of activity needed for optimal health in individuals with spina bifida and the impact of severity of impairment on these variables, however, requires further research.[25]

Recommendations for Teachers, Therapists, and Trainers

Program and Instructional Adaptations

Children with spina bifida may be educated in adapted physical education or general physical education settings, where they will pursue either individualized goals or the same goals and educational standards as their peers without disabilities. Assessment of physical, motor, and cognitive skills and readiness is critical to accommodate the needs of students with spina bifida and to develop appropriate goals.

Physical fitness and the development of team, individual, and lifetime sports skills are the focus of both the general and adapted physical education curriculum for students with and without spina bifida. Activities can be modified to enable individuals with spina bifida to participate safely and fully in sport and physical activity. Prior to making instructional modifications, it is always a good idea to consult with the individual as they often have ideas of what has worked, what might work, and what they would prefer to facilitate their sport and physical activity participation. Allowing the individual to contribute to the planning or implementation of their sport, physical education, physical activity, or therapeutic program can increase perceptions of control, self-determination, and motivation. Broad categories with specific modifications individuals and practitioners may adjust include the equipment, rules, environment, and instruction.

Equipment (taking into consideration any latex allergies first and foremost)
- Lighter bats, rackets.
- Balls that are.
  - Brighter colored.
  - Softer.
  - Larger.
  - Lighter (balloons, beach balls, scarves).
- Shorter handle (paddle, tennis racket).
- Larger head size (on rackets, bats).
- Modified compression (lower density) ball that impacts the flight and loft of the ball.
- Bright color boundary lines, floor markings and targets for contrast.
- Velcro (on balls, targets, for straps).
- Stationary (batting tee) or suspended equipment.
- Light and sound (targets, balls, boundary lines).
- Target height, size, color.

Rules
- Allow extra time, extra attempts, or remove time limits.
- Adjust requirements for performance (e.g., 2 bounces in tennis).
- Serve or inbound ball from a closer distance.
- Allow for a partner to assist.
- Change how points are earned.
- Elimination of defense/defenders.
- Eliminate or extend boundary lines.
- Change size of teams/number of players on a court at one time.

Environment/Space
- Change field size (reduce or increase size if using a wheelchair or partner).
- Create larger boundary area/target to hit balls into.
- Create smaller boundary area to receive balls.
- Shorten distances.
- Create zones for personal safety.
- Larger or lower targets.
- Have back to a wall to stop a ball.
- Consider playing surface.

Instruction
- Break down a task into smaller or easier components to allow the child to do as much of the task independently as possible.
- Use gestures and visual cues.
- Provide demonstration and verbal instruction.
- Physical assistance (partial, full, brailing for students with visual impairments).
- Use peer partner/mentors and paraprofessionals.
- Use sign language.
- Small group and one-on-one instruction.
- Check for understanding/ask questions.
- Provide feedback.

Orthotics and Assistive Devices

Braces or **orthotics** are externally used devices to support the structural and functional growth of the body and keep the legs and feet in proper positioning to facilitate weight bearing in an upright posture, increase range of motion, improve standing, mobility (i.e., stride length, speed), and independence. Upright mobility is also associated with improved bone density, reduced urinary tract infections due to more complete emptying of the bladder, and improved positioning to increase social interaction.[26] Successful orthotic treatment is based on a combination of factors including (a) level of neurological involvement, (b) degree of musculoskeletal impairment, (c) sensory impairment, (d) acquired obesity, (e) existing muscle strength, (f) visual and motor perception impairment, (g) the individual's motivation, and (h) family support. Braces are designed to address different joint problems and are named based on the joints the braces cross or the location of the braces on the body. There are six general types of leg and foot braces commonly used by individuals with spina bifida. They include foot, supramelleolar, ankle–foot, floor reaction, knee–ankle–foot, hip–knee–ankle–foot, reciprocating gait, and dynamic ankle–foot orthoses. Children with spina bifida require frequent changes of their braces as their bodies grow.

For individuals with spina bifida who are ambulatory, there are several different options of assistive devices to help ensure proper body alignment, balance, and less effort during walking. Even for individuals who can walk, wheelchairs may offer the freedom and mobility to engage in sport, physical activity, and activities of daily living that require longer distances, speed, or agility. Proper wheelchair fitting and cushioning is critical to ensure proper body alignment and the prevention of skin breakdown and pressure sores. Forearm crutches may be used to provide balance and can help navigate stairs. Individuals may use a single forearm crutch or two crutches. A crutch has a cuff that fits around the forearm and a handpiece to lean on while walking. Lastly, two types of walkers, reverse walkers, which allow the individual to pull the walker while walking, or forward walkers, which an individual pushes, offer assistance with standing by providing a support base and assist with upright posture and mobility.

Development of Physical Fitness

The development of all components of physical fitness should be the goal of practitioners. Exercise programs should consist of stretching, aerobic exercise, and muscle endurance, and strengthening activities. Stretching activities can assist the proper range of motion for individuals with spina bifida to prevent further injury on the impacted limbs. Individuals with spina bifida who use an assistive device to ambulate tend to have greater energy expenditure and may require more frequent rest due to fatigue. Aerobic and muscle-strengthening exercises can help improve mobility and independence with activities of daily living.

General physical activity guidelines by the National Center for Health Physical Activity and Disability (NCHPAD) for individuals with spina bifida are provided here and are in accordance with the National Physical Activity Guidelines published by the Center for Disease Control and Prevention. The NCHPAD website has sample activity programs to guide practitioners that include both written and visual pictures and videos of how to perform various exercises.

Cardiovascular training guidelines include:
- 20-60 minutes of continuous vigorous aerobic exercise or multiple sessions of short duration (10 min) 3-5 times per week.
- Monitor aerobic exercise using maximal heart rate or rating of perceived exertion. It is important to note that max heart rate may be lower than normal for persons with spina bifida or spinal cord injuries with ratings of perceived exertion reported in the moderate to strong range.
- Beneficial cardiovascular training activities include upper body calisthenics, rowing machines, hand cycles and arm ergometers, functional electrical stimulation-leg cycle ergometers, or adapted sports such as basketball, track, and swimming.

Strength training guidelines include:
- Training all active muscle groups.
- Training three days per week (do not train the same muscle group on consecutive days).
- Strengthen the muscles of the shoulders and upper back to help maintain body posture and balance in a wheelchair.
- Upper body pushing and pressing exercises to strengthen muscles used for transfer and wheeling.
- Pulling and rowing exercises to help prevent shoulder overuse injuries and improve sitting posture.
- Perform wheelchair push-ups keeping the elbows slightly bent every 10-30 minutes during the day holding for 30-60 seconds.
- Leg exercises (for those with leg movement) including knee lifts from a sitting position and foot lifts from a sitting position (straightening the knee) 10 repetitions twice a day. Ankle weights can be added as strength increases.
- Use straps for stabilization and balance in a wheelchair.
- Vary strengthening exercises to reduce overuse injuries including free weights, weight machines, medicine balls, wall pullies, and therabands.
- Flexibility training guidelines should consider:
- Stretching paralyzed muscles including the hamstrings, adductors, and muscles that flex the hip and foot, and that extend the back.
- Lie on stomach to help stretch muscles of the hips and back of thighs.
- Stretch muscles of the chest and front of the shoulders. This is especially important for wheelchair users who may tend to sit and push a chair in a crouched position.
- Stretch shoulders by grasping the elbow of the arm overhead and pulling back to gently

stretch. Stretch the front of the shoulder by placing your hand on a wall with fingers pointed backward with the arm outstretched and lean forward toward the wall.
- Stretch calf muscles to decrease swelling.
- Use passive resistance from therabands, standing in a standing frame, or doing yoga or Pilates.

Sport and Physical Activity Opportunities and Organizations

Persons with spinal cord disabilities, inclusive of spina bifida, are eligible to compete in the Paralympic Games. The sports in the Paralympic games are referred to as Parasports. There are a total of 28 summer and winter sports for persons with a spinal cord disability. Some Parasports are designed and modified only for individuals with paraplegia (e.g., wheelchair basketball, badminton, powerlifting) and other sports accommodate individuals with tetraplegia (e.g., boccia, rugby). The majority of sports in the Paralympic games have classification groups for those with paraplegia and tetraplegia (e.g., athletics, archery, cycling, alpine skiing, ice hockey). There are many recreational sports outside of Parasports (referred to as disability sport or adaptive sports) in which individuals with spinal cord disabilities can participate including but are not limited to hiking, rock climbing, mountain biking, paddling, power soccer, rafting, scuba diving, skateboarding, tai chi, water skiing, and yoga. Move United, an official affiliate of the U.S. Olympic and Paralympic Committee, provides programming, and partners with organizations across the United States to offer more than 60 different adaptive sports. To learn more about the different sports and physical activity opportunities available to persons with a spinal cord disability consult the Move United website (moveunited.org). The National Center on Health, Physical Activity and Disability is a great starting point to look for organizations (nchpad.org/directories/organizations) as is the United Spinal Association Spinal Cord Injury Resource Center. The chapter on disability sport in this textbook also contains information on community and school-based sport organizations for individuals with spinal cord disabilities. Lastly, Sports n' Spokes magazine is devoted to recreation and sport for persons living with a spinal cord disability and other wheelchair users and provides national and international recreation news, opportunities, and information on the latest equipment.

KYPHOSIS, LORDOSIS, AND SCOLIOSIS
Defining Kyphosis, Lordosis, and Scoliosis

In the normal spine there is some degree of kyphosis in the thoracic spine and lordosis in the cervical and lumbar spine. **Kyphosis** is an increase of the normal forward rounding of the spine seen from the sagittal plane. This often gives a hunchback appearance. **Lordosis** is an excessive inward/backward curve of the spine also seen from the sagittal plane. Lordosis often makes the buttocks appear more prominent. It may also be referred to as swayback. **Scoliosis** is a sideways curvature of the spine along the frontal plane. See Figure 19.7 for illustrations of the three diagnoses. With the exception of scoliosis, these diagnoses can be mild in condition and produce no noticeable signs or symptoms; however, more severe cases can cause pain and other symptoms.

Prevalence, Etiology, Pathophysiology, and Management

Kyphosis, lordosis, and scoliosis often occur in conjunction with other physical impairments such as SCI, spina bifida, cerebral palsy, and muscular dystrophy where muscle imbalance and muscle weakness in the torso are often impaired leading to the development of spinal curvatures. We will provide a general overview of these different spinal curvatures in isolation of any association with other physical impairments.

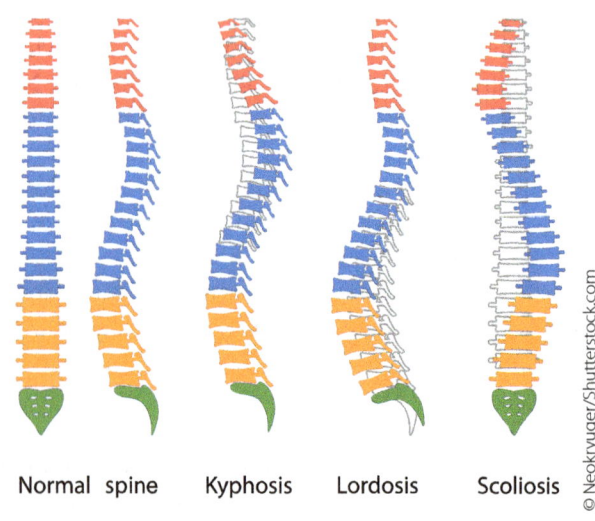

FIGURE 19.7 Types of spinal curvatures.

Kyphosis

Kyphosis occurs when the vertebrae of the spine become abnormally shaped and do not stack as a column. There are three types of kyphosis: postural, Scheuermann disease, and congenital deformities. Postural kyphosis can be seen predominantly in women and can begin around adolescence, but is more predominant in women over 40 years of age with prevalence rates of approximately 20-60% of adults, primarily women 60 years of age or older.[27] Postural kyphosis is caused by a slouching posture that increases the forward curve stretching the extensor back muscles and the posterior ligaments of the spine, weakening the spine over time. Scheuermann disease is also known as juvenile kyphosis and is a structural change in the thoracic spine occurring prior to puberty (usually between 13 and 16 years of age) due in part to changes in the growth plate (areas of new bone growth that determines length and shape of mature bone) during development.[27] There is some research suggesting a hereditary component to Scheuermann disease and is found in roughly 0.4-8% of the population. Lastly, congenital kyphosis is a type of hyperkyphosis (excessive kyphosis) and tends to be the most disabling, rapidly progressive, and is more commonly associated with neurological complications.[27] This type of kyphosis is present at birth with an outward curve of the spine that can become more noticeable with growth. Kyphosis can also come from fractures, osteoporosis, disk degeneration, certain syndromes, and cancer and cancer treatments. Aside from causing back pain, which can range from mild to severe, kyphosis often does not lead to any harmful effects. In more severe situations, kyphosis can lead to fatigue, increased pain with movement, increased forward posture of the head, uneven shoulder height and cause breathing problems, limited physical functions (weakness), loss of sensation, digestive problems, and bowel/bladder incontinence caused by spinal cord compression.[27]

Lordosis

Some of the causes of lordosis are neuromuscular conditions such as spina bifida and cerebral palsy, birth defects, hip or pelvic conditions, previous back surgery, imbalances of postural muscles, and athletic activities. Complications that can arise include chronic back pain, limited mobility of the spine, numbness and weakness, weak bladder control, and inhibited muscle control. Most people with lordosis do not require treatment unless it is a severe case.

Scoliosis

The spine of someone with scoliosis is curved appearing like an S or C with rotation of the vertebrae giving the appearance that the individual is leaning to one side.[28] The cause of scoliosis is unknown though it is

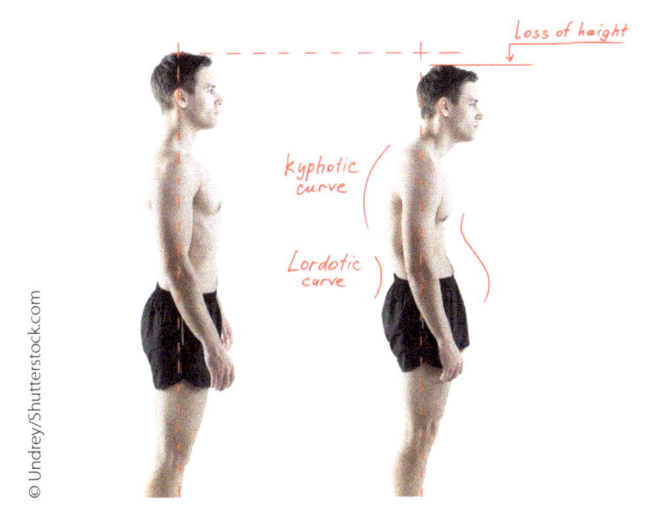

FIGURE 19.8 Kyphotic curve.

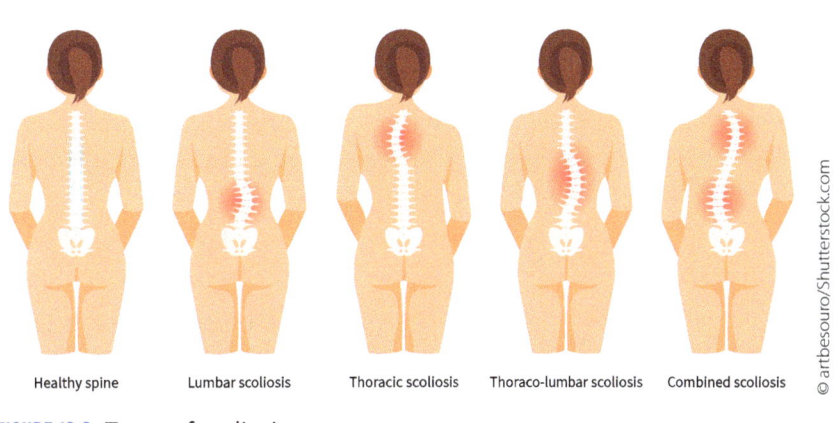

FIGURE 19.9 Types of scoliosis.

thought to have a hereditary component. Other causes of scoliosis include arthritis and osteoporosis.[28] Scoliosis may develop around the age of 10 years, the severity of which can increase with growth throughout adolescence. Other types of scoliosis may be caused by neuromuscular conditions such as cerebral palsy, muscular dystrophy, birth defects, and injuries or infections of the spine. Scoliosis usually causes no pain. However, individuals with more severe cases of scoliosis may experience lung and heart damage, back problems such as chronic pain, and postural issues such as uneven hips and shoulders, prominent ribs, and a shift of the waist and trunk to the side.[28]

Treatment options for all three types of spinal curvature (kyphosis, lordosis, and scoliosis) depend on the cause and severity. Some options include medication for pain management, medication for osteoporosis, physical therapy, bracing, and surgery. If the condition is severe, treatment options may include surgery.

Specific Benefits and Modifications for Sport, Physical Activity, and Exercise

For individuals with atypical postures of the spine (kyphosis, lordosis, or scoliosis), exercise to strengthen the core muscles and back extensor stretching and strengthening can be used to help mitigate some of the symptoms and long-term complications as well as improving overall health. The main concern for practitioners working with individuals with these conditions is to ensure that proper form is used, and that good posture is encouraged.

SPONDYLOSIS AND SPONDYLOLISTHESIS

Spondylosis and spondylolisthesis are conditions related to vertebral bodies of the spine. **Spondylosis** is caused by degenerative changes of the vertebrae such as the development of bone spurs and degeneration of intervertebral discs.[29] This can occur in the cervical, thoracic, and lumbar spine, though damage in the thoracic region frequently does not cause symptoms. Damage or injury in the lumber and cervical regions of the spine tend to be the most common. **Spondylolisthesis** occurs when one vertebral body slips and is not aligned with the adjacent vertebral bodies.[30]

Prevalence, Etiology, Pathophysiology, and Management

Spondylosis

One of the common causes of cervical spondylosis is aging as bones, ligaments, and discs wear down and weaken. Genetics is a risk factor along with spinal injuries and osteoarthritis. Due to this condition, bulging discs and inflammation can cause the compression of nerves, which can lead to chronic pain that can develop into tenderness and muscle spasms.[29]

Spondylolisthesis

There are multiple causes of spondylolisthesis. It can result from a birth defect, hereditary issues, rapid growth during adolescence, sports injuries that overstretch and stress the lower back, or overuse by hyperextension (e.g., weight lifters, tennis players, baseball pitchers). As the vertebrae move closer together, the spinal cord or nerves can be compressed, which can result in localized pain.[30]

These conditions can be treated with conservative therapy, which can include medications to address inflammation and muscle spasms, and physical therapy, light exercise, bracing, and bed rest. If conservative treatments fail or symptoms worsen, surgery might be an option.

Suggested Modifications for Sports, Physical Activity, and Physical Education

The main concern for practitioners working with individuals with these conditions is to ensure that activities match the diagnosis and will not aggravate the condition. This can be achieved by working with the individual's medical team to ensure that contraindicated activities are avoided.

TRANSVERSE MYELITIS AND GUILLAIN–BARRE SYNDROME

Transverse myelitis (TM) and Guillain–Barre syndrome (GBS) are both conditions that affect an individual's nervous system. Both conditions can come from multiple causes and present differently for each individual. Individuals with these conditions may recover but may experience lingering effects. These conditions often present similar to spinal cord injuries and can look comparable.

Prevalence, Etiology, Pathophysiology, and Management

In the United States, it is estimated that 3,000 to 6,000 people develop GBS each year. There is not an estimate of the yearly TM incidence rate since it can be confused with other conditions such as stroke.

Transverse Myelitis (TM)

Transverse Myelitis (TM) is caused by inflammation at a particular level across the spinal cord (hence the word transverse) that affects motor and sensory pathways on both sides of the spinal cord at and below the level of the damage. The exact cause of roughly 60% of cases of TM is not known though 40% of cases may be caused by conditions that affect the spinal cord such as immune system disorders (e.g., multiple sclerosis, lupus), viral infections, bacterial infections, fungal infections, parasites, inflammatory disorders, and vascular disorders.[31] TM can be found across age groups, gender, and race. Much like other spinal cord injuries, damage of the spinal cord will affect function at that level and below. The symptoms of TM may include weakness of the legs and/or arms, sensory alterations, pain, altered sensitivity (numbness, tingling, coldness, burning, sensory loss), and bowel and bladder dysfunction. Following initial treatment of TM using steroids, plasma exchange, or immune based therapies (i.e., immunosuppressant drugs), individuals will partake in long-term rehabilitative therapy. This therapy is focused on helping individuals attain as much functional independence as possible to improve quality of life. Often this comes from working with physical, occupational, and vocational therapists to address needs and create long-term plans to accomplish the goals and needs of the individual.[31]

Guillain–Barre Syndrome (GBS)

Guillain–Barre Syndrome (GBS) is a neurological impairment in which the body's immune system attacks the peripheral nervous system. The causes of GBS are not fully understood, but it is believed that immune function plays a role in its development. Two-thirds of individuals report symptoms of an infection in the six weeks prior to the onset of GBS. Rare cases have been reported after infections such as the flu, Zika virus, and COVID-19. In rare cases, individuals have developed GBS in the days or weeks after receiving certain vaccines. GBS usually begins with tingling and weakness in the extremities, with muscle weakness spreading, and can then lead to paralysis. Following the onset of symptoms, people with GBS may experience difficulties breathing, residual numbness and weakness, heart and blood pressure problems, nerve pain, bowel and bladder issues, blood clots, and pressure sores.

FIGURE 19.10 Kyphotic.

No cure exists for GBS, but some medical treatments can help with the recovery and severity of GBS. Following stabilization, physical therapy will be needed to help with the recovery process along with helping to train individuals about the use of different adapted devices to help with mobility and independence.[32]

Specific Benefits of Physical Activity and Exercise

Individuals with TM and GBS will both benefit from participation in physical activity and exercise. Following the initial onset of symptoms and potential hospital stays, individuals will likely be deconditioned and weak. Regular physical activity will help with the recovery process as well as help to establish a sense of normalcy especially with those who were very active previously. When working with these individuals, it is important to gather their input for appropriate activities and what they feel comfortable performing. As with those with spinal cord injuries, it is important to create a safe environment by encouraging proper form and following direction from medical professionals while ensuring proper use of adaptive equipment needed for the given activity.

CHAPTER SUMMARY

- Individuals with spinal cord disabilities may experience similar symptoms based on the location and the severity of the damage to the spinal cord. Symptoms include:
  1. Weakened or loss of motor and sensory functions below the area impacted by the injury.
  2. Secondary health conditions due to immobility and insensitivity of the impacted body parts including impairment-related pain, pressure sore, bowel and bladder dysfunction, social/emotional health, and other disability related conditions.
- Participation in physical activity can provide health benefits that can reserve remaining body functions and reduce or prevent the further deterioration of the symptoms of health conditions.
- Treatment and plans for physical activity, sports, and physical education should be developed based on each individual's functional level in collaboration with a multidisciplinary team including the individual themselves, family members, therapists, physicians, teachers, and trainer.
- Programs or sports specially designed for individuals with spinal cord disabilities can have maximum benefits through appropriate modifications and adaptations. Suggestions for programs include:
  1. Providing appropriate physical and environmental accommodations.
  2. Modified equipment, rules, environment, and instruction.
  3. Focusing on all aspects of physical fitness, especially flexibility, aerobic capacity, and muscular strength.
  4. Appropriate use of assistive devices (wheelchair or orthotics) to aid the achievement of physical activity goals.

REFERENCES

1. Lin, V. W., & Bono, C. M. (2010). *Spinal cord medicine, second edition: Principles & practice.* Springer Publishing Company.
2. Shepard Center. (2013, April 11). Chapter 2: Anatomy of the spinal cord and how it works [Video]. YouTube. www.youtube.com/watch?v=Gg0F67mnTys&index=2&list=PLdBakfx9g1hY8pP9ohzJimrdh9dpmFpwI.youtube.com/watch?v=Gg0F67mnTys&list=PLdBakfx9g1hY8pP9ohzJimrdh9dpmFpwI&index=3
3. Facingdisability.(n.d.).*Quadriplegia or tetraplegia*.https://facingdisability.com/blog/quadriplegia-or-tetraplegia
4. American Spinal Injury Assocation. (n.d). American Spinal Injury Association (ASIA) impairment scale. www.icf-casestudies.org/introduction/spinal-cord-injury-sci/american-spinal-injury-association-asia-impairment-scale
5. International Paralympic Committee. (2019, December). Explanatory guide to the paralympic classification:

Paralympic summer sports. https://gtimg.tokyo2018.org/image/upload/production/n4fd9qx81mgkd9hjllgd.pdf

6. National Spinal CordInjury Statistical Center. (2021). Facts and Figures at a glance. www.nscisc.uab.edu/
7. Woundsource. (2016, November 23). Pressure injury prevention: Managing shear and friction. www.woundsource.com/blog/pressure-injury-prevention-managing-shear-and-friction
8. Wounds International. (2010). Pressure ulcer prevention: pressure, shear,fricktion and microclmate in context. www.woundsinternational.com/download/resource/6015
9. Claydon, V. E., Steeves, J. D., & Krassioukov, A. (2006). Orthostatic hypotension following spinal cord injury: Understanding clinical pathophysiology. *Spinal cord, 44*, 341–351. https://doi.org/10.1038/sj.sc.3101855
10. University of Pittsburgh Medical Center. (n.d.). Musculoskeletal issues after spinal cord injury. www.upmc.com/services/rehab/rehab-institute/conditions/spinal-cord-injury/education-spinal-injury/musculoskeletal-issues-after-spinal-cord-injury
11. Flint Rehab. (2020, September 16). Understanding muscle atrophy after spinal cord injury: How to regain strength. www.flintrehab.com/muscle-atrophy-due-to-spinal-cord-injury/
12. Lundberg, N. R., Taniguchi, S., McCormick B. P., & Tibbs, C. (2011). Identity negotiating: redefining stigmatized identities through adaptive sports and recreation particiapation among individuals with a disability. *Journal of Leisure Research, 43*(2), 205–225. https://doi.org/10.1080/00222216.2011.1195023
13. Diaz, R., Miller, E. K., Kraus, E., & Fredericson, M. (2019). Impact of adaptive sports particiaption on quality of life. *Sports Medicine and Arhroscopy Review, 27*, 73–82.
14. Center for Disease Control and Prevention. (n.d.). *What is spina bifida?* www.cdc.gov/ncbddd/spinabifida/facts.html
15. Christopher Reeve Foundation. (n.d.). *What is spina bifida.* www.christopherreeve.org/living-with-paralysis/health/causes-of-paralysis/spina-bifida.
16. Spina bifida association. (n.d.). *What is spina bifida.* www.spinabifidaassociation.org/what-is-spina-bifida-2/
17. Center for Disease Control and Prevention. (2020, September 3). Data and statistics on spina bifida. www.cdc.gov/ncbddd/spinabifida/data.html
18. National Institute of Neurological Disorders and Stoke. (n.d.). *Chiari malformation fact sheet.* www.ninds.nih.gov/Disorders/Patient-Caregiver-Education/Fact-Sheets/Chiari-Malformation-Fact-Sheet
19. Spina Bifids Assocation. (n.d.). *Hydrocephalus and shunts.* www.spinabifidaassociation.org/wp-content/uploads/Hydrocephalus-and-Shunts1.pdf
20. Spina Bifida Association. (n.d.). *Spinal cord tethering.* www.spinabifidaassociation.org/wp-content/uploads/Spinal-Cord-Tethering.pdf
21. Hydrocephalus Association. (n.d.). *About hydrocephalus.* www.hydroassoc.org/about-hydrocephalus/
22. Hydrocehalus Association. (n.d.). *Complications of shunt systems.* www.hydroassoc.org/complications-of-shunt-systems/
23. Spina bifida Association. (n.d.). *Learning among children with spina bifida.* www.spinabifidaassociation.org/wp-content/uploads/Learning-among-Children-with-Spina-Bifida1.pdf
24. Spina Bifida Association. (n.d) *Natural rubber latex allergy.* www.spinabifidaassociation.org/resource/latex-2/
25. National Center for Health, Physical Activity and Disability. (n.d.). *Spina bifida: Importance of exercise.* www.nchpad.org/222/1444/Spina~Bifida
26. Apokon, S. D., Grady, R., Hart, S., Lee, A., McNalley, T., Niswander, L., Petersen, J., Remley, S., Rotenstein, D., Shurtleff, H., Warner,. M., & Walker, W. O. (2014). Advances in the care of children with spina bifida. *Advances in Pediatrics, 61*, 33–74.
27. Lam, J. C., & Mukhdomi, T. (2021). *Kyphoisis.* National Center for Biotechnology Information. www.ncbi.nlm.nih.gov/books/NBK558945/
28. Johns Hopkins Medicine. (n.d). *Scoliosis.* www.hopkinsmedicine.org/health/conditions-and-diseases/scoliosis
29. Clevelend Clinic. (n.d.). *Cervical spondylosis.* https://my.clevelandclinic.org/health/diseases/17685-cervical-spondylosis
30. Tenny S., & Gillis C. C.(2021). Spondylolisthesis. National Center for Biotechnology Information. www.ncbi.nlm.nih.gov/books/NBK430767/
31. National Institute of Neurological Disorders and Stroke. (n.d.). Transverse myelitis fact sheet. www.ninds.nih.gov/Disorders/Patient-Caregiver-Education/Fact-Sheets/Transverse-Myelitis-Fact-Sheet
32. National Institute of Neurological Disorders and Stroke. (n.d.). Guillain-Barre syndrome fact sheet. www.ninds.nih.gov/Disorders/Patient-Caregiver-Education/Fact-Sheets/Guillain-Barr%C3%A9-Syndrome-Fact-Sheet